REVEALING
COSMIC
MYSTERIES

ALSO BY H. P. BLAVATSKY

THE SECRET DOCTRINE

ISIS UNVEILED

THE VOICE OF THE SILENCE

THE KEY TO THEOSOPHY

THE LAND OF THE GODS

FROM THE CAVES AND JUNGLES OF HINDOSTAN

THE PEOPLE OF THE BLUE MOUNTAINS

THE DURBAR IN LAHORE

COLLECTED WRITINGS

H. P. BLAVATSKY

REVEALING
COSMIC
MYSTERIES

UNPUBLISHED CONVERSATIONS

Radiant Books
New York

This book contains interviews with H. P. Blavatsky and stenographic reports of the meetings of the Blavatsky Lodge held in London from 20 December 1888 to 20 June 1889. In 1890 and 1891, a highly condensed and heavily edited version of these reports was published as *Transactions of the Blavatsky Lodge*, covering the meetings from December 1888 to mid-March 1889, but in only 110 pages. The report of the meetings on 20 and 27 December 1888 is reproduced here from *Transactions of the Blavatsky Lodge* (1890) because its original manuscript has not survived.

The publisher expresses gratitude to all those who have preserved, discovered, and transcribed the manuscripts of these long-lost stenographic reports and made them available to the public.

Yours Till Death and After, H.P.B. was originally published by William Q. Judge in *Lucifer* in 1891. *Magic* is a compilation of articles originally published by William Q. Judge in *The Path*: "Conversations on Occultism" (1888, 1894, 1895), "Occult Vibrations" (1893), and "Conversations on Occultism with H.P.B." (1894). *Astral Bodies* was originally published by H. P. Blavatsky as "Dialogue Between the Two Editors" in *Lucifer* in 1888. *The Afterlife and the Constitution of Man* was originally published by H. P. Blavatsky as "Dialogue on the Mysteries of the After Life" in *Lucifer* in 1889. *Helena Petrovna Blavatsky* was originally published by Charles Johnston in *The Theosophical Forum* in 1900. *Cosmic Evolution* was originally published by H. P. Blavatsky in *The Secret Doctrine* in 1888.

Table 1 on page 64 is reproduced from *The Key to Theosophy*. Table 2 on page 76 and Diagrams 1, 2, and 3 on pages 434, 462, and 492, respectively, are reproduced from *The Secret Doctrine*.

H. P. Blavatsky's photo on page viii was taken in New York around 1874–1876 by Edsall Photographic Studio. The image of Blavatsky's house at 17 Lansdowne Road, London, on page 92, was drawn by William Q. Judge. The photo of the room where the meetings of the Blavatsky Lodge were held, on page 94, was taken in 1888.

Annotated by Radiant Books, using H. P. Blavatsky's *The Theosophical Glossary* (London: Theosophical Publishing Society, 1892).

Library of Congress Control Number: 2023941418

Published in 2023 by Radiant Books
radiantbooks.co

ISBN 978-1-63994-042-4 (hardback)
ISBN 978-1-63994-043-1 (paperback)
ISBN 978-1-63994-044-8 (e-book)

TABLE OF CONTENTS

"Blessed are the pure-hearted
who have only intuition,
for intuition is better than intellect."

H. P. Blavatsky

YOURS TILL DEATH AND AFTER, H.P.B.

Such has been the manner in which our beloved teacher and friend always concluded her letters to me. And now, I feel ever near and ever potent the magic of that resistless power, as of a mighty rushing river, which those who wholly trusted her always came to understand. Fortunate indeed is that Karma[1] which, for all the years since I first met her, in 1875, has kept me faithful to the friend who, masquerading under the outer *mortal* garment known as H. P. Blavatsky, was ever faithful to me, ever kind, ever the teacher and the guide.

In 1874, in the City of New York, I first met H.P.B. in this life. By her request, sent through Colonel H. S. Olcott,[2] the call was made in her rooms in Irving Place,[3] when then, as afterwards, through the remainder of her stormy career, she was surrounded by the anxious, the intellectual, the bohemian, the rich and the poor. It was her eye that attracted me, the eye of one whom I must have known in lives long passed away. She looked at me in recognition at that first hour, and never since has that look changed. Not as a questioner of philosophies did I come before her, not as one groping in the dark for lights that schools and fanciful theories had obscured, but as one who, wandering many periods through the corridors of life, was seeking the friends who could show where the designs for the work had been hidden. And true to the call she responded, revealing the plans once again, and speaking no words to explain, simply pointed them out and went on with the task. It was as if but the evening before we had parted, leaving yet to be done some detail of a task taken up with one common end; it was teacher and pupil, elder brother and younger, both bent on the one single end, but she with the power and the knowledge that belong but to lions and sages. So, friends from the first, I felt safe. Others I know

---

[1] **Karma** (*Sanskrit*, "action") — the Law of Retribution, the Law of Cause and Effect, or Ethical Causation. There is the Karma of merit and the Karma of demerit. Karma neither punishes nor rewards, it is simply *the one* Universal Law which guides unerringly — and, so to say, blindly — all other laws productive of certain effects along the grooves of their respective causations.

[2] **Henry Steel Olcott** (1832–1907) — the co-founder of the Theosophical Society and its first President from 1875 to 1907. His activities contributed to reviving Buddhism in South Asia.

[3] **Irving Place** — H.P.B.'s place of residence in lower midtown Manhattan, New York, in 1875; her apartment was at 46 Irving Place.

have looked with suspicion on an appearance they could not fathom, and though it is true they adduce many proofs which, hugged to the breast, would damn sages and gods, yet it is only through blindness they failed to see the lion's glance, the diamond heart of H.P.B.

The entire space of this whole publication would not suffice to enable me to record the phenomena she performed for me through all these years, nor would I wish to put them down. As she so often said, they prove nothing but only lead some souls to doubt and others to despair. And again, I do not think they were done just for me, but only that in those early days she was laying down the lines of force all over the land and I, so fortunate, was at the centre of the energy and saw the play of forces in visible phenomena. The explanation has been offered by some too anxious friends that the earlier phenomena were mistakes in judgement, attempted to be rectified in later years by confining their area and limiting their number, but until someone shall produce in the writing of H.P.B. her concurrence with that view, I shall hold to her own explanations made in advance and never changed. That I have given above. For many it is easier to take refuge behind a charge of bad judgement than to understand the strange and powerful laws which control in matters such as these.

Amid all the turmoil of her life, above the din produced by those who charged her with deceit and fraud and others who defended, while month after month, and year after year, witnessed men and women entering the theosophical[1] movement only to leave it soon with malignant phrases for H.P.B., there stands a fact we all might imitate — devotion absolute to her Master.[2] "It was He," she writes, "who told me to devote myself to this, and I will never disobey and never turn back."

In 1888 she wrote to me privately:

---

[1] Theosophy (*Greek*, "divine wisdom" or "wisdom of the gods") — Wisdom-Religion, the substratum and basis of all the world religions and philosophies, taught and practised by a few elect ever since man became a thinking being. In its practical bearing, Theosophy is purely divine ethics; the definitions in dictionaries are pure nonsense, based on religious prejudice and ignorance of the true spirit of the early Rosicrucians and medieval philosophers who called themselves Theosophists.

[2] **Master** — a translation from the Sanskrit *Guru*, "spiritual teacher," and adopted by the Theosophists to designate the Adepts, from whom they hold their teachings.

"Well, my *only* friend, you ought to know better. Look into my life and try to realize it — in its outer course at least, as the rest is hidden. I am under the curse of ever writing, as the wandering Jew[3] was under that of being ever on the move, never stopping one moment to rest. Three ordinary healthy persons could hardly do what I *have* to do. I live an artificial life; I am an automaton running full steam until the power of generating steam stops, and then — goodbye! ... Night before last I was shown a bird's-eye view of the Theosophical Societies. I saw a few earnest reliable Theosophists in a death struggle with the world in general, with other — nominal but ambitious — Theosophists. The former are greater in numbers than you may think, and *they prevailed*, as you in *America will prevail*, if you only remain staunch to the Master's programme and true to yourselves. And last night I saw .˙. [the Master Morya] and now I feel strong — such as I am in my body — and ready to fight for Theosophy and the few *true* ones to my last breath. The defending forces have to be judiciously — so scanty they are — distributed over the globe, wherever Theosophy is struggling against the powers of darkness."

Such she ever was; devoted to Theosophy and the Society organized to carry out a programme embracing the world in its scope. Willing in the service of the cause to offer up hope, money, reputation, life itself, provided the Society might be saved from every hurt, whether small or great. And thus bound body, heart and soul to this entity called the Theosophical Society, bound to protect it at all hazards, in face of every loss, she often incurred the resentment of many who became her friends but would not always care for the infant organization as she had sworn to do. And when they acted as if opposed to the Society, her instant opposition seemed to them to nullify professions of friendship. Thus she had but few friends, for it required a keen insight, untinged with personal feeling, to see even a small part of the real H. P. Blavatsky.

But was her object merely to form a Society whose strength should lie in numbers? Not so. She worked under directors who, operating from *behind the scene*, knew that the Theosophical Society was, and

---

[3] **Wandering Jew** — a Jew who scoffed at Jesus Christ on his way to Calvary and therefore was cursed by the greatest Magi on the Earth to walk the world without any rest until the Second Coming. See Thales of Argos, *The Mystery of Christ* (New York: Radiant Books, 2023), pp. 66–68.

was to be, the nucleus from which help might spread to all the people of the day, without thanks and without acknowledgment. Once, in London, I asked her what was the chance of drawing people into the Society in view of the enormous disproportion between the number of members and the millions of Europe and America who neither knew of nor cared for it. Leaning back in her chair, in which she was sitting before her writing desk, she said:

"When you consider and remember those days in 1875 and after, in which you could not find any people interested in your thoughts, and now look at the wide-spreading influence of theosophical ideas — however labelled — it is not so bad. We are not working merely that people may call themselves *Theosophists*, but that the doctrines we cherish may affect and leaven the whole mind of this century. This alone can be accomplished by a small earnest band of workers, who work for no human reward, no earthly recognition, but who, supported and sustained by a belief in that Universal Brotherhood of which our Masters are a part, work steadily, faithfully, in understanding and putting forth for consideration the doctrines of life and duty that have come down to us from immemorial time. Falter not so long as a few devoted ones will work to keep the nucleus existing. You were not directed to found and realize a Universal Brotherhood, but to form the nucleus for one; for it is only when the nucleus is formed that the accumulations can begin that will end in future years, however far, in the formation of that body which we have in view."

H.P.B. had a lion heart, and on the work traced out for her she had the lion's grasp; let us, her friends, companions and disciples, sustain ourselves in carrying out the designs laid down on the trestle-board, by the memory of her devotion and the consciousness that behind her task there stood, and still remain, those Elder Brothers who, above the clatter and the din of our battle, ever see the end and direct the forces distributed in array for the salvation of "that great orphan — Humanity."

William Q. Judge
June 1891

MAGIC

In 1875, '76, '77 and '78 my intimacy with H.P.B. gave me many opportunities for conversing with her on what we then called "Magic."[1] These useful, and for me very wonderful, occasions came about late at night, and sometimes during the day. I was then in the habit of calling on her in the daytime whenever I could get away from my office. Many times I stayed in her flat for the purpose of hearing as much and seeing as much as I could. Later on, in 1884, I spent many weeks with her in the Rue Notre-Dame des Champs[2] in Paris, sitting beside her day after day and evening after evening; later still, in 1888, being with her in London, at Holland Park,[3] I had a few more opportunities. Some of what she said I publish here for the good of those who can benefit by her words. Certainly no greater practical occultist[4] is known to this century: from that point of view what she said will have a certain useful weight with some.

William Q. Judge
April 1894

---

[1] **Magic** — the great science of communicating with and directing supernal, supramundane Potencies, as well as of commanding those of the lower spheres; a practical knowledge of the hidden mysteries of nature known to only the few, because they are so difficult to acquire, without falling into sins against nature. *White Magic*, or "Beneficent Magic," is divine magic, devoid of selfishness, love of power, ambition or lucre, and bent only on doing good to the world in general and one's neighbour in particular. The smallest attempt to use one's abnormal powers for the gratification of self makes of these powers sorcery or *black magic*.

[2] **Rue Notre-Dame des Champs** — a long and narrow street on the left bank of the Seine River in the 6th arrondissement (district) of Paris. The house at 46 Rue Notre-Dame des Champs was provided for H.P.B. by Marie Sinclair, Countess of Caithness (Duchess of Pomar).

[3] **Holland Park** — an area of Kensington, on the western edge of Central London. H.P.B.'s residence was at 17 Lansdowne Road, where the meetings of the Blavatsky Lodge were held.

[4] **Occultist** — a person who studies occultism.

Occultism (*Latin*, "hidden," "secret") — the totality of sciences that study the secret laws of Nature and the spiritual forces in human beings and the Cosmos, as well as the unfathomed properties of matter and consciousness.

OCCULT TEACHINGS

W.Q.J.:[1] What is Occultism?

H.P.B.: It is that branch of knowledge which shows the universe in the form of an egg. The cell of science is a little copy of the egg of the universe. The laws which govern the whole govern also every part of it. As man is a little copy of the universe — is the microcosm[2] — he is governed by the same laws which rule the greater. Occultism teaches therefore of the secret laws and forces of the universe and man, those forces playing in the outer world and known in part only by the men of the day who admit no invisible real nature, behind which is the model of the visible.

W.Q.J.: What does Occultism teach in regard to man, broadly speaking?

H.P.B.: That he is the highest product of evolution, and hence has in him a centre or focus corresponding to each centre of force or power in the universe. He therefore has as many centres or foci for force, power, and knowledge as there are such in the greater world about and within.

W.Q.J.: Do you mean to include also the ordinary run of men, or is it the exceptions you refer to?

H.P.B.: I include every human being, and that will reach from the lowest to the very highest, both those we know and those beyond us who are suspected as being in existence. Although we are accustomed to confine the term "human" to this earth, it is not correct to confine that sort of being to this plane[3] or globe, because other planets have beings the same as ours in essential power and nature and possibility.

W.Q.J.: Please explain a little more particularly what you mean by our having centres or foci in us.

---

[1] **William Q. Judge** (1851–1896) — the co-founder of the Theosophical Society, editor of *The Path* and author of *The Ocean of Theosophy*. He served as General Secretary of the American Section from 1886 to 1895. In 1890, he was appointed Vice President of the international Theosophical Society.

[2] **Microcosm** (*Greek*, "little Universe") — man, made in the image of his creator, the Macrocosm, or "great" Universe, and containing all that the latter contains.

[3] **Plane** — an extension of space, whether in the physical or metaphysical sense. In Occultism, the range or extent of some state of consciousness, or the state of matter corresponding to the perceptive powers of a particular set of senses or the action of a particular force.

H.P.B.: Electricity is a most powerful force not fully known to modern science, yet used very much. The nervous, physical, and mental systems of man acting together are able to produce the same force exactly, and in a finer as well as subtler way and to as great a degree as the most powerful dynamo, so that the force might be used to kill, to alter, to move, or otherwise change any object or condition. This is the "vril"[4] described by Bulwer-Lytton[5] in his *The Coming Race.*[6]

Nature exhibits to our eyes the power of drawing into one place with fixed limits any amount of material so as to produce the smallest natural object or the very largest. Out of the air she takes what is already there, and by compressing it into the limits of tree or animal form makes it visible to our material eyes. This is the power of condensing into what may be known as the ideal limits, that is, into the limits of the form which is ideal. Man has this same power, and can, when he knows the laws and the proper centres of force in himself, do precisely what Nature does. He can thus make visible and material what was before ideal and invisible by filling the ideal form with the matter condensed from the air. In his case the only difference from Nature is that he does quickly what she brings about slowly.

Among natural phenomena there is no present illustration of telepathy good for our use. Among the birds and the beasts, however, there is telepathy instinctually performed. But telepathy, as it is now called, is the communicating of thought or idea from mind to mind. This is a natural power, and being well-understood may be used by one mind to convey to another, no matter how far away or what be the intervening obstacle, any idea or thought. In natural things we can take for that the vibration of the chord which can cause all other chords of the same length to vibrate similarly. This is a branch of Occultism, a part of which is known to the modern investigator.

---

[4] **Vril** — an explosive substance of enormous destructive power used in Edward Bulwer-Lytton's novel, *The Coming Race.* However, the Force itself is real. It is the terrible sidereal Force, known to and named by the Atlanteans as *Mash-mak.* It is allegorized in the *Vishnu Purana,* in the *Ramayana,* and in other works. This vibratory Force, which, when aimed at an army, would reduce to ashes 100,000 men as easily as it would a dead rat.

[5] **Edward Bulwer-Lytton** (1803–1873) — an English writer and politician.

[6] *The Coming Race* — a science fiction novel by Edward Bulwer-Lytton, published in 1871 and later republished under the title *Vril: The Power of the Coming Race.*

But it is also one of the most useful and one of the greatest powers we have. To make it of service many things have to combine. While it is used every day in common life in the average way — for men are each moment telepathically communicating with each other — to do it in perfection, that is, against obstacle and distance, is perfection of occult art. Yet it will be known one day even to the common world.

W.Q.J.: Is there any object had in view by Nature which man should also hold before him?

H.P.B.: Nature ever works to turn the inorganic or the lifeless or the non-intelligent and non-conscious into the organic, the intelligent, the conscious; and this should be the aim of man also. In her great movements Nature seems to cause destruction, but that is only for the purpose of construction. The rocks are dissolved into earth, elements combine to bring on change, but there is the ever onward march of progress in evolution. Nature is not destructive of either thing or time, she is constructive. Man should be the same. And as a free moral agent he should work to that end, and not to procuring gratification merely nor for waste in any department.

W.Q.J.: Is Occultism of truth or of falsehood; is it selfish or unselfish; or is it part one and part the other?

H.P.B.: Occultism is colourless, and only when used by man for the one side or the other is it good or bad. Bad Occultism, or that which is used for selfish ends, is not false, for it is the same as that which is for good ends. Nature is two-sided, negative and positive, good and bad, light and dark, hot and cold, spirit and matter. The black magician[1] is as powerful in the matter of phenomena as the White, but in the end all the trend of Nature will go to destroy the black and save the white. But what you should understand is that the false man and the true can both be occultists. The words of the Christian teacher Jesus will give the rule for judgement: "By their fruits ye shall know them. Do men gather grapes of thorns or figs of thistles?"[2] Occultism is the general, all-inclusive term, the differentiating terms are *White* and *black*; the same forces are used by both, and similar laws, for there

---

[1] **Black magic** — sorcery; necromancy, or the raising of the dead, and other selfish abuses of abnormal powers. This abuse may be unintentional; yet it is still *black* magic whenever anything is produced phenomenally simply for one's own gratification.

[2] Matthew 7:16.

are no special laws in this universe for any special set of workers in Nature's secrets. But the path of the untruthful and the wicked, while seemingly easy at first, is hard at last, for the black workers are the friends of no one, they are each against the other as soon as interest demands, and that may be anytime. It is said that final annihilation of the personal soul awaits those who deal in the destructive side of Nature's hall of experience.

W.Q.J.: Where should I look for the help I need in the right life, the right study?

H.P.B.: Within yourself is the light that lighteth every man who cometh here. The light of the Higher Self[3] and of the Mahatma[4] are not different from each other. Unless you find your Self, how can you understand Nature?

THE POWER TO KNOW

W.Q.J.: What is the effect of trying to develop the power of seeing in the Astral Light[5] before a person is initiated?[6]

---

[3] **Self** — there are two *Selves* in men: the Higher and the Lower, the Impersonal and the Personal Self. One is divine, the other semi-animal. A great distinction should be made between the two.

[4] **Mahatma** (*Sanskrit*, "great soul") — an Adept of the highest order. Exalted beings who, having attained to the mastery over their lower principles, are thus living unimpeded by the "man of flesh," and are in possession of knowledge and power commensurate with the stage they have reached in their spiritual evolution. Called *Rahats* and *Arhats* in Pali.

[5] **Astral Light** — the invisible region that surrounds our globe, as it does every other, and corresponding, as the second Principle of Cosmos (the third being Life, of which it is the vehicle), to the *Linga-sharira* or the astral double in man. A subtle Essence visible only to a clairvoyant eye, and the lowest but one (namely, the earth) of the Seven Akashic or Cosmic Principles. The Astral Light gives out nothing but what it has received; it is the great terrestrial crucible in which the vile emanations of the earth (moral and physical), upon which the Astral Light is fed, are all converted into their subtlest essence and radiated back intensified, thus becoming epidemics — moral, psychic, and physical.

[6] **Initiation** — the practice of initiation or admission into the sacred Mysteries, taught by the Hierophants and learned priests of the Temples, is one of the most ancient customs. This was practised in every old national religion. In Europe, it was abolished with the fall of the last pagan temple. In the days of old, the Mysteries, according to the greatest Greek and Roman philosophers, were the most sacred of all solemnities as well as the most beneficent, and greatly pro-moted virtue. The Mysteries represented the passage from mortal life into finite ▸

H.P.B.: Seeing in the Astral Light is not done through Manas,[1] but through the senses, and hence has to do entirely with sense-perception removed to a plane different from this, but more illusionary. The final perceiver or judge of perception is in Manas, in the Self; and therefore the final tribunal is clouded by the astral perception if one is not so far trained or initiated as to know the difference and able to tell the true from the false. Another result is a tendency to dwell on this subtle sense-perception, which at last will cause an atrophy of Manas for the time being. This makes the confusion all the greater, and will delay any possible initiation all the more or forever. Further, such seeing is in the line of phenomena, and adds to the confusion of the Self which is only beginning to understand this life; by attempting the astral another element of disorder is added by more phenomena due to another plane, thus mixing both sorts up. The Ego[2] must find its basis and not be swept off hither and thither. The constant reversion of images and ideas in the Astral Light, and the pranks of the elementals[3] there, unknown to us as such and only seen in effects, still again add

---

death and the experiences of the disembodied Spirit and Soul in the world of subjectivity.

[1] **Manas** (*Sanskrit*, "mind") — the mental faculty which makes of man an intelligent and moral being, and distinguishes him from the mere animal; a synonym of *Mahat*. Esoterically, however, it means, when unqualified, the Higher Ego, or the sentient reincarnating Principle in man. When qualified it also means *Buddhi-Manas* or the Spiritual Soul in contradistinction to its human reflection — *Kama-Manas* (*Sanskrit*, "mind of desire").

[2] **Ego** (*Latin*, "self") — the consciousness in man "I am I," or the feeling of "I-am-ship." Esoteric philosophy teaches the existence of two Egos in man, the mortal or personal, and the Higher, the Divine and the Impersonal, calling the former *personality* and the latter *Individuality*.

[3] **Elementals** — spirits of the Elements. The creatures evolved in the four Kingdoms or Elements — earth, air, fire, and water. The Kabbalists call them Gnomes (of the earth), Sylphs (of the air), Salamanders (of the fire), and Undines (of the water). Except for a few of the higher kinds, and their rulers, they are rather forces of Nature than ethereal men and women. These forces, as the servile agents of the Occultists, may produce various effects; however, if employed by "Elementaries" (the disembodied souls of the depraved that lost their chance for immortality) in which case they enslave the mediums — they will deceive the credulous. All the lower invisible beings generated on the 5th, 6th, and 7th planes of our terrestrial atmosphere are called Elementals: Peris, Devs, Jinns, Sylvans, Satyrs, Fauns, Elves, Dwarfs, Trolls, Kobolds, Brownies, Nixies, Goblins, Pinkies, Banshees, Moss People, White Ladies, Spooks, Fairies, etc.

to the confusion. To sum it up, the real danger from which all others flow or follow is in the confusion of the Ego by introducing strange things to it before the time.

W.Q.J.: How is one to know when he gets real occult information from the Self within?

H.P.B.: Intuition must be developed and the matter judged from the true philosophical basis, for if it is contrary to true general rules it is wrong. It has to be known from a deep and profound analysis by which we find out what is from egotism alone and what is not; if it is due to egotism, then it is not from the Spirit and is untrue. The power to know does not come from book-study nor from mere philosophy, but mostly from the actual practice of altruism[4] in deed, word, and thought; for that practice purifies the covers of the soul and permits that light to shine down into the brain-mind. As the brain-mind is the receiver in the waking state, it has to be purified from sense-perception, and the truest way to do this is by combining philosophy with the highest outward and inward virtue.

W.Q.J.: Tell me some ways by which intuition is to be developed.

H.P.B.: First of all by giving it exercise, and second by not using it for purely personal ends. Exercise means that it must be followed through mistakes and bruises until from sincere attempts at use it comes to its own strength. This does not mean that we can do wrong and leave the results, but that after establishing conscience on a right basis by following the Golden Rule,[5] we give play to the intuition and add to its strength. Inevitably in this at first we will make errors, but soon if we are sincere it will grow brighter and make no mistake. We should add the study of the works of those who in the past have trodden this path and found out what is the real and what is not. They say the Self is the only reality. The brain must be given larger views of life, as by the study of the doctrine of reincarnation,[6] since that

---

[4] **Altruism** (*Latin*) — a quality opposed to egoism; actions tending to do good to others, regardless of self.

[5] **Golden Rule** — a moral and ethical principle that advises treating others as you would like to be treated yourself. It can be found in all religions and philosophies.

[6] **Reincarnation** — the once universal doctrine, which taught that the Ego is born on this earth an innumerable number of times. This doctrine of rebirth was believed in by Jesus and the Apostles, as by all in those days, but denied now by the Christians. Nevertheless, the putting on of flesh periodically and throughout ›

gives a limitless field to the possibilities in store. We must not only be unselfish, but must do all the duties that Karma has given us, and thus intuition will point out the road of duty and the true path of life.

W.Q.J.: Are there any Adepts[1] in America or Europe?

H.P.B.: Yes, there are and always have been. But they have for the present kept themselves hidden from the public gaze.

The real ones have a wide work to do in many departments of life and in preparing certain persons who have a future work to do. Though their influence is wide they are not suspected, and that is the way they want to work for the present. There are some also who are at work with certain individuals in some of the aboriginal tribes in America, as among those are Egos who are to do still more work in another incarnation, and they must be prepared for it now. Nothing is omitted by these Adepts. In Europe it is the same way, each sphere of work being governed by the time and the place.

W.Q.J.: What is the meaning of the five-pointed star?

H.P.B.: It is the symbol of the human being who is not an Adept, but is now on the plane of the animal nature as to his life-thoughts and development inside. Hence it is the symbol of the race. Upside down it means death or symbolizes that. It also means, when upside down, the other or dark side. It is at the same time the cross endowed with the power of mind, that is, man.

W.Q.J.: Is there a four-pointed star symbol?

H.P.B.: Yes. That is the symbol of the next kingdom below man, and pertains to the animals. The right kind of clairvoyant can see both the five- and the four-pointed star. It is all produced by the intersections of the lines or currents of the Astral Light emanating from the person or being. The four-pointed one means that the being having but it has not as yet developed Manas.

W.Q.J.: Has the mere figure of a five-pointed star any power in itself?

H.P.B.: It has some, but very little. You see it is used by all sorts of people for trademarks and the like, and for the purposes of organi-

---

long cycles by the higher human Soul (Buddhi-Manas) or *Ego* is taught in the Bible as it is in all other ancient scriptures.

[1] **Adept** (*Latin*, "one who has obtained") — one who has reached the stage of Initiation and has become a Master in the science of Esoteric Philosophy.

zations, yet no result follows. It must be actually used by the mind to be of any force or value. If so used, it carries with it the whole power of the person to whom it may belong.

W.Q.J.: Why is the sword so much spoken of in practical Occultism by certain writers?

H.P.B.: Many indeed of these writers merely repeat what they have read. But there is a reason, just as in warfare the sword has more use for damage than a club. The Astral Light corresponds to water. If you try to strike in or under water with a club, it will be found that there is but little result, but a sharp knife will cut almost as well under water as out of it. The friction is less. So in the Astral Light a sword used on that plane has more power to cut than a club has, and an elemental for that reason will be more easily damaged by a sword than by a club or a stone. But all of this relates to things that are of no right value to the true student, and are indulged in only by those who work in dark magic or foolishly by those who do not quite know what they do. It is certain that he who uses the sword or the club will be at last hurt by it. And the lesson to be drawn is that we must seek for the true Self that knows all Occultism and all truth, and has in itself the protecting shield from all dangers. That is what the ancient Sages sought and found, and that is what should be striven after by us.

MENTAL DISCIPLINE

W.Q.J.: Is there not some attitude of mind which one should in truth assume in order to understand the occult in Nature?

H.P.B.: Such attitude of mind must be attained as will enable one to look into the realities of things. The mind must escape from the mere formalities and conventions of life, even though outwardly one seems to obey all of them, and should be firmly established on the truth that Man is a copy of the Universe and has in himself a portion of the Supreme Being. To the extent this is realized will be the clearness of perception of truth. A realization of this leads inevitably to the conclusion that all other men and beings are united with us, and this removes the egotism which is the result of the notion of separateness. When the truth of Unity is understood, then distinctions due to comparisons made like the Pharisee's,[2] that one is better than

---

[2] **Pharisees** (*Hebrew*, "separated") — a Jewish sect, from the 2nd century BCE to the 1st century CE, known for their strict adherence to religious laws and ›

his neighbour, disappear from the mind, leaving it more pure and free to act.

W.Q.J.: What would you point out as a principal foe to the mind's grasping of truth?

H.P.B.: The principal foe of a secondary nature is what was once called *phantasy*;[1] that is, the reappearance of thoughts and images due to recollection or memory. Memory is an important power, but mind in itself is not memory. Mind is restless and wandering in its nature, and must be controlled. Its wandering disposition is necessary or stagnation would result. But it can be controlled and fixed upon an object or idea. Now as we are constantly looking at and hearing of new things, the natural restlessness of the mind becomes prominent when we set about pinning it down. Then memory of many objects, things, subjects, duties, persons, circumstances, and affairs brings up before it the various pictures and thoughts belonging to them. After these the mind at once tries to go, and we find ourselves wandering from the point. It must hence follow that the storing of a multiplicity of useless and surely-recurring thoughts is an obstacle to the acquirement of truth. And this obstacle is the very one peculiar to our present style of life.

W.Q.J.: Can you mention some of the relations in which the sun stands to us and nature in respect to Occultism?

H.P.B.: It has many such, and all important. But I would draw your attention first to the greater and more comprehensive. The sun is the centre of our solar system. The life-energies of that system come to it through the sun, which is a focus or reflector for the spot in space where the real centre is. And not only comes mere life through that focus, but also much more that is spiritual in its essence. The sun

---

traditions, often characterized by their emphasis on oral law, meticulous observance of rituals and separation from those they considered impious.

[1] "The phantasy," says Olympiodorus (in Plato's *Phaedo*), "is an impediment to our intellectual conceptions; and hence, when we are agitated by the inspiring influence of the Divinity, if the phantasy intervenes, the enthusiastic energy ceases: for enthusiasm and the ecstasy are contrary to each other. Should it be asked whether the soul is able to energize without the phantasy, we reply, that its perception of universals proves that it is able. It has perceptions, therefore, independent of the phantasy; at the same time, however, the phantasy attends in its energies, just as a storm pursues him who sails on the sea."

should therefore not only be looked at with the eye but thought of by the mind. It represents to the world what the Higher Self is to the man. It is the soul-centre of the world with its six companions, as the Higher Self is the centre for the six principles[2] of man. So it supplies to those six principles of the man many spiritual essences and powers. He should for that reason think of it and not confine himself to gazing at it. So far as it acts materially in light, heat, and gravity, it will go on of itself, but man as a free agent must think upon it in order to gain what benefit can come only from his voluntary action in thought.

W.Q.J.: Will you refer to some minor one?

H.P.B.: Well, we sit in the sun for heat and possible chemical effects. But if at the same time that we do this we also think on it as the sun in the sky and of its possible essential nature, we thereby draw from it some of its energy not otherwise touched. This can also be done on a dark day when clouds obscure the sky, and some of the benefit thus be obtained. Natural mystics,[3] learned and ignorant, have discovered this for themselves here and there, and have often adopted the practice. But it depends, as you see, upon the mind.

W.Q.J.: Does the mind actually do anything when it takes up a thought and seeks for more light?

H.P.B.: It actually does. A thread, or a finger, or a long darting current flies out from the brain to seek for knowledge. It goes in all directions and touches all other minds it can reach so as to receive the information if possible. This is telepathically, so to say, accomplished. There are no patents on true knowledge of philosophy nor copyrights in that realm. Personal rights of personal life are fully respected, save by potential black magicians who would take anyone's property. But general truth belongs to all, and when the unseen messenger from one

---

[2] **Principles** — the elements or original essences, the basic differentiations upon and of which all things are built up. We use the term to denote the seven individual and fundamental aspects of the One Universal Reality in Cosmos and in man. Hence, also the seven aspects in the manifestation in the human being — divine, spiritual, psychic, astral, physiological and simply physical.

[3] **Mystic** — in antiquity, one belonging to those admitted to the ancient mysteries; in our own times, one who practises mysticism, holds mystic, transcendental views, etc. Any doctrine involved in mystery and metaphysics, and dealing more with the ideal worlds than with our matter-of-fact, actual universe, is called *Mysticism*.

mind arrives and touches the real mind of another, that other gives up to it what it may have of truth about general subjects. So the mind's finger or wire flies until it gets the thought or seed-thought from the other and makes it its own. But our modern competitive system and selfish desire for gain and fame is constantly building a wall around people's minds to everyone's detriment.

W.Q.J.: Do you mean that the action you describe is natural, usual, and universal, or only done by those who know how and are conscious of it?

H.P.B.: It is universal and whether the person is aware or not of what is going on. Very few are able to perceive it in themselves, but that makes no difference. It is done always. When you sit down to earnestly think on a philosophical or ethical matter, for instance, your mind flies off, touching other minds, and from them you get varieties of thought. If you are not well-balanced and psychically purified, you will often get thoughts that are not correct. Such is your Karma and the Karma of the race. But if you are sincere and try to base yourself on right philosophy, your mind will naturally reject wrong notions. You can see in this how it is that systems of thought are made and kept going, even though foolish, incorrect, or pernicious.

W.Q.J.: What mental attitude and aspiration are the best safeguards in this, as likely to aid the mind in these searches to reject error and not let it fly into the brain?

H.P.B.: Unselfishness, Altruism in theory and practice, desire to do the will of the Higher Self which is the "Father in Heaven," devotion to the human race. Subsidiary to these are discipline, correct thinking, and good education.

W.Q.J.: Is the uneducated man, then, in a worse condition?

H.P.B.: Not necessarily so. The very learned are so immersed in one system that they reject nearly all thoughts not in accord with preconceived notions. The sincere ignorant one is often able to get the truth but not able to express it. The ignorant masses generally hold in their minds the general truths of Nature, but are limited as to expression. And most of the best discoveries of scientific men have been obtained in this subconscious telepathic mode. Indeed, they often arrive in the learned brain from some obscure and so-called ignorant person, and then the scientific discoverer makes himself famous because of his power of expression and means for giving it out.

W.Q.J.: Does this bear at all upon the work of the Adepts of all good Lodges?

H.P.B.: It does. They have all the truths that could be desired, but at the same time are able to guard them from the seeking minds of those who are not yet ready to use them properly. But they often find the hour ripe and a scientific man ready, and then touch his cogitating mind with a picture of what he seeks. He then has a "flash" of thought in the line of his deliberations, as many of them have admitted. He gives it out to the world, becomes famous, and the world wiser. This is constantly done by the Adepts, but now and then they give out larger expositions of Nature's truths, as in the case of H.P.B. This is not at first generally accepted, as personal gain and fame are not advanced by any admission of benefit from the writings of another, but as it is done with a purpose, for the use of a succeeding century, it will do its work at the proper time.

W.Q.J.: How about the Adepts knowing what is going on in the world of thought, in the West, for instance?

H.P.B.: They have only to voluntarily and consciously connect their minds with those of the dominant thinkers of the day to at once discover what has been or is being worked out in thought and to review it all. This they constantly do, and as constantly incite to further elaborations or changes by throwing out the suggestion in the mental plane so that seeking and receptive minds may use it.

RULES IN OCCULTISM

W.Q.J.: Are there any rules, binding on all, in white magic or good occultism? I mean rules similar to the ten commandments of the Christians, or the rules for the protection of life, liberty, and property recognized by human law.

H.P.B.: There are such rules of the most stringent character, the breaking of which is never wiped out save by expiation. Those rules are not made up by some brain or mind, but flow from the laws of nature, of mind, and of soul. Hence they are impossible of nullification. One may break them and seem to escape for a whole life or for more than a life; but the very breaking of them sets in motion at once other causes which begin to make effects, and most unerringly those effects at last react on the violator. Karma here acts as it does elsewhere, and becomes a Nemesis[1] who, though sometimes slow, is fate itself in its certainty.

W.Q.J.: Is it not, then, the case that when an occultist violates a rule, some other Adept or agent starts out like a detective or policeman and brings the culprit to justice at a bar or tribunal, such as we sometimes read of in the imaginative works of mystical writers or novelists?

H.P.B.: No, there is no such pursuit. On the contrary, all the fellow-Adepts or students are but too willing to aid the offender, not in escaping punishment, but in sincerely trying to set counteracting causes in motion for the good of all. For the sin of one reacts on the whole human family. If, however, the culprit does not wish to do the amount of counteracting good, he is merely left alone to the law of nature, which is in fact that of his own inner life from which there can be no escape. In Lytton's novel, *Zanoni*,[2] you will notice the grave Master, Mejnour, trying to aid Zanoni, even at the time when the latter was falling slowly but surely into the meshes twisted by himself that ended in his destruction. Mejnour knew the law and so did Zanoni. The latter was suffering from some former error which he had to work out; the former, if himself too stern and unkind, would later on come to the appropriate grief for such a mistake. But meanwhile he was bound to help his friend, as are all those who really believe in brotherhood.

W.Q.J.: What one of those rules in any way corresponds to "Thou shalt not steal"?

H.P.B.: That one which was long ago expressed by the ancient sage in the words, "Do not covet the wealth of any creature." This is better than "Thou shalt not steal," for you cannot steal unless you covet. If you steal for hunger you may be forgiven, but you coveted the food for a purpose, just as another covets merely for the sake of possession. The wealth of others includes all their possessions, and does not mean mere money alone. Their ideas, their private thoughts, their mental

---

[1] **Nemesis** (*Greek*, "to give what is due") — the goddess of retribution and vengeance in Greek mythology.
[2] ***Zanoni*** — a mystical novel by Edward Bulwer-Lytton, published in 1842. Zanoni and Mejnour are its characters.

forces, powers, and faculties, their psychic powers — all, indeed, on all planes that they own or have. While they in that realm are willing to give it all away, it must not be coveted by another.

You have no right, therefore, to enter into the mind of another who has not given the permission and take from him what is not yours. You become a burglar on the mental and psychic plane when you break this rule. You are forbidden taking anything for personal gain, profit, advantage, or use. But you may take what is for general good, if you are far enough advanced and good enough to be able to extricate the personal element from it. This rule would, you can see, cut off all those who are well-known to every observer, who want psychic powers for themselves and their own uses. If such persons had those powers of inner sight and hearing that they so much want, no power could prevent them from committing theft on the unseen planes wherever they met a nature that was not protected. And as most of us are very far from perfect, so far, indeed, that we must work for many lives, yet the Masters of Wisdom do not aid our defective natures in the getting of weapons that would cut our own hands. For the law acts implacably, and the breaches made would find their end and result in long after years. The Black Lodge, however, is very willing to let any poor, weak, or sinful mortal get such power, because that would swell the number of victims they so much require.

W.Q.J.: Is there any rule corresponding to "Thou shalt not bear false witness"?

H.P.B.: Yes; the one which requires you never to inject into the brain of another a false or untrue thought. As we can project our thoughts to another's mind, we must not throw untrue ones to another. It comes before him, and he, overcome by its strength perhaps, finds it echoing in him, and it is a false witness speaking falsely within, confusing and confounding the inner spectator who lives on thought.

W.Q.J.: How can one prevent the natural action of the mind when pictures of the private lives of others rise before one?

H.P.B.: That is difficult for the run of men. Hence the mass have not the power in general; it is kept back as much as possible. But when the trained soul looks about in the realm of soul it is also able to direct its sight, and when it finds rising up a picture of what it should not voluntarily take, it turns its face away. A warning comes with all such pictures which must be obeyed. This is not a rare rule or piece of information, for there are many natural clairvoyants who know it very well, though many of them do not think that others have the same knowledge.

W.Q.J.: What do you mean by a warning coming with the picture?

H.P.B.: In this realm the slightest thought becomes a voice or a picture. All thoughts make pictures. Every person has his private thoughts and desires. Around these he makes also a picture of his wish for privacy, and that to the clairvoyant becomes a voice or picture of warning which seems to say it must be let alone. With some it may assume the form of a person who says not to approach, with others it will be a voice, with still others a simple but certain knowledge that the matter is sacred. All these varieties depend on the psychological idiosyncrasies of the seer.

W.Q.J.: What kind of thought or knowledge is excepted from these rules?

H.P.B.: General, and philosophical, religious, and moral. That is to say, there is no law of copyright or patent which is purely human in invention and belongs to the competitive system. When a man thinks out truly a philosophical problem it is not his under the laws of nature; it belongs to all; he is not in this realm entitled to any glory, to any profit, to any private use in it. Hence the seer may take as much of it as he pleases, but must on his part not claim it or use it for himself. Similarly with other generally beneficial matters. They are for all. If a Spencer thinks out a long series of wise things good for all men, the seer can take them all. Indeed, but few thinkers do any original thinking. They pride themselves on doing so, but in fact their seeking minds go out all over the world of mind and take from those of slower movement what is good and true, and then make them their own, sometimes gaining glory, sometimes money, and in this age claiming all as theirs and profiting by it.

THE KALI YUGA – THE PRESENT AGE

W.Q.J.: I am very much puzzled about the present age. Some theosophists seem to abhor it as if wishing to be taken away from it altogether, inveighing against modern inventions such as the telegraph, railways, machinery, and the like, and bewailing the disappearance of former civilizations. Others take a different view, insisting that this is a better time than any other, and hailing modern methods as the best. Tell me, please, which of these is right, or, if both are wrong, what ought we to know about the age we live in.

H.P.B.: The teachers of Truth know all about this age. But they do not mistake the present century for the whole cycle.[1] The older times of European history, for example, when might was right and when darkness prevailed over Western nations, was as much a part of this age, from the standpoint of the Masters, as is the present hour, for the Yuga[2] — to use a Sanskrit word — in which we are now had begun many thousands of years before. And during that period of European darkness, although this Yuga had already begun, there was much light, learning, and civilization in India and China. The meaning of the words "present age" must therefore be extended over a far greater period than is at present assigned. In fact, modern science has reached no definite conclusion yet as to what should properly be called "an age," and the truth of the Eastern doctrine is denied. Hence we find writers speaking of the "Golden Age," the "Iron Age," and so on, whereas they are only parts of the real age that began so far back that modern archaeologists deny it altogether.

---

[1] **Cycle** — the ancients divided time into endless cycles, wheels within wheels, all such periods being of various durations, and each marking the beginning or the end of some event, either cosmic, mundane, physical or metaphysical.
[2] **Yuga** (*Sanskrit*, "age") — an epoch, or cycle of Evolution, in Hinduism. There are four Yugas, which follow each other in a series, namely: Krita (or Satya) Yuga, the Golden Age; Treta Yuga, Dwapara Yuga and finally Kali Yuga (*Sanskrit*, "Dark Age") — an age of spiritual decline and ignorance. Esoterically, Kali Yuga ended in 1942. H.P.B. kept secret the actual period for the end of Kali Yuga and used only the information which was available to all. Only in the late 1930s, when researchers themselves were able to understand that the gigantic figures indicated were simply symbols and widely informed the population of India about this, did the Masters confirm — through Helena Roerich , who continued H.P.B.'s mission in the 20th century — the accuracy of those calculations. And on 1 August 1943, the cosmic event occurred that was described in the *Vishnu Purana* as the sign of Satya Yuga's beginning, as cited in *The Secret Doctrine*, vol. 1, p. 378. The four Yugas also correspond to Cosmic Seasons for the Solar System: Spring (Satya), Summer (Treta), Autumn (Dwapara) and Winter (Kali). The global warming and temperature records broken every year on the Earth, as well as similar processes on Mars, Jupiter and Pluto, testify to the fact that we are currently living in the very first phases of Cosmic Spring, although "winter colds" still make themselves felt.

W.Q.J.: What is the Sanskrit name for this age, and what is its meaning?

H.P.B.: The Sanskrit is "Kali," which added to Yuga gives us "Kali Yuga." The meaning of it is "Dark Age." Its approach was known to the ancients, its characteristics are described in the Indian poem the *Mahabharata*.[1] As I said that it takes in an immense period of the glorious part of Indian history, there is no chance for anyone to be jealous and to say that we are comparing the present hour with that wonderful division of Indian development.

W.Q.J.: What are the characteristics to which you refer, by which Kali Yuga may be known?

H.P.B.: As its name implies, darkness is the chief. This of course is not deducible by comparing today with 800 AD, for this would be no comparison at all. The present century is certainly ahead of the middle ages, but as compared with the preceding Yuga it is dark. To the Occultist, material advancement is not of the quality of light, and he finds no proof of progress in merely mechanical contrivances that give comfort to a few of the human family while the many are in misery. For the darkness he would have to point but to one nation, even the great American Republic. Here he sees a mere extension of the habits and life of the Europe from which it sprang; here a great experiment with entirely new conditions and material was tried; here for many years very little poverty was known; but here today there is as much grinding poverty as anywhere, and as large a criminal class with corresponding prisons as in Europe, and more than in India. Again, the great thirst for riches and material betterment, while spiritual life is to a great extent ignored, is regarded by us as darkness. The great conflict already begun between the wealthy classes and the poorer is a sign of darkness. Were spiritual light prevalent, the rich and the poor would still be with us, for Karma cannot be blotted out, but the poor would know how to accept their lot and the rich how to improve the poor; now, on the contrary, the rich wonder why the poor do not go to the poorhouse, meanwhile seeking in the laws for cures for strikes and

---

[1] **Mahabharata** (*Sanskrit*, "great war") — the celebrated epic poem of India (probably the longest poem in the world), which includes the *Bhagavad Gita*, "the Song Celestial."

socialism, and the poor continually growl at fate and their supposed oppressors. All this is of the quality of spiritual darkness.

W.Q.J.: Is it wise to inquire as to the periods when the cycle changes, and to speculate on the great astronomical or other changes that herald a turn?

H.P.B.: It is not. There is an old saying that the gods are jealous about these things, not wishing mortals to know them. We may analyse the age, but it is better not to attempt to fix the hour of a change of cycle. Besides that, you will be unable to settle it, because a cycle does not begin on a day or year clear of any other cycle; they interblend, so that, although the wheel of one period is still turning, the initial point of another has already arrived.

W.Q.J.: Are these some of the reasons why Mr. Sinnett[2] was not given certain definite periods of years about which he asked?

H.P.B.: Yes.

W.Q.J.: Has the age in which one lives any effect on the student; and what is it?

H.P.B.: It has effect on everyone, but the student after passing along in his development feels the effect more than the ordinary man. Were it otherwise, the sincere and aspiring students all over the world would advance at once to those heights towards which they strive. It takes a very strong soul to hold back the age's heavy hand, and it is all the more difficult because that influence, being a part of the student's larger life, is not so well understood by him. It operates in the same way as a structural defect in a vessel. All the inner as well as the outer fibre of the man is the result of the long centuries of earthly lives lived here by his ancestors. These sow seeds of thought and physical tendencies in a way that you cannot comprehend. All those tendencies affect him. Many powers once possessed are hidden so deep as to be unseen, and he struggles against obstacles constructed ages ago. Further yet are the peculiar alterations brought about in the astral world. It, being at once a photographic plate, so to say, and also a reflector, has become the keeper of the mistakes of ages past which

---

[2] **Alfred Percy Sinnett** (1840–1921) — an English journalist and the author of *The Occult World*, which described the phenomena performed by H.P.B., and *Esoteric Buddhism*, which was based on the letters that he received from the Master Koot Hoomi.

it continually reflects upon us from a plane to which most of us are strangers. In that sense therefore, free as we suppose ourselves, we are walking about completely hypnotized by the past, acting blindly under the suggestions thus cast upon us.

W.Q.J.: Was that why Jesus said, "Father, forgive them, *for they know not what they do*"?[1]

H.P.B.: That was one meaning. In one aspect they acted blindly, impelled by the age, thinking they were right.

Regarding these astral alterations, you will remember how in the time of Julian[2] the seers reported that they could see the gods, but they were decaying, some headless, others flaccid, others minus limbs, and all appearing weak. The reverence for these ideals was departing, and their astral pictures had already begun to fade.

W.Q.J.: What mitigation is there about this age? Is there nothing at all to relieve the picture?

H.P.B.: There is one thing peculiar to the present Kali Yuga that may be used by the Student. All causes now bring about their effects much more rapidly than in any other or better age. A sincere lover of the race can accomplish more in three incarnations under Kali Yuga's reign than he could in a much greater number in any other age. Thus by bearing all the manifold troubles of this Age and steadily triumphing, the object of his efforts will be more quickly realized, for, while the obstacles seem great, the powers to be invoked can be reached more quickly.

W.Q.J.: Even if this is, spiritually considered, a Dark Age, is it not in part redeemed by the increasing triumphs of mind over matter, and by the effects of science in mitigating human ills, such as the causes of disease, disease itself, cruelty, intolerance, bad laws, etc.?

H.P.B.: Yes, these are mitigations of the darkness in just the same way that a lamp gives some light at night but does not restore daylight. In this age there are great triumphs of science, but they are nearly all directed to *effects* and do not take away the *causes* of the evils. Great strides have been made in the arts and in cure of diseases, but in the future, as the flower of our civilization unfolds, new diseases will arise and more strange disorders will be known, springing from causes

[1] Luke 23:34.

[2] Julian (331–363) — the last non-Christian Roman emperor from 361 to 363.

that lie deep in the minds of men and which can only be eradicated by spiritual living. *alcoholism?*

W.Q.J.: Admitting all you say, are not we, as Theosophists, to welcome every discovery of truth in any field, especially such truth as lessens suffering or enlarges the moral sense?

H.P.B.: That is our duty. All truths discovered must be parts of the one Absolute Truth, and so much added to the sum of our outer knowledge. There will always be a large number of men who seek for these parts of truth, and others who try to alleviate present human misery. They each do a great and appointed work that no true Theosophist should ignore. And it is also the duty of the latter to make similar efforts when possible, for Theosophy is a dead thing if it is not turned into the life. At the same time, no one of us may be the judge of just how much or how little our brother is doing in that direction. If he does all that he can and knows how to do, he does his whole present duty.

W.Q.J.: I fear that a hostile attitude by Occult teachers towards the learning and philanthropy of the time may arouse prejudice against Theosophy and Occultism, and needlessly impede the spread of Truth. May it not be so?

H.P.B.: The real Occult Teachers have no hostile attitude towards these things. If some persons, who like theosophy and try to spread it, take such a position, they do not thereby alter the one assumed by the real Teachers who work with all classes of men and use every possible instrument for good. But at the same time we have found that an excess of the technical and special knowledge of the day very often acts to prevent men from apprehending the truth.

W.Q.J.: Are there any causes, other than the spread of Theosophy, which may operate to reverse the present drift towards materialism?

H.P.B.: The spread of the knowledge of the laws of Karma and Reincarnation and of a belief in the absolute spiritual unity of all beings will alone prevent this drift. The cycle must, however, run its course, and until that is ended all beneficial causes will of necessity act slowly and not to the extent they would in a brighter age. As each student *lives* a better life and by his example imprints upon the Astral Light the picture of a higher aspiration acted in the world, he *thus aids souls of advanced development to descend from other spheres* where the cycles are so dark that they can no longer stay there.

W.Q.J.: Accept my thanks for your instruction.

H.P.B.: May you reach the terrace of enlightenment.

ON DARK ENTITIES

W.Q.J.: At a former time you spoke of entities that crowd the spaces about us. Are these all unconscious or otherwise?

H.P.B.: They are not all unconscious. First, there are the humdrum masses of elementals that move like nerve-currents with every motion of man, beast, or natural elements. Next are classes of those which have a peculiar power and consciousness of their own and not easily reached by any man. Then come the shades of the dead, whether mere floating shells,[1] or animated elementals, or infused with galvanic and extraordinary action by the Brothers of the Shadow.[2] Last, the Brothers of the Shadow, devoid of physical bodies save in rare cases, bad souls living long in that realm and working according to their nature for no other end than evil until they are finally annihilated — they are the lost souls of Kama-loka[3] as distinguished from the "animated corpses" devoid of souls which live and move among men. These black entities are the Dugpas,[4] the black magicians.

---

[1] **Shells** — a Kabbalistic name for the phantoms of the dead, the "spirits" of the spiritualists, figuring in physical phenomena; so named on account of their being simply illusive forms, empty of their higher principles.

[2] **Brothers of the Shadow** — a name given by the Occultists to sorcerers, and especially to the Tibetan *Dugpas*, of whom there are many in the Bhon sect of the *Red Caps* (Dugpa). The word is applied to all practitioners of black or *left-hand* magic.

[3] **Kama** (*Sanskrit*, "desire") — evil desire, lust, volition; the cleaving to existence.

Loka (*Sanskrit*, "place") — a region or circumscribed place; a world or sphere or plane. The Puranas in India speak incessantly of seven and fourteen Lokas, above, and below our Earth; of heavens and hells.

Kama-loka (*Sanskrit*, "place of desire") — the semi-material plane, to us subjective and invisible, where the disembodied "personalities," the astral forms called *Kama-rupa*, remain until they fade out from it by the complete exhaustion of the effects of the mental impulses that created these eidolons of human and animal passions and desires.

[4] **Dugpas** (*Tibetan*, "Red Caps") — a sect in Tibet. Before the advent of *Tsong-kapa* in the 14th century, the Tibetans — whose Buddhism had deteriorated and been dreadfully adulterated with the tenets of the old *Bhon* religion — were all Dugpas. From that century, however, and after the rigid laws imposed upon the ▸

W.Q.J.: Have they anything to do with the shocks, knocks, bad influences, disintegration of soft material accompanied by noises more or less distinct?

H.P.B.: Yes, they have. Not always, of course. But where they are actually seen at the time preceding such occurrence, they are the agents.

W.Q.J.: Then I am to suppose that if such takes place with me I am the attracting person, the unfortunate channel through which they have come?

H.P.B.: No, you are thoroughly in error there. You are not such a channel in that case. You are in fact the opposite, and the very cause for the temporary defeat of that dark entity. You have mistaken the appearance, the outer manipulation of forces, for the thing itself. If you were their channel, their agent, the cause for their coming and thus making their presence possible, there would be no noise and no explosion. They would then act in and through you for the hurt of others, silently and insidiously. They approach your sphere and attempt to make an entry. The strength of your character, of your aspiration, of your life, throws them off, and they are obliged, like rain-clouds, to discharge themselves. The stronger they are, the louder will be their retreating manifestation. For the time they are temporarily destroyed or, rather, put outside the combat, and, like a war vessel, have to retire for repairs. In their case this consists in accumulating force for a new attack, there or elsewhere.

W.Q.J.: If, then, such loud explosions, with pulverization of wall-plaster and the like, take place, and such an evil entity is seen astrally, it follows that the person near whom it all occurred — if identification due to solitude is possible — was in fact the person who, by reason of inner power and opposition to the evil entity, became the cause for its bursting or temporary defeat?

H.P.B.: Yes, that is correct. The person is not the cause for the entity's approach, nor its friend, but is the safeguard in fact for those who otherwise would be insidiously affected. Uninformed students

---

Gelugpas (yellow caps) and the general reform and purification of Buddhism (or Lamaism), the Dugpas have given themselves over more than ever to sorcery, immorality, and drunkenness. Since then, the word *Dugpas* has become a synonym of "sorcerer," "adept of black magic" and everything vile.

are likely to argue the other way, but that will be due to want of correct knowledge. I will describe to you condensedly an actual case. Sitting at rest on a seat, eyes closed, I saw approach one of those evil entities along the astral currents, and looking as a man. His hands like claws reached out to affect me; on his face was a devilish expression. Full of force he moved quickly up. But as I looked at him the confidence I felt and the protection about me acted as an intense shock to him, and he appeared to burst from within, to stagger, fall to pieces, and then disappeared. Just as the disintegration began, a loud noise was caused by the sudden discharge of astral electricity, causing reactions that immediately transmitted themselves into the objects in the room, until, reaching the limit of tension, they created a noise. This is just the phenomenon of thunder, which accompanies discharges in the clouds and is followed by equilibrium.

W.Q.J.: Can I carry this explanation into every objective phenomenon, say, then, of spiritualistic rappings?

H.P.B.: No, not to every case. It holds with many, but specially relates to the conscious entities I was speaking of. Very often the small taps and raps one hears are produced under the law referred to, but without the presence of such an entity. These are the final dissipations of collected energy. That does not always argue a present extraneous and conscious entity. But in so far as these taps are the conclusion of an operation, that is, the thunder from one astral cloud to another, they are dissipations of accumulated force. With this distinction in mind you should not be confused.

W.Q.J.: Have not colours a good deal to do with this matter?

H.P.B.: Yes; but just now we will not go into the question of colour except to say that the evil entities referred to often assume a garb of good colour, but are not able to hide the darkness that belongs to their nature.

"FORMS" OF ELEMENTALS

W.Q.J.: What principal idea would it be well for me to dwell upon in my studies on the subject of elementals?

H.P.B.: You ought to clearly fix in your mind and fully comprehend a few facts and the laws relating to them. As the elemental world is wholly different from the one visible to you, the laws governing them and their actions cannot as yet be completely defined in terms now used either by scientific or metaphysical[1] schools. For that reason, only a partial description is possible. Some of those facts I will give you, it being well understood that I am not including all classes of elemental beings in my remarks.

First, then, Elementals have no form.

W.Q.J.: You mean, I suppose, that they have no limited form or body as ours, having a surface upon which sensation appears to be located.

H.P.B.: Not only so, but also that they have not even a shadowy, vague, astral form such as is commonly ascribed to ghosts. They have no distinct personal form in which to reveal themselves.

W.Q.J.: How am I to understand that, in view of the instances given by Bulwer-Lytton and others of appearances of elementals in certain forms?

H.P.B.: The shape given to or assumed by any elemental is always subjective in its origin. It is produced by the person who sees, and who, in order to be more sensible of the elemental's presence, has unconsciously given it a form. Or it may be due to a collective impression on many individuals, resulting in the assumption of a definite shape which is the result of the combined impressions.

W.Q.J.: Is this how we may accept as true the story of Luther's[2] seeing the devil?

H.P.B.: Yes. Luther from his youth had imagined a personal devil, the head of the fraternity of wicked ones, who had a certain specific form. This instantly clothed the elementals that Luther evoked, either through intense enthusiasm or from disease, with the old image reared and solidified in his mind; and he called it the Devil.

W.Q.J.: That reminds me of a friend who told me that in his youth he saw the conventional devil walk out of the fire place and pass across

---

[1] **Metaphysics** (*Greek*, "beyond the things of the external material world") — the term to designate that science which treats of the real and permanent being, as contrasted with the unreal, illusionary or *phenomenal* being. It is to forget the spirit and hold to the dead letter, to translate it beyond nature or *supernatural*, as it is rather beyond the natural, visible, or concrete.

[2] **Martin Luther** (1483–1546) — a German priest and theologian, who was one of the initiators of the Protestant Reformation.

the room, and that ever since he believed the devil had an objective existence.

H.P.B.: In the same way also you can understand the extraordinary occurrences at Salem[1] in the United States, when hysterical and mediumistic[2] women and children saw the devil and also various imps of different shapes. Some of these gave the victims information. They were all elementals, and took their illusionary forms from the imaginations and memory of the poor people who were afflicted.

W.Q.J.: But there are cases where a certain form always appears. Such as a small, curiously-dressed woman who had never existed in the imagination of those seeing her; and other regularly recurring appearances. How were those produced, since the persons never had such a picture before them?

H.P.B.: These pictures are found in the aura[3] of the person, and are due to pre-natal impressions. Each child emerges into life the possessor of pictures floating about and clinging to it, derived from the mother; and thus you can go back an enormous distance in time for these pictures, all through the long line of your descent. It is a part of the action of the same law which causes effects upon a child's body through influences acting on the mother during gestation.[4]

W.Q.J.: In order, then, to know the cause of any such appearance, one must be able to look back, not only into the person's present life, but also into the ancestor's past?

---

[1] **Salem** — a city in Massachusetts, notorious for witch trials in the late 17th century.

[2] **Mediumship** — an abnormal psycho-physiological state which leads a person to take the fancies of his imagination, his hallucinations, real or artificial, for realities. No entirely healthy person on the physiological and psychic planes can ever be a medium. That which mediums see, hear, and sense is "real," but *untrue*; it is either gathered from the astral plane, so deceptive in its vibrations and suggestions, or from pure hallucinations, which have no actual existence but for him who perceives them.

[3] **Aura** (*Greek*, "breeze") — a subtle invisible essence or fluid that emanates from human and animal bodies and even things. It is a psychic effluvium, partaking of both the mind and the body, as it is the electro-vital — and at the same time an electro-mental — aura; called in Theosophy the akashic or magnetic aura.

[4] See H. P. Blavatsky, *Isis Unveiled*, vol. 1 (New York: J. W. Bouton, 1877), pp. 390–401.

H.P.B.: Precisely. And for that reason an occultist is not hasty in giving his opinion on these particular facts. He can only state the general law, for a life might be wasted in needless investigation of an unimportant past. You can see that there would be no justification for going over a whole lifetime's small affairs in order to tell a person at what time or juncture an image was projected before his mind. Thousands of such impressions are made every year. That they are not *developed into memory* does not prove their non-existence. Like the unseen picture upon the photographer's sensitive plate, they lie awaiting the hour of development.

W.Q.J.: In what way should I figure to myself the essence of an elemental and its real mode of existence?

H.P.B.: You should think of them as *centres of energy* only, that act always in accordance with the laws of the plane of nature to which they belong.

W.Q.J.: Is it not just as if we were to say that gunpowder is an elemental and will invariably explode when lighted? That is, that the elementals know no rules of either wrong or right, but surely act when the incitement to their natural action is present? They are thus, I suppose, said to be implacable.

H.P.B.: Yes; they are like the lightning which flashes or destroys as the varying circumstances compel. It has no regard for man, or love, or beauty, or goodness, but may as quickly kill the innocent, or burn the property of the good as of the wicked man.

W.Q.J.: What next?

H.P.B.: That the elementals live in and through all objects, as well as beyond the earth's atmosphere.

W.Q.J.: Do you mean that a certain class of elementals, for instance, exist in this mountain, and float unobstructed through men, earth, rocks, and trees?

H.P.B.: Yes, and not only that, but at the same time, penetrating that class of elementals, there may be another class which float not only through rocks, trees, and men, but also through the first of the classes referred to.

W.Q.J.: Do they perceive these objects obstructive for us, through which they thus float?

H.P.B.: No, generally they do not. In exceptional cases they do, and even then never with the same sort of cognition that we have. For them the objects have no existence. A large block of stone or iron offers for them no limits or density. It may, however, make an impression on them by way of change of colour or sound, but not by way of density or obstruction.

W.Q.J.: Is it not something like this, that a current of electricity passes through a hard piece of copper wire, while it will not pass through an unresisting space of air?

H.P.B.: That serves to show that the thing which is dense to one form of energy may be open to another. Continuing your illustration, we see that man can pass through air but is stopped by metal. So that "hardness" for us is not "hardness" for electricity. Similarly, that which may stop an elemental is not a body that we call hard, but something which for us is intangible and invisible, but presents to them an adamantine front.

W.Q.J.: I thank you for your instruction.

H.P.B.: Strive to deserve further enlightenment!

ELEMENTALS AND ELEMENTARIES

W.Q.J.: If I understand you, an elemental is a centre of force, without intelligence, without moral character or tendencies, but capable of being directed in its movements by human thoughts, which may, consciously or not, give it any form, and to a certain extent intelligence; in its simplest form it is visible as a disturbance in a transparent medium, such as would be produced by "a glass fish, so transparent as to be invisible, swimming through the air of the room," and leaving behind him a shimmer, such as hot air makes when rising from a stove. Also, elementals, attracted and vitalized by certain thoughts, may effect a lodgement in the human system (of which they then share the government with the ego), and are very hard to get out.

H.P.B.: Correct, in general, except as to their "effecting a lodgement." Some classes of elementals, however, have an intelligence of their own and a character, but they are far beyond our comprehension and ought perhaps to have some other name.

That class which has most to do with us answers the above description. They are centres of force or energy which are acted on by us while thinking and in other bodily motions. We also act on them and give them form by a species of thought which we have no register of. As, one person might shape an elemental so as to seem like an insect, and not be able to tell whether he had thought of such a thing or not. For there is a vast unknown country in each human being which he does not himself understand until he has tried, and then only after many initiations.

That "elementals ... may effect a lodgement in the human system, of which they then share the government, and are very hard to get out" is, as a whole, incorrect. It is only in certain cases that any one or more elementals are attracted to and "find lodgement in the human system." In such cases special rules apply. We are not considering such cases. The elemental world interpenetrates this, and is therefore eternally present in the human system.

As it (the elemental world) is automatic and like a photographic plate, all atoms continually arriving at and departing from the "human system" are constantly assuming the impression conveyed by the acts and thoughts of that person, and therefore, if he sets up a strong current of thought, he attracts elementals in greater numbers, and they all take on one prevailing tendency or colour, so that all new arrivals find a homogeneous colour or image which they instantly assume. On the other hand, a man who has many diversities of thought and meditation is not homogeneous, but, so to say, parti-coloured, and so the elementals may lodge in that part which is different from the rest and go away in like condition. In the first case it is one mass of elementals similarly vibrating or electrified and coloured, and in that sense may be called one elemental, in just the same way that we know one man as Jones, although for years he has been giving off and taking on new atoms of gross matter.

W.Q.J.: If they are attracted and repelled by thoughts, do they move with the velocity of thought, say from here to the planet Neptune?

H.P.B.: They move with the velocity of thought. In their world there is no space or time as we understand those terms. If Neptune be within the astral sphere of this world, then they go there with that velocity, otherwise not; but that "if" need not be solved now.

W.Q.J.: What determines their movements besides thought — *e.g.*, when they are floating about the room?

H.P.B.: Those other classes of thoughts above referred to; certain exhalations of beings; different rates and ratios of vibration among beings; different changes of magnetism caused by present causes or by the moon and the year; different polarities; changes of sound; changes of influences from other minds at a distance.

W.Q.J.: When so floating, can they be seen by anyone, or only by those persons who are clairvoyant?

H.P.B.: Clairvoyance[1] is a poor word. They can be seen by partly clairvoyant people. By all those who can see thus; by more people, perhaps, than are aware of the fact.

W.Q.J.: Can they be photographed, as the rising air from the hot stove can?

H.P.B.: Not to my knowledge yet. It is not impossible, however.

W.Q.J.: Are they the lights, seen floating about a dark séance[2] room by clairvoyant people?

H.P.B.: In the majority of cases those lights are produced by them.

W.Q.J.: Exactly what is their relation to light, that makes it necessary to hold séances in the dark?

H.P.B.: It is not *their* relation to light that makes darkness necessary, but the fact that light causes constant agitation and alteration in the magnetism of the room. All these things can be done just as well in the light of day.

If I should be able to make clear to you "exactly what is their relation to light," then you would know what has long been kept secret, the key to the elemental world. This is kept guarded because it is a dangerous secret. No matter how virtuous you are, you could not — once you knew the secret — prevent the knowledge getting out into the minds of others who would not hesitate to use it for bad purposes.

---

[1] **Clairvoyance** — the faculty of seeing with the inner eye or spiritual sight. As now used, it is a loose and flippant term, embracing under its meaning a happy guess due to natural shrewdness or intuition, as well as that faculty which was so remarkably exercised by Jacob Boehme and Emanuel Swedenborg. Real clairvoyance means the faculty of seeing through the densest matter (the latter disappearing at the will and before the spiritual eye of the Seer), and irrespective of time (past, present and future) or distance.

[2] **Séance** — a sitting with a medium for phenomena, the materialization of "spirits" and other manifestations.

W.Q.J.: I have noticed that attention often interferes with certain phenomena; thus a pencil will not write when watched, but writes at once when covered; or a mental question cannot be answered till the mind has left it and gone to something else. Why is this?

H.P.B.: This kind of attention creates confusion. In these things we use desire, will, and knowledge. The desire is present, but knowledge is absent. When the desire is well formed and attention withdrawn, the thing is often done; but when our attention is continued we only interrupt, because we possess only half attention. In order to use attention, it must be of that sort which can hold itself to the point of a needle for an indefinite period of time.

W.Q.J.: I have been told that but few people can go to a séance without danger to themselves, either of some spiritual or astral contamination, or of having their vitality depleted for the benefit of the spooks,[3] who suck the vital force out of the circle through the medium, as if the former were a glass of lemonade and the latter a straw. How is this?

H.P.B.: Quite generally this happens. It is called Bhut[4] worship by the Hindus.

W.Q.J.: Why are visitors at a séance often extremely and unaccountably tired next day?

H.P.B.: Among other reasons, because mediums absorb the vitality for the use of the "spooks," and often vile vampire elementaries[5] are present.

W.Q.J.: What are some of the dangers at séances?

---

[3] **Spook** — a ghost, a hobgoblin. Used in the various apparitions in the séance rooms of the spiritualists.

[4] **Bhut** (*Sanskrit*, "gone") — a ghost, phantom; the "astral monad" or body of the deceased personality.

[5] **Elementaries** — properly, the disembodied souls of the depraved; these souls, at some time prior to death, separated from themselves their divine spirits and so lost their chance for immortality. However, at the present stage of learning, it has been thought best to apply the term to the spooks or phantoms of disembodied persons, in general, to those whose temporary habitation is the Kama-loka. Éliphas Lévi and some other Kabbalists make little distinction between elementary spirits who have been men and those beings which people the elements and are the blind forces of nature. Once divorced from their higher triads and their bodies, these souls remain in their *Kama-rupic* envelopes and are irresistibly drawn to the earth amid elements congenial to their gross natures. Their stay in ▸

H.P.B.: The scenes visible — in the Astral — at séances are horrible, inasmuch as these "spirits" — Bhuts — precipitate themselves upon sitters and mediums alike; and as there is no séance without having present some or many bad elementaries — half dead human beings — there is much vampirizing going on. These things fall upon the people like a cloud or a big octopus, and disappear within them as if sucked in by a sponge. That is one reason why it is not well to attend them in general.

Elementaries are not all bad, but, in a general sense, they are not good. They are shells, no doubt of that. Well, they have much automatic and seemingly intelligent action left if they are those of strongly material people who died attached to the things of life. If of people of an opposite character, they are not so strong. Then there is a class which are really not dead, such as suicides, and sudden deaths, and highly wicked people. They are powerful. Elementals enter into all of them, and thus get a fictitious personality and intelligence wholly the property of the shell. They galvanize the shell into action, and by its means can see and hear as if beings themselves, like us. The shells are, in this case, just like a sleepwalking human body. They will through habit exhibit the advancement they got while in the flesh. Some people, you know, do not impart to their bodily molecules the habit of their minds to as great an extent as others. We thus see why the utterances of these so-called "spirits" are never ahead of the highest point of progress attained by living human beings, and why they take up the ideas elaborated day-by-day by their votaries. This séance worship is what was called in Old India the worship of the Pretas[1] and Bhuts and Pishachas[2] and Gandharvas.[3]

---

the Kama-loka varies as to its duration, but it ends invariably in disintegration, as they dissolve like a column of mist, atom by atom, into the surrounding elements.

[1] **Pretas** (*Sanskrit*) — hungry demons in popular folklore; "shells" of the avaricious and selfish man after death; "Elementaries" reborn as Pretas, in Kama-loka, according to the esoteric teachings.

[2] **Pishachas** (*Sanskrit*) — in southern Indian folklore, ghosts, demons, larvae and vampires — generally female — who haunt men. Fading remnants of human beings in Kama-loka, as shells and Elementaries.

[3] **Gandharva** (*Sanskrit*) — the celestial choristers and musicians of India. In the *Vedas*, these deities reveal the secrets of heaven and earth and esoteric science to mortals. They had charge of the sacred Soma plant and its juice, the ambrosia drunk in the temple which gives "omniscience."

I do not think any elementary capable of motive had ever any other than a bad one; the rest are nothing, they have no motive and are only the shades refused passage by Charon.[4]

W.Q.J.: What is the relation between sexual force and phenomena?

H.P.B.: It is at the bottom. This force is vital, creative, and a sort of reservoir. It may be lost by mental action as well as by physical. In fact its finer part is dissipated by mental imaginings, while physical acts only draw off the gross part, that which is the "carrier" (Upadhi)[5] for the finer.

W.Q.J.: Why do so many mediums cheat, even when they can produce real phenomena?

H.P.B.: It is the effect of the use of that which in itself is sublimated cheating, which, acting on an irresponsible mind, causes the lower form of cheat, of which the higher is any illusionary form whatever. Besides, a medium is of necessity unbalanced somewhere.

They deal with these forces for pay, and that is enough to call to them all the wickedness of time. They use the really gross sorts of matter, which causes inflammation in corresponding portions of the moral character, and hence divagations from the path of honesty. It is a great temptation. You do not know, either, what fierceness there is in those who "have paid" for a sitting and wish "for the worth of their money."

W.Q.J.: When a clairvoyant, as a man did here a year ago, tells me that, "he sees a strong band of spirits about me," and among them an old man who says he is a certain eminent character, what does he really see? Empty and senseless shells? If so, what brought them there? Or elementals which have got their form from my mind or his?

---

[4] **Charon** (*Greek*) — the hawk-headed steersman of the boat conveying the souls across the black waters that separate life from death. Charon, the Son of Erebus and Nox, is a variant of the Egyptian *Khu-en-ua*. The dead were obliged to pay an *obolus*, a small piece of money, to this grim ferryman of the Styx and Acheron (the rivers of the underworld); therefore, the ancients always placed a coin under the tongue of the deceased.

[5] **Upadhi** (*Sanskrit*, "that which places its own attributes to something that is nearby") — basis; the vehicle, carrier or bearer of something less material than itself: as the human body is the *upadhi* of its spirit, ether the *upadhi* of light, etc.; a mould; a defining or limiting substance.

H.P.B.: Shells, I think, and thoughts, and old astral pictures. If, for instance, you once saw that eminent person and conceived great respect or fear for him, so that his image was graven in your astral sphere in deeper lines than other images, it would be seen for your whole life by seers, who, if untrained — as they all are here — could not tell whether it was an image or reality; and then each sight of it is a revivification of the image.

Besides, not all would see the same thing. Fall down, for instance, and hurt your body, and that will bring up all similar events and old forgotten things before any seer's eye.

The whole astral world is a mass of illusion; people see into it, and then, through the novelty of the thing and the exclusiveness of the power, they are bewildered into thinking they actually see true things, whereas they have only removed one thin crust of dirt.

W.Q.J.: Accept my thanks for your instruction.

H.P.B.: May you reach the terrace of enlightenment.

ELEMENTALS – KARMA

W.Q.J.: Permit me to ask you again, are elementals beings?

H.P.B.: It is not easy to convey to you an idea of the constitution of elementals; strictly speaking, they are not, because the word *elementals* has been used in reference to a class of them that have no being such as mortals have. It would be better to adopt the terms used in Indian books, such as Gandharvas, Bhuts, Pishachas, Devas,[1] and so on. Many things well-known about them cannot be put into ordinary language.

W.Q.J.: Do you refer to their being able to act in the fourth dimension of space?

H.P.B.: Yes, in a measure. Take the tying in an endless cord of many knots — a thing often done at spiritist séances. That is possible to him who knows more dimensions of space than three. No three-dimensional being can do this; and as you understand "matter," it is impossible for you to conceive how such a knot can be tied or how a solid ring can be passed through the matter of another solid one. These things can be done by elementals.

W.Q.J.: Are they not all of one class?

---

[1] **Deva** (*Sanskrit*, "shining one") — a god, deity, or celestial being, whether good, bad, or indifferent. Devas inhabit the "three worlds," which are the three planes above us. In Hinduism, there are 33 groups or 330 million of them.

H.P.B.: No. There are different classes for each plane, and division of plane, of nature. Many can never be recognized by men. And those pertaining to one plane do not act in another. You must remember, too, that these "planes" of which we are speaking interpenetrate each other.

W.Q.J.: Am I to understand that a clairvoyant or clairaudient has to do with or is affected by a certain special class or classes of elementals?

H.P.B.: Yes. A clairvoyant can only see the sights properly belonging to the planes his development reaches to or has opened. And the elementals in those planes show to the clairvoyant only such pictures as belong to their plane. Other parts of the idea or thing pictured may be retained in planes not yet open to the seer. For this reason few clairvoyants know the whole truth.

W.Q.J.: Is there not some connection between the Karma of man and elementals?

H.P.B.: A very important one. The elemental world has become a strong factor in the Karma of the human race. Being unconscious, automatic, and photographic, it assumes the complexion of the human family itself. In the earlier ages, when we may postulate that man had not yet begun to make bad Karma, the elemental world was more friendly to man because it had not received unfriendly impressions. But so soon as man began to become ignorant, unfriendly to himself and the rest of creation, the elemental world began to take on exactly the same complexion and return to humanity the exact pay, so to speak, due for the actions of humanity. Or, like a donkey, which, when he is pushed against, will push against you. Or, as a human being, when anger or insult is offered, feels inclined to return the same. So the elemental world, being unconscious force, returns or reacts upon humanity exactly as humanity acted towards it, whether the actions of men were done with the knowledge of these laws or not. So in these times it has come to be that the elemental world has the complexion and action which is the exact result of all the actions and thoughts and desires of men from the earliest times. And, being unconscious and only acting according to the natural laws of its being, the elemental world is a powerful factor in the workings of Karma. And so long as mankind does not cultivate brotherly feeling and charity towards the whole of creation, just so long will the elementals be without the impulse to act for our benefit. But so soon and wherever man or men begin to cultivate brotherly feeling and love for the whole of creation, there and then the elementals begin to take on the new condition.

W.Q.J.: How then about the doing of phenomena by Adepts?

H.P.B.: The production of phenomena is not possible without either the aid or disturbance of elementals. Each phenomenon entails the expenditure of great force, and also brings on a correspondingly great disturbance in the elemental world, which disturbance is beyond the limit natural to ordinary human life. It then follows that, as soon as the phenomenon is completed, the disturbance occasioned begins to be compensated for. The elementals are in greatly excited motion, and precipitate themselves in various directions. They are not able to affect those who are protected. But they are able, or rather it is possible for them, to enter into the sphere of unprotected persons, and especially those persons who are engaged in the study of occultism. And then they become agents in concentrating the karma of those persons, producing troubles and disasters often, or other difficulties which otherwise might have been so spread over a period of time as to be not counted more than the ordinary vicissitudes of life. This will go to explain the meaning of the statement that an Adept will not do a phenomenon unless he sees the desire in the mind of another lower or higher Adept or student; for then there is a sympathetic relation established, and also a tacit acceptance of the consequences which may ensue. It will also help to understand the peculiar reluctance often of some persons, who can perform phenomena, to produce them in cases where we may think their production would be beneficial; and also why they are never done in order to compass worldly ends, as is natural for worldly people to suppose might be done — such as procuring money, transferring objects, influencing minds, and so on.

W.Q.J.: Accept my thanks for your instruction.

H.P.B.: May you reach the terrace of enlightenment!

ELEMENTALS – HOW THEY ACT

W.Q.J.: Is there any reason why you do not give me a more detailed explanation of the constitution of elementals and the modes by which they work?

H.P.B.: Yes. There are many reasons. Among others is your inability, shared by most of the people of the present day, to comprehend a description of things that pertain to a world with which you are not familiar and for which you do not yet possess terms of expression. Were I to put forth these descriptions, the greater part would seem vague and incomprehensible on one hand, while on the other many of them would mislead you because of the interpretation put on them by yourself. Another reason is that, if the constitution, field of action, and method of action of elementals were given out, there are some minds of a very inquiring and peculiar bent who soon could find out how to come into communication with these extraordinary beings, with results disadvantageous to the community as well as the individuals.

W.Q.J.: Why so? Is it not well to increase the sum of human knowledge, even respecting most recondite parts of nature; or can it be that the elementals are bad?

H.P.B.: It is wise to increase the knowledge of nature's laws, but always with proper limitations. All things will become known some day. Nothing can be kept back when men have reached the point where they can understand. But at this time it would not be wise to give them, for the asking, certain knowledge that would not be good for them. That knowledge relates to elementals, and it can for the present be kept back from the scientists of today. So long as it can be retained from them, it will be, until they and their followers are of a different stamp.

As to the moral character of elementals, they have none; they are colourless in themselves — except some classes — and merely assume the tint, so to speak, of the person using them.

W.Q.J.: Will our scientific men one day, then, be able to use these beings, and, if so, what will be the manner of it? Will their use be confined to only the good men of the earth?

H.P.B.: The hour is approaching when all this will be done. But the scientists of today are not the men to get this knowledge. They are only pigmy forerunners who sow seed and delve blindly in no thoroughfares. They are too small to be able to grasp these mighty powers, but they are not wise enough to see that their methods will eventually lead to black magic in centuries to come when they shall be forgotten.

When elemental forces are used similarly as we now see electricity and other natural energies adapted to various purposes, there will be "war in heaven." Good men will not alone possess the ability to use them. Indeed, the sort of man you now call "good" will not be the most able. The wicked will, however, pay liberally for the power of those who can wield such forces, and at last the Supreme Masters, who now guard this knowledge from children, will have to come forth. Then will ensue a dreadful war, in which, as has ever happened, the Masters will succeed and the evil doers be destroyed by the very engines, principalities, and powers prostituted to their own purposes during years of intense selfish living. But why dilate on this? In these days it is only a prophecy.

W.Q.J.: Could you give me some hints as to how the secrets of the elemental plane are preserved and prevented from being known? Do these guardians of whom you speak occupy themselves in checking elementals, or how? Do they see much danger of divulgement likely in those instances where elemental action is patent to the observer?

H.P.B.: As to whether they check elementals or not need not be inquired into, because, while that may be probable, it does not appear very necessary where men are unsuspicious of the agency causing the phenomena. It is much easier to throw a cloud over the investigator's mind and lead him off to other results of often material advantage to himself and men, while at the same time acting as a complete preventive or switch which turns his energies and application into different departments.

It might be illustrated thus: Suppose that a number of trained occultists are set apart to watch the various sections of the world where the mental energies are in fervid operation. It is quite easy for them to see in a moment any mind that is about reaching a clue into the elemental world; and, besides, imagine that trained elementals themselves constantly carry information of such events. Then, by superior knowledge and command over this peculiar world, influences presenting various pictures are sent out to that inquiring mind. In one case it may be a new moral reform, in another a great invention is revealed, and such is the effect that the man's whole time and mind are taken up by this new thing which he fondly imagines is his own. Or, again, it would be easy to turn his thoughts into a certain rut leading far from the dangerous clue. In fact, the methods are endless.

W.Q.J.: Would it be wise to put into the hands of truly good, conscientious men who now use aright what gifts they have, knowledge of and control over elementals, to be used on the side of right?

H.P.B.: The Masters are the judges of what good men are to have this power and control. You must not forget that you cannot be sure of the character at bottom of those whom you call "truly good and conscientious men." Place them in the fire of the tremendous temptation which such power and control would furnish, and most of them would fail. But the Masters already know the characters of all who in any way approach to a knowledge of these forces, and They always judge whether such a man is to be aided or prevented. They are not working to make these laws and forces known, but to establish right doctrine, speech, and action, so that the characters and motives of men shall undergo such radical changes as to fit them for wielding power in the elemental world. And that power is not now lying idle, as you infer, but is being always used by those who will never fail to rightly use it.

W.Q.J.: Is there any illustration at hand showing what the people of the present day would do with these extraordinary energies?

H.P.B.: A cursory glance at men in these western worlds engaged in the mad rush after money, many of them willing to do anything to get it, and at the strain, almost to warfare, existing between labourers and users of labour, must show you that, were either class in possession of power over the elemental world, they would direct it to the furtherance of the aims now before them. Then look at Spiritualism.[1] It is recorded in the Lodge — photographed, you may say, by the doers of the acts themselves — that an enormous number of persons daily seek the aid of mediums and their "spooks" merely on questions of business. Whether to buy stocks, or engage in mining for gold and silver, to deal in lotteries, or to make new mercantile contracts. Here on one side is a picture of a coterie of men who obtained at a low

---

[1] **Spiritualism** — the belief that the spirits of the dead return to earth to commune with the living, whether through the mediumistic powers of oneself or a so-called medium. Believers in such communications are simply dishonouring the dead and performing constant sacrilege. It was well called *Necromancy* in days of old.

figure some mining property on the advice of elemental spirits with fictitious names masquerading behind mediums; these mines were then to be put upon the public at a high profit, inasmuch as the "spirits" promised metal. Unhappily for the investors, it failed. But such a record is repeated in many cases.

Then here is another where in a great American city — the Karma being favourable — a certain man speculated in stocks upon similar advice, succeeded, and, after giving the medium liberal pay, retired to what is called enjoyment of life. Neither party devoted either himself or the money to the benefiting of humanity.

There is no question of honour involved, nor any as to whether money ought or ought not to be made. It is solely one as to the propriety, expediency, and results of giving suddenly into the hands of a community unprepared and without an altruistic aim, such abnormal power. Take hidden treasure, for instance. There is much of it in hidden places, and many men wish to get it. For what purpose? For the sake of ministering to their luxurious wants and leaving it to their equally unworthy descendants. Could they know the mantram[1] controlling the elementals that guard such treasure, they would use it at once, motive or no motive, the sole object being the money in the case.

W.Q.J.: Do some sorts of elementals have guard over hidden treasure?

H.P.B.: Yes, in every instance, whether never found or soon discovered. The causes for the hiding and the thoughts of the hider or loser have much to do with the permanent concealment or subsequent finding.

W.Q.J.: What happens when a large sum of money, say, such as Captain Kidd's[2] mythical treasure, is concealed, or when a quantity of coin is lost?

H.P.B.: Elementals gather about it. They have many and curious modes of causing further concealment. They even influence animals to that end. This class of elementals seldom, if ever, report at your spiritualistic séances. As time goes on the forces of air and water still

---

[1] **Mantram** or **mantra** (*Sanskrit*, "instrument of thought") — a sacred or mystical phrase, word, verse, or sound that has spiritual power and is used in spiritual practices, such as meditation or prayer.

[2] **William Kidd** (c.1654–1701) — a Scottish privateer, who was believed to have left buried treasure.

further aid them, and sometimes they are able even to prevent the hider from recovering it. Thus in course of years, even when they may have altogether lost their hold on it, the whole thing becomes shrouded in mist, and it is impossible to find anything.

W.Q.J.: This in part explains why so many failures are recorded in the search for hidden treasure. But how about the Masters; are they prevented thus by these weird guardians?

H.P.B.: They are not. The vast quantities of gold hidden in the earth and under the sea are at their disposal always. They can, when necessary for their purposes, obtain such sums of money on whom no living being or descendants of any have the slightest claim, as would appal the senses of your greatest money getter. They have but to command the very elementals controlling it, and They have it. This is the basis for the story of Aladdin's[3] wonderful lamp, more true than you believe.

W.Q.J.: Of what use then is it to try, like the alchemists,[4] to make gold? With the immense amount of buried treasure thus easily found

---

[3] **Aladdin** — a character in one of the best-known Middle-Eastern folktales in *One Thousand and One Nights*, also known as the *Arabian Nights*. He found an oil lamp containing a wish-granting jinn.

[4] **Alchemy** (*Arabic*, "art of transmutation") — an ancient science that deals with the finer forces of nature and the various conditions in which they are found to operate. Seeking under the veil of language, more or less artificial, to convey to the uninitiated so much of the *mysterium magnum* (great mystery) as is safe in the hands of a selfish world, the alchemist postulates, as his first principle, the existence of a certain Universal Solvent by which all composite bodies are resolved into the homogeneous substance from which they are evolved, which substance he calls pure gold, or *summa materia* (supreme matter). This solvent, also called *menstruum universal* (universal solvent), possesses the power of removing all the seeds of disease from the human body, of renewing youth and of prolonging life. Such is the *lapis philosophorum* (philosopher's stone). Alchemy is studied under three distinct aspects, which admit many different interpretations: the Cosmic, Human, and Terrestrial. These three methods were typified under the three alchemical properties — sulphur, mercury, and salt. Different writers have stated that there are three, seven, ten, and twelve processes, respectively; but they are all agreed that there is but one objective in alchemy, which is to transmute gross metals into pure gold. What that gold, however, really is, very few people understand correctly. No doubt there is such a thing in nature as transmutation of the baser metals into the nobler ones, or gold. But this is only one aspect of alchemy, the terrestrial or purely material, for we sense logically the same process taking place in the bowels of the earth. Yet, besides and ▸

when you control its guardian, it would seem a waste of time and money to learn transmutation of metals.

H.P.B.: The transmutation spoken of by the real alchemists was the alteration of the base alloy in man's nature. At the same time, actual transmutation of lead into gold is possible. And many followers of the alchemists, as well as of the pure-souled Jacob Boehme,[1] eagerly sought to accomplish the material transmuting, being led away by the glitter of wealth. But an Adept has no need for transmutation, as I have shown you. The stories told of various men who are said to have produced gold from base metals for different kings in Europe are

---

beyond this interpretation, there is, in alchemy, a symbolical meaning, purely psychic and spiritual. While the Kabbalist-Alchemist seeks for the realization of the former, the Occultist-Alchemist, spurning the gold of the mines, gives all his attention and directs his efforts only towards the transmutation of the baser *quaternary* into the divine upper *trinity* of man which, when finally blended, are one. The spiritual, mental, psychic, and physical planes of human existence are, in alchemy, compared to the four elements, fire, air, water and earth, and are each capable of a threefold constitution, *i.e.*, fixed, mutable and volatile. Modern chemistry owes its best fundamental discoveries to alchemy; but, regardless of the undeniable truism of the latter that there is but one element in the universe, chemistry has placed metals in the class of elements and is only now beginning to find out its gross mistake.

[1] **Jacob Boehme** (1575–1624) — a great mystic philosopher, one of the most prominent Theosophists of the medieval ages. In his boyhood, he was a common shepherd, and after learning to read and write in a village school, he became an apprentice to a poor shoemaker at Görlitz. He was a natural clairvoyant of most wonderful powers. With no education or acquaintance with science, he wrote works which are now proved to be full of scientific truths; but then, as he says himself, what he wrote upon, he "saw it as in a great Deep in the Eternal." He had "a thorough view of the universe, as in a chaos," which yet "opened itself in him, from time to time, as in a young plant." He was a thorough born Mystic, and evidently of a constitution which is most rare — one of those fine natures whose material envelope impedes in no way the direct, even if only occasional, intercommunion between the intellectual and the spiritual Ego. It is this Ego which Jacob Boehme, like so many other untrained mystics, mistook for God. "Man must acknowledge," he writes, "that his knowledge is not his own, but from God, who manifests the Ideas of Wisdom to the Soul of Man, in what measure he pleases." Had this great Theosophist mastered Eastern Occultism, he might have expressed it otherwise. He would have known then that the "god" who spoke through his poor uncultured and untrained brain was his own divine Ego, the omniscient Deity within himself, and that what that Deity gave out was not in "what measure pleased," but in the measure of the capacities of the mortal and temporary dwelling *It* informed.

wrong explanations. Here and there Adepts have appeared, assuming different names, and in certain emergencies they supplied or used large sums of money. But instead of its being the product of alchemical art, it was simply ancient treasure brought to them by elementals in their service and that of the Lodge. Raymond Lully[2] or Robert Fludd[3] might have been of that sort, but I forbear to say, since I cannot claim acquaintance with those men.

W.Q.J.: I thank you for your instruction.

H.P.B.: May you reach the terrace of enlightenment!

MANTRAMS

W.Q.J.: You spoke of mantrams by which we could control elementals on guard over hidden treasure. What is a mantram?

H.P.B.: A mantram is a collection of words which, when sounded in speech, induce certain vibrations not only in the air, but also in the finer ether,[4] thereby producing certain effects.

W.Q.J.: Are the words taken at haphazard?

H.P.B.: Only by those who, knowing nothing of mantrams, yet use them.

W.Q.J.: May they, then, be used according to rule and also irregularly? Can it be possible that people who know absolutely nothing of their existence or field of operations should at the same time make use of them? Or is it something like digestion, of which so many people know nothing whatever, while they in fact are dependent upon

---

[2] **Raymond Lully** (c.1232–1315/1316) — an alchemist and philosopher, born on the island of Majorca. It is claimed for him that, in a moment of need, he made for King Edward III of England several million gold "rose nobles," and thus helped him to carry on war victoriously. He founded several colleges for the study of Oriental languages.

[3] **Robert Fludd** (1574–1637) — an English physician, astrologer, mathematician and cosmologist.

[4] **Ether** — a term often confused with Akasha and the Astral Light. It is neither, in the sense in which ether is described by physical science. Ether is a material agent, though hitherto undetected by any physical apparatus; whereas Akasha is a distinctly spiritual agent, identical, in one sense, with the *Anima Mundi*. The Astral Light is only the seventh and highest principle of the terrestrial atmosphere, as undetectable as Akasha and real Ether, because it is something quite on another plane. The seventh principle of the earth's atmosphere, as said, the Astral Light, is only the second on the Cosmic scale.

its proper use for their existence? I crave your indulgence because I know nothing of the subject.

H.P.B.: The "common people" in almost every country make use of them continually, but even in that case the principle at the bottom is the same as in the other. In a new country where folklore has not yet had time to spring up, the people do not have as many as in such a land as India or in long settled parts of Europe. The aborigines, however, in any country will be possessed of them.

W.Q.J.: You do not now infer that they are used by Europeans for the controlling of elementals?

H.P.B.: No. I refer to their effect in ordinary intercourse between human beings. And yet there are many men in Europe, as well as in Asia, who can thus control animals, but those are nearly always special cases. There are men in Germany, Austria, Italy, and Ireland who can bring about extraordinary effects on horses, cattle, and the like, by peculiar sounds uttered in a certain way. In those instances the sound used is a mantram of only one member, and will act only on the particular animal that the user knows it can rule.

W.Q.J.: Do these men know the rules governing the matter? Are they able to convey it to another?

H.P.B.: Generally not. It is a gift self-found or inherited, and they only know that it can be done by them, just as a mesmerizer[1] knows he can do a certain thing with a wave of his hand, but is totally ignorant of the principle. They are as ignorant of the base of this strange effect as your modern physiologists are of the function and cause of such a common thing as yawning.

W.Q.J.: Under what head should we put this unconscious exercise of power?

H.P.B.: Under the head of natural magic, that materialistic science can never crush out. It is a touch with nature and her laws always

---

[1] **Mesmerism** — the term comes from Franz Mesmer (1734–1815), a German physician, who rediscovered the magnetic force in man and its practical application towards the year 1775, at Vienna. This magnetic fluid was called *animal magnetism*, and since then, *Mesmerism*. It is a vital current that one person, a mesmerizer, may transfer to another, and through which he induces an abnormal state of the nervous system that permits him to have a direct influence upon the mind and will of the *subject* or mesmerized person.

preserved by the masses, who, while they form the majority of the population, are yet ignored by the "cultured classes." And so it will be discovered by you that it is not in London or Paris or New York drawing-rooms that you will find mantrams, whether regular or irregular, used by the people. "Society," too cultured to be natural, has adopted methods of speech intended to conceal and to deceive, so that natural mantrams cannot be studied within its borders.

Single, natural mantrams are such words as "wife." When it is spoken it brings up in the mind all that is implied by the word. And if in another language, the word would be that corresponding to the same basic idea. And so with expressions of greater length, such as many slang sentences; thus, "I want to see the colour of his money." There are also sentences applicable to certain individuals, the use of which involves a knowledge of the character of those to whom we speak. When these are used, a peculiar and lasting vibration is set up in the mind of the person affected, leading to a realization in action of the idea involved, or to a total change of life due to the appositeness of the subjects brought up and to the peculiar mental antithesis induced in the hearer. As soon as the effect begins to appear the mantram may be forgotten, since the *law of habit* then has sway in the brain.

Again, bodies of men are acted on by expressions having the mantramic quality; this is observed in great social or other disturbances. The reason is the same as before. A dominant idea is aroused that touches upon a want of the people or on an abuse which oppresses them, and the change and interchange in their brains between the idea and the form of words go on until the result is accomplished. To the occultist of powerful sight this is seen to be a "ringing" of the words coupled with the whole chain of feelings, interests, aspirations, and so forth, that grows faster and deeper as the time for the relief or change draws near. And the greater number of persons affected by the idea involved, the larger, deeper, and wider the result. A mild illustration may be found in Lord Beaconsfield of England.[2] He knew about mantrams, and continually invented phrases of that quality. "Peace with honour" was one; "a scientific frontier" was another; and his last, intended to have a wider reach, but which death prevented

---

[2] **Benjamin Disraeli** (1804–1881) — a British statesman and writer who twice served as Prime Minister of the United Kingdom; the 1st Earl of Beaconsfield.

his supplementing, was "Empress of India." King Henry of England[1] also tried it without himself knowing why, when he added to his titles, "Defender of the Faith." With these hints numerous illustrations will occur to you.

W.Q.J.: These mantrams have only to do with human beings as between each other. They do not affect elementals, as I judge from what you say. And they are not dependent upon the *sound* so much as upon words bringing up ideas. Am I right in this; and is it the case that there is a field in which certain vocalizations produce effects in the *Akasha*[2] by means of which men, animals, and elementals alike can be influenced, without regard to their knowledge of any known language?

H.P.B.: You are right. We have only spoken of natural, unconsciously-used mantrams. The scientific mantrams belong to the class you last referred to. It is to be doubted whether they can be found in modern Western languages — especially among English speaking people who are continually changing and adding to their spoken words to such an extent that the English of today could hardly be understood by Chaucer's[3] predecessors. It is in the ancient Sanskrit and the language which preceded it that mantrams are hidden. The laws governing their use are also to be found in those languages, and not in any modern philological store.

W.Q.J.: Suppose, though, that one acquires a knowledge of ancient and correct mantrams, could he affect a person speaking English, and by the use of English words?

H.P.B.: He could; and all Adepts have the power to translate a strictly regular mantram into any form of language, so that a single sentence thus uttered by them will have an immense effect on the person addressed, whether it be by letter or word of mouth.

---

[1] **Henry VIII** (1491–1547) — the King of England from 1509 to 1547.

[2] **Akasha** (*Sanskrit,* "sky") — the subtle, supersensuous spiritual essence which pervades all space; the primordial substance erroneously identified as Ether. But it is to Ether what Spirit is to Matter. It is, in fact, the Universal Space in which lies inherent the eternal Ideation of the Universe in its ever-changing aspects on the planes of matter and objectivity, and from which radiates the *First Logos*, or expressed thought.

[3] **Geoffrey Chaucer** (c.1340s–1400) — an English poet and writer, considered the "father of English literature."

W.Q.J.: Is there no way in which we might, as it were, imitate those Adepts in this?

H.P.B.: Yes, you should study simple forms of mantramic quality, for the purpose of thus reaching the hidden mind of all the people who need spiritual help. You will find now and then some expression that has resounded in the brain, at last producing such a result that he who heard it turns his mind to spiritual things.

W.Q.J.: I thank you for your instruction.

H.P.B.: May the Brahmamantram[4] guide you to the everlasting truth — *Om.*[5]

LAWS GOVERNING ELEMENTALS

W.Q.J.: A materialist[6] stated to me as his opinion that all that is said about mantrams is mere sentimental theorizing, and while it may be true that certain words affect people, the sole reason is that they embody ideas distasteful or pleasant to the hearers, but that the mere sounds, as such, have no effect whatever, and as to either words or sounds affecting animals he denied it altogether. Of course he would

---

[4] **Brahmamantram** (*Sanskrit*) — the mantram of Brahma.

Brahma (*Sanskrit*) — there are Brahma, the neuter, and Brahma, the male creator of the Hindu Pantheon. The former *Brahma*, or *Brahman*, is the impersonal, supreme and uncognizable Principle of the Universe, from the essence of which all emanates and into which all returns; it is incorporeal, immaterial, unborn, eternal, beginningless and endless. It is all-pervading, animating the highest god as well as the smallest mineral atom. The latter Brahma, by contrast, is the male Creator, who exists periodically in his manifestation only and then again disappears.

[5] **Aum** or **Om** (*Sanskrit*) — the sacred syllable; the most solemn of all words in India; the triple-lettered unit; hence the trinity in One. It is "an invocation, a benediction, an affirmation and a promise, and it is so sacred as to be, indeed, *the word at low breath* of occult, *primitive* masonry. No one must be near when the syllable is pronounced for a purpose. This word is usually placed at the beginning of sacred Scriptures and is prefixed to prayers. It is a compound of three letters A, U and M, which, in the popular belief, are typical of the three Vedas, also of three gods — A (Agni), V (Varuna) and M (Maruts) or Fire, Water and Air. In esoteric philosophy, these are the three sacred fires, or the "triple fire" in the Universe and Man, besides many other things.

[6] **Materialist** — not necessarily only one who believes in neither God nor soul, nor the survival of the latter, but also any person who materializes the purely spiritual; such as belief in an anthropomorphic deity, in a soul capable of burning in hell fire, and a hell and paradise as localities instead of states of consciousness.

not take elementals into account at all, as their existence is impossible for him.

H.P.B.: This position is quite natural in these days. There has been so much materialization of thought, and the real scientific attitude of leading minds in different branches of investigation has been so greatly misunderstood by those who think they follow the example of the scientific men, that most people in the West are afraid to admit anything beyond what may be apprehended by the five senses. The man you speak of is one of that always numerous class who adopt as fixed and unalterable general laws laid down from time to time by well-known *savants*, forgetting that the latter constantly change and advance from point to point.

W.Q.J.: Do you think, then, that the scientific world will one day admit much that is known to Occultists?

H.P.B.: Yes, it will. The genuine Scientist is always in that attitude which permits him to admit things proven. He may seem to you often to be obstinate and blind, but in fact he is proceeding slowly to the truth — too slowly, perhaps, for you, yet not in the position of knowing all. It is the veneered scientist who swears by the published results of the work of leading men as being the last word, while, at the very moment he is doing so, his authority may have made notes or prepared new theories tending to greatly broaden and advance the last utterance. It is only when the dogmatism of a priest backed up by law declares that a discovery is opposed to the revealed word of his god, that we may fear. That day is gone for a long time to come, and we need expect no more scenes like that in which Galileo[1] took part. But among the materialistic minds to whom you referred, there is a good deal of that old spirit left, only that the "revealed word of God" has become the utterances of our scientific leaders.

W.Q.J.: I have observed that within even the last quarter of a century. About ten years ago many well-known men laughed to scorn anyone who admitted the facts within the experience of every mesmerizer, while now, under the term "hypnotism,"[2] they are nearly

[1] **Galileo Galilei** (1564–1642) — an Italian astronomer, physicist and engineer, considered the "father of observational astronomy."
[2] **Hypnotism** (*Greek*) — a name given by Dr. Braid to various processes by which one person of strong will-power plunges another of weaker mind into a kind of trance; once in such a state, the latter will do anything *suggested* to him ▸

all admitted. And when these lights of our time were denying it all, the French doctors were collating the results of a long series of experiments. It seems as if the invention of a new term for an old and much abused one furnished an excuse for granting all that had been previously denied. But have you anything to say about those materialistic investigators? Are they not governed by some powerful, though unperceived, law?

H.P.B.: They are. They are in the forefront of the mental, but not of the spiritual, progress of the time, and are driven forward by forces they know nothing of. Help is very often given to them by the Masters, who, neglecting nothing, constantly see to it that these men make progress upon the fittest lines for them, just as you are assisted not only in your spiritual life but in your mental also. These men, therefore, will go on admitting facts and finding new laws or new names for old laws, to explain them. They cannot help it.

W.Q.J.: What should be our duty, then, as students of truth? Should we go out as reformers of science, or what?

H.P.B.: You ought not to take up the role of reformers of the schools and their masters, because success would not attend the effort. Science is competent to take care of itself, and you would only be throwing pearls before them to be trampled under foot. Rest content that all within their comprehension will be discovered and admitted from time to time. The endeavour to force them into admitting what you believe to be so plain would be due almost solely to your vanity and love of praise. It is not possible to force them, any more than it is for me to force you, to admit certain incomprehensible laws, and you would not think me wise or fair to first open before you things, to understand which you have not the necessary development, and then to force you into admitting their truth. Or if, out of reverence, you should say, "These things are true," while you comprehended nothing and were not progressing, you would have bowed to superior force.

W.Q.J.: But you do not mean that we should remain ignorant of science and devote ourselves only to ethics?

---

by the hypnotizer. Unless produced for beneficial purposes, Occultists would call it *black magic* or sorcery. It is the most dangerous of practices, morally and physically, as it interferes with the nerve fluid and the nerves controlling the circulation in the capillary blood-vessels.

H.P.B.: Not at all. Know all that you can. Become conversant with and sift all that the schools have declared, and as much more on your own account as is possible, but at the same time teach, preach, and practise a life based on a true understanding of brotherhood. This is the true way. The common people, those who know no science, are the greatest number. They must be so taught that the discoveries of science which are unillumined by spirit may not be turned into black magic.

W.Q.J.: In our last conversation you touched upon the guarding of buried treasure by elementals. I should like very much to hear a little more about that. Not about how to control them or to procure the treasure, but upon the subject generally.

H.P.B.: The laws governing the hiding of buried treasure are the same as those that relate to lost objects. Every person has about him a fluid, or plane, or sphere, or energy, whichever you please to call it, in which are constantly found elementals that partake of his nature. That is, they are tinted with his colour and impressed by his character. There are numerous classes of these. Some men have many of one class or of all, or many of some and few of others. And anything worn upon your person is connected with your elementals. For instance, you wear cloth made of wool or linen, and little objects made of wood, bone, brass, gold, silver, and other substances. Each one of these has certain magnetic relations peculiar to itself, and all of them are soaked, to a greater or less extent, with your magnetism as well as nervous fluid. Some of them, because of their substance, do not long retain this fluid, while others do. The elementals are connected, each class according to its substance, with those objects by means of the magnetic fluid. And they are acted upon by the mind and desires to a greater extent than you know, and in a way that cannot be formulated in English. Your desires have a powerful grasp, so to say, upon certain things, and upon others a weaker hold. When one of these objects is suddenly dropped, it is invariably followed by elementals. They are drawn after it, and may be said to go with the object by attraction rather than by sight. In many cases they completely envelop the thing, so that, although it is near at hand, it cannot be seen by the eye. But after a while the magnetism wears off and their power to envelop the article weakens, whereupon it appears in sight. This does not happen in every case. But it is a daily occurrence, and is sufficiently obvious to many persons to be quite removed from the realm of fable. I think, indeed, that one of your literary persons[1] has written an essay upon this very experience, in which, although treated in a comic vein, many truths are unconsciously told; the title of this was, if I mistake not, "Upon the Innate Perversity of Inanimate Objects." There is such a nice balancing of forces in these cases that you must be careful in your generalizations. You may justly ask, for instance, why, when a coat is dropped, it seldom disappears from sight? Well, there are cases in which even such a large object is hidden, but they are not very common. The coat is full of your magnetism, and the elementals may feel in it just as much of you as when it is on your back. There may be, for them, no disturbance of the relations, magnetic and otherwise. And often in the case of a small object not invisible, the balancing of forces, due to many causes that have to do with your condition at the time, prevents the hiding. To decide in any particular case, one would have to see into the realm where the operation of these laws is hidden, and calculate all the forces, so as to say why it happened in one way and not in another.

W.Q.J.: But take the case of a man who, being in possession of treasure, hides it in the earth and goes away and dies, and it is not found. In that instance the elementals did not hide it. Or when a miser buries his gold or jewels. How about those?

H.P.B.: In all cases where a man buries gold, or jewels, or money, or precious things, his desires are fastened to that which he hides. Many of his elementals attach themselves to it, and other classes of them also, who had nothing to do with him, gather round and keep it hidden. In the case of the captain of a ship containing treasure the influences are very powerful, because there the elementals are gathered from all the persons connected with the treasure, and the officer himself is full of solicitude for what is committed to his charge. You should also remember that gold and silver — or metals — have relations with elementals that are of a strong and peculiar character. They do not work for human law, and natural law does not assign any property in metals to man, nor recognize in him any peculiar and transcendent

---

[1] **Friedrich Theodor Vischer** (1807–1887) — a German novelist, poet, playwright and writer. In his novel *Auch Einer*, published in 1879, he developed the comical concept of *Die Tücke des Objekts* ("the perversity of inanimate objects").

right to retain what he has dug from the earth or acquired to himself. Hence we do not find the elementals anxious to restore to him the gold or silver which he had lost. If we were to assume that they occupied themselves in catering to the desires of men or in establishing what we call our rights over property, we might as well at once grant the existence of a capricious and irresponsible Providence. They proceed solely according to the law of their being, and, as they are without the power of making a judgement, they commit no blunders and are not to be moved by considerations based upon our vested rights or our unsatisfied wishes. Therefore, the spirits that appertain to metals invariably act as the laws of their nature prescribe, and one way of doing so is to obscure the metals from our sight.

W.Q.J.: Can you make any application of all this in the realm of ethics?

H.P.B.: There is a very important thing you should not overlook. Every time you harshly and unmercifully criticize the faults of another, you produce an attraction to yourself of certain quantities of elementals from that person. They fasten themselves upon you and endeavour to find in you a similar state or spot or fault that they have left in the other person. It is as if they left him to serve you at higher wages, so to say.

Then there is that which I referred to in a preceding conversation, about the effect of our acts and thoughts upon, not only the portion of the Astral Light belonging to each of us with its elementals, but upon the whole astral world. If men saw the dreadful pictures imprinted there and constantly throwing down upon us their suggestions to repeat the same acts or thoughts, a millennium might soon draw near. The Astral Light is, in this sense, the same as a photographer's negative plate, and we are the sensitive paper underneath, on which is being printed the picture. We can see two sorts of pictures for each act. One is the act itself, and the other is the picture of the thoughts and feelings animating those engaged in it. You can therefore see that you may be responsible for many more dreadful pictures than you had supposed. For actions of a simple outward appearance have behind them, very often, the worst of thoughts or desires.

W.Q.J.: Have these pictures in the Astral Light anything to do with us upon being reincarnated in subsequent earth-lives?

H.P.B.: They have very much indeed. We are influenced by them for vast periods of time, and in this you can perhaps find clues to many operations of active Karmic law for which you seek.

W.Q.J.: Is there not also some effect upon animals, and through them upon us, and vice versa?

H.P.B.: Yes. The animal kingdom is affected by us through the Astral Light. We have impressed the latter with pictures of cruelty, oppression, dominion, and slaughter. The whole Christian world admits that man can indiscriminately slaughter animals, upon the theory, elaborately set forth by priests in early times, that animals have no souls. Even little children learn this, and very early begin to kill insects, birds, and animals, not for protection, but from wantonness. As they grow up the habit is continued, and in England we see that shooting large numbers of birds beyond the wants of the table, is a national peculiarity, or, as I should say, a vice. This may be called a mild illustration. If these people could catch elementals as easily as they can animals, they would kill them for amusement when they did not want them for use; and, if the elementals refused to obey, then their death would follow as a punishment. All this is perceived by the elemental world, without conscience of course; but, under the laws of action and reaction, we receive back from it exactly that which we give.

W.Q.J.: Before we leave the subject I should like to refer again to the question of metals and the relation of man to the elementals connected with the mineral world. We see some persons who seem always to be able to find metals with ease — or, as they say, who are lucky in that direction. How am I to reconcile this with the natural tendency of elementals to hide? Is it because there is a war or discord, as it were, between different classes belonging to any one person?

H.P.B.: That is a part of the explanation. Some persons, as I said, have more of one class attached to them than another. A person fortunate with metals, say of gold and silver, has about him more of the elementals connected with or belonging to the kingdoms of those metals than other people, and thus there is less strife between the elementals. The preponderance of the metal-spirits makes the person more homogeneous with their kingdoms, and a natural attraction exists between the gold or silver lost or buried and that person, more than in the case of other people.

W.Q.J.: What determines this? Is it due to a desiring of gold and silver, or is it congenital?

H.P.B.: It is innate. The combinations in any one individual are so intricate and due to so many causes that you could not calculate them. They run back many generations, and depend upon peculiarities of soil, climate, nation, family, and race. These are, as you can see, enormously varied, and, with the materials at your command now, quite beyond your reach. Merely wishing for gold and silver will not do it.

W.Q.J.: I judge also that attempting to get at those elementals by thinking strongly will not accomplish that result either.

H.P.B.: No, it will not, because your thoughts do not reach them. They do not hear or see you, and, as it is only by accidental concentration of forces that unlearned people influence them, these accidents are only possible to the extent that you possess the natural leaning to the particular kingdom whose elementals you have influenced.

W.Q.J.: I thank you for your instruction.

H.P.B.: May you be guided to the path which leads to light!

OCCULT VIBRATIONS

W.Q.J.: It has struck me while thinking over the difference between ordinary people and an Adept or even a partly developed student, that the rate of vibration of the brain molecules, as well as the coordination of those with the vibrations of the higher brain, may lie at the bottom of the difference and also might explain many other problems.

H.P.B.: So they do. They make differences and also cause many curious phenomena; and the differences among all persons are greatly due to vibrations of all kinds.

W.Q.J.: In reading the article [*Aum!*] in *The Path* of April 1886, this idea was again suggested. I open at p. 6, vol. 1:

"The Divine Resonance, spoken of above, is not the Divine Light itself. The Resonance is only the outbreathing of the first sound of the entire Aum. This goes on during what the Hindus call a Day of Brahma, which, according to them, lasts a thousand ages.[1] It manifests itself not only as the power which stirs up and animates the particles of the Universe, but also in the evolution and dissolution of man, of the animal and mineral kingdoms, and of solar systems. Among

---

[1] See *Bhagavad Gita.*

the Aryans[2] it was represented in tbe planetary system by the planet Mercury, who has always been said to govern the intellectual faculties and to be the universal stimulator."

What of this?

H.P.B.: Mercury was always known as the god of secret wisdom. He is Hermes[3] as well as Budha[4] the son of Soma.[5] Speaking of matters on the lower plane, I would call the "Divine Resonance" you read of in *The Path* "vibrations" and the originator, or that which gives the impulse to every kind of phenomena in the astral plane.

W.Q.J.: The differences found in human brains and natures must, then, have their root in differences of vibration?

H.P.B.: Most assuredly so.

W.Q.J.: Speaking of mankind as a whole, is it true that all have one key or rate of vibration to which they respond?

H.P.B.: Human beings in general are like so many keys on the piano, each having its own sound, and the combination of which produces other sounds in endless variety. Like inanimate nature they have a keynote from which all the varieties of character and constitution proceed by endless change. Remember what was said in *Isis Unveiled*,

---

[2] **Arya** (*Sanskrit*, "holy") — originally the title of Rishis, those who had mastered the "Aryasatyani" (four truths) and entered the path to Nirvana or Moksha, the great "fourfold" path.

Aryans — the people of India. The ancient name of Northern India was *Aryavarta* (*Sanskrit*, "land of Aryans"), where the first newcomers from Central Asia settled following the destruction of Atlantis. The Fifth Race of humanity, the present stage of evolution, is also called *Aryan* because it originated in India one million years ago.

[3] **Hermes** (*Greek*) — the God of Wisdom in Greek mythology.

[4] **Budha** (*Sanskrit*, "Wise and Intelligent") — the Son of Soma, the Moon, and of Rokini or Taraka, wife of Brihaspati carried away by King Soma. That act led to the great war between the Asuras, who sided with the Moon, and the Gods who took the defence of Brihaspati (Jupiter), who was their *Purohita* (family priest). This war is known as the *Tarakamaya*. It is the original of the war in Olympus between the Gods and the Titans and also of the war in Revelation between Michael (Indra) and the Dragon (personifying the Asuras).

[5] **Soma** (*Sanskrit*, "extract") — the Moon, and also the juice of the plant of that name used in the temples for trance purposes; a sacred beverage. Soma, the Moon, is the symbol of the Secret Wisdom. In the *Upanishads*, the word is used to denote gross matter (with an association of moisture) capable of producing life under the action of heat.

at p. xvi, vol. 1, "The Universe is the combination of a thousand elements, and yet the expression of a single spirit — a chaos to the sense [physical], a cosmos to the reason [*manas*]."

W.Q.J.: So far this applies generally to nature. Does it explain the difference between the Adept and ordinary people?

H.P.B.: Yes. This difference is that an Adept may be compared to that one key which contains all the keys in the great harmony of nature. He has the synthesis of all keys in his thoughts, whereas ordinary man has the same key as a basis, but only acts and thinks on one or a few changes of this great key, producing with his brain only a few chords out of the whole great possible harmony.

W.Q.J.: Has this something to do with the fact that a disciple may hear the voice of his master through the astral spaces, while another man cannot hear or communicate with the Adepts?

H.P.B.: This is because the brain of a chela[1] is attuned by training to the brain of the Master. His vibrations synchronize with those of the Adept, and the untrained brain is not so attuned. So the chela's brain is abnormal, looking at it from the standpoint of ordinary life, while that of the ordinary man is normal for worldly purposes. The latter person may be compared to those who are colour-blind.

W.Q.J.: How am I to understand this?

H.P.B.: What is considered normal from the view of the physician is considered abnormal from the view of occultism, and vice versa. The difference between a colour-blind signal man who mistakes the lamps and the Adept who sees is that the one takes one colour for another, while the Adept sees all the colours in every colour and yet does not confuse them together.

W.Q.J.: Has the Adept, then, raised his vibrations so as to have them the same as those of nature as a whole?

H.P.B.: Yes; the highest Adepts. But there are other Adepts who, while vastly in advance of all men, are still unable to vibrate to such a degree.

W.Q.J.: Can the Adept produce at his will a vibration which will change one colour to another?

---

[1] **Chela** (*Sanskrit*, "servant") — a disciple, the pupil of a Guru or Sage, the follower of some Adept of a school of philosophy.

H.P.B.: He can produce a sound which will alter a colour. It is the sound which produces the colour, and not the other or opposite. By correlating the vibrations of a sound in the proper way a new colour is made.

W.Q.J.: Is it true that on the astral plane every sound always produces a colour?

H.P.B.: Yes; but these are invisible because not yet correlated by the human brain so as to become visible on the earth plane. Read Galton,[2] who gives experiments with colours and sounds as seen by psychics[3] and sensitives,[4] showing that many sensitive people always see a colour for every sound. The colour-blind man has coming to him the same vibrations as will show red, but not being able to sense these he alters the amount, so to say, and then sees a colour corresponding to the vibrations he can perceive out of the whole quantity. His astral senses may see the true colour, but the physical eye has its own vibrations, and these, being on the outer plane, overcome the others for the time, and the astral man is compelled to report to the brain that it saw correctly. For in each case the outer stimulus is sent to the inner man, who then is forced, as it were, to accept the message and to confirm it for the time so far as it goes. But there are cases where the inner man is able to even then overcome the outer defect and to make the brain see the difference. In many cases of lunacy the confusion among the vibrations of all kinds is so enormous that there is no correlation between the inner and the outer man, and we

---

[2] **Francis Galton** (1822–1911) — an English polymath, explorer, anthropologist and statistician. "Besides Galton's interesting chapter upon this subject, in his *Inquiries into Human Faculty and its Development*, we find in the *London Medical Record* a sensitive describing his impressions in this wise: 'As soon as I *hear* the sounds of a guitar, I *see* vibrating chords, surrounded by coloured vapours.' The piano produces the same: 'coloured images begin to float over the keys.'" See H. P. Blavatsky, "Occult or Exact Science?" *Collected Writings*, vol. 7 (Wheaton, IL: Theosophical Publishing House, 1958), pp. 55–90.

[3] **Psychism** — a term used to denote very loosely every kind of mental phenomena, *e.g.*, mediumship, and the higher sensitiveness, hypnotic receptivity, and inspired prophecy, simple clairvoyance in the Astral Light, and real divine seership; in short, the word covers every phase and manifestation of the powers and potencies of the *human* and the *divine* Souls.

[4] **Sensitive** — a person who has psychical or paranormal abilities. The term was introduced by Carl Ludwig von Reichenbach (1788–1869).

have then a case of aberration. But even in some of these unfortunate cases the person inside is all the time aware that he is not insane but cannot make himself be understood. Thus often persons are driven really insane by wrong treatment.

W.Q.J.: By what manner of vibrations do the elementals make colours and lights of variety?

H.P.B.: That is a question I cannot reply to though it is well-known to me. Did I not tell you that secrets might be revealed too soon?

ON DEVACHAN

This term[1] was not in use at this time. The conversation was about steps on the Path and returning here again. In answer to a question:

"Yes, you have been here and at this before. You were born with this tendency, and in other lives have met these persons [supposed Adept influences], and they are here to see you for that reason."

Later, when definite terms had come into use, the question raised was whether or not all stayed 1500 years in Devachan.

"Well, Judge, you must know well that under the philosophy we don't all stay there so long. It varies with the character of each. A thoroughly material thinker will emerge sooner than one who is a spiritual philosopher and good. Besides, recollect that all workers for the Lodge, no matter of what degree, are helped out of Devachan if they themselves permit it. Your own idea which you have stated, that 1500 years had not elapsed since you went into Devachan, is correct, and that I tell is what Master himself tells me. So there you are."

PRECIPITATION BY MASTERS

In reply to a question on this she said:

"If you think Master is going to be always precipitating[2] things, you mistake. Yes, He can do it. But most of the precipitations are by

---

[1] **Devachan** (*Sanskrit*, "dwelling of the gods") — a state intermediate between two earth-lives, into which the Ego (Atma-Buddhi-Manas, or the Trinity made one) enters, after its separation from Kama-rupa (*Sanskrit*, "body of desires"), and the disintegration of the lower principles on earth. The interval between one's incarnations may vary from a few instances to hundreds of years.

[2] **Precipitation** — the mysterious production of letters sent by the Masters to disciples. H.P.B. explained it in her article 'Precipitation': "Mr. Sinnett sought for an explanation of the process and elicited the following reply from the revered Mahatma, who corresponds with him: 'Bear in mind these letters are not written but impressed, or precipitated, and then all mistakes corrected. … I have to think ▸

chelas who would seem to you almost Masters. I see His orders, and the thoughts and words He wishes used, and I precipitate them in that form; so does * * * and one or two more."

"Well, what of Their handwritings?"

"Anything you write is your handwriting, but it is not your personal handwriting, generally used and first learned if you assume or adopt some form. Now you know that Masters' handwritings, peculiar and personal to Themselves, are foreign both as to sound and form — Indian sorts, in fact. So They adopted a form in English, and in that form I precipitate Their messages at Their direction. Why B——— almost caught me one day and nearly made a mess of it by shocking me. The message has to be seen in the Astral Light in *facsimile*,[3] and through that astral matrix I precipitate the whole of it. It's different, though, if Master sends me the paper and the message already done.

---

it over, to photograph every word and sentence carefully in my brain before it can be repeated by precipitation. As the fixing on chemically prepared surfaces of the images formed by the camera requires a previous arrangement within the focus of the object to be represented, for, otherwise — as often found in bad photographs — the legs of the sitter might appear out of all proportion with the head, and so on — some have to first arrange our sentences and impress every letter to appear on paper in our minds before it becomes fit to be read.' ... Those having even a superficial knowledge of the science of mesmerism know how the thoughts of the mesmerizer, though silently formulated in his mind, are instantly transferred to that of the subject. ... The work of writing the letters in question is carried on by a sort of psychological telegraphy; the Mahatmas very rarely write their letters in the ordinary way. An electro-magnetic connection, so to say, exists on the psychological plane between a Mahatma and his chelas, one of whom acts as his amanuensis. When the Master wants a letter to be written in this way, he draws the attention of the chela, whom he selects for the task, by causing an astral bell (heard by so many of our Fellows and others) to be rung near him, just as the despatching telegraph office signals to the receiving office before wiring the message. The thoughts arising in the mind of the Mahatma are then clothed in words, pronounced mentally, and forced along the astral currents he sends towards the pupil to impinge on the brain of the latter. Thence, they are borne by the nerve-currents to the palms of his hand and the tips of his fingers, which rest on a piece of magnetically prepared paper. As the thought-waves are thus impressed on the tissue, materials are drawn to it from the ocean of *Akasha* (permeating every atom of the sensuous universe), by an occult process, out of place here to describe, and permanent marks are left." See H. P. Blavatsky, "Precipitation," *Collected Writings*, vol. 6 (Wheaton, IL: Theosophical Publishing House, 1954), pp. 118–123.

[3] **Facsimile** (*Latin*) — an exact copy.

That's why I call these things 'psychological tricks.' The sign of an objective wonder seemed to be required, although a moment's thought will show it is not proof of anything but occult ability. Many a medium has had precipitations before my miserable self was heard of. But blessed is the one who wants no sign. You have seen plenty of these things. Why do you want to ask me? Can't you use your brain and intuition? I've sampled almost the whole possible range of wonders for you. Let them use their brains and intuition with the known facts and the theories given."

IF WHITE MAGICIANS ACT, WHAT THEN?

"Look here; here's a man who wants to know why the Masters don't interpose at once and save his business. They don't seem to remember what it means for a Master to use occult force. If you explode gunpowder to split a rock you may knock down a house. There is a law that if a White Magician uses his occult power, an equal amount of power may be used by the black one. Chemists invent powders for explosives and wicked men may use them. You force yourself into Master's presence and you take the consequences of the immense forces around him playing on yourself. If you are weak in character anywhere, the black ones will use the disturbance by directing the forces engendered to that spot and may compass your ruin. It is so always. Pass the boundary that hedges in the occult realm, and quick forces, new ones, dreadful ones, must be met. Then if you are not strong you may become a wreck for that life. This is the danger. This is one reason why Masters do not appear and do not act directly very often, but nearly always by intermediate degrees. What do you say — 'the dual forces in nature'? Precisely, that's just it; and Theosophists should remember it."

DO MASTERS PUNISH?

"Now I'm not going to tell you all about this. They are just; They embody the Law and Compassion. Do not for an instant imagine that Masters are going to come down on you for your failures and wrongs, if any. Karma looks out for this. Masters' ethics are the highest. From the standpoint of your question, They do not punish. Have I not told you that, much as detractors have cast mud at Them, never will the Masters impose punishment? I cannot see why such a question comes up. Karma will do all the punishing that is necessary."

ABOUT ELEMENTALS

"It's a long time ago now that I told you this part would not be explained. But I can tell you some things. This one that you and Olcott used to call * * * can't see you unless I let him. Now I will impress you upon it or him so that like a photograph he will remember so far. But you can't make it obey you until you know how to get the force directed. I'll send him to you and let him make a bell."

[In a few days after this the proposed sign was given at a distance from her, and a little bell was sounded in the air when I was talking with a person not interested in Theosophy, and when I was three miles away from H.P.B. On next seeing her she asked if * * * had been over and sounded the bell, mentioning the exact day and time.]

"This one has no form in particular, but is more like a revolving mass of air. But it is, all the same, quite definite, as you know from what he has done. There are some classes with forms of their own. The general division into fiery, airy, earthy, and watery is pretty correct, but it will not cover all the classes. There is not a single thing going on about us, no matter what, that elementals are not concerned in, because they constitute a necessary part of nature, just as important as the nerve currents in your body. Why in storms you should see them how they move about. Don't you remember what you told me about that lady * * * who saw them change and move about at that opera? It was due to her tendencies and the general idea underlying the opera."

[It was the opera of *Tristan and Isolde*,[1] by Wagner.[2]]

"In that case, as Isolde is Irish, the whole idea under it aroused a class of elementals peculiar to that island and its traditions. That's a queer place, Judge, that Ireland. It is packed full of a singular class of elementals; and, by Jove![3] I see they even have emigrated in quite large numbers. Sometimes one quite by accident rouses up some ancient system, say from Egypt; that is the explanation of that singular astral noise which you said reminded you of a sistrum[4] being shaken; it

---

[1] *Tristan and Isolde* — a famous medieval romance based on a Celtic legend about the forbidden love between the Cornish knight Tristan and the Irish princess Isolde.
[2] **Richard Wagner** (1813–1883) — a German composer, known for his operas.
[3] **Jove** — Jupiter, the Supreme Deity of the Romans, identified with the Greek Zeus.
[4] **Sistrum** (*Greek*) — an instrument, usually made of bronze but sometimes of gold or silver, of an open circular form, with a handle. Four wires were passed

was really objective. But, my dear fellow, do you think I will give you a patent elemental extractor? — not yet. Bulwer-Lytton wrote very wisely, for him, on this subject."

[Riding over in Central Park, New York.]

"It is very interesting here. I see a great number of Indians, and also their elementals, just as real as you seem to be. They do not see us; they are all spooks. But look here, Judge, don't confound the magnetism escaping through your skin with the gentle taps of supposed elementals who want a cigarette."

[In West 34th Street, New York. The first time she spoke to me of elementals particularly, I having asked her about Spiritualism.]

"It is nearly all done by elementals. Now I can make them tap anywhere you like in this room. Select any place you wish."

[I pointed to a hard plaster wall-space free from objects.]

"Now ask what you like that can be answered by taps."

Question: What is my age?

Taps: the correct number.

Question: How many in my house?

Taps: right.

Question: How many months have I been in the city?

Taps: correct.

Question: What number of minutes past the hour by my watch?

Taps: right.

Question: How many keys on my ring?

Taps: correct.

H.P.B.: "Oh bosh! Let it stop. You won't get anymore, for I have cut it off. Try your best. They have no sense; they got it all out of your own head, even the keys, for you know inside how many keys are on the ring, though you don't remember; but anyhow I could see into your pocket and count the number, and then that tapper would give the right reply. There's something better than all that magic nonsense."

---

through holes and jingling pieces of metal attached to the ends. The top of the instrument was ornamented with a figure of Isis or Hathor. This was a sacred instrument used in temples for the purpose of producing magnetic currents and sounds by means of its combination of metals. The priestess usually held it in her right hand during the ceremony of *purification of the air*, while the priests held the sistrum in their left hand, using the right to manipulate the "key of life" — the handled cross or Tau.

SHE PRECIPITATES IN LONDON

In 1888 I was in London and wanted a paper, with about four sentences written on it in purple ink, which I had left in America. I came down to her room where B. Keightley[1] was, and, not saying anything, sat down opposite H.P.B. I thought: "If only she would get me back someway a copy of that paper." She smiled at me, rose, went into her room, came out at once, and in a moment handed me a piece of paper, passing it right in front of Keightley. To my amazement it was a duplicate of my paper, a *facsimile*. I then asked her how she got it, and she replied: "I saw it in your head and the rest was easy. You thought it very clearly. You know it can be done; and it was needed." This was all done in about the time it takes to read these descriptive sentences.

thought forms → energy → matter.

elementals

energy mass — thought forms → energy → matter.

-ive thoughts

destructive elementals

+ve thoughts

kind

elementals

---

[1] **Bertram Keightley** (1860–1944) — an English Theosophist who helped H.P.B. in preparing *The Secret Doctrine* for publication. In 1889, he founded the Indian Section of the Theosophical Society, serving as its first General Secretary from 1897 to 1901.

Table 1. **The Seven Principles of Human Nature**[1]

	SANSKRIT TERMS	MEANING	EXPLANATION
LOWER QUATERNARY (PERSONALITY)	(a) Rupa, or Sthula-sharira	(a) Physical body	(a) The vehicle of all the other principles during life.
	(b) Prana	(b) Life, or Vital principle	(b) Necessary only to *a, c, d,* and the functions of the lower *Manas,* which embrace all those limited to the (*physical*) brain.
	(c) Linga-sharira	(c) Astral body	(c) The *Double,* the phantom body.
	(d) Kama-rupa	(d) The seat of animal desires and passions	(d) This is the centre of the animal man, where lies the line of demarcation which separates the mortal man from the immortal entity.
HIGHER TRIAD (INDIVIDUALITY)	(e) Manas — a dual principle in its functions	(e) Mind, Intelligence: the higher human mind, whose light, or radiation, links the Monad to the mortal man for the lifetime.	(e) The future state and the Karmic destiny of man depend on whether Manas gravitates more downward to Kama-rupa, the seat of the animal passions, or upwards to *Buddhi,* the Spiritual *Ego.* In the latter case, the higher consciousness of the individual Spiritual aspirations of *mind* (Manas), assimilating Buddhi, are absorbed by it and form the *Ego,* which goes into Devachanic bliss.
	(f) Buddhi	(f) Spiritual Soul	(f) The vehicle of pure universal spirit.
	(g) Atma	(g) Spirit	(g) One with the Absolute, as its radiation.

---

[1] In Mr. Sinnett's *Esoteric Buddhism, d, e,* and *f,* are respectively called the Animal, the Human, and the Spiritual Souls, which answers as well. Though the ‣

ASTRAL BODIES

M.C.:[2] Great confusion exists in the minds of people about the various kinds of apparitions, wraiths, ghosts or spirits. Ought we not to explain once for all the meaning of these terms? You say there are various kinds of "doubles" — what are they?

H.P.B.: Our occult philosophy teaches us that there are three kinds of "doubles," to use the word in its widest sense. First, man has his "double" or *shadow*, properly so called, around which the physical body of the *fetus* — the future man — is built. The imagination of the mother, or an accident which affects the child, will affect also the astral body.[3] The astral and the physical both exist before the mind is developed into action, and before the Atma[4] awakes. This occurs when the child is seven years old, and with it comes the responsibility attaching to a conscious sentient being. This "double" is born with man, dies with him, and can never separate itself far from the body during life, and though surviving him, it disintegrates, *pari passu*,[5] with the corpse. It is this which is sometimes seen over the graves like a luminous figure of the man that was, during certain atmospheric conditions. From its physical aspect it is, during life, *man's vital* double, and after death, only the gases given off from the decaying body. But, as regards its origin and essence, it is something more. This "double" is

---

principles in *Esoteric Buddhism* are numbered, this is, strictly speaking, useless. The dual *Monad* alone (*Atma-Buddhi*) is susceptible of being thought of as the two highest numbers (the 6th and 7th). As to all others, since *that* principle alone which is predominant in man has to be considered as the first and foremost, no numeration is possible as a general rule. In some men, it is the higher Intelligence (Manas or the 5th) which dominates the rest; in others, the Animal Soul (Kama-rupa) reigns supreme, exhibiting the most bestial instincts, etc.

[2] **Mabel Collins** (1851–1927) — a British theosophist and author, known for *Light on the Path*, which she wrote under the guidance of the Master Hilarion.

[3] **Astral body** — the ethereal counterpart or double of any physical body — the *Linga-sharira* or *Doppelganger*. The reader must not confuse it with the Astral Soul, another name for the lower Manas, or Kama-Manas, the reflection of the Higher Ego.

[4] **Atma** or **Atman** (*Sanskrit*, "spirit") — The Universal Spirit, the divine Monad, the seventh principle in the septenary constitution of man. The Supreme Soul.

[5] **Pari passu** (*Latin*) — with equal step; side by side.

what we have agreed to call *Linga-sharira*,[1] but which I would propose to call, for greater convenience, "Protean" or "Plastic Body."[2]

M.C.: Why Protean or Plastic?

H.P.B.: Protean, because it can assume all forms; *e.g.* the "shepherd magicians" whom popular rumour accuses, perhaps not without some reason, of being "werewolves," and "mediums in cabinets," whose own "Plastic Bodies" play the part of materialized grandmothers and "John Kings."[3] Otherwise, why the invariable custom of the "dear departed angels" to come out but little further than arm's length from the medium, whether entranced or not? Mind, I do not at all deny foreign influences in this kind of phenomena. But I do affirm that foreign interference is rare, and that the materialized form is always that of the medium's *Astral*, or Protean body.

M.C.: How is this astral body created?

H.P.B.: It is not created; it grows, as I told you, with the man and exists in the rudimentary condition even before the child is born.

M.C.: And what about the second?

H.P.B.: The second is the "Thought" body, or Dream body, rather; known among Occultists as the *Mayavi-rupa*,[4] or "Illusion-body." During life this image is the vehicle both of thought and of the animal passions and desires, drawing at one and the same time from the lowest terrestrial *manas* (mind) and *Kama*, the element of desire. It

---

[1] **Linga-sharira** (*Sanskrit*, "body's image") — the aerial symbol of the body; the astral body of man or animal; the reflection of the man of flesh. It is born *before* and dies or fades out, with the disappearance of the last atom of the body.

[2] **Plastic Soul** — used in Occultism in reference to the *Linga-sharira* or the astral body of the lower Quaternary. It is called the "plastic" and also "Protean" Soul based on its power of assuming any shape or form and moulding or modelling itself into or upon any image impressed in the Astral Light around it, or in the minds of the medium or of those present at séances for materialization. The *Linga-sharira* must not be confused with the *Mayavi-rupa* or "thought-body" — the image created by the thought and will of an Adept or sorcerer; for, while the astral form or *Linga-sharira* is a real entity, the "thought-body" is a temporary illusion created by the mind.

[3] **King John** (1166–1216) — the King of England from 1199 to 1216.

[4] **Rupa** (*Sanskrit*, "form") — body; any form, applied even to the forms of the gods, which are subjective to us.

Mayavi-rupa (*Sanskrit*, "illusory body") — the thought-body, the higher astral form which assumes all forms and every form at the will of an Adept's thought.

is *dual* in its potentiality, and after death forms what is called in the East *Bhut*, or *Kama-rupa*,[5] but which is better known to theosophists as the "Spook."

M.C.: And the third?

H.P.B.: The third is the true *Ego*, called in the East by a name meaning "causal body"[6] but which in the trans-Himalayan schools is always called the "Karmic body," which is the same. For *Karma*, or action, is the cause which produces incessant rebirths or "reincarnations." It is *not* the *Monad*,[7] nor is it *Manas* proper; but is, in a way, indissolubly connected with and a compound of the Monad and Manas in Devachan.

M.C.: Then there are three doubles?

H.P.B.: If you call the Christian and other Trinities "three Gods," then there are three doubles. But in truth there is only one under three

---

[5] **Kama-rupa** (*Sanskrit*, "body of desires") — the subjective form created through the mental and physical desires and thoughts in connection with things of matter, by all sentient beings; a form which survives the death of their bodies. After that death, three of the seven principles — or, let us say, planes of senses and consciousness on which the human instincts and ideation act in turn, namely, the body, its astral prototype and physical vitality — being of no further use, remain on Earth. The three higher principles, grouped into one, merge into the state of Devachan, in which state the Higher Ego will remain until the hour for a new reincarnation arrives; and the *eidolon* of the ex-Personality is left alone in its new abode. Here, the pale copy of the man that was vegetates for a period of time, the duration of which is variable and according to the element of materiality which is left in it, and which is determined by the past life of the defunct. Bereft as it is of its higher mind, spirit and physical senses, if left alone to its own senseless devices, it will gradually fade out and disintegrate. But, if forcibly drawn back into the terrestrial sphere, whether by the passionate desires and appeals of the surviving friends or by regular necromantic practices — one of the most pernicious of which is mediumship — the "spook" may prevail for a period that greatly exceeds the span of the natural life of its body. Once the Kama-rupa has learnt the way back to living human bodies, it becomes a vampire, feeding on the vitality of those who are so anxious for its company.

[6] **Causal body** — this "body" is no body either objective or subjective, but *Buddhi*, the Spiritual Soul. However, Buddhi alone could not be called a "causal body," but becomes so in conjunction with Manas, the incarnating Entity or Ego.

[7] **Monad** (*Greek*, "unity") — the unified triad, Atma-Buddhi-Manas, or the duad, Atma-Buddhi, that immortal part of man which reincarnates in the lower kingdoms and gradually progresses through them to man and then to the final goal — Nirvana.

aspects[1] or phases: the most material portion disappearing with the body; the middle one, surviving both as an independent, but temporary entity in the land of shadows; the third, immortal throughout the Manvantara,[2] unless Nirvana[3] puts an end to it before.

M.C.: But shall not we be asked what difference there is between the *Mayavi-* and *Kama-rupa,* or as you propose to call them the "Dream body" and the "Spook"?

H.P.B.: Most likely, and we shall answer, in addition to what has been said, that the "thought power" or aspect of the *Mayavi* or "Illusion body," merges after death entirely into the causal body or the conscious, *thinking Ego.* The animal elements, or power of desire of the "Dream body," absorbing after death that which it has collected (through its insatiable desire *to live*) during life; *i.e.,* all the astral vitality as well as all the impressions of its *material* acts and thoughts while it lived in possession of the body, forms the "Spook" or *Kama-rupa.* Our Theosophists know well enough that after death the *higher* Manas unites with the *Monad* and passes into Devachan, while the dregs of the *lower* Manas or animal mind go to form this Spook. This has life in it, but hardly any consciousness, except, as it were, by proxy, when it is drawn into the current of a medium.

M.C.: Is it all that can be said upon the subject?

H.P.B.: For the present this is enough metaphysics, I guess. Let us hold to the "Double" in its earthly phase. What would you know?

M.C.: Every country in the world believes more or less in the "double" or doppelganger.[4] The simplest form of this is the appearance of a man's phantom, the moment after his death, or at the instant of death, to his dearest friend. Is this appearance the *Mayavi-rupa?*

---

[1] **Aspect** — the form (*rupa*) under which any principle in septenary man or nature manifests is called an *aspect* of that principle in Theosophy.

[2] **Manvantara** (*Sanskrit,* "age of a Manu") — a period of manifestation, as opposed to Pralaya (dissolution, or rest), applied to various cycles and to the reign of one Manu (the patron or guardian of the mankind cycles in a Manvantara).

[3] **Nirvana** (*Sanskrit,* "blown out") — the state of absolute existence and absolute consciousness, into which the Ego of a man who has reached the highest degree of perfection and holiness during life goes, after the body dies, and occasionally, as in the case of Gautama Buddha and others, during life.

[4] **Doppelganger** (*German,* "double-walker") — a synonym of the "Double" and of the "Astral body" in occult parlance.

H.P.B.: It is; because produced by the thought of the dying man.

M.C.: Is it unconscious?

H.P.B.: It is unconscious to the extent that the dying man does not generally do it knowingly; nor is he aware that he so appears. What happens is this. If he thinks very intently at the moment of death of the person he either is very anxious to see, or loves best, he may appear to that person. The thought becomes objective; the double, or shadow of a man, being nothing but the faithful reproduction of him, like a reflection in a mirror: that which the man does, even in thought, that the double repeats. This is why the phantoms are often seen in such cases in the clothes they wear at the particular moment, and the *image* reproduces even the expression on the dying man's face. If the double of a man bathing were seen it would seem to be immersed in water; so when a man who has been drowned appears to his friend, the image will be seen to be dripping with water. The cause for the apparition may also be reversed; *i.e.,* the dying man may or may not be thinking at all of the particular person his image appears to, but it is that person who is sensitive. Or perhaps his sympathy or his hatred for the individual whose wraith is thus evoked is very intense physically or psychically; and in this case the apparition is created by, and depends upon the intensity of the thought. What then happens is this. Let us call the dying man A, and him who sees the double B. The latter, owing to love, hate, or fear, has the image of A so deeply impressed on his psychic memory, that actual magnetic attraction and repulsion are established between the two, whether one knows of it and feels it, or not. When A dies, the sixth sense or psychic spiritual intelligence of the *inner man* in B becomes cognizant of the change in A, and forthwith apprises the physical senses of the man by projecting before his eye the form of A as it is at the instant of the great change. The same when the dying man longs to see someone; *his* thought telegraphs to his friend, consciously or unconsciously along the wire of sympathy, and becomes objective. This is what the "Spookical" Research Society[5] would pompously, but none the less muddily, call *telepathic impact.*

---

[5] **Society for Psychical Research (S.P.R.)** — a British organization, founded in 1882. In 1884, the S.P.R. issued an accusatory report against H.P.B. based on fabricated evidence. This substantially damaged H.P.B.'s reputation and health. However, in 1986, the S.P.R. issued a press release headlined: "Madame Blavatsky, co-founder of the Theosophical Society, was unjustly condemned, new study›

M.C.: This applies to the simplest form of the appearance of the double. What about cases in which the double does that which is contrary to the feeling and wish of the man?

H.P.B.: This is impossible. The "Double" cannot act, unless the keynote of this action was struck in the brain of the man to whom the "Double" belongs, be that man just dead, or alive, in good or in bad health. If he paused on the thought a second, long enough to give it form, before he passed on to other mental pictures, this one second is as sufficient for the *objectivization* of his personality on the astral waves, as for your face to impress itself on the sensitized plate of a photographic apparatus. Nothing prevents your form, then, being seized upon by the surrounding Forces — as a dry leaf fallen from a tree is taken up and carried away by the wind — being made to caricature or distort your thought.

M.C.: Supposing the double expresses in actual words a thought uncongenial to the man, and expresses it — let us say to a friend far away, perhaps on another continent? I have known instances of this occurring.

H.P.B.: Because it then so happens that the created image is taken up and used by a "Shell." Just as in séance rooms when "images" of the dead — which may perhaps be lingering unconsciously in the memory or even the auras of those present — are seized upon by the Elementals or Elementary Shadows and made objective to the audience, and even caused to act at the bidding of the strongest of the many different wills in the room. In your case, moreover, there must exist a connecting link — a telegraph wire — between the two persons, a point of psychic sympathy, and on this the thought travels instantly. Of course there must be, in every case, some strong reason why that particular thought takes that direction; it must be connected in some way with the other person. Otherwise such apparitions would be of common and daily occurrence.

M.C.: This seems very simple; why then does it only occur with exceptional persons?

---

concludes." Dr. Vernon Harrison, who re-examined the case, finished his report with the words: "I apologize to her that it has taken us one hundred years to demonstrate that she wrote truly."

H.P.B.: Because the plastic power of the imagination is much stronger in some persons than in others. The mind is dual in its potentiality: it is physical and metaphysical. The higher part of the mind is connected with the spiritual soul or Buddhi,[1] the lower with the animal soul, the Kama principle. There are persons who never think with the higher faculties of their minds at all; those who do so are the minority and are thus, in a way, *beyond*, if not above, the average of human kind. These will think even upon ordinary matters on that *higher* plane. The idiosyncrasy of the person determines in which principle of the mind the thinking is done, as also the faculties of a preceding life, and sometimes the heredity of the physical. This is why it is so very difficult for a materialist — the metaphysical portion of whose brain is almost atrophied — to raise himself, or for one who is naturally spiritually-minded, to descend to the level of the matter-of-fact vulgar thought. Optimism and pessimism depend on it also in a great measure. *FTF* .

M.C.: But the habit of thinking in the higher mind can be developed — else there would be no hope for persons who wish to alter their lives and raise themselves? And that this is possible must be true, or there would be no hope for the world.

H.P.B.: Certainly it can be developed, but only with great difficulty, a firm determination, and through much self-sacrifice. But it is comparatively easy for those who are born with the gift. Why is it that one person sees poetry in a cabbage or a pig with her little ones, while another will perceive in the loftiest things only their lowest and most material aspect, will laugh at the "music of the spheres,"[2] and ridicule the most sublime conceptions and philosophies? This difference depends simply on the innate power of the mind to think on the higher or on the lower plane, with the *astral* (in the sense

---

[1] **Buddhi** (*Sanskrit*, "Soul") — Universal Soul or Mind; the spiritual Soul in man (the sixth principle), the vehicle of Atma exoterically the seventh.

[2] **Music of the spheres** — a Pythagorean concept that suggests a harmonious, mathematical relationship between the movements of celestial bodies, such as planets and stars, and the production of music-like sounds or vibrations. Music is the combination and modulation of sounds, and sound is the effect produced by the vibration of the ether. If the impulses communicated to the ether by the different planets may be likened to the tones produced by the different notes of a musical instrument, certain planetary aspects may imply disturbances in the ether of our planet, and certain others rest and harmony.

given to the word by de Saint-Martin[1]), or with the physical brain. Great intellectual powers are often no proof of, but are impediments to spiritual and right conceptions; witness most of the great men of science. We must rather pity than blame them.

M.C.: But how is it that the person who thinks on the higher plane produces more perfect and more potential images and objective forms by his thought?

H.P.B.: Not necessarily that "person" alone, but all those who are generally sensitives. The person who is endowed with this faculty of thinking about even the most trifling things from the higher plane of thought has, by virtue of that gift which he possesses, a plastic power of formation, so to say, in his very imagination. Whatever such a person may think about, his thought will be so far more intense than the thought of an ordinary person, that by this very intensity it obtains the power of creation. Science has established the fact that thought is an energy. This energy in its action disturbs the atoms of the astral atmosphere around us. I already told you; the rays of thought have the same potentiality for producing forms in the astral atmosphere as the sun-rays have with regard to a lens. Every thought so evolved with energy from the brain, creates, *nolens volens*,[2] a shape.

M.C.: Is that shape absolutely unconscious?

H.P.B.: Perfectly unconscious unless it is the creation of an Adept, who has a preconceived object in giving it consciousness, or rather in sending along with it enough of his will and intelligence to cause it to appear conscious. This ought to make us more cautious about our thoughts.

But the wide distinction that obtains between the Adept in this matter and the ordinary man must be borne in mind. The Adept may at his will use his *Mayavi-rupa*, but the ordinary man does not, except in very rare cases. It is called *Mayavi-rupa* because it is a form of illusion created for use in the particular instance, and it has quite enough of the Adept's mind in it to accomplish its purpose. The ordinary man merely creates a thought-image, whose properties and powers are at the time wholly unknown to him.

---

[1] **Louis Claude de Saint-Martin** (1743–1803) — a great French mystic and writer, who pursued his philosophical and theosophical studies at Paris, during the Revolution. He was an ardent disciple of Jacob Boehme.

[2] **Nolens volens** (*Latin*) — whether willing or unwilling.

M.C.: Then one may say that the form of an Adept appearing at a distance from his body, as for instance Ram Lal in *Mr. Isaacs*,[3] is simply an image?

H.P.B.: Exactly. It is a walking thought.

M.C.: In which case an Adept can appear in several places almost simultaneously.

H.P.B.: He can. Just as Apollonius of Tyana,[4] who was seen in two places at once, while his body was at Rome. But it must be understood that not *all* of even the *astral* Adept is present in each appearance.

---

[3] *Mr. Isaacs: A Tale of Modern India* — a novel by Francis Marion Crawford (1854–1909), an American writer. In the novel, Isaacs is a disciple of the initiate Ram Lal, who has various mystical powers and can command the forces of nature. See H. P. Blavatsky, "Mr. Isaacs," *Collected Writings*, vol. 4 (Wheaton, IL: Theosophical Publishing House, 1969), pp. 339–344.

[4] **Apollonius of Tyana** (*Greek*) — a wonderful philosopher born in Cappadocia about the beginning of the 1st century; an ardent Pythagorean, who studied the Phoenician sciences under Euthydemus; and Pythagorean philosophy and other studies under Euxenus of Heraclea. According to the tenets of this school, he remained a vegetarian the whole of his long life, fed only on fruit and herbs, drank no wine, wore vestments made only of plant-fibres, walked barefooted, and let his hair grow to its full length, as all the Initiates before and after him. He was initiated by the priests of the temple of Æsculapius (Asciepios) at Ægae, and learnt many of the "miracles" for healing the sick wrought by the god of medicine. Having prepared himself for a higher initiation by a silence of five years and by travel, visiting Antioch, Ephesus, Pamphylia and other parts, he journeyed via Babylon to India, all his intimate disciples having abandoned him, as they feared to go to the "land of enchantments." A casual disciple, Damis, however, whom he met on his way, accompanied him in his travels. At Babylon, he was initiated by the Chaldees and Magi, according to Damis, whose narrative was copied by one named Philostratus a hundred years later. After his return from India, he showed himself a true Initiate, in that the pestilences and earthquakes, deaths of kings and other events which he prophesied, duly happened. At Lesbos, the priests of Orpheus, being jealous of him, refused to initiate him into their peculiar mysteries, though they did so several years later. He preached to the people of Athens and other cities the purest and noblest ethics, and the phenomena he produced were as wonderful as they were numerous and well attested. After crossing the Hindu Kush, Apollonius had been directed by a king to the *abode of the Sages*, whose abode it may be to this day, by whom he was taught unsurpassed knowledge. His dialogues with the Corinthian Menippus, indeed, give us the esoteric catechism and disclose (when understood) many an important mystery of nature. Apollonius was the friend, correspondent and guest of kings and queens, and no marvellous or "magic" powers are better▸

M.C.: Then it is very necessary for a person of any amount of imagination and psychic powers to attend to their thoughts?

H.P.B.: Certainly, for each thought has a shape which borrows the appearance of the man engaged in the action of which he thought. Otherwise how can clairvoyants see in your *aura* your past and present? What they see is a passing panorama of yourself represented in successive actions by your thoughts. You asked me if we are punished for our thoughts. Not for all, for some are still-born; but for the others, those which we call "silent" but potential thoughts — yes. Take an extreme case, such as that of a person who is so wicked as to wish the death of another. Unless the evil-wisher is a *Dugpa*, a high adept in black magic, in which case Karma is delayed, such a wish only comes back to roost.

M.C.: But supposing the evil-wisher to have a very strong will, without being a *dugpa*, could the death of the other be accomplished?

H.P.B.: Only if the malicious person has the evil eye, which simply means possessing enormous plastic power of imagination working involuntarily, and thus turned unconsciously to bad uses. For what is the power of the "evil eye"? Simply a great plastic power of thought, so great as to produce a current impregnated with the potentiality of every kind of misfortune and accident, which inoculates, or attaches itself to any person who comes within it. A *jettatore*[1] (one with the evil eye) need not be even imaginative, or have evil intentions or wishes. He may be simply a person who is naturally fond of witnessing or reading about sensational scenes, such as murder, executions, accidents, etc., etc. He may be not even thinking of any of these at the moment his eye meets his future victim. But the currents have been produced and exist in his visual ray ready to spring into activity the instant they find suitable soil, like a seed fallen by the way and ready to sprout at the first opportunity.

M.C.: But how about the thoughts you call "silent"? Do such wishes or thoughts come home to roost?

H.P.B.: They do; just as a ball which fails to penetrate an object rebounds upon the thrower. This happens even to some *dugpas* or

---

attested than his. At the end of his long and wonderful life, he opened an esoteric school at Ephesus, and he died aged almost one hundred years.

[1] Jettatore (*Italian*, "throw") — the wielder of the evil eye; a sorcerer.

sorcerers who are not strong enough, or do not comply with the rules — for even they have *rules* they have to abide by — but not with those who are regular, fully developed "black magicians"; for such have the power to accomplish what they wish.

M.C.: When you speak of rules it makes me want to wind up this talk by asking you what everybody wants to know who takes any interest in occultism. What is a principal or important suggestion for those who have these powers and wish to control them rightly — in fact to enter occultism?

H.P.B.: The first and most important step in occultism is to learn how to adapt your thoughts and ideas to your plastic potency.

M.C.: Why is this so important?

H.P.B.: Because otherwise you are creating things by which you may be making bad Karma. No one should go into occultism or even touch it before he is perfectly acquainted with his own powers, and that he knows how to commensurate it with his actions. And this he can do only by deeply studying the philosophy of Occultism before entering upon the *practical* training. Otherwise, as sure as fate — *he will fall into black magic.*

Table 2. Septenary Division in Different Indian Systems

		ESOTERIC BUDDHISM		VEDANTIC PHILOSOPHY	TARAKA RAJA YOGA
BODY		1. Body (Rupa)		Annamaya kosha	Sthulopadhi
		2. Vitality (Prana)		Pranamaya kosha	
		3. Astral Body (Linga-sharira)			
SOUL		4. Animal Soul (Kama-rupa)		Manomaya kosha	Sukshmopadhi
		5. Human Soul (Manas)	Lower Mind		
SPIRIT			Higher Mind	Vignanamaya kosha	
		6. Spiritual Soul (Buddhi)		Anandamaya kosha	Karanopadhi
		7. Spirit (Atma)		Atma	Atma

THE AFTERLIFE AND THE CONSTITUTION OF MAN

H.P.B.: Of course, it is most difficult, and, as you say, puzzling to understand correctly and distinguish between the various *aspects*, called by us the *principles* of the real *Ego*. It is the more so as there exists a notable difference in the numbering of those principles by various Eastern schools, though at the bottom there is the same identical substratum of teaching in all of them.

Student: Are you thinking of the Vedantins?[1] They divide our seven principles into five only, I believe?

H.P.B.: They do; but though I would not presume to dispute the point with a learned Vedantin, I may yet state as my private opinion that they have an obvious reason for it. With them it is only that compound spiritual aggregate which consists of various mental aspects that is called *Man* at all, the physical body being in their view something beneath contempt, and merely an *illusion*.[2] Nor is the Vedanta the only philosophy to reckon in this manner. Lao-Tzu[3] in his *Tao Te Ching*, mentions only five principles, because he, like the Vedantins, omits to include two principles, namely, the spirit (Atma) and the physical body, the latter of which, moreover, he calls "the cadaver." Then there is the *Taraka Raja Yoga*[4] School. Its teaching recognizes only three principles in fact; but then, in reality, their *Sthulopadhi*,[5]

---

[1] **Vedanta** (*Sanskrit*, "end of the Vedas") — a mystic system of philosophy which has developed from the efforts of generations of sages to interpret the secret meaning of the *Upanishads*.

[2] **Illusion** — in Occultism, everything finite (like the Universe and all in it) is called illusion or *Maya*.

[3] **Lao-Tzu** (*Chinese*) — a great sage, saint and philosopher who preceded Confucius. His *Tao Te Ching* (*Chinese*, "Book of the Perfectibility of Nature") is a kind of cosmogony which contains all the fundamental tenets of Esoteric Cosmogenesis.

[4] **Yoga** (*Sanskrit*, "union") — a spiritual practice leading to liberation and enlightenment, as well as to development of spiritual powers, through the union or merger of the individual self with the Universal Self. The highest form of yoga is *Agni Yoga*, which is represented in the book series of the same name, given by Helena Roerich (1879–1955) under the guidance of the Master Morya.

Taraka Raja Yoga (*Sanskrit*) — one of the Brahminical Yoga systems for the development of purely spiritual powers and knowledge which lead to Nirvana.

[5] **Sthulopadhi** (*Sanskrit*) — a principle answering to the lower triad in man, *i.e.*, body, astral form, and life, in the Taraka Raja Yoga system, which names ›

or the physical body in its *Jagrata*[1] or waking conscious state, their *Sukshmopadhi*,[2] the same body in *Svapna*[3] or the dreaming state, and their *Karanopadhi*[4] or "causal body," or that which passes from one incarnation to another, are all dual in their aspects, and thus make six. Add to this Atma, the impersonal divine principle or the immortal element in Man, undistinguished from the Universal Spirit, and you have the same seven, again, as in the esoteric[5] division.

Student: Then it seems almost the same as the division made by mystic Christians: body, soul, and spirit?

H.P.B.: Just the same. We could easily make of the body the vehicle of the "vital Double"; of the latter the vehicle of Life or *Prana*;[6] of *Kama-rupa* or (animal) soul, the vehicle of the *higher* and the *lower* mind, and make of this six principles, crowning the whole with the one immortal spirit. In Occultism, every qualificative change in the state of our consciousness gives to man a new aspect, and if it prevails and becomes part of the living and acting *Ego*, it must be (and is) given a special name, to distinguish the man in that particular state from the man he is when he places himself in another state.

Student: It is just that which is so difficult to understand.

H.P.B.: It seems to me very easy, on the contrary, once that you have seized the main idea, *i.e.*, that man acts on this, or another plane of consciousness, in strict accordance with his mental and spiritual condition. But such is the materialism of the age that the more we explain, the less people seem capable of understanding what we say. Divide the terrestrial being called man into three chief aspects, if you like; but, unless you make of him a pure animal, you cannot do less. Take his objective *body*; the feeling principle in him — which is only

---

only three chief principles in man. *Sthulopadhi* corresponds to the *jagrata*, or waking conscious state.

[1] **Jagrata** (*Sanskrit*, "wakefulness") — the waking state of consciousness.

[2] **Sukshmopadhi** (*Sanskrit*) — in Taraka Raja Yoga, the principle containing both the higher and the lower Manas and Kama. It corresponds to the *Svapna* state.

[3] **Svapna** (*Sanskrit*, "dream") — a trance or dreamy condition; clairvoyance.

[4] **Karanopadhi** (*Sanskrit*, "basis of the cause") — the "causal body" or or what we call Buddhi.

[5] **Esoteric** (*Greek*, "inner") — hidden, secret; intended solely for Initiates with the aim of avoiding use by untrained people that might result in destructive consequences.

[6] **Prana** (*Sanskrit*, "breath") — Life-Principle; the breath of Life.

a little higher than the *instinctual* element in the animal — or the vital elementary soul; and that which places him so immeasurably beyond and higher than the animal — *i.e.*, his *reasoning* soul or "spirit." Well, if we take these three groups or representative entities, and subdivide them, according to the occult teaching, what do we get?

First of all Spirit (in the sense of the Absolute, and therefore indivisible *All*) or Atma. As this can neither be located nor conditioned in philosophy, being simply that which *is*, in Eternity, and as the *All* cannot be absent from even the tiniest geometrical or mathematical point of the universe of matter or substance, it ought not to be called, in truth, a "human" principle at all. Rather, and at best, it is that point in metaphysical Space which the human Monad and its vehicle man, occupy for the period of every life. Now that point is as imaginary as man himself, and in reality is an illusion, a *Maya*;[7] but then for ourselves as for other personal Egos, we are a reality during that fit of illusion called life, and we have to take ourselves into account — in our own fancy at any rate, if no one else does. To make it more conceivable to the human intellect, when first attempting the study of Occultism, and to solve the ABC of the mystery of man, Occultism calls it the *seventh* principle, the synthesis of the sixth, and gives it for vehicle the *Spiritual* Soul, *Buddhi*. Now the latter conceals a mystery, which is never given to anyone with the exception of irrevocably pledged *chelas*, those at any rate, who can be safely trusted. Of course there would be less confusion, could it only be told; but, as this is directly concerned with the power of projecting one's double consciously and at will, and as this gift, like the "Ring of Gyges,"[8] might prove very fatal to men at large and to the possessor of that faculty in particular, it is carefully guarded. Alone the Adepts, who have been tried and can

---

[7] **Maya** (*Sanskrit*, "illusion") — the cosmic power which renders phenomenal existence and the perceptions thereof possible. In Hindu philosophy, that alone which is changeless and eternal is called *reality*; all that which is subject to change through decay and differentiation, and which has therefore a beginning and an end, is regarded as *Maya* — illusion.

[8] **Ring of Gyges** — a magic ring mentioned in Plato's *Republic*. Gyges was a Lydian who, after murdering the King Candaules, married his widow. Plato tells us that Gyges descended once into a chasm of the earth and discovered a brazen horse, within whose open side was the skeleton of a man who had a brazen ring on his finger. This ring, when placed on his own finger, made Gyges invisible.

never be found wanting, have the key of the mystery fully divulged to them… Let us avoid side issues, however, and hold to the principles.

This divine soul or Buddhi, then, is the vehicle of the Spirit. In conjunction, these two are one, impersonal, and without any attributes (on this plane, of course), and make two spiritual principles. If we pass on to the *Human* Soul (*Manas*, the *mens*)[1] everyone will agree that the intelligence of man is *dual* to say the least: *e.g.*, the high-minded man can hardly become low-minded; the very intellectual and spiritual-minded man is separated by an abyss from the obtuse, dull and material, if not animal-minded man. Why then should not these men be represented by two principles or two aspects rather? Every man has these two principles in him, one more active than the other, and in rare cases, one of these is entirely stunted in its growth; so to say paralysed by the strength and predominance of the other *aspect*, during the life of man. These, then, are what we call the two principles or aspects of *Manas*, the higher and the lower; the former, the higher Manas, or the thinking, conscious *Ego* gravitating towards the Spiritual Soul (Buddhi); and the latter, or its instinctual principle attracted to *Kama*, the seat of animal desires and passions in man. Thus, we have *four* principles justified; the last three being (1) the "Double" which we have agreed to call Protean, or Plastic Soul; the vehicle of (2) the life principle; and (3) the physical body. Of course no physiologist or biologist will accept these principles, nor can he make head or tail of them. And this is why, perhaps, none of them understand to this day either the functions of the spleen, the physical vehicle of the Protean Double, or those of a certain organ on the right side of man, the seat of the above mentioned desires, nor yet does he know anything of the pineal gland, which he describes as a horny gland with a little sand in it, and which is the very key to the highest and divinest consciousness in man — his omniscient, spiritual and all embracing mind. This seemingly useless appendage is the pendulum which, once the clock-work of the *inner* man is wound up, carries the spiritual vision of the *Ego* to the highest planes of perception, where the horizon open before it becomes almost infinite…

---

[1] **Mens** (*Latin*) — the mind; in Roman mythology, Mens was the goddess of thought and consciousness.

Student: But the scientific materialists assert that after the death of man nothing remains; that the human body simply disintegrates into its component elements, and that what we call soul is merely a temporary self-consciousness produced as a by-product of organic action, which will evaporate like steam. Is not theirs a strange state of mind?

H.P.B.: Not strange at all, that I see. If they say that self-consciousness ceases with the body, then in *their* case they simply utter an unconscious prophecy. For once that they are firmly convinced of what they assert, no conscious afterlife is possible for them.

Student: But if human self-consciousness survives death as a rule, why should there be exceptions?

H.P.B.: In the fundamental laws of the spiritual world which are immutable, no exception is possible. But there are rules for those who see, and rules for those who prefer to remain blind.

Student: Quite so, I understand. It is an aberration of a blind man, who denies the existence of the sun because he does not see it. But after death his spiritual eyes will certainly compel him to see.

H.P.B.: They will not compel him, nor will he see anything. Having persistently denied an afterlife during this life, he will be unable to sense it. His spiritual senses having been stunted, they cannot develop after death, and he will remain blind. By insisting that he *must* see it, you evidently mean one thing and I another. You speak of the spirit from the Spirit, or the flame from the Flame — of Atma in short — and you confuse it with the human soul — Manas... You do not understand me, let me try to make it clear. The whole gist of your question is to know whether, in the case of a downright materialist, the complete loss of self-consciousness and self-perception after death is possible? Isn't it so? I say: It is possible. Because, believing firmly in our Esoteric Doctrine, which refers to the *post-mortem*[2] period, or the interval between two lives or births as merely a transitory state, I say: Whether that interval between two acts of the illusionary drama of life lasts one year or a million, that *post-mortem* state may, without any breach of the fundamental law, prove to be just the same state as that of a man who is in a dead swoon.

---

[2] **Post-mortem** (*Latin*) — occurring after death.

Student: But since you have just said that the fundamental laws of the after-death state admit of no exceptions, how can this be?

H.P.B.: Nor do I say now that they admit of exceptions. But the spiritual law of continuity applies only to things which are truly real. To one who has read and understood Mundaka Upanishad[1] and Vedanta-Sara,[2] all this becomes very clear. I will say more: it is sufficient to understand what we mean by Buddhi and the duality of Manas to have a very clear perception why the materialist may not have a self-conscious survival after death: because Manas, in its lower aspect, is the seat of the terrestrial mind, and, therefore, can give only that perception of the Universe which is based on the evidence of that mind, and not on our spiritual vision. It is said in our Esoteric school that between Buddhi and Manas, or Ishvara[3] and Pragna,[4] there is in reality no more difference than *between a forest and its trees, a lake and its waters,* just as Mundaka teaches. One or hundreds of trees dead from loss of vitality, or uprooted, are yet incapable of preventing the forest from being still a forest. The destruction or *post-mortem* death of one personality[5] dropped out of the long series, will not cause the smallest change in the Spiritual divine *Ego,* and it will ever remain the same *Ego.* Only, instead of experiencing *Devachan* it will have to immediately reincarnate.

---

[1] **Mundaka Upanishad** (*Sanskrit,* "Mundaka esoteric doctrine") — a Vedic work of high antiquity.

[2] **Vedanta-Sara** (*Sanskrit,* "Essence of Vedanta") — a 15th-century Advaita vedanta text.

[3] **Ishvara** (*Sanskrit,* "sovereign, independent existence") — the "Lord" or the personal god, the divine Spirit in man; the collective consciousness of the manifested deity. A title given to Shiva and other gods in Hinduism.

[4] **Pragna** or **Prajna** (*Sanskrit,* "wisdom") — the Universal Mind; the capacity for perception; a synonym of *Mahat.* While Ishvara is the collective consciousness of the Host of Spiritual Beings, Pragna is their individual wisdom.

[5] **Personality** — the teachings of Occultism divide man into three aspects: the *divine,* the *thinking* or rational, and the *irrational* or animal man. For metaphysical purposes also, he is considered under a septenary division, or, as it is agreed to express it in Theosophy, he is composed of seven principles, three of which constitute the Higher *Triad* and the remaining four the lower *Quaternary.* It is in the latter that dwells the *Personality* which embraces all the characteristics, including memory and consciousness, of each physical life in turn. The *Individuality* is the Higher Ego (Manas) of the Triad, considered as a Unity. In other words, the Individuality is our imperishable *Ego,* which reincarnates and clothes itself in *a new Personality* at every new birth.

Student: But as I understand it, Ego-Buddhi represents in this simile the forest and the personal minds the trees. And if Buddhi is immortal, how can that which is similar to it, *i.e.,* Manas-taijasi,[6] lose entirely its consciousness till the day of its new incarnation? I cannot understand it.

H.P.B.: You cannot, because you will mix up an abstract representation of the whole with its casual changes of form; and because you confuse *Manas-taijasi,* the *Buddhi*-lit human soul, with the latter, animalized. Remember that if it can be said of Buddhi that it is unconditionally immortal, the same cannot be said of Manas, still less of taijasi, which is an attribute. No *post-mortem* consciousness or Manas-taijasi, can exist apart from Buddhi, the divine soul, because the first (*Manas*) is, in its lower aspect, a qualificative attribute of the terrestrial personality, and the second (*taijasi*) is identical with the first, and that it is the same Manas only with the light of Buddhi reflected on it. In its turn, Buddhi would remain only an impersonal spirit without this element which it borrows from the human soul, which conditions and makes of it, in this illusive Universe, *as it were something separate* from the universal soul for the whole period of the cycle of incarnation. Say rather that *Buddhi-Manas*[7] can neither die nor lose its compound self-consciousness in Eternity, nor the recollection of its previous incarnations in which the two — *i.e.,* the spiritual and the human soul, had been closely linked together. But it is not so in the case of a materialist, whose human soul not only receives nothing from the divine soul, but even refuses to recognize its existence. You can hardly apply this axiom to the attributes and qualifications of the human soul, for it would be like saying that because your divine soul is immortal, therefore the bloom on your cheek must also be immortal; whereas this bloom, like taijasi, or spiritual radiance, is simply a transitory phenomenon.

---

[6] **Taijasi** (*Sanskrit,* "radiant," "flaming") — the term used sometimes to designate the *Manasa-rupa,* the "thought-body," also the stars, and the *star-like* shining envelopes. It means the radiant in consequence of the union with Buddhi of Manas, the human, illuminated by the radiance of the divine soul.

Manas-taijasi (*Sanskrit,* "radiant mind") — the *human* reason lit by the light of the spirit; a state of the Higher Ego, which only high metaphysicians are able to realize and comprehend.

[7] **Buddhi-Manas** (*Sanskrit*) — the representation of the divine *plus* the human intellect and self-consciousness.

Student: Do I understand you to say that we must not mix in our minds the noumenon[1] with the phenomenon, the cause with its effect?

H.P.B.: I do say so, and repeat that, limited to Manas or the human soul alone, the radiance of Taijasi itself becomes a mere question of time; because both immortality and consciousness after death become for the terrestrial personality of man simply conditioned attributes, as they depend entirely on conditions and beliefs created by the human soul itself during the life of its body. Karma acts incessantly; we reap in our afterlife only the fruit of that which we have ourselves sown, or rather created, in our terrestrial existence.

Student: But if my Ego can, after the destruction of my body, become plunged in a state of entire unconsciousness, then where can be the punishment for the sins of my past life?

H.P.B.: Our philosophy teaches that Karmic punishment reaches the Ego only in its next incarnation. After death it receives only the reward for the unmerited sufferings endured during its just past existence.[2] The whole punishment after death, even for the materialist, consists therefore in the absence of any reward and the utter loss of the consciousness of one's bliss and rest. Karma — is the child of the terrestrial Ego, the fruit of the actions of the tree which is the objective personality visible to all, as much as the fruit of all the thoughts and even motives of the spiritual "I"; but Karma is also the tender mother, who heals the wounds inflicted by her during the preceding life, before she will begin to torture this Ego by inflicting upon him new ones. If it may be said that there is not a mental or physical suffering in the life of a mortal, which is not the fruit and consequence of some sin in this, or a preceding existence, on the other hand, since he does not preserve the slightest recollection of it in his actual life, and feels himself not

---

[1] **Noumenon** (*Greek,* "to mean") — the true essential nature of being as distinguished from the illusive objects of sense.

[2] Some Theosophists have taken exception to this phrase, but the words are those of the Masters, and the meaning attached to the word "unmerited" is that people often suffer from the effects of the actions done by others, effects which, thus, do not strictly belong to their own Karma, but to that of other people — and for these sufferings, they, of course, deserve compensation. If it is true to say that nothing that happens to us can be anything else than Karma — or the direct or indirect effect of a cause. It would be a great error to think that every evil or good which befalls us is due *only* to *our* own personal Karma.

deserving of such punishment, but believes sincerely he suffers for no guilt of his own, this alone is quite sufficient to entitle the human soul to the fullest consolation, rest and bliss in his *post-mortem* existence. Death comes to our spiritual selves ever as a deliverer and friend. For the materialist, who, notwithstanding his materialism, was not a bad man, the interval between the two lives will be like the unbroken and placid sleep of a child; either entirely dreamless, or with pictures of which he will have no definite perception. For the believer it will be a dream as vivid as life and full of realistic bliss and visions. As for the bad and cruel man, whether materialist or otherwise, he will be immediately reborn and suffer his hell on earth. To enter *Avichi*[3] is an exceptional and rare occurrence.

Student: As far as I remember, the periodical incarnations of Sutratma[4] are likened in some Upanishad[5] to the life of a mortal which oscillates periodically between sleep and waking. This does not seem to me very clear, and I will tell you why. For the man who awakes, another day commences, but that man is the same in soul and body as he was the day before; whereas at every new incarnation a full change takes place not only in his external envelope, sex and personality, but even in his mental and psychic capacities. Thus the simile does not seem to me quite correct. The man who arises from sleep remembers

---

[3] **Avichi** (*Sanskrit*, "uninterrupted hell") — a state: not necessarily after death only or between two births, for it can take place on Earth as well. The last of the eight hells, where the culprits *die and are reborn without interruption* — yet not without hope of final redemption. This is because Avichi is another name for Myalba (our Earth) and also a state to which some soulless people are condemned on this physical plane.

[4] **Sutratma** (*Sanskrit*, "thread of soul") — the immortal and reincarnating principle (the Ego) in conjunction with the Manasic recollections of the preceding lives. Sutratma literally means the Thread-Soul because, like the pearls on a thread, so is the long series of human lives (personalities) strung together on that one thread of the Individuality. Manas must become *taijasi*, the radiant, before it can hang on the Sutratma as a pearl on its thread, and so have full and absolute perception of itself in the Eternity. Too close an association with the terrestrial mind of the human soul alone causes this radiance to be entirely lost.

[5] **Upanishads** (*Sanskrit*, "esoteric doctrine") — the third division of the *Vedas*. They treat very abstruse, metaphysical questions, such as the origin of the Universe; the nature and the essence of the Unmanifested Deity and the manifested gods the connection, primal and ultimate, of spirit and matter; the universality of mind and the nature of the human Soul and Ego.

quite clearly what he has done yesterday, the day before, and even months and years ago. But none of us has the slightest recollection of a preceding life or any fact or event concerning it. I may forget in the morning what I have dreamed during the night, still I know that I have slept and have the certainty that I lived during sleep; but what recollection have I of my past incarnation? How do you reconcile this?

H.P.B.: Yet some people do recollect their past incarnations. This is what the Arhats[1] call Samma-Sambuddha[2] — or the knowledge of the whole series of one's past incarnations.

Student: But we ordinary mortals who have not reached Samma-Sambuddha, how can we be expected to realize this simile?

H.P.B.: By studying it and trying to understand more correctly the characteristics of the three states of sleep. Sleep is a general and immutable law for man as for beast, but there are different kinds of sleep and still more different dreams and visions.

Student: Just so. But this takes us from our subject. Let us return to the materialist, who, while not denying dreams, which he could hardly do, yet denies immortality in general and the survival of his own individuality[3] especially.

H.P.B.: And the materialist is right for once, at least; since for one who has no inner perception and faith, there is no immortality possible. In order to live in the world to come a conscious life, one has to believe first of all in that life during one's terrestrial existence. On these two aphorisms of the Secret Science all the philosophy about the *post-mortem* consciousness and the immortality of the soul is built. The Ego receives always according to its deserts. After the dissolution of the body, there commences for it either a period of full clear

---

[1] **Arhat** (*Sanskrit*, "worthy one," "deserving divine honours") — the name first given to the Jain and subsequently to the Buddhist holy men initiated into the esoteric mysteries. The Arhat is one who has entered the best and highest path, and is thus emancipated from rebirth.

[2] **Samma-Sambuddha** (*Pali*) — a Buddhist mystic term meaning the sudden remembrance of all one's past incarnations, a phenomenon of memory obtained through Yoga.

[3] **Individuality** — one of the names given in Theosophy and Occultism to the human Higher *Ego*. We make a distinction between the immortal and divine and the mortal human Ego which perishes. The latter, or *Personality* (personal Ego), survives the dead body but for a time in Kama-loka; the Individuality prevails forever.

consciousness, a state of chaotic dreams, or an utterly dreamless sleep indistinguishable from annihilation; and these are the three states of consciousness. Our physiologists find the cause of dreams and visions in an unconscious preparation for them during the waking hours; why cannot the same be admitted for the *post-mortem* dreams? I repeat it, *death is sleep.* After death begins, before the spiritual eyes of the soul, a performance according to a programme learnt and very often composed unconsciously by ourselves; the practical carrying out of *correct* beliefs or of illusions which have been created by ourselves. A Methodist will be a Methodist, a Mussulman a Mussulman, of course, just for a time — in a perfect fool's paradise of each man's creation and making. These are the *post-mortem* fruits of the tree of life. Naturally, our belief or unbelief in the fact of conscious immortality is unable to influence the unconditioned reality of the fact itself, once that it exists; but the belief or unbelief in that immortality, as the continuation or annihilation of separate entities, cannot fail to give colour to that fact in its application to each of these entities. Now do you begin to understand it?

Student: I think I do. The materialist, disbelieving in everything that cannot be proven to him by his five senses or by scientific reasoning, and rejecting every spiritual manifestation, accepts life as the only conscious existence. Therefore, according to their beliefs so will it be unto them. They will lose their personal Ego, and will plunge into a dreamless sleep until a new awakening. Is it so?

H.P.B.: Almost so. Remember the universal esoteric teaching of the two kinds of conscious existence: the terrestrial and the spiritual. The latter must be considered real from the very fact that it is the region of the eternal, changeless, immortal cause of all; whereas the incarnating Ego dresses itself up in new garments entirely different from those of its previous incarnations, and in which all except its spiritual prototype is doomed to a change so radical as to leave no trace behind.

Student: Stop! Can the consciousness of my terrestrial *Egos* perish not only for a time, like the consciousness of the materialist, but in any case so entirely as to leave no trace behind?

H.P.B.: According to the teaching, it must so perish and in its fulness, all except that principle which, having united itself with the

Monad, has thereby become a purely spiritual and indestructible essence, one with it in the Eternity. But in the case of an out and out materialist, in whose personal "I" no Buddhi has ever reflected itself, how can the latter carry away into the infinitudes one particle of that terrestrial personality? Your spiritual "I" is immortal; but from your present Self it can carry away into afterlife but that which has become worthy of immortality, namely, the aroma alone of the flower that has been mown by death.

Student: Well, and the flower, the terrestrial "I"?

H.P.B.: The flower, as all past and future flowers which blossomed and died, and will blossom again on the mother bough, the *Sutratma*, all children of one root or Buddhi, will return to dust. Your present "I," as you yourself know, is not the body now sitting before me, nor yet is it what I would call Manas-Sutratma[1] — but Sutratma-Buddhi.[2]

Student: But this does not explain to me at all, why you call life after death immortal, infinite, and real, and the terrestrial life a simple phantom or illusion; since even that *post-mortem* life has limits, however much wider they may be than those of terrestrial life.

H.P.B.: No doubt. The spiritual Ego of man moves in Eternity like a pendulum between the hours of life and death. But if these hours marking the periods of terrestrial and spiritual life are limited in their duration, and if the very number of such stages in Eternity between sleep and awakening, illusion and reality, has its beginning and its end, on the other hand the spiritual "Pilgrim" is eternal. Therefore are the hours of his *post-mortem* life — when, disembodied he stands face to face with truth and not the mirages of his transitory earthly existences during the period of that pilgrimage which we call "the cycle of rebirths" — the only reality in our conception. Such intervals, their limitation notwithstanding, do not prevent the Ego, while ever perfecting itself, to be following undeviatingly, though gradually and slowly, the path to its last transformation, when that Ego having reached its goal becomes the divine *All*. These intervals and stages help towards this final result instead of hindering it; and without such limited intervals the divine Ego could never reach its ultimate goal. This Ego is the actor, and its numerous and various incarnations

---

[1] **Manas-Sutratma** (*Sanskrit*) — the reincarnating Ego.
[2] **Sutratma-Buddhi** (*Sanskrit*) — the spiritual and divine Ego.

the parts it plays. Shall you call these parts with their costumes the individuality of the actor himself? Like that actor, the Ego is forced to play during the Cycle of Necessity, up to the very threshold of *Para-Nirvana*,[3] many parts such as may be unpleasant to it. But as the bee collects its honey from every flower, leaving the rest as food for the earthly worms, so does our spiritual individuality, whether we call it Sutratma or Ego. It collects from every terrestrial personality into which Karma forces it to incarnate, the nectar alone of the spiritual qualities and self-consciousness, and uniting all these into one whole it emerges from its chrysalis as the glorified Dhyan-Chohan.[4] So much the worse for those terrestrial personalities from which it could collect nothing. Such personalities cannot assuredly outlive consciously their terrestrial existence.

Student: Thus then it seems, that for the terrestrial personality, immortality is still conditional. Is then immortality itself *not* unconditional?

H.P.B.: Not at all. But it cannot touch the *non-existent*. For all that which exists as *Sat*,[5] ever aspiring *Sat*, immortality and Eternity are absolute. Matter is the opposite pole of spirit and yet the two are one. The essence of all this, *i.e.*, Spirit, Force and Matter, or the three in one, is as endless as it is beginningless; but the form acquired by this triple unity during its incarnations, the externality, is certainly only the illusion of our personal conceptions. Therefore we call the afterlife alone a reality, while relegating the terrestrial life, its terrestrial personality included, to the phantom realm of illusion.

Student: But why in such a case not call sleep the reality, and waking the illusion, instead of the reverse?

H.P.B.: Because we use an expression made to facilitate the grasping of the subject, and from the standpoint of terrestrial conceptions, it is a very correct one.

---

[3] **Para-Nirvana** (*Sanskrit*) — absolute *Non-Being*, which is equivalent to absolute *Being* or "Be-ness," the state reached by the human Monad at the end of the great cycle.

[4] **Dhyan-Chohans** (*Sanskrit*, "Lords of Light") — the highest gods, answering to the Roman Catholic Archangels. The divine Intelligences charged with the supervision of Cosmos.

[5] **Sat** (*Sanskrit*) — the one ever-present Reality in the infinite world; the divine essence which is, but cannot be said to exist, as it is Absoluteness, Be-ness itself.

Student: Nevertheless, I cannot understand. If the life to come is based on justice and the merited retribution for all our terrestrial suffering, how, in the case of materialists many of whom are ideally honest and charitable men, should there remain of their personality nothing but the refuse of a faded flower!

H.P.B.: No one ever said such a thing. No materialist, if a good man, however unbelieving, can die forever in the fulness of his spiritual individuality. What was said is, that the consciousness of one life can disappear either fully or partially; in the case of a thorough materialist, no vestige of that personality which disbelieved remains in the series of lives.

Student: But is this not annihilation to the Ego?

H.P.B.: Certainly not. One can sleep a dead sleep during a long railway journey, miss one or several stations without the slightest recollection or consciousness of it, awake at another station and continue the journey recollecting other halting places, till the end of that journey, when the goal is reached. Three kinds of sleep were mentioned to you: the dreamless, the chaotic, and the one so real, that to the sleeping man his dreams become full realities. If you believe in the latter why can't you believe in the former? According to what one has believed in and expected after death, such is the state one will have. He who expected no life to come will have an absolute blank amounting to annihilation in the interval between the two rebirths. This is just the carrying out of the programme we spoke of, and which is created by the materialist himself. But there are various kinds of materialists, as you say. A selfish wicked egoist, one who never shed a tear for anyone but himself, thus adding entire indifference to the whole world to his unbelief, must drop at the threshold of death his personality forever. This personality having no tendrils of sympathy for the world around, and hence nothing to hook on to the string of the Sutratma, every connection between the two is broken with the last breath. There being no Devachan for such a materialist, the Sutratma will reincarnate almost immediately. But those materialists who erred in nothing but their disbelief, will oversleep but one station. Moreover, the time will come when the ex-materialist will perceive himself in the Eternity and perhaps repent that he lost even one day, or station, from the life eternal.

Student: Still, would it not be more correct to say that death is birth into a new life, or a return once more to the threshold of eternity?

H.P.B.: You may if you like. Only remember that births differ, and that there are births of "still-born" beings, which are *failures*. Moreover, with your fixed Western ideas about material life, the words "living" and "being" are quite inapplicable to the pure subjective state of *post-mortem* existence. It is just because of such ideas — save in a few philosophers who are not read by the many and who themselves are too confused to present a distinct picture of it — that all your conceptions of life and death have finally become so narrow. On the one hand, they have led to cross materialism, and on the other, to the still more material conception of the other life which the spiritualists have formulated in their Summerland.[1] There the souls of men eat, drink, and marry, and live in a Paradise quite as sensual as that of Mohammed,[2] but even less philosophical. Nor are the average conceptions of the uneducated Christians any better, but are still more material, if possible. What between truncated Angels, brass trumpets, golden harps, streets in paradisiacal cities paved with jewels, and hell-fires, it seems like a scene at a Christmas pantomime. It is because of these narrow conceptions that you find such difficulty in understanding. And, it is also just because the life of the disembodied soul, while possessing all the vividness of reality, as in certain dreams, is devoid of every grossly objective form of terrestrial life, that the Eastern philosophers have compared it with visions during sleep.

---

[1] **Summerland** — the fancy name given by the spiritualists to the abode of their disembodied "spirits," which they locate somewhere in the Milky Way. It is described on the authority of returning "spirits" as a lovely land, having beautiful cities and buildings, a Congress Hall, and museums and libraries for the instruction of the growing generations of young "spirits."

[2] **Mohammed** — the Prophet to whom Quran, the sacred scripture of the Mussulmans, was revealed by Allah (god) himself. The revelation differs, however, from that given by Jehovah to Moses. The Christians abuse the Quran, calling it a hallucination and the work of an Arabian impostor, whereas Mohammed preaches in his scripture the unity of Deity, and renders honour to the Christian prophet *Issa Ben Yussuf* (Jesus, son of Joseph). The Quran is a grand poem, replete with ethical teachings proclaiming loudly Faith, Hope and Charity.

THE MEETINGS OF
THE BLAVATSKY LODGE
17 LANSDOWNE ROAD, LONDON

"Official receptions, weekly meetings, accompanied by learned discussions, with a stenographer behind my back, and sometimes two or three reporters in the corners — all this, as you can easily guess, takes some time. I must specifically prepare myself for every Thursday by studying the materials, because the people who come here are not some ignoramuses from the street, but such people as the electrical engineer Kingsland, Dr. William Bennett and the naturalist Carter Blake. I must be prepared to defend the teachings of Occultism against the adepts of applied science."

— H.P.B.

20 AND 27 DECEMBER 1888

Student: What are the principles which are active during dreams?

H.P.B.: The "principles" active during ordinary dreams — which ought to be distinguished from real dreams, and called idle visions — are *Kama*, the seat of the personal Ego and of desire awakened into chaotic activity by the slumbering reminiscences of the lower Manas.

Student: What is the "lower Manas"?

H.P.B.: It is usually called the animal soul (the *Nephesh*[1] of the Hebrew Kabbalists). It is the ray which emanates from the Higher Manas or permanent Ego, and is that "principle" which forms the human mind — in animals instinct, for animals also dream.[2] The combined action of Kama and the "animal soul," however, are purely mechanical. It is instinct, not reason, which is active in them. During the sleep of the body they receive and send out mechanically electric shocks to and from various nerve-centres. The brain is hardly impressed by them, and memory stores them, of course, without order or sequence. On waking these impressions gradually fade out, as does every fleeting shadow that has no basic or substantial reality underlying it. The retentive faculty of the brain, however, may register and preserve them if they are only impressed strongly enough. But, as a rule, our memory registers only the fugitive and distorted impressions which the brain receives at the moment of awakening. This aspect of "dreams" however, has been sufficiently observed and is described correctly enough in modern physiological and biological works, as such human dreams do not differ much from those of the animals. That which is entirely *terra incognita*[3] for Science is the real dreams and experiences of the higher Ego, which are also called dreams, but ought not to be so termed, or else the term for the other sleeping "visions" changed.

Student: How do these differ?

---

[1] **Nephesh** (*Hebrew*, "breath of life") — generally means *prana* (*Sanskrit*, "life"); in the Kabbalah it is the animal passions and the animal soul. Therefore, *Nephesh* is the synonym of the Prana-Kamic Principle, or the vital animal soul in man.
[2] The word dream means really "to slumber" — the latter function being called in Russian "*dreamatj*."
[3] **Terra incognita** (*Latin*) — unknown territory.

H.P.B.: The nature and functions of real dreams cannot be understood unless we admit the existence of an immortal Ego in mortal man, independent of the physical body, for the subject becomes quite unintelligible unless we believe — that which is a fact — that during sleep there remains only an animated form of clay, whose powers of independent thinking are utterly paralysed.

But if we admit the existence of a higher or permanent *Ego* in us — which Ego must not be confused with what we call the "Higher Self," we can comprehend that what we often regard as dreams, generally accepted as idle fancies, are, in truth, stray pages torn out from the life and experiences of the *inner* man, and the dim recollection of which at the moment of awakening becomes more or less distorted by our physical memory. The latter catches mechanically a few impressions of the thoughts, facts witnessed, and deeds performed by the *inner* man during its hours of complete freedom. For our *Ego* lives its own separate life within its prison of clay whenever it becomes free from the trammels of matter, *i.e.*, during the sleep of the physical man. This Ego it is which is the actor, the real man, the true human self. But the physical man cannot feel or be conscious during dreams; for the personality, the outer man, with its brain and thinking apparatus, are paralysed more or less completely.

We might well compare the real Ego to a prisoner, and the physical personality to the gaoler of his prison. If the gaoler falls asleep, the prisoner escapes, or, at least, passes outside the walls of his prison. The gaoler is half asleep, and looks, nodding all the time, out of a window, through which he can catch only occasional glimpses of his prisoner, as he would a kind of shadow moving in front of it. But what can he perceive, and what can he know of the real actions, and especially the thoughts, of his charge?

Student: Do not the thoughts of the one impress themselves upon the other?

H.P.B.: Not during sleep, at all events; for the real Ego does not think as his evanescent and temporary personality does. During the waking hours the thoughts and Voice of the Higher Ego do or do not reach his gaoler — the physical man, for they are the *Voice of his Conscience*, but during his sleep they are absolutely the "Voice in the desert." In the thoughts of the *real* man, or the immortal

"Individuality," the pictures and visions of the Past and Future are as the Present; nor are his thoughts like ours, subjective pictures in our cerebration, but living acts and deeds, present actualities. They are realities, even as they were when speech expressed in sounds did not exist; when thoughts were things, and men did not need to express them in speeches, for they instantly realized themselves in action by the power of *Kriya-Shakti*,[1] that mysterious power which transforms instantaneously ideas into visible forms, and these were as objective to the "man" of the early Third Race[2] as objects of sight are now to us.

Student: How, then, does Esoteric Philosophy account for the transmission of even a few fragments of those thoughts of the Ego to our physical memory which it sometimes retains?

H.P.B.: All such are reflected on the brain of the sleeper, like outside shadows on the canvas walls of a tent, which the occupier sees as he wakes. Then the man thinks that he has dreamed all that, and feels as though *he* had lived through something, while in reality it is the *thought-actions* of the true Ego which he has dimly perceived. As he becomes fully awake, his recollections become with every minute more distorted, and mingle with the images projected from the physical brain, under the action of the stimulus which causes the sleeper to awaken. These recollections, by the power of association, set in motion various trains of ideas.

---

[1] **Kriya-Shakti** (*Sanskrit*, "power to create") — the power of thought; one of the seven forces of Nature. Creative potency of the *Siddhis* (powers) of the full Yogis.

[2] **Root Race** or **Race** — a stage in the evolution of humanity. This Theosophical term does not refer to any ethnicities. There are Seven Races in total, each of which develops a particular quality in man, solidifying or rarefying the matter clothing his body. Humanity in the first two Races, as well as in the first half of the Third Race, did not have physical bodies — their bodies were of ethereal matter. Those people were sexless beings, not endowed with reason and never dying, for they did not have flesh. They had existed for 300 million years. Eighteen million years ago, in the middle of the Third Race — the Lemurians — the separation of the sexes took place, and people began to conceive their progeny. Humanity received dense physical bodies and began to reflect the Higher Mind. The Fourth Race — the Atlanteans — came into being approximately 4–5 million years ago. But only three sub-races of the Atlanteans evolved on the continent of Atlantis, while the remaining four were in Egypt, Asia, and Europe. The current Fifth Race, known as the Aryan, originated about one million years ago in India. Today, a transition to the next, more spiritual, Sixth Race is in progress.

Student: It is difficult to see how the Ego can be acting during the night things which have taken place long ago. Was it not stated that dreams are not subjective?

H.P.B.: How can they be subjective when the dream state is itself for us, and on our plane, at any rate, a subjective one? To the dreamer (the Ego), on his own plane, the things on that plane are as objective to him as our acts are to us.

Student: What are the senses which act in dreams?

H.P.B.: The senses of the sleeper receive occasional shocks, and are awakened into mechanical action; what he hears and sees are, as has been said, a distorted reflection of the thoughts of the Ego. The latter is highly spiritual, and is linked very closely with the higher principles, Buddhi and Atma. These higher principles are entirely inactive on our plane, and the higher Ego (Manas) itself is more or less dormant during the waking of the physical man. This is especially the case with persons of very materialistic mind. So dormant are the Spiritual faculties, because the Ego is so trammelled by matter, that *It* can hardly give all its attention to the man's actions, even should the latter commit sins for which that Ego — when reunited with its *lower* Manas — will have to suffer conjointly in the future. It is, as I said, the impressions projected into the physical man by this Ego which constitute what we call "conscience"; and in proportion as the Personality, the lower Soul (or *Manas*), unites itself to its higher consciousness, or Ego, does the action of the latter upon the life of mortal man become more marked.

Student: This Ego, then, is the "Higher Ego"?

H.P.B.: Yes; it is the higher Manas illuminated by Buddhi; the principle of self-consciousness, the "I-am-I," in short. It is the *Karana-sharira,*[1] the immortal man, which passes from one incarnation to another.

Student: Is the "register" or "tablet of memory" for the true dream-state different from that of waking life?

---

[1] **Karana-sharira** (*Sanskrit,* "causal body") — it is dual in its meaning. Exoterically, it is Avidya, ignorance, or that which is the cause of the evolution of a human ego and its reincarnation; hence the lower Manas esoterically — the causal body or Karanopadhi stands in the Taraka Raja Yoga as corresponding to Buddhi and the Higher Manas, or Spiritual Soul.

H.P.B.: Since dreams are in reality the actions of the Ego during physical sleep, they are, of course, recorded on their own plane and produce their appropriate effects on this one. But it must be always remembered that dreams in general, and as we know them, are simply our waking and hazy recollections of these facts.

It often happens, indeed, that we have no recollection of having dreamt at all, but later in the day the remembrance of the dream will suddenly flash upon us. Of this there are many causes. It is analogous to what sometimes happens to every one of us. Often a sensation, a smell, even a casual noise or a sound, brings instantaneously to our mind long-forgotten events, scenes and persons. Something of what was seen, done, or thought by the "night-performer," the Ego, impressed itself at that time on the physical brain, but was not brought into the conscious, waking memory, owing to some physical condition or obstacle. This impression is registered on the brain in its appropriate cell or nerve-centre, but owing to some accidental circumstance it "hangs fire," so to say, till something gives it the needed impulse. Then the brain slips it off immediately into the conscious memory of the waking man; for as soon as the conditions required are supplied, that particular centre starts forthwith into activity, and does the work which it had to do, but was hindered at the time from completing.

Student: How does this process take place?

H.P.B.: There is a sort of conscious telegraphic communication going on incessantly, day and night, between the physical brain and the inner man. The brain is such a complex thing, both physically and metaphysically, that it is like a tree whose bark you can remove layer by layer, each layer being different from all the others and each having its own special work, function, and properties.

Student: What distinguishes the "dreaming" memory and imagination from those of waking consciousness?

H.P.B.: During sleep the physical memory and imagination are of course passive, because the dreamer is asleep: his brain is asleep, his memory is asleep, all his functions are dormant and at rest. It is only when they are stimulated, as I told you, that they are aroused. Thus the consciousness of the sleeper is not active, but passive. The inner man, however, the real Ego, acts independently during the sleep of the body;

but it is doubtful if any of us — unless thoroughly acquainted with the physiology of occultism — could understand the nature of its action.

Student: What relation have the Astral Light and Akasha to memory?

H.P.B.: The former is the "tablet of the memory" of the animal man, the latter of the spiritual Ego. The "dreams" of the Ego, as much as the acts of the physical man, are all recorded, since both are actions based on causes and producing results. Our "dreams," being simply the waking state and actions of the true Self, must be, of course, recorded somewhere. Read "Karmic Visions"[1] in *Lucifer,*[2] and note the description of the real Ego, sitting as a spectator of the life of the hero, and perhaps something will strike you.

Student: What, in reality, is the Astral Light?

---

[1] See H. P. Blavatsky, "Karmic Visions," *Collected Writings*, vol. 9 (Wheaton, IL: Theosophical Publishing House, 1962), pp. 318–339.

[2] *Lucifer* (*Latin*, "Light-Bearer") — a monthly magazine published in London from 1887 to 1897. H.P.B explained its name in the following way: "The name of the present magazine — rather equivocal to orthodox Christian ears — is due to no careless selection, but arose in consequence of much thinking over its fitness, and was adopted as the best symbol to express that object and the results in view. Now, the first and most important, if not the sole object of the magazine, is expressed in the line from the 1st Epistle to the Corinthians, on its title page. It is to bring light to "the hidden things of darkness"; to show in their true aspect and their original real meaning things and names, men and their doings and customs; it is finally to fight prejudice, hypocrisy and shams in every nation, in every class of Society, as in every department of life. The task is a laborious one, but it is neither impracticable nor useless, if even as an experiment. Thus, for an attempt of such nature, no better title could ever be found than the one chosen. 'Lucifer' is the pale morning-star, the precursor of the full blaze of the noon-day sun — the 'Eosphoros' of the Greeks. It shines timidly at dawn to gather forces and dazzle the eye after sunset as its own brother 'Hesperos' — the radiant evening star, or the planet Venus. No fitter symbol exists for the proposed work — that of throwing a ray of truth on everything hidden by the darkness of prejudice, by social or religious misconceptions; especially by that idiotic routine in life, which, once that a certain action, a thing, a name, has been branded by slanderous inventions, however unjust, makes respectable people, so-called, turn away shiveringly, refusing to even look at it from any other aspect than the one sanctioned by public opinion. Such an endeavour then, to force the weak-hearted to look truth straight in the face, is helped most efficaciously by a title belonging to the category of branded names." See H. P. Blavatsky, "What's in a Name?" *Collected Writings*, vol. 8 (Wheaton, IL: Theosophical Publishing House, 1960), pp. 5–13.

H.P.B.: As the Esoteric Philosophy teaches us, the *Astral Light* is simply the dregs of *Akasha* or the Universal Ideation in its metaphysical sense. Though invisible, it is yet, so to speak, the phosphorescent radiation of the latter, and is the medium between it and man's thought-faculties. It is these which pollute the Astral Light, and make it what it is — the storehouse of all human and especially psychic iniquities. In its primordial genesis, the Astral Light as a radiation is quite pure, though the lower it descends approaching our terrestrial sphere, the more it differentiates, and becomes as a result impure in its very constitution. But man helps considerably in this pollution, and gives it back its essence far worse than when he received it.

Student: Can you explain to us how it is related to man, and its action in dream-life?

H.P.B.: Differentiation in the physical world is infinite. Universal Ideation — or *Mahat*,[3] if you like it — sends its homogeneous radiation into the heterogeneous world, and this reaches the human or *personal* minds through the Astral Light.

Student: But do not our minds receive their illuminations direct from the Higher Manas through the Lower? And is not the former the pure emanation of divine Ideation — the "Manasa-Putras,"[4] which incarnated in men?

H.P.B.: They are. Individual *Manasa-Putras* or the Kumaras[5] are the direct radiations of the divine Ideation — "individual" in the sense of later differentiation, owing to numberless incarnations. In sum they are the collective aggregation of that Ideation, become on our plane, or from our point of view, *Mahat*, as the Dhyan-Chohans are in

---

[3] **Mahat** (*Sanskrit*, "great principle") — the Universal Cosmic Mind; the first principle of Universal Intelligence and Consciousness; the producer of *Manas*, the thinking principle, and of *Ahankara*, egotism or the feeling of "I am I" (in the lower Manas).

[4] **Manasa-Putras** (*Sanskrit*, "Sons of Mind" or "mind-born Sons") — a name given to our Higher Egos before they incarnated in mankind. In the *exoteric* though allegorical and symbolical Puranas (the sacred and ancient writings of Hindus), it is the title given to the mind-born Sons of Brahma, the *Kumara*.

[5] **Kumara** (*Sanskrit*, "youth") — a virgin boy, or young celibate. The first Kumaras are the seven sons of Brahma born out of the limbs of the god, in the so-called ninth creation. It is stated that the name was given to them owing to their formal refusal to "procreate their species," and so they "remained Yogis," as the legend says.

their aggregate the Word or "Logos"[1] in the formation of the World. Were the Personalities (Lower Manas or the *physical* minds) to be inspired and illumined solely by their higher *alter Egos* there would be little sin in this world. But they are not; and getting entangled in the meshes of the Astral Light, they separate themselves more and more from their parent Egos. Read and study what Éliphas Lévi[2] says of the Astral Light, which he calls Satan and the Great Serpent. The Astral Light has been taken too literally to mean some sort of a second blue sky. This imaginary space, however, on which are impressed the countless images of all that ever was, is, and will be, is but a too sad reality. It becomes in, and for, man — if at all psychic — and who is not? — a tempting Demon, his "evil angel," and the inspirer of all our worst deeds. It acts on the will of even the sleeping man, through visions impressed upon his slumbering brain (which visions must not be confused with the "dreams"), and these germs bear their fruit when he awakes.

Student: What is the part played by Will in dreams?

H.P.B.: The will of the outer man, our volition, is of course dormant and inactive during dreams; but a certain bent can be given to the slumbering will during its inactivity, and certain after-results developed by the mutual inter-action — produced almost mechanically — through union between two or more principles into one, so that they will act in perfect harmony, without any friction or a single false note, when awake. But this is one of the dodges of "black magic," and when used for good purposes belongs to the training of an Occultist. One must be far advanced on the "path" to have a will which can act consciously during his physical sleep, or act on the will of another person during the sleep of the latter, *e.g.*, to control his dreams, and thus control his actions when awake.

Student: We are taught that a man can unite all his principles into one — what does this mean?

---

[1] **Logos** (*Greek*, "word") — the manifested deity with every nation and people; the outward expression, or the effect of the cause which is ever concealed. Thus, speech is the Logos of thought; hence, it is aptly translated by the "Verbum" and "Word" in its metaphysical sense.

[2] **Éliphas Lévi** (1810–1875) — the pen name of Alphonse Louis Constant, a French poet and author of over twenty esoteric books.

H.P.B.: When an Adept succeeds in doing this he is a *Jivanmukta*:[3] he is no more of this earth virtually, and becomes a Nirvanee,[4] who can go into *Samadhi*[5] at will. Adepts are generally classed by the number of "principles" they have under their perfect control, for that which we call will has its seat in the higher Ego, and the latter, when it is rid of its sin-laden personality, is divine and pure.

Student: What part does Karma play in dreams? In India they say that every man receives the reward or punishment of all his acts, both in the waking and the dream state.

H.P.B.: If they say so, it is because they have preserved in all their purity and remembered the traditions of their forefathers. They know that the Self is the *real* Ego, and that it lives and acts, though on a different plane. The external life is a "dream" to this Ego, while the inner life, or the life on what we call the dream plane, is the real life for it. And so the Hindus (the profane, of course) say that Karma is generous, and rewards the real man in dreams as well as it does the false personality in physical life.

Student: What is the difference, "karmically," between the two?

H.P.B.: The physical animal man is as little responsible as a dog or a mouse. For the bodily form all is over with the death of the body. But the real Self, that which emanated its own shadow, or the lower thinking personality, that enacted and pulled the wires during the life of the physical automaton, will have to suffer conjointly with its *factotum*[6] and *alter ego*[7] in its next incarnation.

Student: But the two, the higher and the lower, Manas are one, are they not?

H.P.B.: They are, and yet they are not — and that is the great mystery. The Higher Manas or Ego is essentially divine, and therefore

---

[3] **Jivanmukta** (*Sanskrit*, "liberated while living") — an Adept or yogi who has reached the ultimate state of holiness, and separated himself from matter; a Mahatma, or *Nirvanee*, a "dweller in bliss" and emancipation. Virtually, one who has reached Nirvana during life.

[4] **Nirvanee** (*Sanskrit*) — an emancipated soul, one who has attained Nirvana.

[5] **Samadhi** (*Sanskrit*, "to bring together") — a state of ecstatic and complete trance. He who possesses this power is able to exercise an absolute control over all his faculties, physical or mental; it is the highest state of Yoga.

[6] **Factotum** (*Latin*) — a servant who does all kinds of work.

[7] **Alter ego** (*Latin*) — another self.

pure; no stain can pollute it, as no punishment can reach it, *per se*,[1] the more so since it is innocent of, and takes no part in, the deliberate transactions of its Lower Ego. Yet by the very fact that, though dual and during life the Higher is distinct from the Lower, "the Father and Son" *are one*, and because that in reuniting with the parent Ego, the Lower Soul fastens upon and impresses upon it all its bad as well as good actions — both have to suffer, the Higher Ego, though innocent and without blemish, has to bear the punishment of the misdeeds committed by the *lower* Self together with it in their future incarnation. The whole doctrine of atonement is built upon this old esoteric tenet; for the Higher Ego is the antitype of that which is on this earth the type, namely, the personality. It is, for those who understand it, the old Vedic story of Visvakarman[2] over again, practically demonstrated. Visvakarman, the all-seeing Father-God, who is beyond the comprehension of mortals, ends, as son of Bhuvana,[3] the holy Spirit, by *sacrificing himself to himself*, to save the worlds. The mystic name of the "Higher Ego" is, in the Indian philosophy, *Kshetrajna*,[4] or "embodied Spirit," that which knows or informs *kshetra*,[5] "the body." Etymologize the name, and you will find in it the term *aja*,[6] "first-born," and also the "lamb." All this is very suggestive, and volumes might be written upon the pregenetic and postgenetic development of type and antitype — of Christ-*Kshetrajna*, the "God-Man," the First-born, symbolized as the "lamb." *The Secret Doctrine*[7] shows that the Manasa-Putras or incarnating Egos have taken upon themselves, voluntarily and knowingly, the burden of

---

[1] **Per se** (*Latin*) — by or in itself; intrinsically.

[2] **Visvakarman** (*Sanskrit*, "all maker") — the omnificent and highest Creator and Logos in the *Rig Veda*, the great architect of the world. He is called the "Father of the Gods" and "Father of the sacred Fire."

[3] **Bhuvana** (*Sanskrit*, "world") — a name of Rudra or Shiva, one of the Indian *Trimurti* (Trinity).

[4] **Kshetrajna** (*Sanskrit*, "one who is conscious of the body") — the embodied spirit, the Conscious Ego in its highest manifestations; the reincarnating Principle; the "Lord" in us.

[5] **Kshetra** (*Sanskrit*, "field") — the body as the field of activities.

[6] **Aja** (*Sanskrit*, "unborn," "uncreated") — an epithet belonging to many of the primordial gods, but especially to the first *Logos* — a radiation of the Absolute on the plane of illusion.

[7] H. P. Blavatsky, *The Secret Doctrine: The Synthesis of Science, Religion, and Philosophy*, 2 vols. (London: Theosophical Publishing Company, 1888).

all the future sins of their future personalities. Thence it is easy to see that it is neither Mr. A nor Mr. B, nor any of the personalities that periodically clothe the Self-Sacrificing Ego, which are the real Sufferers, but verily the innocent *Christos*[8] within us. Hence the mystic Hindus say that the Eternal Self, or the Ego (the one in three and three in one), is the "Charioteer" or driver; the personalities are the temporary and evanescent passengers; while the horses are the animal passions of man. It is, then, true to say that when we remain deaf to the Voice of our Conscience, we crucify the Christos within us. But let us return to dreams.

Student: Are so-called prophetic dreams a sign that the dreamer has strong clairvoyant faculties?

H.P.B.: It may be said, in the case of persons who have truly prophetic dreams, that it is because their physical brains and memory are in closer relation and sympathy with their "Higher Ego" than in the generality of men. The Ego-Self has more facilities for impressing upon the physical shell and memory that which is of importance to such persons than it has in the case of other less gifted persons. Remember that the only God man comes in contact with is his own God, called Spirit, Soul and Mind, or Consciousness, and these three are one.

But there are weeds that must be destroyed in order that a plant may grow. We must die, said St. Paul,[9] that we may live again. It is

---

[8] **Christos** (*Greek*, "anointed one") — the Higher Self in man. There are *Chrestos* and *Christos*. Chrestos is a disciple on probation — a candidate for becoming a full Initiate. When he had attained to this through long trials and suffering, and had been "anointed" (*i.e.*, "rubbed with oil," as were Initiates, as the last touch of ritualistic observance), his name was changed into Christos, the "purified," in esoteric or mystery language. In mystic symbology, *Christos* meant that the "Way," the Path, was already trodden and the goal reached; when the fruits of the arduous labour, uniting the personality of evanescent clay with the indestructible Individuality, transformed it thereby into the immortal Ego. "At the end of the Way stands the *Christos*," the *Purifier*, and the union once accomplished, the *Chrestos*, the "man of sorrow," became *Christos* himself. Paul the Apostle knew this, and meant this precisely, when he is made to say, in bad a translation: "I travail in birth again until Christ be formed in you" (Galatians 4:19), the true rendering of which is "…until ye form the Christos within yourselves." Every good individual, therefore, may find Christ in his "inner man" as Paul expresses in Ephesians 3:16, whether he be Jew, Muslim, Hindu, or Christian.

[9] **Paul the Apostle** — an Initiate, the incarnation of the Master Hilarion.

through destruction that we may improve, and the three powers, the preserving, the creating and the destroying, are only so many aspects of the divine spark within man.

Student: Do Adepts dream?

H.P.B.: No advanced Adept dreams. An Adept is one who has obtained mastery over his four lower principles, including his body, and does not, therefore, let flesh have its own way. He simply paralyses his lower Self during Sleep, and becomes perfectly free. A dream, as we understand it, is an illusion. Shall an Adept, then, dream when he has rid himself of every other illusion? In his sleep he simply lives on another and more real plane.

Student: Are there people who have never dreamed?

H.P.B.: There is no such man in the world so far as I am aware. All dream more or less; only with most, dreams vanish suddenly upon waking. This depends on the more or less receptive condition of the brain ganglia. Unspiritual men, and those who do not exercise their imaginative faculties, or those whom manual labour has exhausted, so that the ganglia do not act even mechanically during rest, dream rarely, if ever, with any coherence.

Student: What is the difference between the dreams of men and those of beasts?

H.P.B.: The dream state is common not only to all men, but also to all animals, of course, from the highest mammalia to the smallest birds, and even insects. Every being endowed with a physical brain, or organs approximating thereto, must dream. Every animal, large or small, has, more or less, physical senses; and though these senses are dulled during sleep, memory will still, so to say, act mechanically, reproducing past sensations. That dogs and horses and cattle dream we all know, and so also do canaries, but such dreams are, I think, merely physiological. Like the last embers of a dying fire, with its spasmodic flare and occasional flames, so acts the brain in falling asleep. Dreams are not, as Dryden[1] says, "interludes which fancy makes," for such can only refer to physiological dreams provoked by indigestion, or some idea or event which has impressed itself upon the active brain during waking hours.

---

[1] John Dryden (1631–1700) — an English poet, playwright and translator.

Student: What, then, is the process of going to sleep?

H.P.B.: This is partially explained by Physiology. It is said by Occultism to be the periodical and regulated exhaustion of the nervous centres, and especially of the sensory ganglia of the brain, which refuse to act any longer on this plane, and, if they would not become unfit for work, are compelled to recuperate their strength on another plane or *Upadhi*. First comes the *Svapna*, or dreaming state, and this leads to that of *Shushupti*.[2] Now it must be remembered that our senses are all dual, and act according to the plane of consciousness on which the thinking entity energizes. Physical sleep affords the greatest facility for its action on the various planes; at the same time it is a necessity, in order that the senses may recuperate and obtain a new lease of life for the *Jagrata*, or waking state, from the *Svapna* and *Shushupti*. According to *Raja Yoga*,[3] *Turiya*[4] is the highest state. As a man exhausted by one state of the life fluid seeks another; as, for example, when exhausted by the hot air he refreshes himself with cool water; so sleep is the shady nook in the sunlit valley of life. Sleep is a sign that waking life has become too strong for the physical organism, and that the force of the life current must be broken by changing the waking for the sleeping state. Ask a good clairvoyant to describe the aura of a person just refreshed by sleep, and that of another just before going to sleep. The former will be seen bathed in rhythmical vibrations of life currents — golden, blue, and rosy; these are the electrical waves of Life. The latter is, as it were, in a mist of intense golden-orange hue, composed of atoms whirling with an almost incredible spasmodic rapidity, showing that the person begins to be too strongly saturated with Life; the life essence is too strong for his physical organs, and he must seek relief in the shadowy side of that essence, which side is the dream element, or physical sleep, one of the states of consciousness.

---

[2] **Sushupti** (*Sanskrit*, "deep sleep") — the deep sleep state.

[3] **Raja Yoga** (*Sanskrit*, "royal path") — the system of developing psychic and spiritual powers and union with one's *Higher Self* — or the Supreme Spirit. The exercise, regulation and concentration of thought. Raja Yoga is opposed to Hatha Yoga, the physical or psycho-physiological training in asceticism.

[4] **Turiya** (*Sanskrit*, "the fourth") — almost a Nirvanic state in Samadhi, which is itself a beatific state of the contemplative Yoga beyond this plane. A condition of the higher Triad, quite distinct (though still inseparable) from the conditions of *Jagrata* (waking), *Svapna* (dreaming), and *Sushupti* (sleeping).

Student: But what is a dream?

H.P.B.: That depends on the meaning of the term. You may "dream," or, as we say, sleep visions, awake or asleep. If the Astral Light is collected in a cup or metal vessel by will-power, and the eyes fixed on some point in it with a strong will to see, a waking vision or "dream" is the result, if the person is at all sensitive. The reflections in the Astral Light are seen better with closed eyes, and, in sleep, still more distinctly. From a lucid state, vision becomes translucid; from normal organic consciousness it rises to a transcendental state of consciousness.

Student: To what causes are dreams chiefly due?

H.P.B.: There are many kinds of dreams, as we all know. Leaving the "digestion dream" aside, there are brain dreams and memory dreams, mechanical and conscious visions. Dreams of warning and premonition require the active co-operation of the inner Ego. They are also often due to the conscious or unconscious co-operation of the brains of two living persons, or of their two Egos.

Student: What is it that dreams, then?

H.P.B.: Generally the physical brain of the personal Ego, the seat of memory, radiating and throwing off sparks like the dying embers of a fire. The memory of the Sleeper is like an Æolian seven-stringed harp;[1] and his state of mind may be compared to the wind that sweeps over the chords. The corresponding string of the harp will respond to that one of the seven states of mental activity in which the sleeper was before falling asleep. If it is a gentle breeze the harp will be affected but little; if a hurricane, the vibrations will be proportionately powerful. If the personal Ego is in touch with its higher principles and the veils of the higher planes are drawn aside, all is well; if on the contrary it is of a materialistic, animal nature, there will be probably no dreams; or if the memory by chance catch the breath of a "wind" from a higher plane, seeing that it will be impressed through the sensory ganglia of the cerebellum, and not by the direct agency of the spiritual Ego, it will receive pictures and sounds so distorted and inharmonious that even a Devachanic vision would appear a nightmare or grotesque caricature. Therefore there is no simple answer to the question "What

---

[1] Æolian harp — a musical instrument played by the wind, named after the ancient Greek god of the wind Æolus.

is it that dreams," for it depends entirely on each individual what principle will be the chief motor in dreams, and whether they will be remembered or forgotten.

Student: Is the apparent objectivity in a dream really objective or subjective?

H.P.B.: If it is admitted to be apparent, then of course it is subjective. The question should rather be, to whom or what are the pictures or representations in dreams either objective or subjective? To the physical man, the *dreamer*, all he sees with his eyes shut, and in or through his mind, is of course subjective. But to the *Seer* within the physical dreamer, that Seer himself being subjective to our material senses, all he sees is as objective as he is himself to himself and to others like himself. Materialists will probably laugh, and say that we make of a man a whole family of entities, but this is not so. Occultism teaches that physical man is one, but the thinking man septenary, thinking, acting, feeling, and living on seven different states of being or planes of consciousness, and that for all these states and planes the permanent Ego (not the false personality) has a distinct set of senses.

Student: Can these different senses be distinguished?

H.P.B.: Not unless you are an Adept or highly-trained chela, thoroughly acquainted with these different states. Sciences, such as biology, physiology, and even psychology (of the Maudsley,[2] Bain,[3] and Herbert Spencer[4] schools), do not touch on this subject. Science teaches us about the phenomena of volition, sensation, intellect, and instinct, and says that these are all manifested through the nervous centres, the most important of which is our brain. She will speak of the peculiar agent or substance through which these phenomena take place as the vascular and fibrous tissues, and explain their relation to one another, dividing the ganglionic centres into motor, sensory and sympathetic, but will never breathe one word of the mysterious agency of intellect itself, or of the mind and its functions.

Now, it frequently happens that we are conscious and know that we are dreaming; this is a very good proof that man is a multiple

---

[2] **Henry Maudsley** (1835–1918) — an English psychiatrist.
[3] **Alexander Bain** (1818–1903) — a Scottish philosopher, psychologist and educationalist.
[4] **Herbert Spencer** (1820–1903) — an English philosopher and sociologist.

being on the thought plane; so that not only is the Ego, or thinking man, Proteus,[1] a multiform, ever-changing entity, but he is also, so to speak, capable of separating himself on the mind or dream plane into two or more entities; and on the plane of illusion which follows us to the threshold of Nirvana, he is like Ain-Soph[2] talking to Ain-Soph, holding a dialogue with himself and speaking through, about, and to himself. And this is the mystery of the inscrutable Deity in the *Zohar*,[3] as in the Hindu philosophies; it is the same in the Kabbalah,[4] Puranas,[5] Vedantic metaphysics, or even in the so-called Christian mystery of the Godhead and Trinity. Man is the microcosm of the macrocosm;[6] the god on earth is built on the pattern of the god in nature. But the universal consciousness of the real Ego transcends a millionfold the self-consciousness of the personal or false Ego.

Student: Is that which is termed "unconscious cerebration" during sleep a mechanical process of the physical brain, or is it a conscious operation of the Ego, the result of which only is impressed on the ordinary consciousness?

H.P.B.: It is the latter; for is it possible to remember in our conscious state what took place while our brain worked unconsciously? This is apparently a contradiction in terms.

---

[1] **Proteus** (*Greek*, "first") — a Greek sea god capable of changing his shape; the intangible, omnipotent, and omnipresent "Unknown," indivisible in its Essence, and eluding form, yet appearing under all and every form.

[2] **Ain-Soph** or **Ein Sof** (*Hebrew*, "infinite") — the nameless and limitless One Principle, without form or being, having no likeness with anything else; the Absolute.

[3] **Zohar** (*Hebrew*, "radiance") — a compendium of Kabbalistic Theosophy, which shares with the *Sepher Yetzirah* the reputation of being the oldest extant treatise on the Hebrew esoteric religious doctrines.

[4] **Kabbalah** (*Hebrew*, "to receive") — the hidden wisdom of the Hebrew Rabbis of the middle ages, derived from the older secret doctrines concerning divine things and cosmogony, which were combined into a theology after the time of the captivity of the Jews in Babylon. It treats hitherto esoteric interpretations of the Jewish Scriptures and teaches several methods of interpreting Biblical allegories. Originally, the doctrines were transmitted "from mouth to ear" only; hence, the name *Kabbalah*.

[5] **Puranas** (*Sanskrit*, "ancient") — a collection of symbolical and allegorical sacred writings.

[6] **Macrocosm** (*Greek*, "great Universe") — the Cosmos.

Student: How does it happen that persons who have never seen mountains in nature often see them distinctly in sleep, and are able to note their features?

H.P.B.: Most probably because they have seen pictures of mountains; otherwise it is somebody or something in us which has previously seen them.

Student: What is the cause of that experience in dreams in which the dreamer seems to be ever striving after something, but never attaining it?

H.P.B.: It is because the physical self and its memory are shut out of the possibility of knowing what the real Ego does. The dreamer only catches faint glimpses of the doings of the Ego, whose actions produce the so-called dream in the physical man, but is unable to follow it consecutively. A delirious patient, on recovery, bears the same relation to the nurse who watched and tended him in his illness as the physical man to his real Ego. The Ego acts as consciously within and without him as the nurse acts in tending and watching over the sick man. But neither the patient after leaving his sick bed, nor the dreamer on awaking, will be able to remember anything except in snatches and glimpses.

Student: How does sleep differ from death?

H.P.B.: There is an analogy certainly, but a very great difference between the two. In sleep there is a connection, weak though it may be, between the lower and higher mind of man, and the latter is more or less reflected into the former, however much its rays may be distorted. But once the body is dead, the body of illusion, *Mayavi-rupa*, becomes Kama-rupa, or the animal soul, and is left to its own devices. Therefore, there is as much difference between the spook and man as there is between a gross material, animal, but sober mortal, and a man incapably drunk and unable to distinguish the most prominent surroundings; between a person shut up in a perfectly dark room and one in a room lighted, however imperfectly, by some light or other.

The lower principles are like wild beasts, and the higher Manas is the rational man who tames or subdues them more or less successfully. But once the animal gets free from the master who held it in subjection; no sooner has it ceased to hear his voice and see him than it starts off again to the jungle and its ancient den. It takes, however, some time for an animal to return to its original and natural state, but these lower principles or "spook" return instantly, and no sooner has the higher Triad[1] entered the Devachanic state than the lower Duad[2] rebecomes that which it was from the beginning, a principle endued with purely animal instinct, made happier still by the great change.

Student: What is the condition of the Linga-sharira, or plastic body, during dreams?

H.P.B.: The condition of the Plastic form is to sleep with its body, unless projected by some powerful desire generated in the higher Manas. In dreams it plays no active part, but on the contrary is entirely passive, being the involuntarily half-sleepy witness of the experiences through which the higher principles are passing.

Student: Under what circumstances is this wraith seen?

H.P.B.: Sometimes, in cases of illness or very strong passion on the part of the person seen or the person who sees; the possibility is mutual. A sick person, especially just before death, is very likely to see in dream, or vision, those whom he loves and is continually thinking of, and so also is a person awake, but intensely thinking of a person who is asleep at the time.

Student: Can a Magician summon such a dreaming entity and have intercourse with it?

H.P.B.: In black magic it is no rare thing to evoke the "spirit" of a sleeping person; the sorcerer may then learn from the apparition any secret he chooses, and the sleeper be quite ignorant of what is occurring. Under such circumstances that which appears is the *Mayavi-rupa;* but there is always a danger that the memory of the living man will preserve the recollections of the evocation and remember it as a vivid dream. If it is not, however, at a great distance, the Double or *Linga-sharira* may be evoked, but this can neither speak nor give information, and there is always the possibility of the sleeper being killed through this forced separation. Many sudden deaths in sleep have thus occurred, and the world been no wiser.

---

[1] **Higher Triad** — the three higher principles in man, consisting of Atma, Buddhi and Manas, or Spirit, Soul and Mind.

[2] **Lower Duad** — the combination of Kama-rupa (the fourth principle) and lower Manas (the personal aspect of the fifth principle) after the higher Triad enters Devachan.

Student: Can there be any connection between a dreamer and an entity in "Kama-loka"?

H.P.B.: The dreamer of an entity in *Kama-loka* would probably bring upon himself a nightmare, or would run the risk of becoming "possessed" by the "spook" so attracted, if he happened to be a medium, or one who had made himself so passive during his waking hours that even his higher Self is now unable to protect him. This is why the mediumistic state of passivity is so dangerous, and in time renders the Higher Self entirely helpless to aid or even warn the sleeping or entranced person. Passivity paralyses the connection between the lower and higher principles. It is very rare to find instances of mediums who, while remaining passive *at will*, for the purpose of communicating with some higher Intelligence, some *exterraneous* spirit (not disembodied), will yet preserve sufficiently their personal will so as not to break off all connection with the higher Self.

Student: Can a dreamer be *en rapport*[3] with an entity in Devachan?

H.P.B.: The only possible means of communicating with Devachanees is during sleep by a dream or vision, or in trance state. No Devachanee can descend into our plane; it is for us — or rather our *inner Self* — to ascend to his.

Student: What is the state of mind of a drunkard during sleep?

H.P.B.: It is no real sleep, but a heavy stupor; no physical rest, but worse than sleeplessness, and kills the drunkard as quickly. During such stupor, as also during the waking drunken state, everything turns and whirls around in the brain, producing in the imagination and fancy horrid and grotesque shapes in continual motion and convolutions.

Student: What is the cause of nightmare, and how is it that the dreams of persons suffering from advanced consumption are often pleasant?

H.P.B.: The cause of the former is simply physiological. A nightmare arises from oppression and difficulty in breathing; and difficulty in breathing will always create such a feeling of oppression and produce a sensation of impending calamity. In the second case, dreams become pleasant because the consumptive grows daily severed

---

[3] **En rapport** (*French*) — in harmony; in accord.

from his material body, and more clairvoyant in proportion. As death approaches, the body wastes away and ceases to be an impediment or barrier between the brain of the physical man and his Higher Self.

Student: Is it a good thing to cultivate dreaming?

H.P.B.: It is by cultivating the power of what is called "dreaming" that clairvoyance is developed.

Student: Are there any means of interpreting dreams — for instance, the interpretations given in dream-books?

H.P.B.: None but the clairvoyant faculty and the spiritual intuition of the "interpreter." Every dreaming Ego differs from every other, as our physical bodies do. If everything in the universe has seven keys to its symbolism on the physical plane, how many keys may it not have on higher planes?

Student: Is there any way in which dreams may be classified?

H.P.B.: We may roughly divide dreams also into seven classes, and subdivide these in turn. Thus, we would divide them into:

1. Prophetic dreams. These are impressed on our memory by the Higher Self, and are generally plain and clear: either a voice heard or the coming event foreseen.

2. Allegorical dreams, or hazy glimpses of realities caught by the brain and distorted by our fancy. These are generally only half true.

3. Dreams sent by Adepts, good or bad, by mesmerizers, or by the thoughts of very powerful minds bent on making us do their will.

4. Retrospective; dreams of events belonging to past incarnations.

5. Warning dreams for others who are unable to be impressed themselves.

6. Confused dreams, the causes of which have been discussed above.

7. Dreams which are mere fancies and chaotic pictures, owing to digestion, some mental trouble, or suchlike external cause.

10 JANUARY 1889

Mr. B. Keightley: In the Proem to *The Secret Doctrine*, speaking of space, this is said… [Reads quotation, vol. 1, p. 8.[1]] That is just the few words on the subject of space in the abstract: but the first Sloka[2] of the first Stanza[3] runs as follows: "The Eternal Parent (Space), wrapped in her ever invisible robes, had slumbered once again for seven eternities,"[4] and on this the first question that strikes one to ask is why is the Eternal Parent, or Space, called feminine here?

H.P.B.: Perhaps it is a mistake to do so. But since it is impossible to define Parabrahm,[5] or that which is beyond human conception, therefore once that we speak of that first something which *can be* conceived, we had better say "She." In all the cosmogonies it is the goddess and goddesses that come first, the former one becoming the all immaculate mother from which proceed all the gods. We have to adopt either one or the other gender, as we cannot say *It*. From *It* nothing can proceed, strictly speaking, neither a radiation nor an emanation.

Mr. Keightley: Is that the Egyptian Neith?[6]

H.P.B.: In truth, it is beyond Neith. But it is Neith in one sense.

Mr. Keightley: Then the *It* itself is not the seven-skinned Eternal Father-Mother in this Stanza?

H.P.B.: Assuredly not. The *It* is the beyond, the *meta*, the Parabrahm. This which is, is the female aspect of Brahma, the male.

Mr. Keightley: And that is what is spoken of in the Proem that I read as the "seven-skinned Father-Mother"?

---

[1] "Space is called in the esoteric symbolism 'the Seven-Skinned Eternal Mother-Father.' It is composed from its undifferentiated to its differentiated surface of seven layers. 'What is that which was, is, and will be, whether there is a Universe or not; whether there be gods or none?' asks the esoteric Senzar Catechism. And the answer made is — Space."

[2] **Sloka** (*Sanskrit*, "praise") — a verse in ancient Sanskrit texts.

[3] The discussed Stanzas from the secret *Book of Dzyan* can be found in *Cosmic Evolution* at the end of this book.

[4] *The Secret Doctrine*, vol. 1, p. 35.

[5] **Parabrahm** (*Sanskrit*, "beyond Brahma") — the Supreme Infinite Brahma, the Absolute — the attributeless, the secondless reality; the impersonal and nameless universal Principle.

[6] **Neith** (*Egyptian*) — the Queen of Heaven in Egypt; the first and prime creator, who created the Cosmos and all in it.

H.P.B.: Yes, it becomes that at the first flutter of differentiation. Then the subjective proceeds to emanate — or falls into the objective and becomes what they called the Mother Goddess, from which proceeds the Logos or Father God, the unmanifested. For the manifested Logos is quite a different thing again and is called the "Son" in all the cosmogonies.

Mr. Keightley: Is the first differentiation from the absolute *It* female always?

H.P.B.: It is sexless; but the female aspect is the first it assumes. Take the Jewish Kabbalah. You have "Ain-Soph" which is also the *It*, the infinite, the endless, the boundless, the adjectives used in conjunction with *It* being negatives of every kind of attributes. From *It* the negative, the zero, 0, proceeds number One, the positive which is Sephira[1] or the Crown. The Talmudists[2] say it is the "Torah,"[3] the law, which they call the wife of Ain-Soph. Now see the Hindu cosmogony. There you find that Parabrahm is not mentioned; but only Mulaprakriti:[4] there is Parabrahm and there is Mulaprakriti, which latter is the lining so to say, or the aspect of Parabrahm in the invisible universe. Mulaprakriti means the root of matter, but Parabrahm cannot be called the "root," for it is the rootless root of all that is. Therefore, you must begin with Mulaprakriti, the veil of Brahman as they call it. Take any cosmogony in the world: you will always find it begins thus; the first manifestation is the Mother Goddess, the reflection, the root or the first plane of substance. From, or rather in that Mother Goddess is formed the unmanifested Logos her son and husband at once, as he is called the Concealed Father; and from these two the manifested Logos which is the Son itself — the Architect of all the visible universe.

---

[1] **Sephira** (*Hebrew*, "counting, enumeration") — an emanation of Deity; the parent and synthesis of the ten Sephiroth (the plural form of *Sephira*) when she stands at the head of the Sephirothal Tree of Life; in the Kabbalah, Sephira, or the "Sacred Aged," is the Divine Intelligence (the same as Sophia), the first emanation from the Endless or Ain-Soph.

[2] **Talmudist** — one who studies and follows the Talmud.

Talmud (*Hebrew*, "instruction, learning") — Rabbinic commentaries on the Jewish faith. It contains the civil and canonical laws of the Jews.

[3] **Torah** (*Hebrew*, "Law") — the Law; the Five Books of Moses: Genesis, Exodus, Leviticus, Numbers and Deuteronomy.

[4] **Mulaprakriti** (*Sanskrit*, "root of Nature") — the Parabrahmic root, the abstract deific feminine principle — undifferentiated substance; Akasha; Matter.

Mr. Keightley: The second question is, "What aspect of space, or the unknown deity 'That,' of which you speak further on, is here called the Eternal Parent"?

H.P.B.: Well it is just this androgynous something; the *Svabhavat*[5] of the Buddhists. It is non-differentiated, hence — an abstraction. It is the Mulaprakriti of the Vedantins. If you proceed to make it correspond with the human principles it will be Buddhi; Atma corresponding to Parabrahm. Then comes Mahat which corresponds to Manas.

Mr. Keightley: And so on downwards.

H.P.B.: Yes.

Mr. Keightley: Then what are the seven layers of space? You speak in the Proem of the "Seven-Skinned Father-Mother."

H.P.B.: Plato[6] and Hermes Trismegistus[7] would have regarded this as the *Divine Thought*, and Aristotle[8] would have viewed this "Mother-Father" as the *privation* of matter. It is that which will become the seven planes of Being, commencing with the spiritual and passing through the psychic to the material plane. The seven planes of thought or the seven states of consciousness correspond to these planes. All these septenaries are symbolized by the seven "Skins."

Mr. Keightley: The divine ideas in the Divine Mind? But the Divine Mind is not yet.

H.P.B.: The Divine Mind *is*, and must be, before differentiation takes place. It is called the divine Ideation, which is eternal in its Potentiality and periodical in its Potency, when it becomes *Mahat*,

---

[5] **Svabhavat** (*Sanskrit*, "plastic substance") — the eternal and the uncreated self-existing substance which produces all; the spirit and essence of substance; the plastic essence of matter; "Father-Mother." From it, all nature proceeds and into it, all returns at the end of the life-cycles.

[6] **Plato** (c.420s–348 BCE) — an Initiate into the Mysteries and the greatest Greek philosopher, whose writings are known the world over. He was the pupil of Socrates and the teacher of Aristotle.

[7] **Hermes Trismegistus** (*Greek*, "thrice great Hermes") — the God of Wisdom, Thoth or Thot in Egypt. Hermes Trismegistus is the name of Hermes or Thoth in his human aspect. According to Plato, he "discovered numbers, geometry, astronomy and letters."

[8] **Aristotle** (384–322 BCE) — an ancient Greek philosopher, scientist and polymath who was a student of Plato and a teacher of Alexander the Great.

Anima Mundi[1] or Universal Soul. But remember that, however you name it, each of these conceptions has its most metaphysical, most material, and also intermediate aspects.

Mr. Keightley: What is the meaning of the term "Ever invisible robes"?

H.P.B.: It is, of course, as every allegory in the Eastern philosophies, a figurative expression. Perhaps it may be the hypothetical *protyle*[2] that Professor Crookes[3] is in search of, but which can certainly never be found on this our earth or plane. It is the non-differentiated substance or *spiritual matter*.

Mr. Keightley: Is it *Laya*?[4]

H.P.B.: "Robes" and *all* are in the Laya condition, up to that point from which the primordial substance begins to differentiate, and thus gives birth to the universe and all in it.

Mr. Keightley: Are they called "invisible" because they are not objective to any differentiation of the consciousness?

H.P.B.: Say rather "invisible" to consciousness, if any differentiated consciousness were possible at that stage of evolution. Most assuredly it cannot be seen. Do not you see in the book that even for the Logos Mulaprakriti is only a veil? And it is a veil that the Logos sees, this veil or the robes in which the Absolute is enveloped, but cannot perceive the latter.

---

[1] **Anima Mundi** (*Latin*, "Soul of the World") — the divine essence which permeates, animates and informs all, from the smallest atom of matter to man and god. It is, in a sense, the "seven-skinned mother" of the stanzas in *The Secret Doctrine*, the essence of seven planes of sentience, consciousness and differentiation, moral and physical. In its highest aspect, it is *Nirvana*; in its lowest, the Astral Light. It is of igneous, ethereal nature in the objective world of form (and then ether), and divine and spiritual in its three higher planes. When it is said that every human soul was born by detaching itself from the *Anima Mundi*, it means, esoterically, that our higher Egos are of an essence identical with It, which is a radiation of the ever unknown Universal Absolute.

[2] **Protyle** (*Greek*, "first substance") — the term used by William Crookes to describe the primal substance from which all chemical elements originated.

[3] **William Crookes** (1832–1919) — an English physicist and chemist who discovered thallium, invented the radiometer, and studied cathode rays.

[4] **Laya** or **Layam** (*Sanskrit*, "to dissolve," "to disintegrate") — a point of equilibrium (zero-point) in physics and chemistry. In occultism, that point where substance becomes homogeneous and is unable to act or differentiate.

Mr. Harbottle:[5] Is it correct to call it Mulaprakriti?

H.P.B.: If you speak to a Hindu you will find that what a Vedantin calls Mulaprakriti is called Aditi[6] in the Vedas.[7] The Vedanta philosophy means, literally speaking, "the end of all knowledge." The great difficulty in studying the Hindu systems esoterically is that in India alone there are six schools of philosophy. Now if you analyse these you will find that they agree perfectly in substance. Fundamentally they are identical; but there is such a wealth of names, such a quantity of side issues, of all kinds of details and ornamentations; of sons being their own fathers, and fathers born from their own daughters, that you become lost in all this, as in a jungle. State anything you will from the esoteric standpoint to a Hindu, and if he only wants to he can contradict and prove you in the wrong, from the standpoint of his own particular sectarian view, or the philosophy he accepts. Each of the six schools of India has its own views and its own (to it) peculiar terms. So that, unless you hold strictly to some one school and say so, your special terminology is sure to be misunderstood. It is nothing but splitting hairs, and quarreling about things that have no importance in reality.

Mr. Keightley: Then the same term identically is used in quite a different sense by different philosophies: for instance, Buddhi has one meaning in the esoteric philosophy, and a different meaning in the Sankhya?[8]

---

[5] **Thomas Benfield Harbottle** (1857–1904) — the President of the Blavatsky Lodge from 1887 to March 1889.

[6] **Aditi** (*Sanskrit,* "limitless") — the Vedic name for the *Mulaprakriti* of the Vedantists; the abstract aspect of Parabrahman, though both unmanifested and unknowable. In the *Vedas,* Aditi is the "Mother-Goddess," her terrestrial symbol being infinite and shoreless space.

[7] **Vedas** (*Sanskrit,* "knowledge") — the most ancient and the most sacred scriptures in Sanskrit.

[8] **Sankhya** (*Sanskrit,* "empirical") — the system of philosophy founded by Kapila Rishi, a system of analytical metaphysics, and one of the six *Darshanas* or schools of philosophy. It discourses on numerical categories and the meaning of the twenty-five *tattvas* (the forces of nature in various degrees). This "atomistic school," as some call it, explains nature by the interaction of twenty-four elements with *purusha* (spirit) modified by the three gunas (qualities), teaching the eternity of *pradhana* (primordial, homogeneous matter), or the self-transformation of nature and the eternity of the human Egos.

H.P.B.: And quite a different meaning again in the *Vishnu*[1] *Purana* in which there are seven Prakritis[2] that come from Mahat and the latter is called Maha-Buddhi.[3]

Mr. Keightley: That is again quite different.

H.P.B.: No it is not; fundamentally it is perfectly the same thing, though in every philosophy you will have some other name and meaning given to it.

Mr. Kingsland:[4] Yet we must call it something. Are we to have our own terms?

H.P.B.: I think the best thing you could do would be to coin new English words. If you want to ever become Western philosophers, you had better not take from the Hindus, who will be the first ones to say: "Behold, these Europeans! They take from us all they can, disfigure everything and do no good." Find equivalents for all these terms, coin new English words, and do not depart from them; and then there will be no confusion.

Mr. Kingsland: Does *protyle* come near the term *Laya*?

H.P.B.: There it is. You are obliged to throw yourself on the tender mercies of ancient Greek and other ancient languages, but the modern languages are really too materialistic and I doubt whether you can get any words to express that which you need.

---

[1] **Vishnu** (*Sanskrit*, "all-pervasive") — the second person of the Hindu Trimurti (Trinity), composed of Brahma, Vishnu and Shiva. In the *Rig Veda*, Vishnu is no high god, but simply a manifestation of solar energy, described as "striding through the seven regions of the Universe in *three* steps and enveloping all things with the dust of his beams." Whatever may be the six other occult significances of the statement, this is related to the same class of types as the seven and ten Sephiroth, as the *seven* and *three* orifices of the perfect Adam Kadmon, as the seven principles and the higher triad in man, etc. Later on, this mystic type becomes a great God, the preserver and the renovator, he "of a thousand names — Sahasranama."

[2] **Prakriti** (*Sanskrit*, "Nature") — Nature in general, nature as opposed to *Purusha* — spiritual nature and Spirit, which together are the two primeval aspects of the One Unknown Deity.

[3] **Maha-Buddhi** (*Sanskrit*, "Great Soul") — the Intelligent Soul of the World. The seven *Prakritis* or seven "natures" or planes, are counted from Maha-Buddhi downwards.

[4] **William Kingsland** (1855–1936) — an English engineer, scientist and author; the President of the Blavatsky Lodge from March 1889.

Mr. Ellis:[5] We may as well get it from the Greek as the Anglo-Saxon; all our scientific words are coined either from the Greek or the Latin, and become English only by use. Such a word as *protyle* is not really English at all.

Mr. Keightley: It is just adopted.

H.P.B.: How long? Hardly two years ago?

Mr. Harbottle: If we have one word that answers the purpose, why not use it? Mr. Crookes probably used the word *protyle* on the most materialistic plane of all.

H.P.B.: What he means by it, is primordial homogeneous matter.

Mr. Ellis: Perhaps, just when it is about to enter into the state of differentiation.

H.P.B.: Then certainly it is not "the robes" that he will ever discover, because they are on the seventh plane of matter and he is searching on this one, which is the lowest.

Mr. Keightley: His protyle is "pre-hydrogen."

H.P.B.: Nothing else, and yet no one will ever be able to find it. How many times have the scientists been disappointed. How often have they thought they had come at last to a real atom, protylic and homogeneous, to find it each time a compound thing of two or three elements! But let us go on.

Mr. Keightley: Is there, so to speak, on each of the seven planes, homogeneous matter relatively to that plane? Is it the root of every particular plane?

H.P.B.: There is; only it must be homogeneous only for that plane of perception and for those who are on that plane. If Mr. Crookes is ever able to find the protyle he is after it will be homogeneous for only him and us. The illusion may last for some time, until the Sixth Race perhaps, when mankind will be entirely changed. Humanity is ever changing, physically and mentally and perfecting itself with every Race more, as you know we are acquiring learning, perception and knowledge that we did not have before. Therefore, the science of today is the ignorance of tomorrow.

---

[5] **William Ashton Ellis** (1852–1919) — an English doctor and the translator of Richard Wagner's prose works.

Dr. Williams: I should think it would be a great mistake to adopt any word that has been already adopted by a scientist with another meaning. Protoplasm[1] had once come almost to mean the same thing as protyle does, but they have now narrowed it down.

H.P.B.: And quite right; because protyle, after all, comes from the Greek word *hyle*,[2] and the Greeks used it certainly not as a word belonging to this plane. Besides which it was used in the Chaldean[3] cosmogony, before the Greeks.

Mr. Harbottle: And yet is not *hyle* used to mean "the root of matter" by certain writers?

H.P.B.: It is; but these writers are not very ancient.

Mr. Harbottle: No, but they used it in a sense which rather transcends that. The word *hyle* is now used really as giving very much the same idea that we endeavoured to give when we used the word Mulaprakriti.

H.P.B.: Well, I do not know. There's Dr. Lewins,[4] who calls himself a Hylo-Idealist, if you please; so there is the metaphysical meaning of the word desecrated entirely. So you certainly had better use another term. *Laya* does not mean anything in particular, on that plane or the other, but means a state, a condition. It is a Sanskrit word conveying the meaning of something entirely undifferentiated and changeless, a zero-point wherein all differentiation ceases. That is what it means and nothing else.

Mr. Kingsland: The first differentiation would represent matter on the seventh plane?

H.P.B.: I believe, you can say so.

Mr. Kingsland: That is to say, I suppose that Mr. Crookes' ideal protyle would be matter on its seventh plane.

---

[1] **Protoplasm** — the living substance found in all cells, essential for the functioning and maintenance of life.

[2] **Hyle** (*Greek,* "matter") — primordial stuff or matter; esoterically the homogeneous sediment of Chaos or the Great Deep. The first principle out of which the objective Universe was formed.

[3] **Chaldeans** — at first a tribe, then a caste, of learned Kabbalists. They were the sages, the magians of Babylonia, astrologers and diviners.

[4] **Robert Lewins** (1817–1895) — a British philosopher who developed the atheist theory called *Hylo-Idealism* ("material idealism").

H.P.B.: I do not know Mr. Crookes' ideas about that. I am not sure, but what I understand he wants to find is simply matter in that state which he too calls the "zero-point."

Mr. Keightley: Which would be so to speak the Laya point of this plane.

H.P.B.: I doubt whether he has any idea about other planes at all, and suspect he is perfectly satisfied with this one. What he wants to find here is the protyle atom, this is plain. But what can even he or anyone else know of atoms, something that no one has ever seen. What is an atom to scientists but another "working hypothesis" added to all the rest? Do you know, Dr. Williams?

Dr. Williams: No, indeed I do not.

H.P.B.: But, as a chemist, you must know what they mean by it?

Mr. Kingsland: It is a convenient definition of what they think it.

H.P.B.: But surely they must have come now to the conclusion that it is no convenient definition, no more than their *elements* are. They speak about some sixty or seventy elements, and laugh at the old honest nomenclature of the four and five elements of the ancients, and yet where are their own elements? Mr. Crookes has come to the conclusion that strictly speaking there is no such thing known as a chemical element. They have never arrived yet at a simple or single molecule, least of all, at an atom. What is it then?

Mr. Kingsland: An atom is a convenient term to divide up a molecule.

H.P.B.: If it is convenient to them I have no objection to it. You call also iron an element, don't you?

Mr. Ellis: I think we ought never to forget that it is called the atomic *theory*. It has never been claimed as anything more.

H.P.B.: Aye, but even the word "theory" is now used in a wrong sense, by the modern schools, as shown by Sir William Hamilton.[5] Why should they, once they laugh at metaphysics, use a purely metaphysical term when applying it to physical science? And there are those to whom theory and axiom mean the same thing. So long as their pet theory is not today upset — which happens more often than the leap year — they regard it as an *axiom*; and woe to him, who dares

---

[5] **William Hamilton** (1788–1856) — a Scottish metaphysician.

doubt or even touch it, outside the sacred precincts of the fanes of science!

Mr. Ellis: It is its inventor, Dalton,[1] who called it atomic theory.

H.P.B.: Well, let us proceed.

Mr. Keightley: You speak of seven eternities. What are the seven eternities, and how can there be such a division in Pralaya[2] when there is no one to be conscious of time?

H.P.B.: The modern astronomer knows "the ordinances of heaven" still less than his ancient brother did. Yet the fact, that if asked whether he could bring forth Mazzaroth[3] in his season, or was with "him" who spread out the sky — the astronomer would reply in the negative — prevents him in no wise from speculating about the ages of the sun, moon, and geological times, when there was not a living man with or without consciousness on earth. Why could not the ancients speculate or cognize *backward* and forwards as moderns do?

Mr. Keightley: Why should you speak of seven eternities? Why put it that way?

H.P.B.: Because of the invariable law of analogy. As Manvantara is divided into seven periods so is Pralaya; as day is composed of twelve hours, so is night. Shall we say because we are asleep during night and are not conscious of time, that the hours do not run the same? They pass on and the clocks strike though we may not hear or count them. Pralaya is the "Night" after the Manvantaric "Day." There is no one by and consciousness is *asleep* with the rest. But since it exists and is in full activity during Manvantara, and that it is fully alive to the fact that the law of analogy and periodicity is immutable, and being so that it must act equally at both ends, why cannot the sentence be used?

Mr. Ellis: I should want to know how you can count an eternity.

H.P.B.: Here we are! Because we Westerners are foolish enough to talk about and to speculate on something that has neither beginning

---

[1] John Dalton (1766–1844) — an English chemist, physicist and meteorologist.

[2] Pralaya (*Sanskrit*, "dissolution") — a period of obscuration or repose (planetary, cosmic or universal). The opposite of Manvantara (*Sanskrit*, "age of a Manu") — a period of active life.

[3] Mazzaroth (*Hebrew*, "constellations") — a Biblical Hebrew term found in the Book of Job (38:32), often interpreted as a term for the Zodiac or the Constellations thereof.

nor can end, therefore the ancients must have done the same! I say they did not. No people in days of old has ever meant by "Eternity" beginningless and endless duration. Take the Greeks, speaking of Æons.[4] Do these mean something eternal? No more than their *Neroses*[5] did. They had no word for eternity in the sense we give it. *Parabrahm* and *Ain-Soph*, and the *Zeruana Akerne*[6] of the Avesta[7] represent alone such an eternity — all the other periods are finite. All these were astronomical, moreover, based on tropical years and other enormous cycles — withal, finite and therefore, they are not eternities, but a way of speaking of eternity. It is the word Æon in the Bible that was translated as eternity; and yet it is not only a period but means an angel and a being as well.

Mr. Harbottle: But is it not true to say in Pralaya there is the Great Breath?

H.P.B.: Assuredly, for the "Great Breath" is ceaseless; it is the universal *perpetuum mobile.*[8]

Mr. Harbottle: If so, it is not possible to divide it into periods. It does away with the idea of absolute and complete nothingness. It does seem incompatible that you should speak of any *number* of periods; but if you have the Great Breath you might say there are so many indrawings and outdrawings of the Great Breath.

H.P.B.: And this would make away with the idea of absolute rest, were not this absoluteness of rest counteracted by the absoluteness of motion. Therefore, one is as good as the other. There is a magnificent poem on the Pralaya. I forget the name of its Hindu author. It is written by a very ancient Rishi[9] and he writes and compares that motion of the Great Breath during the Pralaya to the rhythmical motions of

---

[4] Æon or Æons (*Greek*, "age") — periods of time; emanations proceeding from the divine essence, and celestial beings; genii and angels with the Gnostics.

[5] **Neros** (*Hebrew*) — a cycle, which the Orientalists describe as consisting of 600 years. There were three kinds of Neros: the greater, the middle and the less. It is the latter cycle only which was of 600 years.

[6] **Zeruana Akerne** (*Persian*, "Eternal Time") — the Unknown Cause from whose depths come the Light and the Darkness that, through their struggle, form the existence of the present world; the Absolute.

[7] **Avesta** (*Zend*, "Law") — the sacred scripture of Zoroastrianism.

[8] **Perpetuum mobile** (*Latin*) — perpetual motion; an engine that can operate indefinitely without an external energy source.

[9] **Rishi** (*Sanskrit*, "sage") — an Adept; the inspired one.

the ocean. It is a most magnificent picture. It is the only reference on this subject that I know or ever heard of.

Mr. ——: The only difficulty is when the word eternity is used instead of the word Æon.

H.P.B.: Why should I use the Greek word when I can use an English one? I give the explanation in *The Secret Doctrine* by saying the ancients had no such thing as eternity — as commonly understood.

Mr. ——: Still, Æon, to the ordinary English reader, would not mean eternity.

H.P.B.: We have quite enough of foreign words; I have tried to avoid and put them into English.

Mr. Harbottle: Æon, to most European Christian readers, does mean eternity, as they have translated it as "for ever and for ever."

Mr. Ellis: That always involves a beginning at least.

Mr. Harbottle: No, "for ever and ever" backwards and forwards.

Mr. Ellis: It is sempiternal. It has a beginning, but it has no end. If you make a thing plural you divide it. There you make a point of beginning and a point of end. You will always make a division.

Mr. Harbottle: Then you agree with the seven eternities.

Mr. Ellis: I think it is only a word that may be taken up by one of the daily papers. I do not think there is any difficulty in the least. The meaning of it is that there are seven concurrent phases, going on at the same time. It is division of time laterally. That is what I meant, if you can understand it. That is what I wanted to know, if you count it in that way.

H.P.B.: I count it in such a way as to translate as best I can the real meaning of a very difficult and abstruse text, and then to give the interpretations that I was taught and have learned. It is just as you say; because if you read my explanations, there you will find the same thing.

Mr. Keightley: Before we leave the subject, I would ask, is the relation of Pralaya and Manvantara strictly analogous to the relation between sleeping and waking?

H.P.B.: In a certain sense only, of course. It has that relation, if you take it in the abstract. During night we all exist and we are, though we sleep and may be unconscious of so living. But during Pralaya everything disappears from the phenomenal universe and merges in the noumenal. Therefore, *de facto*[1] there is a great difference.

Mr. Keightley: You remember you gave us a very remarkable thing about sleep, saying that "it was the shady side of life." Then is the Pralaya the shady side of cosmic life?

H.P.B.: You may call it so. It is a time of rest. Even cosmic matter, indestructible though it be in its essence, must have a time of rest, its Laya condition notwithstanding. The absoluteness of the eternal all-containing one essence has to manifest itself equally, in rest and activity.

Mr. Keightley: The next question is on Sloka 2. "Time was not, for it lay asleep in the infinite bosom of duration."[2] The first point is what is the difference between time and duration as here used?

H.P.B.: Duration *is*: it is neither a beginning nor an end, nor time, as its very name implies, though we may divide it into Past, Present and Future. What is time? How can you call that "time" which has neither beginning or an end? Duration is beginningless and endless; time is finite.

Mr. Keightley: Duration is the infinite, and time the finite conception?

H.P.B.: Time can be divided, duration cannot; therefore the word duration is used.

Mr. Kingsland: The only way you can define time is by the motions of the earth.

H.P.B.: But, you can define time in your conception also, can't you?

Mr. Kingsland: Duration, you mean?

H.P.B.: No, time; for as to "duration" there is no such thing as splitting it, or putting landmarks on it. It is impossible.

Mr. Kingsland: But we can define time by certain periods.

H.P.B.: But not duration, which is the one real eternity. In this finite and phenomenal universe, of course you can. All you can do is to divide time in duration and take illusions for realities.

Mr. Kingsland: But without that you would not be able to define time at all.

---

[1] **De facto** (*Latin*) — in fact; actually.
[2] *The Secret Doctrine*, vol. 1, p. 36.

H.P.B.: Why not? The natural division of time is night and day.

Mr. Kingsland: The essential idea of duration is existence, it seems to me.

H.P.B.: Existence has limited and definite periods, and duration is a thing which has neither a beginning nor an end. While it is something perfectly abstract and contains time, time is that which has no duration. Duration is just like space. Space as an abstraction is endless; but in its concreteness and limitation, space becomes a representation of something. Of course you can call space the distance between this book and that table or between any two points you may imagine. It may be enormous, or it may be infinitesimal, yet it will always be space. But all such specifications are divisions in human conceptions. In reality, space is what the ancients called Deity itself.

Mr. Keightley: Then time is the same as space. They are one in the abstract.

H.P.B.: As two abstractions they may be one; yet I would say duration and space, not time and space.

Mr. Keightley: You get time and space with differentiation, time being the subjective character corresponding to space, the objective, one being the objective and the other being the subjective side of all manifestation.

Mr. Harbottle: They are the only attributes of the infinite, really. But attribute is a wrong word, inasmuch as they are coextensive with the infinite; but then that is also a difficult word.

Mr. Ellis: How can you say that? They are nothing but the creations of your own intellect. They are nothing but the forms in which you cannot help conceiving things. How can they be called attributes? Take cause and effect, they are nothing but the way in which you think of things. If you had a different brain you would think about things in a different way.

H.P.B.: And now you speak as a Hylo-Idealist would. We do not speak of the phenomenal world, but of the noumenal universe. It is without space and time, but still there is duration and abstract space. In the Occult Catechism[1] it is asked: "what is the thing which always

---

[1] **Catechism** (*Greek*, "to teach orally") — a summary or manual of teachings and principles, often in a question-and-answer format.

is, which you cannot imagine as not 'being,' do what you may." The answer is — Space. For, there may be not a single man in the universe to think of it, not a single eye to perceive it, not a single brain to sense it, but still space *is* — and you cannot make away with it.

Mr. Ellis: Because you cannot help thinking of it.

H.P.B.: My or your thinking has nothing to do with it. Space exists there where there is nothing and must exist in full vacuum as elsewhere.

Mr. Ellis: The philosophers have reduced it to this. They say they also are nothing but attributes, nothing but accidents.

H.P.B.: Buddha[2] says better than this still. He says speaking of Nirvana, that Nirvana, after all, is also an illusion.

Mr. Ellis: You would not call eternal space and duration the only attributes of the Infinite?

H.P.B.: I would not give to the Infinite any attributes at all. That only which is finite and conditioned can have attributes.

Mr. Keightley: You touched upon a question that is put here. Time and space in modern philosophy are conceived of, as you said, simply as forms of the human physical brain, and as having no existence apart from human intellect, as we know it. Thence arises this old question: "We can conceive of no matter that is not extended" (in consequence of that faculty or that peculiarity of mental faculty), "no extension that is not extension of something. Is it the same on the higher planes, and if so, what is the substance that fills absolute space, and is it identical with that space?" You see, that brings to a focus the question.

H.P.B.: "Is it the same on another plane?" Now how can I answer your query? I never travelled in absolute space, as far as I know. All I can give you, is simply the speculations of those who had a thousand

---

[2] **Buddha** (*Sanskrit*, "Enlightened") — the highest degree of knowledge. To become a Buddha, one has to break through the bondage of sense and personality; to acquire a complete perception of the Real Self and learn not to separate it from all other selves; to learn, by experience, the utter unreality of all phenomena of the visible Cosmos foremost of all; to reach a complete detachment from all that is evanescent and finite, and live while yet on Earth in the immortal and the everlasting alone, in a supreme state of holiness. This degree of enlightenment was reached by Gautama, the Prince of Kapilavastu.

times more brains than I, or any of you have. Some of you would call them vagaries. We don't.

Mr. Ellis: Does not he answer his own question in the question itself?

H.P.B.: How?

Mr. Ellis: He presupposes that that is the only way in which the intellect can think.

Mr. Keightley: I say on this plane our intellect is limited. In this way we only conceive of matter extended.

Mr. Ellis: If your soul or anything else could conceive, we will imagine for a moment, in another form. You cannot get an answer in words to that, can you? Your intellect has to understand those words. Therefore intellect, not being able to conceive in any other way, cannot get an answer in any other way.

H.P.B.: On this very same plane, there are not only the intellects of men. There are other intellects, and intelligences, call them whatever you like. The minds of animals, from the highest to the lowest, from elephant down to the ant. I can assure you that the ant has in relation to its own plane just as good an intellect as we have. If it cannot express it to us in words, it yet shows high reasoning powers, besides and above instinct, as we all know. Thus finding on this plane of ours so many and such varied states of consciousness and intelligences, we have no right to take into consideration or account only our own human consciousness, as though there were no other. Nor can we, beyond accepting it as a fact, presume to decide how far animal and insect consciousness goes.

Mr. Hall:[1] Why not? Natural science can find it out.

H.P.B.: No, it cannot. It can speculate and guess but will never be able with its present methods to acquire any certitude for such speculation. If Sir John Lubbock[2] could become an ant for a while, and think as an ant, and remember it when returning to his own sphere of consciousness then would he know something for certain; not otherwise.

---

[1] **Roger Hall** — a member of the Esoteric Section of the Theosophical Society.
[2] **John Lubbock** (1834–1913) — an English politician, banker and archaeologist, the author of *Ants, Bees and Wasps*.

Mr. Keightley: The ant's conceptions of time and space are not our own conceptions.

H.P.B.: And therefore, if we find such conceptions that are not our conceptions and that are entirely on another plane, we have no right to deny *a priori*[3] the existence of other planes of which we may have no idea but which exist, nevertheless, planes higher and lower than our own by many degrees.

Dr. Williams: May I suggest on that point that every animal is more or less born with its faculties? Man is born the most helpless and ignorant of all and progresses, so far as we know, forever, in the acquisition of the enlargement of his intelligences. That seems to be the most practical difference between the intelligence of all animals and man.

Mr. Ellis: Have you ever seen a dog taught to sit on its hind legs?

Dr. Williams: Whenever animals are put beyond the influence of civilization they always return without exception to the primitive and prior condition into which they were born. This shows that they have no capability of holding on longer than they are under the influence of civilization.

Mr. Ellis: They would lose a great deal. But how are we to know they have not developed before? If they were put in different circumstances, of course they would lose a great deal.

Dr. Williams: So far as our experience goes, we know the terms on which they were, and very clearly too.

Mr. Ellis: We know they can be taught, therefore they resemble man. If we put man back out of civilization what does he become? Nothing but the animal.

H.P.B.: To say that animals have no intelligence is the greatest fallacy in the world. How shall science explain to us the facts that there is no animal or insect which cannot be taught to remember, to obey the voice of the master. Why, take a flea. He will fire a gun, and he will draw water, and he will do all kinds of tricks.[4] If a flea has an intellect, what must it be with others which are more developed? How can we say that the animals have got no intellect?

---

[3] **A priori** (*Latin*) — without examination or analysis; before experience.

[4] In the 19th century, "flea circuses" were sideshow attractions.

Mr. ——: They have not got the quality of thinking.

H.P.B.: They have not got the quality of reasoning, and yet they have.

Mr. ——: A horse will pull a string and fire off a cannon, but he does not know anything about the objects of it.

H.P.B.: This is a question that has never been satisfactorily answered, because it is simply our organization and our human conceit that causes us to make of man a king of all the animals. I say there are animals compared to which a mortal man is the lowest of the animals. There is not a dirtier animal in the world than man, and I say it is a great insult to any animal to go and compare him to a man. I would object if I were an animal. You cannot find any man who is as faithful as a dog. It shows feeling and affection. It does not show reasoning power, but it does show intelligence, feelings and memory. It is just the same as a man.

Mr. ——: Look at the birds that pull up their own water.

Mr. ——: But you cannot compare that with human intelligence.

H.P.B.: I think in all probability an ant has a thousand times more intellect than a man, if we take the proportionate size.

Mr. ——: It is well-known that any intelligent donkey, if he is left with only a door between him and the garden where he can get the things he might have to eat, will open it; he will pull down the handle of the door. Again, look at the way cats that are out at night act. In many a house that I have been in, the cats knock at the windowpane with their heads on the balcony in front; and look at the way dogs will pull the bell sometimes. Surely that is reasoning enough.

H.P.B.: Go and compare a child and a kitten, if you please, when they are born; what can a child do? And a cat, immediately it stands on its legs, goes eating.

Mr. Harbottle: That is, I think, what Dr. Williams meant just now when he said, "The animal is born more or less with all its faculties, and generally speaking does not gain on that, while man is gradually learning and improving." Is not that really the point?

Dr. Williams: That is exactly the point.

H.P.B.: Of course man is a perfected animal. He is a progressive animal.

Mr. Ellis: Is not it a question of degree and surroundings?

H.P.B.: We look upon the animals, as the men of science look upon us.

Mr. Harbottle: I think it is fair to say that the animal intelligence cannot be denied, and simply to add that the intelligence of the animal is of a different plane to anything we humans can appreciate. And so will it go higher and higher. That which transcends the human intelligence we cannot pretend to understand in any way. That answers that question as put there.

Mr. ——: But does not one of the great distinctions between the animal and the human intelligence be in the fact that human beings can, to some extent, work with abstract thought, while the animal can only work in the concrete? That is to say, that the animal can largely be taught and apparently will reason from it in conjunction with the fact that it may get food or something that it likes; whereas a human being can actually argue from facts and by means of imagination create the surroundings.

Mr. Ellis: How do you teach a child? By giving it a lump of sugar stick, or else smacking it. The child passes as you know by physiology through all the stages of every other class of animals, and therefore they are passing through the same stages as the animals are in now.

Mr. Harbottle: We have rather wandered from the point I think.

Mr. Keightley: The question is, is there any consciousness or conscious being to cognise and make a division of time at the first flutter of manifestation?

H.P.B.: I should think not.

Mr. Keightley: In the way that Subba Row[1] speaks of the first Logos he implies…

H.P.B.: That the Logos kept a diary, or what?

Mr. Keightley: He implies both consciousness and intelligence.

H.P.B.: Well I am not of Subba Row's opinion. You forget one thing, he spoke about the Logos without saying whether it is the first or second he spoke about, the unmanifested or the manifested Logos.

---

[1] **T. Subba Row** (1856–1890) — an Indian lawyer and early member of the Theosophical Society, who was against the publication of *The Secret Doctrine* and eventually turned against H.P.B.

Several times he calls it Ishvara, so it is not the unmanifested Logos, because Ishvara was never Narayana.[1] You may call it whatever you like, but it is not the highest Logos, because that from which the manifested Logos is born is that which is translated by me there "the Eternal Father-Mother." In the *Vishnu Purana* they call it the egg of the world, and this egg of the world is surrounded by seven skins or layers or zones — call it whatever you like — it is that which is given in the Purana as the Golden Egg. This is the Father-Mother, and in this Golden Egg is born Brahma, the male, which is in reality the second Logos, or the third, according to the enumeration adopted, not the highest — that is to say the point which is everywhere and nowhere. Mahat comes afterwards. Mahat is something between the third and fourth, it fluctuates, you understand, because it contains the physical germs in it and the whole roots of all the physical universe. At the same time it is a universal Divine Mind.

Mr. Keightley: It is the first manifestation, then?

H.P.B.: It is the third but it overlaps the fourth.

Mr. Harbottle: Then the first Logos is the first point within the circle.

H.P.B.: The first point, because there is the circle, the circle which has neither limit nor boundaries, nor can it have a name nor attributes, nor anything, and this point which is put there, is the unmanifested Logos. Which is simultaneous with that line you draw across the diameter. The first line is the Father-Mother and then comes from that Father-Mother the second Logos, that is to say, the manifested word. For instance, in the Hindu Puranas, it is said (and the Orientalists have said a good deal about that also) that the first production of Akasha is sound. Now Akasha is just what is called there the Mother or the Father-Mother (call it whichever you like), and sound means there simply speech or expression of the unuttered thought; and it is the Logos, that which the Greeks and Platonists called the Logos, and is just that which is sound and which made Dr. Wilson[2] and many

---

[1] **Narayana** (*Sanskrit*, "mover on the Waters") — a title of Vishnu, in his aspect of the Holy Spirit, moving on the Waters of Creation. In esoteric symbology, it stands for the primeval manifestation of the life-principle, spreading in infinite Space.

[2] **Horace Hayman Wilson** (1786–1860) — an English Orientalist who translated the *Vishnu Purana* and was the first person to translate the *Rig Veda* into English.

other Orientalists say, "What fools these Hindus are!" They speak of Akasha, which is, according to our showing, Chaos, and from this Chaos they make sound proceed. It means just that which was adopted subsequently by St. John, the Evangelist, who speaks about the Logos, saying just the same thing in other words.[3]

Mr. Keightley: On the subject of time this question has been put "What is the consciousness which takes cognizance of time?" Is the consciousness of time limited to the plane of waking physical consciousness or does it exist on higher planes? Is the consciousness or sense of succession, limited purely to our present plane? Or does it exist on higher planes?

H.P.B.: Whose consciousness? Why, you must tell me, of whom you are talking — whose consciousness is limited?

Mr. Keightley: Our own. All our consciousness is succession. We have a succession of ideas or succession of thought. Haven't we?

H.P.B.: Then who is there to think like that?

Mr. Keightley: You speak of time. "Time was not." Time to our minds conveys this idea of succession.

H.P.B.: And if time *was not*, it can convey no such idea. Time was not means that there was duration only and not time, because no one was there to make time or the division of time. That which was not, how can it have any consciousness or any aspect of consciousness? What does it mean, all this?

Mr. Keightley: This question really applied to a later subject. You speak thus of time: "Time is only an illusion produced by the succession of our states of consciousness as we travel through eternal duration, and it does not exist where no consciousness exists."[4] Then the question which is put is, is the consciousness of time, in our sense of the word, limited only to our present plane of waking consciousness, or does it exist on any other planes?

H.P.B.: It cannot exist because even in sleep it does not exist. You have been answering it to yourselves how many times, when we have been talking about dreams.

[3] See H. P. Blavatsky and G. R. S. Mead, "Notes on the Gospel according to John," *Collected Writings*, vol. 11 (Wheaton, IL: Theosophical Publishing House, 1973), pp. 482–503.

[4] *The Secret Doctrine*, vol. 1, p. 37.

Mr. ——: Seeing that the "Gods" have a beginning and an ending, they must exist in time.

H.P.B.: They exist in space and time. Duration cannot be divided.

Mr. Harbottle: But the word succession applies to them.

Mr. ——: But is there not a consciousness which can take cognizance of it?

H.P.B.: Certainly the universal mind can.

Mr. ——: Then the idea exists there.

H.P.B.: I don't think so. In the Absolute there cannot exist the same division of time as in our conception. I would say there is a consciousness there, but I don't think time has got anything to do with it. Can you say that the sea has also a conception of time in its rhythmical striking of the shore, in the movement of the waves and so on? To my mind, the Absolute can have no consciousness, or not a consciousness such as we have here, and that is why they speak as they do about the Absolute. It has neither consciousness, nor desire, nor wish, nor thought, because it is absolute thought, absolute desire, absolute all — just what the *Daily News*[1] laughed at from not understanding the true definition of the Absolute. They said — I don't remember how the phrase went there in the *Daily News*, do you, miss?

Miss ——: I do not.

H.P.B.: They laughed at "Be-ness"[2] and yet there is no other way in this world of translating the word *Sat* but by Be-ness, because it is not existence, for existence implies something that feels that it exists. Existence must give you the idea of having a beginning, a creation,

---

[1] "The Secret of all Things," *Daily News* (10 January 1889), p. 5.

[2] **Be-ness** — a term coined by Theosophists to render more accurately the essential meaning of the untranslatable word *Sat*. The latter word does not mean "Being," for it presupposes a sentient feeling or some consciousness of existence. But, as the term *Sat* is applied solely to the absolute Principle, the universal, unknown, and ever unknowable Presence, which philosophical Pantheism postulates in Cosmos, calling it the basic root of Cosmos, and Cosmos itself — "Being" was no fit word to express it. Indeed, the latter is not even, as translated by some Orientalists, "the incomprehensible Entity"; for it is no more an Entity than a non-Entity, but both. It is, as said, absolute *Be-ness*, not *Being*, the one secondless, undivided, and indivisible All — the root of all Nature visible and invisible, objective and subjective, to be sensed by the highest spiritual intuition but never to be fully comprehended.

and an end, it is just what Gautama Buddha says about Nirvana — or if not Buddha, it is [...].[3] He says Nirvana does not exist, but it *is*. Try to make what you can of this Oriental metaphysical conception. Still it is there, it exists and all the philosophy is built on it.

Mr. Ellis: The Hebrew Jehovah[4] was "I am."

H.P.B.: He calls himself so. So is the Ormuzd[5] of the Persians, too. Every one of us is [...] the "I am that I am."

Mr. Duncan: Be-ness has some connection with the word "to be."

H.P.B.: Yes, but it is not that. No word, my dear Mr. Duncan, can apply better than that, better than the word Be-ness. It is a word we have coined, and we have coined it correctly, I think. It is the only thing that renders the Sanskrit word *Sat*. It is not existence, it is not being, it is absolute Be-ness.

Mr. Harbottle: It is both being and non-being.

H.P.B.: Well then, how can you explain that better? We cannot conceive it. Our intellects are limited and finite and language is far more finite and conditioned than we are. So how can we explain that which we can only conceive by our highest intuition?

Mr. Ellis: The Germans understand it at once because they have a word they use every day, that is the word "sein." "Sein," of course, means "to be," and "das sein" means, of course, what you mean by the word Be-ness. I am sure nobody would have said that was absurd, only you cannot use German words. No German would call this word absurd, but a frivolous Englishman would.

H.P.B.: Well now, you Englishmen invent a word that would answer to that "sein" there.

Mr. Ellis: One is constantly meeting with the absolute poverty of our language for purposes of translation. In German one or two words may require twenty for perfect translation.

---

[3] [...] means that stenographers could not understand a word.

[4] **Jehovah** (*Hebrew*) — a Hebrew name for the God of Israel.

[5] **Ormazd** or **Ahura Mazda** (*Persian*, "Lord of Wisdom") — the Supreme God-Creator in Zoroastrianism. He is symbolized by the Sun, as being the Light of Lights.

H.P.B.: Now look at Max Müller.[1] Why, he makes a mess of it positively, as the English language must have at least 40 or 50,000 words more invented or coined to express a part of that which the Sanskrit language expresses.

Mr. Ellis: We have no methods of doing what they do in the Sanskrit. They couple two words together and you have the whole meaning of a sentence. If we want to express that same quality I have found over and over again you have to put about twenty words. You cannot do it in one or two.

Mr. Duncan: I think that last question had reference to the consciousness of time.

H.P.B.: Oh, this is all finite beginning and ending, so you cannot find any correspondence between that and real duration or real abstract space, for it is not, it cannot be localized. There is such a thing as time; it has a beginning and an end.

Mr. ——: Yes but are we conscious of it?

H.P.B.: No, even the Devachanee is not conscious of it.

Mr. ——: But he is conscious of a succession of states of consciousness.

H.P.B.: No, all is present to the Devachanee. There is no past, because he would recall it and regret it, and there is no future because he would be anxious to have it. Devachan is a state of bliss in which everything is present; that is why they say the Devachanee has no conception and no idea of time; to him everything is just a real and vivid dream.

Mr. ——: He can have no idea of time in as much as there is nothing to measure it by.

H.P.B.: To him it is not a dream, but to us it is a dream. When we dream everything is present and we enjoy the greatest bliss.

Mr. ——: In a dream also we may dream a lifetime in half a second, yet we are conscious of succession of states of consciousness. Events take place one after the other.

---

[1] **Max Müller** (1823–1900) — a German Orientalist. He was the editor of *Sacred Books of the East*, a 50-volume set of English translations of Oriental sacred scriptures.

H.P.B.: After the dream, not during the dream. During the dream you will be conscious of nothing of the kind. You will perhaps forget there is such a thing as succession of states of consciousness. You will forget it surely.

Mr. Ellis: If you were describing a picture to somebody you could not give him all that picture at once, you have to give him first one part of the picture then another, although you have it all in your mind.

H.P.B.: Yes, you have it all before you all the time.

Mr. Keightley: That is the last question.

17 JANUARY 1889

Mr. A. Keightley:[1] Stanza 1 continued, Sloka 3: "Universal mind was not, for there were no Ah-hi[2] to contain it."[3] This Sloka seems to imply that the universal mind has no existence apart from the Ah-hi, but in the commentary you state that during the Pralaya, "the 'universal mind' remains as a permanent possibility of mental action, or as that abstract absolute thought, of which mind is the concrete relative manifestation,"[4] and that the Ah-hi are the vehicle for divine universal thought and will. "They are the intelligent forces that give to Nature her 'laws,' while themselves acting according to laws imposed upon them by still higher powers; … [They are] the hierarchy of spiritual beings through which the universal mind comes into action."[5] This commentary suggests that the Ah-hi are not themselves the universal mind, but only the vehicle for its manifestation.

H.P.B.: Universal mind and absolute mind are one. Are they not? Very well, that only implies that as there are no finite differentiated minds during Pralaya, therefore it is just as though there were no mind at all, if there is nothing to contain it, or to perceive it. That is the meaning. There is nothing to reflect or contain the ideation of the absolute mind, therefore *it is not*, because everything outside of the absolute and immutable Sat, or the Be-ness, is necessarily finite and conditioned, since it has a beginning and end, and here is something with no beginning and no end. Therefore since the Ah-hi *were not*, there was no universal mind, because you must make a distinction between the absolute mind which is ever present, and its reflection in the Ah-hi at the first flutter of Manvantara. The Ah-hi are on the highest plane; they are those who reflect the universal mind collectively, and begin the work of evolution of all the lower forces until they come, throughout the seven planes, down to our lowest plane.

Mr. A. Keightley: Then the Ah-hi and the universal mind are necessary compliments of one another?

---

[1] **Archibald Keightley** (1859–1930) — an English physician and Theosophist; the nephew of Bertram Keightley.
[2] **Ah-hi** (*Senzar*) — Celestial Beings; Dhyan-Chohans; "Wise Serpents" or Dragons of Wisdom.
[3] *The Secret Doctrine*, vol. 1, p. 37.
[4] *The Secret Doctrine*, vol. 1, p. 38.
[5] *The Secret Doctrine*, vol. 1, p. 38.

H.P.B.: Not at all. Universal mind, or absolute mind, always *is*, whether during Manvantara or during Pralaya; it is immutably one. But since the term Ah-hi means the highest Dhyanis — the Logoi perhaps — those which begin, which are the creation — or evolution, not creation, because everything is an emanation; since the Ah-hi were not, there was no universal mind, because it was the absolute dormant, latent mind, and it was not differentiated in the collectivity of these Dhyanis.

Mr. Harbottle: It was, rather, absolute consciousness.

H.P.B.: It was absolute consciousness which is not consciousness. What is consciousness? Further on you make a question: "Can consciousness exist without any mind?" But it will come in time. You had better proceed, unless you have some other questions to ask. For instance, let us represent to ourselves, if you can do such a thing, that universal mind is a kind of vacuum, but vacuum with latent consciousness in it. You just suppose you pump out all the air you can from some vessel, there is a vacuum. You cannot represent yourselves in that particular vessel as a vehicle: there is the vacuum; but break these vessels that contain this *soi-disant*[6] vacuum; where shall you look for it? It has disappeared, it is everywhere and nowhere. It is something, yet it is the absence of something. It is entirely a homogeneous thing. This is what is supposed to be a vacuum, I think. Dr. Williams, how would you describe vacuum?

Dr. Williams: Absolute vacuum is a figment, really.

H.P.B.: It is a figment which is a negative thing. It is the supposed place where nothing exists.

Dr. Williams: It is absence of air, I should think.

H.P.B.: You break those vessels and nothing exists, therefore universal mind is not, because there are no vehicles to contain it.

Mr. A. Keightley: The first question is, can you give us a definition of the universal mind, which will solve the difficulty?

H.P.B.: Well, I think I have just done so.

Mr. A. Keightley: Quite so. Then number 2. "What are the higher powers which condition the Ah-hi?"

---

[6] **Soi-disant** (*French*) — so-called.

H.P.B.: Well I don't call them powers at all; it is simply a manifestation of the periodical law, the universal law, which becomes by turns active or inactive. This is that law of periodical manifestation which creates them, which emanates them. I always use the word create, which is a very bad and wrong word to use, for there is no creation.

Mr. A. Keightley: Then the power, which is higher than the Ah-hi, is the law which necessitates manifestation.

H.P.B.: Just so; periodically, when the hour strikes, it comes, and they appear into manifestation. They are on the first rung of manifestation, after which it goes on gradually shaping itself more and more.

Mr. B. Keightley: It should really be *the* law, and not *a* law.

H.P.B.: The law and not a law. I give it to you from the standpoint of esoteric, or eastern teaching. If physical science objects, just say so, and I will try to repent. Who of you has an objection to make?

Mr. Kingsland: The grand difficulty is to account for this law.

H.P.B.: You want to go beyond even the first manifestation, beyond what they call the Supreme Cause; you want to go beyond that. You try to understand first the Supreme Cause, as they call it, and I can assure you, you won't understand it; it is all a figment, all our imagination. We try to do the best we can, but it does not stand to reason at all. We do not even approach this absolute, this merely logical speculation which dates from thousands and thousands of years. If physical or modern science can say or invent something better, let it do so, but it has not done it yet. There are gaps and flaws everywhere, and at every moment one thing breaks its nose, and another comes, and then they jump over the wall and imagine some other speculation; that again in its turn breaks its nose, and that is all it is.

Mr. Kingsland: Would not cosmic mind be a better term than universal mind in this case?

H.P.B.: No; cosmic mind would take in the third degree. Cosmic mind is simply confined or limited to the manifested universe.

Mr. Kingsland: Quite so. In that sense it seems the passage is intended.

H.P.B.: Cosmic mind is quite a different thing from universal ideation. It is just the manifestation of that mind during the Manvantaric period of activity. But universal ideation knows no change. It was, always was, is, and will be. I never said it does not exist: it does not exist for our perception, because there were no minds to perceive it. Universal mind was not because there was no one to perceive it. One is latent and the other is active. One is a potentiality.

Mr. Kingsland: The universal mind was in the absolute, but it was cosmic mind that was not.

H.P.B.: Yes, but we speak here about manifestation. I cannot go and invent things; I am obliged to translate just as the Stanzas give it in the book.

Mr. Kingsland: That is the manifestation.

H.P.B.: Well, let us call it cosmic mind, if you like it better.

Mr. Kingsland: I only think there is a confusion between universal mind and absolute mind.

H.P.B.: If you say universal mind, it is absolute, but if you say cosmic mind, that is another thing.

Mr. Kingsland: Then you can't say that it was not.

H.P.B.: Cosmic ideation was not, but universal mind was.

Mr. Kingsland: Quite so.

H.P.B.: How can I put that it was not? I am obliged to translate as it is, and then to give all the commentaries. I didn't invent them. If I were inventing it, I might put it otherwise.

Mr. Kingsland: If you say universal mind was not manifested, you get over the difficulty.

H.P.B.: Those who have written this do not concern themselves with the manifested universe. This relates to the highest, and does not deal yet with the universal matter, it deals with the universe of ideation of consciousness and so on.

Mr. Kingsland: It deals with the first manifestation.

H.P.B.: You had better send your protest to those who have written this thing, because I can't help it.

Mr. Kingsland: No, it is the English translation. Do you see what I mean, Harbottle?

Mr. Harbottle: I see what you mean.

Mr. Mead:[1] It is the same thing looked upon from different points of view.

Mr. Harbottle: I think we are apt to use the word cosmic as applied to the manifested universe in all its forms. This does not touch anything of the sort. This is the first absolute consciousness or non-consciousness, and I think it really does mean that the absolute consciousness could not be that universal mind because it was not to be expressed, it could not be expressed, there was no expression for it. That is what I take to be the meaning of it.

Mr. Kingsland: There was no expression for it; but it was there.

Mr. Harbottle: It was there and it was not there.

H.P.B.: Because the Ah-hi were not, to the persons who can conceive of it; since there was nothing and no one to conceive of it, how could it be? It was not. You must remember the peculiar mode of expression used by the Easterners. They express it always allegorically, always figuratively. You cannot ask them to express in scientific language which says so much and means so little.

Mr. Kingsland: When you say it was not, you mean it was not in the absolute.

H.P.B.: I beg your pardon. I say it was not, simply.

Mr. Harbottle: If you can say it was, that would be taking a very one-sided view of what we mean by *Sat*. That would be equivalent to saying that *Sat* was being.

Mr. Mead: I think the question hangs on the time referred to altogether. It involves the question of time, and no time then existed.

Mr. Harbottle: I think it goes even farther back than that. I think it is all inherent in the meaning we attribute to the word *Sat*, which is as I say both being and non-being.

Mr. Kingsland: I don't think there is any confusion in our minds, it is in the terms.

H.P.B.: Just read this over again, will you?

Mr. A. Keightley: "What are the higher powers which condition the Ah-hi?"

---

[1] **George Robert Stow Mead** (1863–1933) — an English historian, writer and translator, who was the first to translate *Pistis Sophia* into English from its Latin version.

H.P.B.: No, no, not that. I mean the thing to which Mr. Kingsland takes objection.

[Mr. A. Keightley then read the passage: *The Secret Doctrine*, Stanza 1, Sloka 3 and commentary.]

H.P.B.: It ought to be higher "power" not "powers."

Mr. Kingsland: First you say it was, and then it was not.

H.P.B.: I didn't say that. The Absolute must be always, it is a perfect impossibility for it to be otherwise. The Absolute is a thing which must be taken tacitly. If there is such a thing as absolute something and not something, an absolute unknown or unknowable, then it must always have been and always be. It is impossible it should go out of the universe. This is a tacit assumption.

Mr. Kingsland: But if you take it as it is written there, "universal mind was not," it treats of it as if it were a manifestation. But mind itself is not a manifestation.

H.P.B.: Mind is a manifestation, universal mind is not the same thing; let us call it an ideation. Cosmic ideation was as soon as the Ah-hi appeared and continues throughout the Manvantara. But this is universal absolute ideation, and *is* always and cannot get out of the universe, whereas cosmic ideation was not and the only mistake is that I did not put cosmic. But why should I? I cannot put things out of my own head; I just translate as it is. There are many, many verses that come between, that I have left out altogether. It may be this would be better.

Mr. B. Keightley: Also, I think the term cosmos is used almost throughout *The Secret Doctrine* in reference chiefly to the solar manifested universe, and is not taken in the sense as referring to that which precedes.

H.P.B.: I think we shall only deal with "cosmos" as our solar system. I think I say it in some place there, at least I so remember. I have a recollection that I have been writing about it.

Mr. A. Keightley: I think I see Kingsland's objection, he means to say this expression is liable to cause a certain amount of confusion because, just as Madame Blavatsky has now expressed it, the universal mind always *is* and never can be. But that which is identical with what we call cosmic ideation was not, because the Ah-hi were not there to perceive it.

H.P.B.: And, as there was no manifestation, it was an impotentiality.

Mr. A. Keightley: First you say universal mind was not and then you say universal mind is always a permanent thing and always is.

H.P.B.: Because I try to explain the Stanza. I know the meaning, I know the spirit too, not the dead letter, I don't take the dead letter; I give it as it is, and then I give the spirit of it.

Dr. Williams: Does not the expression, "universal mind," convey, itself, that idea?

Mr. B. Keightley: I think it is implied in the word, "mind."

H.P.B.: We are obliged to use it.

Mr. Harbottle: Unless you call it consciousness.

H.P.B.: It is absolute consciousness. But it is not consciousness as we understand it.

Dr. Williams: If you get rid of all predicates, everything has been done that can be done. You say the Absolute is. If you say more than that you approach perception, and that is manifestation.

Mr. Harbottle: You cannot attribute mind to the Absolute until you have got something capable of perception radiating from the Absolute, in which case it is correct to say that the universal mind was not.

Mr. Kingsland: It is correct in one sense but creates confusion.

H.P.B.: But what can we do? Do you want to change it? Now it is printed, what can you do?

Mr. Kingsland: We cannot do anything, now it is printed.

H.P.B.: Then why do you break my heart?

[Laughter.]

Mr. Harbottle: You asked him to object, really.

H.P.B.: But what can we do now? I think about 20 persons have broken their heads about it when they were preparing the thing, even the great metaphysical Fawcett,[1] because I have been asking all of them. Is there anything according to Herbert Spencer or any of your

---

[1] **Edward Douglas Fawcett** (1866–1960) — an English mountaineer, philosopher and novelist. He assisted H.P.B. in writing and compiling quotations from scientific works for *The Secret Doctrine*.

scientists which you can object to? "No," they said "it is perfect," and now you find flaws! Well, let us pass on.

Mr. A. Keightley: "To what cosmic plane do the Ah-hi here spoken of belong?"

H.P.B.: To the first, the second, and the third. Because it is a triad, a manifested triad, a reflection of the non-manifested. Taking the triad in the sense that Pythagoras[2] gives it, it disappears in the darkness and the silence. Taken in this sense it is the only thing, as there is Atma, Buddhi, Manas — well, all, the first, second and third planes — the Ah-hi belong to these planes.

Mr. A. Keightley: That is to say the Ah-hi belong to the cosmic planes which correspond to Atma, Buddhi, Manas.

H.P.B.: Just so, they correspond.

Mr. B. Keightley: Then this question cannot arise, that Atma, Buddhi, Manas…

H.P.B.: I know, the two are on the same plane.

Mr. B. Keightley: They are successive emanations; you get the Atma, Buddhi in man, before Manas makes its appearance.

H.P.B.: But we do not speak of man now, if you please, we speak in general that these correspond. Don't you go and mix up man with it now. We speak of the macrocosm simply, at the beginning when there was the first flutter of Manvantaric dawn, and then evolution begins.

Mr. B. Keightley: The question I want to put exactly is this: Are those three planes simultaneous emanations or do they emanate one from the other?

---

[2] **Pythagoras** (c.570–c.495 BCE) — the most famous of mystic philosophers, born at Samos. He seems to have travelled all over the world, and to have culled his philosophy from the various systems to which he had access. Thus, he studied the esoteric sciences with the *Brachmanes* of India, and astronomy and astrology in Chaldea and Egypt. After returning, he settled in Crotona, in Magna Grecia, where he established a college to which, very soon, went all the best intellects of the civilised centres. His father was one Mnesarchus of Samos, and was a man of noble birth and learning. It was Pythagoras who was the first to teach the heliocentric system, and who was the greatest proficient in geometry of his century. It was he also who created the word *philosopher*. As the greatest mathematician, geometer and astronomer of historical antiquity, and also the highest of the metaphysicians and scholars, Pythagoras has won imperishable fame. He taught reincarnation as it is professed in India and much else of the Secret Wisdom.

H.P.B.: I suppose one from another, but I could not tell you that. Don't ask me questions I cannot answer.

Mr. B. Keightley: That is the question that is now meant here.

H.P.B.: Do you really want to apply mechanical law to cosmogony as it is in the metaphysical minds of the Orientals? You won't get much if you come to apply space and time because there was no space and no time, so how can you ask me this question?

Mr. B. Keightley: Well, then, that settles the question.

H.P.B.: After this comes the question of the reflection of the triad in space and time, therefore, how can you apply anything mechanical?

Mr. B. Keightley: That is what I wanted you to say. I got what I wanted.

Mr. A. Keightley: Question 4. "Have these Ah-hi been men in previous Manvantaras or will they become so?"

H.P.B.: They will become men in subsequent Manvantaras.

Mr. A. Keightley: Then do they remain permanently on this very exalted plane during the whole period of the Manvantara?

H.P.B.: Of the 15 figures?[1] No, they pass through all the planes until they become on the third plane Manasa-Putra, the sons of Manas or mind. They are arupa.[2] On the higher planes these Ah-hi are arupa, that is to say formless, bodiless, without any substance, without anything, they are breaths. On the second plane they first approach to *rupa* or to form. Then on the third they become Manasa-rupa,[3] those who become incarnated in men.

Mr. A. Keightley: Then is that stage taken in one Manvantara or are those various stages?

H.P.B.: It is. It is all the same thing, only a distinction is made. On every plane they reach they are called by other names.

Mr. A. Keightley: Quite so.

---

[1] 311,040,000,000,000 years.

[2] **Arupa** (*Sanskrit*, "formless") — formless or bodiless, as opposed to **Rupa** (*Sanskrit*, "form") — a form or shape in any degree of visible or invisible manifestation. For example, thoughts do have a certain form, although invisible, while ideas are formless.

[3] **Manasa-rupa** (*Sanskrit*, "body of mind") — the vehicle of the reincarnating Ego.

H.P.B.: There is more and more differentiation because what we talk about is the homogeneous substance, which we call substance from our conceit, because it cannot be any substance which we can conceive of. Later they become substance, if you like.

Mr. A. Keightley: Then the Ah-hi of this Manvantara…

H.P.B.: They do not exist any more, if you please. They have become long ago Planetary, Solar, Lunar, and lastly, incarnating Egos. Read *The Secret Doctrine*, you will see the thing there.[4]

Mr. A. Keightley: I understood you to say they did not become men in this Manvantara.

H.P.B.: The 15 figures apply to the solar system. The first answers relate to the beginning of the whole objective universe, but after that, when you begin to speak about the Father-Mother, then it relates to our objective universe and to the solar system only because our teaching does not busy itself at all with things outside. At least those things that I have selected. I could not go and select the whole thing. I have only taken that which relates to our solar system. I have just taken two or three just to show the general idea, and then skipped over whole Stanzas and came to the point. I have said there are some 60 Stanzas passed over. I would have had compliments from the *Daily News* if I had translated the whole of it.

Mr. B. Keightley: Then on the re-awakening, will the men of one Manvantara have to pass through a similar stage to the Ah-hi stage in the next Manvantara?

H.P.B.: In many, many Manvantaras at the end of the tail of the serpent; when the tail will be in the mouth of the serpent, I might say. What have you got the ambition of becoming? An Ah-hi, or what? You will have time, my dear fellow, to do many things before you become an Ah-hi.

Mr. A. Keightley: "A man can choose what he shall think about, can the analogy be applied to Ah-hi?"

H.P.B.: No, because a man has free will and the Ah-hi have no free will. They have a collective will. They are obliged to act simultaneously. It is one law that gives them the impulse and they have to act just according to that law. I do not call it free will. Free will can exist

---

[4] See *The Secret Doctrine*, vol. 1, p. 38.

only in man, in a man who has a mind with consciousness, which acts and makes him perceive things not only within himself but outside himself also. These Ah-hi simply are forces; you don't take them to be men, do you? They are not human beings.

Mr. A. Keightley: No, but I take them to be conscious agents in the work.

H.P.B.: Conscious in so far that they act within the universal consciousness. The Manasa-Putra is a different thing when they come on the third plane.

Mr. Hall: Can the Ah-hi be said to be enjoying bliss?

H.P.B.: Why should they enjoy bliss or enjoy non-bliss? What have they done to do so? I don't think they enjoy anything of the kind. They cannot smoke cigarettes, even, when they like. Why should they enjoy bliss? What extraordinary ideas you have! You can enjoy bliss only when you have known what suffering is.

Mr. Hall: I was making a distinction in my mind between bliss and happiness.

H.P.B.: I thought it was the same thing; you can have neither happiness nor bliss if you have not known suffering and pain.

Mr. Hall: I was thinking of bliss as the state of the Absolute.

H.P.B.: You suppose the Absolute is bliss? The Absolute can have no condition, no attribute, nothing at all. The Absolute is conditionless; that is the first thing to learn about the Absolute. It is only that which is finite and differentiated which can have some attribute or something of the kind.

Dr. Williams: How can they be said to be conscious intelligences in as much as intelligence is such a complex thing?

H.P.B.: Because the English language does not furnish us with a better word. I admit the word is very inadequate, but the English language is not the Sanskrit language. If it were written in Sanskrit you would not find a single objection, but what can you do with the English language or any other European language?

Dr. Williams: There may not be one word, but I should think a collection of words would express anything.

H.P.B.: Oh, then try, if you please, to do so!

Dr. Williams: It seems to me from what I can gather from your elucidation that it really means a force which is a unity, not a complex action and reaction of several forces — which would be implied in the word intelligence or anything which implies complexity — but rather it is that simple force, almost. The noumenal, the aspect of phenomenal force, would at least express better what is meant by that.

H.P.B.: Well, I don't know. You take one flame and represent yourselves a flame and it will be unity. But the rays which will proceed from that flame, they will become complex and do all kinds of things and will be seen to act each one on its own line.

Dr. Williams: But they only become complex when they find receptacles in lower forms.

H.P.B.: Just what they do find. The lower they descend the more they find it. But it is all one; it is simply the rays which proceed from one; and more and more do they proceed to differentiate until they become fully conditioned and fall down here in this world of ours, with its thousands and millions of inhabitants — as Carlyle[1] said, "most of them fools."

Dr. Williams: Well, the Ah-hi, then, considered as a primary essence, would be a unity.

H.P.B.: Certainly, because they proceed from unity. It is the first of the seven rays, as they call it.

Mr. A. Keightley: Then they are the reflection of unity.

H.P.B.: What are the prismatic rays, if you please, if not one single white ray? From the one they become three, from the three they become seven, because there is a prismatic scale of colours.

Mr. A. Keightley: Seven, but they are still one when they are moving rapidly over each other.

H.P.B.: To our perception, quite so. They become seven just in the same way, there if you please take the analogy.

Mr. A. Keightley: Next question. You say that during deep sleep "mind is not" on the material plane; but it is implied that during this period mind is active on another plane. Can you give us a definition of the characteristics which distinguish mind in the waking state from mind during the sleep of the body?

---

[1] **Thomas Carlyle** (1795–1881) — a British essayist, historian and philosopher.

H.P.B.: Well, I suppose there is a great difference between the two. You see, the reason in higher minds sleeps, but the instinctual mind is awakened. That is the difference. The reason of the higher mind, in the physical man, is not always the same. Today I have been looking at a book and I learnt at last the great difference between cerebrum and cerebellum. I was always mixing them up in my mind, I was not sure of them, and this morning I on purpose went to look and I at last learnt that this is the cerebellum [pointing to the head] and this the cerebrum. The one sleeps when the other is awake, and if you ask an astrologer,[1] he will give you a magnificent idea. I don't know where it is stated, but the brain is all in seven, and he separated them and put all the planets that answer to those portions. Now here you will find the earth, the sun, and the moon, here at the back of the head; and this part sleeps and rests when the other is awake.

Mr. A. Keightley: Then what do you mean by instinctual mind?

H.P.B.: You see, it passes from a plane which we regard as an illusion. Now, for instance, this plane in which we are proceeding is called reality; we call it illusion, but we say that this part going to sleep, and this part of the brain having no more a definite function, it is the other one that begins and carries away man on the Astral — which is still more deceptive, because it is all the emanations of everything that is bad. It preserves no record. The great serpent, it is called. Now if the higher mind sleeps there you will have a perception of the dreams and you can bring back when you awake the recollection of them — this pretence of dreams, but I think we have been discussing dreams quite enough — and unless it is that, you will have all these chaotic dreams because you have all these dreams with this peculiar part of your brain, the cerebellum.

Mr. B. Keightley: One thing that question was meant to cover was this: for instance, the fundamental conditions of the mind in the waking state are space and time.

H.P.B.: Yes.

---

[1] **Astrology** (*Greek*, "account of the stars") — the science which defines the action of celestial bodies upon mundane affairs, and claims to foretell future events from the position of the stars. Its antiquity is such as to place it among the very earliest records of human learning. It remained, for long ages, a secret science in the East, and its final expression remains so to this day.

Mr. B. Keightley: Do they exist for the Manas, the mind, during the sleep of the physical body?

H.P.B.: No.

Mr. B. Keightley: So there you get at any rate one very marked distinction between the manifestation of man on the two planes of consciousness.

H.P.B.: There may be something approximate, some hallucination of space and time; but certainly it is nothing real. We have been talking about it many times, and have seen that in one second you may live through the events of thirty years, as some dreams prove to you. Therefore there is no conception, no possibility of conceiving of division of time.

Mr. B. Keightley: Or of space.

H.P.B.: They are both in duration or eternity; they are not in time.

Mr. A. Keightley: Next question: It has been stated that Manas (mind) is the vehicle of Buddhi, but the universal mind has been spoken of as Maha-Buddhi. Can you define for us the distinction between Manas and Buddhi as applied in a universal sense, and Manas and Buddhi as manifested in man?

H.P.B.: Well, cosmic Buddhi is the vehicle of Mahat, that is to say, in the sense of Buddhi being Prakriti and this is Prakriti; at least it descends in the seven planes, that is the difference, and the Buddhi of man proceeds from the highest Akasha. He does not go on the highest plane until he comes to the most objective plane. Maha-Buddhi is used there in the same sense as Prakriti in its seven manifestations.

Mr. B. Keightley: But is the vehicle of Mahat, the universal mind? Does the Manas in man proceed from the universal mind too?

H.P.B.: Yes it proceeds from Akasha — Buddhi, I mean, or Manas. The Manasa-Dhyanis[2] are the same Ah-hi I just told you of on a lower plane.

Mr. B. Keightley: Because, of course, one would naturally think, as Mahat is the universal mind, that Manas in man proceeds from the universal mind.

---

[2] **Manasa-Dhyanis** (*Sanskrit,* "Lords of Mind") — the Solar Ancestors of man; those who made of man a rational being by incarnating in the senseless forms of semi-ethereal flesh of the men of the Third Race.

H.P.B.: It is just the same Prakriti in its last manifestation. It is what in the Kabbalah is called Malkuth,[1] the Bride of Heavenly Man — well, earth, everything earthly, or atomic.

Mr. B. Keightley: i.e., the plane of objective consciousness, in fact, waking consciousness.

Mr. A. Keightley: Question 8. "Can there be consciousness without mind?"

H.P.B.: There we come to the great question. Consciousness — what is it? It is only the faculty of the mind, is not it? It is that which permeates the mind or the Ego, and causes it to perceive that such a mind has action, that such a thing is so — is not that it? How do you explain it otherwise? Consciousness is not a thing *per se.* It is a faculty of the mind. That is what Hamilton will tell you and what all the Eastern idealists will tell you. They cannot tell you anything else. It is a thing inseparable from mind — unless it is the mind of an idiot, of course you won't have any consciousness.

Mr. A. Keightley: You say the fashion nowadays amongst philosophers is to speak slightingly…

H.P.B.: We know that, of course.

Mr. A. Keightley: …of the idea of making mind an entity.

H.P.B.: Of course, but mind is still the soul. It is perfectly synonymous with soul. Those who don't believe in soul certainly will tell you that there is no such thing as consciousness apart from brain, and once the brain is dead and the man is dead, there is no consciousness. The Nihilists,[2] the Atheists and the Materialists will tell you so. If you believe in mind, mind is the soul or the Ego. What kind of a soul is that if it has not any consciousness?

Mr. A. Keightley: But they accept consciousness.

H.P.B.: But not after the death of man, while we accept consciousness after death, and say the real consciousness and the real freedom of the Ego or the soul begins only after the physical death of man. It

---

[1] **Malkuth** (*Hebrew,* "kingdom") — the Kingdom, the tenth Sephira, corresponding to the final H of the Tetragrammaton or IHVH. It is the Inferior Mother, the Bride of Adam Kadmon (the "Heavenly Man" not fallen into sin); also called the Queen.

[2] **Nihilism** (*Latin,* "nothing") — views that existence is meaningless and all values are baseless.

is then that it is no longer impeded by terrestrial matter that it is free, that it can perceive everything.

Mr. A. Keightley: Because they confine their consciousness to the sense of perception.

H.P.B.: That is what they do, and we don't. It is the difference between us.

Mr. Hall: When you say the physical death of man, do you mean the permanent death?

H.P.B.: What other death is there for a man?

Mr. Hall: I don't know whether it is the fact that you meant us to take it that after each death the soul is free and can proceed without being hampered by the body.

H.P.B.: You make a too subtle distinction. What is it you are talking about?

Mr. Hall: If you mean when a man ceases to incarnate, that is another thing.

H.P.B.: When does he cease? When he becomes Nirvanee, when you are dead and no Hall will exist any more, but your Ego will. The Roger Hall will have become one of the dresses that your Ego has thrown off to assume another in a certain time.

Mr. Hall: But then why should the Ego be anymore able to perceive things than it is at present?

H.P.B.: Because it is not impeded by matter, by gross matter. Can you see what is behind that door unless you are a clairvoyant? There, there is no impediment of matter and the soul sees everything. It goes into Devachan, its own place, and afterwards it must reincarnate. But there are cases when they don't go into Devachan, that is what we are fools enough to believe in.

Mr. Hall: It would not apply to every physical death.

H.P.B.: We do not speak about exceptions, they only prove the rule; we speak about the average death.

Mr. B. Keightley: There is a moment of freedom of that mind, I take it, between the actual death and the time when the Ego proceeds to the Devachanic state.

H.P.B.: We can only go by analogies. When I am dead, I will come and tell you, if I can. I do not think I will, but there are others who have been in trances, which is just as good as death, and there are those yogis[1] who were, for instance, 40 days buried.

Mr. Hall: Those yogis are exceptions.

H.P.B.: Their consciousness can live and the body is — I do not say dead, but any doctor will tell you, it is dead.

Mr. Hall: But all these are exceptions. I was asking whether it applied to every physical death, because if at the ordinary physical death of ordinary man his Ego must go along of itself, then it is not impeded in Devachan by the illusory bliss as it is by the illusory matter.

H.P.B.: Don't let us mix up these things or we will never end here.

Mr. A. Keightley: Then we come to the 4th Sloka. "The seven ways to bliss were not. The great causes of misery (Nidana[2] and Maya) were not."[3] The question is, what are the seven ways to bliss?

H.P.B.: Well, they are practically faculties, of which you will know more later on, perhaps, if you go a little deeper into esotericism.

Mr. A. Keightley: Then the seven ways are not actually mentioned?

H.P.B.: No, they are not mentioned in *The Secret Doctrine*, are they? They are not, I should say not.

Mr. A. Keightley: I don't think they are. Then the question is: "Are the four truths of the Hinayana[4] School the same as the four truths mentioned by Edwin Arnold[5] in his book *The Light of Asia*?"

H.P.B.: Almost the same. He mentions something which is somewhat different from it.

Mr. A. Keightley: The first is of sorrow, the second is of sorrow's cause, the third of sorrow's ceasing and the fourth is the way.

H.P.B.: What do you understand by Edwin Arnold's explanation?

Mr. B. Keightley: Read the passage please, Arch. [Mr. A. Keightley then read the passage indicated, *The Light of Asia*.]

---

[1] Yogi (*Sanskrit*) — a devotee, one who practises the Yoga system. There are various grades and kinds of Yogis, and the term has now become, in India, a generic name to designate every kind of ascetic.

[2] Nidana (*Sanskrit*, "cause") — the cause of existence, or a chain of causation.

[3] *The Secret Doctrine*, vol. 1, p. 38.

[4] Hinayana (*Sanskrit*, "Smaller Vehicle") — a School of the Northern Buddhists, opposed to the *Mahayana* (*Sanskrit*, "Greater Vehicle") in Tibet. Both schools are mystical.

[5] Edwin Arnold (1832–1904) — an English poet and journalist.

H.P.B.: All this is theological and all this exoteric;[6] this is what you can find in all the volumes that any Buddhist priest will give you; but there is far more explanation, of course, in Aryasanga's[7] works, though that is the esoteric too. Arnold took it from the Singhalese Buddhism.[8]

Mr. A. Keightley: Then do these four truths: the first of sorrow, the second of sorrow's cause, the third sorrow ceasing and the fourth the way, do they represent the four noble truths esoterically?

H.P.B.: Yes, I think they do. You will find Buddhism all about them.

Mr. B. Keightley: What do they really stand for?

H.P.B.: It would take too long and it has no relevancy to this Sloka. It would take much too long. It is impossible to tell you now. It would take several evenings to explain to you one of them thoroughly.

Mr. Harbottle: Then we will put them down for the future.

Mr. B. Keightley: I am not sure it would not be a profitable thing to take up next time.

---

[6] **Exoteric** (*Greek*) — outward, public; the opposite of esoteric or hidden.

[7] **Aryasanga** (*Sanskrit*) — a direct disciple of Gautama Buddha, the founder of the first Yogachara School (Mahayana).

[8] **Buddhism** — Buddhism is now split into two distinct divisions: the Southern and the Northern Buddhism. The former is said to be the purer form, having preserved more religiously the original teachings of the Lord Buddha. It is the religion of Sri Lanka, Thailand, Myanmar and other places, while the Northern Buddhism is confined to Tibet, China and Nepal. Such a distinction, however, is incorrect. If the Southern Buddhism is nearer, in that it has not departed — except perhaps in some trifling dogmas due to the many councils held after the death of the Master — from the public or *exoteric* teachings of Sakyamuni, the Northern Buddhism is the outcome of Siddharta Buddha's esoteric teachings, which he confined to his elect Bhikshus and Arhats. In fact, Buddhism in the present age cannot be justly judged either by one or the other of its exoteric popular forms. Real Buddhism can be appreciated only by blending the philosophy of the Southern division and the metaphysics of the Northern Schools. If one seems too iconoclastic and stern, and the other too metaphysical and transcendental, even to being overgrown with the weeds of Indian exotericism — many of the gods of its Pantheon having been transplanted under new names to Tibetan soil — it is entirely due to the popular expression of Buddhism in both divisions. Correspondingly, they stand in their relation to each other as Protestantism to Roman Catholicism. Both err by an excess of zeal and erroneous interpretations. Though neither the Southern nor the Northern Buddhist clergy have ever departed from truth consciously, still less have they acted under the dictates of *priestocracy*, ambition, or with an eye to personal gain and power, as the two Christian Churches have.

H.P.B.: I am not sure that it would be. You had better follow the Slokas. You are not going to follow that, because the four noble truths meant one thing for the priests of the yellow robes, and meant different things to the mystics. The one acts on the dead letter, just the same as our priests will act on the canons of the Church, and the mystics have got nothing to do with it.

Mr. A. Keightley: Can you give us any idea for the moment?

H.P.B.: I cannot, I am not an exoteric Buddhist. Ask Olcott. He is the man to know all these things. He is a very pious Buddhist and I am not. I am nothing pious.

Mr. A. Keightley: Then I put this question now, "Is the eightfold path the same as the seven ways to bliss?"

H.P.B.: Yes.

Mr. A. Keightley: "Are Nidana and Maya the (great causes of misery) aspects of the Absolute?"

H.P.B.: Is that number 4?

Mr. A. Keightley: That is number 4.

H.P.B.: Now what can Nidana, I ask myself, and Maya have to do with each other? Nidana means the concatenation of cause and effect. The twelve Nidanas are the enumeration of the chief causes which produce material for Karma to strike you very heavily. Maya is simply an illusion. Now what has Nidana to do with Maya? I cannot understand what analogy, what idea one has in common with the other. If you take the universe as an illusion, a Maya, then certainly the Nidanas as being in the universe are included in the Maya, but apart from that, what has one thing to do with the other?

Mr. B. Keightley: Then why do you class them together in that way?

H.P.B.: They are two distinct things. Maya is an illusion. You think yourself a very grand fellow, that you can go and compete with any Ah-his, and any of the [...]. But you make a fool of yourself and then comes Nirvana and shows it to you. It is just then, I think, that the man cannot take into his own head that he is not separate from the one and he goes and thinks himself a very great man in his own individuality, and he is nothing at all. He is still one in reality. It is nothing but Maya, an illusion; but taking this Maya, it is illusion or ignorance that brings us to commit all the acts which awaken the Nidanas, which produce the first cause of Nidana; this cause having been produced, the effects follow and there is Karma. Of course Nidanas and the production of bad Karmic effects and Maya are at the root of every evil. If we knew what we are we would not do such things. Everyone of us thinks he or she is a unit and something very grand in the eyes of all the authorities upstairs that you may think of; we are simply a drop of water in the ocean, not to be distinguished from another drop in the ocean, that is all we are. This sense of separateness is at the root of all evil. You know, there is no correspondence, no analogy, except the one I gave just now.

Mr. Harbottle: The only possible analogy is that they both of them are synonymous with manifestation, inasmuch as there cannot be any manifestation without the production of Nidanas on the one hand and Maya on the other.

H.P.B.: You think you can produce something but in reality you cannot produce anything at all.

Mr. Harbottle: The instant one single chain of a causation is started by any manifestation whatever, there is the Nidana.

H.P.B.: Now let us say: I have dressed myself in a red dress, I go out and because I am dressed in a red dress I have produced a cause, and a bull goes for me because I irritated his nerves; there is the Maya of the bull and there is the Nidana I have produced. So you can put two and two together. It is just an illusion which makes us produce the most Nidanas.

Mr. Harbottle: "Are Nidana and Maya aspects of the Absolute," is the exact form of the question.

Mr. B. Keightley: The question really ought to be separated; the question is to ask, first of all, is Maya an aspect of the Absolute?

H.P.B.: It cannot be an aspect of the Absolute. It is an aspect of the differentiation, if you put it this way. If Maya means an illusion, everything that is differentiated is an illusion also, but it cannot be an aspect of the Absolute.

Mr. Harbottle: Maya is a manifestation surely.

H.P.B.: Certainly; the Absolute cannot have any manifestation whatever, it can have reflection at best.

Mr. B. Keightley: In one of the old articles in *The Theosophist*, Maya is described as the cause of manifestation. I forget by who.

H.P.B.: Perhaps by some Hindu.

Mr. B. Keightley: By some good Hindu metaphysician. I am not sure if it was not Subba Row himself. He describes Maya as the cause of differentiation.

H.P.B.: If there were no Maya, there would be nothing — no differentiation.

Mr. Harbottle: But if there were no differentiation, there would be Maya so you cannot put one before the other, can you?

Mr. B. Keightley: But you are taking Maya as the cause of differentiation, therefore the moment you get behind differentiation, where is the Maya? Madame Blavatsky said that even Nirvana is a Maya.

Dr. Williams: Maya is a collective term meaning all manifestation.

H.P.B.: Certainly; they say that every thing is an illusion, because, first of all no two persons in the world see things in the same way. They may see it alike on general principles, but they won't see it altogether in the same way. And secondly, that which has a beginning and an end is not a reality, and, being less than the wink of the eye, it is an illusion, a momentary deception of the senses. This is why they call it an illusion. They call reality only that which ever was, is, and will be, which cannot be, now, that absolute consciousness or what they call Parabrahm, or what in Kabbalah is called Ain-Soph.

Dr. Williams: The term, it seems to me, applies to the complex points of differentiation. Differentiation applies to the unit and the other term applies to the collection of units.

Mr. B. Keightley: Yes, that is the way to explain it.

H.P.B.: Now I must ask Mr. Kingsland to bring in his objections.

Mr. Kingsland: It is Dr. Williams' turn.

H.P.B.: Do make it a little lively. Don't go to sleep, all of you. This won't be any illusion.

Dr. Williams: I notice one thing as you passed along the explanation. I do not quite understand what the idea was at the back of it. I think the expression would lead to a misunderstanding of what the real facts are. That is with reference to the cerebellum and cerebrum as being, respectively, the organ of the higher mind and lower mind.

H.P.B.: I never said higher mind and lower mind. I said this one acted during the waking hours; for instance, with everyone of us now, what acts is the front part — I think you call it cerebrum. Well, the other is active simply when this part sleeps and rests and becomes, so to say, inert — well, it is paralysed. Then the dreams begin and the mind begins to live and to feel and to be conscious with that part of the brain that is astrologically. I don't know if it is so, scientifically, and I don't presume to say, because there is no atom of science in me; I simply say that which the Occultists say and which the Kabbalists say, and all kinds of hallucinated lunatics in general. That is what I tell you.

Mr. Harbottle: You have described the back part as the instinctive.

Dr. Williams: That is the word I wanted.

H.P.B.: "Instinctual." Yes.

Dr. Williams: Of course, I want to avoid if possible making the appearance of any discrepancy. I stand as a go-between, between the two to reconcile, if possible, the two statements. Leave that for a moment or so and take an animal. An animal is supposed to have an instinctive mind, but the cerebellum is the organ of vegetative life. It simply controls the functions of the body, nothing more.

H.P.B.: But yet it acts during sleep.

Dr. Williams: The sensual mind is the mind to which the senses open, and there can be no thought, no ideation, no anything of which we predicate intellect or instinct anywhere, except in that part of the brain into which the senses do go, and that is the cerebrum.

H.P.B.: I said it is the organ of instinctual animal function and these functions will reflect themselves in the dreams to produce the dreams. And unless the higher Ego takes in hand the plane of the material [...] the dreams will have no sequence, even, because those dreams that we remember and that really have something in them are produced by the vision of the higher Ego. They are not produced by anything else. Every dog dreams, and certainly we cannot say a dog has prophetic dreams.

Mr. A. Keightley: Is not the cerebellum what you may call the organ of habit?

H.P.B.: Well, if I say instinctual, it comes to the same thing.

Mr. A. Keightley: Except that habit is very often referred to what we may call the present phase of existence and instinct to a past phase of existence.

H.P.B.: Whatever its name, the only thing that functions during night is cerebellum and not the cerebrum, because the dreams or the emanations — I don't know how to express it — well, those instinctive feelings which are felt here are just recollections of what took place. I told you my dream the other day. The thing gets distorted, and at the moment you awake you have a dream, and you have a thing that is half mixed up with all those feelings that were acting during sleep, and so on. If this part (the front brain) acted during sleep, then we would have consecutive dreams, because now we sit here we do not dream. We think, you understand, and we have all kinds of dreams awake, but there is some consecutiveness in them; we can think what we like and just make it clear. We can invent pictures, or, for instance, a man will be writing a novel; but in a dream you don't do that, just because it is *that* part which acts.

Dr. Williams: The consecutiveness is brought about entirely by the coordinating faculty. I do not know that scientific men have attempted to determine what part of the brain it is.

H.P.B.: It does not act in sleep.

Dr. Williams: But the cerebrum certainly does act, and the proof of it is this: that the nearer we approach the waking sleep, the more vivid our dreams become.

H.P.B.: Just so; *when* you are awakening, but not before.

Dr. Williams: When we are awakening, it is cerebrum which is coming into consciousness.

H.P.B.: It is just like something that has been very much heated during the day and which will emanate or irradiate during the night, but not at all because there is something acting there; it is the energy of the brain that comes out unconsciously.

Mr. Harbottle: Didn't you describe it just a moment ago as being that portion of the brain which received the impression of the senses? Is not it exactly during sleep when we receive such impressions? The reception of a very vivid impression.

Dr. Williams: Of course, you cannot reproduce anything except from that portion of the brain where it has been registered. The cerebellum does not receive and register impressions through the cerebrum.

Mr. Harbottle: It is because the senses are producing no impressions at all that we sleep, really.

Mr. B. Keightley: Not quite "no impressions at all," because if you make a noise over a sleeping man he will awake, and very likely will be able to trace his dream to the sense of oppression which awoke him.

Mr. Harbottle: Don't you think that seems to show, from the very fact that brain activity is required to register it, that the brain must be brought into activity again? Or in other words, he must be woke up.

Dr. Williams: All that you are describing is the function of the cerebrum.

H.P.B.: You have no consciousness of the activity of the cerebrum and it acts mechanically.

Mr. B. Keightley: One notices it often in ordinary life.

H.P.B.: In dreams, in the same way the memory comes into play. You must have a memory and perception of this thing, and if you catch one glimpse of it, maybe you will be able to reconstruct the dreams. I knew persons who could reconstruct their dreams in the most extraordinary way; if they only caught one little bit, it was enough. They would just throw themselves into a kind of negative state, and little by little it would come to them again, so that they could pump out again these things that were present unconsciously; but those persons are very rare. The average person dreams what is perfect nonsense, dreams of digestion, of nervous disturbances, etc., but I speak with respect to dreams that really are dreams.

Dr. Williams: It cannot be a matter of any importance. Still, I think if it should go out as it is, it would be very severely criticized. Whether this is a matter of any consequence, I don't know.

H.P.B.: If we were to write like all the blessed sages in the world, we should be pitched into. "The Theosophical Society," they say, "is absurd." It is a jumble, it has hallucinations, it is this, that, and the other; what can you do?

Dr. Williams: I suppose the Theosophical Society and yourself, as well, desire so far as possible to avoid giving them occasion for such remarks.

H.P.B.: It is no use to sit under an umbrella the whole of your life.

Mr. A. Keightley: One does not want to give them a handle they can seize hold of.

Mr. B. Keightley: Your old simile for the sleep of the brain was a very good one, the flickering embers of the fire just dying down. If you reverse that and suppose a current of air passes over the slumbering embers…

Dr. Williams: That would be a beautiful illustration of it.

Mr. B. Keightley: That is the true analogy; then you get it.

H.P.B.: I do not know if this is put down.

Mr. B. Keightley: The point of it is this: you get a factor or two, as it were. These waking sparks in the cerebrum, the brain, just beginning to awake, combined with the activity that has been going on all night in the cerebellum, which in its turn is fading below the plane of consciousness.

H.P.B.: Were you here, Dr. Williams, when we talked about that? I have it all in the little book. I have been writing considerably in it. It is not notes such as I have taken here. There I have been writing whole pages.

Mr. A. Keightley: Does the cerebellum ever permanently stop working?

H.P.B.: No, but it is perfectly lost in the functions of the cerebrum, which is, just as Dr. Williams says, connected more with — what do you call it — vegetative life.

Mr. B. Keightley: The stimuli which proceed from the cerebellum during waking life fall, all of them, below the waking consciousness. The field of consciousness being entirely occupied by the cerebrum till it goes to sleep, when the stimuli from the cerebellum begin to form the field of consciousness.

Dr. Williams: You say all consciousness must necessarily reside in the cerebrum. I am speaking now of the ordinary dream state, that the ordinary dream state must always be connected with more or less activity of the cerebrum. Of course, when we say it sleeps, there is not an absolute paralysis, there is circulation of the blood. It is simply the withdrawal of the ordinary, normal amount of blood that occupies it during waking hours. Just in that state there are a great many stages.

Mr. Harbottle: Then if dreams are the beginning and the end of sleep, they occur practically at the particular moment when the cerebrum is going to sleep, and deep sleep is temporary paralysis.

Mr. B. Keightley: I don't think it is strictly true that the cerebrum is the only seat of consciousness.

H.P.B.: No, but it is that which polishes the ideas and makes them perfect — coordinates them, but the other does not. It simply gives conscious desires and so on.

Dr. Williams: They say a sensitive plant has consciousness. I meant coordinating consciousness.

Mr. B. Keightley: Du Prel[1] cites some very curious experiments showing there is a kind of local consciousness.

Dr. Williams: That is what they call reflex connection?

Mr. B. Keightley: He goes further than that in the cases of clairvoyants who perceive through the stomach. He cites a number of well authenticated cases that were experiments of his own, in that direction, in which he shows that the threshold of consciousness is capable of a very wide range of variation, very much wider than we are accustomed to attribute to it, both upwards and downwards.

Mr. A. Keightley: The point I was about to raise is this. You get your cerebrum acting from the point of your consciousness at the beginning and end of sleep. Very well then, in the intervening period, a period of deep sleep, the consciousness of the man is not lost; that goes on.

Mr. B. Keightley: The consciousness of the man is then inherent in the higher Ego.

Mr. A. Keightley: But the brain is not a sufficiently sensitive registering organ under those circumstances.

Mr. B. Keightley: No; except what is impressed upon it at the moment of awakening, and that is liable, of course, to get mixed up with the suggestions and stimuli and sensations that have been going on during the night in the cerebellum.

---

[1] **Baron Carl Du Prel** (1839–1899) — a German philosopher.

Mr. A. Keightley: Now, query: The cerebellum has sometimes been called the coordinating organ of the physiological senses.

Mr. B. Keightley: Of the sense of sight, do you mean?

Mr. A. Keightley: Coordinating organ — I want to query whether it is possible for the cerebrum to be the coordinating organ of ideas?

Mr. B. Keightley: As opposed to sensations?

H.P.B.: Sensations. I suppose the animal also will have its sensations coordinated. If you give it a name in man, it is a different thing. In man there are the ideas, whereas an animal has nothing of the kind. It is simply an instinctual feeling; the animal does not think.

Mr. A. Keightley: Well, but roughly speaking, you have the animal with his sensation, which sensation is transmitted to the brain, if there is anything to be done with it for the first time. That process is repeated, until finally there is a sort of course of action determined, giving a repetition of the sensation. Ultimately, the end of it is that the cerebellum appears to act as an organ which will entail a definite course of action following a similar sensation without the creature taking a conscious part in the process. Is not that supposed to be the function of the cerebellum?

Dr. Williams: Yes.

Mr. A. Keightley: Then, you see, the cerebrum has taken its part and the cerebellum takes its part during the waking hours. Very well then; then we come to another part of it. Is it possible for the cerebrum to be a coordinating organ of ideas, as the cerebellum is a coordinating organ of action?

H.P.B.: Well, really, I don't know physiology enough for it, I can tell you. I don't know all the scientific things and I have read a good deal of what Huxley[1] was saying about the evidence of one lobe and another lobe. I say he has a theory which I cannot make head or tail of, just to reconcile it with occult theories, with what we are taught.

Dr. Williams: I don't think you could understand him. I think Huxley is ultra materialistic.

H.P.B.: He speaks about things most peculiarly. I read him several times and I think if I read it ten times, I could not understand it either. It may be very scientific physiologically, but in reality, as well

---

[1] Thomas Henry Huxley (1825–1895) — an English biologist and anthropologist.

as I could check it by my own experience in dreams, all that I see in sleep etc., I could not make head or tail of it. I don't see it is that at all.

Mr. B. Keightley: If you tickle a sleeping man gently, he will make a movement to brush it away, but without waking. Therefore the stimulus goes to the cerebellum and the mechanical action is produced. Arch's point was this: does the cerebrum, the forebrain, act in the same way with regard to the ideas? Does that establish a coordination between ideas?

H.P.B.: I believe it does. It cannot be otherwise.

Dr. Williams: I should say it could not be otherwise.

Mr. Harbottle: Well I think we might make it now general.

24 JANUARY 1889

Mr. A. Keightley: The first question arises from what was stated at a previous meeting, when you said that it would take too long. We want to know if you will give us some explanation of the four and seven truths, even if it takes all the evening, as you said it would be too large a subject to deal with at the same time as others.

H.P.B.: Well, I will answer as follows: Everything about the four truths you can find in *The Buddhist Catechism*[1] or any of the exoteric books, but I do not think you are ready, anyone of you, for the esoteric explanation of them; therefore I had better ask you to postpone this.

Mr. A. Keightley: Can anything that is esoteric be found in these exoteric books?

H.P.B.: You can find it in any manual of Buddhism; in Olcott's book, for instance. There is nothing occult about it.

Mr. A. Keightley: Then how far is that exoteric side to be taken for anything real?

H.P.B.: It is real, because in the Buddhist church they practise it, and certainly the high priests know the truth about it, and they do not take the exoteric forms literally. As to the small fry and the laymen, they do.

Mr. A. Keightley: Then how far has that any value?

H.P.B.: It has a great value, because it is a discipline and it helps them to lead a good life and to have their mind fixed always on the spiritual.

Mr. A. Keightley: Then we pass on. *The Secret Doctrine*, Stanza 1, Sloka 5. "Darkness alone filled the boundless All." Is "darkness" the same as the "Eternal Parent: Space," spoken of in Sloka 1?

H.P.B.: How can it be the same thing? To me, Space is something already with attributes, at least in potentiality; it is differentiated matter, and "darkness" is something of which no attributes can be predicated, surely, for it is chaos; it is the Absoluteness. How can it be the same?

Mr. A. Keightley: But then is "darkness" there used in the sense of the opposite pole to light?

---

[1] *The Buddhist Catechism* — H. S. Olcott's work, published in 1881.

H.P.B.: Yes, the opposite pole to manifestation. "Darkness" means something that is perfectly void of any attributes or qualities — all negative.

Mr. B. Keightley: It is not opposed to light, then, but opposed to differentiation?

H.P.B.: There is no light yet.

Mr. B. Keightley: But it is really taken as the symbolism of negativeness.

H.P.B.: It is taken as that which you can find in the Bible, the void, "Tohu-va-bohu"[2] as they call it, the "chaos"; as it is said: "everything was darkness, and on the darkness the spirit of God was."[3] Just the same as in that sense. There was nothing in it — in the Universe.

Mr. Kingsland: Is it that there is no light, or simply nothing to manifest it?

H.P.B.: There is nothing to manifest it. It is not darkness as absence of light, but it is darkness as Absoluteness[4] in the absence of any manifestation.

Mr. Kingsland: Quite so; just the same as the Universal Mind we were discussing last time?

H.P.B.: Just so.

Colonel Chowne:[5] Then it says: "Light proceeds from Darkness."

H.P.B.: After that. First comes light. Light is the first Logos — call it whatever you like — it is the non-manifested Logos. In the second Logos it is not the Creator, but the light. In the *Vishnu Purana* they do not call it even Brahma, because Brahma is an aspect of Vishnu in the *Vishnu Purana*. What they say is, it is Vishnu — all. Vishnu *is* and *is not.*

Mr. A. Keightley: Then what is the difference there between the derivations of Vishnu and Brahma, the spreading and the pervading?

---

[2] **Tohu-va-bohu** (*Hebrew*) — a phrase from Genesis 1:2: "And the earth was without form, and void."

[3] A paraphrase of Genesis 1:2.

[4] **Absoluteness** — when predicated of the Universal Principle, it denotes an abstraction, which is more correct and logical than to apply the adjective "absolute" to that which can have neither attributes nor limitations.

[5] **Colonel Chowne** — he and his wife were members of the Esoteric Section of the Theosophical Society and personal friends of H.P.B.

H.P.B.: In the *Vishnu Purana* you will find Vishnu spoken of as the Absolute "No-Thing," as the Ain-Soph, that which is perfectly unknown, endless and incomprehensible. The Heavenly Man is its vehicle to manifest itself in the Universe when the Ain-Soph becomes that celestial man. Just in the same way we deal with Vishnu in the *Vishnu Purana*, who will be spoken of as the Absolute; and then one of his aspects will be Brahma, the male, not the neuter, and after that he becomes everything. In the Veda you won't find Vishnu prominently mentioned, nor Brahma. Vishnu is named in the Veda, but is not mentioned as anything of a high order. As to Brahma, he is not mentioned at all.

Mr. A. Keightley: Then that quotation, "For Father, Mother and Son were once more One"?

H.P.B.: Means that all *that*, the creative forces and the causing forces — if I may use the expression — and the effect of this cause is the Universe. Again, in the undifferentiated condition all was merged into one and was One. The Absolute is during the Pralaya, always.

Mr. A. Keightley: Second. What are the different meanings of the terms: Father, Mother and Son? For in the Commentary you explain them (a) as Spirit, Substance, and the Universe; (b) as Spirit, Soul and Body; (c) as the Universe, the Planetary Chain,[1] and Man.

H.P.B.: Well, so they are. I think I have explained entirely. What can I say more? Unless you anthropomorphize[2] them and make ideals of them, and deities, and put them as the Father, Mother and Son, as put all kinds of goddesses and gods. I do not see how I can explain it in any other way.

Mr. A. Keightley: Then take the last items of the series: I suppose "Son," "Substance," "Body" and "Man" correspond?

H.P.B.: Certainly they do.

Mr. A. Keightley: Then why are "Father-Mother" linked together? And then the correspondence comes, "Spirit and Substance"; "Spirit and Soul"; and the "Universe and the Planetary Chain"; and the third term in the series seems to proceed from the other two.

---

[1] **Planetary Chain** — the septenary structure of a planet, which consists of seven bodies, globes, or spheres, similarly to that of man.

[2] **Anthropomorphism** — the act of endowing God or the gods with a human form and human attributes or qualities.

H.P.B.: I put all the examples because it can be applied to anything. It can be applied to a planetary chain, it can be applied to the solar system, it can be applied to the whole Cosmos or anything you like. It is simply a figure of speech — a metaphor.

Mr. A. Keightley: But I think the point that I was meaning was this: you have Father and Mother and then you have the Son. The sentence seems to mean that the Son is distinct from the Father and the Mother, and that ultimately, in Pralaya, the Son is merged back again into the Father and Mother in a closer union.

H.P.B.: Remember, I do not speak about the period preceding what they call in common parlance "Creation." I speak about the time after matter was differentiated, but before it began to assume form. I say in *The Secret Doctrine* I do not touch the thing which was pre-natal — if you can say that of the Cosmos. I do not touch this at all. Father-Mother simply means here the differentiated primeval substance, protyle, when it began to differentiate and became positive and negative, the active and the passive, and the Son, the production of the two, is the Son of the Universe, that is to say, of the universal forms.

Mr. A. Keightley: Then the ultimate state is the Laya state of Father, Mother and Son?

H.P.B.: Laya is that which remains during Pralaya, but also that which, in the manifested universe, is at the terminus of all matter. It is the zero-point. Now ask Mr. Bulaki Rama[3] what Laya means. He knows and will explain it to you a great deal better than I. I say it is non-differentiated matter, the zero-point, as Crookes calls it. I don't know how to describe in any other way, that point where indestructible substance becomes homogeneous, entirely and absolutely homogeneous, that is to say, and not objective.

Mr. A. Keightley: Then is that the point you are speaking of here, just at the time when the Father, Mother and Son become once more One?

H.P.B.: Yes, but I don't know, I don't think it is in *The Secret Doctrine*. I simply make reference to that which was before the Father-Mother period. If there is Father-Mother, then certainly there is no such condition as Laya.

---

[3] **Bulaki Rama** — a Sanskrit scholar.

Mr. B. Keightley: Father-Mother are later than the Laya condition.

H.P.B.: Certainly, individual objects may be in Laya, but the universe cannot be in Laya when Father-Mother appear there, as it is said in this Stanza.

Mr. A. Keightley: That is the point I was meaning. Where the Son and the Father and the Mother reunite, there can be no differentiation at all.

H.P.B.: Certainly, it is the Laya, but not at that point you are talking about.

Colonel Chowne: You explained it once as the essence.

H.P.B.: It is the essence, it is that which exists and does not exist, it is space. Now, for us, space is a word which has no meaning unless we limit and condition it; but in reality, space is the most abstract thing, and space containing all is just that unknown deity which is invisible and which we cannot understand, which we can but intellectually sense. What do they call it in Sanskrit, "dis," isn't it? The "ten divinities" that are in space. It is written "dis."

Mr. Bulaki Rama: "Desha,"[1] you mean, the "Ten Divinities" of space.

H.P.B.: It is just what I have been talking about. They pronounce like "sh" what we pronounce as "s," for instance, they would say "shloka" for what we call "Sloka."

Mr. B. Keightley: Is Fohat[2] one of the three — Father, Mother, and Son — or what is it?

H.P.B.: Fohat is a manifestation. You mix up in the most extraordinary way the first Logos and the second Logos. The first is the unmanifested potentiality of Father, Mother and Son and of everything. It makes a triangle, that which is so dealt with by the Pythagoreans. You mix up the second Logos, which is the collectivity of the creators, or

---

[1] **Desha** (*Sanskrit*, "space") — a place or environment; land; country.
[2] **Fohat** (*Tibetan*) — a term used to represent the active (male) potency of the Shakti (female reproductive power) in Nature. The essence of cosmic electricity. An occult Tibetan term for *Daiviprakriti* (primordial light), and in the universe of manifestation, the ever-present electrical energy and ceaseless destructive and formative power. Esoterically, it is the same, Fohat being the universal propelling Vital Force, at once the propeller and the resultant.

what they call in Greek Demiurgi,[3] the builders of the universe, or simply the masons.

Mr. B. Keightley: I only want to get as clear as we can the sense in which the term is used in *The Secret Doctrine.*

H.P.B.: I use it in many senses in *The Secret Doctrine.* If you ask me such a thing I cannot remember in what sense I use it in such and such a page, but I can tell you in general what it means.

Mr. A. Keightley: Question 3. Can you give us the equivalents of these terms (Father, Mother and Son) in (a) the Vedantic, and (b) in the Sankhya phraseology?

H.P.B.: No, sir, I do not teach you the Vedanta or the Sankhya. It will only confuse you, and make matters worse. Let us hold to the esoteric philosophy, without mixing up the Sankhya and other philosophies with it. There are many things which are identical, but now, since we learn Occultism, I do not see why I should go and speak on it. This is, I know, a knotty question. I am perfectly sure of it.

Mr. A. Keightley: Question 5. During Manvantara, when the "Son" is in existence or awake, do the Father and Mother exist independently, or only as manifested in the Son?

H.P.B.: This is a thing which tickled me very much when I read it. I cannot understand, unless you want to become polytheists and idolaters, how anyone can offer such a question as that. How can a Father and Mother be independent of the Son? Are the Father and Mother two entities of the male and female persuasions and the Son the product of these two entities? Why, it is all one, it seems to me. How can we anthropomorphize in such a way in metaphysical questions? Well, look here, I cannot tell you any better than this, that they are, if you like, centripetal and centrifugal forces. This is the Father-Mother. That which they produce is the Son. I cannot say any better, because this gives you the whole thing.

Mr. B. Keightley: And that is the point; because in our mental conceptions we had conceived of the centripetal and centrifugal forces as existing independently of the effects they produce. We regard the effects in ordinary thinking as secondary to these two forces.

---

[3] **Demiurge** (*Greek*, "Creator") — the Artificer; the Supernal Power which built the universe.

H.P.B.: Well, you are very wise in the West. You are great pundits,[1] a thousand times more so than any of these benighted pundits in the East. I am not one of them, but I am very near to them in my heart. But still you do not know anything about it, and you cannot bring me any of your Herbert Spencers, or your other scientists, who know anything about it. They do not understand the thing as we do; they do not understand it aright, because you think about centripetal and centrifugal forces not as to any effect they produce. Therefore you think when there are no effects they will exist the same, do you, and they will produce no effect? They will be effectless. But why should you go and conceive a thing upside down? If these centripetal and centrifugal forces exist they must be producing effects, because there is nothing aimless in nature, and if they exist they produce effects. When there are no more effects the Forces do not exist either.

Mr. Kingsland: They exist as separate entities for mathematical purposes.

H.P.B.: Oh, for mathematics, but in nature and in science it is a different thing. We divide also a man into seven principles. We do not mean that in man there are seven skins or seven entities, or seven souls or, as Gerald Massey[2] thought, seven devils. They are only aspects of the one and nothing else. It certainly does not mean that. I see that you have been reading a good many books in your British Museum, but you are not accustomed to the way of expression — well, to this metaphorical form of speech of theirs. I do not know how it is, but I have been brought up from childhood in this way; and in the Georgian and Armenian times there was always this metaphorical mode of expression. In Persia they won't say a single word.

Mr. A. Keightley: Then we pass on to Sloka 6. "The universe, the Son of Necessity, was immersed in Paranishpanna.[3] ... The causes of existence had been done away with."[4] If the "causes of existence" had been done away with, how did they come into existence again? For

---

[1] **Pundit** (*Sanskrit*, "learned") — an expert in a particular subject.

[2] **Gerald Massey** (1828–1907) — an English poet and writer.

[3] **Paranishpanna** (*Sanskrit*, "perfect") — Para-Nirvana; the Absolute Perfection to which all Existences attain at the close of a great period of activity, and in which they rest during the succeeding period of repose. In Tibetan it is called *Yong-Grub*.

[4] *The Secret Doctrine*, vol. 1, pp. 42, 44.

you state in the Commentary that the chief cause of existence is the desire to exist, and it has been just stated that the Universe is the Son of Necessity.

H.P.B.: What a contradiction indeed; it is extraordinary. "The causes of existence had been done away with" refers to the past Manvantaras or age of Brahma, but the cause which makes the wheel of Time and Space run into eternity, which is out of time and space (now try and understand me) has nothing to do with finite cause or that which we call Nidanas. What has one thing to do with the other? That is a little bit of criticism which I could not understand. I received it very humbly with very great gratitude, but I thought to myself of the person who wrote it. I do not think he will ever be a rival to Schopenhauer,[5] or anyone like him. That was my intimate opinion. What is contradictory there.

Mr. A. Keightley: Nobody has said it is a contradiction.

H.P.B.: But read it, if you please. It is a very great contradiction. I want all of you to remark that.

Mr. A. Keightley: It is the contrast here. If the causes of existence had been done away with, how did they come into existence again? And there you answer that by saying that one Manvantara had disappeared into Pralaya and that the cause which led the previous Manvantara to exist is behind the limits of space and time, and therefore causes another Manvantara to come into being.

H.P.B.: Yes, because that cause is immutable and has nothing to do with the *causes* of this terrestrial plane produced by finite and conditioned being. And we say *that* cause is immutable and it can be in no sense a finite consciousness or desire. It postulates an absurdity to give to the Absolute desire or consciousness or necessity. If you don't understand it, read it, and you will see it is so. I say it is no more natural to predicate of the Absolute, or to charge the Absolute with desire or thought, than it is to say, for instance — how did I put it here — than the striking of the hours in a clock proves the desire of the clock to strike. Now you say: "Yes, the clock is wound up." I say the universe is wound up. The only difference is that this one is wound up in space and time, and the other is out of space and time, that is to say, in eternity; therefore, it is one and the same thing. Whoever

---

[5] **Arthur Schopenhauer** (1788–1860) — a German philosopher.

has something to say against it, let him come and say it, and I will see what objection there is. There I am charged positively with the most absurd idea, as if the Absolute could have any desire or feel necessity, is not it so? Read it all over again.

Mr. A. Keightley: Well, it is divided into two or three different headings. [Reads again.]

H.P.B.: Well I don't find "the blind will" of Schopenhauer so very stupid; it is a thousand times more philosophical than the philosophy of the ruler who created man. Doesn't it accuse me of contradiction? Well, not me, but the Sloka there.

Mr. B. Keightley: No, I don't think so. It seems to me to ask for an explanation.

H.P.B.: How can I explain why, when I am sitting down, I am not standing up? What can I say?

Mr. A. Keightley: It practically reduces the whole matter to "what is the cause in the Absolute of differentiation?"

Mr. B. Keightley: The difficulty is you cannot postulate…

H.P.B.: Ah! It is a very easy question to ask, you understand. I know you don't ask, but many ask. Fawcett asked it. He wants to ask what is the cause that propels or compels Parabrahm to create. Parabrahm is not a cause. It is not even the Absolute, as I say, but Absoluteness. Now, how can we know the cause that propels Parabrahm to create? That which is behind all the veil of matter is incomprehensible, and no finite intellect can conceive it. Well, we can perhaps have a slight conception in our hazy ideas that there may be such a thing, but we don't understand it, and to come and ask for the cause is perfectly ridiculous. Look at what Subba Row says in his lectures; it is perfectly true. He says that even the Logos — the first, not the second — cannot see Parabrahm. He sees simply the veil of matter, Mulaprakriti. So you see what it must be; then how can you know the cause, when we have no idea of Mulaprakriti, even? It is simply a conception, and it is just as Buddha said: "What is Nirvana? It is nowhere." "Then it is not, it does not exist?" "No, it does not exist, but it *is*." Well, just the same with that. Nirvana itself is a Maya. You will come always to the old question, unless you can conceive of such a thing as an eternal, endless, perpetual motion machine which you will call the universe — though properly we cannot call it a machine. We cannot call that a machine which is unlimited, limitless. But if you can conceive even of such an idea, you will never conceive of the Absolute in the way you do. You just try to imagine space in nature without giving it limits or form or anything. Understand my idea, and just try to imagine two forces: the centripetal and the centrifugal, which periodically must emanate from *It*. Just as the clock must strike so this strikes and emanates periodically. When it has done striking it goes to sleep again. Try to imagine that and then you will have perhaps a notion. I tell you what was in my conception in the beginning. I had the perpetual motion machine. Mind you, it is not that I say, and certainly not that I would go and advocate, the automatic creation of the materialists; never. But it is for the purpose of giving a shape to it, and to allow people to conceive of it, because otherwise, you cannot.

Mr. B. Keightley: It is a peg to hang your mind upon.

H.P.B.: Yes, you must have a peg; therefore, imagine a perpetual motion machine which has no form and which is endless. Well, you can, with a little imagination, have these two forces which appear and disappear periodically.

Mr. Gardner:[1] What portion of the machine is Parabrahm?

H.P.B.: What! Put him to bed! Please give him a pillow! Mr. Gardner, my dear man! Shame him, if you please, let him blush — Parabrahm, why, it is all. If there is one mathematical point in the universe where Parabrahm is not, then you had better go to bed, because it does not exist. It is not the present it is eternal. Oh! Do explain, somebody else, will you, please? Tell him some verses from the Veda to refresh him — anything you like.

Mr. A. Keightley: Supposing you take your conception of a machine. If ultimately you work out your conception of the universe, you bring yourself back to plain, simple, centrifugal and centripetal forces.

H.P.B.: With intelligence, *plus* intelligence; that will be another kind of "machine."

Mr. A. Keightley: Very well, call that the primary differentiation, and get that back to Parabrahm.

---

[1] **Frederick Leigh Gardner** (1857–1930) — an English stockbroker and bookseller who belonged to various societies.

H.P.B.: Why should it get back to Parabrahm? It will get back to Parabrahm when the universe has finished its Age of Brahma, its cycle.

Mr. A. Keightley: Very well, then, you get your primary differentiation, and you postulate then that you must have a cause, the great first cause, the Absolute.

H.P.B.: No, I beg your pardon. The great First Cause is not the Absolute, never call it that; the great First Cause is the first unconscious radiation or emanation. Call it what you like, you know English better than I do. That which periodically manifests itself as light.

Mr. B. Keightley: The unmanifested Logos, in fact.

H.P.B.: Yes, the unmanifested Logos, if you like, but never Parabrahm. It is the causeless cause of all, and Absoluteness cannot be a cause. That is the great difficulty.

Mr. B. Keightley: Look at the paradox. You will say on the one hand that Absoluteness cannot be a cause, and you call it in the same breath a causeless cause.

H.P.B.: Because, in the first place, the English language is very poor, and in the second place, human language is almost as poor. And then, with our finite language, our finite brains, our finite conception, it is impossible to put in form that which is formless. How can you go, and presume to put it in language? Look at Herbert Spencer, he also calls it the First Cause, and he mixes it up with Absoluteness. Why, this is a very great philosophical mistake, at least in the eyes of the Vedantins. Certainly it is the greatest mistake.

Mr. A. Keightley: What I am getting towards is this, that you get back to your unmanifested Logos, and behind that, whatever attribute you chose to apply, you have Parabrahm.

Mr. B. Keightley: As the root.

H.P.B.: Look here, if you want to have the Vedantin theory, there is Parabrahm and Mulaprakriti. They are the same; only, Mulaprakriti is an attribute — it is a primordial, undifferentiated matter. We can conceive of such a thing, knowing there is such a thing, if we take it a little limited, that is of limited size or space; but we cannot conceive of that which is beyond that matter, that is to say, which is not even spirit, which is metaspirit, and is a thing inconceivable to the human intellect, and we can only barely sense it in our conceptions. We cannot put it in any definite words. This is the thing I want to impress upon you. Now Mr. Gardner thought Parabrahm was *something*; Parabrahm is *no thing*. Not *nothing*, it is Ain-Soph, the Endless. It is not *a thing* which is all and nothing, for it is Be-ness, and not non-being. Now try to understand this philosophically.

Mr. Kingsland: But it is still the First Cause, isn't it?

H.P.B.: It is the root of all, the causeless cause, the root of everything. And the First Cause, the unmanifested Logos, is that which will be the cause of everything in the universe.

Mr. Kingsland: You don't use the term "causeless" in the sense of cause-that-is-not-a-cause for anything else, but you use it in the sense of a cause that has not a cause behind it.

H.P.B.: It is a universal potentiality of that which will become potency. That is to say, if there is a difference in the English language between potentiality and potency. Is there?

Mr. B. Keightley: Certainly there is, distinctly.

Mr. Kingsland: That overcomes your objection, then.

Mr. B. Keightley: Yes, I only put it as a paradox of expression.

H.P.B.: They call it the rootless root; that is to say, it has no root because it is causality itself — causation.

Mr. Kingsland: It has no root, but it is the root of everything.

H.P.B.: It is the spiritual basis of all cause, which Mulaprakriti certainly is not. They say Akasha has only one attribute, and it is sound, in the *Vishnu Purana*. What is sound? It is Logos, that is to say, the sensuous representation of something. You see, it is very difficult for me to tell you. I speak English like a Spanish cow, and I am very sorry for it, but I cannot speak better, though I try to explain it as well as I can.

Mr. A. Keightley: Is it possible, as a speculation, as an entirely speculative thing, to conceive that after the universe has gone back into the Parabrahmic condition, that there should be to that Parabrahmic condition a Para-Parabrahmic.

H.P.B.: It is what they say — Para-Parabrahmic, that is the expression they use in philosophy. Don't they?

Mr. Hall: It is the old story about veil behind veil.

H.P.B.: No, it is not that. It is that nothing is behind the veil but nothingness — the root of all.

Mr. A. Keightley: Otherwise, you don't get back to infinity.

H.P.B.: Well, infinity is Sat, and Sat is Parabrahm, and Parabrahm is Absoluteness; it is immutability.

Mr. B. Keightley: You see, you can't have the fallacy of an endless chain of the hen from the egg, and the egg from the hen and so on backwards. You must come to a stopping point somewhere.

Mr. A. Keightley: Must you? That is the question.

H.P.B.: You can conceive of it. If you train your intellect to be always aspiring and striving after the beginning of things, then you can.

Mr. B. Keightley: Can you go back?

H.P.B.: If you take the Aristotelian method you cannot go on, and you will be lost in a maze of all kinds of speculations which will be fruitless. But if you begin with the universals, taking the method of Plato, then I think you can, because then having once travelled on that road you can far more easily backtrack, and beginning from the particulars ascend to the universals. Then your method will be splendid; not quite on the lines of the men of science, but still it is good for something.

Mr. B. Keightley: But what I understand Arch was putting was this: behind that cause you have one cause, and behind that another cause, behind that another, and so on *ad infinitum*.[1]

H.P.B.: Is it so, Arch?

Mr. A. Keightley: It is partly that. Well it is this: the subject seems to me so big that you can't get the right expression.

H.P.B.: But "causeless cause" puts a stop to it, because that means there is no cause behind it and that it had no cause, because it is cause itself. Why, for instance, do we say that the Absolute cannot think, nor can it desire, nor can it have attributes? Why, I have been saying to you a thousand times it has no consciousness. It has no desire because it is absolute desire; "It" being the Absoluteness. How can you have the smallest thing that is not in *It*? But we can't say that anything is an attribute of *It*.

---

[1] **Ad infinitum** (*Latin*) — to infinity; endlessly.

Mr. B. Keightley: Certainly not.

H.P.B.: Because an attribute is something finite, and this is infinite. So a stop is put to our speculations, by these words: "causeless cause" and "rootless root." And I think it is the most remarkable, suggestive and graphic expression I ever saw.

Dr. Williams: I think it says everything that can be said.

H.P.B.: Take the Vedanta. I don't know of any philosophy in the world higher than that philosophy.

Mr. A. Keightley: Then we come to section b, question 6.

Mr. B. Keightley: I think you can pass over those; they have been practically dealt with. We have just been discussing them. Pass on to the next one.

H.P.B.: Oh no, he has not done. There is a, b, c, and d of that.

Mr. A. Keightley: [Reads] "To conceive of either a necessity or a desire in the Absolute is to destroy the Absoluteness of the Absolute, or to reduce it to the 'blind will' of Schopenhauer."

H.P.B.: Well, I have answered that question. It is not at all to reduce it to the "blind will" of Schopenhauer, but the "blind will," as far as I can express it, it is expressed perfectly; that which appears to us as "blind will" is absolute — well, not intelligence; but yes, absolute intelligence, absolute wisdom or knowledge, or absolute consciousness.

Mr. A. Keightley: (b) "If this desire is attributed to the Logos, it can only exist subsequent to the emergence of the Logos."

H.P.B.: I say no desire is attributed to Logos number one. That is what I said to you before.

Mr. A. Keightley: (c) "If it is said to exist as a latent potentiality in the Logos during Pralaya, then there must be a cause that makes it pass from latency into activity. Whence then the impulse to manifestation?"

H.P.B.: That is the old original question. We come again to the first principles. It is old Fawcett, who wants absolutely that someone should leave their visiting card at the door of Parabrahm and ask him what impels him to such capers, to create the universe. How can we answer that? It is a perfect impossibility. The potentiality, it says, if it exists in the Logos, it exists in everything. It exists in you, it exists in this fan and everywhere. Once we have approached the Pralaya — well, certainly we are in it, and it exists everywhere — but why should "the impulse" be absolutely limited to the Logos? There is again a thing which shows he has not been thinking on these Eastern lines.

Mr. A. Keightley: "The visible that was, and the invisible that is, rested in eternal non-being, the One Being."[1] Question 7. What is the meaning of the expression, "the visible that was, and the invisible that is"?

H.P.B.: "The visible that was" means the universe of the past Manvantara, which had dropped into eternity and was no more. Very well; and "the invisible that is" means the eternal, present and ever invisible deity. It is abstract space, absolute Sat, and then we go over again what we have been talking about. It is very simple that; I don't see why the question is asked.

Mr. B. Keightley: It was really to find out from what point of view you were speaking in that Sloka, whether of the past Manvantara or not.

H.P.B.: Certainly, the past Manvantara. "The visible that was," was no more, "and the invisible that is" in this is certainly that which was, and that which will be in everything.

Mr. A. Keightley: Then we get to Sloka 8.[2] "Alone the one form of existence stretched boundless, infinite, causeless, in dreamless sleep; and life pulsated unconscious in universal Space, throughout that All-Presence which is sensed by the opened eye of the Dangma."[3] Does then this "eye" open upon the Absolute, or is the "one form of existence" and the "All Presence" here mentioned other than the Absolute?

H.P.B.: Well, but the eye of Dangma being open and all that — I suppose everyone ought to see that it is again a metaphorical way of expressing the thing. You may open your eyes, and anyone can open his eyes on the Absolute, but the question is, "shall we see It"? It is not said that the eye saw, it says it "sensed." Now, if it is said that on opening the eye Dangma saw the Absolute, then it would be a fallacy and an absurdity, but it is said "sensed," if you please.

Mr. B. Keightley: It is not taken in that sense. What was meant by the question was, is it through this open eye that we do receive such

---

[1] *The Secret Doctrine*, vol. 1, p. 44.
[2] *The Secret Doctrine*, vol. 1, p. 46.
[3] **Dangma** (*Sanskrit*, "purified soul") — a Seer and an Initiate; one who has attained full wisdom.

sense, or such feeling, or such consciousness, whatever you take it to be?

H.P.B.: Do you take it for your own eye?

Mr. B. Keightley: No, for the highest spiritual faculty.

H.P.B.: There was no Dangma at that time, therefore nobody could see it. What other questions have you, then?

Mr. A. Keightley: What is "dreamless sleep"?

H.P.B.: "Dreamless sleep" is a sleep without dreams, I suppose. I certainly cannot give you a better definition than that. Who can?

Mr. A. Keightley: What does it mean?

H.P.B.: A dreamless sleep means a sleep without dreams.

Mr. B. Keightley: But that simply describes its state in relation to waking consciousness.

H.P.B.: In what particular is it? What is it about the dreamless sleep? I would like to know to what page it refers, what I have been talking about.

Mr. B. Keightley: It is part of that Sloka.

H.P.B.: I remember very well. I use the expression, only I don't see what there is. It means that there can be no presentation of the objects you can see in the universe, and therefore it is a "dreamless sleep."

Mr. B. Keightley: What you say here is this. [Reads passage from *The Secret Doctrine*, vol. 1, p. 47.]

H.P.B.: I think that I have explained it, and what can I explain more?

Mr. Kingsland: It implies there is something very active going on in that state of dreams. I think what you want to know is, what is that which is active going on?

Mr. B. Keightley: A greater degree of activity.

Mr. Kingsland: What they want to get at is, what is that activity?

H.P.B.: I surely cannot give you what is the activity of the causeless cause. I can tell you what is the activity in man. Therefore I am obliged to say I did not graduate as high as that. Man is a microcosm of the macrocosm. It means all the spiritual faculties behind matter. Matter being asleep and resting, we are more active than ever, though we cannot see with our spiritual eyes. But this belongs to the question of dreams, it does not belong at all to this series of questions.

Mr. B. Keightley: It is deeper than a state of dreams; it is further back still.

H.P.B.: There are no dreams on the physical plane. I said to you here that it is when we do not dream about anything that we dream the most. Not only that, but we act the most, and we live on an entirely different plane from this one, and our life is a thousand times more active. Our existence, rather, is a thousand times more varied; and it would be a nice thing if we could bring it back.

Mr. Kingsland: How do we act?

H.P.B.: We cannot take it, certainly, as we act on a physical plane, since that plane we are then on is Arupa, when here we are Rupa.

Mr. Hall: Do we generate Karma in that condition?

H.P.B.: No, we do not. A man generates Karma every time he moves, with the exception of the activity of his highest faculties.

Mr. Hall: Therefore it is the higher faculties which operate.

H.P.B.: And therefore you come to the dreams again. If you dream, for instance, you slew somebody, and you slew him asleep, that even affects your idea, and you dream you are killing a man. Do you know, it may so happen that you will really kill a man, and the man will die, if you see it in the dream. Don't try it, because you may do a nice little bit of black magic if it succeeded. If you had success, it might kill the man.

Mr. Kingsland: Now we are speaking about dreams that come back to consciousness?

H.P.B.: No, you can begin in consciousness and end unconsciously. The more it goes into the regions of the spiritual, the more it will be potent, and the easier you will kill the man.

Mr. B. Keightley: And the less you will remember about it.

Mr. Kingsland: Do you mean to say you can dream you have murdered a man, and not remember it at all, and that dream would be a potential force which might make you murder the man?

H.P.B.: It is your desire in the dream to hurt somebody. If you are neither an Adept nor a black magician nor anything of the kind, nor a Jadoo,[1] you cannot do it while you are awake, but in the dream life you are no more impeded by the limits of matter and of your senses, and that which limits you when you are awake. Then you can produce effects just the same as a hypnotizer could kill one of his subjects. You have such a potency in you that you can kill a man at a distance, by thinking you are killing him.

Mr. Hall: But he must be asleep.

H.P.B.: Not a bit of it. *You* must be asleep, not he.

Mr. Kingsland: Then the question is whether those actions produce Karma.

H.P.B.: That is what I say. On the lower plane, they will produce Karma; but if you are in your higher spiritual senses, you won't kill a man at all. There you have not got those passions, and where you have not got them, by wanting to kill a man in the high spiritual regions you would kill yourself — because you are not separate from any man in creation, as your mind is not separate from the *All*.

Mr. Kingsland: In these dreamless sleeps it is only the higher principles which are active.

H.P.B.: We are talking about what Hall asked about, potentiality.

Mr. Kingsland: In every case we were referring to dreamless sleep.

H.P.B.: Dreamless sleep you may not remember. But from the next lower state you may remember, and do a good deal of mischief.

Mr. A. Keightley: Then, question 10. What portion of the mind and what principles are active during dreamless sleep?

H.P.B.: Now, please, leave this. This will make us go on till twelve o'clock, wool gathering. It belongs, my dear fellow, to these other things. We discussed dreams for four or five evenings, you know.

Mr. A. Keightley: We have no record of it.

H.P.B.: I have a record, excuse me. I can repeat it to you. I will take the same things and answer you.

Mr. A. Keightley: Then that closes these questions.

Colonel Chowne: There is one thing you talked about: you said there was no other way of expressing how light came except by a cause, and that cause was darkness.

---

[1] **Jadoo** (*Hindi*) — sorcery, black magic, enchantment.

H.P.B.: Darkness so far that we don't know anything about it, and it is perfect darkness for us; we cannot discern anything behind that, it is impossible.

Colonel Chowne: But how does the light come?

H.P.B.: In consequence of an immutable law which manifests itself periodically. Just as I say the clock strikes and shows the hours without being conscious of it at all. Now, the clock is an automatic thing, and the other is a thing which has absolute consciousness. Therefore, to us it is no better than clockwork, because we cannot see how the intellect works.

Mr. A. Keightley: Then darkness and light in that Stanza are not used as pairs of opposites.

H.P.B.: No, no; I use darkness because there is no other word suitable. If you say chaos and take that, immediately you create all kinds of confusion. Immediately you will have thoughts of chaotic matter and all kinds of anomalies. Therefore, I use the word darkness, which is a great deal better.

Colonel Chowne: The light that you refer to is not the physical light that we think of?

H.P.B.: Oh, no! The light means, well, the first potentiality of all — the first flutter in undifferentiated matter which throws it into objectivity and into a plane which is nearer to manifestation than the other. That is the first light. Light is figuratively used.

Mr. A. Keightley: But then, also later in *The Secret Doctrine,* in the more scientific part, you state that light is only made visible by darkness, or rather darkness is the original thing and light is the result of the presence of objects in the objective world.

H.P.B.: If there is no sun, there would be no light, certainly, in the objective world.

Mr. A. Keightley: But I mean if there were no objects, there would be nothing to reflect the light.

H.P.B.: Take two rays of light, and they will produce darkness.

Mr. A. Keightley: Take a globe of water and pass an electric beam through it. The electric beam is perfectly dark, unless there are objects in the water, in which case you get specks of light.

H.P.B.: Yes, that is a good illustration.

Mr. B. Keightley: You cannot see the light, it passes through the water perfectly invisible.

Mr. Kingsland: You cannot see light itself. But light may be manifested to another sense, as something quite different, may it not?

Mr. B. Keightley: Yes, because, after all, the light is only differentiation of vibration.

H.P.B.: You can have the sense of light in the taste or hearing; in all your senses you can have it, or you can, for instance, in the hearing have the sense of taste and have the sense of seeing; why, look at the clairvoyants, they are perfectly asleep. They are in a trance, moreover, and you come and put a letter upon them and the clairvoyant reads it. How is that?

Mr. A. Keightley: That is an extra sense.

H.P.B.: It is not an extra sense. It is simply that the sense of seeing can be shifted. It passes into the sense of touch.

Mr. A. Keightley: Is not the sense of perception the beginning of the sixth sense?

H.P.B.: Oh, yes, but that goes a little further. This is simply the shifting of the physical sense of sight into the sense of touch, nothing else. Now those clairvoyants will, blindfolded, read to you a letter; but if you ask them what will be the letter that I will receive tomorrow, that is not written yet, the clairvoyant will not tell you. But the sense you are talking about (the sixth sense) will, because it is there before you. That is quite a different thing. One is manifestation on the physical plane, and the other on the spiritual plane.

Mr. B. Keightley: You have an instance of this shifting of one sense into a another when you happen to take some very fiery extract into your mouth. It will produce the sense of a flash of light before your eyes.

Mr. A. Keightley: For instance, if you put the two poles of an electric battery together in your mouth, you will get a flash of light in your eyes and you get a metallic taste in your mouth.

Colonel Chowne: If you knock your head against a wall, you get a flash of light in your eyes, too.

Mr. A. Keightley: That is the sense of touch transferred into the stimulation of the optic nerves.

H.P.B.: This is very interesting, and you ought to collect as many facts as you can about those phenomena on the physical plane. Then you could go higher and use the phenomena which are in correspondence. You know what I mean, until we come to the highest that we can have.

Mr. B. Keightley: Now a blind man, too, gets practically the sense of sight transferred into the sense of touch. And besides that, he develops a very definite sense of locality which is independent of the sense of touch. For instance, he will find his way about a town or about a house which he knows without touching the objects to localize himself.

H.P.B.: Certainly, he sees by the other senses.

Mr. B. Keightley: But how does he see? Which of the senses helps him to get at it?

Mr. A. Keightley: But even when in possession of all the senses, physiologists have worked on the idea of a sense of direction.

Mr. Hall: Yes. There certainly must be one.

H.P.B.: Dr. Williams, what do you say to that?

Dr. Williams: I don't know anything about the sense of direction. I have not heard anything of it.

Mr. A. Keightley: It is supposed to refer to the semi-circular canals in the ear.

Dr. Williams: Senses of direction — that one might hear a sound, do you mean?

Mr. A. Keightley: No. Suppose that part of the brain is removed in an animal. As long as the animal is standing still and not moving, every function goes on perfectly naturally. If it once begins to move, even in places where it is most familiar, the idea of direction is lost. For instance, a canary in which this has happened, or there is some disease of the semi-circular canals, or any, will not be able to find its way to its food if these canals have been interfered with. The sense of direction is entirely lost.

Mr. B. Keightley: But all the control over the muscles is perfectly intact; it does not stagger about.

Mr. A. Keightley: No; it simply cannot go straight. That is very interesting. You will find it, really, in any physiological book of late years which deals with the functions of the brain.

Mr. B. Keightley: Where are they situated?

Mr. A. Keightley: Close behind the ear.

Mr. B. Keightley: Then it must be connected with the sense of hearing.

H.P.B.: I am afraid physiology is very much at sea as to the most elementary questions about the senses and so on; it goes and denies *a priori* the possibility of super-senses, if I may call them so, and does not know a single thing about the most simple matters, about that which one has experience of every day of one's life. It does not know anything about the touch and the sight.

Mr. A. Keightley: Don't you think it would be a thing for some future Thursday, if you would take the senses and give us some principles to work upon?

H.P.B.: I would have all the physiologists sitting on me, if I did. Not in public you know.

Mr. A. Keightley: But you are not in public. You are only in the Blavatsky Lodge.

H.P.B.: I am not learned enough to undertake such a thing as that.

Mr. B. Keightley: I think you could do it, if you tried. We should be content with the little elementary things, but I think you could give us the others, if you tried.

Mr. A. Keightley: At present, one works blindly in connection with these things, and often sets about working on matters which really are of no use, and have to be completely unlearned again.

H.P.B.: What does physiology say about it? You see, I am more capable of detecting mistakes if I see them; if I read a book on physiology, or if I hear somebody talk. It is a great deal easier for me to find the mistake than to come and tell you anything about the thing, because not knowing physiology or your technical terms, and not being sure how far they have progressed with their illusions and hallucinations, I do not know where to begin.

Mr. A. Keightley: I shall be very happy to supply you with books.

Dr. Williams: He can supply illusions enough.

H.P.B.: Can you tell me, Dr. Williams, what they say in physiology about it?

Dr. Williams: They say a great deal.

H.P.B.: Do they say anything about this?

Dr. Williams: The only thing they say worth consideration is — or rather the deduction that may be made from what they do say is — every sense may be resolved into the sense of touch. You may call that the coordinating sense, and the deduction is made from their embryological investigations, which show that the sense of touch is the first and primary sense, and that all others have been evolved from that, since sight and sound and taste, everything, are simply more highly specialized or differentiated forms of touch. I know of nothing worthy of consideration.

H.P.B.: If you go to the trouble of reading the *Anugita*[1] and the conversation between the brahmin[2] and his wife, I can assure you, he teaches very good things to his wife there, and very philosophically. You won't lose your time. He [Mr. Keightley] can lend it to you, if you like. Really, it is worth reading, and the brahmin speaks there about the seven senses. All the time he talks about the seven senses. It is translated by Max Müller. "Mind and Understanding" are the two extra senses, and I say it is very badly translated, because it does not mean that in Sanskrit at all. I think the first sense, you understand, is sound, on the top of the ladder, on the last rung on the terrestrial plane. Maybe they will win their case by touch, but I do not think it is so.

Mr. B. Keightley: By touch they mean skin, sensibility.

H.P.B.: Do they call skin, also, the eye that sees?

Mr. B. Keightley: No, they say the eye that sees is formed of one of the nerves of the skin.

Mr. A. Keightley: No, the eye is the outgrowth of the brain.

H.P.B.: And that is all that they say, the physiologists. They do not make much progress, it appears.

Dr. Williams: I meant that that to me seems to be the only thing worth thinking very much about. That deduction is founded on the beginning of the very lowest forms of life, the first differentiation of that which results in the organ of sight, a simple pigment cell which is more sensitive to light than the other cells. I am not sure that there

---

[1] **Anugita** (*Sanskrit*, "continuation of Gita") — part of the ancient epic of the *Mahabharata*.

[2] **Brahmin** — a member of the highest social group (caste) in Hindu society.

is no harmony between the most advanced physiology and that proposition of yours.

H.P.B.: The sense of sound is the first thing that manifests itself in the universe. Then after that, sound, certainly, is in correspondence with colours or sight; that is the second thing. Well, I think you have got enough for tonight.

Dr. Williams: I think the sense of sound always passes into the sense of sight. I do not think we can have any conception of anything unless it does.

H.P.B.: If you could only see clairvoyantly a person playing a piano, you would see the sound as plainly as you hear it. If you allow yourself to sit there in your own normal state and listen, of course you will hear the sound, but if you only can concentrate your ideas; just paralyse your sense of sound — you can even put cotton in your ears — you will see the sound and how much better you can see it, and detect every little note and modulation that you could not do otherwise. You cannot hear at a distance, but you can see at a distance.

Dr. Williams: Do you mean you see it as a sort of rhythmic movement?

H.P.B.: You see it if you are accustomed to it. Now let us take an illustration. For instance, to hear a person sing on the stage, you must be within a limited distance from the stage, in a place where the acoustic properties are good and where the sound travels freely. But now you just imagine yourself that you have a very good sight, and you sit there and a *prima donna*[3] will sing, say in Kensington Gardens;[4] you can see it if there is no impediment. You will hear it with your sight better than you will see with your ears. That is paradoxical, but it is perfectly occult and true. Note this.

Mr. B. Keightley: Supposing you stop your physical ears and watch clairvoyantly the plane, and allow your clairvoyant hearing, so to speak, to operate at the same time. Clairvoyant sight would translate itself into hearing on the same plane.

H.P.B.: One would merge into the other. You can taste sound, if you like, too. There are sounds which are exceedingly acid, and there are sounds which are exceedingly sweet, and bitter, and all the scale of

---

[3] **Prima donna** (*Italian*, "first lady") — the leading female singer in an opera.
[4] **Kensington Gardens** — a Royal Park of London.

taste, in fact. This is no nonsense, I say it seriously, and you will find it so if you want to know about the super-physical senses.

Mr. A. Keightley: Then, do you get the same extension of smelling into touch?

H.P.B.: Yes, you may reverse entirely and shift one sense into the other, and you may make it a great deal more intense and do anything you like. Now in the Vedas it is said — or is it in the Upanishads, I think it is the Upanishads — they speak about seeing a sound. I don't know if I did not mention it in *The Secret Doctrine.* Oh! I wrote an article[1] in *The Theosophist*[2] about it. There is something either in the Upanishads or the Vedas.

Mr. Bulaki Rama: Yes, there is several times a mention of seeing a sound, but we think it is in the metaphorical sense.

H.P.B.: Now you want to take it so, because you are in the England universities.

Mr. B. Keightley: Instead of being the sons of Brahma!

Dr. Williams: I wonder if anyone has read a story in the last number of *Harper's Magazine,*[3] a story of a sailor who had been cast away on an island in one of the Archipelagoes, in the South Seas, and finds a race of people who have entirely lost the art of talking. They understand each other and see what they think, but they regard sound as a very gross way of communicating thought. It is a very interesting little sketch.

H.P.B.: It would be a "Palace of Truth." You could not say then, "How happy I am to see you," and send them to all kinds of disagreeable places in your mind. They communicated in such a way as that in the olden times. Their thoughts took objective form.

Mr. A. Keightley: They hit each other in the eye with the thought.

Dr. Williams: He says he found it a powerful incentive to moral elevation.

[Laughter.]

---

[1] See H. P. Blavatsky, "Occult or Exact Science?" *Collected Writings*, vol. 7 (Wheaton, IL: Theosophical Publishing House, 1958), pp. 55–90.

[2] *The Theosophist* — a monthly journal, published by the Theosophical Society in India since 1879.

[3] Edward Bellamy, "To Whom This May Come," *Harper's New Monthly Magazine*, vol. 78 (February 1889), pp. 458–466.

H.P.B.: They could not fib, then. You could not say a falsehood. How nice it would be to go into a drawing room of Mrs. Grundy's[4] and just to know that they must communicate their thoughts. It would be the sweetest thing in the world! How many compliments would be exchanged! Well gentlemen, what else? Once I am dead I won't be worth much, so take your last chance before I die. Gardner has subsided.

Mr. Gardner: No, I was thinking, "before you took your dreamless sleep."

H.P.B.: We should know more about the senses and could just exchange thought and all kinds of things simply by scratching our noses. We would understand each other. This business would be thought transferring. It would be a very nice thing.

Mr. B. Keightley: It is a very curious thing, that transference of sense localities in parts of the body. For instance, as a rule, with the mesmeric clairvoyant, the sense of sight is transferred to the pit of the stomach and it won't operate in any other part of the body. Though sometimes it is at the back of the head.

Colonel Chowne: There is some centre of nerves there.

H.P.B.: You will learn that.

Mr. Gardner: Sometimes it works through the forehead.

Mr. B. Keightley: Generally the pit of the stomach or the back of the head.

H.P.B.: They never tried it here, at the back of the head. [Pointing.]

A Lady: They tried it through the feet.

Mr. B. Keightley: I never heard of seeing through the feet, though certainly the sense of sight is one they have experimented with the most.

Colonel Chowne: You mean a blind man is supposed to read colours. I do not see how he distinguishes red from blue.

H.P.B.: The colours, you see, he can know. For instance, a deaf man can be looking at the sounds; he can see because it gives him a kind of sound. Of course he does not hear it as a sound, but it is transferred

---

[4] **Mrs. Grundy** — a character with conventional standards of propriety in Thomas Morton's play *Speed the Plough* (1798). She represents a personification of public opinion and one's fear of judgement from society.

to his mind as a something that is sound, really. Though it cannot be expressed. You could not understand it, of course.

Mr. Hall: Deaf and dumb people very often like to put their hands on a piano while it being played, so that the vibration may be communicated to their brains.

Mr. B. Keightley: Then there is the well-known case of a blind man, who always associated sounds with colours. He had a conception, red, which he associated with brass instruments, the trumpet particularly. Red always suggested to his mind the trumpet.

H.P.B.: It is extremely interesting, this association of sounds and colours by vibration, and then it is a very scientific thing, as I think somebody speaks about it. Now, for instance, the sounds have got so many modulations and vibrations. And light is just the same way.

Dr. Williams: Sound begins at fifteen vibrations a second and runs through a very limited scale, so far as the ear is capable of conceiving it. The vibrations increase in intensity, and then comes the sense of heat. The different senses seem to take up one scale of vibration, of which all these different manifestations consist. You go on with the sense of heat until you get a dull redness, and there you get light, and so you run through the whole gamut. It passes out of light, then call it the chemical rays that passes beyond colour and produces chemical changes.

H.P.B.: Isn't there a difference in the prismatic colours? They are seven, and then there is something, I forget how they call it, a measurement.

Mr. B. Keightley: A wavelength.

H.P.B.: I don't know how they call it. There are only five of them seen, or three. Is it an instrument that was invented, that these seven colours reduce themselves to five, then to three and then one?

Mr. B. Keightley: No, there are three primary colours. These other seven are formed from combinations of those. First you get five…

H.P.B.: No, I speak about some instrument.

Mr. Kingsland: Perhaps the spectroscope.

H.P.B.: No, not that. I read that they had invented an instrument which could give not only the radiation of colours but the reduction of colours, and that seven colours passed through some 77 shades until merged into one white, you know.

Mr. Hall: Is that the helioscope?[1]

Mr. Kingsland: It is only a matter of combining again after they are once dispersed by means of the prism.

H.P.B.: Oh, but it is the seven colours, where in their, so to say, gradation or shading, instead of being seven they become perhaps seventy-seven times seven?

Dr. Williams: I think it was some adaptation for showing the ratio, rather, of wavelength and colour to rate vibration. That would be an almost indefinite number of vibrations, of course.

H.P.B.: But they must be counted. I speak about that because it will always come back to the three and the four and the seven.

Mr. Hall: Some people associate the different kinds of colour with different kinds of pain.

H.P.B.: It is very easy. When you have neuralgia, there must be some colour you cannot look at without terrible pain.

Dr. Williams: Insane persons are treated sometimes by means of colour.

H.P.B.: Now did you ever think why bulls are irritated at the red colour? Do you know it gives them terrible pain? It enters somehow or other through their sight into the brain, and makes them perfectly crazy. It gives them physical pain.

Mr. Gardner: Is that why they wear red coats in hunting?

Mr. Kingsland: They don't hunt bulls!

Mr. Gardner: Oh! I thought you said "wolves."

H.P.B.: Some colours do give pain. There are some sensitive persons who cannot look at very bright colours, they feel positively nervous at some combinations of colours, they cannot bear it.

Dr. Williams: I think it is the most interesting question of science.

H.P.B.: But I think the far more interesting question is to see the result of various combinations in the occult spheres. Now you will see one result on the terrestrial plane; but if you were to follow it up and see what are the results produced in the invisible sphere, well, it

---

[1] **Helioscope** (*Greek*, "looking at the sun") — a device used to observe the sun.

is invisible but still, some of the effects will become objective. Though the causes which are set in motion will be invisible, you will see the effects.

Dr. Williams: It is always far more interesting to investigate any question from the point of view of principles before descending into particulars.

H.P.B.: I believe the only exact science that you have is mathematics, and mathematics proceeds in this way.

Dr. Williams: Yes, from first principles to details.

H.P.B.: Certainly, it is not quite the Aristotelian way that you can use in mathematics.

Dr. Williams: I do not think science would object to this more than this: "Be sure of your first principles. If you know what they are, then there would be no difficulty."

H.P.B.: But how about they who don't know what they see before their noses? They only see that which they think they see, and then they are obliged to give them up, because they see they are mistaken. Why are the men of science so very, very conceited?

Dr. Williams: Well, I think it all grows out of the idea that man in a certain way creates everything from himself, that he has no relation to any higher power than himself, and he regards himself as the highest power in the universe.

H.P.B.: Is it conceit?

Dr. Williams: I should say almost supreme conceit.

H.P.B.: How about our grandfathers? For the scientists want us to have a grandfather common with the ape; that is supreme degradation.

Mr. B. Keightley: No, they may think this: "Look how gloriously we have progressed in a few thousand years."

Mr. Hall: Like a self-made man who is always referring to the time when he came to London with twopence in his pocket.

H.P.B.: How do you know there are not self-made apes in the forest? We do not know anything about it. I have seen apes who are very wise. I have seen many; I love apes. I have a great tenderness for them, and I think they are better than men are. It is a fact.

31 JANUARY 1889

Mr. A. Keightley: The first question is in connection with Sloka 6, Stanza 1. [Reads passage from *The Secret Doctrine*, vol. 1, p. 42.] Now, with reference to the "Seven Lords," question 1 runs: "Since confusion is apt to arise in the correct application of the terms, will you please distinguish between Dhyan-Chohans, Planetary Spirits,[1] Builders and Dhyani-Buddhas?"[2]

H.P.B.: Yes; but you know, really, it will take a volume if you want to know all the hierarchies and every distinct class of angels among the Dhyan-Chohans, the Planetary Spirits, the Dhyani-Buddhas, the Builders, etc. Now, Dhyan-Chohan is a generic name for all Devas, or celestial beings. They are one and all called Dhyan-Chohans. Now, a Planetary Spirit is the ruler of a planet, a kind of personal God, but finite; that is the difference you see. A Planetary Spirit is the one that has to rule and watch over each globe of a chain, or every planet, and there is some difference between those who are over the great sacred planets, and those over small chains like ours, because the earth has never been one of the sacred planets — never. It was simply taken as a substitute, like the moon and the sun, because the sun is the central star. And the moon has never been a sacred planet. It is dead long ago.

Mr. A. Keightley: But does the earth belong to a chain which belongs to the train of one of the sacred planets?

H.P.B.: Oh no, not at all. The earth has its own chain. Then there are six companions which are not seen, which are on three different planes.

---

[1] **Planetary Spirits** — primarily the rulers or governors of the planets. As our earth has its hierarchy of terrestrial planetary spirits, from the highest to the lowest plane, so has every other heavenly body. In Occultism, however, the term *Planetary Spirit* is generally applied only to the seven highest hierarchies corresponding to the Christian archangels. These have all passed through a stage of evolution corresponding to the humanity of earth on other worlds, in long-past cycles. Our earth, being as yet only in its Fourth Round, is far too young to have produced high planetary spirits. The highest Planetary Spirit ruling over any globe is, in reality, the "Personal God" of that planet and far more truly its "over-ruling providence" than the self-contradictory Infinite Personal Deity of modern Churchianity.

[2] **Dhyani-Buddhas** (*Sanskrit*) — they "of the Merciful Heart." These have again a secret meaning.

Mr. Kingsland: Are none of those other six, one of the sacred planets?

H.P.B.: No, sir, not one, and it is not feasible.

Mr. Kingsland: Then how are we to distinguish between them?

H.P.B.: The seven sacred planets of antiquity were the planets which astrologers take now, minus the sun and the moon, which are substitutes.

Mr. Harbottle: And plus two that we do not know.

H.P.B.: Yes, of which one is an intra-Mercurial planet, which they are trying to find and cannot. They wanted to call it Vulcan,[1] or to give it a name before it was found out; they think they have found it, but they are not sure. Some say there are several, others one, but they do not know. When they find out they will know that it is one of the secret planets. And the other one is what I cannot explain. It was as the substitute of this planet that the moon was taken, and it was seen at a certain hour of the night just as though it was near the moon, but it was not; it is this planet which was not known at all. I think sometimes they do not give the name, but as to my astronomical ideas, I would not trust them.

Mr. Harbottle: It is not Herschel,[2] is it?

H.P.B.: I thought it was at one time, and yesterday evening I was thinking a good deal about it, but I am not sure. If I were to see, or if it were possible to have a planisphere[3] of the heavens to see at certain hours of the night, as astronomers must have it, I would have recognized it; but if it is not Herschel, I could not tell you.

Mr. Harbottle: But the modern astronomers say about Herschel that it is a planet which has an almost unexpected and what we should call an occult influence upon things; and they, having recently discovered Herschel, assign exactly the sort of attributes to Herschel in astrology that one should expect of the secret planet.

---

[1] **Vulcan** (*Latin*) — the ancient Roman God of Fire, both destructive and purifying.

[2] **Herschel** — Uranus. In Britain, it was sometimes referred to as *Herschel* in honour of its discoverer, William Herschel (1738–1822), a German-British astronomer and composer.

[3] **Planisphere** — a circular map or chart used to display the stars and constellations visible in the night sky for a specific location and time.

H.P.B.: That is why I thought it was so, but I am not sure, and I cannot tell you until I have seen the planispheres. But as far as the name is concerned, you cannot go by the Sanskrit in order to know what is the name. I do not know well enough beyond this, that it is an occult planet, which is seen at a certain hour of the night, directly, as though near the moon.

Mr. Kingsland: Every night?

H.P.B.: I am not sure whether it is every night. I know it was so, and that it had a sacred day, also.

Mr. Gardner: It moves very slowly.

H.P.B.: And, mind you, the motion is retrograde. Therefore I do believe it is Herschel; but I would not swear to it.

Mr. B. Keightley: If you do away with the moon as one of the astrological planets, you would have to attach to one of the others the influence which is at present ascribed to the moon, and the question is, whether that can be done.

H.P.B.: What is said is this, that the influence of this secret planet passes through the moon, *i.e.*, the occult influence of this secret planet; but whether it passes so that it comes in a direct line, or how, I cannot explain. That is for your mathematicians to know better than I can.

Mr. Harbottle: Then, if that were so, you would find the influence of Herschel would be very strong indeed when it was in conjunction with the moon, as the astrologers call it.

Mr. Kingsland: Are these seven planets all on the same plane as ourselves?

H.P.B.: Certainly.

Mr. Kingsland: Then I presume there is a separate plane belonging to each of those.

H.P.B.: Yes, you find it in *The Secret Doctrine.*

Mr. A. Keightley: Are there minor chains belonging to these sacred planets? You say the earth has never been one of the sacred planets, and it has a chain.

H.P.B.: It has a chain and many others have chains, which have not been discovered, but will be discovered just as much as the earth's. That is one of the smallest planets, as you know yourselves.

Mr. Kingsland: What makes the others sacred or secret?

H.P.B.: I suppose because they have occult influences.

Mr. Harbottle: But then the seven are on a different hierarchy, as it were, to the planetary spirit of the earth?

H.P.B.: Oh, yes. The planetary spirit of the earth is what they call the terrestrial spirit and is not very high. The planetary spirit has nothing to do with the spiritual man. It has to do with the things of matter with the cosmic beings — they are cosmic rulers, so to say, and they form into shape and fashion things. They have everything to do with matter, but not with spirit. With spirit it is the Dhyani-Buddhas who have to do. It is another hierarchy that has to do with that, and I am explaining it to you here.

Mr. Harbottle: These seven planetary spirits, as we should use the phrase, have really nothing to do with the earth, except incidentally.

H.P.B.: They have everything to do with the earth, materially.

Mr. Kingsland: They have to do, in fact, with man in his higher part.

H.P.B.: They have nothing whatever to do with the spiritual man.

Mr. Kingsland: Have they anything to do with the fifth principle?

H.P.B.: They have something to do with the fourth principle but with the three higher principles they have nothing to do whatever. I have not finished yet. You asked me what were the things, and I tell you. First, Dhyan-Chohans was a generic name for all the celestial beings. Second, the Builders are a class called by the ancients Cosmocratores,[1] the builders. They are builders simply, like the celestial masons who shape under the orders of the architect, so to speak. They are but the masons to the grand architect of the universe.

Mr. Kingsland: Are they not the planetary spirits, then?

H.P.B.: What, the Builders? Well, they are, but of a lower kind.

Mr. A. Keightley: Do they act under the planetary spirit of the earth?

H.P.B.: Well, no. The planetary spirit of the earth is not a bit higher, unless he is one who has attained his rank, so to say, earlier than the others, and therefore he is considered the chief of them. Mind you,

---

[1] **Cosmocratores** (*Greek*, "Builders of the Universe") — the world architects, or the Creative Forces personified.

I tell you that which is said not in the exoteric religions (though in some, of course, you may learn it), but in the esoteric teaching.

Mr. Harbottle: But are not the Builders of various classes when considering the solar system or the universe as a whole or any one particular planet? I mean, are there not Builders absolutely terrestrial, in the same way that there are builders of the solar system and the universe?

H.P.B.: Most assuredly.

Mr. Kingsland: Then the terrestrial Builder is a planetary spirit?

H.P.B.: Yes, but a very low kind. What is our earth compared to Jupiter, for instance (well, we won't speak of the solar angels)? It is nothing but a speck of dirt or mud.

Mr. Harbottle: But it has its hierarchy.

H.P.B.: Of course it has, all of them have. This will be shown to you here. They are reflected in the intelligence of the G.A.O.T.U.,[2] which is simply Mahat, the Universal Mind. There comes again the third. Well it is said distinctly, the planetary spirits are those who watch over planets and globes of a chain such as that of our earth. Now, fourth, you spoke about Dhyani-Buddhas. They are the same as the higher Devas. In India they are what are called Bodhisattvas[3] in the Buddhist religion, but exoterically they are given only as five whereas there are seven. Why they do so is because exoterically they take it "*à la lettre,*"[4] but they represent the Seven. And it is also said in *The Secret Doctrine,* "the five Buddhas who have come, and two who are to come in the Sixth and Seventh Races."[5] Now, esoterically, their president is Vajra-sattva,[6] and he is called the Supreme Intelligence, and the Supreme

---

[2] **G.A.O.T.U.** — a Masonic abbreviation that stands for "Grand Architect of the Universe."

[3] **Bodhisattva** (*Sanskrit,* "he, whose essence has become intelligence") — those who need but one more incarnation to become perfect Buddhas, *i.e.,* to be entitled to Nirvana. In the metaphysical sense, *Bodhisattva* is a title given to the sons of the celestial Dhyani-Buddhas.

[4] **À la lettre** (*French*) — to the letter.

[5] *The Secret Doctrine,* vol. 1, p. 108.

[6] **Vajrasattva** (*Sanskrit,* "Diamond Mind") — the name of the Buddha of Supreme Intelligence, the sixth Dhyani-Buddha (of whom there are but five in the popular Northern Buddhism) — in the Yogachara school, the latter counts seven Dhyani-Buddhas and as many Bodhisattvas — the "mind-sons" of the former.

Buddha, and Vajradhara[1] which is again higher than the [...], because he is as much above [...] as Parabrahm is above Brahma or Mahat. It is the same difference. Or as, for instance, the Dhyani-Buddha is higher than the Manushi Buddha,[2] the Human Buddha — which is the same difference. The Dhyani-Buddhas are one thing exoterically and another thing in occultism. Exoterically, each is a Trinity. [Continues reading from her own notes.] That is the difference between Dhyani-Buddhas and the others. The Dhyani-Buddhas are those who remain from a previous Manvantara on a planet which is not as high as ours, which is very low; and the others have to pass through all kingdoms of Nature, through the mineral kingdom, the vegetable kingdom, and the animal kingdom.

Mr. Kingsland: Then the Dhyan-Chohan is prehuman, and the Dhyani-Buddha is posthuman.

H.P.B.: They are all Dhyan-Chohans.

Mr. A. Keightley: Well, the planetary spirit.

H.P.B.: That is a creature in this period.

Mr. A. Keightley: Prehuman?

H.P.B.: How do you mean prehuman?

Mr. A. Keightley: Will be a human.

Mr. Kingsland: Dhyani-Buddhas have been men.

H.P.B.: And the Dhyani-Buddhas were before, and they will not be men on this, but they will be something higher than men, because at the end of the Seventh Race it is said they will come and incarnate on earth.

Mr. Kingsland: Will they be what corresponds to man on a higher plane?

H.P.B.: I don't know, but they will come in the Seventh Round,[3] because all humanity will then become Buddhas, or Devas. They are the emanations or the reflections of the Manushi Buddha, the Human

---

[1] **Vajradhara** (*Sanskrit*, "Diamond-holder") — the Supreme Buddha, the ultimate primordial.

[2] **Manushi Buddhas** (*Sanskrit*) — Human Buddhas, Bodhisattvas, or incarnated Dhyan-Chohans.

[3] **Round** — a cycle of Evolution, consisting of Seven Races. There are Seven Rounds in total. The humanity of the planet Earth is currently in the Fourth Round. The term *Round* may also refer to a Race, because each Race consists of ›

Buddhas. Not necessarily Gautama Buddha, for he is a Manushi Buddha, a human Buddha, a saint — whatever you like to call it.

Mr. A. Keightley: Question 2. "Does the planetary spirit in charge of a Globe go into Pralaya when his Globe enters Pralaya?"

H.P.B.: The planetary spirits go into Pralaya at the end of the Seventh Round, not after every one of the rounds, because he is in charge of the Globe, and has to watch the workings of the laws even during the *status quo*[4] condition of the Globe when it goes into its time of rest, that is to say, during its interplanetary Pralaya. I explain everything in *The Secret Doctrine*, and this is explained somewhere there.

Mr. Harbottle: I don't remember it.

Mr. B. Keightley: I don't think you put it in print.

H.P.B.: Maybe. Then they must have left it out. Or perhaps it is the third or fourth volume. I remember I have written it. There is the third volume; it is full of the Buddhas, Devas, and things.

Mr. A. Keightley: Well then, if anything is missed out of *The Secret Doctrine*, we will say it is in the third volume.[5]

H.P.B.: No, really, I could show it to you, it is in the third volume. I know I have written it.

Mr. A. Keightley: Then Question 3. "Does the Dhyani, whose province it is to watch over a Round, watch over, during his period of activity, the whole series of Globes, or only over a particular Globe?"

H.P.B.: I have explained this just now. Each of them has his own Globe to watch, but there are seven planetary spirits, and it is Dhyani-Buddha. You make a mistake there.

Mr. A. Keightley: I said Dhyani.

---

seven sub-races, which form a Small Round, or Ring. That is, the current change of Races is also the change of Small Rounds.

[4] **Status quo** (*Latin*) — the current state of things; the present situation or condition.

[5] Volume 3 of *The Secret Doctrine* has never been published. What was published posthumously in 1897 was just a collection of H.P.B.'s unfinished articles. According to H. S. Olcott and W. Q. Judge, she was to write *five* volumes in total. However, humanity appeared not to be prepared for the Highest Knowledge: H.P.B. was severely criticized, which contributed to ill health and her untimely demise. Therefore, after her passing, the almost completed manuscripts of Volumes 3 and 4 mysteriously disappeared, and Volume 5 had never been commenced.

H.P.B.: Here it is said when the All and planetary, and the Dhyani-Buddhas and all who will appear on earth in the Seventh Round when all humanity will have become Buddhas and Devas, their sons, and they will be no more trammeled with matter, there is a difference between planetary and the other. [Continues reading from her own notes.] Mind you, in the Kabbalah you will see always mention of the three higher planes, of which they speak with great reluctance. Even there they will not go as far as that, they simply give you the Triad: Chokmah[1] (or whatever they call it) and Binah,[2] the male and female intelligence, or wisdom and intelligence. And this Binah in the Kabbalah is called the Jehovah, and a female, if you please.

Mr. Kingsland: It says here that the Dhyani is to watch successively every one of the rounds. A little confusion arose there.

H.P.B.: But Dhyani is a generic name, as I said to you. It is an abbreviation of Dhyan-Chohans, that is all, but not of Dhyani-Buddhas. Dhyani-Buddhas are quite a different thing. If I said it, it is a very great mistake, a *lapsus linguae*[3] to which I plead guilty very often — as I have just said 28 was 5 times 7.

Mr. A. Keightley: Question 4. Is there any name which can be applied to the "Planetary Spirit," which watches over the entire evolution of a planetary chain?

H.P.B.: Which one is it?

Mr. A. Keightley: Number 4.

H.P.B.: I had two or three pages written out, but perhaps it is better that I should not read it. There is nothing at all, it simply explains why we do not worship them.

Mr. Harbottle: Well, let us have it; it is a very interesting point, that.

H.P.B.: This is why we go against the idea of any personal extra-cosmic[4] god. You cannot worship one such god, for "the gods are

[1] **Chokmah** (*Hebrew*) — Wisdom; the second of the ten Sephiroth, and the second of the supernal Triad.
[2] **Binah** (*Hebrew*) — Understanding; the third of the ten Sephiroth, the third of the Supernal Triad; Supernal Mother and "the great Sea."
[3] **Lapsus linguae** (*Latin*) — a slip of the tongue.
[4] **Extra-cosmic** — outside of Cosmos or Nature. A nonsensical word invented to assert the existence of a *personal* god independent of, or outside, Nature *per se*; for as Nature, or the Universe, is infinite and limitless there can be nothing outside it. The term is coined in opposition to the Pantheistic idea that the whole ▸

many," is said in the Bible. Therefore you have to choose either to worship many, who are all one as good, and as limited, as the other, which is polytheism and idolatry; or do as the Israelites have done — choose your one tribal god. [Continues reading from notebook.] Now this, in the Bible, is what is said: "The gods are many, but the God is one."[5] Why? Because it is their own god that they have chosen. With the end of Pralaya he disappears, as Brahma does, and as all other Devas do. That is to say, he is merged in the Absolute, because he is simply one of the rays, which, whether the highest or the lowest, will all be merged into the Absolute. And therefore we do not worship and we do not offer prayers to them, because if we did we should have to worship many gods; and if we address our prayers to the one Absolute, then I do not think the one Absolute has got ears to hear us. That is my opinion. It may be atheistical and I may appear a very great infidel, but I cannot help it.

Mrs. Williams: What objection would there be to worshipping many gods?

H.P.B.: I do not see any objection, but it would be a tiresome thing. You would not have time to pay them all compliments. It would be rather a monotonous thing.

Mrs. Williams: You spoke of it as being idolatrous. I wanted to find out whether in your mind it was so.

H.P.B.: Not at all. I say if we have to offer prayers to some personal god, then we must believe in many gods, and we must offer prayers to many or to none, because why should we have a preference? We do not know whether it is the best or the worst we may fall upon. It may be one who is not at all very perfect.

Mr. B. Keightley: Besides, we should make the others jealous.

H.P.B.: Besides, we have a god within us, every one of us. This is a direct ray from the Absolute; every one of us is the celestial ray from the one — well, I do not find any other word but the Absolute and the Infinite. Now then, number 4.

Cosmos is animated or informed by the Spirit of Deity, with Nature being but the garment and matter the illusive shadows of the real unseen Presence.
[5] A paraphrase of 1 Corinthians 8:5–6.

Mr. A. Keightley: Is there any name which can be applied to the Planetary Spirit, which watches over the entire evolution of a Planetary Chain?

H.P.B.: No name, unless you make of it the generic name since he is not alone but seven. [Continues reading from her notebook.] If you give him this name it will be a very good name, I think. It will be scientific and it will answer the purpose, but you are at liberty to give any name you like. What is in a name? "Choose you the daily gods you duly worship,"[1] says Joshua.[2]

Mr. A. Keightley: Is there any name applied to it in the Sanskrit?

H.P.B.: Look here, the Vaishnavas worship Vishnu, the Shaivas worship Shiva,[3] the other — how do you call them? — the Krishnaites worship Krishna,[4] and so on. Everyone has a god of his own. Everyone chooses his own tribal god, or anything they like, or their racial god, and they are happy.

Mr. Harbottle: But such a god as Vishnu is the synthesis of the seven.

H.P.B.: One is the creator, so called, though he certainly did not create matter out of nothing, but the universe out of something. The other is a preserver and the third is a destroyer; but being that, he is the highest, because that which destroys, regenerates, and because you cannot have a plant growing without killing the seed. Therefore, he destroys to give a higher form, you understand.

Mr. A. Keightley: Then these three questions: the name of the "Planetary Spirit," and "Is there a name which can be applied to the Planetary Spirit watching over a Round?" Also, "Is Brahma the correct

---

[1] A paraphrase of Joshua 24:15.

[2] **Joshua** — the leader of the Israelite tribes who succeeded Moses.

[3] **Shiva** (*Sanskrit*) — the third person of the Hindu Trinity (the Trimurti). He is a god of the first order, and in his character of Destroyer, he is higher than Vishnu, the Preserver, as he destroys only to regenerate on a higher plane. He is born as Rudra, the Kumara, and is the patron of all the Yogis, being called, as such, Mahadeva (*Sanskrit*, "Great God").

[4] **Krishna** (*Sanskrit*) — the most celebrated Avatar (divine incarnation) of Vishnu, the Saviour of the Hindus and their most popular god. He is the eighth Avatar, the son of Devaki, and the nephew of Kansa, the Indian King Herod, who, while seeking for him among the shepherds and cow-herds who concealed him, slew thousands of their newly born babes. The story of Krishna's conception, birth, and childhood are the exact prototype of the New Testament story.

term to use concerning the Planetary Spirit of one Globe during one Round, or would Manu[5] be the more correct term?" In this sense is Manu identical with Brahma?

H.P.B.: You have jumped to number 6.

Mr. A. Keightley: I put those three together, because they really practically come together. We wanted to distinguish a Planetary Spirit in a Chain of Worlds from the Planetary Spirit over one Globe, which really rules one Globe, and thirdly to ask whether Brahma is the correct term to use.

H.P.B.: Of the universe they would never say Brahma. They would say Manus, and they are the same as Brahma; and then the rest of them, sometimes they are reckoned the seven, sometimes ten, according to what they are talking about. And this is in the esoteric meaning in the Puranas.

Mr. A. Keightley: There is a special class of Planetary Spirits which deal with a Chain.

H.P.B.: There are Rishis, and the Manus are those who are over every Round.

Mr. A. Keightley: Then are the Manus and the Rishis the same?

H.P.B.: They are just the same — Rishi or Manu. What is Manu? Manu comes from Man, to think — the thinking intelligence. Now just the same as this [...], which is the intelligence, or this [...] is considered the supreme intelligence, and he and Brahma are one. Take the *Vishnu Purana*; take any Purana which will give you exoterically these things. They give the real thing, and they invent many things just as blinds. But you will find a good many things which you will never find in the other scriptures. They will come and ornament things, and yet the fundamental truths are there.

Mr. A. Keightley: I want to avoid, if possible, all these blinds with regard to these names.

H.P.B.: The Brahmins will pitch into us after that. Why shall I give them names? Am I a Roman Catholic priest, to come and baptize them, and give them all different names? For me they are ideations. I am not going to give them names. If I told you the real occult names,

---

[5] **Manu** (*Sanskrit*) — the fourteen Manus are the patrons or guardians of the race cycles in a Manvantara, or Day of Brahma. The primeval Manus are seven; they become fourteen in the Puranas.

it would not make you any the wiser. You are sure to forget them the first moment.

Mr. Harbottle: But it helps us to place them.

H.P.B.: Then let us take the Prismatic Idea: let us call them the Red God and the Orange God and the Yellow God and the Blue and the Green.

Mr. Harbottle: Very well, but in regard, for instance, to that seven in one, what relation do they bear to the Sephiroth?[1]

H.P.B.: They are three and seven. They are ten in all, but the higher is considered the greatest, and the seven, the god descending into matter.

Mr. Harbottle: What relation is there between that seven and the seven we were speaking of?

H.P.B.: The Planetary Spirits? None.

Mr. Harbottle: Are they the Planetary Spirits?

H.P.B.: Well, I would not call them that. You never find a single name which is not Angelic. Take the Kabbalah. They call it the third Sephiroth, as being intelligence; his angelic name is [...], and he is called Jehovah, and this, that and the other, and the book goes on and gives the thing. How it is called, you cannot understand it. But, you see, all of them start from one point, and make a kind of broken ray, coming from one focus. Shall we then in this way give names to all of them?

Mr. Harbottle: No, but I think we might understand what they are, and what relation they bear to names which we do know at present.

---

[1] **Sephiroth** (*Hebrew*, "emanations") — the ten emanations of Deity; the highest is formed by the concentration of the Ain-Soph Aur, or the Limitless Light, and each: Sephira produces by emanation another Sephira. The names of the Ten Sephiroth are: 1. Kether — the Crown; 2. Chokmah — Wisdom; 3. Binah — Understanding; 4. Chesed — Mercy; 5. Geburah — Power; 6. Tiphereth — Beauty; 7. Netzach — Victory; 8. Hod — Splendour; 9. Jesod — Foundation; 10. Malkuth — the Kingdom. The conception of Deity embodied in the Ten Sephiroth is a very sublime one, and each Sephira is a picture to the Kabbalist of a group of exalted ideas, titles and attributes, which the name but faintly represents. Each Sephira is called either active or passive, although this attribution may lead to error as passive does not mean a return to negative existence and the two words only express the relation between individual Sephiroth and not any absolute quality.

The Sephiroth is a name which is particularly familiar, and if one can have an idea that they are in the seventh Sephiroth, we might know.

H.P.B.: They are just the Cosmocratores on a higher plane, but yet the last hierarchy, Malkuth coming to earth, and this is the perfect hierarchy.

Mr. Harbottle: Then the sevenfold or prismatic gods which preside over the Planetary Chains will be something lower.

H.P.B.: Certainly they will; because they are not the Watchers, you know.

Mr. Harbottle: I have got what I wanted.

H.P.B.: If you tell me what you want, I will say, but why are you so inquisitive, tell me?

Mr. Harbottle: Only because I think one looks for these analogies all through, and when the analogies do not seem to fit, you are puzzled. The only way to attempt to understand them is to see one analogy running through them.

H.P.B.: Do you want to compare them with the Kabbalah?

Mr. Harbottle: Yes, but not in detail, because I do not know enough about its details. One wants to know the relation, as it were, of the Planetary Chain to the Cosmos, and secondly, of the spirits ruling the Planetary Chains to the spirits of the Cosmos, and so on.

H.P.B.: It is the [...] in its collectivity, and this includes the seven lower Sephiroth. And it becomes another thing, for it becomes the bridegroom of the bride, Malkuth.

Mr. A. Keightley: Then we pass on to the Stanza following:[2] "But where was the Dangma when the Alaya[3] of the Universe (Soul as the basis of all, Anima Mundi) was in Paramartha[4] (Absolute Being and Consciousness which are Absolute Non-Being and Unconsiousness) and the Great Wheel was Anupadaka?"[5] Does Alaya mean that which is never dissolved, being derived from "a" and "Laya"?

---

[2] *The Secret Doctrine*, vol. 1, p. 47.

[3] **Alaya** (*Sanskrit*, "abode") — the Universal Soul. Identical with *Akasha* in its mystic sense, and with *Mulaprakriti*, in its essence, as it is the basis or root of all things.

[4] **Paramartha** (*Sanskrit*, "highest truth") — the absolute existence.

[5] **Anupadaka** (*Sanskrit*, "self-existing") — born without any parents or progenitors. A term applied to certain self-created gods and to the Dhyani-Buddhas.

H.P.B.: Well, in this book they are very rough. I have just strung them together. They are simply notes. Alaya is the living sentient or active Soul of the World. [Continues reading from her notes.] Now, the Laya means the negation or Layam, as they call it, because it is that which is perfect non-differentiation. It is perfectly homogeneous and it is negative, inactive, and has no attributes. And Alaya is the Soul of the Universe.

Mr. A. Keightley: Then practically this Stanza means "Where was the Dangma, when the Alaya of this universe was in Laya."

H.P.B.: There is Bulaki Rama, who will give you the true explanation. Because I give you the Hindu things simply on analogy. I do not profess to teach it. What I give is occultism and the occult doctrine and I try to make, for example, to the Hindus and those who have read Hindu books, the thing more clear. I just give you the analogy, but there is a Sanskrit scholar. How would you explain it?

Mr. Bulaki Rama: Laya means that which is absolutely nothing, from the root *li*, to disappear, and Alaya means not alive.

H.P.B.: Just what I give you here. One is manifested and fully active and the other has disappeared from the realm of manifestation and fallen into Non-Being. So, then, I have given them correctly.

Mr. A. Keightley: Then it is different exactly from what we put down in the question as being, *e.g.*, never dissolved.

H.P.B.: Certainly not, because it is non-differentiation. Alaya means latent. At the end of Manvantara, when Pralaya sets in, certainly the Alaya will become Laya and fall into nothing. There will be the one Great Breath only. It is most assuredly dissolved. It *is* eternally, throughout the Manvantaras, but the Laya is nothing, it is the thing which is a negation of all. Just the same as the Absolute, the Parabrahm; it is and it is not.

Mr. B. Keightley: Alaya is simply two negatives put together to make a positive. You can get at it in that way.

Mr. Bulaki Rama: Laya means to disappear forever, and therefore it is not negative.

H.P.B.: That is to say, it is nothing; it is just like Ain-Soph. What is Ain-Soph? No-thing. It is not a thing; that is to say, it is nothing, the zero point.

Mr. Harbottle: It is neither negative nor positive.

H.P.B.: Hence Alaya is the one active life in Jivatma,[1] while Laya is the life, latent. One is absolute life and Be-ness, and the other is absolute non-life and non-Be-ness. So you see it is perfectly the opposite.

Mr. A. Keightley: Then the next question is asked in these words, "Page 50, Alaya is the one life, the one life is Jivatma. Are then Alaya and Jivatma identical?"

H.P.B.: I should say that they were. I do not see any difference. Anima Mundi — that is Jivatma, the Soul of the World, the living soul. Jiva[2] is life. For the matter of that, every life has got its Jiva, but this is the Jivatma, the one Universal Soul. I think so, at least. May be you will tell me otherwise, but it seems to me that Alaya and Jivatma are one.

Mr. Bulaki Rama: Certainly.

H.P.B.: How would you translate "Atma"?

Mr. Bulaki Rama: Well, it means that which is present.

Mr. A. Keightley: What is the difference between Atma and Jiva?

H.P.B.: Jivatma is the life everywhere, that is, Anima Mundi, and Atma simply is — well, as he explains it.

Mr. B. Keightley: It is your All-presence.

Mr. Kingsland: Then it can only be Jivatma during Manvantara.

H.P.B.: Certainly. At least, the Vedantins say so; after that all becomes Parabrahm, and Parabrahm is beyond our conception. It is something we cannot certainly go and speculate about, because it has no attributes. It is all and nothing, nothing in our conceptions, or our ideas.

Mr. A. Keightley: Stanza 2: "Where were the Builders, the luminous sons of Manvantaric Dawn? In the Unknown Darkness in their Ah-hi (Chohanic Dhyani-Buddhic) Paranishpanna. The producers of form (rupa) from no form (arupa), the root of the world — the Devamatri[3] and Svabhavat, rested in the bliss of Non-Being."[4] Question 9. "Luminous Sons of Manvantaric Dawn." Are these the perfected human

---

[1] **Jivatma** (*Sanskrit*, "spirit soul") — the one universal life, generally; but also the divine spirit in man.

[2] **Jiva** (*Sanskrit*, "life") — Life, as the Absolute; the Monad also or "Atma-Buddhi."

[3] **Devamatri** (*Sanskrit*, "mother of the gods") — a title of Aditi, Mystic Space.

[4] *The Secret Doctrine*, vol. 1, p. 53.

spirits of the last Manvantara or are they on their way to humanity in this or a subsequent Manvantara?

H.P.B.: They are the primordial seven rays from which will emanate, in their turn, all the other luminous or non-luminous lives, whether angels or devils, men or apes. These are the seven rays from which will come all the flames of being and everything in this world of illusion. The seven logoi.

Mr. A. Keightley: Yes, exactly. Then question 10.

H.P.B.: There you go again. Because I wanted to explain to you here that some are this and some are something else. "Some have been, others will become." [Continues reading from her notebook.] Everything, therefore, is there in the seven rays. You cannot say which, because they are not yet differentiated and therefore are not yet individualized.

Mr. Harbottle: And within these are both prehuman and posthuman.

H.P.B.: Exactly. That is a very much earlier stage. This belongs all to the precosmic times, it does not belong to the after state. It is precosmic, before there was a universe.

Mr. A. Keightley: What puzzles one is talking of the negation, [...], first of all, and then speaking of the luminous sense. One gets accustomed to the recurrence of terms which are intracosmic, in contradistinction to precosmic.

H.P.B.: It is only after the differentiation of the seven rays and after the seven forces of Nature have taken them in hand and worked on them that they become one, the cornerstone of the temple; the other the rejected stone of clay or piece of clay. After that begins the shifting and the sifting and the differentiation and everything, and the sorting of things, but this all belongs to the precosmic period. Therefore it is very difficult. These answers are for those who are perfectly familiar with the occult philosophy, and as they proceed, I do not take them one after the other. There are breaks of forty Stanzas, and there are Stanzas that I would not be permitted to give. What can I do? I do the best I can. There are things they would not permit for anything to be translated. I wish I could. It is no fault of mine. Therefore are our teachers called egoists, and selfish, because they do not want to give the information to the Fellows of the Royal Society, who would appreciate it so much! Who would sense it, and who would drag it in the mud, and laugh at it as they do everything else. Now then, question 10.

Mr. A. Keightley: "Builders — our Planetary System." By our Planetary System, do you mean the solar system, or the chain to which our Earth belongs?

H.P.B.: The Builders are those who build or fashion things. [Continues reading from her notebook.] By Planetary System, I mean the solar system. I suppose it is called the solar system. I would not refer thus to that as the Planetary Chain. I would call the latter simply a chain. And if I say Planetary System, it is the solar system; if I say Planetary Chain, it is the Chain of Worlds. I do not know whether I am right in so using it. This one is our planet, the root, the lowest one, but the others are not, because they are not seen. They are spheres, globes; they are not on our plane.

Mr. B. Keightley: It is the old mistake about Mars and Mercury.

H.P.B.: My dear sir, I have shown it in *The Secret Doctrine*. If Mars and Mercury belonged to our chain, we would not see them, we would not know anything about them. How could we see that which is not on our plane? It is perfectly impossible. Now, then comes a thing which pertains more to physics and chemistry and all that than anything else, but still you can, I suppose, learn something from that.

Mr. A. Keightley: Stanza 2. In reference to what is said on page 54 of oxygen and hydrogen combining to form water, would it really be correct to say that what we perceive is, in reality, a different "element," if the same substance? For example, when a substance is in the gaseous state, it is the element of air which is perceived; and when combined to form water, oxygen and hydrogen appear under the guise of the element of water. Would it be correct to say that when we get it in the solid state — ice — we then perceive the element of earth? Would a clairvoyant perceive oxygen and hydrogen separately in the water?

H.P.B.: There are two or three things I do not recognize at all. It must be Mr. Harte,[1] who has put his finger in the pie. You remember at the beginning you wanted to make it more plain, and I have been crossing it out as much as I could. I can recognize in a minute what is mine and what is not. He begins to make comparisons, and I don't

---

[1] **Richard Harte** (1840–1903) — an Irish journalist who assisted H.P.B. with the *Lucifer* and *The Theosophist* magazines, as well as with *The Secret Doctrine*.

see at all the object of the comparison. I think it is all correlations, and I don't see how we can say this or the other. They have made a most absurd objection to calling the earth and water and fire and air elements, because they say they are composed of elements. Now they begin to find out that they do not approach even to an element in their chemical analysis, and that such a thing as an element can only exist in their imagination. They cannot get at an element which is really an element. Do what they will, they will find more and more that the element of today will become the two elements of tomorrow. This is a world of differentiation; therefore, if we call water an element, we have a perfect right so to do, because it is an element. It is something which does not resemble anything else, it is not like fire or air or earth. These are all the states of one and the same element, if you like, of the one element in Nature. These are various manifestations in various aspects, but to our perceptions they are elements. Now they go and quarrel: "Shall we call it an element?" and then they say that oxygen and hydrogen do not exist any more, since they have correlated and become something else; but if you go and decompose water, immediately you have the two elements reappearing. Do they pretend to create something out of nothing?

Mr. B. Keightley: No, they say they do not understand.

H.P.B.: It proves that they are latent, and it is a fallacy to say they do not exist. They disappear from our plane of perception, from our senses and sight, but they are there. There is not a single thing that exists that can go out of the universe.

Mr. Kingsland: Oxygen and hydrogen are all differentiated states of something. When they are combined to form water we lose sight of them as distinct differentiations, but if we could follow them with our inner sight, should we still see them?

H.P.B.: Most assuredly, because the test gives it to you. Not a very experienced person is required to test water, and if that person knew something of oxygen and hydrogen, that person would tell you immediately which predominates. That is the test which will give you the real thing, but of course it must be an occultist. But they are there. They may be all the same — but they are not, if you please. They will take a drop of water and decompose it and they will find so and so, but then the analysis or instrument cannot detect which is more intense than the other. The proportion will become the same, but it won't be the same in the intensity or taste. This is an occult thing — I mean the intensity of one thing or the other. An occultist, if he were really so, would tell you even the plane from which it comes, too. Well, I don't want to tell you more, because it would seem like a fable, and you would not understand.

Mr. Gardner: For instance, the water when I was going up Snowdon[1] tasted very pure.

H.P.B.: Most assuredly, that water which you will get on the Himalayas will be quite different from the waters you drink in the valleys and the plains. There is nothing physical without its subjective moral and spiritual aspects, and so on.

Mr. Kingsland: We cannot decompose the water without getting a definite quantity of oxygen and a definite quantity of hydrogen. You say one may be more intense than the other.

H.P.B.: Intense in quality, not in quantity.

Mr. Gardner: The quality of the oxygen?

H.P.B.: Yes, sir.

Mr. Kingsland: But that is not perceived.

H.P.B.: You don't perceive the presence of the soul in man, at least the men of science don't, but we do; that is the difference. How can you go and argue with a man of science?

Mr. Kingsland: We are dealing with the most physical plane.

H.P.B.: Never mind. The physical plane cannot exist nor give you any correspondence nor anything without having the spiritual mixed with it, because otherwise you cannot go to the root of things. When your men of science tell me they are acting on the physical plane, and say metaphysics is all nonsense, I see that their science is really perfectly honeycombed with metaphysics. The scientists cannot go beyond matter; beyond the things they perceive, it is all speculation.

Mr. Harbottle: The reason we cannot distinguish in this way as to quality and intensity is because we have no perception of the three higher elements. If we had, we should at once distinguish.

H.P.B.: Certainly. Mr. Harbottle has just hit the nail on the head. I don't want to enter into it, because I shan't be understood.

---

[1] **Snowdon** (*Old English*, "snow hill") — the highest mountain in Wales.

Mr. Gardner: What do you mean by the term intensity?

H.P.B.: I mean intensity.

Mr. B. Keightley: You know whether a taste is intense or not.

H.P.B.: Now, you will take a drop of vinegar — let us come on the lowest plane — and you will know this vinegar weighs so much. You will take the same weight of another vinegar, and it will be quite different, but the weight will be the same.

Mr. Gardner: Well, the strength.

H.P.B.: Call it strength, if you like. I call it intensity.

Mr. Harbottle: It shows itself in the absence or presence of the essence.

Mr. Kingsland: That can be analysed chemically.

Mr. Harbottle: Yes, but there is something behind that.

Mr. Kingsland: There is nothing corresponding to that intensity in the molecule of oxygen and hydrogen, in the case of these we can analyse with our chemical methods.

H.P.B.: I will tell you a better thing yet, if you go on the occult principle. We are not Christians, we do not believe in the doctrine of transubstantiation as it is taught in the church, we are occultists, and yet, I say there is such a thing as transubstantiation on the occult plane, and that if it comes to this, if the priests, the Roman Catholic priests, were not such stupid fools, they would give a very good reply. They would say: "We take bread and wine, and we say that it changes by a kind of miracle or a mystery into the flesh and blood of Christ." Very well, then; once they take Christ to be one with the Absolute (which they do, I don't know how they arrange it), then they are perfectly right. In this bread and wine there is as much of the Absolute, and I tell you that in every drop we swallow, and every morsel we eat, there is as much of Parabrahm as there is in anything, because, everything coming from the one Absolute it is impossible it should not be there. Transubstantiation is that which takes away for the time being — whether on the plane of illusion, or on the plane of senses — which takes away one quality of a thing, and makes it appear as though it were another. The bread and wine changes, and becomes flesh and blood. With a hypnotized person, you may give him a tallow candle and he will exclaim, "What delicious chocolate."

The hypnotized person does not believe. If he were not hypnotized, he would be choked unutterably. And if we go on to the plane of realities, then really, once they say their Christ is one with the Absolute, they are logical in maintaining the doctrine of transubstantiation, for the bread and wine becomes his flesh, because it is flesh and blood; if you want to anthropomorphize. Certainly a Vedantin would not say such a thing, but they act very logically, and that is all. Now I have told you a thing of which I did not like to speak, because I may hurt the feelings of any Roman Catholic who may be among you. I don't like to hurt the feelings of anybody. (Bert looks very pale, you see.)

Mr. A. Keightley: Is this question possible to answer? Is it utterly nonsensical to say, when you speak of a gas, you perceive the different elements in that gas, as distinguished from its liquid condition?

H.P.B.: It is in the liquid condition, and yet you detect the gas in this liquid condition, you detect it clairvoyantly.

Mr. A. Keightley: For instance, oxygen ordinarily is in a gas; by various processes it is reduced to a liquid and solidified. The question really means this: when you find it in the gaseous condition, is it the element of air in the oxygen, the occult element of air which is perceived; and again the occult element of water which is perceived in the liquid condition, and the occult element of earth in the solid?

H.P.B.: Most assuredly. You have first of all fire — not the fire that burns there, but the real fire that the Rosicrucians[1] talk about, the one flame, the fire of life. On the plane of differentiation it becomes fire in whatever aspect you like; fire from friction or whatever it is, it is fire. Very well, after that it produces the heat in the liquid and then you pass through the element of water and from the liquid it becomes gas. You must know better than I, speaking of the physical things. Then from the gas, the two gases mix up and produce water. You take simply a drop of water and follow it. When solid it becomes ice. When ice is liquefied it becomes water, this water becomes vapour, ether, anything you like; and then it entirely disappears in the universal flame, which of course you physicists won't speak about. The universal flame — you

---

[1] **Rosicrucians** — the name was first given to the disciples of a learned Adept named Christian Rosenkreuz, who flourished in Germany, circa 1460. He founded an Order of mystical students who maintained their secrecy, but traces of them have been found in various places every half-century since then.

call it inter-ether, but follow it like that and there it is. It is the element which appears to you here, and to say that this gas is not there or these two are not there I should say is a fallacy. The only thing we can say is that the gases have passed from the plane of the objective into the plane of the subjective.

Mr. Kingsland: It seems to me that it is only possible with the physical senses to see one element at a time, and therefore we are quite right to say if anything is in a liquid state that what we perceive is the element of water.

H.P.B.: Perfectly. There you are perfectly right, and an occultist will answer you so. He will say as I tell you: it has disappeared from the plane of the objective and appeared on the plane of the subjective.

Mr. A. Keightley: Then all substances on the physical plane are really so many correlations or combinations of these elements and ultimately of the one element.

H.P.B.: Most assuredly, if you only realized this: how many times I have spoken to you about this, that the first thing to realize is the existence of One and only One, *i.e.,* of the Absolute. You have to start from universals to the particulars. You cannot proceed on your Aristotelian system, you will never come to anything. You will come to grief and confusion, and you will be always knocking your heads against stone walls, and your heads will come out second best. How can you come and begin a thing? On its appearance you have to go to the primal motor and beyond that to the spiritual cause.

Mr. Kingsland: How could we do that before we are initiates?[1]

H.P.B.: I beg your pardon, there is no need to become initiates. There is something beyond matter, but the men of science laugh at metaphysics, and they say, "fiddlesticks for your metas," and yet I say they are always dealing with metaphysics; that is what they do.

Mr. Kingsland: You can start with that hypothesis.

---

[1] **Initiate** — the designation of anyone who was received into and had revealed to him the mysteries and secrets of Occultism. In times of antiquity, those who had been initiated into the arcane knowledge taught by the Hierophants of the Mysteries, and in our modern days, those who have been initiated by the Adepts of mystic lore into the mysterious knowledge, which, notwithstanding the lapse of ages, has yet a few real votaries on Earth.

H.P.B.: If you permit metaphysics in your hypothesis, and you do not believe in metaphysics, what is your hypothesis worth? Take, for instance, ether. Now, in *Webster's Dictionary*, what do they call it? "A problematical or hypothetical agent of so and so, which is not yet believed in." They take it as just a necessity, and yet you build on that ether the whole theory — axiomatic, mind you, your axiomatic teachings of light, and your vibrations. What right have you to do it? If you base yourself on a phantom of your imagination, a physical consciousness that it is such a thing, I call it humbug and sham.

Mr. Kingsland: You want us to go further back.

H.P.B.: I want men with something like brains, but not men with brains only on the physical plane that they cannot see beyond. They have not got feelers or antennae.

Mr. Kingsland: How can you, by getting a something which is hypo-hypothetical, so to speak, arrive at more knowledge by working on what you do not know?

H.P.B.: You don't work on your own inventions, you work on the wisdom of the ages. And if during these 100,000 years or so all the men of the best intellects said all the same and found out this, and their Adepts and their wise men said the same thing over and over again, there must be more truth in that than in the speculations of the few.

Mr. B. Keightley: I think the position is summed up in this way. Physical science is…

H.P.B.: Nothing but a conceit.

Mr. B. Keightley: The whole basis of occultism lies in this, that there is latent within every man a power which can give him true knowledge, a power of perception of truth, which enables him to deal first hand with universals, if he will be strictly logical and face the facts and not juggle with words. Thus he can truly proceed from universals to particulars by the effect of the innate spiritual power which is in every man, and with certainty, not as a hypothesis. It is a hypothesis only as regards our physical senses.

Mr. Kingsland: But how is he to get at that except through initiation?

Mr. Harbottle: A man has consciousness, or has not.

H.P.B.: He has it inherent in him, it is simply the method of your education together with these ideas that they took into their heads "that we will not proceed in such a way, that we will take the Aristotelian method and the Baconian method, and there never was a man in antiquity who was capable or worthy of untying our shoestrings." And therefore you see they do take one hypothesis after the other. There is not a single thing that will be said in science that is not purely hypothetical. From your Sir William Thomson,[1] who said of something: "I have come to the conclusion that it does not exist more than 50,000,000 years ago," and then said: "I am of opinion it existed 80,000,000 years ago." Between 80 and 50,000,000 there is a difference. Huxley goes and says a certain thing takes a thousand years; another one will go and say something else, while another says, "I am not disposed to admit such a thing." Why, my dear sir, Plato was a match for any one of your greatest philosophers of the day. Such sages as Plato — I don't speak about Socrates,[2] but I think Plato could beat all the Schopenhauers, and Herbert Spencers, and Hartmanns[3] and all the *tutti quanti*[4] that the 19th century is so proud of. And if he proved that you could not get at knowledge unless you began from universals and speculated down to particulars, and found the thing on the terrestrial plane, I suppose he was more right than you are. We had intelligence, we had knowledge, we had most extraordinary knowledge before. What have we got now?

Mr. Kingsland: It is only in the last few years that we have had the privilege of learning this.

H.P.B.: You had the privilege nearly 1,900 years ago. You knew it all. It was only in the 5th century that you succeeded in destroying every temple. You have been hunting the occultists and have been acting so that those who knew went away, hid themselves and never came near the civilized minds. Everything was destroyed; your poor scientists are nothing but the children of the reaction, and the men of science who have eyes will not see, and will not permit that anyone in antiquity was greater than themselves. You go and read your best men from Oxford and Cambridge. When they speak about Plato, they say, "Oh! He did not know anything about the circulation of the blood.

---

[1] **William Thomson (Lord Kelvin)** (1824–1907) — a British mathematician, mathematical physicist and engineer.
[2] **Socrates** (c.470–399 BCE) — a Greek philosopher.
[3] **Eduard von Hartmann** (1842–1906) — a German philosopher.
[4] **Tutti quanti** (*Italian*) — every single one; one and all.

Pythagoras — well, he knew a little bit of arithmetic, but we are the kings, you know, and the gods in the 19th century." And it has led to something very beautiful, your civilization — the highest morality, to begin with.

Mr. B. Keightley: The whole point lies in this: as to the way you are going to set to work to build your hypothesis. Suppose you are hypothesis building, which I don't expect. I am quite sure, not by the physical senses, but by the use of strict logic and strict reasoning, you can form a basis of thought. If you look at Schopenhauer and read him carefully, and Hartmann and others, you will find that step-by-step they have come to the same bases of thought as have been adopted in India, particularly in the Vedantin system.

Mr. Kingsland: By the inductive method.

Mr. B. Keightley: No, though they pretended to do it by the inductive method. They started by an intuition. Schopenhauer got the idea, it came upon him like a flash. He then set to work, having got his hypothetical idea and started with the broad basis of facts. He got his facts together, and so, you reading his book are nicely led up to reach the point which came to him as a flash. But he did not get it by the inductive method. He says he did not.

H.P.B.: Every fact you get you do get by intuition, you get it by a flash.

Mr. B. Keightley: Every scientist of the 19th century, from the time science has become anything like science, has said the same thing, that he has made his great discoveries not by a system of classifying facts in the nice Baconian method, but by having the facts in his mind.

Mr. Harbottle: Darwin[5] especially says so. He gives you the moment at which the idea first occurred to him, and it was in comparing some of the physical flora and fauna.

Mr. Kingsland: But they had been working for years, if the idea came to them apparently in the form of intuition…

Mr. Harbottle: But they might have been quite unconsciously working up to it in various ways. If you read what Darwin says himself, you will come to the same conclusion as I did, that the thing came to him almost as a finished idea.

---

[5] **Charles Darwin** (1809–1882) — an English naturalist, geologist and biologist.

H.P.B.: All of them come just in that way: intuitionally.

Mr. Harbottle: I cannot quote it, I wish I could, but I will turn it up.

H.P.B.: There is somewhere a book which says that all the greatest discoveries that have ever been made in the world came just like flashes of lightning, everything, even to the law of gravitation. How did Newton[1] discover that? Through the apple.

Mr. Kingsland: If you have no knowledge of universals, how are you to proceed from universals to particulars? What knowledge of universals has this century, we will say? They have got no knowledge of the law of God, that is the highest ideal of the universe.

H.P.B.: A very high one, yes.

Mr. B. Keightley: But they have not carried out the canon which was laid down, that their ideas should be tried by strict logic.

Mr. Kingsland: Excuse me, Herbert Spencer does not.

H.P.B.: Herbert Spencer calls it the First Cause, and he calls it the Absolute and I will show it to you in his *First Principles*.[2] He calls the Absolute "the First Cause" in three lines. Well, the First Cause cannot be the Absolute because the First Cause is the first effect.

Mr. Kingsland: That only proves to me that a man who may be considered to be one who has the highest intellect has no knowledge of universals.

H.P.B.: Because he has been made to study on your methods.

Mr. Kingsland: How can the poor fellow help that?

H.P.B.: You take Solomon Ben Judah,[3] the great philosopher, who was a Jew, one of the greatest men living, he whose works have been refused by the French Academy — I don't know what you call it, the French University. They proclaim them heretical, because they say he was an Aristotelian, and Aristotle was not then in odour of sanctity. This Aristotelian has more spirituality in him than any of the great men of science that I ever read about. Because he explains Kabbalah just in the way that *The Secret Doctrine* would explain it. In the most

[1] Isaac Newton (1642–1726/27) — an English mathematician, physicist, astronomer, alchemist, theologian and author.
[2] Published in 1862, the first volume of *A System of Synthetic Philosophy*.
[3] **Solomon ibn Gabirol** or **Solomon ben Judah** (1021/22–1090) — an Andalusian poet and Jewish philosopher.

spiritual way he explains it, and yet he is called an Aristotelian, and why? Because he had an intuition. He is one of the greatest of the poets.

Mr. Kingsland: But you are not really answering my objection. There may be a man here and there who has this intuition, but the ordinary mortals who treat of our political economy, and our methods of improving our dwellings and all the rest of it, how can they obtain the knowledge of these particulars, when they have practically no idea of universals?

Mr. Harbottle: It seems to me that the real objection to the lines adopted by modern science lies in the fact that in every case when they make a so-called discovery, they jump at it. They go a long way ahead and argue downwards, and they are very often completely wrong. What I mean is this, most of their detail work comes after the idea of their main scheme has occurred to them, and they then make the details fit in if they won't do so of themselves. Instead of taking the logical test and commencing with universals and then seeing if it agrees with the particulars, they work backwards and they make the particulars agree with the false conception, and they won't permit anybody to start a little higher up and argue down to them, and according to their particulars. That is really why occultism and science are at loggerheads.

H.P.B.: The thing that they say is: "Oh! look at science; everything they have said is perfectly correct. Everything is brought there and the cases are shown and so on and they are dovetailed together" — I say because they are syllogisms. They began, if you please, by inventing a proposition; they will come to the conclusion that it is dovetailed, but it is not. That the first proposition is the correct one. It may be anything. I may come and say: "a horse has the head of a serpent, therefore all horses are with serpent's heads," and it would be a scientific proposition because I put it myself, which is perfectly incorrect.

Mr. Harbottle: You see, they, most of them, start with a universal, only it happens to be a negative.

Dr. Williams: I think Mr. Kingsland's point is this, that while it is a perfectly true principle, yet before the mind is open to receive universals, it must have facts as a basis for the universals, otherwise it could not exist.

H.P.B.: Well, mind being a microcosm, I suppose he would have some means of getting to the macrocosm.

Dr. Williams: It seems to me that the two go always hand in hand.

H.P.B.: I touch this thing. Why do I touch it? Because I have a hand. What makes the hand to move? Will power, whatever you like. From where does it come? Go and follow it out in that way, and if you follow from these particulars to your own universals, then after a few times you will be perfectly able to begin and take first the universals, and then having come to something, make your hand the head of it.

Dr. Williams: That is what I say: you first have to trace your hand and from that you may predict many things; but you must have your facts first. If you begin with a child, you do not begin teaching him as the very first thing some universal fact, because you cannot.

Mr. Kingsland: You see, H.P.B. blames the scientists of today. I instance Herbert Spencer as a man who has got as near the Absolute as any of our modern men, and she is down on him; if a man like he is so far wrong, what are all the rest of us to do?

H.P.B.: Shall I tell you, and give you good advice? Try to be a little less conceited, you men of science, that is the way to begin. Try not to think yourselves the only intelligences that have ever been developed in this universe and that all the rest are fools, and that the ancients did not know anything at all, and don't go and consult what the ancients said, because they study classics very well. How many ideas have I traced in your modern science which have never been acknowledged to their proper source and which were stolen bodily from ancient science? I could write, if they only took one of my articles, in one of your great reviews, I can assure you, and I would put them to shame. I have traced five or six modern inventions which I can trace as easily as you like to the old men of science who existed thousands of years ago.

Mr. Harbottle: There is a great deal in Lucretius.[1] Lucretius is full of modern science.

Mr. B. Keightley: I think the practical answer to your question is this: not to deny with quite such dead certain as your modern men do.

Mr. Kingsland: I do not say they could not find universals if they tried to look for them.

---

[1] **Titus Lucretius Carus** (c.99–c.55 BCE) — a Roman poet and philosopher.

H.P.B.: Let them be agnostics,[2] but don't let them be bigots.

Mr. B. Keightley: You take a man like Huxley. The first thing he will say is: "I know that that is not so." You say to him anything — that, for instance, in every material thing we see there is a psychic side; in another way, that the thing exists on a different plane of consciousness. He will say, "I know that is not so" before you have got the words out of your mouth, almost.

H.P.B.: There is a man of science — and he is a great man of science in America — who pitches into me in the *American*.[3] He says it is all chaos, and he goes on and he is obliged to say: "Yes, it is true, but why does she show such animus to the men of science, if she quotes them?" But I quote them just to break their heads with the weapons furnished by the older men of science. He sends to us the most stupid things. He sends his journal in which he speaks about it. Some men of science who write in the journal wanted, it may be, that I should be exposed, but they only showed their own ignorance.

Mr. A. Keightley: Does not the difference between the men of science who talk about the particulars and you who talk about universals consist in this: that the man of science, as a general rule, depends purely upon his reason and his observation to deal with the facts of his physical consciousness? The practice of working from universals depends upon the intuition, which proceeds from a higher plane of consciousness, but as the man of science declines to admit anything but that which he can touch with his physical senses, he will insist on negativing anything else.

H.P.B.: He steps off from the platform of agnosticism, which is perfectly his right, but he has no right to come and dogmatize on his own plane of matter. If he said: "It is not the province of physical science to go beyond physicals; it may be, or it may not be on the physical; to every appearance it is so and so," then we should say: "Very well; we bow to you; you are a very great man; you find every faculty in the hind leg of a frog, and all sorts of things"; but why does he say: "There is nothing beyond that," and everyone who comes and says beyond

---

[2] **Agnostic** — a word first used by Professor Huxley to indicate one who believes nothing which cannot be demonstrated by the senses.

[3] *Scientific American* — an American popular science magazine, in print since 1845.

that there is knowledge he will come and pitch into? Mind you, I had a very great respect for science when I was in my green age, between twenty and thirty. The men of science were then my gods.

Dr. Williams: I do not think the great representative men of science take that ground. They did in the past, and there are some who occupy a lower sphere who do today. Spencer, for instance, whenever he is brought face to face with a thing which may be true or not true simply says, "it may be."

H.P.B.: But you take the best of them. He certainly is one of the greatest intellects; I do not mean to say at all because he says something flapdoodle somewhere that he is not a great man of science — he is. But when you say that Huxley does this thing or Tyndall,[1] or when you say any fellow of the Royal Society, I say no, I have seen a good many of them, and with the exception of Crookes and of Wallace[2] I never found one who would not call the other a madman. Do you suppose the others do not call Crookes a madman? They say: "He is cracked on one point." So they say about Wallace. Have they the right to say that of such a man of science, that he is cracked because he believes in things beyond matter? They have no such right at all.

Dr. Williams: I do not know what the smaller men say because I never care to read what they write.

H.P.B.: Look at Huxley; look at the tone of regret he adopts. Didn't they say that Zöllner[3] died a madman? Look at the French scientists, they all say he did. All the Germans say the same: "Softening of the brain." "He died in consequence of the fact that he happened to believe in the phenomenal form."

Mr. Kingsland: But that is something like blaming a schoolboy for not applying the calculus.

Mr. Harbottle: That is equivalent to saying that the scientists are deficient in principles.

Mr. B. Keightley: They are only that because they choose to make themselves so, and they choose deliberately to be dogmatic.

---

[1] **John Tyndall** (1820–1893) — an Irish physicist.
[2] **Alfred Russel Wallace** (1823–1913) — an English naturalist, explorer, geographer, anthropologist, biologist and illustrator.
[3] **Johann Karl Friedrich Zöllner** (1834–1882) — a German astrophysicist.

Mr. Kingsland: The best of them do not deal in dogmatic negatives.

H.P.B.: I do not know. Look at Huxley and such men. They deal greatly in dogmatic negatives. I do not call Tyndall a very great man of science. He is a popularizer and a compiler. I call Huxley a great man of science, and there is not one more bitter than Huxley, not one.

7 FEBRUARY 1889

Mr. A. Keightley: Sloka 3, Stanza 2. "The hour had not yet struck; the ray had not yet flashed into the Germ; the Matri-Padma[1] had not yet swollen." "The ray of the 'Ever-Darkness' becomes, as it is emitted, a ray of effulgent life or light, and flashes into the 'Germ' — the point in the Mundane Egg, represented by matter in its abstract sense."[2] Question 1. Is the point in the Mundane Egg the same as the point in the circle — the unmanifested Logos?

H.P.B.: Never; the point in the circle is that which we call the unmanifested Logos. The manifested Logos is the triangle, and I have said it many times. Does not Pythagoras speak of the never manifested Monad which lives in solitude and darkness, which, when the hour strikes, radiates from itself number 1? This number 1, descending, produces number 2, and number 2, number 3, the 3 forming a triangle, the first full geometrical figure in the world of forms. It is this triangle which is the point in the Mundane Egg, and which, after gestating, starts from the egg and forms a triangle and not the point in the circle, for the point in the circle is the unmanifested Logos.

Mr. A. Keightley: That is what I thought.

H.P.B.: Brahma-Vach-Viraj[3] in the Hindu philosophy, and it is Kether,[4] Chokmah and Binah in the Sephirothal tree.[5] The one Logos is the potential, the unrevealed cause; the other the actus, or in other

---

[1] **Matri-Padma** (*Sanskrit*, "mother-lotus") — the womb of Nature.

[2] *The Secret Doctrine*, vol. 1, p. 57.

[3] **Vach** (*Sanskrit*, "speech") — the mystic personification of speech, and the female *Logos*, the female creator, being one with Brahma, who created her out of one-half of his body, which he divided into two portions; she is also one with Viraj who was created in her by Brahma. In one sense, Vach is "speech" by which knowledge was taught to man; in another, she is the "mystic, secret speech" which descends upon and enters into the primeval Rishis, as the "tongues of fire" are said to have "sat upon" the apostles. Esoterically, she is the subjective Creative Force which, emanating from the Creative Deity (the subjective Universe, its "privation," or *ideation*) becomes the manifested "world of speech," *i.e.*, the *concrete expression of ideation*, hence the "Word" or Logos.

Viraj (*Sanskrit*, "shining") — the male Logos, created in the female portion of Brahma's body (Vach) by that god.

[4] **Kether** (*Hebrew*) — the Crown, the highest of the ten Sephiroth; the first of the Supernal Triad.

[5] **Sephirothal tree** — the Kabbalistic Tree of Life, consisting of the ten Sephiroth.

words, the Monad evolving, from its invisible self, the active effect which in its turn becomes a cause on a lower plane. Now discuss the matter. Who has any objections? Collect your combativeness and go on, gentlemen. Has no one any objections to offer? Do ask, Mr. President.

Mr. Harbottle: Well, in a sense, the second question bears upon it, because it illustrates, or at least it will settle the question, as to the exact plane of differentiation with which the whole of this Sloka is dealing as I take it. Ask the second question.

Mr. A. Keightley: 2. "What is the Ever-Darkness, in the sense used here?"

H.P.B.: Ever-Darkness means the ever-unknowable mystery, behind the veil even of the Logos.

Mr. A. Keightley: Parabrahm, in fact.

H.P.B.: Parabrahm; even the Logos can see only Mulaprakriti. It cannot see that which is beyond the veil; that is the "Ever-Unknowable Darkness."

Mr. A. Keightley: What is the ray, then, in this connection?

H.P.B.: The plane of the circle whose face is black and whose point in the circle is white; but white figuratively, because certainly it has no colour. The first possible conception in our minds of the invisible Logos. Ever-Darkness is eternal and the ray is periodically flashed out of its central point through the germ. The ray is withdrawn back into the central point and the Germ grows into the second Logos, the triangle within the Mundane Egg. If you don't understand still, you just offer me any questions, and I will try to answer them.

Mr. Harbottle: The difficulty we were all in when we were reading this Sloka the other day and considering it was, that we were doubtful whether it really referred to the same epoch of manifestation as the earlier portion, as the first Stanza, for instance.

H.P.B.: There is the beauty of these Stanzas, and I will tell you afterwards, later in the questions.

Mr. Harbottle: I may say, I think most of these questions are intended to bring out this point, that is to say, whereabouts we are.

Mr. B. Keightley: Because the Mundane Egg seems to be really the third stage. At any rate, not earlier than the third.

H.P.B.: The first stage is when the point appears within the dark circle, within that unknowable darkness.

Mr. Harbottle: May I interrupt you for one moment — that point being the unmanifested Logos?

H.P.B.: Yes. The second stage is when, from that white point, proceeds the ray which darts and produces the first point, which in the Zohar is called Kether or Sephira, then produces Chokmah and Binah, the first triangle, which is the manifested Logos. And yet, from this manifested Logos will go the seven rays, which in the Zohar are called the lower Sephiroth, and which in our system are called, well, the Primordial Seven, from which there will proceed innumerable series of hierarchies. They simplify the thing and take simply the four planes and the worlds and so on. That is all. This does not explain anything.

Mr. Kingsland: What you say is that the triangle is what you here refer to as the Germ in the Mundane Egg?

H.P.B.: Yes.

Mr. B. Keightley: The Mundane Egg being used in a very much wider sense than that of terrestrial — being the Universal Egg, so to speak.

H.P.B.: There is the Universal Egg and the Solar Egg; they refer to it, and of course you must qualify it and say what it is.

Mr. B. Keightley: Abstract form is the same, whatever scale you take it on.

Mr. Harbottle: Being the eternal feminine, really.

H.P.B.: No, no. There is no eternal female principle, and there is no eternal male principle. There is the potentiality of both in one only, a principle which cannot be even called spirit.

Mr. Harbottle: Put it thus, then: abstract form being the first manifestation of the female principle.

H.P.B.: The first manifestation, not of the female principle, but of the ray, that proceeds from the central point, which is perfectly sexless; this ray produces first that which is the potentiality united of both sexes, but is not yet either male or female sex. That differentiation will come later when it falls into matter, when the triangle becomes a square. The first tetraktys.[1]

Mr. Harbottle: Then the Mundane Egg is as sexless as the ray?

H.P.B.: It is undifferentiated primordial matter.

Mr. Harbottle: One is in the habit of associating matter with anything to which the name of female is applied.

H.P.B.: Matter certainly is female, because it is receptive of the ray of the sun which fecundates it, and this matter produces everything that is on its face; but that is quite a different thing. This is on the lowest plane.

Mr. Harbottle: This is substance, rather than material.

Mr. B. Keightley: And substance is of no sex.

H.P.B.: Do you know what is matter? The synonym of matter is mother, and mother comes from matter, they are interchangeable.

Mr. A. Keightley: Then what I want to understand is this: You have the ray, which ultimately starts the manifested Logos, or the Germ within the Mundane Egg. Does the Mundane Egg exist, then, in any way, excepting potentiality, before this first triangular — if you may call it so — Germ is started by this ray?

H.P.B.: What is the egg, the Mundane Egg, or Universal Egg, call it whatever you like, whether on the principle of universality, or on the principle of a solar system? The egg means the ever-eternal, existing, undifferentiated matter, which is not strictly matter as we ordinarily use the term, but which, as we say, is the atoms. The atoms are

---

[1] **Tetraktys** or **Tetrad** (*Greek*, "four") — the sacred "Four" by which the Pythagoreans swore, this being their most binding oath. It has a very mystic and varied signification, being the same as the Tetragrammaton (the four-lettered name of God). First of all, it is Unity, or the One under four different aspects; then it is the fundamental number Four, the Tetrad containing the Decad, or Ten, the number of perfection; finally it signifies the primeval Triad (or Triangle) merged in the divine Monad. The Ineffable Name IHVH — one of the Kabbalistic formula of the 72 names — can be arranged in the shape of the Pythagorean Tetrad. The mystic Decad, the resultant of the Tetraktys, or the 1+2+3+4=10, is a way of expressing this idea. The One is the impersonal principle "God"; the Two, matter; the Three, combining Monad and Duad and partaking of the nature of both, is the phenomenal world; the Tetrad, or form of perfection, expresses the emptiness of all; and the Decad, or sum of all, involves the entire Cosmos.

indestructible; and matter is destructible in *form*, but the atoms are absolutely indestructible.

Mr. Gardner: Do you mean to say that the atoms are not yet crystallized?

H.P.B.: I do not speak about chemical atoms. I speak about the atoms of occultism, which certainly no chemist has ever seen. They are mathematical points. If you read about the Monads of Leibniz,[1] you will see what it is, this atom.

Mr. A. Keightley: Then may one say the Germ is the active point within the Alayic condition of substance?

H.P.B.: The Germ is simply a figurative way of speaking. The Germ is everywhere. Just as when one speaks of the circle whose centre and circumference is everywhere and nowhere; because, given the proposition that the circle is endless, surely it is infinite, and you cannot place the circumference anywhere, or put any centre to that which is limitless. It is simply a way of talking, just to bring to your conception something more clearly than you could otherwise imagine it. Just the same with the Germ. They call it the Germ, and the Germ is all the Germs, that is to say, the whole of Nature: the whole creative power that will emanate, that they call Brahma or any name you like. For on every plane it has got another name.

Mr. A. Keightley: Then you practically answer the third question. "What stage of manifestation is symbolized by the Mundane Egg?"

H.P.B.: I say the Mundane Egg is on the plane of differentiation, the first stage if you like; but from the plane of non-differentiation it is the third, as I just told you. The Egg represents the just differentiated cosmic matter in which the vital creative Germ receives its first spiritual impulse, and potentiality becomes potency. I think that is answered.

Mr. Harbottle: Yes.

Mr. B. Keightley: That is a very good phrase, "potentiality becomes potency"; it just expresses the difference between the first and the second Stanzas.

---

[1] **Gottfried Wilhelm Leibniz** (1646–1716) — a German mathematician, philosopher, scientist and diplomat. *The Monadology* is one of his best known works.

H.P.B.: That is my difficulty, you see, I don't know English well enough to come and explain it to you.

Mr. A. Keightley: Question 4. "Is the Matri-Padma here spoken of the eternal or the periodical Egg?"

H.P.B.: The eternal, of course; it will become periodical only when the ray from Logos number one will have flashed from the latent Germ in the Matri-Padma, which, you understand, is the Egg, the womb of the universe, as it is called. You would not call eternal the physical germ in the female, but rather the latent spirit of the Germ concealed within the male cell in Nature. In all the creations of plants or animals, it is just the same. Take it on analogy or on the method of correspondence, it is just the same.

Mr. B. Keightley: Sloka 4. "But, as the hour strikes and it becomes receptive of the Fohatic impress of Divine Thought (the Logos or the male aspect of the Anima Mundi, Alaya) — its heart opens."[2] Question 5: Does not "Fohatic impress of Divine Thought" apply to a later stage of differentiation, strictly speaking?

H.P.B.: Now look here, this involves a very difficult answer. I wish you would give all your attention to it. Understand once for all, for if you understand clearly this thing, it will prevent your putting many, many questions which are perfectly useless, and you will understand them better also. You see, I have explained to you as well as I can, now try and correct me, if you please, if I don't explain clearly. They want to say that Fohat is a later manifestation. Very well. I answer that Fohat is, as a full-blown force or entity, a later development. Fohatic as an adjective may be used in any sense, Fohat as a noun springs from a Fohatic attribute. Do you understand this now? No electricity will be developed or generated from something where there is no electric power. But before electricity, or a certain kind of electricity, is developed, you can speak about the electric impulse and electric impress, cannot you? I say Fohatic, because Fohatic has got a special meaning in the esoteric teaching; and I will first give you the meaning here. It comes afterwards, you know. The Divine Principle is eternal and gods are periodical.

---

[2] *The Secret Doctrine*, vol. 1, p. 58.

Mr. B. Keightley: In other words, the Fohatic principle — to translate it into a different term — the Fohatic principle is eternal, but Fohat is an entity or a god.

H.P.B.: Or, as a synthesis of this force on our plane of differentiation, it is periodical and is limited, and it comes later.

Mr. Harbottle: The Fohatic principle produces Fohat instead of arising from it.

H.P.B.: It is the Shakti[1] or Force of the Divine. Fohat and Brahma are all one thing. They are various aspects of the Divine Mind.

Mr. B. Keightley: Have you written nothing more about that there?

H.P.B.: Not here. It is too easy a thing to write anything about. It comes in the next question.

Mr. A. Keightley: "In the commentary on Stanza 2, is it not your aim to convey some idea of the subject by speaking of the correspondences on a much later stage of evolution? For instance, is not 'Fohat' in the sense used here the synthesis of the primordial seven, and therefore appearing at a much later stage than that of the first manifestation of the Alaya?"

H.P.B.: It is so, most assuredly; but then you were told more than once that the commentaries busy themselves but with the evolution of our solar system in this book. The beauty and the wisdom of the Stanzas are in this, that they may be interpreted on seven different planes, the last reflecting in its grossly differentiated aspect, and copying on the universal law of correspondences, or analogy, all that it sees before in the beginning. Every plane is a reflection and a copy of another plane. As it took place in the definite, undifferentiated plane, so it took place on the second, on the third, on the fourth, and so on. Now these Stanzas represent all of them, and the student who understands well the gradual development, so to speak, and the progressive order of things, will understand perfectly to which it applies. If we talk about the higher divine world, we shall talk just in the same way, because in *The Secret Doctrine* that I give to the world and to your great critics, I certainly give it as applied to the solar system, and even this they do not understand. They call it idle talk, so why shall I go

---

[1] **Shakti** (*Sanskrit,* "power") — the active female energy of the gods; in popular Hinduism, their wives and goddesses; in Occultism, the crown of the Astral Light; Force and the six forces of nature synthesized; Universal Energy.

and bother my brains to go into something more on the higher plane? This is not for the profane, let us make a difference, we must draw a line of demarcation somewhere.

Mr. Forsyth: Then are we to understand, madam, that the whole of the writing in *The Secret Doctrine* has reference only to the solar system, as we understand the solar system?

H.P.B.: It has reference to that chiefly. The second volume is simply the development of life on our earth, not even in the solar system, for the thing is so tremendous that it would require 100 volumes to write all this. Sometimes I make remarks about larger questions, but as a whole the exposition begins and ends on this earth and with the development of life from the first day of Manvantara. You see how they are confused even on this terrestrial plane; so what would it be if I mixed up the evolution of life on Neptune, or beyond the solar system? Why, they would not understand a word. The esoteric doctrine teaches all that, but then it is not in a few months you can learn. You have to study for 20 or 30 years, and according to your capacity it will be given to you, because a man may be spirit-blind just as he is colour-blind on this plane, and I know unfortunately too many of those who are perfectly spirit-blind.

Mr. Harbottle: But yet the Stanzas up to the point we have reached them do deal with the awakening from the Pralaya.

H.P.B.: Most assuredly; but after that, when I come and say that so many Stanzas are left out, then it begins with the solar system.

Mr. Harbottle: That is really the point I wanted to get at, whether the second Stanza was still entirely dealing with that awakening from the Maha-Pralaya. We have not come to the point you mention yet, have we?

H.P.B.: Certainly not, but as it deals with this awakening on all the planes, you can apply it to any plane, because one covers the other.

Mr. Harbottle: Because, we are feebly and vaguely attempting to apply it to the highest plane of which we have the faintest idea.

Mr. B. Keightley: There is also this, that the Stanzas deal with the abstract, and the commentaries are applied more particularly to the solar system.

H.P.B.: But the Stanzas contain seven meanings, and every one of them may be applied to the highest, and the second, the third, and so on to the seventh plane of matter. But certainly I speak more about the four lower planes. As you will see there, when we come to the part about the moon and the evolution of the stars and so on, there I speak more about the solar system. I limit myself to that in the commentaries. Not in the Stanzas, because I have rendered them just as they are.

Mr. Kingsland: I think we are making a little mistake in this way. Instead of following the process entirely out on the first plane, and then taking it on to the lowest plane, we are supposing it takes place on the higher plane, and we immediately jump down on the lower, instead of following the whole process on one plane.

H.P.B.: Perfectly so; but it did not begin on a Thursday, and it won't end on a Thursday. The creation began on Monday, didn't it — because Sunday is the day of rest?

Mr. B. Keightley: Because he took his day off on Sunday.

H.P.B.: Sabbath[1] breaking, I call it.

Mr. Harbottle: No, Sabbath is Saturday.

H.P.B.: You call it Sabbath, it is no fault of mine. Well, then, we will go on. Moreover, you have to learn the etymology of the word Fohat. There is where it becomes difficult to understand. It is a Turanian compound word. "Pho"[2] is the word. "Pho" was once and is derived from the Sanskrit "bhu," meaning existence, or rather the essence of existence. Now, "Swayambhu"[3] is Brahma and man at the same time. "Swayambhu" means self-existence and self-existing; it means also Manvantara. It means many, many things according to the sense in which you take it, and one must know exactly whether the accent is on the "m" or on the "u," or where it is, for therein lies the difference. Take "bhu." It means earth, our earth. Take "Swayambhu." It means divine breath, self-existence, that which is everlasting, the eternal breath. To this day in China, Buddha is called "Pho."

A Lady: Is not the first meaning, breath?

---

[1] **Sabbath** (*Hebrew*, "rest") — the seventh day of the week (Saturday) for Jews and the first day of the week (Sunday) for Christians.

[2] **Pho** (*Chinese*) — the inner essence of something; the animal soul in man.

[3] **Swayambhu** (*Sanskrit*, "self-existent") — an epithet for self-born or self-manifested deities, such as the Trimurti of Brahma, Vishnu and Shiva or Manu.

H.P.B.: It is not. It is self-essence. It is very difficult for me to translate it to you. Look at the Sanskrit dictionaries. They will give you 100 etymologies, and they won't know what it is. It is existence, it is self-evolution, it is earth, it is spirit, everything you like. It depends on the accent, and how it is placed. That is a very difficult thing. In this sense, certainly it comes from bhu and sva. Now, they don't pronounce the "b" generally, it is "Pho," which is bhu or Budha, which means wisdom. Fohat comes from Mahat, and it is the reflection of the Universal Mind — the synthesis of all the seven and the intelligences of all the seven creative builders or cosmocratores. Hence the word, you understand — for life and electricity are one in our philosophy. I told you, I think, Mr. Kingsland, that they say life is electricity, and the one life is simply the essence and the root of all the electric phenomena that you have in this world on this manifested plane.

Mr. Harbottle: If "Sat" is the potentiality of being, "Pho" is the potency of being — the very next thing.

H.P.B.: That is very good. Just repeat it.

Mr. Harbottle: If "Sat" is the potentiality of being, "Pho" is the potency of being itself, the next to "Sat."

H.P.B.: That is so, and it is a very good definition indeed.

Mr. A. Keightley: Can you explain more fully the process by which Horus[4] or any other god is born *through* and not *from* an immaculate source? Can you render in clearer language the distinction between "through" and "from" in this sense? The only explanation given is rendered in the unintelligible mathematics of the *Source of Measures.*[5]

---

[4] **Horus** (*Egyptian*) — the last in the line of divine Sovereigns in Egypt, the son of Osiris and Isis. He is the great god "loved of Heaven," the "beloved of the Sun, the offspring of the gods, the subjugator of the world." At the time of the Winter Solstice (our Christmas), his image, in the form of a small newborn infant, was brought out from the sanctuary for the adoration of the worshipping crowds. As he is the type of the vault of heaven, he is said to have come from the *Maem Misi*, the sacred birthplace (the womb of the World), and is, therefore, the "mystic Child of the Ark" or the *argha*, the symbol of the matrix. Cosmically, he is the Winter Sun. A tablet describes him as the "substance of his father" Osiris, of whom he is an incarnation and also identical with him. Horus is a chaste deity.
[5] See James Ralston Skinner, *Key to the Hebrew-Egyptian Mystery in the Source of Measures Originating the British Inch and the Ancient Cubit* (Philadelphia: D. McKay Co., 1876).

H.P.B.: If mathematics is unintelligible, what can my poor, unfortunate English teach you better? Because mathematics alone can express that which it is impossible to express in words, in such poor words as mine are.

Mr. B. Keightley: I think I should prefer your words to the mathematics.

H.P.B.: That is a compliment, of course.

Mr. B. Keightley: I quite agree with it.

H.P.B.: The author of the Source of Measures is a very great Kabbalist. I have got a very great regard for him, and he is one of my pupils, and he knows a thousand times more than I do. In mathematics I am the biggest fool that ever was created. Two and two will seem to me five. I laboured under the impression that 5 times 7 was 28.

Mr. Kingsland: Then do not be surprised if we cannot make anything of it.

H.P.B.: I get mixed up sometimes on this plane, but you have not got always to pull yourselves down by the tail as I have. I have got my own region. Now listen to this, and I will try to give it as well as I can. On the first plane of differentiation there is no sex, but both sexes exist potentially in the primordial matter, as I have before explained to you. Now that mother which I just told you was the same as matter is not fecundated by any act in space and time, but fertility or productiveness is inherent in it. Therefore, that which emanates or is born out of that inherent virtue is not born *from* but *through* it. That is to say, that virtue is the sole cause that the something manifests through it as a vehicle, whereas on the physical plane the mother is not the active cause but the passive effect, rather, and the agent of an independent cause. Now listen: even in speaking of the mother of their God, Christians will show her first fecundated by the Holy Ghost and say Christ is born from her, whereas Christ is not born "from" but "through" her. Lightning may manifest itself through a board, pass through it, but the chip of wood from the hole made by the thunderbolt proceeds from the wood plank. Do you see the difference? "From" implies and necessitates a limited and conditioned object *from* which it can start, *from* which something starts, this act having to take place in space and time. "Through" applies to eternity as much as to anything else, as much as to something limited. The Great Breath, for instance, thrills *through* space, which is endless, and is "*in*" not "*from*" eternity. Do you understand the difference?

Mr. Kingsland: Would not a good illustration be the case of a ray of light passing through a crystal and becoming seven colours? You say it is an immaculate medium?

H.P.B.: It is an immaculate medium. It is not that this medium is fecundated, it is not that, it passes through, it is the vehicle, therefore the Matri-Padma; the first scene is called born from an immaculate matter, which is the root of the immaculate conception in the Christian religion, because it is taken from that the immaculate matter. He is not born *from* her but *through* her, and Christians if they understand well their own dogmas would not say he is born *from* the Virgin Mary, but *through* her, if they wish to make an incarnation of Jesus; there is the great difference. But, for instance, the Roman Catholics have materialized the idea in such a way that they positively made a goddess of her, and drag her at the same time in the mud; and made of her a simple woman, instead of explaining. They don't preserve the original idea. They do not say, as they should, that she was such a virtuous woman that she was chosen to be the mother of that in which God incarnated. But by saying she is a goddess, they imply a false idea, and that they do consider her as a goddess is shown by their adoration. And as a goddess, what merit has she got? No merit at all. She need be neither virtuous, good, bad, nor indifferent. It is supposed that she gives birth to gods. I say the religions have materialized this divine abstract conception in the most terribly materialistic way. Speaking of spirituality, there is nothing more materialistic and coarse in this world than the religions, Christian, Brahmanical, anything — except the Buddhist, which is not a religion but a philosophy. They have all dragged down divinity to the lowest depths of degradation. Instead of trying and rising to a divinity, they try to drag down the Logos, just as in America I have seen the negroes in Methodist Churches get into such a state of excitement that they will jump up and do all kinds of things, and then with their umbrellas they will try to catch Jesus and say, Come here, Jesus! Come here, Jesus! It is positive blasphemy. I have seen it once, and it disgusted me.

Mr. Forsyth: And they fall down on the floor.

H.P.B.: Oh! You have seen it too. I am very glad you can corroborate my statement.

Mr. Forsyth: Yes, they fall down and foam at the mouth.

H.P.B.: Now comes a question, gentlemen, a strange question, a mathematical one.

Mr. A. Keightley: "How does the triangle become the square; and how does the square become the six-faced cube?"

H.P.B.: In occult Pythagorean geometry, the tetrad is said to combine within itself all the materials from which Cosmos is produced; that is the Pythagorean rule. The point or 1 extends to a line that make 2, the line to a superficies, 3; the superficies or triad or triangle is converted into a solid or 4 or the tetrad, by the point being placed over it.

Mr. B. Keightley: A pyramid, it is a four-pointed figure.

Mr. Kingsland: It is a four-sided figure.

Mr. Harbottle: It is a four-sided figure.

Mr. ——: Is it pyramidical?

H.P.B.: Yes, but it must have something on it. We will see how it is transformed into the pentagon and the pentagon into the six. The square becomes after that a cube, and so on.

Mr. A. Keightley: But a pyramid is not a square.

H.P.B.: The base of it is.

Mr. Harbottle: No, it is a triangle turned into a pyramid.

H.P.B.: Excuse me, there are four faces. My dear sir, I don't speak to you about the figures. They asked me about the square. They do not speak about the cube here, they speak about the cube afterwards.

Mr. Kingsland: Isn't it built on a square, and then it becomes the four things.

Mr. Gardner: The four sides coming up to the apex.

Mr. Harbottle: You may have a three-faced pyramid.

H.P.B.: I don't speak here of that, it will come later. You can take Pythagoras by the beard if you can get him.

Mr. Kingsland: Do you mean a triangle becomes a tetraktys?

H.P.B.: I say it becomes the tetraktys because matter is square always. It is always a plane square, and once that the triangle falls into it, you have the seven. Allow me a pencil and I will draw it for you. There is the triangle, and it is inscribed between four lines.

Mr. B. Keightley: We shall see as we go on. You get a plane square, then the moment you add another point, a fifth point outside that, you get your pyramid or square-based pyramid.

Mr. Kingsland: We want to know how you get your square, first.

Mr. ——: How do you get from the triangle to the square?

H.P.B.: I can't show it to you, but in mathematics it exists. It is not on this plane of matter that you can square the circle. We know what it means to square the circle, but the men who spent years trying to square the circle are shut up in lunatic asylums. On this plane you cannot think of squaring the circle, but we can. It is quite a different thing.

Mr. Harbottle: Éliphas Lévi takes it in this way: he takes the first eternal as representing the triangle, and the synthesis of the three forming a fourth point; but I don't see myself how that brings one any nearer to matter. I think he puts it that way in his works. Does he not?

Mr. B. Keightley: The point becomes the line two, the line becomes a plane superficies three, then you have the triangle or the first plane figure.

H.P.B.: And the superficies or triangle is converted into a solid of four, or the tetrad, by the point being placed over it.

Mr. B. Keightley: Then that is the triangular pyramid.

H.P.B.: But then it becomes again another thing to make the cube out of the square. It will become a triangular pyramid, but it will come on the base of the square.

Mr. Harbottle: At the same time, what one wanted to get at was that the first four stages ought to have produced, and according to that process did produce four dimensions — if you take the point, line, superficies, and solid, you have 1, 2, 3, and 4. But, of course, if you take the ordinary plane square, you are simply altering a mathematical figure, still of the same dimensions.

H.P.B.: You can't understand the thing unless you have this conception very clearly in your mind: that the first real figure that you can conceive of and that can be produced in this world of ours is a triangle.

The point is no figure at all, nor the "2," for which the Pythagoreans had the greatest contempt, because it cannot form any figure. You can do nothing with them, you cannot make of two lines a figure. The first one then is the triangle, and this is taken as a symbol of the first manifested Logos; the first in this world of manifestation. I think this is as plain as can be.

Mr. Harbottle: And further; the first possible solid is the four-sided figure with four angles, four sides, each plane side contained by three lines. It is not the square, it is the pyramid; it is the three-sided pyramid.

H.P.B.: [...] which is the point itself [...] produces, or is one. It goes to the left or the right, it produces Chokmah, the wisdom. He makes this plane, which is a horizontal plane of matter, and produces intelligence, Binah, or the Mahat, and then returns back into the first. There are the four, if you like. It is not the concrete quaternary; I don't know these names. It is still the Tetraktys, and this is called the Tetragrammaton[1] in the Kabbalah. It is called that, because it is the first thing. The triangle falling into matter, or standing on matter, makes the four, that is to say, spirit, matter, male and female. That is the real significance of it. This number contains both the productive and the produced numbers; this is why it is sacred. Now, it is the spirit, will, and intellect which form the triangle animating the four lower principles, and then come the seven principles which we speak of in Theosophy. They are the same that Pythagoras spoke about, the seven properties in man, and even the Rosicrucians took it. The square becomes the cube when each point of the triangle becomes dual, male and female. The Pythagoreans said once 1, twice 2, and there ariseth a tetrad having on its top the highest unity, which becomes the pyramid whose base is a plane tetrad; divine light resting on it

---

[1] **Tetragrammaton** (*Greek*, "four letters") — the four-lettered name of God, its Greek title: the four letters are in Hebrew "yod, he, vau, he," or in English capitals, IHVH. The true ancient pronunciation is now unknown; the sincere Hebrew considered this name too sacred for speech, and in reading the sacred writings he substituted the title "Adonai," meaning Lord. In the Kabbalah, the letter I is associated with Chokmah, H with Binah, V with Tiphereth, and H final with Malkuth. Christians in general call IHVH Jehovah, and many modern Biblical scholars write it Yahveh. In *The Secret Doctrine*, the name Jehovah is assigned to Sephira Binah alone. The IHVH of the *Kabbalah* has but a faint resemblance to the God of the Old Testament.

makes the abstract cube. Now take six solid or concrete squares, they make a cube, don't they? And the cube unfolded gives you the cross or the vertical four, barred by the horizontal three. Four here and three will make seven, because you count again the central square, as you know (I have given it in *The Secret Doctrine*), making our seven principles or the Pythagorean seven properties in man. And this is the cross, the symbol of Christianity, which is the vertical male and the horizontal female. It is spirit and matter, and at the same time it is the most phallic symbol there is.

Mr. B. Keightley: Isn't that rather excluded, because the vertical is four, while the horizontal is three?

H.P.B.: My dear sir, that which is above is itself below, but the below is seen as in a looking glass reversed. I told you it is four and divine; on the divine plane it becomes four, and material on the plane of matter, for matter is four also. That which is three and divine here is, for instance, the three higher principles in man becoming the nothing yet. It is nothing yet, it is simply the first thing which will become something. You must always take this, that it will be reversed and will be like the reflection in the looking glass, for your right arm will appear to you your left.

Mr. B. Keightley: Therefore you get your three and your four interchanged.

H.P.B.: Just so.

Mr. B. Keightley: Question 9: "What is meant by Astral Light in the middle paragraph of page 60?"

H.P.B.: It means an infernal misprint of the printer, who just put "has" instead of "lies," and also carelessness of the bright but not quick-eyed editors. They just ask in the most innocent way what it means. It means an infernal mistake of the printer and an oversight on your part for which I ought to have skinned you if I had seen it.

Mr. B. Keightley: You saw the proofs too; you are in the same boat.

H.P.B.: Read it; see if it has any sense.

Mr. A. Keightley: [Reads passage from *The Secret Doctrine*, vol. 1, p. 60.]

Mr. B. Keightley: That *has* means *lies*, that is what it is.

Mr. A. Keightley: But "has" has distinctly a meaning.

H.P.B.: It has not, because Astral Light expands. What is "has," then, if you please?

Mr. Harbottle: You can say a thing has something between it and another thing.

Mr. Forsyth: What do you wish to say then, madam?

H.P.B.: I would say it expands. It is a misprint, I can assure you. Look at my manuscript.

Mr. Forsyth: I would like you to think of a word and let us know decidedly what word it is.

H.P.B.: If they say it is correct, they are English and I am not.

Mr. Harbottle: "Is spread." It has that meaning to me.

H.P.B.: Will you kindly read this, Mr. Forsyth, because I take it for a misprint, and I know I would never put this sentence.

Mr. B. Keightley: You would often say this room has a door between it and the next.

H.P.B.: But there is nothing there relative to "has."

Mr. B. Keightley: The Tetragrammaton.

Mr. Forsyth: "Has" means possession.

Mr. Harbottle: We did not ask that question.

H.P.B.: What is meant by Astral Light is explained in questions 10 and 11. Why are you so very impatient, all of you?

Mr. Kingsland: I don't think we misunderstood the meaning of that.

H.P.B.: Oh you are very, very pundit-like, all of you.

Mr. Harbottle: I don't understand what it means, but I understand what you mean to convey.

H.P.B.: What can be meant by Astral Light? The Astral Light is the great deceiver.

Mr. B. Keightley: We seem to have gone suddenly from the stage of the first manifested Logos, and landed ourselves on the other side of the plane of Astral Light and Tetragrammaton.

H.P.B.: Now, what do you mean? Allow me. "Thus is repeated on earth the mystery enacted, according to the seers, on the divine plane." [Continues reading from passage in *The Secret Doctrine*, vol. 1, p. 60.] That is to say, the second Logos becomes a Tetragrammaton, the triangle and the four. I think it is as plain as can be. "It is now in the 'Lap of Maya' or illusion and between itself and the Reality *has* the Astral Light," etc. Now, why did you come and pitch into me in my old age and dishonour me? I believe this thing is the most clear of all the blessed paragraphs that are here in the book. Is it, or not? I put it to the justice of those here. You see how I am ill-treated.

Mr. Forsyth: It is a shame, madam. I think your interpretation, "lies" in place of "has," has a somewhat different meaning to the general reader. It certainly to me has a slightly different meaning.

H.P.B.: Maybe it is more English, but I would not put it.

Mr. Forsyth: If you put it in classic English, "has" is strictly a matter of possession.

H.P.B.: I suppose they understand it just as it is. What is it Mr. Kingsland just proceeded to scold me for?

Mr. Kingsland: I do not think it has been perfectly made clear yet how the three becomes the four.

Mr. Harbottle: Yes, I think it has. I think the explanation of that is that the "four" really and truly means what we call the third dimension of space, and consequently is Maya — the Tetragrammaton, in one sense. You mean a different sort of four, and if it can do that, obviously there is Maya and the highest triangle. It answers itself, that use of the pyramid to explain the four.

H.P.B.: Just so.

Mr. Kingsland: Is the Astral Light used there in the sense of Maya?

H.P.B.: Most assuredly. When you come there to a certain passage where I speak of the seven principles and the moon and all that, I show there are only four planes, that the three which are above do not belong to our terrestrial chain or to the chain of any planet. You do not know anything about it. You can't speculate. I am not a high Adept. I am a poor old woman very ill-treated here. We speak only of the four planes that we can conceive.

Mr. B. Keightley: We apologize to you, but the explanation of the whole thing is the pyramid.

Mr. Harbottle: It explains it all, because we get in that four what we could not see at all, the third dimension of space, and consequently Maya. One is apt to look on the Tetragrammaton as above Maya.

H.P.B.: Did you read my article in *The Theosophist* on the Tetra-grammaton?[1] The Kabbalists say something else, but in my sight the Tetragrammaton is not very high. I have been just answering Mr. Subba Row. He said: "How can it be seven principles?" I said: "I am not going to worship the Tetragrammaton. I do not see why I should. I do not worship differentiated things." "I know only of the Absolute and perfectly homogeneous. I can invent for myself any kind of conceptions and flapdoodles." The Tetraktys by which the Pythagoreans swore was quite a different kind of tobacco, if you please, quite another thing. You just take the third chapter of Genesis and the beginning of the fourth and you find there the Tetragrammaton. You find Eve and Adam and Jehovah, who becomes Cain. That is what you find. There is the Tetragrammaton. That is the first one which is symbolized. Then comes at the end of the fourth chapter already the human conception, and there is Enoch and there is Seth, and to him was born a son, Enos. And it is written in the real Jewish scrolls, "From that time man began to be male and female," and they have translated it in the authorized — James's version — "From that time man began to call upon the Lord." I ask you if you can translate it like that, when in the real Hebrew you see men began to be called "Jod-he-vah." That is always so, you know. They say one thing in the Hebrew scriptures and they translate it as another. They do not take into consideration the fact that the people had all symbolical and figurative language. Then they will never come and see this difference: it is always "Lord God," or "God," or "Jehovah" and all that, nothing else, and even "Jehovah" says to Moses that he never was called by the name Jehovah. Centuries and thousands of years before that there is Abraham, who builds an altar to "Jehovah." Is it so, or not?

Mr. Harbottle: In the revised version, they translate Elohim[2] as "Lord" in the first chapter.

H.P.B.: They have no right to translate Elohim as "God" in the singular. It means "Lords" and "Gods." Everything there is in the plural. They cannot go against the facts. They translate Abel and say it is the "son of Eve." I say fiddlesticks! I say it was a daughter of Eve for Abel

[1] See H. P. Blavatsky, "Tetragrammaton," *Collected Writings*, vol. 8 (Wheaton, IL: Theosophical Publishing House, 1960), pp. 140–159.
[2] **Elohim** or **Alhim** (*Hebrew*, "gods") — a name for God in the Hebrew Scriptures.

is the female aspect of Cain. When they separate, the first separation is shown in the first verse of the fourth chapter, when Cain was born unto Eve, and she said there, it is translated: "I have gotten a man from the Lord," though it doesn't mean this. It means what Ralston Skinner[3] showed perfectly; it means Jehovah, male and female kind. Abel comes afterwards and is female, and then comes the separation of sexes. And then they say he kills Abel, and he doesn't kill him at all — he marries him. That is the whole of it. I am obliged to tell you these things, if you are to learn. History is history and facts are facts.

Mr. A. Keightley: How does Astral Light come between Tetragrammaton and "reality"?

H.P.B.: How do I know? It is there. That is answered.

Mr. A. Keightley: What is "reality" in this context?

H.P.B.: That which has neither form, colour, limitation, attributes, nothing. A number that is nothing, it is all; it is the Absolute. Now, this, if I have not said it 120 times, I have not said it once.

Mr. Harbottle: The whole of these questions have arisen out of a misunderstanding of the word Tetragrammaton. Now I think we understand what Tetragrammaton is.

Mr. B. Keightley: It is simply humanity, as far as I know it. Man.

H.P.B.: No, it is rather different — I do not call it so. It is Malkuth, when the bridegroom comes to the bride on earth; then it becomes humanity.

Mr. B. Keightley: After the separation.

H.P.B.: The seven lower Sephiroth must be all passed through. The Tetragrammaton becomes more and more material.

Mr. B. Keightley: And then after the separation he is completely Tetragrammaton.

H.P.B.: Then he becomes an M.P. or a Grand Master of all the Masons.

Mr. Kingsland: In one sense the Astral Light is between the four lower planes and the three higher ones.

H.P.B.: Between Tetraktys and Tetragrammaton there is an immense difference. The difference is because Pythagoras swore by the Tetraktys of the invisible Monad, which comes and having produced

---

[3] **James Ralston Skinner** (1830–1893) — an American attorney and author.

the first point and the second and the third retires afterwards into the darkness and everlasting silence, *i.e.*, into that of which we cannot know anything. It is the first Logos, and this is the Tetraktys. There is the point. The point comes, that is 1. He produces the first point, the second, third, and fourth. Or if you take it from the point of matter, there is the horizontal plane of the triangle and there is the second side, the third and the point. Éliphas Lévi says many things to which certainly I will never consent, and he knew very well he was bamboozling the public. He simply laughed at people.

Mr. Harbottle: At the same time he gives that idea of the formation of the four, inasmuch as he suggests it is the first triangle and the synthesis of it. You may perfectly well take the Monad which forms the 1, the 2, the 3 and retires into the darkness. At any rate it is not a great extension of the idea, and therefore I say he is really describing the Tetraktys.

H.P.B.: And I just showed it to you. You take the point in the circle and you proceed and make a triangle from the lower point and take the plane of matter and you proceed like that, it becomes the reverse. He takes it on a lower plane.

Mr. B. Keightley: That is how the confusion has arisen in our minds. Éliphas Lévi is speaking of the Tetraktys as the Tetragrammaton.

H.P.B.: In the preliminary rules to the Esoteric Section[1] I said: "please, all those who want to study the eastern esoteric science, have the kindness not to belong to any society except the Masonic societies,[2] which are perfectly harmless, to the Masonic societies or to the Odd Fellows, but you must not belong to any of the occult societies, that teach you after the western methods." Very well; this morning I

---

[1] **Esoteric Section** — an inner section of the Theosophical Society founded in October 1888 for the deeper study of esoteric philosophy.

[2] **Freemasonry** — a centuries-old fraternal organization based on a system of moral and ethical teachings. It uses symbols and allegory derived from the tools and practices of stonemasonry. Just like the Rosicrucians, the Knights Templar, and other mystical orders, this society was first designed to protect and spread secret knowledge among those who could use it for the benefit of humanity, often guided by the Masters of Wisdom. The first Grand Master and founder of Masonry was Enoch, also known as Hermes. The founding fathers of the United States were Freemasons. However, over time, this organization, just like all others founded by the Masters, lost all connections with Them and today operates as any other created by people.

received an insult. Mr. Westcott[3] writes to me and says: "I am a fellow of the Theosophical Society, and am I going to be blackmailed and sent like a black sheep out of the fold because I have belonged to a society." I said: "My dear fellow, I have got nothing to do with you. You don't belong to my Esoteric Section; you are welcome to belong to anything you like." Now you see the enormous confusion it produces in you, simply because you have read Éliphas Lévi. What shall it be with others who study in other societies, which will go and say that the Tetragrammaton is the highest divinity? You will have such a confusion that you will never learn anything of the one or the other, and the consequence will be that you will be in the most fearful state of confusion. I said you may belong to the Masonic societies, but not to the occult societies. I am perfectly sure I have got enough to do. Whether there are 300 members or 30, I don't care. It will be useless trouble to teach and teach and find they won't understand it.

Mr. Harbottle: We have no more formal business tonight.

---

[3] **William Wynn Westcott** (1848–1925) — a co-founder of the Hermetic Order of the Golden Dawn.

14 FEBRUARY 1889

Mr. A. Keightley: The first verse, Stanza 3. "The last vibration of the seventh eternity thrills through infinitude. The Mother swells, expanding from within without like the bud of the lotus."[1] (Commentary, the first three sentences.) Question 1. Does the commencement of time as distinguished from Duration correspond to the appearance of the second or manifested Logos?

H.P.B.: Is it the first question, this?

Mr. A. Keightley: Yes.

H.P.B.: You see, it was not there. I answer the question which was written there. It doesn't seem to meet it. You say: "How is it that the mother swells," and so on, if there is a difference between Duration and time, or to what time it corresponds, to what period? That is the question isn't it?

Mr. A. Keightley: [Reads the question again.]

H.P.B.: Certainly it does not correspond, because you see that when the Mother swells, it is a good proof that the differentiation has set in; and while, when Logos number one radiates through primordial or undifferentiated matter in Laya, there is no action in chaos. Thus there is a great difference between those. There is no time at this stage. There is no time. There is neither space nor time when the first thing begins, and it is all in space and time once it is differentiated. The last vibration of the seventh eternity is the first one announcing dawn, and it is this last vibration which is the synonym of the unmanifested Logos at the time of the primordial radiation. It is Father-Mother, potentially; and when the second Logos emanates the third, has it become the Virgin Mother: then only. Do you understand the difference?

Mr. A. Keightley: I understand the difference between these two, but I do not see how it applies to time and Duration.

H.P.B.: When the first Logos appears, there is neither time nor space. Duration is always; it is eternal; but there is neither time nor space; it is outside time and space. This last, seventh vibration means just the same as if it was said: the first Logos radiated. That is to say, the ray emanated from the Absolute — or radiated rather, because nothing

---

[1] *The Secret Doctrine*, vol. 1, p. 62.

emanates from the Absolute. Therefore, this term, the last vibration of the seventh eternity, applies to the moment or period, whatever it is, when the first Logos appears, when the first light appears. Therefore it is certainly not the time of the second Logos.

Mr. B. Keightley: The question as put there was whether time appears; whether you can speak of time from the moment when the second Logos, the unmanifested-manifested Logos, appears.

H.P.B.: Most assuredly, because then time begins. It is what he told me that made me answer, because I could not understand your question when I read it first. I thought you meant that the word "time" could not be applied to the seventh vibration, or you mixed up the first and the second Logos. It was written in a way that I could not understand. Certainly there is an immense space of time between the two. One is just at the last moment when it ceases to be outside of time and space, and the second is when space and time begin — periodical time.

Mr. B. Keightley: Space and time as periodical manifestations begin with the second Logos.

H.P.B.: When it is said the Mother swells like the lotus or the bud, it means that it has begun already — because it could not have happened before. Before there is no action possible and no quality applied to anything. It is impossible to see it here, at least in our philosophy. The divine ray, Logos number one, is the abstract parent, while Logos number two is at the same time his mother's son and her husband. Now, if you go and study the cosmogonies and the theogonies of all the peoples you will find in the Egyptian, in the Indian and the Chaldean, everywhere, that the second Logos, the creative Logos, is spoken of as his mother's husband and his mother's son. Now, for instance, Osiris[2] is the son and husband of Isis, and Horus is the son

---

[2] **Osiris** (*Egyptian*) — the greatest God of Egypt, the Son of Seb (Saturn), celestial fire, and of Neith, primordial matter and infinite space. This shows him as the self-existent and self-created god, the first manifesting deity (the third Logos), identical with Ahura Mazda and other "First Causes." For as Ahura Mazda is one with, or the synthesis of, the Amshaspends, so Osiris, the collective unit, when differentiated and personified, becomes his brother Typhon, his sisters Isis and Nephtys, his son Horus and his other aspects. The four chief aspects of Osiris were: Osiris-Phtah (Light), the spiritual aspect; Osiris-Horus (Mind), the intellectual *manasic* aspect; Osiris-Lunus, the Lunar or psychic, astral aspect; ▸

and the husband and the father too. It is all interchangeable. Just the same with Brahma; Brahma is the father, the husband and the son of Vach. You understand the difference — when he differentiates.

Mr. A. Keightley: That is to say, that the first differentiation is everything, practically.

H.P.B.: Most assuredly. It is only on the second plane that this Mother becomes the Virgin Mother, because before that it has no qualification, none whatever, no adjective.

Mr. Kingsland: In other words, you would say there is no differentiation with the first Logos. The differentiation only begins with the second, and therefore the first Logos is outside of time and space, and time and space begin with the second.

Mr. A. Keightley: The second question refers to the words: "One is the abstraction or noumenon of infinite time (Kala)."[1] Is this the "Duration" referred to in Stanza 1: "Time ... lay asleep in the infinite bosom of Duration," or is it the potentiality of time?

H.P.B.: I have been just explaining it. Duration has always potential time in it, in itself. Duration is Eternal time which had neither beginning nor end. Time is something, and that is why they say in the eastern philosophy, "Time is the son of Duration, its child."

Mr. A. Keightley: Yes, exactly.

H.P.B.: Infinite time.

Mr. A. Keightley: At once with the second Logos you proceed out of Duration into time, and time is therefore periodical, while Duration is eternal.

H.P.B.: Just so, as I have just been saying. Periodical time is the child of eternal Duration. Well, has anyone questions to ask? Let them ask, if they have anything, because after that it won't be understood again. Have you anything to ask, Mr. Kingsland?

Mr. Kingsland: No, I think I have not.

---

and Osiris-Typhon, physical, material, therefore passional turbulent aspect. In these four aspects, he symbolizes the dual Ego — the divine and the human, the cosmico-spiritual and the terrestrial.

Isis (*Egyptian*) — the goddess Virgin-Mother; personified nature; the female reflection of Osiris.

[1] **Kala** (*Sanskrit*, "time") — time, fate; a cycle and a proper name.

Mr. Scott-Elliot:[2] You mentioned radiation and emanation. One has never any distinct idea. What is the difference between radiation and emanation?

H.P.B.: Enormous. Radiation is the unconscious action, so to say, of something from which something radiates, but emanation is — well, it supposes already something that emanates out itself consciously. Now radiation can come from the Absolute; emanation cannot. Nothing can emanate from it.

Mr. Scott-Elliot: Radiation comes from the Absolute.

H.P.B.: Yes, the first radiation, when the Logos radiates. The first ray, that of which it is said in the Bible: "Let there be Light, and Light was."[3] The first divine light, this is radiation. It radiates; but emanating means emanating one from the other — how shall I say — from one being to another being, that is the difference. I make this difference because I do not know how to translate it in any other way. We have a word for it in the occult language, but it is impossible to translate it into English.

Mr. Scott-Elliot: Then there is a closer connection between that which has emanated and that from which it emanates than there is between that which radiates and that from which the radiation takes place.

H.P.B.: No. You see, the radiation — if it radiates, it is sure, sooner or later, to be withdrawn again. Emanation emanates and may run into other emanations and it is separated; that is a different thing. It may be, of course, that at the end of the cycle of times it will also be withdrawn into the one Absolute. But meanwhile, during the cycle of changes and the cycle of change of forms, this will be an emanation. And it is in my mind the same as evolution — of course, in another sense, but it is exactly the same thing. One thing evolves from the other and one thing emanates from the other, with the change of forms and substance and so on.

Mr. A. Keightley: Number 3. Page 63, line 5. Is not Astral Light used here in a different sense from that on page 60, line 22? Please

---

[2] **William Scott-Elliot** (1849–1919) — an investment banker and the author of *The Story of Atlantis* (1896) and *The Lost Lemuria* (1904).
[3] Genesis 1:3.

enlarge upon this idea of prototypes existing, before becoming manifest upon the material plane.

H.P.B.: Yes, certainly. Well, Astral Light is a very wide term. As I said, I use this because to use another would be to make the book still more incomprehensible, and heaven knows that they are complaining quite enough of its being very difficult to understand already. I have tried to avoid all such words, and I have put Astral Light in general. Now suppose I had said and given to you the difference — that Astral Light is used here as a convenient term for one very little understood, "the realm of Akasha or primordial light manifested in the divine ideation." Now, suppose I had to use this very long phrase. Very few would understand it, I would have to explain what is divine ideation, I would have to explain what is the Akasha; I would have to explain the difference between Akasha and Ether, and so on. Therefore, I use it simply as a term that everyone understands. Astral Light is everywhere. It may be from the highest plane to the lowest plane, it is always Astral Light, at least according to the Kabbalists. All the Kabbalists call it so, from the days of the alchemists and the Rosicrucians. Astral Light must be accepted here as a generic term for universal and divine ideation reflected in the waters of space or chaos, which is the Astral Light proper. That is to say, the Astral Light is like the mirror of the highest divine ideation, but it is all reversed, because it is a plane of illusion and everything is topsy-turvy there. In the divine thought everything exists and there was no time when it did not so exist, so that it is impossible to say that anything came out, because this divine mind is Absoluteness and everything was, is, and will be in it. At least, according to our philosophy, it is the undifferentiated — I will not say field — but the noumenal abstract space which will be occupied, the field of primordial consciousness. It is the field, however, of latent consciousness which is coeval with the Duration of the first and unmanifested Logos — which is the light which shineth in darkness, which is in the Gospel, is the first word used there; which comprehends it not. When the hour strikes for the second Logos then from the latent potentiality radiates a lower field of differentiated consciousness, which is Mahat. It is called Mahat in the *Vishnu Purana* and all the other Puranas, or the collectivity of those Dhyan-Chohans of which Mahat is the representative. Now do you understand the thing that you have been asking the last time?

Mr. Kingsland: Not altogether. What is the relation between Astral Light used in that sense and Fohat?

H.P.B.: Fohat is in the Astral Light because it is everywhere until the fourth plane, but the Astral Light doesn't go to the fifth plane. Then begins the Akasha. You see, we call Astral Light that which mirrors all the upper planes of consciousness, matter, being, call it whatever you like.

Mr. Kingsland: When you say that the Astral Light contains the prototype of everything, does it contain not only the prototype, but does it contain it in a sequence of events in the same way that we have sequence of events on the physical plane?

H.P.B.: There is a great difference between how this Astral Light reflects all kinds of things and how the other reflects them, because the first ones, the highest ones, are eternal. The Astral Light is periodic. It changes not only with the great Manvantara but it changes with every period, with every cycle. The Astral Light will change with every tropical year,[1] if you like.

Mr. Kingsland: Then everything that exists on this plane exists first of all in the Astral Light?

H.P.B.: No, it exists, first of all, in divine ideation on the plane of divine eternal consciousness and nothing can exist or take place on this plane if it does not exist there.

Mr. Kingsland: And then, further, it is reflected on the Astral Light.

H.P.B.: But it is reflected topsy-turvy; that is why we call it illusion. It is from the Astral Light that we take our prototypes. The evolution takes its prototypes from the Astral Light, but the Astral Light takes its representation from the upper ones and gives them entirely upside down. Just like a looking-glass, it will reverse everything. Therefore we call it illusion.

Mr. Kingsland: Therefore, both we ourselves and Nature get our ideas from the Astral Light in whatever we produce?

H.P.B.: They cannot get them, and those who go mentally beyond the Astral Light, those are they who see the truth and can sense it.

---

[1] 25,868 years.

Otherwise, they will never see it. If they do not go beyond the Astral Light they will be always in that ocean of illusion or deception, of self-ideation which is good for nothing, because once we begin to think we see things really with our eyes of senses, with our physical eyes, we won't see anything at all.

Mr. B. Keightley: There really seem to be three stages. First, divine ideation reflects itself in [...], the highest Akasha beyond the Astral Light.

H.P.B.: Which is the eternal, full of divine consciousness, which being Absolute consciousness cannot differentiate, cannot have any qualities, cannot act, but it is only that which is reflected from it or mirrored that can act, because the unconditioned and the infinite can have no relation with the finite and conditioned. Therefore it is our medium from which we take our "middle Heaven," as the Gnostics[1] called it, the middle space, on which is Sophia Achamoth.[2] The Gnostics all spoke about the middle space, which was the region of Sophia Achamoth, not the Sophia the Divine Sophia, but the Sophia Achamoth, the mother of all the evil spirits, the seven spirits, the builders of the Earth. And the Gnostics said it was these ones that built, and that therefore the God of the Bible was one of those wicked spirits. This is what they said, the Gnostics, Valentinus[3] and Marcion[4] and so on.

---

[1] **Gnostics** (*Greek*) — the philosophers who formulated and taught the Gnosis (*Greek*, "knowledge"). This spiritual and sacred knowledge could only be obtained by Initiation into Spiritual Mysteries of which the ceremonial "Mysteries" were a type. They flourished in the first three centuries of the Christian era. The following Gnostics were eminent: Valentinus, Basilides, Marcion, Simon Magus, etc.

[2] **Sophia** (*Greek*, "Wisdom") — the female *Logos* of the Gnostics; the Universal Mind; and the female Holy Ghost, with others.

Sophia Achamoth (*Greek*) — the daughter of Sophia. Esoterically and with the Gnostics, the elder Sophia was the Holy Spirit (female Holy Ghost) or the Power of the Unknown, and the Divine Spirit; while Sophia Achamoth is but the personification of the female aspect of the creative male Force in nature; also the Astral Light, or the lower plane of Ether.

[3] **Valentinus** (c.100–c.180) — an early Gnostic who received the writings of Mary Magdalene from the disciple of John the Apostle, but greatly distorted them. Therefore, only the Initiated are able to correctly understand his teachings.

[4] **Marcion** (c.85–c.160) — a devout Christian, as long as no dogma of human creation came to mar the purely transcendental and metaphysical concepts and the original beliefs of the early Christians.

Mr. B. Keightley: They had three heavens, then?

H.P.B.: I wish somebody could translate this thing. I have it entirely in Latin. It is the Pistis of Sophia.[5] If only somebody could translate this!

Mr. B. Keightley: I think Roger Hall knows it.

H.P.B.: But it must be given entirely in the Kabbalistic language. You know nothing of the Kabbalah, and you won't be able to do it; it wants somebody who knows Kabbalah well. I can't ask Mathers[6] to do it, because he will do it in his own Kabbalistic way. There will be eternity in the way and there will be St. Joseph[7] and everything. Therefore I can't give it to him. I must get somebody who knows Latin and at the same time who knows Kabbalah well enough to translate. There you will see this middle space and the upper middle space and the seven heavens that they spoke about. You see, if you only study the early Christian Fathers and compare that with what is said now with the theological teachings, why, you see there is just the same difference as there is between the teachings of Ammonius Saccas[8] and the teachings of Mr. Spurgeon.[9] They believed in the seven heavens and the seven planes, they talked about the incarnation. I will show it to you in the teachings of the Church Fathers, beginning with Alexandrinus[10] and ending with any of them. Then, after the 6th century, there begins our own flapdoodle church, theology which disfigures everything, which

---

[5] **Pistis Sophia** (*Greek*, "Faith of Sophia") — a sacred book of the early Gnostics or the primitive Christians. See H. P. Blavatsky, "Pistis Sophia: Commentary and Notes," *Collected Writings*, vol. 13 (Wheaton, IL: Theosophical Publishing House, 1982), pp. 1–81.

[6] **Samuel Liddell MacGregor Mathers** (1854–1918) — a co-founder of the Hermetic Order of the Golden Dawn.

[7] **Joseph** — the husband of Mary, the Mother of Jesus.

[8] **Ammonius Saccas** (175–242) — a great and good Greek philosopher who lived in Alexandria, Egypt. He was the teacher of Plotinus and the founder of the Neo-Platonic School of the Philalethians or "lovers of truth." He was of poor birth and born of Christian parents, but endowed with such prominent, almost divine goodness as to be called Theodidaktos, the "God-taught." He honoured that which was good in Christianity, but broke with it and the Churches at an early age, being unable to find in Christianity any superiority over the old religions.

[9] **Charles Haddon Spurgeon** (1834–1892) — an English Baptist preacher.

[10] **Clement of Alexandria** (c.150– c.215) — a Christian theologian and philosopher.

becomes more and more Pagan,[1] which takes not, mind you, the Pagan ideas of the higher initiates, but of the mob, the rabble. You see they always come and say I go against Christianity. I never go against Christ or the teachings of Christianity of the first centuries, but I go against this terrible perversion of all the truths. There is not a single thing they have not disfigured, and in such a way that you cannot name a rite, whether in the Roman Catholic or the Episcopal or Protestant Churches, that cannot be traced directly back to the rites of the pagan mob. Not at all of the mysterious initiates, but the pagan mob, simply, at the time when they were so persecuted, and when they wanted to save the scriptures of the initiation, and they had to compromise and come to terms, and they had come to terms with the Fathers of the church, who were very ignorant. They were either very learned or very ignorant. Now let us take Augustine; they call him the greatest man and the wisest. I say he is as ignorant as can be, and then they went and made a kind of *olla podrida*[2] out of these Pagan rites and the little things of the initiations. I am going to give it all in *Lucifer*,[3] the rites of ritualism in masonry and the church, and I am going to give it in five or six numbers. I think it will be very interesting for the masons, and for others too, because I show the origin, and I show it on the authority of the manuscripts and the old classics, and they cannot say I have invented it.

Dr. Williams: I was talking with a bishop of the Church of England last week, and he admitted that if the Church wanted to continue its integrity it would have to go back to the teaching of the early Christian fathers.

H.P.B.: But they will have to give up the temples and everything. The early Christians until the beginning of the 3rd century would not hear of temples, or rites, or ceremonies, or churches or anything of

---

[1] **Pagan** (*Latin*) — meaning, at first, no worse than a dweller in the country or the woods; one far removed from the city-temples, and therefore unacquainted with the state religion and ceremonies. The word *heathen* has a similar significance, meaning one who lives on the heaths and in the country. Now, however, both have come to mean *idolaters.*

[2] **Olla podrida** (*Spanish*) — a miscellaneous mixture.

[3] See H. P. Blavatsky, "The Roots of Ritualism in Church and Masonry," *Collected Writings*, vol. 11 (Wheaton, IL: Theosophical Publishing House, 1973), pp. 62–101.

the kind. That which is called a church in Paul is simply a gathering and an assembly in a room; there were no churches, no rites, nothing at all. You know what this Felix[4] says: he says, "you say that we are not pious because we have not temples, and this, that, and the other, but we cannot have a temple, for where is the temple that is large enough to contain the Almighty and the Absolute?" This is his argument, that went dead against the temples. Therefore, if your bishop wants to return, he will have to make away with every church and temple, and every chapel. They have to go to the endowment of Jesus. When you pray, don't go into the synagogues and do as the Pharisees do. Go into the room and pray. This is the meaning of it. Surely there is not the slightest comparison between what Jesus or Christ taught you, and what the Church is doing, not the smallest similitude. It is like two different things. It says one thing and you do another; and you call yourselves Christians, when you are all nothing but the most paradoxical people in creation. I mean all Christendom, I don't mean only England.

Dr. Williams: I think the world is coming to it very fast now.

H.P.B.: If I can help it a bit, I am perfectly ready to do anything. I can assure you I am perfectly ready to do anything, even to be cut into a thousand pieces, I don't care; for this is the curse. It is Church cant!

Mr. Kingsland: They would have to have meetings on the model of the Blavatsky Lodge.

H.P.B.: Well, at the Blavatsky Lodge they don't teach anything but good. They don't teach you anything of the vices. It is not a self-admiration society. At the Blavatsky Lodge you hear from me very disagreeable truths, but I think they do not do you any harm, do they? I say I am a very poor specimen of anything good, but I will say as the Lutheran preacher did: "do as I tell you, don't do as I do."

Dr. Williams: What is the first manifestation of the Astral Light proceeding downward towards matter?

H.P.B.: From the Astral Light? Already it will be on the fourth, third and second planes — from which of the planes do you mean? You take *The Secret Doctrine* and you see the four planes. It is useless to speak about that which cannot be given in any language.

---

[4] **Marcus Minucius Felix** (died c.250) — a Roman Christian apologist.

Mr. Kingsland: I think what Mr. Williams means is, what is that which makes the reflection become potentiality?

Mr. Williams: What is the first manifestation proceeding out from the Astral Light towards the plane of manifestation? I mean manifestation on the material plane.

H.P.B.: My dear Dr. Williams, I must ask you first, do you speak about theogony?[1] Do you speak about the physical forces? On what plane do you want me to tell you this? Because, if you speak about the theogony, I may say there are all the builders that proceed from it, the builders of the cosmic terrestrial world.

Dr. Williams: But the different planes are all inter-reality are they not?

H.P.B.: Certainly, but what is this Astral Light? All these intelligences, which are already from the son of chaos,[2] in matter and all these builders of the lower world proceed from it. All the seven elements, of which you know only five so far, or four.

Mr. A. Keightley: Then, there you are speaking of two distinct planes: the cosmic plane, and that which applies particularly to our earth. I suppose you would say, then, there were as many divisions of the Astral Light, if one may so speak of it, as there are planetary systems.

H.P.B.: Most assuredly.

Dr. Williams: Did you use the term there in our abstract sense, in the sense of unity?

---

[1] Theogony (*Greek,* "birth of the gods") — the genesis of the gods; that branch of all non-Christian theologies which teaches the genealogy of the various deities.
[2] Ilda-Baoth ("child of chaos," "child from the Egg") — the Son of Sophia Achamoth, the proud, ambitious and jealous god, and impure Spirit. She begot him by looking into the chaos of matter. He is the creator of our physical globe (the earth), according to the Gnostic teaching in the *Codex Nazaraeus* (the Evangel of the Nazarenes and the Ebionites). The latter identifies him with Jehovah, the God of the Jews. Ilda-Baoth is "the Son of Darkness" in a bad sense and the father of the six terrestrial "stellar," dark spirits, the antithesis of the bright Stellar spirits. Their respective abodes are the seven spheres, the upper of which begins in the "middle space," the region of their mother Sophia Achamoth, and the lower ending on this earth — the seventh region. Ilda-Baoth is the genius of Saturn, the planet; or rather the evil spirit of its ruler.

H.P.B.: I use terms mostly in that sense. At least, in my mind it all comes to that, I am afraid. But when we begin talking about the plane of differentiated matter and the evolution on earth, of course I am obliged to go into details.

Dr. Williams: Really, the idea at the back of the question was whether it manifests simultaneously in many different ways, or whether there is some sort of emanation from the Astral Light which constitutes a higher degree of potentiality from which various forms in the physical universe proceed, or the physical forces proceed. Or whether they proceed simultaneously in many different forms from this unity.

H.P.B.: I think the question will be answered in the following question.

Mr. B. Keightley: I think it is covered by the question of the prototypes.

H.P.B.: Now, question 4 is answered in the third.

Mr. A. Keightley: Question 4 is: "Is there an evolution of types through the various planes of the Astral Light or do all possible types exist in the Divine Thought?"

H.P.B.: Certainly, no possible types, nothing can be there, that does not exist in the Divine Thought.

Mr. A. Keightley: In that case (that there is an evolution) would it be correct to say that actual Astral prototypes of physical forms only exist on the lowest plane of the Astral Light?

H.P.B.: Yes, because this is the world of forms, and there there are no forms. You cannot come and make the comparison there. It is the world of forms, and there is the world Arupa.

Mr. B. Keightley: You have not read the keynote of the thing.

H.P.B.: Number 4 is answered in the third. Number 5 is answered here. The existence of physical forms on the Astral plane — their prototypes can best be compared to the noumenal germ from which will proceed the phenomenal germ which will finally become the acorn. Now, do you understand this thing?

Dr. Williams: No, I am afraid I do not.

H.P.B.: That first it can be compared to a noumenal germ; from the noumenal germ there comes the phenomenal germ and that germ becomes the acorn. Now, just to show you the different prototypes on different planes and how one thing is evoluted from the other. From the acorn will grow an oak and this oak as a tree may be of a thousand forms, all varying from each other. You see, all these forms are contained in the acorn, and yet from the same acorn the form that the oak will take depends already on extraneous circumstances, on physical forces at work, and all kinds of things. You know it is impossible to speak about this. The germ is there, but you cannot speak about form. And it is contained in the phenomenal germ and the noumenal germ.

Dr. Williams: Does the noumenal germ exist in the Astral Light? Can that in any way be said to be an emanation from the Astral Light?

H.P.B.: It is. The noumenal germ does not exist in the Astral Light but beyond, above. It is already a physical germ that exists in the Astral Light, the physical germ. That is to say, the prototype, what Aristotle calls the privation of matter.

Dr. Williams: Do you understand this prototype of the developed oak tree exists or does it develop with the physical oak tree? And is not the development of the physical oak tree the result of the developed prototype?

H.P.B.: Surely it is, but we cannot give it a form and expression here. We know that nothing can be here unless it is found in another higher plane, and from one plane to another it must proceed. From the highest it comes to the lowest and must have its development; only here it has its last consolidation of forms and development of forms. And this I tell you further: it is such a difficult subject that I do not think any one of you, even those who study Occultism, can understand it, and this is that the real Vedantin philosopher will tell you that even the oak or the tree that grows from the germ has its karma, and that whatever way it grows it is the result of karma. Now, try to understand that.

Mr. A. Keightley: Does that mean, then, that supposing you have an oak tree, the privation of the oak tree is a perfect example of a tree growth?

H.P.B.: Yes; but who had done the privation; who has traced it out?

Mr. A. Keightley: That is the Divine Thought, as I understand it.

H.P.B.: I beg your pardon. It is the Dhyan-Chohan, the builders on the lower plane, and as they draw it, it is their karma for having drawn it.

Mr. A. Keightley: But I thought they could not draw, apart from the natural evolutionary law.

H.P.B.: It is sometimes in such extraordinary forms that it is a thing of intention. We can't see it, but it is so.

Mr. Kingsland: Do you mean they actually draw it as it will be when the tree is full grown, before the tree is full grown?

H.P.B.: Just so, as the astral body of every man, woman, and child must exist before the physical body grows over it, and the physical body takes the shape of the astral form. The Hindus will tell you the gods, Brahma, Vishnu, Shiva are all under karmic law. They all say the same. You read the Hindu books, you will find it. All that which is at the end of Pralaya to die, so to say, to end in a certain form, is under karmic law.

Mr. Kingsland: That is closely connected with the phenomena of prediction. How is it that somnambulists are able to predict certain events that take place?

H.P.B.: Because they see it in the Astral Light.

Mr. B. Keightley: You get this state. The Dhyan-Chohan first of all takes that, the noumenal idea of it, or reflects it from the Divine Mind, as I understand; that, of course, is perfect in the Divine Mind, it is perfection. But as the Dhyan-Chohan takes it or reflects it in himself and transmits it again in the astral plane he modifies it, of course, either intentionally or otherwise — according to what I do not know, but either intentionally or otherwise — so that you get then the oak tree modified somewhat from perfection.

H.P.B.: This is why the Rosicrucians and all the Kabbalists of the Middle Ages spoke about spirits, that every species, every tree, everything in nature, every kingdom of nature has its own elements, its own Dhyan-Chohans, or what they call the elemental spirits.

Mr. Hall: Would the Dhyan-Chohans be the Hamadryads?[1]

H.P.B.: It is the Greeks who call them so.

---

[1] **Hamadryads** (*Greek*, "one with tree") — nymphs or spirits of trees in Greek mythology.

Mr. B. Keightley: Then, when you have, for instance, oaks, you have many different variations of oaks, each differing very considerably from each other. Are they, so to speak, differentiations of a single idea in the Divine Mind, differentiated in a thousand forms?

H.P.B.: They are the broken rays of one ray, and on every plane they are broken. As they pass through the seven planes they are all broken on each plane into thousands and millions, until they come to the world of forms; and every one breaks into an intelligence on its own plane, because every plant has an intelligence. It is no use to come and say that there are only sensitive plants which feel, and all that. If botanists could have the slightest — we won't say Kabbalistic ideas, but real clairvoyant powers or intuition — they would see that there is no plant that has not got its own intelligence, its own purpose of life, its own free will. It cannot, of course, walk or perambulate or move, but it has its own purpose of life. It can do this, the other, or the third. It can be receptive or non-receptive. It can close its petals or unclose them, it has its own ideation — each little blade of grass.

Mr. B. Keightley: Its own intelligence on its own plane.

H.P.B.: And this intelligence is not the plant, it is that Dhyan-Chohan, or let us call it elemental, that incarnates in it. It all seems as though we are a pack of fools, believing in all this. The Kabbalists laugh at this belief of nymphs and sylphs and gnomes and all that, but this is perfectly true, this is an allegorical way of talking; there is not a thing in this universe that is not animated, and all these atoms go to form a thing. They are the product of a kind of intelligence of its own, a cosmic intelligence that acts.

Mr. Hall: I think botanists practically admit all that.

H.P.B.: Only for the sensitive plants.

Mr. Hall: Look at the way they admit plants will grow towards the light; that implies it.

H.P.B.: Look at the great piety of the solar flower — of the sun-flower. It will always turn to the sun. Why, it is considered in the East a very pious yogi among the flowers, especially as it is clothed in yellow, and they have a great respect in some parts for it.

Mr. Scott-Elliot: But surely the words Dhyan-Chohan and elemental are not convertible. We have always understood Dhyan-Chohan as referring to the providers of the whole system.

H.P.B.: Dhyan-Chohan applies to everything. You call it Dhyan-Chohan, but you cannot call them Dhyani-Buddhas.

Mr. Scott-Elliot: I have always understood it to be a Dhyani-Buddha.

Mr. Kingsland: We had it all explained last Thursday.

Mr. Scott-Elliot: Then these elementals, all the creation, are they on their way to animal life, those that animate plants, say?

H.P.B.: Just the same, and the animals are on their way to humanity, and humanity on their way to Devas or the highest Dhyan-Chohans. We have used the words promiscuously because no one has taken the trouble to learn it from the ABC to the last letter. We always have spoken of the Dhyan-Chohans without going into details, and these are the details that will give you the correct idea. Otherwise, you will be at sea, and you will never understand it.

Mr. A. Keightley: Then I suppose you can speak of evolution from the prototypal world, through the elemental kingdom up to minerals and animals and human beings in the elemental world, as well as on the other parts.

H.P.B.: Just the same below, so it is above.

Mr. A. Keightley: But at the same time, are they separate or are they one and the same thing?

H.P.B.: Well, they are separate as you are separate from another man who may be walking now in Regent Street.[1]

Mr. Hall: Is it not that we are just the material shadows of our astral prototypes?

H.P.B.: We are; and the astral prototypes are the shadows of their higher prototypes, which are the Dhyans, up to the Dhyani-Buddha.

Mr. A. Keightley: Could you use the term in this way: that there is an elemental which is connected with us in the astral world, we ourselves being separated from that elemental in the astral world; that the elementals are represented in this astral world, and so are we, but we are in addition represented in the physical?

H.P.B.: We are in the Divine World also.

---

[1] **Regent Street** — a major street in the West End of London.

Mr. B. Keightley: No, I will tell you how it is. Our body — the cells of our physical body — have of course their astral correspondence, which you might call elementals. Those are not ourselves, but we must have as human beings our humanity, so to speak, on the astral plane, apart from the animal elementals which are the correspondencies of the physical body.

Mr. A. Keightley: That is what I meant.

Mr. B. Keightley: The animal elementals on the astral plane.

H.P.B.: These are questions of immense difficulty. They are such abstruse questions that one answer will elicit another question and then this question elicits ten questions more. It is a thing to which you Europeans are not at all accustomed. It is a train of thought that you could not follow unless you began from the beginning, and were trained as the Eastern people are trained, especially now the yogis, who begin a systematic course of training for the development of metaphysical ideas, and so on. It is a very difficult, abstruse subject, this. You see, it is not enough to come and have a very flowery tongue, and to express yourself well and to have a flow of language. You must first of all pass into the heads or the brains of those who listen to you a clear representation of what a thing is in reality. Unless you do that you will be listening to a very nice metaphysical speech, as I know many friends of ours have done and get nothing out of it. You have to know and understand everything and how it stands in relation to another thing, and you have to begin from the beginning and pro-ceed from the universals to particulars. And then it will be extremely difficult for you to understand anything on the higher planes. This is a question that we had already.

Mr. A. Keightley: There is another question arising out of that that I wanted to ask you. I was talking to a man not very long ago who said that there had been a communication from a sort of intelligence which signed itself "Chela," and it was written by means of a medium. That medium, according to the intelligence, was not very amenable. It varied, the condition varied, and so did the communications. But one sentence which was used struck me as rather curious. It said: "First of all you have to get the brain in a proper receptive condition, then when that brain is in a proper receptive condition, it stimulates the muscles of the hand to follow out the letters which are traced in a subtle medium." Probably he meant the letters in the Astral Light; that is to say, there seemed to be a double action. First, there was a tracing of the letters. Secondly, there was an impression on the brain to stimulate the nerves and the muscles and all the rest of it, to follow the tracings with pen and ink or pencil of that which was traced in the Astral Light. Is that a true representation of the way such things are done?

H.P.B.: When you trace it from the Astral Light, your brain may go to sleep, and need simply have the will to copy that without giving it a thought, whether it is good, bad or indifferent, wise or foolish.

Mr. A. Keightley: But that is an actual thing. Supposing for instance that this physical writing here was previously traced in the Astral Light. Were I a medium, my hand would follow the tracings with the pencil in the Astral Light with the physical pen and ink.

H.P.B.: Most assuredly, but certainly you must see it, and seeing, of course you must have a certain process going on in your brain.

Mr. A. Keightley: According to this explanation, apparently there was the double process going on — not only the sight but the stimulation of the brain to follow this tracing.

H.P.B.: "Stimulation" — I don't understand the use of it. If you don't want to do it, then perhaps your brain would be stimulated to do it. I cannot understand it.

Mr. A. Keightley: That was the explanation of the medium not being particularly amenable.

H.P.B.: Well, let us have question 6.

Mr. A. Keightley: Page 63, line 22. "Is Manu a unity of human consciousness personified into one human comprehension, or is he the individualization of the Thought Divine as applied for Manvantaric purposes?"

H.P.B.: Oh! It is about the root Manus and the Seed Manus. It is about the fourteen you are talking.

Mr. A. Keightley: [Repeats the question.]

H.P.B.: Well, didn't we speak of it last time, or the time before last? You asked me, I think, whether Manu and those builders were the same. That is at least the spirit, and whose duty it was to watch over the planet; and I told you then there were seven of them. Don't you remember this? It is just the same. Well, do you want to know what Manu is, and what he represents, or do you want simply, metaphysically, to know what kind of consciousness he has or how many consciousnesses he represents? Again, I don't understand that.

Mr. A. Keightley: It means this — is Manu what you may call the primary thought, which is separated into a variety of intelligences in the physical world? That is to say, is Manu the thing from which intelligences proceed on earth in diversity, or is he the synthesis of divers intelligences?

H.P.B.: He is not. He is the beginning of this earth; from Manu humanity is born. He was the only one who remained, and the others, who came with him, they have gone somewhere else. And, you see, he creates humanity by himself. He creates a daughter to himself, and from this daughter there is the evolution of humanity of the soul, mankind. Now, Manu is a unity, which contains all the pluralities and their modifications. The name "Manu" comes from the word "man," to think; it is a Sanskrit word, and thought in its actions and human brains is endless. So it is Manu which is and contains in itself all these forms that will be developed on earth from the particular Manu. Every Manvantara has its own Manu. Every [...] has its own Manu. From this Manu the Manus of all the Kalpa[1] Manus will be such.

Mr. A. Keightley: Then, practically, Manu is in the position with regard to humanity as a prism is to a single ray of white light.

H.P.B.: I would call it the white light which contains all the other lights, and then passes through the prism of differentiation and evolution.

Mr. A. Keightley: Then, that is the decomposing prism. Then, Manu has no relation to a uniting prism, if we may so use it, the prism of reunion.

H.P.B.: Going to one Manu, no. The Manu is simply the Alpha of something differentiated, which, when it comes to the Omega, that something disappears. It is Omega, and then you pass onward.

Mr. A. Keightley: Then, that is practically what I mean.

H.P.B.: Except, perhaps, Swayambhu.

---

[1] **Kalpa** (*Sanskrit*, "formation," "creation") — the period of a mundane revolution, generally a cycle of times.

Mr. Kingsland: Can't you say it stands in relation to each Manvantara the same as the first Logos?

H.P.B.: Yes, on the physical plane it is just in the same relation as if you take it on this, on the physical plane. It will be just that as it stands on the universal plane.

Mr. B. Keightley: Now, look at it for a moment. From the side of consciousness, you may say all the cells of the human body have each their own individual consciousness, but yet there is the unit of consciousness which is the man — well, is the analogy applicable to the Manu?

H.P.B.: I think it is — very well.

Mr. B. Keightley: Is the Manu a unit of consciousness which remains a unit?

H.P.B.: It is the latent, or it contains in itself all that.

Mr. B. Keightley: Which remains a unit in spite of differentiation. There is the unit of consciousness in a man, but still there are all the cells of his body which are individualized to a certain extent. But the unit of consciousness of man still persists.

H.P.B.: Yes, just that. I think it is a very good analogy.

Mr. B. Keightley: Because I want to get at the point whether the Manu represents a single consciousness — if I may make the phrase, one, a unit.

H.P.B.: But do you suppose that your consciousness is a single consciousness? Why, your consciousness is a reflection of thousands and millions of consciousnesses.

Mr. B. Keightley: But still it is united in a focus.

H.P.B.: But still this contains all consciousnesses which you have absorbed, and no one has got one alone. I don't know what you mean by that, that your brain is a focus. Of course, it is there. Manu is, as I say, meaning to think. It is the thinking man.

Mr. Hall: Has Manu, then, an individuality?

H.P.B.: Well, I don't know. It has no individuality in the abstract sense.

Mr. Scott-Elliot: All the consciousnesses that you have been talking about, are they the hosts of the Dhyani-Buddhas who are concentrated in the ray of the one man?

H.P.B.: Oh, no. The Dhyani-Buddhas are on the higher plane. They have nothing to do with our dirty household work of our earth. It is just as you will put, for instance, somebody as a great governor in the house, and then this governor will have nothing to do with the work of the kitchen maids. Of all that, he does not know anything. He governs simply a place. Or let us take the Queen, if she were not a constitution, or anyone, an emperor. In such an example, that is the thinking man, it has nothing to do with what the subalterns do. If you understand me, this is a thing which belonged to that mind. To that ruler, they are under the sway of that ruler, and yet that ruler is not cognizant of them. So it is with the Dhyani-Buddha that has come and emanated from him and all that. But he has nothing to do with them. It is just like the millions of cells that do something automatically or the foot which steps there without thinking about it. Every one thing has got its allotted duty to perform, but the Dhyani-Buddha is the supervisor. I gave it all to you about two Thursdays ago.

Mr. B. Keightley: Not quite what you have given now.

H.P.B.: Very well, then. Of course, if we go on with the conversation you will hear new things for 365 days in the year, because the subject is immense. I cannot express myself. My dear Mr. Scott-Elliot, I tell you, as I grow older the worse I begin speaking English. I begin to be in despair. I have the more thoughts in my head and I can express them less and less. It is very difficult for me to express it. I can write it but to speak it is very difficult.

Mr. A. Keightley: Then Manu is a unit of consciousness which differentiates into a multitude.

H.P.B.: It is.

Mr. A. Keightley: Then is Manu pre-Manvantaric? What I am wanting to get at is this.

Mr. Kingsland: What becomes of Manu at the end of the Manvantara?

H.P.B.: Manu is not individuality. It is not one. It is the whole of mankind.

Mr. Scott-Elliot: The whole of mankind?

H.P.B.: Certainly, it is not an individual. The Hindu will come and tell you Manu is an individual, but I say it is perfect nonsense.

Manu is that, the forefathers, the Pitris,[1] the progenitors of mankind, as it is called.

Mr. B. Keightley: In other words, it is a name applying to the Monads which come from the Lunar Chain.

H.P.B.: Why are they called the Lunar? Because the moon is said — of course, in defiance of all astronomy — to be the parent of the Earth; and these are the Monads. They progressed and passed through the First Round, and then it is they who, having become the first men, the Manus give birth to others by evolving their astral selves. They give birth to humanity, they give birth to the animals, and to all kinds of things. So in the Puranas they say for instance such and such a high yogi gave birth to all the serpents or all the birds — this, that, and the other — you see it there.

Mr. Scott-Elliot: What I wanted to express was the perfected humanity of one Round becomes the Dhyan-Chohans, or the Dhyani-Buddhas of the next Manvantara, and are the guiding rulers of the universe.

H.P.B.: But what do you call Manvantara? We call Manvantara seven Rounds; and this is a small, little Manvantara, of our globe.

Mr. Scott-Elliot: What bearing has Manu on the hosts of the Dhyani-Buddhas?

H.P.B.: He has no bearing at all. The hosts of the Dhyani-Buddhas evolve a lower set of Dhyani-Buddhas, these Dhyani-Buddhas a third, and so on. There are seven of them, though in Tibet they take only five Buddhas — after that they begin to be Cosmocratores, the builders (call them whatever names you like, they have all got special names in the Sanskrit) — then the builders of the Astral Light; and it is an endless hierarchy of one kind of Dhyanis evoluting another kind of Dhyans. Every one becomes more consolidated, more material, until it comes to the builders of this universe, some of which are Manus, the Pitris and the Lunar ancestors. It has a task, to give birth to men; and they give birth by projecting their astral shadows, and the first humanity (if humanity it can be called) are those Chhayas[2] of those

---

[1] **Pitris** (*Sanskrit*, "fathers") — the ancestors, or creators of mankind. They are of seven classes, three of which are incorporeal, *arupa*, and four corporeal.

[2] **Chhaya** (*Sanskrit*, "shadow") — the astral image of a person in esoteric philosophy.

Lunar ancestors over which physical nature begins building the physical body, which first begins to be formless; then the Second Race begins to be more and more formed. Then they are sexless; then they become bisexual; and then hermaphrodites, and then they separate and go all kinds of ways for the propagation of mankind. This is all given in *The Secret Doctrine.*

Mr. Scott-Elliot: Then, talking of Manvantara, the Manvantara is the period which is embraced by the seven rounds of seven planets.

H.P.B.: The Manvantara of our planetary chain.

Mr. Scott-Elliot: But I see you talk in *The Secret Doctrine* of a minor Manvantara.

H.P.B.: There is a minor Manvantara, and there is a major Manvantara, and there are various kinds of Manvantaras.

Mr. Scott-Elliot: Or rather, I thought Manvantara meant the circle, a single round of the seven worlds, and that Kalpa represented the total seven rounds of the seven worlds.

H.P.B.: Minor Manvantara means between two Manus, but as I show also there, there are fourteen Manus in reality. There are seven Root Manus at the beginning of the round and Seed Manu, as it is called, at the end of the round. Therefore they make fourteen. There are two Manus for each round, but these Manus are simply figures of speech — they are symbols of the beginning of humanity and the end, and the Manus are simply synonymous with the Pitris, the fathers, the progenitors of mankind, the Lunar ancestors. These are Manus.

Mr. Scott-Elliot: What would you call the duration of a minor Manvantara?

H.P.B.: If you take the exoteric duration, it is one thing. I could not tell you.

Mr. B. Keightley: Manvantara simply means the period of activity. You may speak about it as twelve hours of daylight and Pralaya of the night, or you may speak of Manvantara as the individual life of man.

H.P.B.: There are seven kinds of Pralaya and seven kinds of Manvantara, and they are all mentioned, from the *Vishnu Purana* to the last ones; all kinds of Pralayas and Manvantara also.

Mr. B. Keightley: It simply means a period of activity and it is not limited in any of the Theosophical writings. It is never used in a definite sense as meaning a definite period of years; you have to gather from the context what period is spoken of a specific period of time.

Mr. Scott-Elliot: During which the rays circle round the seven globes.

Mr. B. Keightley: You have to gather from the context what the extent of the Manvantara that is spoken of is, but you cannot go very far wrong, because what applies on one scale applies to the smaller scale, just as you take it.

Mr. A. Keightley: Question 7, page 64, second paragraph. "Is 'water' as used here purely symbolical or has it a correspondence in the evolution of the elements?"

H.P.B.: I speak about the water here simply in this way. You see, you make a great mistake, all of you, in confusing the universal elements with the terrestrial elements. Now, again, I do not speak about the chemical elements, I speak simply about the elements as they are known here, that we have been talking the last time about. We had a long conversation about it. But the universal elements, I would call them the noumena of the terrestrial elements. They are cosmic elements. Cosmic does not apply to our little solar system. Cosmic is infinite. I have in my head always the infinitude.

Dr. Williams: Are they identical with the elementals, or is that something entirely different?

H.P.B.: Elementals are simply the creatures produced for the various species in differentiation. That is to say, every differentiation of matter produces and evolves a kind of a force of an intelligence — well, anything you like — that which the Kabbalists and the Rosicrucians called elemental spirits, nature's spirits. They chronologized those things. But we say there is an intelligence, in every one there is a force. Hartmann[1] there writes about undines, and he believes they

---

[1] **Franz Hartmann** (1838–1912) — a German medical doctor, theosophist, astrologer and author. In the 1880s, he received a manuscript written by H.P.B. and published it in 1887 as *An Adventure Among the Rosicrucians* under the pseudonym "A Student of Occultism." In 1910, Hartmann republished the book with a new title: *With the Adepts.* However, in his preface, he acknowledged that he was not its original author, but that it "has been gathered from notes handed to me by a friend, a writer of considerable repute." Being fascinated by elementals, he did add his own fantasies to the story. In 2022, the book was published under the name of its true author as *The Land of the Gods* without his false additions.

are real creatures. It is a little bit too much to believe in sylphs, they are creatures of our imaginations, and they do not exist by themselves.

Mr. Hall: Would not they exist to the person who believes in that seriously?

H.P.B.: Every one of us can believe in elementals which they create for themselves. There are some who create this or that. This is what the spiritualists do, if you please. You can create an elemental, but this elemental will have no existence outside your vitiated imagination. It will be an intelligence, but the form you will give it, and the attributes you will give it, will be of your own creation, and this is the horrible thing.

Mr. Hall: And it weakens you physically.

H.P.B.: It will make a lunatic of you. It evaporizes you. This is why most mediums end in the lunatic asylums or get drunkards for life. Look at Kate Fox.[1] Look at Charles Foster[2] and all the great mediums, in fact. They are all half crazy.

Mr. A. Keightley: But then there, "water" is used as actually the first cosmic element.

H.P.B.: It is. It is called water, darkness; chaos is called water. "The waters of space" means you can have water. What is water? What is matter? Matter is in one of the three states: solid, fluid or gaseous. Very well, and in occult things there are four states more, there are seven states. But if you only speak and you say I shall limit our conversation only to this plane, if you take it as water in three states, as matter in its three states, you will understand perfectly what I mean.

Mr. A. Keightley: But what I am working at is this: water is used as the one element originally in the cosmic sense, and then finally on the terrestrial plane, water is preceded by ether, fire and air.

H.P.B.: But ether contains in itself fire and water and air and everything, all the elements, all the seven. And this ether which is the hypothetical agent of your physical science is the last form of Akasha. Therefore you can judge.

It briefly mentions the higher kinds of elementals who guard the approaches to the Abodes of Shambhala. The subject of higher orders of elementals and their rulers still represents the secret behind seven seals.

[1] **Kate Fox** (1837–1892) — an American medium.

[2] **Charles H. Foster** (1838–1888) — an American medium.

Mr. B. Keightley: But the point, really, of that question was this: as to whether the term water is applied to the cosmic, first matter, apparently from which everything evolves.

H.P.B.: Because it is not yet solid matter. That is why, as we know it, we cannot go and speak about that if we do not show it on this plane — something that we know, that we can conceive and understand. Now, space instead of water in the scriptures of any Bible some other word was used that we cannot understand, some word that has no meaning to us. That is why they call it water, because it has not the solidity of matter.

Mr. B. Keightley: Supposing that we knew anything about ether, it might just as well be called ether.

H.P.B.: Most assuredly, the moist principle — what is it the philosophers call it? "The hot and moist principle," from which proceed all things. "The waters of space" — you read this expression in all the scriptures and the Puranas and even in the Bible, and everywhere it is the same thing.

Mr. B. Keightley: It is from the "waters of space" that Sophia Achamoth proceeds.

H.P.B.: It proceeds from this Astral Light.

Mr. B. Keightley: Sophia Achamoth proceeds from the "waters of space."

H.P.B.: Moses says it requires earth and water to make a living soul. Understand it, if you like — and it is very easy — that is to say that man is a living soul, that the Nephesh is of a dual element. It partakes of the middle pre-astral of the psychic and of the metaphysic.

Mr. B. Keightley: It is really, then, the root, the Astral Light.

H.P.B.: That which is all the prototypes of everything on earth.

Mr. A. Keightley: Verse 3, Stanza 3. Are the virgin-egg and the eternal-egg the same, or are they different stages of differentiation?

H.P.B.: In its prototypal form as the eternal-egg and not the virgin-egg, the virgin-egg is already differentiated.

Mr. A. Keightley: You say in one sense it is absolute eggness.

H.P.B.: In one sense it is, but not in another sense. In this sense of the inner nature of its essence, it is the eggness, just as I say; but in the sense of its form in which it appears for its purposes of differentiation and evolution, it becomes a virgin-egg. It is all a metaphorical way of speaking. I say it is just the same. The eternal-egg is a pre-differentiation in a Laya condition; at that moment (before differentiation) it can have neither attributes nor qualities. The virgin-egg is already qualified, therefore differentiated, but it is the same, just as I told you. Everything is the same, nothing is separated from the other in its abstract essential nature. But in the world of illusion, in the world of forms, of differentiation, we seem all to be various persons and to be different things and all kinds of subjects. Well, whoever has got questions to ask, let them. I think there are many questions, I think, that you ask me over and over again, questions from another aspect; and it is the same aspect.

Mr. A. Keightley: When we ask you questions from the different points of view, it all serves to explain things. Then we are able to put them before you in the light in which we may understand them.

Dr. Williams: When you were speaking of writing from an appearance which is the Astral Light, can you explain anything more of that phenomena? If there is a writing in the Astral Light from which the medium writes, does not that imply form in the Astral Light?

H.P.B.: No, I would not say it is a form. It is something that assumes a form for the time being and takes a form which is comprehensible to the medium.

Dr. Williams: The medium sees or perceives something, otherwise there would be nothing from which he would write.

H.P.B.: Most assuredly, it takes that. The potential energy, the essence of the thing, assumes a form which is comprehensible to the medium.

Mr. Hall: It assumes form in his own brain only.

H.P.B.: And he sees it. Now, for instance, a sentence will be uttered in a language which is perfectly unknown to the medium, which the medium has never heard. This medium will see the thing repeated in the Astral Light not in the language that he or she does not understand, but in the language which is its own language. When two persons speak, let us say an Adept speaks with his chela, that chela does not understand the language of the Adept or the Adept the language of the chela on the physical plane, yet they understand each other because every word that is uttered is impressed on the brain, if you like — no language, the language of thought.

Mr. Scott-Elliot: No language is necessary.

Mr. Hall: You ask anybody who knows one or two languages equally well, you nearly always find he is unable to tell you in which he thinks.

H.P.B.: I am perfectly unable to say in what language I think sometimes. Very likely I can just perceive, you know, that I think in some language.

Dr. Williams: Is not that a lack of concentration upon the subject of thought itself? If one were to concentrate their minds it seems to me they must inevitably think in one or other of the languages in which they are equally familiar.

Mr. B. Keightley: No, because the more concentrated your thought, the less you think in words.

Mr. Hall: It is only when the man reflects afterwards, and then he has to give a certain form to his thoughts. And then he takes one of the languages which he knows.

Dr. Williams: Is thought anything until it assumes form?

Mr. B. Keightley: You can certainly have formed thought apart from words.

H.P.B.: How do the dumb and the deaf think, in what language?

Dr. Williams: Well, there is something which stands with them for words. The signification in their minds is precisely the same.

H.P.B.: Sometimes deaf and dumb persons will be taught a language by the process that they have invented. And after that, when they are able to communicate their thoughts to people, they cannot say in what language they thought. They had no guide.

Dr. Williams: But words are simply symbols to express qualities. We perceive the qualities in various ways and the words simply stand as symbols for the qualities. Now, they have another set of symbols and those symbols convey to their consciousness the same qualities that words do to ours, so that it actually comes to the same thing.

H.P.B.: But you said one must think in a special language.

Dr. Williams: And they think by their sign language.

Mr. Hall: I think not, because you cannot think the language until you have formed it.

H.P.B.: When you speak, do you follow the ideas that take form in your thinking? You don't think, you just speak as it comes to you, especially a man who is accustomed to speak easily.

Mr. Kingsland: You generally think too rapidly for speech at all.

H.P.B.: But this thinking does not at all take place in a language.

Dr. Williams: Do we think at all, then?

H.P.B.: We could not speak and give expression to thought if we did not think.

Dr. Williams: That is what I am trying to analyse. There is something which precedes, and speech is the external symbol which first exists in the mind.

Mr. Hall: That is the real thought.

H.P.B.: It is abstract thought.

Mr. Hall: A man would never have to look for words. When he thoroughly understands his subject, he knows all the things he wants to talk about; and then he is at a loss for words to translate the idea.

Miss Kenealy:[1] Speech is precipitated thought, just as one may have chemical solution, and thought is that solution. Speech is solution precipitated.

H.P.B.: I think this is a good definition.

Miss Kenealy: One thinks ideas, not words.

H.P.B.: What form do these thoughts take in the brain? I know I could not follow, I could not say what I think. I think and I will say it, but I cannot say in what form they have come in my brain.

Mr. A. Keightley: Then you don't think in symbols?

H.P.B.: If I want to think something, I want to meditate it, but when I talk simply, as I talk now, I don't give a thought to that — thought!

Dr. Williams: I don't mean that you watch the mechanical processes that are going on in your brain, but I mean thought must take a concrete form until it is used in speech; otherwise, naturally, there could be no speech.

H.P.B.: I can only judge by my own experience.

---

[1] **Miss Kenealy** — the daughter of Edward Vaughan Kenealy (1819–1880).

Mr. Kingsland: But when you are meditating — for instance, without any attempt to put them into words — when you simply think about a thing, meditate about it — that is the question.

Dr. Williams: Then I should say we are thinking or we are not thinking. We may make the mistake that was attributed to a certain extent to Washington, who went always about with his head down and his hands behind his back. Somebody said he was a very deluded man, he thought he was thinking. And it seems to me we are either thinking or not thinking. And in meditation we either have thoughts or we do not have thoughts. Now the moment we have a thought, that is a concrete form in the mind, but it is, as the lady remarked, a precipitation, so to say, from the realm of ideas. An idea is not a thought, it is something entirely different; and ideas precipitate themselves into thought.

Mr. B. Keightley: But I think you can certainly have thought that is not expressed in words.

Dr. Williams: I don't think you can. The moment ideas are precipitated into thought, then you can speak. We fail to distinguish between the realm of feeling and emotion and thought. Feeling and emotion is only one of the sources. They are really identical. Feeling is only one of the sources of ideas which are precipitated into thought.

Mr. Hall: Dr. Williams takes entirely a different idea of what thought is from what I think the rest of us would take it.

Mr. Kingsland: You classify thought in a different way.

Mr. B. Keightley: [To H.P.B.] When you are thinking out an article, do you think it out in words?

H.P.B.: Never.

Dr. Williams: If you don't think in words, where do the words come from?

Mr. B. Keightley: They come afterwards.

Dr. Williams: From what do they come?

Mr. B. Keightley: For instance, Madame Blavatsky writes an elaborate article like one she has been writing now. Well, I know from the way in which that article was written, the draft of that article, the outline of it, the distinct sequence of the ideas and so on must have existed in her mind — not in words, before she put pen to paper.

Dr. Williams: Oh, of course. I understand there exist in memory the materials.

Mr. B. Keightley: No, no. The plan, the idea of the article — how it was to be put, what facts were to be brought in — but not if you asked her to write down on paper the plan on which she was going to write her article.

Mr. Kingsland: Dr. Williams wants to draw a distinction between an idea and a thought.

Dr. Williams: I have something else, that was simply this — there is a time in the evolution of thought when things become manifested to consciousness; now what exists prior to that? That was the point I was after all the while. Prior to anything taking form in human consciousness, can we predicate anything of it at all?

H.P.B.: Well, let us say I am a carpenter, and I want to build or construct something — well, let us say a cabinet — how do I do it unless I am told to do so and so? If I am left to my own resources, I begin thinking it will be so and so. But this thought is not created in my brain; it is that I have put myself *en rapport* with a certain current which makes my thought draw from that privation of the thing which I am going to do in the Astral Light. Now, do I express it so that you understand it?

Mr. Kingsland: Supposing a person finishes his argument. You know in a moment what you are going to say. You know exactly what it is, though you take five minutes to answer it, you thought it in five seconds.

Dr. Williams: Thought is instantaneous. You have got to go through what takes time when it precipitates itself, so to say, in the realm of space and time. Then the movements of the mouth take the time.

Mr. Kingsland: But surely you knew in a moment what answer you were going to give.

H.P.B.: Dr. Williams, believe me, perhaps I will say a very great absurdity, and perhaps not. As I understand the thing, it seems to me that thought is a perfect sponge, and that it imbibes into itself from the Astral Light. And the more the capacity of this sponge to imbibe, to absorb ideas that are in the Astral Light, the more you will have ideas. Now, persons who are dull, it is because their brains are not sponge-like as that of others. They are very hard sponges through which it passes with great difficulty. But our thoughts — we call them our own, it is only the form into which you put them that is our own — but the beginning, the origin of that thought, has existed from all eternity. It must be somewhere either in this or on the plane of divine ideation. We cannot invent anything that was not or is not.

Mr. Kingsland: It is just that your brain has managed to catch it.

H.P.B.: A man who is very intelligent and a man who is very stupid, it is simply the capacity of his physical brain; and he is capable to start his ideas. I am speaking now occultly.

Dr. Williams: What then would be your definition of a thought?

H.P.B.: You must ask me something easier. I am not a speaker, I cannot give it to you in good language. I see it and understand it, but I cannot express it.

Miss Kenealy: Thought is a faculty of the higher brain and speech is a faculty of the lower brain, to a great extent automatic and mechanical.

H.P.B.: Yes, but there is something beyond that. It is the definition on the physical plane. But you must go beyond.

Mr. B. Keightley: You get to this question: what is the power in speech which makes it convey ideas? Because it actually exists. I know in reading other languages, and you might see it in English. It often happens to me in reading German. If I am reading German, particularly out-of-the-way books, I come across a word I have never seen before. It is not a compound of any words that I know, yet in reading that I shall get an accurate idea of the word. I have often tested it by hunting it up and found I have got from the word itself...

Miss Kenealy: A sort of correspondence.

Mr. Kingsland: It is the word standing in the context.

H.P.B.: Tell me another thing. How is it that a person of average intelligence, or very intelligent, who will be able to speak and write and all that, comes to an illness, there comes something — well, physiological reasons, and the brain is so plugged up that it is impossible — it cannot evolute a single idea, the person can neither think nor write nor express anything. That shows there is something, that there is a physiological reason which shuts up the avenues through which all the ideas from the Astral Light pass. Is it so or not? I ask these ladies who have been studying physiology.

Mr. B. Keightley: Everyone feels sometimes that one's brain is packed with cotton wool, and there is not an idea of any kind in it.

Dr. Williams: I remember several years ago an article of mine was criticized by a scientific materialist, and he said it made him feel as though ants were crawling through his brain. It must have been congested through his effort to understand it.

Mr. Hall: Don't you think when a person sees a word which he does not know, and yet gets a clear idea of it, that it is because he is in a certain way in a magnetic rapport?

H.P.B.: With the man who wrote, or what?

Mr. Hall: With the ideas of the man who wrote it; and that he gets it from the Astral Light.

H.P.B.: But as Mr. Kingsland says just now, it is perhaps because of what precedes and follows. The general sense of the sentence makes one guess at the word.

Miss Kenealy: Is there not a direct correspondence between thought and words? I think there is.

Mr. B. Keightley: Between thought and sound. Not necessarily between thought and words, as there is an element of the arbitrary in words.

H.P.B.: You see, this is why I say that human testimony is such an unreliable thing. For instance, we are talking and there are two persons in the room. A person may be saying to me something. In 99 cases out of a 100 that person will be saying to me one thing and I will understand it in my own way. And though perhaps I will understand the thing and remember, yet there will be something that will not represent in my brain that which that person said. That is why it is impossible to go and repeat what another said to you, because you will not repeat the very words, which you do not retain in the memory; but you repeat simply the suggestions of your own thought, with variations.

Dr. Williams: Some individuals remember words and repeat them verbatim. They used to do that in the ages past much more than they do now, the necessity for that having passed away. We remember now the first principles which underlie communications, and we may use different words in expressing those principles, but yet we do correctly convey the principles which were communicated to us. I think it has grown out of the necessities of the times, of the changed way in which we acquire knowledge and communicate it. But I think the test of every human mind, the test of truth, must come back to a knowledge of its own constitution. I do not say any other possible test for the truth to the individual mind, except a greater or less degree of knowledge of its own constitution. And this very subject of thought and mind seems to me goes right back to the very root of it all. If we listen to beautiful music or if we look at a beautiful picture, we may not have a thought about them; and yet we are thrilled, and that is all emotional. That is pure feeling. And so I think it is very often we mistake a thrill of feeling for a thought, or a series of thoughts. So I would make that distinction between feeling and thought and between ideas and thought. The moment anything comes into thought, the mind having coordinated the material out of which that comes into thought, then it takes form; and then it is capable of speech. And therefore, when we think anything, we can express it in speech.

21 FEBRUARY 1889

Mr. B. Keightley: First are some additional questions on some points that we just touched upon last time. Stanza 3, Sloka 2: "The vibration sweeps along," etc. [Reads from *The Secret Doctrine*, vol. 1, p. 63.] The first question is: How are we to understand the expression that the vibration touches the whole universe and also the germ? For does not the germ mean the germ of the universe not yet called into existence?

H.P.B.: Now, will you put me this very long speech in very short sentences, for I don't understand what you mean here. Maybe I have misunderstood you far more than you have misunderstood me.

Mr. B. Keightley: Not having put the question, I cannot say.

H.P.B.: Whoever has put the question, let him rise and explain.

Mr. Kingsland: I think the question has reference to the explanation with reference to the germ, that the universe has not yet come into existence, because the germ being only the germ in the primordial triangle…

H.P.B.: Then what do you mean when you say the unmanifested universe? Is not the universe eternal?

Mr. Kingsland: We do not use the term here — unmanifested universe.

H.P.B.: Do you say manifested? No.

Mr. Kingsland: We do not use either.

H.P.B.: If you do not use either, it means unmanifested universe, for here both are purely abstract terms. The universe does not mean the Cosmos or world of forms, but the formless space, the future vehicle of the universe which will be manifested. Otherwise how could we speak, as we do, of the unmanifested universe? The same for the germ. The germ is eternal and must be so if matter — or rather the undifferentiated atoms of future matter — are said to be indestructible and eternal. That germ therefore is one with space, as infinite as it is indestructible, and as eternal as abstract space itself. Now do you understand? The same again for the word vibration. Who can imagine that the term is meant here for a real audible sound? Why, it is figurative.

Mr. Kingsland: Yes, but is it not figurative in the same sense that the emanation from the first triangle is figurative?

H.P.B.: Not at all. It is figurative; but speaking of the universe, how can I say anything else? Shall I say, "the space in which will be the universe"?

Mr. Kingsland: Does not the vibration correspond to the point, the unmanifested Logos?

H.P.B.: It does. But it is from darkness, which means here the "beyond," beyond the first Logos, even. That is what it means.

Mr. Harbottle: Is it the ray from the eternal Logos that is the vibration?

H.P.B.: No, no, no. Read the thing again and it will make them understand.

Mr. B. Keightley: The first Sloka was this. [Reads again from *The Secret Doctrine*, Stanza 3, Sloka 2.]

H.P.B.: Well, all this is figurative.

Mr. Kingsland: And the whole Sloka refers to the period before there is any manifestation whatever.

H.P.B.: Most assuredly. It refers to the abstract things, to the potentiality of that which will be. Space is eternal, as is repeated many times in *The Secret Doctrine*. Space is something that will be whether there is a manifested universe or an unmanifested universe. This space is synonymous with the universe. It is synonymous with the "waters of space," with everything, with eternal darkness and with Parabrahm, so to say.

Mr. Kingsland: Then this vibration is before even differentiation begins.

H.P.B.: There I am just telling you. You read this second question.

Mr. B. Keightley: Question 2. Is not the germ here, the point in the circle, the first Logos?

H.P.B.: Precisely, and the central point being everywhere, the circumference of the circle is nowhere. This means that all such expressions are simply figures of speech. I think this proves it.

Mr. B. Keightley: Is that all you have?

Mr. Harbottle: I think one sometimes does not quite see how apparently fresh terms are to be referred back to the old ones; but I think that explains it.

Mr. Kingsland: It seems to be jumping back a little bit. Whereas we began to be catching on to differentiation, now we seem to go back.

Mr. Harbottle: The first Stanza is negative and the second positive, in a sense. Almost the whole of the first Stanza says: "There was not this, there was not that, nor the other. It is simply a description of the nothingness or the all"; whereas with the second Stanza we begin at once with that which precedes differentiation, the first movements as it were.

Mr. B. Keightley: Speaking of that which *will be* positive, in fact.

Mr. Harbottle: Is not it rather that?

H.P.B.: Most assuredly. Perfectly so, just so, that is what I have been saying.

Mr. Harbottle: But it really refers to the same points.

Mr. B. Keightley: Then the third Sloka: "Darkness radiates light."[1] Question 3. Is this equivalent to the first Logos becoming the second Logos?

H.P.B.: Now, you see this question, if you only look back over the transactions, has been answered more than once. Darkness as a general rule refers only to the unknown totality, the absoluteness. It is all a question of analogy and comparisons. Contrasted with eternal darkness, the first Logos is light certainly; contrasted with the second, or manifested, Logos, the first is darkness and the second is light. All depends upon where you locate that or another power, on what plane and so on. Now, is this clear?

Mr. B. Keightley: Yes, and I am very glad the question has been asked because it has brought a general explanation.

H.P.B.: If I were to answer from every standpoint, it would not be two but 22 volumes. How is it possible to answer more than in general terms?

Mr. B. Keightley: Question 4. The phrase is: "Darkness radiates light, and light drops one solitary ray into the waters." Why is light

---

[1] *The Secret Doctrine*, vol. 1, p. 64.

represented as dropping one ray? How is this one ray represented in connection with the triangle?

H.P.B.: Because howsoever many powers may appear to us on this plane, brought back to their first, original principles they will all be resolved into unity. We say seven prismatic colours, don't we, but they proceed all from the one white ray and they will be drawn back into this ray, and it is this one solitary ray which expands into the seven rays on the plane of illusion. It is represented in connection with the triangle, because the triangle is the first geometrical figure on the third dimensional plane; and we cannot come and give figures which can only be represented on planes of which we have no conception or idea. Therefore we are obliged to take that which has a certain aspect here on this plane. It is stated in Pythagoras, as also in the oldest Stanzas, that the ray which Pythagoras called the Monad descended from no place, *Aloka*,[2] like a falling star through the planes of non-being into the first world of being, and gave birth to number 1. Then, descending to the right following an oblique direction, it gives birth to number 2. Then, turning at a right angle, it begets number 3, and from thence re-ascends at an oblique angle (do I make use of the right expression?) to number 1 back again; from whence it disappears once more into the realm of non-being. These are the words, I do not know how to translate better — that is to say, it starts, it shoots, then having passed through innumerable worlds of non-being and formless worlds, where no form can exist, it proceeds and creates the point first. Then it proceeds to the right in an oblique direction and creates number 2. And having created number 2 it returns and creates number 3, and thence returns to number 1, and from this it disappears into non-being again.

Mr. B. Keightley: Where does the right angle occur?

Mr. Harbottle: Is there a right angle? It is an equilateral triangle.

Mr. Kingsland: It is an acute angle.

H.P.B.: What do you call, if you please, a horizontal like that [drawing with pencil on a sheet] when it arrives here [indicating], is it not a right angle? I meant that obliquely. I had in my mind a different thing.

Mr. Gardner: It would be 45 degrees.

---

[2] **Aloka** (*Sanskrit,* "no place") — the region of non-entity, beyond the reach of life and matter.

H.P.B.: [Describes the angle meant with a pencil on paper.]

Mr. B. Keightley: The point really to get at is this: in the conception of it, are the sides of the triangle imagined as being equal, so that it is a perfectly symmetrical triangle?

H.P.B.: It is a triangle just as Pythagoras gives it.

Mr. B. Keightley: It is rather an important point, because you know that the right angled triangle is a very important figure in geometrical science, and Pythagoras was the discoverer of that very wonderful proposition.

H.P.B.: Of the hypotenuse, but that is not this. Then we will please put horizontal instead of right.

Mr. Hall: But horizontal what? You cannot have an imaginary horizontal.

H.P.B.: In this I cannot follow you. I am no pundit in geometry, mathematics, or anything like that.

Mr. Kingsland: It is a line at right angles to the radius, starting from the point.

Mr. Hall: Is it an equilateral triangle?

Mr. Kingsland: Yes.

Mr. B. Keightley: The moment you think of a point and the line descending from it, you have an imaginary horizontal right angle to the first line.

Mr. Hall: Then this ray first of all descends.

Mr. B. Keightley: Not vertically.

H.P.B.: First of all it descends vertically. It shoots like a falling star, as is said, and then it goes in the oblique direction; and then it goes in the horizontal direction, and then it returns like that, obliquely, as he says, and rises again.

Mr. Hall: I understand that.

H.P.B.: That is just what Pythagoras gives in the old books, for Pythagoras studied in India and he was called the Yavanacharya.[1] All the books are full of the traditions of the Greek teacher, because he was a teacher in many things for them also and he learned with the

---

[1] **Yavanacharya** (*Sanskrit*, "Ionian Teacher") — the name of Pythagoras in India, where he studied esoteric sciences.

Brahmins, with the initiated, and he taught the uninitiated a good deal. Everyone says it was Pythagoras. Many traditions speak of him as going again into the country and the west and teaching this, that, and the other. I have been reading many things. He is called the Yavanacharya, the Greek teacher.

Mr. Kingsland: Then do you say when this one ray forms a triangle that it has begun to differentiate?

H.P.B.: Most assuredly. The triangle is the first differentiation, of the one ray. Certainly, it is always the same ray, and from this ray come the seven rays; and the seven may be as the one that started from the unknown to the known, and then produced the triangle.

Mr. Kingsland: After it has got to the apex and formed a triangle, do you say it has begun to differentiate?

H.P.B.: Then it begins to differentiate.

Mr. Kingsland: Then the one solitary ray here is simply equivalent to the point.

Mr. Hall: I want to put one question. You say: "all the planes of non-being"; how can there be planes of non-being?

H.P.B.: There are, but it is too long to explain it now. There are planes of non-being. I understand your objection perfectly, but it is so.

Mr. B. Keightley: Then again in a sense there is something (of course quite in a different sense from what we use the word here), something you can call differentiated, though not as we know the term.

H.P.B.: I understand that is the whole question. It is not "differentiated," but yet there are planes. To us, the lowest appear differentiated, but there, it is just that which is non-being to us, which is being and matter to others. It is all analogies. We cannot come and reach with our finite intellect that which is pure, undifferentiated first principle. It is perfectly impossible, not only on this plane, but on the 77th plane.

Mr. Hall: Then you can say in an instance of this kind, you never can reach any plane where there would not be a higher.

H.P.B.: I can assure you, you won't. You must get disembodied first, and then you must be again embodied 77 million times. I would like to know, how can something finite understand that which is infinite? It is all human speculation, my dear sir, let there be the highest intellect in the world, the highest initiated Adept. It is as Masters said: that the highest Dhyan-Chohans of the solar system can have no conception of what is in the higher systems — in those still higher than our solar system. It is a perfect impossibility, because, however high they may be (we may call them personal gods and far more than personal gods), still they are finite. They are not the unity — the Absolute. And the time will come when they have to dissolve, in whatever manner they may do so, whether cremated or buried, I don't know, but there will be a time when the end comes for them.

Mr. Hall: Then, is there a finite point you might call, in a sense, the absolute finite point of the journey of all?

Mr. B. Keightley: Final point? You see, you cannot bring in any way whatever the Absolute in connection with the finite.

H.P.B.: It makes me despair that most of them must go beyond, they must touch, they must hear, they must sense, and in a way conceive it with one of their five physical senses, otherwise very few will understand. It is, my dear sir, the effect of your education from your childhood. All of you are brought up in a kind of material atmosphere, and you must have everything put before you so that it speaks to one of your senses, otherwise you cannot understand it. Even the God you believe in, you make something finite, you make him feel anger, you make him feel goodness, you make him smell sweet, and you make this, that, and the other of him and all kinds of things, just as though this God was a gigantic man and nothing more.

Mr. Hall: I mean this: when at the end of the Manvantara for the whole universe, so to speak, when everything gets reabsorbed into the Absolute, then when Maha-Pralaya[1] is over, and a fresh Maha-Manvantara[2] begins, might you not say in a sense there was, if I may use the term, a special point?

---

[1] **Maha-Pralaya** (*Sanskrit*, "great dissolution") — the opposite of Maha-Manvantara, the Night following the Day of Brahma. It is the great rest and sleep of all nature after a period of active manifestation; orthodox Christians would refer to it as the "Destruction of the World."

[2] **Maha-Manvantara** (*Sanskrit*, "great age of a Manu") — the period of universal activity. Manvantara implying here simply a period of activity, as opposed to Pralaya, or rest — without reference to the length of the cycle.

H.P.B.: But all this depends on which Maha-Pralaya you speak of. Is it that which refers to this little speck of dirt which we call our planetary chain, or is it the Maha-Pralaya of the whole universe?

Mr. Hall: Of the whole universe.

H.P.B.: What do we know of it? Why, in comparison with the Hindus, nothing. They just put 15 zeroes to show it.

Mr. B. Keightley: How can you answer the question? How can you ask it?

Mr. Kingsland: Have you read this last pamphlet on Parabrahm?[3]

Mr. Hall: No.

Mr. Kingsland: You would not ask it if you had. Read that and then you have the question answered. It is all there.

Mr. B. Keightley: Yes, it is all there.

H.P.B.: Let us hold to that which we can conceive. Don't let us go beyond the limits, not only of the universe, but the Cosmos; and let us hold to our solar system. And that is more than we can understand or conceive of in all our lives. As everything is "as below, so above," and as this is the first axiom in the occult sciences, therefore you can draw your analogies as much as the power of every man will allow him. That is all the advice I can give you. Some may go far beyond this, others cannot go as far as that. Everyone can conceive, but let us hold to this solar system, and it will be enough for the time being. Otherwise, we will go wool-gathering, and nothing will come out of it.

Mr. Kingsland: After this last pamphlet, I really think we ought to draw a line at this particular subject.

H.P.B.: Because the first thing will be that some of you gentlemen will have brain fever, and then I shall have the misery of seeing some of you shut up in a lunatic asylum. I can assure you it is so, and this thing can happen.

Mr. B. Keightley: I will give Hall a prescription. If he wants to understand the meaning of his own question, I will ask him to sit down for half an hour and write the figure one, and then go on for half an hour making zeroes after it. When he has done that I will ask him

---

[3] See Amaravella [Edouard Coulomb], "Parabrahm," *Theosophical Siftings*, vol. 1 (1888–1889).

to state in words the figures he has written down, and when he has done it, I will tell him that is the first and second Maha-Manvantara he is talking about.

Mr. Hall: But in theory would not there be…

H.P.B.: Oh, theory! There you are.

Mr. Harbottle: Take analogies, not theory.

Mr. B. Keightley: Sloka 4. [Reads from *The Secret Doctrine*, vol. 1, p. 66.] Question 5: "Is the 'Radiant Essence' the same as the Luminous Egg? What is the root that grows in the Ocean of Life"?

H.P.B.: You see, this is again the same thing. You don't make the slightest allowance for the metaphorical mode of expression. You are all the same, if you please. There must be a certain solidarity. What one says, another will say. I don't make any distinction whatever there, so you are answerable one for the other. Of course the Radiant Essence is the same as the radiant or Golden Egg of Brahma. "The Root that grows in the Ocean of Life" is the potentiality that transforms into objective differentiation, like the universal, subjective, ubiquitous, undifferentiated germ, or the eternal potency of abstract nature. Now, is it so? Is it plain? And the "Ocean of Life" is the "One Life," "Paramatma"[1] when the transcendental supreme and secondless soul is meant. "Jivatma" when we speak of the physical and animal, or rather, differentiation of Nature's soul — expressions all found in the Vedantin philosophy. Now try to remember, Paramatma and Jivatma are the same identically, and even the soul of a man and of an animal, a Nephesh, is just the same; but there is a distinction. One is the supreme subjective soul of the secondless, and the other is already in the manifested universe. Jivatma, that is to say, is the life that gives being to the atom, and the molecule, and the man, and everything in creation — plant, mineral, and so on.

Mr. Harbottle: And the other is the potentiality; potency and potentiality express the difference.

Mr. B. Keightley: Then you say in the commentary, speaking about the Radiant Essence: "from an astronomical point of view," etc. [Reads from *The Secret Doctrine*, vol. 1, p. 67, b.] Question 6. "Is the Radiant

---

[1] **Paramatma** (*Sanskrit*, "Supreme Spirit") — the Supreme Soul of the Universe.

Essence, Milky Way, or World-Stuff,[2] resolvable into stars or atoms, or is it non-atomic?"

H.P.B.: In its precosmic state, of course, the Radiant Essence is non-atomic, if by atoms you mean molecules or compound units. For where have you seen a real atom that you could show me? An atom is simply a mathematical point with regard to matter. It is what we call in occultism a mathematical point.

Mr. B. Keightley: It has position, it has location.

H.P.B.: It has location, certainly, but not a location as you understand it, because a real atom cannot be on this plane.

Mr. B. Keightley: That I understand.

H.P.B.: Then how can you ask? Just when you go on to this plane, you must go outside time and space.

Mr. Kingsland: An atom cannot, but a molecule can.

H.P.B.: What do you chemists call an atom?

Mr. Kingsland: This ought to be "resolvable into stars or molecules," not "into atoms." Now if you read it in that sense it will be all right.

Mr. B. Keightley: Then: "is it resolvable into stars or molecules, or is it non-molecular?"

H.P.B.: Most assuredly, because this world-stuff from one plane to another goes and forms everything that you see, all the stars and all the worlds, and so on.

Mr. Kingsland: Then when may it be said to be sufficiently differentiated to call it molecular?

H.P.B.: Molecular, as you call it, is only simply on this our globe. It is not even on the other globes of our planetary chain, it does not exist in the same way. The others are already on another plane.

Mr. Kingsland: Is not the ether, for instance, molecular?

H.P.B.: I don't know. It may be molecular; yes, in its lower or lowest strata, then it may be. But the ether of science, that science suspects, is the grossest manifestation of Akasha. When it penetrates something, or forms something, it may be molecular, because it takes

---

[2] **World-stuff** — Primordial Matter in its first form, the Radiant Essence, the eternal substance, out of which worlds are formed.

on the shape of it. Now, remember that ether is in every blessed thing that you can think of; there is not a thing in the universe where ether is not. Therefore we say it takes a shape, but not outside of the gross matter, which is also that ether, only crystallized. What are we, what is matter, but crystallized ether? This is what matter is.

Mr. Kingsland: Then the ether is on its way to a lower differentiation, on its way from Akasha, and it will become ether in this Manvantara or a future Manvantara — what we now know as the physical atoms.

H.P.B.: Most assuredly that is so, but not in this Manvantara.

Mr. B. Keightley: I don't know if I am right, but the difference as I understand it between atom and molecule, strictly speaking, is this: that a molecule must be composed of several atoms. The idea it conveys to one is that.

Mr. Harbottle: It need not, there are also non-atomic molecules.

Mr. Kingsland: That is only a chemical term.

Mr. B. Keightley: And an atom is only one.

H.P.B.: May I tell you a thing and try to impress it upon you? You take a molecule, and fancy to yourselves that this molecule is an independent being *per se*. The seventh principle of every molecule will be the atom of which you speak. But you cannot catch it in your scales or your retorts or your chemical combinations. Now do you understand what we mean by atom? The atom is the seventh principle of every molecule, the finest, the smallest that you can find in this world. Why, what is one of the names of Brahma? It is "atom." He is called atom, and at the same time that he is an atom, he is the whole.

Mr. Gardner: Is it Atma?

Mr. Kingsland: Now you are saying it in a purely metaphysical sense. It is very important it should be distinguished from the way in which chemists use it.

H.P.B.: But you are all taking your ideas and the correctness of your language from how the chemists use it. I am the biggest ignoramus in the world in regard to chemistry. Why should I go and stuff my head with the speculations of today, when tomorrow I may have to throw them off, and take up some other speculations? You have not come to that point that there is one single thing you can feel perfectly sure of, that it is there, and that the truth will remain. It is an axiom that the truth, or the axiom of today, is the error of tomorrow.

Mr. B. Keightley: I think it would be a good thing if you can give us — not from our standpoint, but from the occult standpoint — the definition of atom and molecule, simply that we may understand.

H.P.B.: Look here, to do such a thing as that you have to make a glossary and dictionary of occult terms. For instance, such a glossary as we have now, trying to give some correct conception of words which the Orientalists use without knowing what they mean; and therefore enlarge the ideas, giving them more definitions, more meanings, and trying to do something for the better and clearer comprehension of the people. But if we began now to use the terms from the occult standpoint, none of you would understand a word, because you have not got a conception of the thing itself. You have to study first the science and just penetrate yourself with all these things that do really exist on the occult side of Nature, before you can understand those terms. What is the use? Now give one question please, and let me try to see if I can answer you, so that I may see whether you understand it or not. What is it that you want?

Mr. B. Keightley: We want to know about this atom.

H.P.B.: I am quite ready.

Mr. Kingsland: If the atom is such an abstract metaphysical conception of a single metaphysical point, how is it that we can speak of molecules as being composed of atoms?

H.P.B.: I never said that. A molecule, one of these that you speak of, is composed of an enormous quantity of other molecules that you cannot see, and each one is composed of as great a number again and the atom is — that which you call atom, I don't know in what sense, is some fiction of your imagination. But what we call an atom is simply the seventh principle of the molecule, as of everything else — of the smallest molecule you can find.

Mr. Kingsland: On this plane, take one of the metals, take iron. There is such a thing as the smallest molecule of iron, that is to say, a thing which cannot be divided without losing its molecular properties.

H.P.B.: What does it become, and why do you call iron an element? Why do you cheat the public and call it an element?

Mr. Kingsland: What does it become?

H.P.B.: If it loses its molecular property and becomes something else, what is that something else?

Mr. Kingsland: I suppose…

H.P.B.: But science must not suppose. I ask science.

Mr. Kingsland: No, no, we are talking occultly, we are trying to get at what occultism teaches.

H.P.B.: When it becomes non-molecular, it becomes resolved into one of its principles, of which you know nothing. There is not the smallest speck in this world, which has not got its seven principles. Mind you, what for us is the smallest atom on the plane of reality is something very objective indeed.

Mr. B. Keightley: You see, the scientific idea of atom or molecule, particularly of a molecule (because the idea of atom is very vague), has not got anything to do with bulk, whether it is visible under a microscope or not. Their definition is this: if you break up a molecule of iron, it will no longer show the properties on the physical plane that we know have characterized it. It enters a certain chemical combination in a particular way.

H.P.B.: Certain, certain and certain, that is all.

Mr. Harbottle: Because they do not know.

H.P.B.: Then why should they go and dogmatize? We say it is the principles; let us say the astral body.

Mr. B. Keightley: I am not speaking of what happens beyond.

H.P.B.: The chemists will not see the astral body of that which is not molecular.

Mr. B. Keightley: The chemical idea of the thing is entirely — and we understand it to be entirely — limited to this point. They do not know what happens to the thing afterwards, and that is what I am trying to get some idea of, what occultism says about it, because there science simply folds her hands and says, "I don't know."

Mr. Harbottle: Isn't it just as much a death of the molecule of iron as the losing of the physical body is called death on the physical plane? The remaining principles being there all the same, but minus the body. So the molecule is the earthly principle.

Mr. B. Keightley: Iron is not itself properly and occultly an element at all. It does not deserve the name.

Mr. Harbottle: It is an element in one sense. It is not an element in the sense in which we speak of the four or seven elements. It is an element in the sense in which Crookes uses it. It is an element in the scientific sense — formed of the protyle or the undifferentiated matter. In that sense it is an element because it has certain definite properties.

H.P.B.: It is the elemental principle; therefore it is that they do not go beyond that. If you told me at once that they analyse or break up any molecule of iron and that it becomes two other things, that you could call elements. I would say: very well then, we have only to give a name, and then you will have something to speak about. But if they come and tell me it becomes nothing, why, go to bed!

Mr. B. Keightley: So far, science has not succeeded in breaking up the molecule of iron.

H.P.B.: Then if it has not succeeded, why then does it speak about it? They don't do so, and they speak of what could be done.

Mr. B. Keightley: Crookes says there is a probability that some day or another they will succeed.

H.P.B.: Then we will talk of it. So far they have not done it, and why should we talk about it?

Mr. Kingsland: Occultism says it is possible to do it; we want to know what will become of it when it is done?

H.P.B.: It won't be one principle; it will be several principles. It passes from the plane of objectivity to the plane of subjectivity.

Mr. Harbottle: The molecule is the final production in the differentiation of matter, and if you can destroy that said molecule, in the sense in which the scientists would use that phrase, you are simply going back into the undifferentiation.

H.P.B.: Take the smallest grain of sand and try to break it up and see what it is. You cannot get at the first principles and the origin of things on this plane, and Crookes will be looking for it for 30,000 years, and he won't be able to find anything, for it is impossible to see anything of the kind on this plane.

Mr. Harbottle: It cannot be done on this plane. You must be on another plane before you can do it. What Crookes has done with certain other metals is a very different thing. He has simply found there that people have been mistaken in thinking they were homogeneous. That is a very different thing.

Mr. B. Keightley: No, no! His theory — whether it is true or not I have no means of judging — goes a great deal further than that. He says that what are called elements — iron and so on, oxygen, hydrogen and so on — are, if I may use the phrase, points of stable equilibrium in the differentiation of protyle. He gives that curved picture, and he shows how all these elements representing different stages of more or less stable equilibrium succeeding each other in density or in some property come one after the other. Then the question is, what idea is it proper to attach to these points, which go at present in chemistry by the name of elements, looking at them in Crookes' sense? That is to say they are not elemental bodies, but they represent these points of stable equilibrium, certain stages in the evolution of matter on this plane.

H.P.B.: I am not able to coin a word.

Mr. Harbottle: You said something to us about the three first gases the other day, some little time ago, which may bear upon it. There is something in *The Secret Doctrine* about it.

Mr. B. Keightley: We want to agree upon some word we can apply to these things that at present are called elements.

H.P.B.: Shall we call it Anu?[1] That means atom, but it is the name of Brahma.

Mr. B. Keightley: What I want is to name these bodies which exist on this physical plane which possess these characteristics.

Mr. Harbottle: If you call them chemical elements, that answers the purpose.

H.P.B.: I think so; what name can we give? People will say we have a jumble.

Mr. Harbottle: If we say chemical elements, we know perfectly well we don't mean fire, water, earth and air.

Mr. B. Keightley: As long as it is said that the term chemical elements is not used with any idea that they are elemental bodies, but

---

[1] **Anu** (*Sanskrit*, "atom") — a title of Brahma, who is said to be an atom just as is the infinite universe. A hint at the pantheistic nature of the god.

simply these stages of evolution, according to Crookes' view. We can adopt that phrase.

H.P.B.: They are the false noses of the molecule.

Mr. B. Keightley: That is rather an idea, that.

Mr. Harbottle: You could not exactly call them the false noses of the elements.

H.P.B.: Well it is not a mask, it is a false nose.

Mr. B. Keightley: The whole position is that we don't know what they are.

Mr. Hall: They are considered apparent, anyway, by chemists.

Mr. Harbottle: I think the phrase best for them is, "chemical elements."

Mr. B. Keightley: Have you got any more about the radiant essence, or did you read it all?

H.P.B.: Yes, I read it all. It is number 7 already we are at.

Mr. B. Keightley: You refer here, speaking about the World-stuff and the primordial matter, to the Hindu allegory of the "Churning of the Ocean of Space." Question 7. Can you give us an idea of how the analogies of "churning the ocean," "the cow of plenty," and "the war in heaven" are related to each other and to the cosmogonic process?

H.P.B.: Now fancy only this: I have got to give a thing which begins at non-being and ends at the end of the Maha-Pralaya, and I have got to give it in one of the séances at the Blavatsky Lodge in five minutes. How is it possible to put such a question as that? If you gave me one-twentieth part of the first question, I may be able to do it. In the first place, do you know what the "churning of the ocean" means with the Hindus?

Mr. B. Keightley: I know the story, the allegory.

H.P.B.: But what does it mean in reality? It simply means an allegorical representation of the unseen and the unknown primeval intelligences, the atoms of our occult science, fashioning and differentiating the shoreless ocean of the radiant essence. It means that it is the atoms which are churning the ocean, and that they are differentiating the matter. It is simply an allegorical representation.

Mr. B. Keightley: It refers also to a process you mention later on, of the vortical movements.

H.P.B.: Most assuredly; but this is one of the details. I speak of the general aspect of the thing. This is the allegorical representation of that period. Now to give the analogies between the "churning" and "war in heaven" is rather difficult. This war began at the first vibration of Manvantaric dawn and will end at the blast of the last trumpet. That is to say, the "war in heaven" is going on eternally. Theologians may have taken one period and made of it all kinds of things, *e.g.*, the fall of man — the picture that is given in the Revelation, which has entirely another meaning in reality — but this war in heaven is going on eternally.

Mr. Harbottle: As long as there is differentiation, there must be war.

H.P.B.: You cannot say otherwise. It is just as light and darkness fighting and trying each to overcome the other. Differentiation means contrast, and contrasts will be always fighting.

Mr. Harbottle: But there are various stages of the war in heaven, referred to under different names.

H.P.B.: Most assuredly, there is the astronomical and the physical, and the war in heaven, when the first Manvantara begins in general; then for everyone every time there is a war in heaven. There is a war in heaven of the fourteen Manus who are supposed to be the presiding genii[1] of our Manvantaric plane, the Seed Manus and the Root Manus. The war in heaven means that there is a struggle and an adjustment, because everything tends to harmonize and equilibrate; everything must equilibrate before it can assume any kind of shape. The elements of which each one of us is composed are always fighting, one crowding out the other; and we change every moment, just as some of your men of science say. Or as one says when he is sick: "I am not anymore the man I was; I am quite a different man." It is quite true. We change every seven years of our lives, sometimes becoming worse than we were before.

Mr. Harbottle: Then there really does not seem to be much analogy between that churning and the other, because that is a special process.

---

[1] **Genii** (*Latin*) — a name for Æons, or angels, with the Gnostics. The names of their hierarchies and classes are simply legion.

H.P.B.: It refers to the churning by the Gods, when the Nagas[2] came and some of them stole of the Amrita,[3] and there was war between Gods and Asuras,[4] and the Gods were worsted. This refers to the first portion, to the extension of the universe and the differentiation of primordial, primeval matter.

Mr. Hall: Even literally, "churning" means differentiation.

H.P.B.: Oh, my dear Hall, you are a pundit! But churning means also something else. There are seven symbolical meanings to everything, not one. This is only cosmogonically speaking, that is what it refers

[2] **Naga** (*Sanskrit*, "serpent") — the name in the Indian Pantheon of the Serpent or Dragon Spirits, and of the inhabitants of *Patala* (hell). But Patala means the *antipodes* and was the name given to America by the ancients, who knew and visited that continent before Europe had ever heard of it. In Esotericism, however, this is a nickname for the "wise men" or Adepts in China and Tibet; the "Dragons" are regarded as the titulary deities of the world and of various spots on the earth, and the word is explained as meaning Adepts, yogis, and saints. The term has simply reference to their great knowledge and wisdom. The Naga is ever a wise man, endowed with extraordinary magic powers, in South and Central America as in India, in Chaldea as also in ancient Egypt. In China, the "worship" of the Nagas was widespread. The Nagas are regarded by the Celestials as the tutelary Spirits or gods of the five regions or the four points of the compass and the centre, as the guardians of the five lakes and four oceans. This, traced to its origin and translated esoterically, means that the five continents and their five Root Races have always been under the guardianship of "terrestrial deities," *i.e.*, Wise Adepts. The tradition that Nagas washed Gautama Buddha at his birth, protected him and guarded the relics of his body when dead, points again to the Nagas being only wise men, Arhats, and no monsters or Dragons.

[3] **Amrita** (*Sanskrit*, "immortal") — the ambrosial drink or food of the gods; the food giving immortality. The elixir of life churned out of the ocean of milk in the Puranic allegory. An old Vedic term applied to the sacred Soma juice in the Temple Mysteries.

[4] **Asuras** (*Sanskrit*, "breath") — exoterically, elementals and evil gods, considered maleficent; demons and no-gods. But esoterically — the reverse. For in the most ancient portions of the *Rig Veda*, the term is used for the Supreme Spirit, and therefore the Asuras are spiritual and divine. It is only in the last book of the *Rig Veda*, its latest part, and in the *Atharva Veda*, and the *Brahmanas*, that the epithet, which had been given to Agni, the greatest Vedic Deity, to Indra and Varuna, has come to signify the opposite of gods. *Asu* means breath, and it is with his breath that Prajapati (Brahma) creates the Asuras. When ritualism and dogma got the better of the Wisdom Religion, the initial letter *a* was adopted as a negative prefix, and the term ended by signifying "not a god," and Sura only a deity. But in the Vedas, the Suras have ever been connected with *Surya*, the Sun, and regarded as *inferior* deities, devas.

to, but there are others, too. You can remember in Revelation that there is a thing in the 12th or the 8th chapter when the woman comes.

Mr. B. Keightley: Yes, and Saint Michael and the dragon.

H.P.B.: This I do not want to deal with now. Ask as many questions as you like.

Mr. B. Keightley: Question 8. In what sense can numbers be called entities?

H.P.B.: When there is no intelligence, when they are meant for digits, then certainly they are nothing but symbols, signs to express an idea. They must be intelligent entities. Then what is your idea of asking this? What did you think about it?

Mr. B. Keightley: I don't know who put the question, really.

H.P.B.: Whose question was that?

Mr. Coulomb:[1] Mine. I wanted to know what was the meaning of numbers.

H.P.B.: Why don't you look at the fingers of your hand? You would see that you had five on one hand and five on the other.

Mr. Coulomb: But they are not intelligent.

[Laughter.]

H.P.B.: You do lose your time in making useless questions.

Mr. B. Keightley: Those are all the written questions.

Mr. Hall: I should like to know how you vivify numbers.

H.P.B.: I do not vivify them at all. That is how I vivify them.

Mr. Hall: How do you attract the intelligence into them?

H.P.B.: Ask another time, early in the morning. No doubt there are many things you would like to know.

Mr. Hall: That can be done.

H.P.B.: How they do like to ask questions that are positively — well, they begin nowhere and end nowhere!

Mr. Harbottle: I fancy Mr. Hall wants to know wherein lies the occult value of numbers.

---

[1] **Edouard Coulomb** — a French Theosophist who wrote under the pen name Amaravella. Should not be confused with Emma and Alexis Coulomb, who took money from Christian missionaries to fabricate evidence for an accusatory report against H.P.B. by the Society for Psychical Research.

H.P.B.: Have patience, and you may learn it.

Mr. Hall: I did not ask so much as that.

Mr. Harbottle: But you expressed your question in that direction. That is a very interesting question.

H.P.B.: You had better go and begin by the ABC of the question, and just ask the first questions, and I will answer you. Don't come and ask me right in the middle of a thing. You must ask me in order, and I am perfectly ready to answer you.

Mr. Harbottle: Are all numbers that we have or can get all to be reduced to their various relations to the first seven rays? They all do fit in, don't they, in some way?

H.P.B.: All, yes, all; because the seven are seven principles, but the first one counts for ten. So it is with the Sephiroth; if you take the seven lower Sephiroth and the three higher, it makes ten. That is the perfect number.

Mr. Harbottle: So that all those combinations, all possible combinations, will belong to one or other of the rays.

H.P.B.: Surely, the white ray, and then after that, its gradations come and form the first one. You take the prism; in what order do you have the colours, do you remember? The colours are given. So it begins and you can see how it is.

Mr. Kingsland: Why is the radiant essence here spoken of as seven inside and seven outside?

H.P.B.: Because it has seven principles on the plane of manifestation and seven principles on the plane of non-manifestation. Can I say to you anything better? What cross-examiners you are.

Mr. Kingsland: Not cross!

H.P.B.: No, *cross-examiners.*

Mr. B. Keightley: There you get back to the planes of non-being.

H.P.B.: I can assure you if you only took the trouble to read the things and immediately form a conception in your head, it would bring you to the correspondences and analogies, and you would understand it without putting any of these questions; because, as I say, it is an axiom and a rule you must not depart from: as below so it is above, as above so it is below. Only put it on another plane and it comes to the same thing.

Mr. B. Keightley: To my mind this idea has become absolutely plain, that what we refer to as non-being and non-manifestation is to be understood as only referring to our intelligence and our intellect and to us. It is very evident you cannot speak of and you don't refer in *The Secret Doctrine* to *absolute* non-being and *absolute* non-manifestation at all.

H.P.B.: I refer to absolute non-being from the standpoint of our finite and relative intellects. This is what I do, but not at all what it would be, because that which is for us absoluteness, perhaps if you go on the plane higher, it will be something relative for those on the plane above.

Mr. B. Keightley: And if you go more above, it will become something more relative. In fact, with our intellects we are in too great a hurry to get to the Absolute and so draw a line.

H.P.B.: You are all in too much of a hurry, and if you go on splitting hairs your brains will become like a homogeneous jelly. It is a very dangerous thing, this. Try to go one after the other and not miss any of the rungs of the ladder, or else it will lead you into some very extraordinary places.

Mr. Kingsland: I was wondering how far that would apply to the molecules that we were just discussing.

H.P.B.: It applies to the molecules just the same. The lowest one will apply to that plane where the molecules are seen and tested by your chemists.

Mr. Kingsland: But the seven outside would not refer only to this plane of matter.

H.P.B.: It does, and the seven inside. Those that are beyond are beyond. We might just as well say 49, or multiply the seven *ad infinitum*. It is simply said to cover the ground, and so there are seven outside and seven inside — seven outside, that is to say, those that go down below; and seven inside, those we are not concerned with, because we would not understand much, because we do not know anything about them. But it does not at all limit the thing to 14. [After a pause.] Well, everyone waits and nobody speaks.

Mr. Johnston: I did not clearly understand what was meant by the war in heaven. Can there be something in a place of bliss which can amount to war?

H.P.B.: War in heaven means simply in space. If you talk of heaven from the Christians standpoint, of course, it will be heaven and the golden harp.

Mr. Harbottle: Or if you take even the Latin *caelum.*[1]

Mr. Hall: Or take the original vehicle — it means space.

Mr. B. Keightley: It is only in England, particularly in the churches, that the idea of heaven as a place of bliss exists. The word itself has no such meaning attached to it.

H.P.B.: Why, the Most High in heaven means simply the sun. It has meant it before *Christianity*, and it meant it after *Christianity*. For four or five centuries they had no higher idea of God, I can assure you, than the sun. Let them come and say now that it was a symbol and a visible sign and so on. I say that they had no higher conception. I do not mean the initiates, I mean the people — the *hoi polloi*[2] — the masses. There is no fitter symbol in the world than the sun; the sun gives life and radiance and everything, light and being and health, and it is the Most High in heaven.

Mr. Johnston: I thought it referred to the Christian conception.

H.P.B.: After that the sky, which is the Dyaus,[3] the Sanskrit Dyaus, became the God, and this God was as the Law-Giver. The Son and the sun in the heavens became the Father in heaven, while "Heaven" became the abode of the Father, and he was humanized or anthropomorphized.

Mr. Johnston: I see now in what sense it is used.

Mr. B. Keightley: You will find all about the war in heaven in *The Secret Doctrine*, second volume.

H.P.B.: You will see what it is, because it has great reference to the evolution of mankind, of the intelligence of mankind, when man sprang from the animal — not from an animal, I mean not from one of the Darwinian ape-ancestors, but simply from an instinctive mass

---

[1] **Caelum** — heaven.

[2] **Hoi polloi** (*Greek*) — the masses.

[3] **Dyaus** (*Sanskrit*, "heaven") — the Vedic God of the Sky; the unrevealed Deity, or that which reveals Itself only as light and the bright day — metaphorically.

of matter — and when he became endowed with intellect. Then you will see the meaning of the war in heaven, when it is said that the angels fought, or in other words, they incarnated in humanity.

Mr. Harbottle: Now you have a special aspect of it, one of the many.

H.P.B.: Yes, the metaphysical aspect, one of the seven. There is the astronomical aspect and all kinds of aspects. Why is it, if you please, that they give in the churches bread and wine? Why is it that you have the Communion of bread and wine? Simply because it was an offering to the sun and to the earth. The earth was supposed to be, metaphorically speaking, the Bride or the wife of the sun and the sun fecundated the earth, and there was the wine and the bread. It is one of the oldest pagan ceremonials and festivals, which finally came to be adopted by the theologians in the church. It was a purely pagan festival. It was in one place called the mysteries of Proserpine,[1] and in another place called by another name and so on. And then it came and landed in the church, and became a sacrament. There is the sun, there is the earth, there is humanity — the humanity which is not sun but son, which is the third. And there they made all these ceremonials and these mysteries.[2] I am going to give in *Lucifer* the roots of ritualism

---

[1] **Proserpine** or **Persephone** — in Roman and Greek mythology, the daughter of Zeus who was abducted by Pluto (Hades), the god of the underworld, and made his wife and queen, but allowed her to leave the underworld for six months each year, from the beginning of Spring to the end of Summer. Therefore, in certain contexts, Proserpine stands for *post-mortem* Karma, which is said to regulate the separation of the lower from the higher principles: the *Soul*, as *Nephesh*, the breath of animal life, which remains for a time in Kama-loka, from the higher compound *Ego*, which goes into the state of Devachan, or bliss.

[2] **Mysteries** — celebrations of initiation and observances, generally kept secret from the profane and uninitiated, in which the origin of things, the nature of the human spirit, its relation to the body, and the method of its purification and restoration to higher life were taught by dramatic representation and other methods. Physical science, medicine, the laws of music, and divination were all taught in the same manner. The Sacred Mysteries were enacted in the ancient Temples by the initiated Hierophants for the benefit and instruction of the candidates. The most solemn and occult Mysteries were certainly those which were performed in Egypt by "the band of secret-keepers." As Plato and many other sages of antiquity affirm, the Mysteries were highly religious, moral and beneficent as a school of ethics. In short, the Mysteries were, in every country, a series of dramatic performances, in which the mysteries of cosmogony and nature, in general, were personified by the priests and neophytes, who enacted the part of various gods and goddesses, repeating supposed scenes (allegories) from their ▸

and modern masonry, on church ritualism and modern masonry, and you will read it all in the next *Lucifer*. I begin a series of articles.

Mr. Gardner: Do you mean the sun represented it?

H.P.B.: No, I don't mean that at all. The sun represented the father and the moon the mother. And after that humanity represented the Son and the wine and the bread were productions of the earth and were made sacred, if you please, in those solar ceremonies. They were offered to all the solar gods, to Bacchus[3] and to Apollo[4] and to everyone; "this is my flesh and this is my blood," and so it is. Perhaps I hurt the feelings of some Christians here. Which of you is a Christian? I think you are all blue infidels, as far as I can see, and nobody is hurt much. Speak, any of you who feel hurt in their Christian feelings.

Mr. Hall: No, there is no Peter here.

H.P.B.: Because you ask me and I am obliged to tell you what I know. If there was a clergyman, here perhaps I would abstain. No, I don't think I would, because he has no business to come here if he does not want to hear things not to his advantage.

Mr. Gardner: There is a question I should like to ask you. You referred to it in the second volume of *The Secret Doctrine*, on the Pyramids.

H.P.B.: The Pyramid again has something to do with the Son.

---

respective lives. These were explained in their hidden meaning to the candidates for initiation, and incorporated into philosophical doctrines.

[3] **Bacchus** (*Greek*) — exoterically and superficially the god of wine and the vintage, and of licentiousness and joy; but the esoteric meaning of this personification is more abstruse and philosophical. He is the Osiris of Egypt, and his life and significance belong to the same group as the other solar deities, all "sin-bearing," killed and resurrected; *e.g.*, as Dionysus or Atys of Phrygia (Adonis, or the Syrian Tammuz), as Ausonius, Baldur, etc. All these were put to death, mourned for, and restored to life. Bacchus is murdered, and his mother collects the fragments of his lacerated body as Isis does those of Osiris, and so on. Dionysus Iacchus, torn to shreds by the Titans, Osiris, Krishna, all descended into Hades (hell) and returned again. Astronomically, they all represent the Sun; psychically they are all emblems of the ever-resurrecting Soul (the Ego in its reincarnation); spiritually, all the innocent scape-goats, atoning for the sins of mortals, their own earthly envelopes, and in truth, the poeticized image of Divine Man, the form of clay informed by its God.

[4] **Apollo** (*Greek*) — the Greek God of the Sun and light, truth and prophecy, healing and diseases, poetry and music, and more.

Mr. Gardner: You say man is represented by 113, numerical value. Do you mean that is the Hebrew of the word man?

H.P.B.: Yes, in the Kabbalah, it is. It is Kabbalistically the value of the Hebrew characters.

Mr. B. Keightley: According to Mr. Ralston Skinner.

Mr. Harbottle: But 113 adds up to 5; and the five-pointed star represents man always.

H.P.B.: It represents man by the letters, because the Hebrew word means man; if you take every letter and if you take the corresponding number and if you put these numbers together, it gives you 113.

Mr. Gardner: The numerical value of the Hebrew letters.

H.P.B.: Certainly, of the Hebrew letters. It does not mean at all the Sanskrit letters. I never said it did. Every system has got its own calculation. In Hebrew it is quite a different thing. If you take all the signs of the Zodiac and if you put them together and sum up the numbers, every sign of the Zodiac will give you a name of the twelve sons of Jacob.[1]

Mr. Gardner: It is man in Hebrew. It is not man in English.

H.P.B.: No, but the English language has not invented the language of the Kabbalah. It takes the property of other persons and then sets itself up as very high.

Mr. Gardner: And then I fancy there is a misprint here. You say 113 over 2. It has got 133 over 2.[2]

H.P.B.: Maybe there is a misprint. I am not answerable for that.

Mr. Keightley: I think it is in a quotation from Ralston Skinner.

H.P.B.: Ralston Skinner is a Mason and an extraordinary Kabbalist.

Mr. B. Keightley: It is a mistake reproduced from a mistake of his.

H.P.B.: Just as I have taken it, so it is. If I had paid attention to it, I would not have done it.

Mr. Gardner: Then you take from the top of the great step to the ceiling of the Great Pyramid of Giza.

H.P.B.: These you can all find from Smyth.[3] Ralston Skinner has elaborated it, but yet Ralston Skinner is perfectly mistaken in this,

---

[1] See Genesis 35:23–26.
[2] *The Secret Doctrine*, vol. 2, p. 466.
[3] **Charles Piazzi Smyth** (1819–1900) — an Italian-born British astronomer.

because he speaks of things as though really such a thing as the temple of Solomon ever existed, or the ark of Noah, and so on. Why, it never existed in those measurements.

Mr. Gardner: And that coffer in the King's Chamber[4] has never been removed.

H.P.B.: I saw it there a few years ago. It is one with the floor as far as I could see. I am not sure, though.

Mr. Gardner: And do you know whether that is anything occult, that niche in the Queen's Chamber?[5]

H.P.B.: Everything has got its significance and everything relates to mysteries, to the mysteries of initiation. It was the great temple of the official initiation.

Mr. B. Keightley: Smyth's opinions are completely knocked on the head. They are not correct because of Petrie,[6] who was rather a pyramidalist before he went out there, spent months most carefully verifying all Piazzi Smyth's measures, and he knocked them on the head by proving all the measurements are wrong.

H.P.B.: But Ralston Skinner does not take Smyth, and I have taken him out of it. For the last three years I have been in correspondence with him, and I said take care. It is so and so. I gave him the correspondences as it was in the Chaldean and as it was really in the Indian teaching, and he took my suggestions and he found three or four mistakes. And I have got any quantity of his manuscripts in which he gives his ideas; but he is not sure of his facts, and he is carried on by an idea. Now he has changed his ideas in the new book that he wants me to write an introductory chapter to.

Mr. B. Keightley: You see, all these fellows are very apt to get crazy after a fixed idea.

---

[4] **King's Chamber** — one of the three main chambers inside the Great Pyramid of Giza in Egypt. It is located closer to the centre of the pyramid. The King's Chamber has a red granite sarcophagus, but it was found empty when it was first opened by archaeologists.

[5] **Queen's Chamber** — one of the three main chambers inside the Great Pyramid of Giza in Egypt. It is situated below the King's Chamber, and it is smaller in size. It contains a similar but smaller granite sarcophagus.

[6] **Flinders Petrie** (1853–1942) — a British Egyptologist.

H.P.B.: You cannot learn anything unless you are perfectly impartial and have not got a hobby. Otherwise you are sure to get mixed up and you will come and not bring your speculations to fit your facts but your facts to fit your speculations.

Mr. Gardner: Isn't it true that some of these men were seeking to find out other chambers in it, and one of them held up a light in such a position that no breeze from outside could touch it, and yet the candle flickered and he came to the conclusion that there must be other chambers. And shortly afterwards a message came from the Khedive[1] to tell him to discontinue his researches.

H.P.B.: The Khedive is a donkey in these sciences; he is not even a Mason. He is a very nice young man.

Mr. Gardner: He might have the idea of doing so.

H.P.B.: The idea of what?

Mr. Gardner: These ideas coming at the right moment.

H.P.B.: I knew him when he ran about without trousers, a child of five years. I know him perfectly well. He was a very nice child, and he is become a very nice young man. But I can assure you he has nothing mystical in him.

Mr. Hall: I think Mr. Gardner means he might have been put up to do it by somebody.

H.P.B.: His father, yes. His father with all his great vices, with all his immorality, Ismail Pasha,[2] was a man who had a streak of mysticism in him. He always had the Bedouins[3] with him and the monks, and he knew some men who were extremely learned. But this one knows nothing; he was brought up by English and French nurses in the harem of his several mothers.

Mr. Kingsland: And he is not even a Mason.

Mr. B. Keightley: It is an interesting question to know this, whether these secret places, these chambers, do exist underneath the Pyramids.

H.P.B.: Certainly they do.

---

[1] **Mohamed Tewfik Pasha** (1852–1892) — the viceroy (Khedive) of Egypt and Sudan.

[2] **Ismail Pasha** (1830–1895) — the Khedive of Egypt and ruler of Sudan; the father of Tewfik Pasha.

[3] **Bedouins** (*Arabic*, "desert-dwellers") — nomadic Arab tribes.

Mr. B. Keightley: They must be protected in some way.

H.P.B.: They are protected in all kinds of ways. They are protected by the greediness of the Arabs and they are protected in many, many ways. And the thing is that unless they go and turn off the Nile at a certain spot, they will never get to them. They have to turn off the Nile and get to the iron door that exists to the present day, and has not been opened for 2,000 years. There is a Mason that knew it, a Mason named [...], who was the Venerable of the Lodge.

Mr. Gardner: At the Cairo Lodge.

H.P.B.: One of your Lodges, your real true blue Masonic Lodges.

Mr. Hall: How could an iron door last 2,000 years?

H.P.B.: Why could not an iron door last not only 2,000 years, but 20,000 years?

Mr. Gardner: Would not it rust?

H.P.B.: It would not rust. Perhaps there are several incredulous; I say it exists.

Mr. B. Keightley: His point is any iron door however thick would have rusted through in a thousand years.

H.P.B.: It would not be destroyed.

Mr. B. Keightley: Yes, eaten through, perfectly porous.

H.P.B.: My dear sir, I tell you it is protected.[4] It is not a door of such iron as you would take from a smith. Just as they do with their mummies, if mummies have lasted, then I suppose an iron door could.

Mr. B. Keightley: What is interesting is that the others are so infernally greedy; if they knew anything about it they would go for the things that are there.

H.P.B.: They do not know it. I spoke to Maspero;[5] he is a Fellow of the Theosophical Society. I passed the whole day with him in Cairo.

---

[4] The great American seer, Edgar Cayce (1877–1945), said that under the paws of the Sphinx was a secret entrance leading to the "Hall of Records" of Atlantis. The research of various scientists using radar and seismological methods at the end of the 20th century demonstrated that there are indeed a cavity and tunnels. However, further research was suddenly forbidden, and now the Egyptian government officially prohibits conducting any kind of research around the Sphinx. Obviously, this prohibition is not accidental.

[5] **Gaston Maspero** (1846–1916) — a French Egyptologist.

I asked him about all the papers that he ever found. Maspero is the Director of the Boulaq Museum.[1]

Mr. B. Keightley: Which, by the by, is to be no more at Boulaq.

H.P.B.: He was there, then, and we sat there between the tombs and the old mummies, and he was telling me of some of the things he has discovered. And he said, "never could I give it to the world, because I would lose my situation." Because Marriette Bey[2] tried to do it, and he was not listened to, and the academy said some very disagreeable things about all kinds of secrets that are there. He found a whole room, he told me — and this thing is known, by the by — and this room was full — Maspero discovered it — it was full of all kinds of retorts and alchemical things and those utensils that the alchemists used; and several parchments he found that he has read and deciphered; enough to see that they had all these alchemical secrets. And he found even some powders and things that he feels sure was the powder to make gold. He found it in this room which exists there to this day. I was going there, only Mrs. Oakley[3] could not stop.

Mr. Gardner: That is near Luxor.[4]

Mr. B. Keightley: What is he going to do with all his collection when he dies?

H.P.B.: He is a very young man about 38 or so. He is no more than 38 years of age.

Mr. Gardner: What post does he hold over there?

H.P.B.: Director of the Museum at Boulaq in Cairo. He is one of the most learned of the Egyptologists.

---

[1] **Boulaq Museum** — the former name of the Egyptian Museum, which, from 1858 to 1891, was located in Boulaq (a district of Cairo).

[2] **Auguste Mariette** (1821–1881) — a French archaeologist and Egyptologist.

[3] **Isabel Cooper-Oakley** (1854–1914) — an English Theosophist and the author of *The Comte de Saint-Germain: The Secret of Kings.*

[4] **Luxor** ("Light of Divine Fire") — an ancient city in Egypt, formerly known as Thebes. In Thebes was the Theban Sanctuary, also known as the Brotherhood of Luxor. This Brotherhood was to provide knowledge, as well as to develop and expand people's consciousness, with emphasis on the mind and the human intellect, in order to help humanity take a step towards the heart.

28 FEBRUARY 1889

Mr. B. Keightley: Stanza 3 continued, Sloka 5. "The root remains," etc. [Reads from *The Secret Doctrine*, vol. 1, p. 68.] What is meant by saying that these remain?

H.P.B.: I beg your pardon. Those are Mr. Kingsland's. Well, let them be first. It is Mr. Kingsland who asks this, and I am going to answer him first. All right, let them be. Now, "that these remain." It means that whatever is, and whatever the plurality of the manifestation is, is all one element, one, that is what it means. It is always summed up in one.

Mr. B. Keightley: It really means they are different aspects of the one element.

H.P.B.: Of the one, certainly.

Mr. Kingsland: It would appear from that that it means almost that they remain without differentiation.

H.P.B.: Oh, no, don't pitch into the style if you can't say anything better. You see, I tried to translate as well as I could, you know, as close to the original as possible.

Mr. B. Keightley: Then speaking in the Commentary of Curds you say: "The curds are the first differentiation," etc. [Reads from *The Secret Doctrine*, vol. 1, p. 69.] Are we to suppose that the Milky Way is composed of matter in a state of differentiation other than that with which we are acquainted?

H.P.B.: Most assuredly it is; it is the storehouse of the materials out of which the new stars, planets and all bodies are produced. You cannot have matter in that state on earth here. It is impossible; it is quite a different kind of matter.

Mr. Harbottle: It is protyle.

H.P.B.: Oh, no, it is not protyle. It is less but it is quite different. It is positively a storehouse of all kinds of materials, which when it comes on to the earth, let us say, or into our solar system, it is entirely differentiated. Besides that, the matter that you have beyond the solar system is entirely in a different state of differentiation.

Mr. Kingsland: The matter we see here we see entirely by reflected light. Do we see the Milky Way by the light we make ourselves?

H.P.B.: Most assuredly; you cannot see otherwise; it is impossible, you cannot. When they come and take the measurements of stars, and the distances, and all that, I say it is impossible it should be correct, because you must always allow a certain margin for the effect of optical delusions and so on.

Mr. Gardner: Refraction.

Mr. Kingsland: Then from an astronomical point of view is the Milky Way outside altogether of the stellar system?

H.P.B.: It is really and entirely another state of matter, and matter is, as I say to you, the material out of which everything will be made.

Mr. Harbottle: But outside as regards state, not as regards position?

H.P.B.: No.

Mr. B. Keightley: Because, for instance, they have just been making very wonderful photographs of the nebulas, the great nebula of Andromeda, etc.

Mr. Kingsland: Is that matter in the same state as the Milky Way?

H.P.B.: I could not tell you; I am not learned enough for it. But it is quite a different state of matter altogether.

Mr. Gardner: What about the planets?

H.P.B.: Oh, the planets are a different thing. You cannot find anything in the planets that there is not on earth.

Mr. Kingsland: Then the Milky Way, we may take it, radiates its own light. It is analogous to the state of matter that is in the sun.

H.P.B.: It is the "World-stuff," as I call it. You cannot call it by any other name. I say to you again I am not learned enough to tell you the difference. I do think there is a difference between the nebulas and the real Milky Way which you see, just as though it was like a highway of dust, like a film.

Mr. Kingsland: In other words, the nebulas are more differentiated.

Mr. Harbottle: But some of the nebulas are resolvable.

Mr. B. Keightley: But they are clusters of stars; they are not true nebulas at all.

Mr. Harbottle: It has never been proved there is no nebula.

Mr. B. Keightley: The Andromeda.

Mr. Harbottle: In other words, you have not yet succeeded in resolving it.

H.P.B.: Well, yes; but I cannot believe in it. I think if it is not today, tomorrow it will be proven that it has not been resolved or resolvable. It seems to me it is all simple theory — that it turns out something else, as many times we have been mistaken already.

Mr. B. Keightley: Then this matter, "Radiant and Cool"?

H.P.B.: You just forgive it, if you please.

Mr. B. Keightley: As it stood originally, it is "This matter, which, according to the revelation received in the primeval Dhyani-Buddhas,"[1] etc. [Reads.]

H.P.B.: "Radiant" it ought to be, and it is put "radical." They have made of primordial matter something political. They have got politics on the brain! I never put "radical." I put "radiant and cool," I can assure you. I could find the manuscripts and I could show you it is so. It is one of these mistakes of the printers and sub-editors and so on. There is another thing I wish to ask. Why does Mr. Kingsland say this was seen probably by the First Race, and so on?

Mr. B. Keightley: He says — this matter appearing "when seen from the earth," etc. — Mr. Kingsland asks: Would not this be to the perception of the First Race and not to our present physical senses?

H.P.B.: I say no.

Mr. Kingsland: No; that is answered now by the first question.

H.P.B.: Certainly, because we see just in this way.

Mr. B. Keightley: Then Sloka 6. "The root of life," etc. [Reads *The Secret Doctrine*, vol. 1, p. 69.] The first question put is: "What are the various meanings of the term 'fire' on the different planes of Cosmos?"

H.P.B.: Now, you see, there is a question again that they put me! I have to give about the 49 fires on every plane, and there are seven times seven — seven planes. I have got to give this very *easy* explanation, if you please. Now, how is it possible? Hold to something and ask a definite question. Fire is the most mystic of all elements, as the most Divine, and to give even a small percentage of its meanings in their various applications on even one plane, let alone on the different

---

[1] *The Secret Doctrine*, vol. 1, p. 69.

planes of Cosmos, is perfectly impossible. Now, shall I give you on one plane, in the solar system?

Mr. B. Keightley: Please.

H.P.B.: Very well; take, for instance, the solar fire on our plane alone. Fire is the father of light, light the parent of heat and of air, vital air, says the occult book, and the absolute deity can be referred to as darkness, the dark fire. Then the first progeny of Light is truly the first self-conscious God, for what is light but the world-illuminating and life-giving deity? Light is Time, what from an abstraction has become a reality. Now, this is what you could not understand. Do you understand the meaning of it? Light is Time, which Time from an abstraction has become a reality. If there were no light you would not have time.

Mr. B. Keightley: Because you would have no point.

Mr. Harbottle: Darkness is duration.

H.P.B.: And there is no time in duration except in Manvantaras. No one has ever seen real primordial light, the one true light, but what we see is only its broken rays or reflections, which become denser and less luminous as they descend into form and matter. Do you really think with the physicists that it is the sun which is the cause of Light? We say (see *The Secret Doctrine*) that the sun gives nothing from himself, because he has nothing to give. He is a reflection and no more; a bundle of electro-magnetic forces, one of the countless milliards of knots of Fohat. Now, I want you to remember this expression, "knots." Fohat is called the thread of primordial light, the thread of Ariadne,[1] indeed, in this labyrinth of chaotic matter. This thread runs down and down through the seven parent planes and ties itself occasionally on its way into knots. This is how they explain it in the occult books. Every plane being septenary — hence the 49 mystical and physical forces — the big knots form stars and suns and systems, the smaller planets. It is, of course, a metaphor, but the electro-magnetic knot of our sun and its forces are neither tangible nor dimensional, nor yet material or even molecular, as, for instance, common electricity is.

---

[1] **Ariadne** — in Greek mythology, the Daughter of King Minos of Crete who gave to Theseus, a divine hero and the founder of Athens, the thread that helped him escape the Labyrinth.

Now, saying not molecular, I say that which Helmholtz[2] says, but I will just say what we mean by saying electricity is molecular. It is a reflection, as I say the sun is; the sun absorbs, psychicizes, and vampirizes his subject within his system. He gives out nothing *per se*. Now, how unutterably foolish it is to say that the solar fires are being consumed or extinguished. Were it so, would not the sun, while losing its heat and flames, be also losing something of its dimensions or magnitude? Do you think so? Is it possible? Must we think, then, that the sun is at the bottom a kind of round disc, made of some inconsumable asbestos, which, once the pitch around it is consumed, will get extinguished? Why, it would be that. If the solar fires were to go out you would see the sun shrinking or diminishing.

Mr. Kingsland: We need not necessarily suppose that would take place within any observable time.

H.P.B.: I do not know if they say it goes with such rapidity as that. Listen to Sir William Thomson and you will learn what he says. The sun, it is said, does not give out anything, it doesn't take anything; it feeds and works within its own system; it vampirizes from all the planets and from everything that comes within it, and sometimes very likely it is almost impossible that anything should come into the sun from without the solar system. This is what is taught now. I do not give you my ideas; they are very heterodox, they are perfectly unscientific. I show you what the Occult Sciences say. They do not allow that the planets have been formed or ejected out of the sun, as the modern theory goes. They say it was not so, that the sun is not even what they say. There are no fires, there is nothing tangible in it; it is merely a reflection, a reflection of this. It is called a bundle of magneto-electric forces.

Mr. ——: Do not the occultists accept Laplace's theory?[3]

Mr. B. Keightley: That the solar system is originally a nebula, more or less, an enormous spherical mass of very diffuse matter which is revolving round its axis at a very great rate. There are differences, because according to Laplace's theory, you get this globular mass spinning very fast. In consequence of its rotation it breaks up into rings.

---

[2] **Hermann von Helmholtz** (1821–1894) — a German physicist and physician.
[3] **Pierre-Simon Laplace** (1749–1827) — a French mathematician, mechanic, physicist and astronomer.

Gradually, owing to small changes, those rings get condensed and form planets. If they do not form planets they form meteors.

H.P.B.: Do you mean to say he says it is from that Milky Way we have been talking about just now? Then it is the "World-stuff," and it goes into eternal rotation. It begins by suns and after having made the big knots it comes in the smaller ones, and so on.

Mr. B. Keightley: The point of that theory is that all these planets round the sun are formed from these rings; but elsewhere, in *The Secret Doctrine*, you state that before a heavenly body of any kind settles down to sober family life as a planet it is first a comet and goes careering through space. Well, that is quite contrary to Laplace altogether.

H.P.B.: Laplace is not an occultist, but yet there is something very near what you state. I never studied Laplace in my life.

Mr. ——: This is the nucleus of the whole system.

Mr. B. Keightley: No, no, no, that is not Laplace's theory.

Mr. ——: Yes, he thought all those rings were thrown out from the periphery of the mass.

Mr. B. Keightley: No, in consequence of the rapid rotation. There are points of minimum and maximum velocity. These are not shown mathematically. There are certain points at which the rings are unequal. The space between two rings is left void by this process of condensation. Then if there is anything of that kind which disturbs the equilibrium of one of those rings it will gradually break up. But there is no idea of things being thrown off from the sun.

Mr. ——: I do not mean it exactly in that sense; I meant outside.

Mr. Harbottle: May I ask one question which I think bears upon that? Does the sun survive several series of planetary existences? For instance, in *The Secret Doctrine* you say that the present earth is the daughter of the moon.

H.P.B.: Daughter, yes. I know what you want to say. Of course it is. Our Pralaya is quite a different thing, a very different one from the Solar Pralaya, of course.

Mr. Harbottle: Because that, in itself, answers the suggestions that the present planets are thrown off from the sun during the formation of the sun itself, and is itself a contradiction of Laplace's theory.

H.P.B.: I say that Laplace's theory looks like ours, because we say everything comes from the Milky Way, and that it begins when the Manvantaric dawn of the solar system begins, and that it goes on. And they show Fohat running like a thread; and these threads sometimes get entangled in a knot, and the central star, the solar system, begins the little knots, and so on.

Mr. Harbottle: Then the theory must be taken very generally, and certainly not specifically, as applied to our solar system as it at present exists. In that case that would simply mean the sun was, so to say, slightly older than the rest of the planets.

Mr. B. Keightley: It is said elsewhere that all the planets have been comets. I am not sure, but there is a suggestion, and I am not certain how far it is intended to go, that all the planets have been suns before they settled down to planetary life.

H.P.B.: And every planet will become that which the moon has become now. And every time it will become like the moon: it will shoot out its principles and make another planetary chain as ours is. Our earth is very, very young, and such moons as ours there are but we don't see them because they are nearly faded out. This one is already quite old. When they come and tell me that that moon is a bit of the earth, and that it was shot out, I say it is perfect nonsense. "When the day was only two hours old," I think that is what they say. And now they have been making the calculation that to make the day 23 hours instead of 24 would require something like 600,000,000 of years.

Mr. Kingsland: You say the electro-magnetic emanation from the sun is neither molecular nor dimensional.

H.P.B.: I will just explain this here. The sun has but one distinct function. He gives the impulse of life to all that moves and breathes and has its being within its light. It is stated in *The Secret Doctrine* that the sun is the throbbing heart of the system. You remember, each throb is an impulse. Very well, but this heart is invisible: no astronomer will ever see any more than you, I, or anyone else, that which is concealed is that heart. And that which we see and feel are simply the apparent flames and fires, and they are only the nerves that govern the muscles of the solar system. Now, did I express myself well? They are not the muscles, they are the nerves, the impulses. This is a real occult theory.

Mr. Kingsland: But now there must be the material base in the sun.

H.P.B.: There is, but we do not see it. The sun as we see it is simply the reflection. It is simply the reflection of that which exists, a bundle of electro-magnetic forces — whatever it is. You see, they call it the heart, but it is not the heart, the heart is concealed. What we see is simply — well, let us say all the planets and everything are the muscles, and that which we see are the nerves that give the impulse, you understand.

Mr. Harbottle: Actually, we don't see the material core, the centre, but simply, its surroundings, its envelope.

H.P.B.: Just so, the radiance that it throws off. But we can never see the real thing.

Mr. Gardner: And the sun spots?

H.P.B.: That I have explained in *The Secret Doctrine.* Now, for the impulse; I speak of it not as a mechanical impulse, but a purely spiritual one. What I would call nervous impulse, if I make use of the right word.

Mr. B. Keightley: Yes, that is to say, not an impulse thought of as a vibration on the physical plane, of the physical nerve fibre, but that which underlies that in the same way that a sound is different from the vibration.

H.P.B.: Now you ask about the various meanings of the term "fire" in *The Secret Doctrine.* Under this term the occultists comprehend all. Fire is the universal deity and the manifesting God life; fire is ether, and ether is born of motion, and motion is the eternal, direct, invisible fire. Again, light sets in motion and controls all in nature, from that highest primordial ether down to the tiniest molecule in space. Remember this occult axiom: motion is the Alpha and the Omega of that which you call electricity, galvanism, magnetism, sensation, moral or physical thought, and even life on this plane. It is motion which is the Alpha and the Omega of all that, and motion is simply the manifestation of fire, what we call the dark fire. All cosmical phenomena were therefore referred to by the occultists and the Rosicrucians as animated geometry. You will find it always referred to as animated geometry — every cosmic phenomenon, every polar function is only a repetition of primeval polarity. Every motion begets heat, and ether in motion is heat. When it slackens its motion, then cold is generated, for cold is ether in a latent condition. Mind you I give you the Kabbalistic terms and simply translate the things. Within the seven principal states of nature are the three positive and three negative principles synthesized by the primordial light. They are six states. The three negative states are: first, darkness, second, cold, third, vacuum or the nothing. The three positive states are: first, light on our plane, second, heat, third, all nature or everything in nature. Thus fire is the unity of the universe. Pure fire without fuel is Deity at the upper rung. Cosmic fire or that which calls it forth is every body and atom of nature in the manifested nature. Name me one thing which does not contain latent fire in itself, and then you can contradict me. Everything is fire, but fire under various forms.

Mr. Kingsland: In fact, it has as many differentiations as matter.

H.P.B.: Because fire you can never come and analyse as you do with air and water and say that is composed of such and such things. You know, broadly speaking, it is combustion, but fire is the one great mystery of this universe, and it is everything, and this fire is what they call Deity. And I say that the fire worshippers who worship the sun are a thousand times more philosophical than we, for this is the one great symbol that can be understood. I do not say the sun is such a very great unity in the universe, but in our solar system it is the ambassador, the representative of the real creative force or Deity, principle, call it whatever you like; you understand my meaning. Now listen: when we say that fire is the first of the elements, it is only the first in our visible universe. This fire of which we speak, which everyone of us knows under its various forms, and that fire that we all know even on the highest plane of our solar universe, the plane of globe A and G. In one respect fire is only the fourth, for the occultists say, and even the medieval Kabbalists say, that to our human perception and even that of the highest angels or Dhyan-Chohans, the universe, deity, is darkness, and from this darkness the first appearance of Logos is — what do you think? It is not light; it is weight, air, or ether, the first thing that weighs, that cannot be seen, and yet it weighs in its primordial state. Then the second is light, the third, heat, and the fourth, fire. The fire that we know, mind you; I don't speak about the universal fire, that is a different thing. Now, will you please put the questions plainly, because I am rather tired of them. I want really serious questions. I get mad over these questions and I want to put things that I can only put when I am mad.

Mr. B. Keightley: Now that question of weight suggests a thing that would be very interesting. It is said over and over again in the [...] theosophy that the scientific theory of gravity is untrue. Well now what do you mean, what does an occultist mean when he speaks of weight? Does he mean attraction?

H.P.B.: Well I don't know, weight is weight, how can I explain it otherwise?

Mr. Harbottle: Does weight exist without gravity?

H.P.B.: Well it is gravity in the occult sense; it is not gravity as you call it on the Newtonian principle. We can explain it and do simply as attraction and repulsion. This weight is all because it throws out, it goes in circuit and absorbs again and it all proceeds to create all the universe and everything that is below. It always is this weight which you cannot say is above or below or on the right side or the left. This weight is something within but not within as to size, but within as to perception, differentiation and everything.

Mr. Kingsland: It is the same thing as we had previously, the expanding from within, without.

Mr. Harbottle: The real point seems to be that if gravity is simply attraction and repulsion, that it must be the first of the attributes, so to say, of any differentiation whatever. As soon as you have two things, they must be pulverized.

H.P.B.: Surely.

Mr. Harbottle: And therefore they may be pulverized in darkness.

H.P.B.: How can you explain otherwise the comets that go against the law of gravitation, how can you? It has been seen hundreds of times, comets in most cases go with their tails right against gravitation.

Mr. B. Keightley: They go and flap their tails in the face of the sun, in fact.

H.P.B.: It is an insult to the sun and the sun sits quiet.

Mr. ——: I thought those tails were a certain gas.

H.P.B.: Even gases have some weight. I know it from the blood poisoning. Well, what is the fourth question?

Mr. Gardner: I should like to ask about the question of weight with regard to that triangle. You told us…

H.P.B.: This is out of the programme.

Mr. B. Keightley: Number 3, you have practically answered. It is this, what are the meanings of "water" in the same applications?

H.P.B.: Well, water being composed of 1/9 of hydrogen (a very inflammable gas, as we are told, and without which no organic body is found), of 8/9 of oxygen (which we are told produces combustion when too rapidly combined with a body), what is water but one of the forms of primordial fire, in a cold or latent and fluidic form? It is nothing else. This is in reality what water is.

Mr. B. Keightley: It is the cold state.

H.P.B.: The cold and fluidic state of fire. It is the female aspect of fire, as matter is the female aspect of spirit.

Mr. Kingsland: Is there any connection between the numbers?

H.P.B.: Most assuredly. Numbers and colours, everything is connected. This, if you please, is esoteric.

Mr. B. Keightley: Question 4. Are fire and water the same as Kwan-Shai-Yin[1] and Kwan-Yin?[2]

H.P.B.: Reverse the question and ask are Kwan-Shai-Yin and Kwan-Yin the same as fire and water, or rather are the latter the symbols of these, and I will say yes: but what does it mean? The two deities in their primordial manifestation are the Dyadic or dual God, the sexual nature and Prakriti.

Mr. B. Keightley: Then Sloka 7: "Behold O Lanoo,"[3] etc. [Reads from *The Secret Doctrine*, vol. 1, p. 71.] The question is number 5. Will you give us the terms corresponding to the three Logoi amongst the words Oeaohoo,[4] Oeaohoo, the younger, Kwan-Shai-Yin, the Kwan-Yin, father-mother, fire and water, bright space and dark space?

---

[1] **Kwan-Shai-Yin** (*Chinese*) — the male logos of the Northern Buddhists and those of China; the manifested god.

[2] **Kwan-Yin** (*Chinese*) — the female logos; the Mother of Mercy.

[3] **Lanoo** (*Sanskrit*) — a disciple, the same as *chela*.

[4] **Oeaohoo** — the occult name for the "seven-vowelled" ever-present manifestation of the Universal Principle; "Father-Mother of the Gods," or the "Six in One," or the Septenary Root from which all proceeds. In one sense, Oeaohoo is the Rootless Root of All; hence, one with Parabrahman; in another sense, ‹

H.P.B.: No I won't. [Laughter.] Have you not just read it is Oeaohoo, the younger, the three stars? Why did I put the three stars "whom thou knowest now as Kwan-Shai-Yin"? You know it is that, well enough — or shall I give you a series of quadruple stars? If I put three stars it is not that I did not know the things, it is because I cannot give it. What is the end of Sloka 7, Stanza 3 [reads passage from *The Secret Doctrine*, vol. 1, p. 71], the one manifested into the great waters? Think over it and you will understand all that is permitted to you to understand here, is there. Fire is spirit-matter. This water stands for matter. Fire stands for the solid spirit, water for the one manifested element. Fire is heat, water, moisture; you understand the difference between heat and moisture. One is male, the other, female, the creative element here on earth, or the evolutive principles within, or the innermost principles. "Within," we say; all of you illusionists would say above, I just said to you there is no above. I believe the qualificative terms, dark space and bright space, give you the key quite sufficiently. I cannot give you any more. Therefore, there are the stars. I don't know it myself.

Mr. B. Keightley: Question 6. What is the veil which Oeaohoo the younger lifts from East to West?

H.P.B.: The veil of reality. The honest and sincere curtain or act drop-lifted or made to disappear in order to show the spectators the illusion we call stage scenery, actors and all the paraphernalia of the universe, which is a universe of illusion. Is this clear?

Mr. B. Keightley: The veil of Maya, in other words.

H.P.B.: I beg your pardon. It shows us Maya and lifts up and shows us the veil of reality. He makes it disappear, just to show us the illusions that are on the stage. Mr. Smith playing Othello[1] or anything else is a sham; it is only illusion and nothing else. I think this perfectly clear.

Mr. B. Keightley: Question 7. What is the "upper space" and "shore-less sea of fire"?

---

it is a name for the manifested One Life, the eternal living Unity. All depends upon the accent given to these seven vowels, which may be pronounced as one, three, or even seven syllables, by adding an *e* after the final *o*. This mystic name is given out, because without a thorough mastery of the triple pronunciation, it remains forever ineffectual.

[1] **Othello** — a character of William Shakespeare's tragedy of the same name.

H.P.B.: The "upper space" is the space within, as I just said, or the universe as it first appears from its Laya state, a "shoreless" expanse of spirit or "sea of fire."

Mr. B. Keightley: Question 8. Are the "great waters" here the same as those on which "darkness moved?"

H.P.B.: Well, I wish to say one thing, that "darkness moved," you put here in quotes. I don't remember to have put anywhere that darkness moves. I don't know on what darkness can ever move. I don't know what they have been doing. I have heard of a darkness which was upon the face of the deep or the great waters, but even in Chapter 1, Genesis it is distinctly stated, verse 2, that darkness was, and that that which moved upon the face of the waters was not darkness but the Spirit of God. Now see esoterically the meaning of these two verses in Genesis. They mean that in the beginning, when Cosmos was yet without form, and chaos, or the outer space, that of illusion, was still void, darkness alone was. Now if you take Kalahamsa,[2] the dark swan or the swan of eternity (it is interchangeable), and at the first radiation of the dawn the Spirit of God, which means Logos number 1, began to move on the face of the great waters of the deep; therefore, if we want to be correct, and if not clear, let us ask are the great waters the same as the darkness spoken of in *The Secret Doctrine?* I will answer in the affirmative. Kalahamsa reads in a dual manner. Now, exoterically, if you speak about Kalahamsa, I took them to task in *The Secret Doctrine* (and I was perfectly right) for putting such a thing as that, that Kalahamsa was Parabrahm. It is not so, but esoterically it comes to that. Exoterically it is Brahma, which is the swan or the vehicle in which darkness manifests itself to human comprehension, but esoterically it is darkness, itself the ever unknowable absoluteness which becomes the vehicle of Brahma the manifested. For under the illusion of manifestation — that which we see and feel and which comes under our sensuous perception, as we imagine — is simply that which we

---

[2] **Kalahamsa** (*Sanskrit,* "swan in and out of time") — a mystic title given to Brahma (or Parabrahman). It is an ancient symbol of the "First Cause," which had no name in the beginning and was later depicted in thinkers' imaginations as an ever invisible, mysterious Bird that dropped an Egg into Chaos, and this Egg became the Universe. Thus, in becoming the Swan of Eternity at the beginning of each Grand Cycle of Evolution, Brahma lays a Golden Egg; this typifies the great Circle, itself a symbol of the Universe and its spherical bodies.

neither hear, feel, see, taste or touch at all: a gross illusion and nothing else. Now, is this too metaphysical?

Mr. B. Keightley: I follow it.

H.P.B.: But I want the others to follow it. You are here always.

Mme. Tambaco: I think it seems clear.

Mr. B. Keightley: Question 9. In what sense can electricity be called an entity?

H.P.B.: In what sense shall I explain once for all so as not to have the same question repeated over and over again every Thursday? In what sense can I explain it to you? How many times have I explained it, and yet you come back? Electricity in a lamp is one thing. Fohat is the cause of that one spark in its millions of aspects, or the said spark in the lamps is quite another thing. Which do you want me to explain? Fohat is not electricity and electricity is not Fohat. Fohat is the sum total of the universal cosmic; electricity is an entity, because entity is that which is from the Latin root *ent*, "being," of *esse*, "to be" and which exists for us, if not independently, by itself, apart from us. Fohat is an entity, but electricity is a mere relative signification. If taken in the usual scientific sense, Fohat is spoken of as cosmic electricity — as the sun is said to get in one's eyes or face or in one's garden, but surely it is not the sun that gets into one's eyes or face. The sun is an entity, and you would hardly call the effect of one of its beams an entity. Electricity is the molecular principle in the physical universe, and here on earth, because, being generated as it is in every disturbance of molecular equilibrium, it then becomes, so to say, the kama-rupa of the object in which such disturbance takes place. Rub amber and it will give birth to a son whose name is Fohat, if you like it, on the lower plane, because in one sense Fohat means birth or life from an apparently inanimate object. Rub a nettle between your thumb and finger and you will obtain by the grace of Fohat an effect or a son in the shape of boils and blisters on them. That is also Fohat. All is electricity, it is all an electric thing, from the nettle up to the lightning that kills you, it is just the same. It is simply the aspect of that one universal fire, and this one aspect is electricity. It is everything, but in various shapes.

Mr. ——: Do you mean to say there is only one force in Nature?

H.P.B.: In reality there is only one, and on the manifested plane it shows itself in millions and millions of various forms.

Mr. Gardner: Is the electricity in the nettle the same as what we have in the batteries?

H.P.B.: Most assuredly not.

Mr. Kingsland: The electricity that you generate, for instance, in rubbing amber, would you say that was both molecular and dimensional?

H.P.B.: Well, it is molecular, because it is the kama-rupa of the amber that acts; and certainly if it is to produce some distortions of the equilibrium it must produce something, because you cannot produce something in nothing. Mind you, electricity you will call an effect. I say the effect is molecular.

Mr. Kingsland: On the amber?

H.P.B.: Very well; but electricity, what is it? It is the effect of that which is molecular by itself. It is an entity, for electricity is the whole world of atoms in a certain state and under certain conditions.

Mr. Kingsland: Is there, for instance, emanated from the amber, matter in any state of differentiation?

H.P.B.: That which emanates from the amber is that which, unfortunately, your microscope won't see. But it *is* molecular.

Mr. B. Keightley: But it is visible to the appropriate senses.

H.P.B.: Positively. It is estimated that there are some insects that would see it and you would not. If you had, for instance, the white ants that are in India, the most impudent of all creatures — and nothing in the world will make them get out of your way — they immediately will scatter like I don't know what, because they perceive that.

Mr. Gardner: Simply rubbing a piece of amber?

H.P.B.: Or there is a tree in India which you will rub, and if you rub it, they will never approach it.

Mr. Harbottle: If you can describe it as a kama-rupa, that answers the question.

H.P.B.: I cannot explain it in any other way; it is the kama-rupa, the disturbing influence which comes and disturbs the equilibrium. I cannot explain it any better than that.

Mr. Gardner: You mean the astral envelope of the amber?

Mr. B. Keightley: No, no, the fourth principle. Now, question 10. "You say that 'Fohat is cosmic electricity'[1] and the son. Is electricity, or Fohat, then, the same as Oeaohoo the younger, or the third Logos?"

H.P.B.: Electricity is the work of Fohat, but Fohat is not electricity. The throwing in one shape or the other of molecules into new combinations of forms into new correlations or disturbances of the equilibrium, as you call it, in general is the work of Fohat, the emanation of the seven sub-logoi. I advise you not to talk much of the seven-voweled deity. I am sorry I wrote and published it at all, I am very sorry, for there they began to tear it to pieces and speak about it just as though it were a potato. It is the combined active principle, the electric force, life, everything that comes out and emanates from those entities.

Mr. B. Keightley: Question 11. Sloka 8: "Where was the germ," etc. [Reads from *The Secret Doctrine*, vol. 1, p. 77.] The question is: "Is the spirit of the flame that burns in thy lamp our Heavenly Father or Higher Self?"

H.P.B.: It is neither the Heavenly Father nor the Higher Self. "The spirit of the flame" is simply speaking about the real bona fide lamp, and not at all metaphorically. It is neither one thing nor the other. He asks simply, the teacher, "where is the spirit of the flame that burns in thy lamp" — in any lamp, but not of gas, certainly.

Mr. B. Keightley: Now question 12. "Are the elements the bodies of the Dhyan-Chohans?"

H.P.B.: It is a perfectly useless question, because, read the symbolism in *The Secret Doctrine* and you will find the question. I cannot give it to you in talking as well as I have written it. Why don't they read it; why come and ask this?

Mr. B. Keightley: Then Question 13. "Are hydrogen, oxygen, ozone and nitrogen the primordial elements on this plane of matter?"

H.P.B.: They are. On other planes, even volatile ether, I think you call it that — never mind. I want to show that which is the most volatile would appear as the mud at the bottom of the River Thames, or on the bridges. Every plane has its own colours, sounds, dimension of

---

[1] *The Secret Doctrine*, vol. 1, p. 76.

space, etc., etc., quite unknown to us on this plane. And as we have, for instance, the ants, they have quite other perceptions of colour and sounds. Those who are intermediary creatures, a kind of transitional state between two planes, so on the plane above us, there are creatures, no doubt with senses, and faculties known to the inhabitants there, but unknown to us. They will probably play the same part as the ants play here, because the ants come from a lower sphere.

Mr. B. Keightley: Just emerging.

H.P.B.: Yes.

Mr. B. Keightley: That is the last of these questions.

Mr. Kingsland: Does not the perceptive power of the ant — for instance, the way in which it differs from our perceptive powers of colour — simply depend upon conditions, physiological conditions?

H.P.B.: It may be, but the wise people say otherwise. They say they can hear sounds we can certainly never hear; therefore, physiology has nothing to do with it whatever, because they do not hear with the ears as we do.

Mr. B. Keightley: They haven't got any.

Mr. ——: You can scarcely say they hear them, they sense them.

H.P.B.: They have a perception of that which we have not, on whatever plane it may be, whatever thing it may be.

Mr. Kingsland: Then we have a perception of that which they have not.

H.P.B.: Most assuredly, you are higher than they, but I say we will be the ants on the sphere above.

Mr. Kingsland: But how do you use the terms higher and lower in that sense, if they see and hear something that we do not, and we see and hear something that they do not?

H.P.B.: I mean high in general. I do not say in this particular instance. I simply say we are higher in general, that the earth is on a higher plane than the one from which the ants come.

Mr. Kingsland: Are they not on the same plane?

Mr. B. Keightley: I think it simply means earlier and later in the history of the evolution, a later and in one sense more advanced stage of evolution. The ants will pass through a stage, passing through the human stage we are in now, whereas we shall not. In that sense we are higher.

H.P.B.: I think that for you gentlemen who are electricians it is the most interesting thing, occultism, on account of its suggestiveness. It gives you ideas that you can never get from physical science.

Mr. Kingsland: I thought you meant that the ants might have the perception of a higher plane than we have.

H.P.B.: I never said that. I said they had perceptions of sounds which may be perhaps — well, I won't say how many millions, but which are within — which are not at all on our plane, which we could not hear under any circumstances.

Mr. B. Keightley: But I think we might follow up that amber and the idea of electricity as a particular state of matter. It throws a great deal of light on the subject.

Mr. Kingsland: Well, of course there is a molecular disturbance of the amber.

Mr. B. Keightley: That is to say, of the molecules on the physical plane.

Mr. Kingsland: But then, electricity to be manifested must be manifested outside the molecular substance of the amber.

Mr. B. Keightley: That is a point that is rather curious to get at. We imagine we create the electricity by rubbing the molecules of a physical piece of silk against the molecules of a physical piece of amber; that is the way we look at it.

H.P.B.: We simply give the conditions to the electricity, which is latent in it, to come out.

Mr. Kingsland: Is there anything corresponding to an emanation from amber?

H.P.B.: There is.

Mr. Kingsland: Or is it a molecular disturbance causing a molecular disturbance in the aura of the amber?

H.P.B.: No. I say it is latent in amber as it is latent everywhere, and giving it certain conditions, that which is within and which is latent in the amber will get into a fight with the electricity which is outside, and then there will be a disturbance produced. You simply change the conditions.

Mr. Kingsland: Is the electricity intermolecular, and is it mani-fested in the same way that you could have a sponge which is perfectly molecular? Does the amber contain electricity in the same sense?

H.P.B.: I am afraid to answer. I don't understand the question. I cannot answer you. I cannot take it in well.

Mr. Harbottle: It seems if you use the phrase, kama-rupa, that would be the best. I should consider that would be the same thing as saying it was intermolecular.

Mr. B. Keightley: But, you see, you have got your sponge and water — both matter on the same plane — but your electricity and your amber are matter on three different planes apart. That is to say, if you take the physical molecules of your amber as the first or lowest, the molecules of your electricity are on the same plane.

H.P.B.: Certainly, the kama-rupa, the fourth plane, that is what I tried to explain to you: kama-rupa. I am not a scientist, I am not at all an electrician or anything of the kind.

Mr. Kingsland: I thought you were using kama-rupa metaphysically.

H.P.B.: Not at all; perfectly physically.

Mr. B. Keightley: The great difference that I notice in the whole view of physical phenomena taken by occult science as distinguished from physical science is this: that in ordinary physical science we are in the habit of looking for the cause of things that we see. We rub a piece of amber and electricity is produced. The occult science will say by rubbing a piece of amber you produce conditions through which electricity, which exists latent and ready to manifest itself, can manifest itself on your physical plane.

H.P.B.: I find a far greater mistake that you all make in science, and it is the most vital mistake. It is by dividing animate from inanimate things and saying that there is such thing on the earth as a perfectly inanimate object. There is not an atom which is inanimate, not one. It is simply the most vicious kind of expression that I ever heard.

Mr. Kingsland: It is a very sensible distinction on our plane.

Mr. Harbottle: Organic and inorganic.

H.P.B.: But there is nothing inorganic in this world; inorganic from your point of perception, but it is occultly speaking.

Mr. B. Keightley: Let us go into that question. What is the scientific definition or distinction drawn by science between organic and inorganic?

H.P.B.: Occultism would say to you, a dead man is more alive than ever.

Mr. B. Keightley: Please don't suggest to Kingsland.

Mr. Kingsland: Ask Dr. Williams.

Dr. Williams: I think he wants to get Mr. Kingsland's idea of the matter. I suppose he has got some particular motive.

Mr. Kingsland: But it is all pro bono publico.

Dr. Williams: I don't know but what you thought he had some personal idea.

Mr. B. Keightley: I thought he probably had some clear notion in his mind.

Mr. Kingsland: If you carry it down to the lowest forms, one shades into the other.

Mr. B. Keightley: Is there any definition to be given what distinguishes it? What is the characteristic according to modern science?

Mr. Kingsland: What is the characteristic between you and a lump of wood?

Mr. Harbottle: You take the two extremes. Science has to admit there is the possibility of an entity or a substance to which they cannot assign either of the words with confidence. I say entity or substance.

Mr. B. Keightley: The only distinction I have ever heard put forward is this, the distinction of nutrition. Science will generally show — Mr. Williams, will you correct me if I am wrong?

Dr. Williams: That is purely an arbitrary one.

Mr. B. Keightley: But simply, the only criterion that is put forward as really distinguishing organic from inorganic is the function of nutrition.

Dr. Williams: I think the latest scientific views recognize no dividing line anywhere. There is no place where you may draw the line, and so this belongs on one side and that on the other.

Mr. B. Keightley: Even if you go down into the mineral kingdom, because you find in the phenomena of producing crystals you get some which is to all intents and purposes nutrition.

H.P.B.: I should like to know, if there was no nutrition for the inorganic substances, how they could change. The fact of their changing and crumbling down shows to you there is a growth, and that it is perfectly organic, as organic as anything else, only under other conditions. Have you ever thought that on this plane of ours there are seven planes? It is subdivided. This perhaps you have never been taught yet, that even on this plane of physical perception there are seven planes.

Mr. Kingsland: There are seven planes of matter?

H.P.B.: I define it so in the mineral kingdom and in the animal kingdom. There are planes for all. Just as I spoke of the ants, just in the same analogy there are the other things. When they come and speak to me about inanimate things, I say fiddlesticks, there is no such thing as that, it is impossible, because there is not a thing in this world that is perfectly inorganic — I don't say it in the dogmatic sense, I mean inorganic — that is not susceptible to decay and ending. Everything grows and everything changes. Everything that changes is organic; it has the life principle in it, and it has all the potentiality of the higher lives.

Dr. Williams: That certainly seems to me to be the universal idea, that there are various manifestations of life on the physical plane, and the quality of that manifestation depends entirely on the molecular relationship of the matter itself. There is no such thing in any abstract sense, as putting matter in one plane under one condition and in another plane under another condition.

H.P.B.: What is matter? Matter is simply a form of more or less crystallized and objective spirit, that is all, nothing else; and what is spirit? There is neither spirit nor matter there. They are all kinds of aspects of one and the same element in this life, if life is universal. I say there is not a point in the shoreless universe. How can there be such a thing as an inorganic atom or anything. I think Kant[1] says perfectly correctly. He is one of the physiologists I prefer the most, because he is so very fair in his matters, he opens so many doors

---

[1] **Immanuel Kant** (1724–1804) — a German philosopher.

to everything, to the possibilities. There is nothing dogmatic about him. I read very little of him, but the little makes me think he is one of the fairest I know. When he speaks about the distinctions between organic and inorganic, he says, just as we occultists say, that there is no such thing in this world as something inorganic. And you take, if you please, Huxley or any of the big bugs of science, and they will come and talk about the organic and inorganic, just as though they were the fathers of everything and they had created the universe. It is perfectly ridiculous.

Dr. Williams: What would you say was the relationship of fire on the different planes? Could you say anything of the relationship which fire on the lowest plane bears to fire on the highest?

H.P.B.: It is beyond our fine perceptive faculties. There is an unbroken relation, because one proceeds from the other. It is a falling into matter and a forming into density.

Dr. Williams: That is precisely the point I was after, if the one was the inner essential life of the other. If fire on the fourth plane was the inner essential life of fire on the third plane, and so on downwards.

H.P.B.: If you speak on the planetary chain, then it will be the seventh on our plane. That is to say, it will become the Atma. It corresponds to Atma on our plane, and we cannot see Atma, but if you can imagine yourself living on the A and B planets, so it is on the spheres A and Z, then it will become "Pho."

Dr. Williams: I was thinking more especially of the seven planes into which human life was divided.

Mr. Harbottle: Speaking with reference to what was said about electricity being the fourth principle; the kama-rupa of the amber.

Dr. Williams: Yes.

Mr. Harbottle: There one would say the change from planet to planet was a molecular change, probably.

H.P.B.: Then the molecules of the change also on the other planes.

Mr. B. Keightley: There is a great deal of that in Keely's[1] inter-etheric ideas.

H.P.B.: He cannot bring it out altogether, because he is neither an occultist nor an orthodox scientist, and he will keep to his own

---

[1] **John Worrell Keely** (1837–1898) — an American inventor.

prejudices, but otherwise he is a very grand man and discoverer. What do they say of him, Mr. Fullerton,[2] in America?

Mr. Fullerton: There have been difficulties growing out of the constitution of his company, and various things of that kind which led to a suspicion of dishonesty. That is the popular impression.

H.P.B.: He was too sanguine in his expectations. He thought he could just take Parabrahm by the coat-tails and show him to the public. It is a perfect impossibility. I said it from the first, it could not be. I said it always. It was perfectly useless.

Mr. Gardner: He won't stick to one thing.

H.P.B.: He wants to go on too much and too high, and therefore he will have failures always, because if he were to hold only to those few things he has found out, really he would have the greatest success, and he could bring to himself and on his side all the men of science, but he won't do it. He wants to go so much into the metaphysical that although the physicists don't want to confess it, they cannot follow him on to the plane of science. It is impossible, because then they will become Roger Bacons,[3] not Crookeses.

Mr. B. Keightley: He says if you make the proper conditions, you can cause the manifestation of something which lies concealed between the molecules of the most attenuated physical bodies. And then he gets a series of these attenuations with this matter, whatever it is, which is intermolecular. For physical matter is molecular itself, and between its molecules there is again something which is also molecular.

H.P.B.: Ad infinitum.

Mr. B. Keightley: And so you get exactly what we say about the ether; that is four stages up his ladder, and the conditions we produce

---

[2] **Alexander Fullerton** (1841–1913) — the first General Secretary of the American Theosophical Society from 1895 to 1907.

[3] **Roger Bacon** (1214–1292) — a very famous Franciscan monk who lived in England. He was an Alchemist who firmly believed in the existence of the Philosopher's Stone, and was a great mechanician, chemist, physicist and astrologer. In his treatise on the *Admirable Force of Art and Nature,* he gives hints about gunpowder and predicts the use of steam as a propelling power, describing besides the hydraulic press, the diving-bell and the kaleidoscope. He also made a famous brazen head fitted with an acoustic apparatus which gave out oracles.

in the manifestations of ordinary electricity are simply parallel to those he employs for his.

H.P.B.: Unfortunately for us, the physicists will not accept anything of the kind. Otherwise, they have only accepted the possibility that there must be something so attenuated and so invisible to our objective eyes that goes on living after us. Then they would see how very easy it is to conceive of those astral bodies who live in their astral body, and live just as much as we do, and they have all their principles put together and they can travel very easily to the fourth plane and act in this little universe of ours just as easily as we do without any body. And I can assure you it is the most blessed condition in the world, for there you have neither gout nor rheumatism nor anything.

Mr. B. Keightley: Nor clothes, nor breakfast to eat, nor anything.

H.P.B.: And every time that there are mediums, as the spiritualists say, they are really not so. I can assure it is, because there will be Nirmanakayas[1] and then they will know the truth. But here they are a little bit perplexed and they will go into their own habits and so on. It is physical matter which is in their way. It is the easiest thing to understand, this.

Dr. Williams: Has not Sir William Thomson got very near Keely's idea in his "Extra Mundane Corpuscles"?

H.P.B.: Yes, he has read a very great deal of the ancient and Greek classics, but he wants to bring them all to his own ideas, to his own established theories. You see, the trouble with him is he jumps from

---

[1] **Nirmanakaya** (*Sanskrit*, "emanation body") — the state of Masters or Initiates, who have advanced along the path of comprehension of Truth and purified themselves to the extent that they have risen above even the divine illusion of *Devachan*. They have achieved the supreme enlightenment, which enables them to enter the Seventh and the Highest Plane, called *Nirvana*, to experience bliss. However, they voluntarily sacrifice themselves and decline to go to Nirvana because, in this case, they will be forever separated from the Earth and be unable to help humanity. Therefore, such Masters continue to live in the higher Subtle or Astral spheres of the Earth to guide and protect humanity. They maintain all their body-principles, except their physical and lower astral bodies, and they reside in the robe of conscious immortality. Nevertheless, they are able to create those two lower bodies should they need to incarnate themselves among people to carry out specific tasks on the Earth.

one conclusion to another. Today he says the incrustation of the earth begins 15,000,000 ago; after tomorrow he will come and say something else, and laugh at himself. I judge from lectures. I never read yet three consecutive lectures without Sir William Thomson contradicting himself on every point. Is that exact science? I call it exact flapdoodle. It is not exact science at all.

Dr. Williams: It always seems interesting when such a man gets hold of such a simple truth.

H.P.B.: He disfigures it in such a way, and he wriggles it so that he distorts it out of recognition. Crookes is a thousand times more hopeful than he. Crookes is magnificent as a man of science.

Mr. Harbottle: Crookes doesn't really speak out. For the scientists he has to dress up in materialistic language what is to him something very much metaphysical.

Dr. Williams: I have no doubt about that.

Mr. Harbottle: If one reads those lectures of his, especially "The Genesis of the Elements"[2] and others, with a little insight into it and into his own way of thinking, you see that at once.

H.P.B.: I am very sorry we separated without any cause; but you see there is a black cat between us, a black cat on two legs, and I know him. Crookes has been giving ideas that are not quite orthodox about me. He says: "Oh, the old lady is getting old and is falling into her dotage. She used to know something, but now she has given out everything and knows nothing." I am very glad he thinks so, because he would otherwise have bothered me out of my life. I made him ring the two astral bells himself. Just the last time I touched him myself. He had his hand in the glass that stood there and they produced two distinct astral bells, and therefore he knows this thing which he can do also, but he wanted me to give him the key to it. I said: "If you behave yourself, I will," but he did not behave himself, and so he did not get it. And on that he was made to believe...

Mr. Harbottle: That you hadn't got a key?

H.P.B.: That I was a poor medium.

---

[2] See William Crookes, *Genesis of the Elements* (London, 1887).

Mr. B. Keightley: Did you ever see, Dr. Williams, those illustrious Elihu Vedders?[1] Do you remember that frontispiece,[2] that great wall? Does it suggest the idea of the knots of Fohat?

Dr. Williams: Yes; it was not so much a wall as a skein.

Mr. Keightley: It was the quatrains of Omar Khayyam.[3]

H.P.B.: This is an occult thing, about the knots.

Mr. Keightley: The frontispiece is a great skein.

Dr. Williams: I think I could draw it for you. [Draws the "skein."]

H.P.B.: It is something like centripetal and centrifugal action.

Dr. Williams: I daresay the nebulas do assume the same forms, but he has taken that as the author of an opera does. It runs through the poem as the *motif*,[4] so to say.

Mr. B. Keightley: An extraordinary effect it produces, drawn with a beautiful sweep.

Mr. Harbottle: Curiously enough, it is the ordinary Japanese representation, in their rough sketches, of cloudscapes; single lines running into a sort of knot, both in carving and in drawing. I have plenty of their woodcarvings, in which a bank of clouds is given in that way.

H.P.B.: It is the old occult idea, what we called Fohat; they give it another name, and the Parsis[5] give it another name, but he is the knot-tier. When he has made the Laya point, he begins in another place; and all the visible universe is formed like that, and all come dragging from that Milky Way, all this world-stuff dragging out, and beyond the Milky Way they say it is the Father-Mother.

Mr. Kingsland: Does that Milky Way stuff get drawn into our stellar system, that being more differentiated in forming new systems?

---

[1] **Elihu Vedder** (1836–1923) — an American symbolist painter, book illustrator and poet.

[2] See Edward FitzGerald, translator, Elihu Vedder, illustrator, *The Rubaiyat of Omar Khayyam* (Boston: Houghton, Mifflin & Co., 1884).

[3] **Omar Khayyam** (1048–1131) — a Persian philosopher, mathematician, astronomer and poet.

[4] **Motif** (*French*, "pattern") — a recurring theme, subject, or idea in a work of art, literature, music, or design.

[5] **Parsis** or **Parsees** — Zoroaster's followers of Persian descent, now settled in India, who remained true to the religion of their forefathers — the sun- and fire-worship.

H.P.B.: It is the inexhaustible storehouse, and this cannot be exhausted.

Mr. Gardner: The quantity is a constant one?

H.P.B.: Always. There is not a given quantity, but it is inexhaustible, for it has neither beginning nor end.

Mr. B. Keightley: It emerges at one side to Father-Mother.

H.P.B.: All these are words, but if we speak from the physical standpoint, it is everywhere — not above our heads, our globe revolving. We say it is everywhere.

Mr. B. Keightley: Why do we see it as a limited thing running across a particular tract of the sky?

H.P.B.: Because we see that which can be seen; that and the other exists nevertheless. We see that which is more contracted, and the rest we do not see, because it is lost in such immensity that certainly no eye — even of a Dhyan-Chohan, or one of the Salvation Army that has a golden harp and plays — can see; no one.

Dr. Williams: Did I understand you correctly in speaking of the sun and the planets and the moon? At one time you spoke of them all in connection, that the planets had at some time been in the same condition that the sun is now in, and that they would at some time be in the condition that the moon is now in.

Mr. B. Keightley: They pass through the sun stage, then they become comets, then planets, then dead bodies, etc.

Dr. Williams: That would give the idea that the sun itself is approaching the state of the planet, and by and by it would reach the condition that the moon is in, and really lose its heat.

H.P.B.: The sun is not a planet, it is a central star.

Mr. B. Keightley: It is a different stage of things altogether.

Dr. Williams: Then the planets were really not suns in the same sense that our sun, the centre of our solar system, is a sun?

H.P.B.: There were suns, but it is a different kind of suns. This one is a reflection, simply.

Dr. Williams: If you were considering the close of the solar Pralaya might it not be that as it approached the consummation of that period it might be effected in that way?

H.P.B.: Most assuredly, it will. It will begin by getting less and less radiant and giving less and less heat; and it is not that which we see. That will lose fire, but it will be that behind, and these are the flames and the nerves, which is merely a reflection, and they will die out and disappear, because it has no consistency, the sun. It is nonsense to come and speak about the sun in this way; it is perfect fancy, because we see simply a reflection of all kinds of electro-magnetic forces — the real furnace of the solar system, where all the fires are. And these forces are Life, and Light, Heat, Electricity and everything, all the different correlations, that which we give different names to. This is one thing. They are just the same as the one thing of the whole universe is there. This is only in our solar system.

Dr. Williams: They must be evident, certainly.

Mr. B. Keightley: After the next solar Pralaya, that which now is the sun will, if I understand *The Secret Doctrine* correctly, become in a following Manvantara of some kind, a comet.

H.P.B.: Yes, in the following Pralaya, but it will never become a comet during the life of our little planetary chain.

Dr. Williams: The point I was after was that this outbreathing and inbreathing is not sudden, but a gradual process. There is no point between the beginning of the outbreathing and the end of the inbreathing, and therefore the sun might approach to the fullness of its forces and then would begin a gradual decadence of its forces.

H.P.B.: There is a magnificent thing described in the *Vishnu Purana*. It is an exoteric thing, full, of course, of allegories, which on their face show themselves very ridiculous and absurd. But it is full of very philosophical meaning, and this thing — when the Pralaya comes and when the seven rays begin to be absorbed — it is described in the most superb way. I wish somebody would translate it into English verse. Wilson gives it, but he makes the most terrible mistakes, and such that poor Fitzedward Hall,[1] his editor, gives more footnotes than text. "Dr. Wilson's mistakes, but he didn't have the benefits in his time that we have," and this, that, and the other. And certainly being a Reverend he could not do it otherwise. He had always to fight for his Jehovah.

---

[1] **Fitzedward Hall** (1825–1901) — an American Orientalist and philologist.

Dr. Williams: Well, there is, is there not, matter in its elementary state?

H.P.B.: Behind, not in what you see; that is merely a reflection. Well, imagine yourself that this cannot be seen, and you see only the reflection in the looking-glass.

Dr. Williams: In star analysis they get the lines showing — I do not know how many — elements they have succeeded in isolating in the sun, but a certain number.

Mr. B. Keightley: That question was answered by saying it was the effect of the atmosphere of finely divided cosmic dust, which has now been recognized by science as falling gradually to the earth, and which acts upon the light of the sun; that according to occult science the formation of the solar lines takes place in the earth's atmosphere and is not a phenomenon due to the sun at all.

Mr. Harbottle: Would not the same thing apply to every star spectra?

Mr. B. Keightley: Certainly, all round.

Mr. Gardner: But they differ very much.

Mr. B. Keightley: As far as I understand what was said in those letters, they do not say that the emanation, whatever it is, the vibrations proceeding from the sun and the stars are of the same nature, but they say that the phenomena that we take to prove the presence of iron and sodium in the sun are not due to the presence of those substances in the sun, as we know them, but due to the action upon the sun's rays of the atmosphere, of cosmic dust which surrounds the earth. That is the point that is meant.

H.P.B.: Because they say this atmosphere is three miles forming.

Mr. B. Keightley: Three hundred.

H.P.B.: Oh! I imagined it was two or three miles.

Mr. B. Keightley: I tell you how they have got to that. They find the meteorites are at least 200 miles.

H.P.B.: Oh, it is three miles where you can breathe, I think, three miles of breathable air, but not atmospherical. When it approaches it, of course it differentiates and it gives quite different optical illusions. This I remember.

Mr. B. Keightley: They say they do not know quite what the atmosphere is, but it is at least 200 miles, because these meteorites get inflamed. It is very difficult to see where the boundary line really is.

Mr. Harbottle: It depends upon what you mean by atmosphere.

H.P.B.: I thought the atmosphere was what you could breathe. What is the other?

Mr. B. Keightley: All that they say is that these meteorites are observed to take fire at a certain height, at least 200 miles above the surface of the earth, that means to say there is something that produces friction; they rub against something.

H.P.B.: Too much Fohat.

Mr. B. Keightley: That would be another way of explaining the same thing.

Mr. Kingsland: Then it is pure hypothesis that it is the friction of the atmosphere?

Mr. B. Keightley: Purely, but that is the accepted hypothesis at the present moment.

H.P.B.: For today, and on Saturday it will be changed.

Mr. B. Keightley: That one has been held the longest.

7 MARCH 1889

Mr. Harbottle: Stanza 3, Sloka 10. "Father-Mother spin a web," etc. [Reads from *The Secret Doctrine*, vol. 1, p. 83.]

Mr. A. Keightley: Question 1. "You state that Spirit and Matter are the opposite ends of the same web; last Thursday you spoke about such opposites as light and darkness, heat and cold, void and space and fullness of all that exists. In what sense are these three pairs of opposites associated with matter and spirit?"

H.P.B.: I think in that sense everything in the universe is in association with it, with every spiritual matter, because there is always either one or the other that predominates in every subject that you can think of.

Mr. A. Keightley: Then do light, heat, and void correspond with matter, darkness, cold, etc.?

H.P.B.: What is it, which question do you put now?

Mr. A. Keightley: The first question.

H.P.B.: Pure matter is pure spirit. It cannot be understood even if admitted by our finite intellects. Of course you cannot see either pure matter or spirit, because they are perfectly one in occultism.

Mr. Harbottle: They are the noumena of the opposites.

H.P.B.: There is but one thing, call it element, force or god, anything you like, it is always one. This is what occult science teaches; and after differentiation come all and everything that is. With regard to this question I can only say that neither light nor darkness as optical effects are matter, nor are they spirit, but both are the qualities of ether, the intermediate agent in the manifested universal universe, for ether is dual. Ether is not as science knows it, but ether, as it really exists — that ether of which the ancient philosophers speak — is dual, because it is the earliest differentiation on our plane of manifestation of consciousness. It is dual in the objective, and dual as the middle Akasha in the subjective universe. In the former case, it is pure differentiated matter; in the latter, elemental. In other words spirit becomes objective matter, and objective spirit eludes our physical senses...

Mr. A. Keightley: Are the other elements beyond ether more differentiated than ether? Are they triple and quadruple?

H.P.B.: What do you call beyond ether? Ether is universal.

Mr. A. Keightley: For instance, the five elements are ether, air, fire, water and earth.

H.P.B.: The ether which is an element is certainly not the ether that science speaks about.

Mr. A. Keightley: No, I am not alluding to science in this particular. You stated there are five elements developed in accordance with the races.

H.P.B.: Yes. The fifth is not developed yet, that which the ancient Greeks called Zeus,[1] that they call the deity of all. Of course, if they spoke in one sense, it was; if in another sense, it was not. Now, the Zeus of Homer[2] certainly was not Akasha in all his Don Juanic[3] peregrinations.

Mr. Harbottle: Isn't it rather true to describe those elements as the different stages?

H.P.B.: Of course. Now that physical science has given the name of elements to everything it believes to be homogeneous and finds after a time it is esoteric, of course this is different; but otherwise I don't see it. The elements are those which are manifested here as the element of fire, the element of water, or the element of earth and so on. They are certainly elements because they are entirely distinct from each other, though there is not an element that has not got some other element in it. It is simply that one aspect predominates.

Mr. A. Keightley: That is the point I was meaning. Are there three main aspects, say, in fire?

H.P.B.: What three main aspects? You may make three. Ether is dual, certainly, because ether is the first differentiated celestial fire, as we call it.

Mr. A. Keightley: Is there a triple aspect in the element next below ether in differentiation?

H.P.B.: You must not mix ether with the others. Ether is an element which follows the four elements that we admit and accept, and the

---

[1] **Zeus** (*Greek*) — the Father of the gods. *Zeus-Zen* is Æther; therefore, Jupiter was called *Pater Æther*.

[2] **Homer** (born c.8th century BCE) — a Greek poet, the author of the *Iliad* and the *Odyssey*.

[3] **Don Juan** — a fictional Spanish character who is typically portrayed as a seducer of women in various literary works.

æther is its abstract or general sense. One you will spell "ether" and the other "æther."[4]

Mr. Harbottle: When you speak of the dual ether, you speak of the Æther of the Greek.

H.P.B.: Certainly. That is why they made all the other gods androgynous. They made the god or the goddess just as the Hindus had: it is the two aspects of the deity, and every one of them is certainly or does certainly belong to ether. You may call them solar or lunar gods;[5] they are the gods of the ether. They all return to that first element, to the god of Brahma, from which they emanated.

Mr. Kingsland: Do you call that dual because it is the middle point, so to speak, between spirit and matter that is mentioned in the Stanza?

H.P.B.: Yes, because otherwise it will be no more on the higher planes, it will become Akasha.

Mr. Kingsland: It is exactly the intermediate point.

---

[4] **Æther** (*Greek*) — with the ancients the divine luminiferous substance which pervades the whole universe, the "garment" of the Supreme Deity, Zeus, or Jupiter. In Esotericism, Æther is the third principle of the Cosmic Septenary; the Earth being the lowest, then the Astral Light, Ether and Akasha the highest.
[5] **Lunar Gods** — the Fathers (Pitris) or the lunar ancestors. They are subdivided, like the rest, into seven classes or Hierarchies. In Egypt although the moon received less worship than in Chaldea or India, still Isis stands as the representative of Luna-Lunus, "the celestial Hermaphrodite." Strangely enough, while the modern connect the moon only with lunacy and generation, the ancient nations, who knew better, have, individually and collectively, connected their "wisdom gods" with it. Thus, in Egypt, the lunar gods are Thoth-Hermes and Chons; in India, it is Budha, the Son of *Soma*, the moon; in Chaldea, Nebo is the lunar god of Secret Wisdom, etc. The wife of Thoth, *Sifix*, the lunar goddess, holds a pole with five rays or the five-pointed star, symbol of man, the Microcosm, in distinction from the Septenary Macrocosm. As in all theogonies, a goddess precedes a god, on the principle most likely that the chick can hardly precede its egg — in Chaldea, the moon was held as older and more venerable than the Sun, because, as they said, darkness precedes light at every periodical rebirth (or creation) of the universe. Osiris, although connected with the Sun and a Solar god, is nevertheless born on Mount *Sinai*, because *Sin* is the Chaldeo-Assyrian word for the moon; so was Dio-Nysos, god of Nyssi or *Nisi*, which latter appellation was that of Sinai in Egypt, where it was called Mount Nissa. The *crescent* is not — as proven by many writers — an ensign of the Turks, but was adopted by Christians for their symbol before the Mahommedans. For ages, the crescent was the emblem of the Chaldean Astarte, the Egyptian Isis, and the Greek Diana, all of them Queens of Heaven, and it finally became the emblem of Mary the Virgin.

H.P.B.: Yes. It plays the same relation between the cosmos and the moon, our little earth, as Manas plays between the Monad and the body, just in the same way as it is mentioned in *The Secret Doctrine.*

Mr. B. Keightley: Then what were you driving at about the triple aspect?

Mr. Harbottle: That was only, I think, because Arch was somewhat misunderstanding the way in which H.P.B. was using the word ether.

H.P.B.: You look at the Orientalists — they translate invariably Akasha as ether. I say nothing can be more erroneous than that, because ether is something which science suspects of being particled or something equivocal. What do they call it? Some strange name — "hypothetical agent" and so on. And of course it must be something particled, since it says if it were not matter it could not do the functions that it does in the eyes of science. And Akasha is a perfectly homogeneous thing. It is the rootless root of all, it is Mulaprakriti, it is the rootless root of Nature, that which is perfectly unknown to us.

Mr. A. Keightley: That is the Akasha in its highest aspect.

H.P.B.: Yes, but not ether. Ether is the Astral Light of the Kabbalists. It is devilish infernal sight, as they call it, it is Astral Light in its earliest aspects.

Mr. Harbottle: Arch is confusing again æther and ether.

Mr. A. Keightley: No, I am not. There we get a distinction between ether, the fifth element of those five.

H.P.B.: It is not yet developed, and therefore you can hardly call it an element. It is to be developed with the Fifth Race.

Mr. Kingsland: Then that is the lowest aspect of Akasha.

H.P.B.: Yes. It is the lowest aspect to us who are the lowest aspect of all kinds of beings and of the celestial aristocracy. Of course it appears very grand, because as the proverb says: "a little eel by itself imagines itself a Himalaya." So we do in our conceit, but it is a very low thing.

Mr. Kingsland: But that ether you were speaking of is actually what science calls the hypothetical medium which transmits light.

H.P.B.: Yes, and poor science does not know whether to believe it or not.

Mr. Kingsland: Still, there it is.

H.P.B.: Well, what is question 2?

Mr. A. Keightley: In Stanza 3, Sloka 10, it is said: "Brahma as 'the germ of unknown darkness' is the material from which all evolves and develops."[1] Goethe[2] is quoted as expressing the same idea in the lines "Thus at the roaring loom of Time I ply, and weave for God the garment thou see'st him by."[3] It is one of the axioms of logic that it is impossible for the mind to believe anything of that of which it comprehends nothing. Now, if this "material" above mentioned, which is Brahma, be formless, then no idea concerning it can enter the mind, for the mind can perceive nothing where there is no form. It is the "garment" or the manifestation in form of God which we see or perceive, and it is by this and this alone that we can know anything of him. Question 2: What is the first form of this material which human consciousness can recognize?

H.P.B.: Well, do you direct the question psychically or physiologically, or as a question coming from materialistic science, physical science?

Dr. Williams: Purely as a question of no significance to me, whatever materialists or any sect believe. I use the word materialists in quotation points, desiring you to use the word just as you did in your own sense.

H.P.B.: In my sense I would not pay the slightest attention to materialistic science. I do not believe in this materialistic science. I say they are very great in small details, but on the whole they do not satisfy anyone.

Dr. Williams: I don't use the word material in the sense in which Huxley uses it, or any of those.

H.P.B.: I want you to say in what sense you use it. I say the first sense in which we can imagine matter, or that which is in our conception of matter — that is to say, the most refined of all, the mother as we call it, the primordial. I will say it is a circle, because in all the occult books, in all the teachings and philosophies, it is impossible to imagine one's self any other first form than that of a circle. It is impossible in

---

[1] *The Secret Doctrine*, vol. 1, p. 83.
[2] **Johann Wolfgang von Goethe** (1749–1832) — a German poet, playwright, novelist, scientist, statesman and theatre director.
[3] A passage from Goethe's *Faust*, translated by Thomas Carlyle in *Sartor Resartus* (London: Chapman and Hall, 1869), p. 53.

the Aristotelian logic, it would be a [...] of that; but as we deal with metaphysics, and from the standpoint of the Adepts in the occult sciences, then I must answer you just as occultism says. If you take, for instance, in the physical science, we will say the first geometrical figure is a triangle, but this is on the manifested plane. It is not in the world of abstraction. The first thing that you see is certainly a circle. Now this circle you can either limit or take it just according to the capacities of your conceptions and of your intuition, and you can make it limitless, all depends upon your powers of conceiving things. You can expand it *ad infinitum*, make of it a limitless circle — not only in words, in which you will say a circle is something, the circumference is everywhere and so on, you know the well-known saying — but I don't use any other figure than that. Does that satisfy you? They make us conceive of a circle first of all, and this circle which is all, and embraces all and has no plane. Let us imagine something that is — well, as large as we can imagine it — and you might expand and extend *ad infinitum*. If we contract it to our conceptions, it is because we want to make it conceivable to the finite intellect.

Dr. Williams: I suppose it would be a safe thing to say that the finite intellect cannot conceive of anything except what is finite.

H.P.B.: I beg your pardon: there are moments that you can conceive far beyond that, which your physical brain can conceive. Certainly you cannot conceive it if you simply hold to the matter and to this manifested universe, but there are moments that you can conceive far more; in your dreams you can conceive of things that you cannot when you are awake.

Dr. Williams: I understand that, but my point was after all it would be a finite conception, because the conception of a finite being.

H.P.B.: No, because this circle of light and of everything is not a being; and then you can conceive it limitless, certainly. If it is limitless you can go and search for limits, but you can conceive it is limitless. Let us say it will only apply to the manifested universe, to the objective; even that, certainly, to the astronomer must appear limitless, if they are accustomed to look through their telescopes, and do as they have to do. It must appear limitless to them.

Dr. Williams: They always think from the standpoint of space and time. That is why they say it is not limitless.

H.P.B.: That is where they limit their intellect. Once they go beyond that, they break their noses and nothing comes out of it.

Dr. Williams: When you get beyond space and time, have not you got beyond all circles of form?

H.P.B.: Most assuredly. Then you have no need for symbols and signs. Everything is in such a way then that it is impossible to express it in words.

Dr. Williams: Then that just brings us right back to the point of the question, and that was what the first form was which comes within the range of human consciousness and finite consciousness. It is not, it seems to me, so much a question of what we may imagine as what we are bound to think by the loss of the constitution of the human mind.

H.P.B.: It is a circle, I say again. It is proved Kabbalistically and occultly that the first thing you may imagine when you want to imagine something is a circle.

Dr. Williams: That is exactly the point I wanted to reach.

H.P.B.: Those who tell you the biggest absurdity in science tell you you can square the circle, positively square it, and make of it any figure you like for it's in all in all.

Mr. Kingsland: Isn't it a sphere, rather than a circle?

H.P.B.: Circle or sphere, call it what you like. Of course it is a sphere — it has circumference but no plane.

Mr. A. Keightley: Then what is the next figure you get after the circle?

H.P.B.: If you begin, the first figure will be a triangle.

Mr. B. Keightley: The circle is the central point first; then the triangle.

H.P.B.: The first figure is no figure: the circle with the point; it is simply primeval germ, and it is the first thing you imagine at the beginning of differentiation. But the triangle is the one you have to conceive of, once that matter begins to differentiate, once you have passed the zero point, the Laya. It is this I wanted to say, it is just this. Brahma is called an atom, Anu, because atom could not be an atom, because it is for us an atom that we don't see, we simply imagine it is a kind of mathematical point and so on, but in reality an atom can be extended and made absoluteness. It is the germ. It is not the atom from the standpoint of the physicists or the chemists, it is from the occult standpoint. It is the infinitesimally small and totally Brahma. It may be the unknown limited quantity, a latent atom during Pralaya, active during the life cycles, but one which has neither circumference or plane, only limitless expansion. Therefore also the circle is but the geometrical symbol in the subjective world and it becomes the triangle in the objective. That is my answer, and it is finished. So do you understand now?

Mr. A. Keightley: I don't see how it becomes a triangle in the objective. That is what puzzled me always.

H.P.B.: If that circle is limited it would be a very difficult thing. Then there would be two things having no relation to each other, unless you put the triangle in the circle.

Mr. A. Keightley: That of course is a figure one has always seen.

H.P.B.: How is it in *The Secret Doctrine*? It is a circle, and the point then becomes the plane and with that the triangle; and this plane has nothing to do with what we imagine. It is that boundary from which begins the manifested universe. When you want to follow into cosmogony and theogony then you have to imagine the triangle, because from this first triangle, if you take this Pythagorean definition, it begins descending, as I explained to you last time, then coming back on itself, making the plane and then going up again and disappearing in darkness. That is it.

Mr. A. Keightley: Then Sloka 11, question 3. Is the word "expand" here used in the sense of differentiating or evolving, and "contract" in that of involution? Or do these terms refer to Manvantara and Pralaya? Or again, to a constant vibratory motion of the world-stuff or atoms? Are this expansion and this contraction simultaneous or successive?

H.P.B.: It is translated word for word, this, and it is all certainly figurative, metaphorical, and so on, and therefore you must not take in the literal sense everything; because you must allow something for the Eastern way of expressing it. Their Stanzas are as old as man, but this is thinking man.

Mr. A. Keightley: [Reads the question again.]

H.P.B.: The Web means here, the ever existant primordial matter — pure spirit to us — the matter out of which the objective universe or universes are evolved. It means that when the breath of fire of father is upon it, it expands. That is to say, a subjective material, it is limitless, infinite, eternal and indestructible. When the breath of the mother touches it, when the time for manifestation comes, and it has to come into objectivity and form, it contracts, for there is no such thing as something material and with a form, and yet limitless. You understand, the fire, it stands here for father. It is that ever unknowable principle, which fecundates that matter, this primordial matter or the mother, and then taking a form — of course it will take a form and become limited. The universe is limitless, but yet everything that has form in it is finite. Well, this is why it is said to contract, contract — that is to say, become something less — maybe the expression is not a happy one.

Mr. B. Keightley: It means to become limited.

H.P.B.: That is what I want to say. *Now,* the critics are many, but the helpers were few when I wrote the thing. That is the mischief of it.

Dr. Williams: It is not the literal interpretation of any of the Stanzas, but only the ideas that are underneath them that we want.

H.P.B.: Oh, yes, the literal; I try to translate word for word.

Dr. Williams: But it is not that I insist upon, at all; it is the ideas that are underneath that.

Mr. Kingsland: What we took it for is this, that when the breath of mother touched it, then the sons dissociated and scattered, and returned to the bosom, the end of Pralaya; but it is the opposite way about.

H.P.B.: You can take it in any way. You can take it as the end of Pralaya, or the other way.

Mr. Kingsland: It is when the breath of mother touches it they contract and come into manifestation.

H.P.B.: Yes, and at the end of Pralaya they contract again and become less and less and less. And then they become dissociated and disintegrated and they fall into that which they were at first.

Mr. Kingsland: Wouldn't you say at the end of Pralaya they expanded?

Mr. Harbottle: The "contraction" here is the same thing as scattering.

H.P.B.: I always took it in one sense.

Mr. Kingsland: We thought dissociating and scattering referred to the Pralaya.

H.P.B.: Oh no, it refers to the differentiation.

Mr. B. Keightley: "To return into their mother's bosom at the end of the great day."[1]

H.P.B.: You see, you have to know the inherent powers of every atom. You have to know what really matter is on this plane, and what matter is before it is differentiated. Now, there; I have tried to give you the explanation. I don't know whether I have succeeded or not. Now, for instance, take that proposition of Sir Isaac Newton, *viz.,*[2] that every particle of matter has the property of attraction for each other particle, etc. You know the well-known proposition. Very well. It is correct from one aspect. Then also there is Leibniz. He speaks about the Monads and says every atom is a universe in itself, which acts through its own inherent force. This is also true, but one speaks from the standpoint of psychology, and the other from that of physical science; and both say that which has neither beginning nor end, because it does not explain anything. It is a perfect impossibility. It is only occultism that comes and reconciles the two and shows that there is something else in it. They are incomplete. Man also is an atom having attraction and repulsion in him, because he is the microcosm of the macrocosm. But would it be true to say that because of that force he moves and acts independently of every other, or could act and move, unless there were a greater force and intelligence than his own to allow him to live and move? I speak about that high element of force and intelligence. That is to say, your physical science says that every atom has its inherent force in itself, and that there is no extra cosmic matter — a thing for which you pitch into me, Dr. Williams, because you say science will not allow the extra cosmic force.

Dr. Williams: I didn't mean to put it in that sense.

H.P.B.: No, but you will read it afterwards. Your physical scientists, as far as I understand them — it seems to me I understand them to say that every atom has its own inherent force in itself, and this is what makes Haeckel[3] say, for instance, that matter has created itself,

---

[1] *The Secret Doctrine*, vol. 1, p. 83.

[2] **Viz., videlicet** (*Latin*) — namely; that is to say.

[3] **Ernst Haeckel** (1834–1919) — a German zoologist, naturalist and philosopher.

that it gave itself a kick and did everything by itself. There is nothing else. Very well, I have no objection to that. But there is something else, therefore there is a force inherent in the atom, and one which acts on the atom, and this is that which I wanted to explain to you. Now one of my objects in *The Secret Doctrine* is to prove that planetary movements cannot be accounted for satisfactorily by the sole theory of gravitation, and this leads me to say that besides force acting in matter there is also that other force which acts on matter. Take, for instance, a sponge. Maybe the sponge will be a very bad simile, but still it will give the idea of what I want to show. Take a sponge, it is soaked through and through in seawater. Every atom of it is, so to say, a dried atom or particle of seawater, yet the waves around it will toss and guide it. Now these waves are the same as those inside it, as those which created it, and which even have created that sponge which has become objective matter and perfectly specific matter. It is just the same with every atom in the universe. What I seek to express then is this: when we speak of modified conditions of spirit-matter, which is in reality force, and call them by various names, such as heat, cold, light, darkness, repulsion, attraction, electricity, magnetism and so on, all these for the occultists are simply names and expressions of difference in manifestation of one and the same force, which is always dual, at least in differentiation, but not in specific differences of force. For all such differences in the objective world result only from the peculiarities of the differentiation of matter on which the one free force acts, helped in this by that portion of its essence which we call imprisoned force. Now I must tell you that the force is one, but it differs in its aspects according to whether it is on the manifested plane, where it is encased and imprisoned in an atom or in any form that you can imagine, or whether it is this free force which I have just tried to show you, as in the illustration of the sponge. There is the other force which is absolute totality, that force is not a force only, it is all, it is life, it is consciousness. But all this is absolute, and all this not having any relation to the finite, certainly, of course, we cannot regard it or compare it with the things that we see in the manifested universe. You understand my idea, Dr. Williams?

Dr. Williams: Yes, I think I do. This is rather anticipating the questions which are to follow.

H.P.B.: That is not my fault.

Dr. Williams: But how are we to know anything about the universal force which lies behind or above or outside of them?

H.P.B.: We can never know it on the physical plane.

Dr. Williams: How are we to get any idea of it?

H.P.B.: Study occultism.

Dr. Williams: That is it. What has occultism to say about it?

H.P.B.: It says that everything you see around, that you can comprehend or conceive of, all this comes from that one absolute force. You have either to believe in a personal God who does so and so — well, of course, as the good clergyman teaches — or you have to believe that there is one absolute totality, incomprehensible, which Herbert Spencer calls the unknowable and refers to it as "He" and the "just cause" (which is very philosophical!), or you have to choose. Logically, it cannot be anything else, because nothing can come out of nothing; everything must come from something. This something cannot be limited; if it were, it would be a personal God.

Mr. B. Keightley: It would come from something itself.

H.P.B.: It would just be the fairy hen that lays the egg, and the egg has existed before that hen, and it has produced that hen. Go on if you can understand that.

Dr. Williams: I quite see the logic of that, and I also see that it is absolutely necessary to postulate the "Absolute," something which is back of all manifestation which has no relation to us; but having postulated that, how is it possible to go any further than that? Because the moment we go further than that we begin to talk about manifestation. We can postulate an Absolute of which we can conceive absolutely nothing.

H.P.B.: Philosophy postulates nothing. It postulates its existence, not its being. It does not say it exists, it does not say it is a being, it simply says it is. Now remember what [...] said to the king, that great [...] when he asked him about Nirvana. He said it is nowhere. It exists nowhere. What is Nirvana? It is nothing. Then Nirvana, he says, does not exist. No, it does not. Then, he says, what are you talking about? He said it is, but it does not exist, it is a state; imagine one absolute state, and this is that consciousness.

Dr. Williams: I see that as a necessity of logic when it applies simply and solely to the Absolute, or to that which forever transcends human consciousness. But the moment we leave that it is different. I want to know how it is possible to talk about the condition of a thing which is not a thing. That is what I cannot comprehend.

H.P.B.: "Nights and days of Brahma," have you ever studied them?

Dr. Williams: Yes.

H.P.B.: Very well. How do you imagine, for instance, a dark night and a man or men sleeping in a kind of dead sleep — let us say that dead men are like that, let us leave aside all other men. Let us say that a man is like in a dead faint, in one of those swoons; there is no remembrance. You may be five or six hours and it appears one second. Let us think of that, and yet there it comes: there is no consciousness, nothing at all, but from that consciousness of non-being a man becomes and begins thinking immediately what he is. Can you imagine that? It is very unsatisfactory analogy, but there is something in it.

Dr. Williams: Yes, I can imagine anything which comes within the range of human consciousness, but that does not seem to me to touch the point at all. We first postulate an Absolute, of which we admit we can have no conception whatever; then we begin to talk about qualities — of this which transcends human consciousness.

H.P.B.: No, we do not begin to talk about that at all; it is that absoluteness, according to the Eastern philosophy. It is that absoluteness, which, when the hour strikes of the life-cycle of the day of Brahma, which has qualities which were latent in it, and dormant, which were in the Laya condition, at the zero point of everything, all negative, which awaken, so to say. And from that they begin gradually one after the other to form the one whole what we call the divine ideation. We call it the divine thought, that which Plato called the eternal idea. Then after that there begins the differentiation. How many times have I been explaining it is not one? That is why the Brahmins, who are certainly the greatest philosophers in the world, postulate seven creations and at the end of the seventh begins that which I tried to explain to you here. And they have a name for every creation. I speak of those in *The Secret Doctrine* on all the planes and through all the planes of consciousness. And until it comes there — and then you may say from the seventh creation, our creation (I call it creation, it ought to be called evolution), then, only begins the differentiation and the fall of spirit into matter. But this goes on gradually, millions and millions of years; and when they come and speak to me about 7,000 years, I say fiddlesticks, and that is all I can say, because seven times seven millions would not cover it.

Mr. B. Keightley: It strikes me, Dr. Williams, that the logic of the position is this if the Absolute is the abstract totality in some form or another. Every object of our consciousness, whether, so to speak, an idea or anything else, must have its root in that Absolute, must come from that, in some way or another. Therefore, ultimately there must be latent, or merged in the Absolute during the time of Pralaya, the essential roots of everything which ever is, has been, or will be manifested.

Dr. Williams: Oh, I quite grant all that.

Mr. B. Keightley: Then comes in what H.P.B. was saying, that you take up the first thing of those qualities. Behind that manifestation you cannot say anything at all.

Dr. Williams: Is not that just what has been done all through *The Secret Doctrine*? Are not there postulates made there of that which has no form, of that which is above form and yet which is in the first absolute, the Absolute?

H.P.B.: Most assuredly, I speak of it as eternal darkness, then on the second plane begins the motion; this is right that motion begins something else, and so on, until it descends, until the seven. Finite intellect cannot reach that; therefore, it has to come to begin on that stage when the first flutter of differentiation begins in the primordial matter, which is eternal.

Dr. Williams: That is the point: what the first manifestation was, and how we came to have any consciousness of it, and how it is possible to have any consciousness.

H.P.B.: It is the experience of ages and ages, of all the seers. Either you have to admit that there are such people in the world as seers or there are not. If there are, then the experience of one checks the other. They never said to each other how it was. Those who had the capacities of seers were put to the test, and if they happened to say in their utterances that they know how to produce it, and if the later one happened to say just the same things as the other said, I suppose there is some probability that it is so.

Dr. Williams: I am quite willing to admit that there is not much that comes within the range of my consciousness, but that which does, if I would be honest with myself, I must hold to, quite irrespective of what anybody has said about it.

Mr. Harbottle: It seems to me the difficulty in these intermediate stages is this: in a sense, they are positive conceptions. The conception of the Absolute is a negative one, and therefore, it is comparatively easy to us. The intermediate stages are not within the range of our finite intellect, but nevertheless they are positive conceptions.

Mr. Yeats:[1] Everything which is within the range of the Absolute must be within our consciousness?

Dr. Williams: Yes, that is exactly the point. The gentleman has stated it.

H.P.B.: Of course, you don't study here the esoteric things. But those who study the Esoteric Instructions[2] will understand what I mean. Isn't it said, if we go on a lower analogy — the birth of a child, if you take, or the birth of any animal — take this and you will find it corresponds admirably. There is not a missing link. It corresponds with things which are known to science — you understand what I mean — and these are facts which are not to be gainsaid. It is impossible; it is a perfect proof because it dovetails with everything that science has so far had any proofs of.

Mr. Kingsland: It seems to me that Dr. Williams' questions amounts to this: he wants to know how we can get at or appreciate what it is that acts upon matter.

H.P.B.: It is the inherent force which covers the whole ground of consciousness and life and everything that you can think of; and at the same time there is a consciousness which acts on it. And these are the things I am going to give you the proofs of, now that your science is at loggerheads with itself.

---

[1] **William Butler Yeats** (1865–1939) — an Irish poet, dramatist and writer, considered a driving force of the Irish Literary Revival; a Nobel Prize laureate in Literature.

[2] See H. P. Blavatsky, "Esoteric Instructions," *Collected Writings*, vol. 12 (Wheaton, IL: Theosophical Publishing House, 1980), pp. 513–713.

Dr. Williams: Here is another way of putting it. We have to begin at the beginning, at the Absolute. Then we have next the manifestation of the Absolute. The moment you have the manifestation of anything, you have an idea, you can predicate something about it; but if you go back to anything in which you can predicate nothing, you will never come to the Absolute. Now how is it possible to say anything or predicate a condition of that which transcends consciousness?

H.P.B.: But we don't postulate anything about it. We say this transforms itself through the planes, the various planes of manifestation, until it reaches this plane of objective scientific perception — even scientific — and that those things that you know are forces in nature, as they can prove to you. There is something beyond; and this is proven by that that even the laws of Newton and Kepler[1] can be perfectly contradicted and proven to be wrong. And this is what I have been preparing here, because with your question I felt like an old war-horse that gets the smell of powder. And I just put to you the explanation.

Mr. Kingsland: I think Dr. Williams seems to suppose that if you pass our plane of consciousness you get to the Absolute.

H.P.B.: Oh, no, not at all. This passes through a plane that we can have some idea of. For us it is perfectly invisible. The men of science don't want to admit it, just because they cannot smell it or touch it, or hear it, or bring it to be perceived with their senses.

Dr. Williams: I daresay the following question will help us somehow.

H.P.B.: This imprisoned force and the free force — the worker, within, or the inherent force — ever tends to unite with its parent essence, that which is outside. And thus the mother acting within causes the web to contract, and the father without to expand. That is another explanation to you; this it is which your men of science call gravity, and we men of ignorance, or fellows, call the work of the universal life-force, spirit-matter, which is one outside space and time, and dual within space and time. This is work of eternal evolution and involution or of expansion and contraction. There: I answer every one of your objections and your questions. Do I or not? This is that dual force; and then you will come to the centripetal and centrifugal

---

[1] Johannes Kepler (1571–1630) — a German astronomer, mathematician, astrologer and natural philosopher.

forces, which will prove to you it must be so, simply because I base myself on the mistakes of science, which are glaringly demonstrated by all the astronomers and physicists, and yet they won't admit them. But they are, if you please, like the Church clergyman — they know the mistakes and the impossibilities, but won't admit them. So your men of science, they find something that does not dovetail that upsets entirely their theory. But they are too lazy to go and invent another theory. It is very comfortable to go and invent some flapdoodle and then go on *ad infinitum*. Anything they say of course the *hoi polloi* will swallow.

Mr. A. Keightley: Then question 4.

Mr. B. Keightley: Before you pass on to that there is this. You say the inner force, the imprisoned force, causes contraction, and the father or external force, expansion.

H.P.B.: That is to say, that force which works inside or something which has form works, and has always to unite itself with that other force which is absolute; and therefore this force tends to take a form. By that action it assumes a form, whereas the other tries to expand and has no form.

Mr. Kingsland: Would not a very good example be the case of a lump of ice in water? It is an expansion of the same material as the water, but the force makes it contract and form into ice, which is something in the manifested plane; and it is always tending to go back again.

H.P.B.: And what forms the ice, your scientists don't say. They are right in the detail, but not in the general explanation.

Mr. A. Keightley: [Reads again question 4.]

H.P.B.: That is a nice question, "when." When the imprisoned force and intelligence inherent in every atom of differentiation — as of homogeneous matter — arrives at a point when both become the slaves of that intelligent force which we call Divine free will, represented by the Dhyani-Buddhas. When the centripetal and centrifugal forces of life and being are subjected to by the one nameless force, which brings order in disorder and establishes harmony in chaos then. I cannot tell you anything else. How can I name to you the precise hour and time in a process, the duration of which is perfectly, and which the Hindus and the Buddhists, as you know, put in figures.

Mr. A. Keightley: The object of the question was at what stage of the process. Now, question 5. What is meant by the web becoming radiant when it cools?

H.P.B.: Just that which is said in the paragraph two of the comments which follow the Stanza.

[The President reads the passage from *The Secret Doctrine*.]

Mr. A. Keightley: Then, question 6. Stanza 3, Sloka 11. The first paragraph of the commentary needs elucidating in reference to the part which heat plays in the forming and breaking up of the element, and also of the worlds in globes. In it is stated first that "great heat breaks up the compound elements and resolves the heavenly bodies into their one primeval element."[1] This heat apparently is already existing in a "focus or centre of heat (energy) of which many are carried about to and fro in space."[2] What are these centres of heat? Are they visible or invisible in our plane of matter? What is the "body" referred to, which may be either "active or dead?" Is the disintegration by heat, here referred to, that which takes place in our plane and with which we are familiar in chemistry?

H.P.B.: Then you see I went to the other thing, and then I answered Dr. Williams entirely on that — the thing where you say something that is in your question 6. That is what I say you have mixed up. You go on to the end, and it will be a great deal better — to the end of that number 6.

Mr. A. Keightley: That is the end of number 6.

Dr. Williams: I think it has relation to Fohat.

H.P.B.: [After reading question 6.] No, it is not that which I answered. There is the confusion that I spoke of to you, because I know I speak of science here.

Dr. Williams: It is the second statement, madam, that you refer to. I remember it.

Mr. A. Keightley: [Reads the second statement.]

H.P.B.: I have just answered till then. I say that science is so afraid to raise her theories into her axioms. And why does she play Penelope[3]

[1] *The Secret Doctrine*, vol. 1, pp. 83–84.
[2] *The Secret Doctrine*, vol. 1, p. 84.
[3] **Penelope** — a character in Homer's *Odyssey*, known for her fidelity to her husband Odysseus.

and do today that which she would not do yesterday? Show to us that the law holds good with regard to the entirety of planetary representatives, and that they can be and are produced in accordance with the law, and then I may say that you are right. We maintain that in this case neither the laws of Newton nor of Kepler will hold good. Take the first and second law of Kepler,[4] communicated in the Newtonian law as given to us by Herschel, as just stated. He says that under the influence of such attractive force you will urge two spherical gravitating bodies towards each other; they will, when moving to each other and each other's neighbourhood, be deflected into an orbit concave to each other and describe, one about the other regarded as fixed, or both around the common centre of gravity, curves, whose forms are those figures known in geometry by the general name of conic sections. It will depend upon the particular circumstances of velocity, distance and attraction which of those curves shall be described — whether an ellipse, a circle, a parabola or a hyperbola — but one of these it must be. Now, there is one of the theories of science which you have raised into an axiom. Now this axiom of science can be upset in the most easy way possible, by proving that of these things that take place in the phenomenon of the planetary motion, that everything goes against that. This will make you smile, of course, but when everything is given to you and proven to you, you will say this is not a vain boast but it is perfectly that which occultism claims. Now, what science says is that the phenomenon of the planetary motion results from the action of the two forces, the centripetal and the centrifugal. Is it so? And they assure us that a body falls to the ground; first, in a line perpendicular to still water; and secondly, it does so owing to the law of gravity or centripetal force. Do they say so? Now, I am going to prove to you this axiom — to prove to you what a fallacy it is. Now, a very learned occultist shows the following: that if we trust these laws, we shall find as obstacles in our way among other things, first, that the path of a circle is impossible in the planetary motion — perfectly impossible, if left to that inherent force. Second, that the argument as to the third

---

[4] Kepler's first law of planetary motion: "The orbit of a planet is an ellipse with the Sun at one of the two foci." The second law: "A line segment joining a planet and the Sun sweeps out equal areas during equal intervals of time."

law of Kepler,[1] namely, that the squares of the periodic times of any two planets are to each other in the same proportion as the cubes of their mean distances from the sun, gives rise to this curious result of the permitted libration on the eccentricities of planets. Now, the said forces remaining unchanged in the nature, this can only arise, as he says, from the interference of an extraneous cause. He also proves that the phenomenon of gravitation or of falling does not exist except as the result of a conflict of forces. It is not gravity, it is a conflict of forces. It can only be considered as an isolated force by way of mental analysis. He asserts moreover that the planet's atoms or particles of matter are not attracted towards each other in the direction of right lines connecting their centres, but rather forced towards each other in the curves of spirals closing upon the centres to each other; also that the tidal wave is not the result of attraction, but simply of this conflict of forces. All this, as he shows, results from the conflict of imprisoned forces, from that which in the eyes of science is antagonism, and what is affinity and harmony to the knowledge of the occultists. Now, these things, if you wanted me to prove them, would take me about two days to prove, but I will draw for you all the geometrical things to prove to you that these things are not rare exceptions, but that they form the rule in the planetary motions. Where is, after that, your Newtonian and your Kepler propositions?

Mr. Kingsland: Is that esoteric, or is that public.

H.P.B.: Not at all; some of the things may be exoteric.

Mr. Kingsland: Is it sufficiently exoteric to be proved to the satisfaction of a man of science.

H.P.B.: The men of science laugh at it, and won't accept it. I think I have given it quite enough in *The Secret Doctrine.*

Mr. Kingsland: Can it not be demonstrated mathematically?

H.P.B.: Mathematically, I think it can. Look at those proofs I have given in my "tugs of science" in *The Secret Doctrine.* Have you read them all?

Mr. B. Keightley: You have not given a detailed proof of that, of this particular point; it would be an awfully good thing to do.

---

[1] Kepler's third law: "The square of a planet's orbital period is proportional to the cube of the length of the semi-major axis of its orbit."

H.P.B.: Oh, thank you! If I were to give you all the proofs I could give, life would not be sufficient.

Dr. Williams: I think you misunderstood my position; I quite understand why you got mad now.

H.P.B.: I thought you laughed at me, saying science would say so and so.

Dr. Williams: I am not here for that. I don't care what any astronomer thinks. I know very well they quarrel among themselves.

H.P.B.: I quarrel not with you, but with science. It was what was suggested to me by you. You say so coolly, science will say this or that. I say fiddlesticks to science.

Mr. A. Keightley: You have not answered Dr. Williams' question at all.

H.P.B.: My dear sir, I tell you, you have mixed up the things. I have answered the whole of it. I felt very much excited and mad. Very well now, put the question.

Mr. A. Keightley: This is question 8. Statement to this question: In the commentary on Sloka 11 of the same Stanza, it is stated that: "Fohat, gathering a few of the clusters of Cosmic matter (nebula) will, by giving it an impulse, set it in motion anew, develop the required heat, and then leave it to follow its own new growth."[2] Such a statement as this makes it necessary for us to abandon all of those great generalizations or conclusions which modern science prides itself upon having reached, *viz.*: the persistence and uniformity of force and the consequent orderly changes in the universe by antecedent and sequence. Science would say that it is inconceivable that an extra-cosmic force, that is, a force not forever immanent within matter, should break into the cycle of evolution on any point, and after a period of activity, again leave matter to its own devices. Science would say that creation, or the bringing of form within the range of our conscious perception, is the result of that something to which it has given the name Force. It would further say that the force which first brought matter within the range of perception must persistently remain within that matter as its sustaining and actuating principle, otherwise it would instantly pass from the range of perception or cease to be, so far as we are concerned.

---

[2] *The Secret Doctrine*, vol. 1, p. 84.

If it is once admitted that there is such a force imminent in matter, then the introduction into it of that which has not always been within it is an inconceivability of thought. Moreover, such an hypothesis would be wholly unnecessary, because all of the movements and activities of matter are completely understood without it. Question 8. Is Fohat to be understood as synonymous with force, or that which causes the changing manifestations of matter? If so, how can Fohat be said to "leave it to follow its own new growth," when all growth depends upon the indwelling force?

H.P.B.: All growth depends upon the indwelling force, because on this plane of ours it is this force alone which acts consciously in our senses. The universal force cannot be regarded as a conscious force, because you would forthwith make of it a personal God. It is only that which is enclosed in form, and limited as to form and matter — I don't know how to express myself well — which is conscious of itself on this plane. That which is limitless and absolute, as this free force or will is, cannot be said to act understandingly, but has but one sole and immutable law of life and being. Fohat is therefore spoken of as the synthetic motor power of all the imprisoned life forces put to give a medium between the Absolute and the conditioned forces. He, so to speak, is the cement between the two, as Manas is the connecting link between the gross matter of the physical body and the Divine Monad which animates it. It is powerless to act upon it directly in the First Race.

Dr. Williams: That bears directly upon the question.

H.P.B.: Very well, now, 9.

Mr. A. Keightley: Are you not going to touch upon number 6, then?

H.P.B.: Six? I have been alluding to all the time.

Mr. A. Keightley: [Reads question 6 again.]

H.P.B.: No, sir, it is not that. It is a thing which cannot be explained to you. On the things that take place here, it is a perfect impossibility.

Mr. A. Keightley: Then what are those centres of heat?

H.P.B.: They are the centres, those from which, for instance, Keely draws his inter etheric force, Laya centres. Heat is paradoxical. It would not be heat to us. There is the negation of heat.

Mr. Kingsland: I thought they might be related to the knots of Fohat that you spoke about last time.

H.P.B.: This is quite a different thing. Now, 9.

Mr. A. Keightley: Will you do anything with question 7?

H.P.B.: I gave you all this about question 7.

Mr. A. Keightley: This is question 7. Could extreme cold produce the same dissociating effect as extreme heat, as Mr. Sinnett seems to convey in *Esoteric Buddhism*,[1] page 200? I will read the passage in *Esoteric Buddhism*. [Reads passage, p. 200.]

H.P.B.: Well, this is correct enough.

Mr. A. Keightley: The question actually is, "would the effect of cold be sufficient to cause a conglomerated mass like the earth to fly apart into separated particles."

H.P.B.: No, it would not.

Mr. B. Keightley: It is not a question of cold but a question of death — loss of life.

Mr. A. Keightley: That is Flammarion[2] whom Mr. Sinnett quotes as being correct.

H.P.B.: Correct in some things, but I remember perfectly well that the Master said he was not correct in other things. But Sinnett wants to bring all under the sway of science; and Flammarion, perhaps, is more for him than anyone else. I have been answering this question that he has been asking about Sinnett. It is question 11, because I find it 11 here on your type thing. Now you must go to 9. This will lead to eternal confusion.

Mr. B. Keightley: All these things must be put into the report.

Mr. A. Keightley: Statement to question 9. Following out the thought already presented in the foregoing statements that Force is unity or One manifesting in an unlimited variety of ways, we find it impossible to understand another statement in the commentary, *viz.*: that "there is heat internal and heat external in every atom," or as it is sometimes spoken of, latent and active heat, or dynamic kinetic heat. From my own standpoint these terms involve a contradiction. We have a perception of matter actuated by force in a peculiar way and to this

---

[1] See A. P. Sinnett, *Esoteric Buddhism* (New York: Houghton, Mifflin & Co., 1889).

[2] **Camille Flammarion** (1842–1925) — a French astronomer and author.

particular phenomenon we have given the name *heat*. Heat, then, on the physical plane, is simply matter in motion. But there is heat in a more interior or occult sense. Yes, and how is it perceived on these higher planes of consciousness? By virtue of the same law which prevails here, because the truth of the unity of force is a universal truth, and therefore perceived in the same or similar way on all planes of consciousness. If there be heat in a more interior or occult sense than physical heat, it must be perceived by some higher or more interior sense than over present physical senses, and it must be perceived *by virtue of its activities on whatever plane it manifests.* That there may be activities and perception of activities on any plane there must be both percipient and objective *forms.* We thus see that the law of heat, on any plane of existence, is the same. Three conditions are necessary, *viz.,* the actuating force, the form which is actuated, and that which perceives the form in motion. The terms latent heat, potential heat, or dynamic heat are misnomers, because *heat,* whether on the first or on the seventh plane of consciousness, is the perception of matter or *substance* in motion. Question: Is the discrepancy between the above statement and the teaching in *The Secret Doctrine* apparent or real? If real, at what point in the scientific teaching does the error come in?

H.P.B.: He who offered this question, and regards them as contradictions and discrepancies, can certainly know nothing of occult sciences. Why should heat be on another plane than ours, the perception of matter or substance in motion? Why should an occultist accept the conditions as a *sine qua non*?[1] First of the actuating force, second the form which is actuated and third that which perceives the forming motion, as this of heat? All this is Spencerianism,[2] pure and simple. An occultist would say on the seventh plane the form will disappear, and there will be nothing to be actuated upon. The actuating force will remain in solitary grandeur — that is to say, according to the Spencerian phraseology. It will be at once the object and the subject, the perceiver and that which is perceived. How can you imagine on the seventh plane it would be the same thing? The terms used are no discrepancies or contradictions, but so many symbols borrowed from physical science in order to render all the processes more clear to the

---

[1] **Sine qua non** (*Latin*) — something absolutely essential.

[2] **Spencerianism** — the system of thought developed by Herbert Spencer.

student. I am sorry I cannot go into this tonight, or any Thursday night, but a practical occultist will understand well my meaning. These questions are, I suppose, met before the end of *The Secret Doctrine*. In the third part I explain everything and if you read this, all these questions will be answered. They are met before you come to the third part; there I answered them entirely. There is no error at all there. Those who understand the symbols used know well what is meant; in fact, all the speculations of heat and force relate to and correspond with every principle in man, and this is why I brought them. Because every one of them corresponds with one of the principles, and I use them simply as symbols. Because if I used other expressions, nobody would understand me.

Dr. Williams: Very well. Of course, connected with every expressed word or thought, there are certain ideas, and it is only the ideas which underlie them that I want. I don't care for the form of expression at all. It is only the idea that underlies the words I wanted to get at. Let us take the fourth or fifth plane, there is something which corresponds to heat on the material plane.

H.P.B.: As you go and ascend on the planes, you find that everything merges more and more into unity, and therefore on the fourth or fifth plane certainly there is no such thing as heat and no contrast between heat and cold. Because it becomes more and more one; it tends to unity.

Dr. Williams: You speak of heat centres.

H.P.B.: Now, for instance, when I speak of heat centres, they are the centres which in the physical science would be the zero point, the negation. It would be nothing, and yet these are just that, because they are spiritual, because it is spirit.

Dr. Williams: Well, on whatever plane we speak of anything, it does not make any difference; we speak of it because we perceive something that we know; if we don't perceive it, we have nothing to say about it.

H.P.B.: Which changes entirely.

Dr. Williams: Is there anything on the third plane which anyone can perceive, which the occultist will perceive?

H.P.B.: With his mind's eye; and then he will need no form and no symbol or objective thing, because he does not see objectively. He sees only the essence and the root of things, and with senses that do not pretend to this plane. Those are the senses that I have been speaking about, when we spoke about dreams.

Dr. Williams: I admitted all the third, that the perception of anything on any plane above matter must proceed on some sense which is higher than matter.

H.P.B.: The word "perceived" is a word which conveys the wrong impression. It is "sensed" and not "perceived."

Dr. Williams: Do you wish me to understand it is impossible to gain any idea?

H.P.B.: On the physical plane, no; but if you go one plane higher, then you will perceive in another way. On the third plane you will "sense" the thing with those senses that you have no idea of on the fourth, and so on, until you come to the last plane where the higher Adept cannot penetrate.

Dr. Williams: I can perceive things which have no relation to this plane at all; but anything I can perceive, I can predicate something of, but it has no relation to space and time.

H.P.B.: Most assuredly it has none, and yet it is linked, it is united and linked indissolubly with this plane — that which has no relation to space or time.

Dr. Williams: Well, the apparent discrepancy — to go back a little into the second statement of the question — is this: there is brought before the mind's eye the beginning of the creation of the physical universe; there is matter in a homogeneous condition, and it was brought into that homogeneous condition because of an actuating force, otherwise it never could have reached that condition. Let us make a comparison. Let us suppose I have a trough or groove constructed for the rolling of a billiard ball, and I know if I strike with a mallet on that which would turn the scale at two ounces, it is sufficient force to send that ball eight feet. What is the necessity of our introducing as an explanation any force — which I compare to an extra-cosmic force — to that which has already received an impulse which will send it eight feet?

H.P.B.: And do you suppose it would proceed to act in this way if it did not have an inherent force which you represent, and which has an analogy to the force outside?

Dr. Williams: But you speak there of Fohat coming in at that point, and doing something and then leaving.

H.P.B.: I have no right to say more. There are things I cannot explain, which I try to make you understand — that there is force outside and a force inside; that no billiard ball is just that.

Mr. Kingsland: Is that force outside acting continuously?

H.P.B.: Most assuredly. If you leave a billiard ball, and if it is there three or four years, I don't think you would find much of it at the end.

Dr. Williams: In our conception of the universe, and it seems through all the investigations of the ages, this one thing remains true, because it is a universal truth — it has no reference whatever to the discrepancies of science, it is a universal truth — and that is this: the persistence of force, that force is everywhere persistent, though you never get the manifestation.

H.P.B.: This proves what we say, because it is absolute, because it is ever present. But they don't know the force, they don't know what it is. Can they explain to you what is force? If they want to gainsay what we say, let them explain what is force. Let them explain why their theories are a bundle of contradictions.

Dr. Williams: I am only speaking self-evident truth.

H.P.B.: That is that they will come and speak to you about the persistence of force — which no occultist will deny — but what is that force? They are perfectly unable to tell you. Before it was all matter, matter reigned supreme. After that, matter has been kicked out — there was a revolution, if you please, among the scientists. They rebelled and they enthroned "Force," and now they look at force and say, "Who are you?"

Mr. Kingsland: The occultists will say: "Force is not persistent on this plane." Speaking of science, he says that science says, force is persistent on this plane.

H.P.B.: It is persistent, certainly, because it is eternal and absolute; and it is given here under various forms and aspects, but it is not the force as it is on the seventh plane, but it certainly is persistent. But what is that force, I ask you? We say what it is. It is an absolute totality; it is the "unknowable" of Herbert Spencer. But then you see science will not admit that there is a force which acts outside of the atom, that there is an intelligent force; they will say it is all blind force. This is what they will say — force inherent, a mechanical force.

Dr. Williams: I cannot conceive of anything blind, or intelligent force, but I must conceive of force acting on matter.

Mr. B. Keightley: But that is not the point Dr. Williams was after. Dr. Williams is still troubled about the statement in *The Secret Doctrine*: if Fohat leaves the nuclei, the nebulous masses, to follow their own growth.[1]

H.P.B.: This is the fault of your learned brother. I have got the things here, and I answer it.

Mr. Kingsland: Fohat will set it in motion anew, and then leave it to follow its own growth.

Mr. B. Keightley: That Dr. Williams understands to be in contradiction to the law of forces.

H.P.B.: I tell you, all the questions here are mixed up, and I cannot find where it is. But I can tell you without looking because I know very well what I have been writing about. It is not a contradiction at all, it leaves everything. How is it expressed? It leaves the…

Mr. Kingsland: It leaves it to follow its own growth.

H.P.B.: Well, I must show it to you, because I have been writing it. All growth depends upon the indwelling force, because on the plane of ours it is this force alone — it is not that it leaves them to themselves, but Fohat acts consciously, and it is only that which acts in the inherent force which acts consciously. It cannot be expressed in any other way. It is not that the forces ceases to act, but it is that one acts consciously and the other unconsciously. The universal force cannot be regarded as a conscious force, because it would forthwith make of it a personal God. It is only that which is enclosed in form and a limitation of matter, which is conscious of itself on this plane of ours. That which, limitless and absolute, has the free force, or will, cannot be said to act understandingly, but has one immutable law of life and being. And therefore it is said that Fohat leaves them alone

---

[1] *The Secret Doctrine*, vol. 1, p. 84.

to do as they please. That is to say, that they will henceforth — this force acting in every atom will be in the eternal conflict with the force outside — well, not conflict, but harmony, as we would call it. Therefore, there is no discrepancy at all.

Dr. Williams: I did not say there was.

Mr. B. Keightley: When Fohat gives them an impulse and leaves them to themselves it means, in other words, that the outside force, or Fohat, the universal force, becomes limited in form.

H.P.B.: It does not become limited in form.

Mr. Harbottle: It becomes differentiated.

H.P.B.: The universal force cannot be said to act consciously because it acts everywhere as an immutable law. Therefore they are said to act for themselves. I don't know how the expression goes — "the indwelling force."

Mr. B. Keightley: The phrase used is, that Fohat gives them an impulse.

H.P.B.: Yes, it is the atom, the medium between that unconscious force and that conscious force. Having established the centripetal and centrifugal forces, he leaves them. Now, this is no discrepancy; without Fohat, it is impossible, because one is the absolute, and the other is the limited. They are the two extremes — there would be no connection, and Fohat connecting, being the universal force of life in that which puts into motion the things, and gives the impulse, he is said to come. You must make some allowance for the Eastern mode of expression. I tell you I have been translating word for word.

Mr. Harbottle: But Fohat is not the absolute immutable force, it is the synthesis of the seven rays.

H.P.B.: Not at all; he is the connecting medium between the absolute and that, since he represents all the Divine mind.

Mr. Kingsland: I asked that question; whose agent is Fohat in this case? The agent of the law. He is the representative of that, of all these Dhyan-Chohans as we call them, the Manasa-Putra, which means the eternal mind.

Mr. Harbottle: It is quite clear but difficult to express, and not very easy to see.

H.P.B.: Well, it is my unfortunate English, but I defy any man with the greatest command of the English language even to come and express these abstruse things so that people could understand them.

Mr. A. Keightley: Statement to question 10. It is then further stated in the commentary that under the influence of Fohat "the required heat" is developed in order to give "*it*" the necessary impulse to follow a new growth. If "*it*" has already been dissociated by heat, how does it require more heat for the new growth? What is this new growth? What is the "*it*" here referred to, is it the "*body*" mentioned a few times before, or is it the "few clusters of cosmic matter" which Fohat has gathered together? Under what guidance does Fohat act in these cases? What is the process by which a globe passes into Pralaya? Does it do so *in situ*[1] so to speak, that is to say, still remaining part of a planetary chain and maintaining its proper position in relation to the other globes? Does the dissociation by means of heat play any part in the passage of a globe into Pralaya?

H.P.B.: Well, I answer here, all this has reference to disrupted atoms from forms becoming Arupa, that is to say, formless — from forms becoming formless. It has no reference to a special thing or some phenomenon here. It refers simply to the disruption of atoms, and once that they return to their primordial element, then Fohat begins again to turn them into use, that is to say, the vital electricity.

Mr. Harbottle: To build them up into their aggregations.

H.P.B.: Certainly just the same as anyone does here. The atoms fly off, and half becomes a cabbage and so on.

Mr. Harbottle: Until that combination is built up. It is no conscious force in itself. It requires Fohat to combine it.

H.P.B.: It requires Fohat to put it into form, to give it a number, a geometrical aspect, a colour, a sound; all these that it should acquire consciousness.

Mr. Harbottle: I think that explains it.

Mr. A. Keightley: Then, question 11. In the passage of a globe into Pralaya, does it remain "*in situ,*" i.e. still being part of a planetary chain, and maintaining its proper position in relation to the other globes?

---

[1] **In situ** (*Latin*) — in the natural, original, or proper position or place.

Does the dissociation by means of heat play any part in the passage of a globe into Pralaya?

H.P.B.: I think this is in *Esoteric Buddhism*, and it is explained there in the obscuration of the planets. Of course, when one of the globes of a planetary chain goes into obscuration, heat retires from it — it remains *status quo*. It is just like the sleeping beauty: it remains so, until it is awakened by a kiss. It is like a frozen paralysed thing, it remains as it is. There is no disruption, but there is no correlation going on, no renovation of atoms, no life.

Mr. Kingsland: And does it pass through the stage in which the mind is now?

H.P.B.: No, no; it will return again when its time comes, because, mind you, there is the planetary chain in every globe. One after the other passes into obscuration.

Mr. A. Keightley: Is that period of obscuration really and genuinely what is ordinarily meant by Pralaya?

H.P.B.: It is the Pralaya of the globe, but the globe above us will go on into activity.

Mr. A. Keightley: Is it a Pralaya of the globe, or is it a Pralaya only of the things upon the globe?

H.P.B.: No, it is a Pralaya of the globe, when it goes into obscuration — Pralaya of everything, of every atom.

Mr. A. Keightley: Take, for instance, the earth at the present moment, supposing this member of this particular chain went into obscuration. At the present moment it probably is visible to Mars. We will say, would the earth still continue to be visible?

H.P.B.: Certainly, it would continue to be visible. It would be just like the moon. You think the moon is a dead planet, because it has no more trees and that. It is a soulless planet, dead spiritually, but not dead — well, if you please, do not speak to me about it. It is a thing that Sinnett received on his fingers for asking too many questions. I know you are all dangerous fellows.

Mr. Kingsland: When our earth goes into Pralaya, it will become like the moon.

H.P.B.: I think it has become like the moon already. We are all lunatics, everyone of us here; mankind has become a perfect lunatic.

Mr. A. Keightley: Statement to question 12. In Sloka 11 the sons are spoken of as dissociating and scattering, and this appears to be opposed to the action of returning to their mother's bosom at the end of the "Great Day." Does the dissociating and scattering refer to the formation of the globes from the universally diffused *world-stuff*? In other words, emerging from a state of Pralaya? What is meant by the expanding and contracting through their own selves and hearts, and how is this connected with the last line of the Sloka: "they embrace infinitude"?[1]

H.P.B.: That has been answered. The dissociating and scattering refers to Nitya Pralaya[2] in general. I explained to you what Nitya Pralaya is, so you may explain it in your turn. You brought it to me the other day. I explained to you what it was. It is an eternal and perpetual Pralaya which took place ever since the worlds were created, ever since there was something on the globes. It is going on always, and ever will be going on.

Mr. Harbottle: It is death, simply — death in the sense of change.

H.P.B.: We are all of us in Nitya Pralaya. None of us has got the atoms that he or she had on entering the room an hour ago, and in an hour more, we will all be entirely changed.

Mr. A. Keightley: It is atomic change and nothing else.

H.P.B.: Yes. Nothing else. All the change is Nitya Pralaya.

Mr. A. Keightley: Question 13. What is meant by the expanding and contracting "through their own selves and hearts," and how is this connected with the last line of the Sloka: "they embrace infinitude?"

H.P.B.: It is just an Eastern metaphor in figurative language, meaning that which was already said — through their own inherent force

---

[1] *The Secret Doctrine*, vol. 1, p. 83.

[2] **Nitya Pralaya** (*Sanskrit*, "perpetual dissolution") — the constant and imperceptible changes undergone by the atoms which last as long as a Maha-Manvantara, a whole age of Brahma, which takes 15 figures to sum up. A stage of chronic change and dissolution, the stages of growth and decay. It is the duration of "Seven Eternities." There are four kinds of Pralayas, or states of changelessness. The Naimittika, when Brahma slumbers; the Prakritika, a partial Pralaya of anything during Manvantara; Atyantika, when man has identified himself with the One Absolute synonym of Nirvana; and Nitya, for physical things especially, as a state of profound and dreamless sleep.

imprisoned and each striving collectively to join in the universal forces, "embraces infinitude." This is, I think, very clear.

Mr. A. Keightley: Question 14. What is the relation between density and the "weight" of which you spoke last Thursday as the first quality manifested in matter?

H.P.B.: Density even in its first degree has a film, imparts weight. I believe one cannot exist without the other. If there is density, there is weight, certainly; that is the relation. Now 15.

Mr. A. Keightley: Question 15. What is the relation between electricity and (a) physical magnetism, (b) animal magnetism, and (c) hypnotism?

H.P.B.: I think this is a very long question, and we had better postpone it. One can be applied to the physical things, and the other is a thing which you could not apply. You could not apply hypnotism to this box, but you could apply electricity to it. The relation between them is that electricity is the mother of all these on the plane of manifestation, and Fohat is the father of all. Electricity is the mother of all the forces in mental and physical phenomena. First of all, and on what you call phenomenal matter, neither can act on a mineral or chemical element without Fohat, who turns about and acts upon the molecules, and the molecular cells of your brains. I think that is quite enough.

14 MARCH 1889

Mr. A. Keightley: Stanza 4, Sloka 1.

Mr. B. Keightley: [Reads passage from *The Secret Doctrine*, vol. 1, p. 86.]

Mr. A. Keightley: Question 1. Are the "Sons of the Fire" the subdivisions of the third Logos, or are they subdivisions of the Universal Mind? Are these two synonymous?

H.P.B.: You mean to say that you understand that the "Sons of the Fire" are simply a hierarchy of angels, or what?

Mr. A. Keightley: I understand that the "Sons of the Fire" are the various hierarchies comprised in the subdivision of the third Logos.

H.P.B.: The modern "Sons of the Fire," that is to say, those of the Fifth Race and sub-race, are called so simply because by their wisdom they belong to the hierarchies, which are nearer to it, of the "divine sons of the fire mists," the highest planetary Chohans or angels. But the "sons of the fire mists" who are spoken of here in the Stanza as addressing the "sons of the earth," are the royal king's instructors, who incarnated on this earth to teach nascent humanity. They belong as kings to the divine dynasties of which every ancient nation — India, Chaldea, Egypt, Homeric Greece, etc. — has preserved the tradition in some form or another. The subdivisions of the second Logos are unknown quantities, my dear sir, and those of the first or unmanifested Logos never existed except as a unity.

Mr. A. Keightley: My question was the third Logos.

H.P.B.: What is it you ask?

Mr. A. Keightley: I say, are these subdivisions of the third Logos?

H.P.B.: Certainly; they must be, because the subdivisions of the second Logos are unknown quantities. Those of the first never existed except as a unity, therefore, they must be necessarily of the third. They cannot be anything else. It is the first manifested point.

Mr. A. Keightley: Then what relation have they to the universal mind?

H.P.B.: What relation have they? Which ones?

Mr. A. Keightley: These hierarchies.

H.P.B.: They belong to the hierarchies that I have been explaining to you many, many times, beginning by the "fire Chohans," and the "fire angels," then the "ether angels," the "air angels," the "water angels," and the "earthly angels." The seven lower Sephiroth are the earthly to the seven hierarchies of the seven elements, of which five you know, and two you don't.

Mr. Kingsland: It would appear from what you say there, they also correspond to the races?

H.P.B.: Most assuredly, they correspond to the divine dynasties. Where would be the intellectual races with brains and thought if it were not for these hierarchies who incarnated it?

Mr. A. Keightley: Then the "Sons of the Fire" are these divine instructors?

H.P.B.: In this sense they are. They are king's instructors — those divine dynasties that the Chaldeans and the Egyptians and the Hindus have thus taken; even to the Greeks they are divine dynasties.

Mr. A. Keightley: Then so far as human beings are concerned, the "Sons of the Fire" are the highest incarnated on earth, as the "sons of the fire mists" are the highest in the celestial sphere.

H.P.B.: Yes, but they are also the "Sons of the fire mists," as the Hierophants[1] were called in the days of old.

Mr. A. Keightley: Are not they and the "divine dynasties" almost identical? That is to say, they must have been in connection; they were king initiates.

H.P.B.: Yes, and they were moreover [...], all of them; they were incarnations. So the occult doctrine teaches of those celestial hierarchies who came and incarnated in man, that they were the highest of those. You see the most puzzling thing before an audience that has been brought up in the belief that for every baby that is born there

---

[1] **Hierophant** (*Greek,* "one who explains sacred things") — the discloser of sacred learning and the Chief of the Initiates. A title belonging to the highest Adepts in the temples of antiquity, who were the teachers and expounders of the Mysteries and the Initiators into the final great Mysteries. The Hierophant represented the Demiurge (Creator), and explained to the postulants for Initiation the various phenomena of Creation that were produced for their tuition. In Hebrew and Chaldaic, the term was *Peter,* the opener, discloser; hence the Pope as the successor of the hierophant of the ancient Mysteries, sits in the Pagan chair of St. Peter.

is a soul, immediately produced by God, and this is a thing which is extremely puzzling: nobody seems to take in that philosophical idea that nothing can come out of nothing, not even the breath of God, at least not of an anthropomorphic God. Of a deity, of course, I understand, because everything is breath, divine essence; but I mean this God that comes and breathes over a child that is born, even a child of sin, this is a thing which is most puzzling.

Mr. A. Keightley: I think the great difficulty in that case is to realize that the underlying soul is one, as distinct from the separated bodies.

H.P.B.: How is it distinguished? It cannot be distinguished from that underlying soul, because it permeates every atom of the human body, and everything in the universe. There is not an atom of mud that is not permeated by the divine soul. If it were otherwise, it would not be infinite. You must have it infinite or you cannot admit the other thing.

Mr. A. Keightley: That is the difficulty — the idea of the individuality as compared with the one underlying reality.

H.P.B.: Can you tell me about this lamp? This fire in it, is it an individual fire?

Mr. A. Keightley: So far, yes. Certainly, I should say so.

H.P.B.: Certainly, it is not. It is individual so long as it is in the lamp and it is confined to a vessel; but if you take it from there, it is not in any way any other fire than the one universal fire which is on earth — at least in our solar system. This you may bet your bottom dollar upon, there is no other. Mind you, I don't say it is of the same essence. It is of the same, though in another form. Just the same for the souls and for the monads.

Mr. A. Keightley: There I get the analogy, but the difficulty in all distinctions is to disabuse one's mind of the idea that that is a separate piece of fire.

H.P.B.: He who wants to be an occultist has not to separate himself from anything in this world. And the moment he separates himself from any vessel of dishonour, he cannot belong to any vessel of honour. It is a perfect impossibility. You must either think of yourself as an infinitesimal something, not even individual, but a part of the one whole; or you are illusions, you are nobodies, and you will go out like breaths and leave no trace behind you. You are separate, so far as illusions are concerned. You are distinct bodies, every one of you, and you are marching about in masks furnished to you by "Maya." Can you claim one single atom in your bodies which is your own? Can you stop a set of atoms? You do not pay even the slightest attention to them. What are you? Is it your own intellect or soul, or spirit? Everything from the spirit down to the last of the atoms is a part of the whole. It is a link. You break one and then everything goes into annihilation. A link cannot be broken, it is impossible.

Mr. B. Keightley: You see, you get a series of vehicles increasing in grossness, so to speak, as you proceed from spirit into matter, so that with each step downward you get more and more the sense of separateness developed, until you get lower down. And yet that cannot exist, because if there was a real and complete separation between any two human beings they would not be able to understand or communicate with each other in any sort of way.

Mr. A. Keightley: Certainly; I am not arguing against the fact.

Mr. B. Keightley: But I am only putting that forward as a fact.

Mr. A. Keightley: Question 2: Are the "Sons of the Earth" simply human beings? If not, what?

H.P.B.: This question has just been answered. It is covered by the first answer.

Mr. A. Keightley: Then there is the passage: "The Fire, the Flame, the Day, this bright fortnight,[1] the six months of the Northern Solstice departing (dying) in these, those who know the Brahman (yogis) go to Brahman," etc., page 86.

H.P.B.: It is from the *Bhagavad Gita.*[2]

Mr. A. Keightley: Question 3. Will you give an explanation of these terms? What is the meaning of the sentence?

H.P.B.: The meaning is given plainly enough in the commentary of *The Secret Doctrine.* If you did not pay attention to it, you tell me and I will try to explain it to you more fully. Will you read this thing?

---

[1] **Bright fortnight** — according to Helena Roerich's explanation, it is the period of the waxing moon, while the "dark fortnight" is the period of the waning moon.
[2] **Bhagavat Gita** (*Sanskrit*, "Lord's Song") — a portion of the *Mahabharata*, the great epic poem of India. See Chapter VIII.

Mr. B. Keightley: [After reading from *The Secret Doctrine*, vol. 1, p. 86.] And then you go on to speak about the different hierarchies, but you do not explain the statement in the quotation, that those departing at that period would go to Brahman, or in the other case would go to the lunar light.

H.P.B.: It means that the "devotees" are divided into two broad classes, those who reach Nirvana, and either accept or don't accept it (because they have the option of remaining on earth, at least in the atmosphere of doing good, or they have the option of going selfishly to plunge themselves into Nirvana and not caring for the world), and those who do not do so and have not reached Nirvana. Now the first ones will never be reborn in this Maha-Kalpa[1] or the hundred years of the age of Brahma — and which means 15 figures; and those who don't reach Nirvana on earth, as Buddha and others did. It is all symbolical and metaphorical and easy enough to understand. I suppose "the Fire, the Flame, the Day, the bright fortnight of the moon" are all symbols of the highest absolute deity; those who had any such state of absolute purity as this symbol shows to be go to Brahman, that is to say, they have a right to Nirvana. On the other hand, Smoke, Night, dark fortnight, etc. are all symbolical of matter and of ignorance. And those who die in such state of incomplete purification must of course be reborn. Only the homogeneous or pure and unalloyed spirit can become spirit and go to Brahman. It is as plain as can be that these are nothing but metaphors.

Mr. A. Keightley: Then what is the meaning of saying they are the highest deities or names of various deities?

H.P.B.: Because the hierarchies belonging to such are there connected correspondentially with the dark fortnight and the bright fortnight and the others that you read. Besides, I say it all pretends to esotericism. I never heard esotericism talked on a Thursday night before.

Mr. A. Keightley: It is a sort of transcendental astrology.

H.P.B.: It is para-metaphysics. Now question 4.

Mr. A. Keightley: You have already answered that. Question 4. What is the distinction between the yogis who do not return and the "devotees" who do return?

---

[1] **Maha-Kalpa** (*Sanskrit*) — the great age.

H.P.B.: Such is the distinction of the yogis who do not return on this earth — oh, I have answered this.

Mr. A. Keightley: Question 5.

Mr. B. Keightley: [Reads Sloka 2.]

Mr. A. Keightley: Then there are the two quotations in the commentary which follow: "The First Primordial are the highest beings on the scale of Existence." "The Primordial proceed from Father-Mother."[2] Question 5. Is Father-Mother here synonymous with the third Logos and not with Svabhavat in Darkness, as before, since it is now manifested and differentiated existence, "whereas the other manifested Quaternary and the seven proceed from the Mother alone"?[3]

H.P.B.: Now you have put there two questions, to which I will give you two answers. The first primordial seven are born from the third Logos. This is before it is differentiated into the mother, when it becomes pure primordial matter in its first primitive essence — father, mother, potentially. All this is explained very plainly in the comment (a) of Sloka 2. Read it over, every word is explained there.

Mr. B. Keightley: [Reads passage from *The Secret Doctrine*, vol. 1, p. 88.]

H.P.B.: Now I will tell you. You asked what is synonymous there.

Mr. A. Keightley: Is Father-Mother here synonymous with the third Logos and not with Svabhavat in Darkness, as before, since it has now manifested and differentiated existence, "whereas the other manifested Quaternary and the seven proceed from the mother alone"?

H.P.B.: It is synonymous now with the third Logos, and Svabhavat is light, or manifestation. It is called both; it is perfectly interchangeable. As it was synonymous earlier with darkness, there it is Svabhavat in light, and in darkness the "first primordial" are always to be understood as the rays of the third Logos, not otherwise. They are the direct emanations of the secret [...], because we reckon twice over. Father-Mother, Parabrahm, Mulaprakriti, the eternal ideal, the dual ideal potency in our mind and the Logos born from it are eternal. It is simply the difference between the existence — or simply the idea

---

[2] *The Secret Doctrine*, vol. 1, p. 88.
[3] *The Secret Doctrine*, vol. 1, p. 88.

in esse[1] and the idea *in actu*.[2] I thought I had explained it perfectly well there.

Mr. B. Keightley: But one wants to come back, to know whether he understands it correctly.

H.P.B.: I thought you understood it correctly. Now, 6 is a continuation of this.

Mr. A. Keightley: Yes; question 6. What is Mother and what is Father in this sentence?

H.P.B.: Mother becomes the immaculate Mother only when differentiation is complete, otherwise there would be no such qualification. No one would speak, for instance, of pure spirit as an immaculate something, for it cannot be otherwise. Immaculate spirit becomes simply matter. So the immaculate mother shows to you that where qualification is possible, it is matter and it is lower; therefore the mother is the immaculate matter which begins the hierarchy. That will end by humanity and man, because it must begin by something which Father-Mother cannot be. They are in the beginning ideally potential; then in potentiality it becomes mother alone, because what is mother? Take the etymology of the word, and you will find it is simply matter, and this matter is the primordial matter which is alone, and after that, of course, the immaculate mother. The idea of the immaculate mother comes from that, because the spirit is invisible.

Mr. A. Keightley: Then one gets rather into difficulties in trying to understand the thing, because here you have the third Logos, which is Father-Mother in manifestation, isn't it?

H.P.B.: You will have time, if you please, to be confused and perplexed. You will find something more difficult, yet they are all interchangeable. Now, you see, it is just the same as though you were to take to task a chemist because he would show to you some compound or chemical preparation, and he would give you this name, and then he would call something by another name; but they are all one and all different. This is a thing you have to learn. It is the order of proceeding. You cannot go further because you would simply cobweb your head with perfectly useless things, unless you want to become

---

[1] **In esse** (*Latin*) — actually existing.
[2] **In actu** (*Latin*) — in action; in practice.

a metaphysical Vedantin and go and give lectures upon it. I tell you, you will only confuse yourself and nothing more.

Mr. A. Keightley: My only object is to find out what is meant.

H.P.B.: What are you? You think you are — you are not at all. It is conceit. You are a part of humanity, though you are Archibald Keightley; and what is humanity? Humanity is a part of thousands of millions of humanity that passed away. It is a piece of dirt, nothing else. And what is the world? It is a little speck of dirt in the Universe. You cannot come and have this spirit of separateness — though you be an Englishman and a Conservative.

Mr. A. Keightley: When one is an illusion one wants to understand one's relation.

H.P.B.: An illusion is an illusion. If you thought you understood it, you would be perfectly disenchanted.

Mr. A. Keightley: Sloka 3, page 91. Question 7. It is on page 91 that the sentence occurs. [Reads.] Can you explain to us the principle of permutation by which 13514 becomes 31415? Page 91.

H.P.B.: I tell you everything is possible to God, and that if it is his sweet will that 2 and 2 should make 5 you know he will do it in a moment.

Mr. B. Keightley: [Reads passage from *The Secret Doctrine*, vol. 1, p. 91.]

H.P.B.: As I said in my comment, we are not concerned at present with the process, which means that it cannot be given exoterically and publicly. That is said in so many words before on the page that you have just read the Sloka from, yet I don't mind explaining a little more, which I will do as much as I can. The set of figures must have the same meaning as the various cycles and ages of the first born, the 15 figures. 311, a great many more or less, and I don't know what. Never mind. I will try to give it to you and make you understand. Now, the Rabbis[3] called the circle (what we call Parabrahm) Achod,[4]

---

[3] **Rabbi** (*Hebrew*, "master") — originally a teacher of the Secret Mysteries, the Kabbalah; later, every member of the priestly caste became a teacher and a Rabbin.

[4] **Achod** or **Echod** (*Hebrew*) — the masculine name for the One represented as the collective aggregate, or totality, of the principal Creators or Architects of this visible Universe. The feminine name is Achath or Echath, also meaning "One."▸

the One or Ain-Soph. On the lower plane of the fourth it becomes
Adam Kadmon,[1] the manifested seven and the unmanifested ten, or
the complete Sephirothal tree, which are the three and the seven lower
ones, and the synthesis which makes the perfect ten. The Sephiroth,
therefore, are the same as the Elohim. Now, the name of the latter
written in Hebrew, Alhim, is composed of five letters. These letters
or their values in numerals being placed upon a circle can be shifted
or transmuted at will, as they could not be, were they applied to any
other geometrical figure. The circle is endless and has neither beginning nor end. Now, the literal Kabbalah is divided into three parts,
as all know, or methods, the third of which is called Temurah,[2] or
the permutation. According to certain rules, one letter is replaced by
another. The Kabbalistic alphabet is divided into two equal parts, each
letter or numeral of one corresponding to the same number or letter in
the sister half. It is a difficult process, and by changing alternately the
letters one from the other, there are about, some say, 22 combinations.
I have heard there are far more than that. In one case there are 22; there
are four more in other combinations within combinations, at least as
my Rabbi explained. Now if you make a circle in such a way (if I had
a table, I would just draw it here), if you make the circle, the perfect
circle, and inscribe within these letters, A L H E or I and M, Elohim,
and take their numerical values, it will yield to you either 13514 — I
left out something. Read this whichever way you like. And you may
read it as 13514 or 31415, which is the value of the astronomical *pi*

"Achath-Ruach-Elohim-Chiim" in the Sepher Jezirah and elsewhere denotes the
Elohim as androgynous at best, the feminine element almost predominating, as
it would read: "One is She the Spirit of the Elohim of Life."

[1] **Adam Kadmon** (*Hebrew*) — Archetypal Man; Humanity. The "Heavenly Man"
not fallen into sin; Kabbalists refer it to the Ten Sephiroth on the plane of human
perception. In the Kabbalah, Adam Kadmon is the manifested Logos corresponding to our Third Logos; the Unmanifested being the first paradigmic ideal
Man, and symbolizing the Universe *in abscondito* (in secret), or in its "privation"
in the Aristotelean sense. The First Logos is the "Light of the World," the Second
and the Third — its gradually deepening shadows.

[2] **Temurah** (*Hebrew*) — one of the three ancient methods used by Kabbalists to
reveal hidden meanings in sacred texts. The other two methods are *Gematria*
and *Notarikon*. Temurah involves replacing letters in a word or phrase with
other letters according to specific rules. Gematria assigns numerical values to
Hebrew letters and words. Notarikon is a technique of forming new words by
taking the initial or final letters from a longer word.

or the constant coefficient number, value, circumference of a circle whose diameter is one. That is a very plain thing in astronomy, that is to say, the five males-females or the ten (because each one of them is a male-female and it makes five) are ten resolving themselves into one. Not only can the numbers be replaced at will by the Temurah, but the Sephiroth, being synonymous with the Elohim, and of the ten words or the Dabarim.[3] These are all found inscribed numerically in the circle. Look at this for instance: there is the circle, which is the one, and there is the line, the straight line, the perpendicular line, which is the line of the first Logos. Then if you make another, and if you draw this line, this will be the plane of matter where will be the second Logos, and then there is the third. They are the seven creations. Nobody has ever remarked it, because they take literally every word of the Kabbalah, and they take literally every word of the Bible. Whose fault is that? It is perfectly well defined, and I promised to show to you my answer to prove it. It is the same thing, but nobody has read it to the present day. They have taken it positively, literally, the circle and its dividing line and the prototype of ten, the sacred number — that is to say, infinite or passive unmanifested, and the infinite active or the Logos. The numerals of the Dabarim, the Sephiroth, which are in Hebrew Sephir, which means cipher or figures, are all inscribed within the two, and yield the values of their names. It all comes out anagrammatically, and so it does with all the Sanskrit names. You may take the circle, and if you put all the letters in Hebrew, of course, of the Sephiroth, Elohim, or our Dhyan-Chohans or of the Builders, anything, it will just give to you the same thing always. It will come out the pi. Why? Because those digits, or the small figures, if you take out, of course, the noughts they are subservient to the circumference and the diameter to the one in the circle. This is very plain; but how extraordinary it is that they should have adopted for the astronomical thing such a thing as that, which if you translate them, they make Elohim. If you translate it (not as we take it, geometrically), it gives the number and the names of the Dhyan-Chohans, their real secret esoteric name, with all of them. But only, instead of putting in letters and numerals as the Hebrews do, we put them in geometrical figures,

---

[3] **Dabarim** (*Hebrew*, "words") — the Ten Words, which are the ten Sephiroth, the Three and the Seven, the Numbers and the Emanations of the Heavenly Light, which is both Adam Kadmon and Sephira.

and it comes to the same — a line, a triangle, a [...], and a cube, 1234 — until it comes to the digits 9 and 10, the three higher ones, and the seven lower ones. So, do you understand it now?

Mr. B. Keightley: I suppose the actual transformation is one of those anagrammatical transformations, in the way which the order of the digits has been shifted here.

H.P.B.: Dr. Westcott has done it very nicely here.[1] Now you should take this, because you can see it very nicely.

Mr. Gardner: When you say it represents the name of the Dhyan-Chohans, do you mean to say the names in Sanskrit?

H.P.B.: Also in Sanskrit just the same, because it all comes from India through Chaldea.

Mr. Gardner: You mean the numerical value of the name.

H.P.B.: All the numbers are the same. You take it in Greek, and it will give you the same value, because it has been adapted so cunningly, so ingeniously, that it is impossible to do it better. If you are inclined to believe that the Patriarchs and the Jews were the first ones, then of course you are welcome to do it. I keep to my own views, and I am for the Hindus. Being a true blue heathen myself, I am for the Hindus.

Mr. A. Keightley: Question 8. Will you give some explanation concerning the various hierarchies mentioned here? The terms are frequently used later on, and explanation in contrast as here would be very useful.

H.P.B.: I believe I have done so now quite enough. I have given it quite enough. You pass on to 9, because you are very fond of repeating the same questions over and over again.

Mr. A. Keightley: Sloka 4, page 95.

Mr. B. Keightley: [Reads passage from *The Secret Doctrine.*]

Mr. A. Keightley: Question 9. "What is the connection between the life-winds and the senses, and the connection of the intelligences with the latter?"

H.P.B.: There — a question to answer for one woman alone! Life-winds, or the various modes of inbreathing and outbreathing and changing thereby the polarity of one's object and state, and con-

---

[1] See William Wynn Westcott, *Numbers: Their Occult Powers and Mystic Virtue* (London: Theosophical Publishing Society, 1890).

sciousness, and principles and so on is all esoteric, of course, but what can I tell you more? It being esoteric, the connection between the intelligences — and I suppose by the intelligences, you mean the Dhyan-Chohans — and the senses is all given in the Esoteric Instructions, numbers 1 and 2, if you know what that means. It is all given, the correspondencies. Now, why should you come and make me speak here of things that are perfectly explained? I don't know.

Mr. A. Keightley: Because it is elucidation of points in *The Secret Doctrine.*

Mr. B. Keightley: One point is that in *The Theosophist* the life-winds have been explained not as breath at all but as forces operating in the body, having nothing to do, apparently, with the actual in and out breathing.

H.P.B.: I never heard that *The Theosophist* was anything but an exoteric exposition of things. You won't find in *The Theosophist* [...], and he who thinks that the [...] can perform miracles, and find a yogi, will find himself very much mistaken indeed, because here, where they will call a thing, perhaps, a table, it will mean a kind of juice of a plant; and when he says put your right leg in such a posture, it means you have to turn your cheek or your eye to a certain star. It is perfectly all blind and nothing else. You have to take yogi theosophy and give it word for word, and he who relies upon it will make a sore yogi, I can assure you.

Mr. A. Keightley: Now 10. What is the meaning of "The Sparks of the Seven are subject to and servants of the first, second, third, fourth, fifth, and sixth, and the seventh of the Seven"? Page 93.

H.P.B.: I have explained it to you. The sparks mean here sparks or monads or the higher intelligences as much as the human sparks, or monads, or the higher intelligences. It means just as I told you. It can be applied on the plane below or the plane above; it relates to the circle and the digits I have just shown you. It is the equivalent to saying in mathematical astronomy that the figures 31415 are all subject to the circumference and diameter, as I told you, of a circle. Think over it and I suppose you will see it. It is no use going over the old ground again; they are all subjects, that is what it means. And in the same way, all these hierarchies are subject to the circle which represents the symbol I. It is the symbol I of the absolute infinite circle; that is all.

Mr. A. Keightley: Now 11. Why is Sarasvati,[1] the Goddess of Speech, also called the goddess of Esoteric Wisdom? If the explanation lies in the meaning of the word Logos, why is there a distinction between the immovable mind and movable speech? Is mind equivalent to Mahat, or to the higher or lower Manas?

H.P.B.: Because and for the same reason that Logos or word is called incarnate wisdom in the Holy Bible, in the Book of God. "Light shining in darkness,"[2] also. Is it so? The distinction lies between the immovable or eternal immutable all, and the movable speech or Logos, that is to say, the periodical and the manifested. The Logos is not an eternal, only a [...]. It becomes manifested only in the Manvantaric periods periodically; therefore it cannot be referred to as the one eternal or the immovable, for he is very much moveable, but moves from the subjective and the unknown. Mind is an abstraction. It can relate to the Universal or the individual Mind, to the Mahat or the higher human Manas, because that which is desire or instinctive impulse in the lower Manas becomes thought in the higher, and consciousness. The former finds expression in acts, the latter in words. Do you understand? Therefore, even in your laws the assault is more severely punished than mere thought. That is a very unpoetical simile, but still it will open your eyes. This is again food for thought to the wise. Do you understand the difference? It is a perfect impossibility not to. You find it in the fourth gospel in the first chapters, which are Platonic and esoteric.

Mr. A. Keightley: Then does this mean that there is a further meaning to that allegory that you put there, to speech and mind going and having a dispute?

H.P.B.: Yes, it is from the *Anugita* again. Certainly it is, and the Brahmin gave the definition and shows what it is, and he reconciles them.

Mr. A. Keightley: He says neither is superior to the other; but speech having been uttered, and going and asking the question was rare also.

---

[1] **Sarasvati** (*Sanskrit*, "flowing one") — the same as Vach, wife and daughter of Brahma produced from one of the two halves of his body. She is the goddess of speech and of sacred or esoteric knowledge and wisdom.
[2] John 1:5.

H.P.B.: And he snubs very prettily the speech.

Mr. A. Keightley: And then he talks about moveable and immoveable speech.

H.P.B.: Yes, it is purely esoteric, all this. Now 12.

Mr. A. Keightley: Page 92. We know that "God geometrizes,"[3] but, seeing that there is no personal God, will you explain why the process of formation should be by dots, lines, triangles, cubes, and why a cube should then expand into a sphere? Finally, why, when the sphere leaves the static state, the inherent force of Breath sets it whirling.

H.P.B.: Certainly. There is God standing here simply (as with Plato) for the plural forces or rays emanating from the one and the Absolute; therefore, law is meant here. We say here law geometrizes, but in the day of Plato, *"hoi polloi"* would not certainly have understood, and therefore they used the word God. Why it should be so, I cannot tell certainly, because the Absolute did not unfortunately take my counsel; or perhaps, as I was part of him, if I had not been such a lazy woman, I might have heard. But I didn't, so how can I tell you such a thing as that? I don't think anyone in any book of wisdom would tell you such a thing as that. Now for instance, where you speak about the cubes and lines, and triangles: if you forget what you have learned in the simple, elemental physics, you just observe the snowflakes, the only things besides crystals which show you all the geometrical aspects existing in Nature. This you certainly cannot contradict. Look at the water, if you would observe [...] that is one thing you can do; and if you open any book of Tyndall you will find it. Now, heat affects the atomic particles of matter in a liquid state. What is heat, but the modification of the particles? It is a physical, or perhaps a mechanical law, that particles which are in motion of themselves become spheroidal. This is law, from a globe or planet down to a drop of rain; as soon as motion stops, the spheroidal shape alters and becomes a flat drop. But if it is passing through all the previous forms, that is to say, as soon as action ceases, as Tyndall teaches you, the drop becomes invariably an equilateral triangle, a hexagon, then cubes or squares coming out of the ends of the hexagon. You will see the six-pointed plane you see immediately forming cubes, and all kinds of things like that. In a lecture of his — something on ice, on the formation of

---

[3] A postulate attributed to Plato.

particles in the ice, if I remember right — Tyndall, having observed the breaking up of ice particles in a large mass of ice through which he passed heat rays by electricity, assures us that the first or primary shape the particles assume is always triangular or pyramidal. Then they become cubical, and finally assume the form of hexagons, etc., etc.; I could not tell you where it is, but I know I know it, because it is just the thing that is taught in the occult doctrine. It is a law, and certainly there is no mistake about it — a law in Nature. Or take a snowflake, you find all these geometrical shapes in it.

Mr. Kingsland: Then as to that experiment of breaking up the piece of ice with a ray of heat. Can you tell us how it is that in examination through the reflection on a screen you see vegetable forms, the forms of ferns and plants?

H.P.B.: Most assuredly. They only show their astral bodies, which are preparing to form plants and all that. Ice is a species of matter which contains all the prototypes of matter in its future forms. It would not be seen there if you observed it on the surface, but when it comes to their forces and everything which will be, then you find that one ring throws off the ring that will become the future ring. This is all one link into another. I am very glad you know this experiment.

Mr. Kingsland: Yes, but it requires something else besides water to make these forms. He takes a large block of ice, and throws a very powerful ray on this ice and onto a screen, and this ray dissolves through. And on the screen you see these ferns and plumes.

H.P.B.: Don't you see triangles, hexagons, and cubes, and you see the ferns and plants, because it throws off the astral bodies — that which is contending in those particles of ice, because ice is matter? You see, if you think about it, you remember that ferns, that that class of plants, particularly ferns, that you most commonly see on a screen are to a large extent built up of geometrical figures. It is in Nature. It is impossible otherwise. Law geometrizes or God geometrizes. Why could we not call Law God, or vice versa? It is just the same.

Mr. B. Keightley: The fact of the matter being that these geometrical figures or mathematical figures are a part of the human law of thought, because they exist in the universal mind from which they proceed, and of which human mind is itself a reflection, a microcosm, I suppose.

H.P.B.: Now, 13.

Mr. A. Keightley: Sloka 5, page 99. Do numbers and geometrical figures represent to human consciousness the laws of action in the Divine Mind?

H.P.B.: They do, most assuredly. How can it be otherwise? There is no chance evolution of forms, nor is there any so-called abnormal appearance or cosmic phenomenon due to haphazard circumstances, but is always a stray something on our earth, either at its beginning or its end (not of the earth, but of its phenomena). For instance, meteors. Now, what are meteors? What does science say about them, that they fall from the Moon or the Sun, or what?

Mr. B. Keightley: One of two hypotheses. One is that they are the fragments of a broken-up planet, and the other is that these rings of matter from which the planets are supposed to be formed, on the hypothesis of Laplace, instead of the ring forming a single planet, owing to various circumstances, the matter consolidates into comparatively small lumps, and the meteor streams are the tracks of these rings of more or less diffuse matter.

H.P.B.: Of course, because the breath is always at work; even during Pralaya it never stops — that breath that I call motion. Perhaps during Pralaya it produces no results because there is no one to see those results. And if there were they would see results perfectly unexpected and which their finite intellect would not comprehend, surely. We call this very proudly Pralaya, but we do not know what we are talking about. We say there is nothing worth blowing for that breath.

Mr. Kingsland: Can't you tell us something more about meteors?

H.P.B.: Perhaps I may tell you at the end here. I think I have been writing at the end about it.

Mr. A. Keightley: Sloka 5, page 99.

Mr. B. Keightley: Which is... [Reads passage from *The Secret Doctrine*.]

Mr. A. Keightley: Astronomically, is there an explanation of Martanda's[1] rejection?

H.P.B.: I do not believe that there is. Astronomers can hardly look beyond their direct mathematical calculations, let alone what takes

---

[1] **Martanda** (*Sanskrit*) — the Vedic name of the Sun.

place in or around our Sun at the beginning of his young life. The Sun is several Manvantaras older than all these planets. His rejection means that when bodies or planets begin to form from his rays or his magnetic rays, or heat, then that attraction had to be stopped, for otherwise he would have swallowed back all his progeny, like Saturn is fabled to have done. I do not mean by progeny that all the planets were thrown out from the Sun; it is simply under his rays that they grow. Aditi is the ever-equilibrizing Mother Nature, or Space, on the purely spiritual and subjective plane; she is the Shakti, the female power or potency of the fecundating spirit, and it is for her to regulate the behaviour of the Sons born in her bosom. The allegory is a very suggestive one. Now, if you turn to question 15, I will tell you what these things mean.

Mr. A. Keightley: Were all the planets in our solar system first comets and then suns?

H.P.B.: They were not comets, certainly, nor planets in our solar system, but comets in space in the beginning. They began life as wanderers over the face of the infinite Cosmos. They detached themselves from the common storehouse of already prepared material ready for use, which is the Milky Way, for the Milky Way is nothing more nor less than that World-stuff, all the rest in space being crude material as yet. Now let me explain to you this. This Milky Way is just the prepared material ready for use. Whereas all the other that we do not see, which consists in these clouds of particles that we can never see any of the atoms of, that is the crude material not prepared yet.

Mr. A. Keightley: Then the process of formation is going on at the present time from the Milky Way.

H.P.B.: Positively, and having set on their long journey, those comets first settled in life where their conditions were prepared for them by Fohat. That is to say, where the conditions of equilibrizing and polarity were and beginning actually to form themselves into suns, each of them (mind you, in space, not in our solar system, it didn't exist then) then, each sun, when its Pralaya arrived, disrupted into millions and billions of fragments. Each of those fragments rolled to and fro in space, collecting fresh materials as it rolled on like an avalanche does until it was stopped by the laws of attraction and repulsion and its own weight (why it should be weight, I do not know; I simply translate you what is said in the occult books), and became a planet. After having disrupted, each fragment became a planet in our or some other system — beyond our telescopes, of course. The fragments of our Sun will be just such planets after our solar Pralaya. He was a comet once upon a time, at the beginning of Brahma's age — not day, don't confuse; then he fixed himself where we see or perhaps, rather, ought to see him in London. When he dies he will burst asunder, and his atoms will be whirled in space, æons upon æons, as those of comets and meteors until each is caught up in the vortex of the two forces and placed in some higher and better system. Now, this is a thing which I told you last Thursday, when I was telling you about these two forces acting, the imprisoned and the free forces, that which produced the thing. And this you have to learn the correspondences of and how it acts — that it begins, for instance, by colour and goes on to sound and so and so — I need not detail. When it reaches the earth, when the two forces begin to act, and everything, it is just the same; as it is above so it is below, and as it is below so it is above. Let us hope that the astronomers of the future systems will be more fitted to appreciate Nature than they do now. Thus, the Sun will live in his children as a parent — as each one of us will live in his children (if we have any, of course). This will show to those of you who are prepared to accept the occult teachings that the modern astronomers who have brought out that hypothesis to which they refer as the Nebula Theory have begun by the wrong end. Had they said that the future planets or planetary systems will be the fragments shot out from the body of our Sun, they would be right; as it is they are wrong. Moreover, when the day comes, the semblance or reflection of the Sun's ray, therefore, will first of all fall off like a veil from the true Sun — for no mortal will see it, because every being with eyes will become blind. It is an impossibility to see the real Sun, because there would not be such a thing as an eye left in the world, and everything would be burnt in a moment. This reflection or veil is a kind of safeguard of nature, and a very wise one; take it off, disperse this veil for one second, and all the planets in the system — everything — would be reduced to a handful of ashes. Because, take the Sun's rays and explain to me — you will speak about reverberation and all that — why is it that you catch the most terrible sunstrokes when there is the most foggy weather? Of course, on the physical plane I know what you will say.

Mr. B. Keightley: I do not think anybody does know or has properly explained that.

H.P.B.: Those able men of science will say it is the most ignorant thing in the world, but you will see it is a thousand times more probable and logical than to accept those 397,000 hypotheses which are only born to die, and which do not dovetail and do not cover the whole ground; and this, as I show to you, if you work out the system, you will find it covers the whole ground. This is a known fact. Now, gentleman, you may ask me any questions you like.

Mr. B. Keightley: As you have traced the stages of comet and sun and then the fragments of the Sun becoming planets, when the planets have lived their life and die, is that their final dispersion?

H.P.B.: We will bury them and write a magnificent epitaph, and we will ask George William Childs[1] in Philadelphia to prepare some verses.

Mr. A. Keightley: Then practically, the planets in the solar system are very much older than the Sun itself?

Mr. Kingsland: It is the opposite way.

H.P.B.: It is the Sun which is a great deal older, because the Sun is the Sun yet. When it becomes disrupted you just go and put together the figures.

Mr. A. Keightley: I understood you to say that the planets in this particular system are fragments of suns that had previously existed.

H.P.B.: They have been suns; they have been disrupted, and every fragment of such a disrupted sun has become a planet.

Mr. Kingsland: That Sun might have belonged to any other system far away.

H.P.B.: There are millions and millions of systems. What is the use of your talking about this little horizon?

Mr. Kingsland: Do you say this earth of which this is composed came originally from the Milky Way?

H.P.B.: But mind you, you know what it is: there was the focus, that was prepared material, and it was in the Milky Way; and when it throws off its principles, it comes and animates, so to say, one of those things from the ready material.

---

[1] **George William Childs** (1829–1894) — an American publisher.

Mr. A. Keightley: And these are the results of building on the imperishable centres.

H.P.B.: Yes, on the Laya centres.

Mr. Kingsland: Then is that Milky Way, as astronomers suppose, so far outside the limits of the solar system, or is that only an appearance? The astronomers suppose that the Milky Way lies far beyond the distance of the furthest fixed stars that we can see; is that actually the case, or is that a deceptive appearance?

H.P.B.: My idea is it is a deceptive appearance; it is very deceptive, because this thing that we see, it is only because it is at a distance that we see it, but this thing actually exists everywhere, in the atmosphere and everywhere. It is not that there is a particular thing at such and such a distance, so many miles away; it is perfect nonsense, because it is everywhere, though only at a certain distance we see it.

Mr. Kingsland: If you take only a foot section you do not see it.

H.P.B.: Just that. It is the same with every bit. This is what we call the prepared world-stuff which is ready for use, which has been differentiated and redifferentiated and combed out and everything has been done to it. And the other is simply everything that is otherwise. And the space which is between this inter-Milky Way space is nothing but ready material.

Mr. Kingsland: Can you tell us why they should appear more or less in the shape of a ring, instead of all round with equal density?

H.P.B.: I suppose there must be some reason. It must take absolutely some geometrical figure and space. You know, this is why with Pythagoras, geometry was the first sacred science which had to be studied and known before one could join the Pythagorean school; they had to study geometry and music, first of all. Now they ask, why music? Because of the sounds, you understand, the correspondences, that is why. You go and read the sacred science and you will find they had to know, among other things, mathematics, geometry and music. They had to know all these.

Mr. Kingsland: We want something more about the meteors.

H.P.B.: They ask me as though I were first cousin to the meteors, or the mother-in-law, or something like that.

Mr. Kingsland: I thought you had something more about it in your notes.

H.P.B.: I do not want any notes; I know what you are going to say without notes. It is only a few "happy thoughts" I book there.

Mr. Kingsland: I want to know what is the occult explanation of the meteors.

H.P.B.: Why, didn't I explain to you enough? Who is it that is dissatisfied?

Mr. B. Keightley: Are the meteors these fragments streaming through space, or what are they?

H.P.B.: In my humble opinion, I do not make much difference between a comet and a meteor. A meteor is something which is a dead comet, or something like that.

Mr. Kingsland: Are we right in supposing the meteors get their incandescence by coming into contact with our atmosphere?

Mr. B. Keightley: Well, there is one of the things: meteors have no tails.

H.P.B.: They are corpses.

Mr. Kingsland: What makes them incandescent?

H.P.B.: It is the nature of the beast, I suppose.

Mr. B. Keightley: We only see them when they come very close to the earth.

H.P.B.: You tell me why the comets are the cheekiest people you ever met with. They always cheek the Sun and snub him; they wag their tails against the Sun in all defiance of gravity, and the poor Sun stops and looks there in amazement and cannot help it. You tell me that, you gentlemen physicists and men of science.

Mr. A. Keightley: Perhaps it is a tone of contempt.

H.P.B.: They will penetrate right through in the most terrible way, and go into his drawing room and bedroom and come out of the kitchen and then go and wag their tails in defiance of all gravity. And the men of science will come and say: "Gravity! It cannot be; it is an immutable law." Is it? I am glad to hear it.

Mr. B. Keightley: What is the explanation of this extremely light-minded behaviour?

H.P.B.: You make their acquaintance and ask them. I have no right to give out their secrets. It only puts there is no gravity, there is no such attraction and repulsion.

Mr. A. Keightley: Why should the tail be repelled?

H.P.B.: Because the Sun is not congenial to the tail. It has got quite enough of its own electricity and its own magnetic heat and doesn't want to spoil its complexion.

Mr. A. Keightley: You speak in *The Secret Doctrine* of the mysterious planet in connection with the moon. Does the moon act to that planet as a kind of veil in the same way as the things of the Sun?

H.P.B.: I think there is something — not behind the Moon, because the Moon is not motionless as the Sun, the Sun is always on the same spot — but the moon has not got such an electric thing. The moon has only magnetic power over the earth.

Mr. A. Keightley: I thought it might be an analogy.

Mr. B. Keightley: The moon has its own independent orbit; it doesn't cover any one point of space constantly.

H.P.B.: There are some planets, or something (I do not know what) they do not pay much attention to, because it is not their time yet to appear. They may appear.

Mr. Kingsland: Between Mercury and the Sun?

H.P.B.: Oh, it is surely the planet between Mercury and the Sun. It was the beginning of the Fourth Race and then it went off. Just the same as if you take the Pleiades; it was seen very well once, and now it is seen no more. You can hardly see it in the telescopes, but Maia[1] was a bright one and a chief one, the nurse of Arcas.[2]

Mr. Gardner: That was the seven Pleiades.

H.P.B.: They say it is because she married below her station and she was ashamed to show herself. They say it in the Greek mythology,

---

[1] **Maia** (*Greek*) — one of the seven daughters of Atlas and Pleione in Greek mythology, after whom the seven stars of the Pleiades were named; the mother of Hermes. Maia was the brightest of the stars in the constellation.

[2] **Arcas** (*Greek*) — the son of Zeus and Callisto in Greek mythology, whom Maia raised.

that she made a *mésalliance*;[1] she was a kind of Princess Louise,[2] she married one of her subjects. But these Pleiades are the most occult constellations that exist.

Mr. Gardner: More than Mercury?

H.P.B.: Oh, more. They are connected with nearly all the aristocracy. They are very occult, because they are connected with all the Rishis, too; they have an interchange of thought with the Rishis.

Mr. Hall: "The sweet influence of the Pleiades."[3]

H.P.B.: If you read those allegories of the Hindus in the astronomy books, you see they had secrets and knowledge which really the moderns cannot think of approaching.

Mr. Gardner: Which old books do you refer to?

Mr. Keightley: The Puranas.

H.P.B.: Even the Puranas. But you read the old astronomical books.

Mr. A. Keightley: Then about the Sun following slowly after the planets, turning upon itself, the actual revolution of the Sun itself.

H.P.B.: Now, there is a thing! This is the most extraordinary thing, how they knew this. See what Bailly says about that.[4] There is not one second's difference if it is so, it is as the Hindus give it, because it is so mathematically correct; they have remarked it and they said because such and such constellations were in conjunction, and so on.

Mr. Hall: Why do we only see one side of the moon?

H.P.B.: Because she doesn't want to show the other; because perhaps she has not combed her hair. I can only tell you what I have learnt, I can't invent.

Mr. A. Keightley: You don't tell us all you know.

H.P.B.: I do not see why I should. We should have nothing for next Thursday.

---

[1] **Mésalliance** (*French*) — a marriage or union between individuals of unequal social, economic, or cultural backgrounds.

[2] **Princess Louise** (1848–1939) — the sixth child and fourth daughter of Queen Victoria and Prince Albert.

[3] Job 38:31.

[4] **Jean Sylvain Bailly** (1736–1793) — a French astronomer and mathematician.

Mr. Gardner: You were saying something about the Rishis of the Ursa Major.[5]

H.P.B.: The seven stars, and they are married. The Rishis are the husbands of the Pleiades.

Mr. Gardner: But which one made the *mésalliance*?

[Loud laughter.]

H.P.B.: The one which hides herself.

Mr. A. Keightley: Gardner, you must not talk celestial scandal!

H.P.B.: It was Electra.[6]

Mr. Gardner: Is *he* the one?

H.P.B.: It was a *she*! What an infidel! Well, I think you ladies and gentlemen can all talk now, and I will faithfully answer your questions.

---

[5] **Ursa Major** or **the Great Bear** — a constellation in the northern sky.
[6] **Electra** (*Greek*) — one of the Pleiades.

21 MARCH 1889

Mr. A. Keightley: Stanza 4, Sloka 6. "Then the Second Seven, who are the Lipika[1] produced by the three (Word, Voice, and Spirit)."[2] Question 1. Can you explain to us the relation of the Lipika, the "Second Seven," to the "Primordial Seven," and to the first "Sacred Four"?

H.P.B.: I think it is rather a difficult thing to do. I think that if I explain to you, who know very little of the Sanskrit books, that which you have access to — for instance, these various systems of the Gnostics that you can easily get in the British Museum — you would understand it better. Now, I have taken from one something just to show to you this difference, and make you understand it better. If you study the Gnostic system of the first centuries of Christianity, from that of Simon Magus[3] down to the highest and noblest systems — the Valentinians[4] — you will comprehend better the relation you want me to explain. All these systems are derived from the East. That which we call the Primordial Seven and the Second Seven are called by Simon Magus, for instance, the Æons. The Valentinians call them the Æons, and many others, the primeval — the second and the third series of Syzygies,[5] I think it is — it is a Greek name. They are graduated emanations ever descending lower and lower into matter from that primordial principle that is called fire. Simon Magus calls it fire and we call it Svabhavat, as behind that fire the manifested, the Silent Deity, stands with him as with us — that which is, was and ever will be. Therefore, take this fire, as he calls it, and that will be the root from which all these various powers and hierarchies descend. Therefore, since his doctrine is almost one with our cosmogony (and that you don't seem to see to this day, the philosophy or process of emanation), permit me to quote to you the words of Simon Magus,

---

[1] **Lipikas** (*Sanskrit*, "scribes") — the celestial recorders, who record every word and deed said or done by man while on this earth. They are the agents of Karma — the retributive Law.

[2] *The Secret Doctrine*, vol. 1, p. 103.

[3] **Simon Magus** — a Samaritan Gnostic and Thaumaturgist, called "the great Power of God."

[4] **Valentinians** — the followers of Valentinus, a Gnostic teacher.

[5] **Syzygy** (*Greek*, "yoked together") — a Gnostic term, meaning a pair or couple, one active, the other passive. Used especially of Æons.

as quoted from his work by the author of *Philosophumena*.[6] He says: "From the permanent stability and personified immutability, fire and this manifested principle, which immutability does not preclude activity, as the second form is endowed with intelligence and reason, who are (Mahat), it (the fire) passed from potentiality of action to action itself. From those series of evolutions were formed six beings, or the emanations from the infinite potency they were formed in Syzygies. That is to say, they are radiated out of the flame two by two, one being the active and the other the passive principle." Then Simon named Nous[7] and Epinoia,[8] or spirit and thought, and many others; and Logismos[9] and Enthumesis,[10] reasoning and reflection. Now, Simon shows the relation you want to know by saying as follows: "In each of the six primitive beings, the Infinite potency was in its totality, but it was there in potentiality only, not innate. It had to be established therein through an image, that of paradigm, in order that it should appear in all its essence, virtue, grandeur, and effects; for only then could it become like unto the parent potency, infinite and eternal. If on the contrary it was not conformed by or through the image, that potentiality could never become potency or pass into action but was lost for lack of use, as it happens to a man who, having an aptitude for grammar or geometry, does not exercise it; it gets lost for him just as if he never had it."[11] Now, one of these, which he calls Nous, spirit, and the other are one, he says, and inseparable. The system is too long

---

[6] See Patricius Cruice, translator, *Philosophumena sive haeresium omnium confutatio* [Philosophumena or the Refutation of all Heresies] (Paris: Imprimerie Royale, 1860).

[7] **Nous** (*Greek*, "mind") — a Platonic term for the Higher Mind or Soul. It means Spirit, as distinct from animal Soul (*psyche*); divine consciousness or mind in man: *Nous* was the designation given to the Supreme Deity (third Logos) by Anaxagoras (c.500–c.428 BCE), a famous Greek philosopher. Taken from Egypt, where it was called *Nout*, it was adopted by the Gnostics for their first conscious Æon, which, with the Occultists, is the third Logos, cosmically, and the third principle (from above), or *manas*, in man.

[8] **Epinoia** (*Greek*, "thought," "invention," "design") — a name adopted by the Gnostics for the first passive Æon.

[9] **Logismos** (*Greek*, "reasoning") — a name adopted by the Gnostics for the third active or male Æon.

[10] **Enthumesis** (*Greek*, "reflection") — a name adopted by the Gnostics for the third passive or female Æon.

[11] *Philosophumena sive haeresium omnium confutation*, pp. 249–251.

and too complicated to give it here. Suffice it to say that he shows that whether his Æons belong to the superior, middle or lower world, they are all one except in material density, which determines their outward manifestation and the results produced and the real essence which is from their mutual relations, which are established from eternity, as he says, by immutable laws. The same, therefore, for the Lipika and the Second Seven or the Primordial Seven, whatever name we may give them for the sake of our own comprehension, which seems to necessitate a name or label in each case to enable us to recognize one from the other. Now, this first, second, third or primordial seven or Lipika is all one; therefore, how can I tell you what relation they are in? When once they emanate from one plane onto another it will be just the same, the repetition — as it is above so it will be below. That is the only relation. They are all simply differentiated in matter in density, but not in qualities. And the same qualities descend unto the last plane, which is our plane, and which shows man endowed just with the same potentiality, if he knows how to develop it as the highest Dhyan-Chohan. I quote it just on purpose to show you, because you can go and read it. In the British Museum you have the book, and there are many things which really will show to you that our doctrine is as old as can be. It is perfectly the occult doctrine in many things. Of course, it changes its name and all kinds of things; but it gives a very good definition of the nature and essence of these Æons only. For instance, he gives six of them, that is to say, three pairs of two each — the seventh being the fourth which descends from one plane to another.

Mr. A. Keightley: Then practically, the synthesis is on the plane above.

H.P.B.: Yes, just that.

Mr. Harbottle: Then really these sevens are all identical, except that they are manifest on different planes. So that the Lipika are the same things as the Primordial Seven, except that the Primordial Seven are not manifest. They are the potentiality of manifestation.

H.P.B.: They are the first, but they are four, mind you, and have proceeded from Mahat, as I will show you. The Lipika are those who, in the Kabbalah, are called the four recording angels. In India they call them the four Maharajahs,[1] those who record every thought and deed of man. It is the book of life, as St. John calls it in Revelation.[2]

Mr. Harbottle: But they are called the seven in that passage, I think, of *The Secret Doctrine*. But that really means that the four are on the plane of the second seven. It does not mean that they are precisely the second seven.

H.P.B.: Just so. And the seven are simply seventy times seven; it is the seven hierarchies, the seven various degrees. And at the four corners of the world, these Lipikas are posted just to put down on the superior Astral Light the record of all our actions, deeds, words and everything.

Mr. Harbottle: On the lowest plane of all, they are the cardinal points.

H.P.B.: They are directly connected with Karma, and they are connected with what the Christians call the Last Day of Judgement. And in the East it is called the Day after Maha-Manvantara, when they come all to receive what is called in Sinnett's *Esoteric Buddhism* the Judgement.

Mr. A. Keightley: "The Day Be-With-Us,"[3] isn't it?

H.P.B.: Yes, when everything becomes one. But with every Manvantara they become more and more, the Absolute becomes more and more. Not only is it absolute intelligence, absolute consciousness and everything (because on our plane it is non-consciousness, non-being), but everyone will feel himself more; still every individuality knows itself. This may be a mysterious thing, but I tell you that which we are taught. Very often we are confronted with the statement: "you talk about Nirvana. What is Nirvana? It is an extinction, it is just like a flame that is blown out from the candle; there remains nothing.

---

[1] **Maharajahs** (*Sanskrit*, "great king") — the four great Karmic deities with the Northern Buddhists placed at the four cardinal points to watch mankind.

[2] See Revelation 3:5, 13:8, 17:8, 20:12, 20:15, 21:27, 22:19.

[3] **Great Day Be-With-Us** — the period of Rest, or Para-Nirvana. It corresponds to the Day of the Last Judgement of the Christians. This is the day when man, freeing himself from the trammels of ignorance, and recognizing fully the non-separateness of the Ego within his Personality — erroneously regarded as his own — from the Universal Ego (Anima Supra-Mundi), merges thereby into the One Essence, to become not only one with "Us," the manifested universal Lives which are one Life, but that very Life itself.

Nirvana — 'the flame out.'" I had how many times to have disputes and discussions about that. I said it is not that at all. It is that every particle of matter, of that which may have form in our conception or be conditioned or limited, everything disappears to make room for one homogeneity,[1] and for the one absolute spirit. But this spirit is not at all; it is non-consciousness for us, but it is absolute consciousness there.

Mr. A. Keightley: Question 2. What relation have the Lipika to Mahat?

H.P.B.: That relation, that the Lipika are a division of the four degrees taken from the septenates that emanated from Mahat. This is what we have been talking about. The latter is as Simon Magus's four, the Mahat, the secret and the manifested or the divine ideation made to witness for itself in the subjective universe through the subjective forms we see upon it. You may call it evolution or creation or whatever you like. What other relation can they have, except that of being wheels within wheels? They are workers on their own plane. If you ask me what relation the Lipika have with humanity, with men, then I have just told you what it was: they are the recorders.

Mr. A. Keightley: Then the Lipika are on the same plane as Mahat.

H.P.B.: They are the sons of Mahat, as they call them. Certainly, they are immediately under the absolute plane of divine ideation. But even that is a very risky thing to say, because immediately it suggests to you that it is like a staircase, and there are stories in the house, one below and the other above. But it is not so at all; it would be a very erroneous conception. It is everywhere and nowhere, just as when we were speaking about the circle and the point and circumference and all that, because it is not a thing above or below, and the right or the left. It is as I have been explaining many times, something which is — well, it may be in one place and yet they are the seven planes, they are states. And being states other than ours, of course they are invisible and perfectly incomprehensible to us, and each state does not know the people of the other state.

Mr. Harbottle: But still, it would not be right to describe them as being on the same plane as Mahat.

---

[1] **Homogeneity** — that which is of the same nature throughout, undifferentiated, non-compound, as gold is *supposed* to be.

H.P.B.: Certainly not.

Mr. Harbottle: Mahat is the synthesis of the plane above the Lipika.

H.P.B.: Certainly, and the Lipika are in the middle of the plane on the four quarters, that is to say, the higher ether or the higher Astral Light and the lower Akasha. Akasha certainly goes beyond the seventh.

Mr. Harbottle: Can you tell us exactly how they would correspond with the archetypal worlds of the Kabbalists? Is it between that and the next?

H.P.B.: The Kabbalists have only four worlds and we have seven, because they leave out entirely the three upper ones and begin counting simply the archetypal world, which is the highest Astral Light. Just the four, there it is; but the others are left in silence, and they are not spoken about.

Mr. Harbottle: The Lipika really are on the plane which is above the archetypal world.

H.P.B.: Together they are on that plane, because their world begins where our globe A begins. And if you take *The Secret Doctrine*, you find there the division of the four planes. You see four planes; it begins there just above our sphere. Their archetypal world goes down, they have got only four worlds.

Mr. B. Keightley: That places, so to speak, the Lipika in relation to the kabbalistic conception and to the evolution perfectly. They are on the highest plane corresponding to the highest plane of our chain of globes.

H.P.B.: What is the use of talking a language no one would understand and cannot even conceive of?

Mr. A. Keightley: Question 3. What is the difference made here between Word, Voice and Spirit?

H.P.B.: The same as between Atman, Buddhi and Manas. In one sense, spirit emanates from the unknown darkness into the mystery of which none of us can penetrate. That spirit — call it the Spirit of God that moves on the face of the waters, if you like, or primordial substance — the spirit mirrors itself in these waters and produces thereby the first flutter of differentiation in the homogeneousness of primordial matter. This is the voice, the first flutter of differentiated matter, if you like, in this sense manifestation number one. And from that voice emanates the word or Logos, that is to say, the definite and objective expression of that which has hitherto remained in the depths of the concealed thought. Of course we cannot begin here about colours and sounds and all that, but I tell you kabbalistically, and kabbalistically you will find that. And mind you the one that mirrors itself in space is the third Logos; they call it the unknown.

Mr. A. Keightley: Then speaking there as you spoke, the Logos there is the subdivided seven Logoi.

H.P.B.: Yes.

Mr. A. Keightley: And the voice is the synthesis of the Logos?

H.P.B.: It is just like saying, as we say in the esoteric thing, the colour, the sound, and numbers. Well, the Logoi ought to stand for numbers, then, in this sense, or the numbers will come after that when they divide the hierarchies.

Mr. Gardner: What stands for the colour?

H.P.B.: Well, you try to dream of it.

Mr. A. Keightley: Sloka 6 continued, etc. "The rejected Son is One, the 'Son-Suns' are countless."[1] Question 4. Is this sentence to be understood in the light of the explanations given on page 99 (c)? And if so, why is the "Rejected One" mentioned again here in connection with the "Second Seven"?

H.P.B.: I have been reading the whole page, and I don't know what you mean. Where do I speak of the second seven? Unless it is the planets that you mean, in which case it would not be the second seven, it would by the seventy-seventh seven, because they are on the material plane.

Mr. B. Keightley: It is in this stanza. The stanza speaks of the second seven, and then goes on in the next sentence to speak of the "Rejected One," and you have been speaking about the "Rejected One" in an earlier part of the stanza.

H.P.B.: But you forget I have been skipping an innumerable number of times not only lines, but whole stanzas. You know perfectly well I have given you only about twelve in the first and about 42 in the second.

---

[1] *The Secret Doctrine*, vol. 1, p. 103.

Mr. B. Keightley: The thing is to find out whether there has been a gap there.

H.P.B.: Certainly you will find gaps. I just try to explain as much as I can. It says there the Son is one and the "Sons-Suns" are many. It does not mean our Sun. It means the Spiritual Sun.[2] You read it there.

Mr. A. Keightley: Is the Spiritual Sun also the Rejected One?

H.P.B.: No, no, no. I say here it is said somewhere there that the Son and the "Son-Suns" are countless.

Mr. A. Keightley: It is the "Rejected One."

H.P.B.: But it is this "Rejected One"; they are not the "Son-Suns." I don't call the planets the "Son-Suns." I speak in general. The Spiritual Sun is one, but the "Son-Suns" are countless, and it does not refer at all to the planets.

Mr. A. Keightley: Then has not it an equal application to the planets as well?

H.P.B.: It may be something like that, but they are not any more suns now. They were suns. In other places I speak about this. I have read it very well.

Mr. B. Keightley: It was in the stanza, that quotation; that is what puzzled me about it.

H.P.B.: Oh yes. You will be puzzled more than once, you know.

Mr. A. Keightley: Stanza 5, Sloka 1. "The Primordial Seven, the first Seven Breaths of the Dragon of Wisdom, produce in their turn from their holy circumgyrating Breaths the Fiery Whirlwind."[3] Question 5: Can you explain in any way the necessity of each entity in becoming divine to pass through matter to self-experience?

H.P.B.: Well perhaps a sufficient reason might be found for it in the very nature of your question. This progress to a Divine state is but the first step, from our earth, at least, to Divine absorption. Now, the

---

[2] **Spiritual Sun** — a central body in the Milky Way, a point unseen and mysterious, the ever-hidden centre of attraction of our Sun and System. This invisible source of Supreme Fire is located behind the constellation of Hercules, towards which the Solar System is moving. As the cycle of seasons on the Earth is caused by the Earth's orbit around the Sun, so Cosmic Seasons are determined by the Solar System's orbit around the Spiritual Sun in the Universe. It is the Spiritual Sun's slow approach that causes global warming on the Earth and other planets.

[3] *The Secret Doctrine*, vol. 1, p. 106.

latter means that each entity will become Absoluteness when it reaches it — that is to say, that which contains all, and therefore every earthly experience, including the very strange question which is now offered (because, really, it is a very strange question). How could that Absoluteness become one, unless it contained every experience — that is to say, every stage and state of mind on the scale or ladder of collective experiences of beings? When you answer this, then I shall be able to proceed. Now answer me, how is it possible that Absoluteness, once that you reach it, there should be one single experience that would not be contained in it, including even the question that you put to me? It must be there.

Mr. A. Keightley: But it was there before.

H.P.B.: It was there in [...], as Simon Magus would say. It was in Divine ideation. When in Divine ideation it comes into Absoluteness. Divine ideation is not Absoluteness, it is the first manifestation of Absoluteness, and is Absolute. It is not the Absoluteness.

Mr. A. Keightley: Then the whole process of one Maha-Manvantara, that Divine ideation, after the previous Maha-Pralaya, shall become Absoluteness to again emanate another Divine ideation?

H.P.B.: Most assuredly, because we all change. With every Maha-Manvantara we become entirely different, and everything becomes different. We cannot say we will be a little better, or have more rosy cheeks, or longer noses. We shall be entirely something we cannot conceive of. We are that which we are only in this Manvantara, which lasts some trillions and trillions of years. That is the teaching, at least. I don't know anything about what we shall become. Therefore, I only know what we are now.

Mr. A. Keightley: That introduces a curious idea, that the Absolute of one Maha-Manvantara is different from the Absolute following it.

H.P.B.: Not at all. It is the same Absolute, only from this Absoluteness there are things which have been and things which are, but have not yet been, you understand, that which was is in that; that which will be is not yet, but it is still, it exists, but has not returned into Absoluteness. I don't see how you cannot understand it?

Mr. A. Keightley: That sounds as if there was in the Absolute a series of paradigms.

H.P.B.: It is on our manifested plane that I speak to you, about the Mahat which is born. Mahat has a beginning in the beginning of a Manvantara, therefore it must have an end. I speak to you about Divine ideation, not in its Absoluteness before manifestation, but the first flutter of manifestation, the first differentiated, when this Mahat is born of Brahma, as they say in the *Vishnu Purana*. Now, that is quite a different thing. Absoluteness does not differentiate the one never-to-be-known ideation. We speak now on the plane of manifestation at every Manvantara.

Mr. Kingsland: Then Mahat is ever becoming, but never does become the Absolute.

H.P.B.: The Mahat is the Absolute of our Manvantara, if you like to say so. Perhaps you will find a better expression. I don't say that I am Herbert Spencer, to come and invent new words. I simply try to tell you as I understand it.

Mr. Harbottle: It is an Absolute which is not an Absolute. It is an Absolute which is limited.

H.P.B.: The Absolute cannot be limited.

Mr. Harbottle: I know it cannot, really; at the same time, it is not the Absolute Absolute: there is that behind which contains the past, present, and future.

H.P.B.: That which they call fire, which is deity, from Simon Magus to the last, and we say in our philosophy it is this which was, is, and will be; and yet this which was, is and will be, is yet, has a beginning in every Manvantara before emanation begins. Now, every Æon becomes also, and is called in its turn that which was, is, and will be. So you take *Philosophumena*, you read the definition given by Simon Magus. Then take a better thing, take Valentinus, who was one of the highest philosophers, and one who explained it the best. You will see he calls it that which is, was, and will be. Every Æon will thus have a beginning, and an end. Therefore, they are all emanations of the Absolute; they are not themselves Absolute.

Mr. Kingsland: Then in what sense do they become the Absolute?

H.P.B.: We are the Absolute, too. The spirit in us becomes the Absolute, but it is on its pilgrimage, it is this circumgyration.

Mr. Kingsland: In what sense do they become Absolute? Because it would appear from that in the next Manvantara, they have to pass to an experience.

H.P.B.: Because you cannot have anything which does not contain the Absolute. If it did not contain the Absolute it could not be anything and could not exist. There is not an atom in this world that has not got the Absolute in it.

Mr. Kingsland: When you speak of the Absolute in that sense, you don't mean the rootless root.

H.P.B.: I do mean it.

Mr. Kingsland: But this Mahat becomes the rootless root.

H.P.B.: Mahat is but a name which people have invented to show the emanation of a certain Manvantara in the Divine ideation. Now, we must call it Absoluteness, we cannot call it anything else, because the philosophy of such terms is not very easy.

Mr. Kingsland: What is it that has to evolve?

H.P.B.: The illusion and nothing more, and that illusion more or less illusionary.

Mr. Kingsland: Then that has no relation to the Absolute.

H.P.B.: I beg your pardon, it has. It is because the Absolute evolves one thing, and we with our finite and little brains see another thing. We are not only colour-blind, we are truth-blind, and we are everything-blind, and we must take these things as they present themselves, but it is not the Absolute.

Mr. B. Keightley: Did you ever think out, Kingsland, the mathematical point of a limit?

H.P.B.: What is a mathematical point? Does it exist? Is there such an animal in nature as a mathematical point? You see, we are obliged to use such expressions. How can you come and — well I cannot invent a phraseology — how can you express that which is inexpressible?

Mr. Kingsland: Well, of course, to our finite minds it is, we admit that, but we try to elucidate that one point. What is it that evolves?

H.P.B.: A Vedantin would tell you that it is an illusion, a Maha-Maya.[1] That is why they call it illusion, because it lasts but a "wink of

---

[1] **Maha-Maya** (*Sanskrit*, "great illusion") — the great illusion of manifestation. This universe, and all in it in their mutual relation, is called the great Illusion or ➤

the eye," though it may last millions of years for us. What is there in Eternity which has a beginning and an end which is of consequence? It is expressed in the Bible that a thousand years is as a "wink of the eye" to the Lord, but I say it is perfect nonsense to speak of thousands of years. You speak of trillions and even higher than that, and then you won't be nearer the truth. Eternity is eternity, it cannot be divided, so as to say: half eternity and quarter of eternity, for then it cannot be eternity.

Mr. A. Keightley: Question 6. Are the atoms — in the occult sense of the term — eternal and indestructible, like the Monads of Leibniz, or are they dissolved during Pralaya?

H.P.B.: Now look at this question, if you please. This proves that the atoms are in your conceptions somethings, when there is no such thing in this world as atoms, except as mathematical points, as I say. The atoms, whether representing the Monads of Leibniz or the eternal and indestructible mathematical points of substance which our occult doctrine teaches, can neither be dissolved during Pralaya nor reform during Manvantara. The atoms do not exist as appreciable quantities of matter on any plane. They are mathematical points of unknown quantity here. And whatever they are or may be on the seventh plane, each is and must be logically an absolute universe in itself, reflecting other universes and yet it is not matter and it is not spirit. Now, will you understand this? This is to say that which is Mahat or divine ideation, a sum total, and is a conceived fraction. Now when I speak of fraction, please don't allow your materialistic conceptions to imagine that Absolute can be divided into parts or pieces. The Absolute is everywhere, even in the smallest molecules of matter. It can neither be pressed into the infinitesimal part, nor enlarged into a limitless cosmos; it is both. And so much the worse for us who have not enough of the metaphysical element to understand the explanation. How could Brahma be called, Anu for instance — an atom — if it was not something of the kind that I tried to explain to you? If it could be conditioned or limited by space or time or anything? The atom is and is not. The atom is the mathematical point, the potentiality in space; and there is not, I suppose, a space in this world that is not an atom. If you call it molecule, it is a different thing. But if you speak

---

Maha-Maya. It is also the usual title given to Gautama the Buddha's Immaculate Mother — Mayadevi, or the "Great Mystery," as she is called by the Mystics.

about the atoms of Democritus[1] it is a different thing. Maybe he has been giving it in a very materialistic way, but if you speak about the atom, that which we call Anu, then certainly they have no substance that we know of.

Dr. Williams: Then what would you say was the ultimate constitution of the ordinary gases, like hydrogen and oxygen?

H.P.B.: Everything is an atom, but what are these atoms? We cannot see them, we cannot smell them or divide them; atoms are something science has accepted simply as hypothesis.

Dr. Williams: Most of them are detected by some one or other of the senses, if you admit that the gases do exist in the atomic form.

H.P.B.: Yes, if you call them molecules — the molecules that you have not yet come to, that Crookes has tried to divide and subdivide and he could not catch them, because every one of them might be divided *ad infinitum* — but when that becomes homogeneous, then you find these molecules become atoms. They may be the atoms of Democritus or somebody else, but they are not the atoms of esoteric science. It is quite a different thing.

Mr. A. Keightley: Question 7. In Occultism, are the true atoms conceived of as "particles" or as something nearer to what we may call "Vortex-Atoms"?[2]

H.P.B.: I know nothing of "Vortex-Atoms," first laughed at by science when they were talked of by [...]; and now, it appears, Sir William Thomson accepts them. If you mean those of Sir William Thomson, I don't know anything at all about them. Pass to 8.

Mr. A. Keightley: Sloka 2. "They make of him the messenger of their will. The Dzyu[3] becomes Fohat; the Swift Son of the Divine sons,

[1] **Democritus** (c.460–c.370 BCE) — a Greek philosopher, who formulated the atomic theory of the universe.

[2] **Vortex theory of the atom** — the 19th-century theory by William Thomson, in which atoms were envisioned as tiny vortex rings or knots of swirling, incompressible fluid-like substances, similar to smoke rings. These vortex rings were thought to represent the fundamental building blocks of matter.

[3] **Dzyu** — the one Real (Magical) Knowledge, or Occult Wisdom; which, dealing with eternal truths and primal causes, becomes almost omnipotence when applied in the right direction. Its antithesis is Dzyu-mi, that which deals with illusions and false appearances only, as in our exoteric modern sciences. In this case, Dzyu is the expression of the collective Wisdom of the Dhyani-Buddhas.

whose sons are the Lipika, runs circular errands."[4] Question 8. Does this mean that the Lipika are the Sons of Fohat, or are they the Sons of the Primordial Seven?

H.P.B.: This means that they are the Sons of Fohat, as a personification of Mahat, the Manasa-Putras or "sons of the universal intelligences," and it means that the Lipika are the Sons of the "Primordial Seven." Whether the Lipikas' marriage certificate is illegal will be next asked, I suppose. I would not wonder, because, for instance, what can I answer you to this? They are the sons; they cannot be the Sons, it is simply an expression used. "The Sons of Fohat" means just as the sons of Lipika, it is simply one coming down from above to below, and that is all.

Mr. A. Keightley: Sloka 3. "He is their guiding spirit and leader. When he commences work he separates the sparks of the lower kingdom (*mineral atoms*) that float and thrill with joy in their radiant dwellings (*gaseous clouds*), and forms therewith the germs of wheels…"[5] Question 9. What is meant by the "mineral atoms" spoken of here? For the stanza seems to refer to a period before even the "Wheels" were formed or placed.

H.P.B.: It means that which is to become in this Manvantara; and the "mineral atoms," that which was set apart for it in eternity; that is what it means and nothing else. You see, if the writers of the stanza were not born out of time they would learn to express themselves better; but really, I think it is impossible to satisfy you and to give you all these explanations. Now, those who wrote the stanzas wrote them just as they would write them in those times; they are perfectly philosophical, but if you come and ask every little thing, and want it to be expressed in Macaulean[6] English, it cannot be done.

Mr. Kingsland: Have not those "mineral atoms" been through a previous state of evolution in a previous Manvantara?

H.P.B.: Most assuredly. Nothing is lost, and they have been in thousands and millions of forms.

---

[4] *The Secret Doctrine*, vol. 1, p. 107.
[5] *The Secret Doctrine*, vol. 1, p. 116.
[6] **Thomas Babington Macaulay** (1800–1859) — a British historian and politician, who introduced English into the educational system of India, considering it to be far superior to Sanskrit and other ancient languages.

Mr. Kingsland: In this Manvantara they have reached the mineral kingdom.

H.P.B.: Yes, and they have been modeled and remodeled in the furnace of nature for millions and millions of years.

Mr. Kingsland: Can you tell us what will be the next stage of those "mineral atoms" in the next Manvantara?

H.P.B.: No, I don't know anything at all about them.

Mr. Kingsland: Will they remain as "mineral atoms" all through Manvantara?

H.P.B.: I don't know. They have got to evolute like everything else, to something else.

Mr. B. Keightley: I wish we could get at anything like a definite conception of what is meant in occultism by the term, atom.

Mr. A. Keightley: Question 10. Commentary (a). Do the six stages of consolidation here mentioned refer to six stages of matter on each plane?

H.P.B.: Yes they do, I suppose so. I wish you would meet on Tuesdays and try to ask some questions which should not be always going round and round the same thing. I believe all these questions I must have answered dozens and dozens of times. You all present the same questions in other forms, and it is an eternal squirrel's work around the wheel. Now, if you go over what has been written, you will see it is so. It is impossible, if we want to have it from all aspects, we must have hundreds and hundreds of volumes.

Mr. B. Keightley: There is that question we have been on the verge of a number of times, as to the true conception from the point of view of esoteric philosophy of atoms. It really lies at the root of a great deal of the difficulties. That is what I thought we should have spent most of the time over, because it is a very wide subject.

Mr. Kingsland: What distinction is there from the occult standpoint between an atom and a molecule?

H.P.B.: I have told you, and I cannot say anymore. Molecule you know, and atom you don't know. I cannot say anything more than what I have said.

28 MARCH 1889

Mr. A. Keightley: On page 101, line 18, it is stated that the Sun is merely the elder brother of the planets — but on page 103 it is stated that the planets were all comets and suns in their origin, and would therefore appear to be older than the Sun. What is therefore the real meaning of these statements?

H.P.B.: So far as our planetary system is concerned, the Sun is the oldest member in it. His place was fixed — as is seen by the language of the stanzas — at a very early period of the Manvantara, but the planets reached their places at a much later period. These planets were dethroned suns, comets, etc. Each of them was at some time the central star, the sun in its own system, but of a lower order than this one, and in a previous Manvantara. In the same way so will our Sun become a planet in another Manvantara, only and also in another and higher system than ours. First he will be broken into innumerable fragments, which will form comets and meteors; these will be scattered through space to be ultimately drawn together by the Fohatic affinity. Well, any questions?

Mr. Kingsland: Then what becomes of the planets in this planetary chain? Are they absorbed in the Sun?

H.P.B.: No, they are not.

Mr. A. Keightley: Then what will become of the physical basis of these planets?

H.P.B.: What do you mean by "They will be absorbed in the Sun"? They are not thrown out of the Sun. Occultism teaches there is no such thing as that. Why, it is the modern theory of science that the planets are thrown off from the Sun. They were never thrown off — and then they will be absorbed again in the Sun. They will be disintegrated in the Manvantara. They will scatter into fragments and go into some higher life, into a higher system.

Mr. A. Keightley: Will the solid bodies of the planets in our system disintegrate into small fragments?

H.P.B.: Just the same as the earth — of course they will.

Mr. B. Keightley: You say somewhere, in speaking of the Moon, that the other planets have also had satellites, which stood to them as the Moon stands to the earth, but they faded out or disappeared altogether.

H.P.B.: Some of them on the secondary plane. I told you many times that there were seven sacred planets in occultism, and that these seven sacred planets had nothing to do with us. There are seven, two of which or three of which are not known yet, and I suppose will never be known, because two of them will never appear; they have disappeared since that time. I told you the Sun was not a planet, because it was a central star. Our earth is not, because we are living on it. It is a planet for others, but not for us; but it was the star which is seen between Mercury and the Sun. I don't know whether it is this one which the astronomers have seen.

Mr. B. Keightley: But when the Moon finally disappears it is not, so to speak, broken up violently according to the modern scientific idea, but rather disintegrates slowly, following the analogy of the human body.

H.P.B.: If the Pralaya does not catch it; but if the Pralaya sets in, then there is an end of it.

Mr. A. Keightley: Is it exactly as if it had a charge of dynamite inside and all burst up into fragments.

H.P.B.: Everything goes into space, and there is all the material of which one world is composed — not the world, the earth only, but the planetary system. All this, of course, will go into chaos again and begin its wanderings in space until it reforms in another Manvantara, a higher world, and the Sun itself will be even nothing but a planet in some higher world.

Mr. Kingsland: But not necessarily the integral parts of it as it now stands. Then how near is that expression in *Esoteric Buddhism*, that particles of matter greatly lose their force of cohesion?

H.P.B.: I suppose it is speaking about the temporary Pralayas.

Mr. Kingsland: Just as we have a tidal wave which becomes an earthquake, because the particles lose their force of cohesion and disintegrates in that way.

H.P.B.: I don't remember it. I mean to say as I don't think that the Pralaya is meant.

Mr. Kingsland: In what way does the material go off into space?

H.P.B.: It scatters, I suppose.

Mr. Kingsland: By reason of their losing their force of cohesion?

Mr. B. Keightley: That, of course, is due from the violent explosion, so to speak, which disintegrates the Sun at the end of the solar Manvantara. It is a different process. Is that so, H.P.B.?

H.P.B.: I suppose so. Now the next.

Mr. A. Keightley: Can you also add to this by explaining what you state in *The Secret Doctrine* as to the behaviour of comets to the Sun?

H.P.B.: Well, the behaviour of comets to the Sun is caused by the difference in density of the head and the tail. If science did not insist so dogmatically on its pretended laws of gravity, it would accept our explanation, which satisfies every condition. That is to say that we do not believe in the law of gravity as it is, but in attraction and repulsion. And if it is once accepted, then we should find it leaves no gaps and it explains many things that are not to be explained now on the hypothesis of science. Postulate instead of gravity the twin forces of attraction and repulsion, and many phenomena will be explained. In this case the Sun exerts a very much more powerful influence of attraction upon the head of the comet, which is approximately solid, than it does upon the tail of the comet, which though enormous in size is a phenomenon of vision, not of our perception. Consequently, it is perfectly that that which is most attracted will always be nearest to the Sun. You know what we spoke about, that the comets act most impudently towards the Sun, and that instead of following the law of gravity they turn tail and go off making faces at the Sun.

Mr. Kingsland: And actually flap their tails in the face of the Sun.

Mr. A. Keightley: They almost stare him out of countenance.

H.P.B.: Just in the same fashion, a man endeavouring with bladders upon his feet to walk upon the water will be drowned — his legs, which are necessarily the heaviest, will be buoyed up by the bladders. In addition to this is the fact that the tail of the comet is so attenuous, corresponding to the soul or spirit of gas, that it approaches in condition to the radiant robes of the Sun. Hence there is also a repulsive force exerted upon the tail of the comet by reason of the somewhat smaller polarities. Now you understand what I mean by this. You see, I don't know what the men of science say about the matter of the comet's tails. I know it is not matter, and it cannot be called matter. It is not matter that falls under the perceptive faculties, so to say, of the men of science here; they could not, if they had a bit of it, do anything with it. It is perfectly impossible. It is the spirit or the soul of gases, if that expression can be allowed. Certainly it is dreadfully unscientific, and all those who have been brought up in scientific reverence, of course, will be much shocked. Many will be; but I don't teach it out of my head. I teach simply that which the occult sciences teach. It remains now to be proved who is right, ancient wisdom or modern wisdom. It is a duel between them.

Mr. B. Keightley: A rather daring representative of modern wisdom suggested the idea that the tail of the comet is not matter at all, but is an optical illusion, produced in some way (which he did not attempt to explain) by some electrical action of the solid nucleus of the comet…

H.P.B.: Whoever he is, he is a very wise man, because it is almost what we say. It is a phenomenon of vision.

Mr. B. Keightley: Upon the matter through which the head of the comet was travelling, and its direction, was dependent upon some other things that I do not exactly remember.

H.P.B.: It is not quite so, because there is something; but it is not matter.

Mr. B. Keightley: But then, that is it. The difficulty of the explanation is in this: supposing, however, ethereally, and then you suppose the matter of the comet's tail to be the velocity with which it travels when, for instance, it approaches the Sun — and the tail is streaming away from the Sun — the body of the head of the comet reaches a point there, and the tail must move with enormous velocity, something too much to be expressed by figures.

Mr. Kingsland: Like a ray of light flashed round your eyes.

Mr. B. Keightley: Just as if you flashed a ray of light through a mirror.

H.P.B.: Not to the velocity or vibrations of the violet ray of which we spoke the other day.

Mr. B. Keightley: That is our vibrations in an actual transference of matter.

H.P.B.: How does motion manifest itself — the eternal motion, the inbreathing and the outbreathing which never will begin and never had an end? Those vibrations are certainly one of the causes of that manifestation of the motion in its various phases.

Mr. ——: How should we take the tail of the comet as visible, if it does not consist of matter?

H.P.B.: How would you say if you were shown a kind of thing — how do you explain those things the astronomers show — a shadow? It is not tangible and yet you see it; it is a reflection.

Mr. B. Keightley: How do you see the image of the Moon and the star?

H.P.B.: There is one thing occultism teaches and it is this, that there is not a single body in that part of the universe which is or which may be perceived by astronomy under the strongest telescope that is not a reflection. There is not a single planet which they see, really, as a planet. It is simply a reflection, neither is the Sun seen. It is simply the reflection and the screen, a veil thrown over it; and so it is the same with the planets. They may go and speculate till Doomsday[1] and say they see canals and they see mountains and rivers and all kinds of things, but all this is optical illusion, nothing else; nothing but reflections, because the real ones are not seen.

Mr. Kingsland: But to have a reflection you must have something which is reflected from it and that must in every case be matter.

H.P.B.: Most assuredly. Everything is matter.

Mr. Kingsland: Then is the tail of the comet matter in that sense?

H.P.B.: No, because the tail of the comet is rather a reflection thrown off. There is the enormous size of it, and this is more of optical illusion than anything else.

Mr. Kingsland: Is it not self-luminous?

H.P.B.: It is not.

Mr. A. Keightley: What is the relation of the tail of the comet to the nucleus?

H.P.B.: Oh, don't ask me this. I am not a man of science, and I could not come and tell you this. I cannot go and invent. You wise men of the West ought to tell me what it is. And once you tell me the cause,

---

[1] **Doomsday** — the day of the Last Judgement in Christianity.

I will proceed and give you a little more. I suppose you astronomers ought to know better.

Mr. A. Keightley: I don't see that.

H.P.B.: Then I am not ashamed to say I don't know, either. I am glad they confess they don't know. There are, however, a few things they say they don't know.

Mr. Atkinson: Is not the relation rather like that of a ship travelling through the water, leaving a luminous trail behind her?

H.P.B.: That is a very good suggestion. It leaves a luminous trail because this friction produces it. This is a very good suggestion.

Mr. Kingsland: Then the tail of the comet does not always correspond with its orbit?

Mr. B. Keightley: This has brought back to my mind the suggestion I was speaking about before, that the luminous appearance caused by attraction in the other is owing to some peculiarity in the action of the Sun upon the waves, upon the vibrations so produced. They are so affected by the Sun that they appear to us to be an extension of the line which joins the nucleus of the comet at any moment. But the detailed explanation of that I do not know.

Mr. Atkinson: The head of the comet, the nucleus of the comet, acts simply like a lens; and where the tail is curved it is simply due to refraction through the nucleus.

Mr. B. Keightley: Refracted through the nucleus and forming a long tail; really refracted from fire particles of matter.

Mr. Atkinson: Round the substance of the Sun.

Mr. A. Keightley: Stanza 5, Sloka 1. "The Fiery Whirlwind."[1] Question 2. On page 107, the "Fiery wind" is stated to be the cosmic dust, etc., and in this sense one would understand it to be the nebula — is this correct?

H.P.B.: Cosmic dust and nebula are one. We say the reason why there seem to be aggregations, which we call nebula, is that in those regions the force of affinity is at work on the formation of the future suns, planets and worlds. What you call nebula is not only in the region known as the Milky Way, but it is everywhere. Didn't I tell you last time that it was in this room and everywhere? It is around

---

[1] *The Secret Doctrine*, vol. 1, p. 106.

dust here in the streets of London as much as it is beyond the most distant and visible stars. It is universal stuff, called world-stuff by some astronomers. To illustrate my meaning by physical examples, we don't see the dust in the air of a room at ordinary times, but supposing that the floor is swept so as to largely increase the amount flying in the air; it becomes at once visible, forms itself into clouds according to the currents of air, etc. Now pass a beam of sunlight into a dark room through a shutter, and the whole of the room is at once alive with the movements of the dust. In exactly the same way as the dust moves, and is collected by the currents of air in the room, so is the cosmic dust moved and collected by the Fohatic currents of affinity and attraction in the higher space, until it appears at the distance from us as the nebula with which science is familiar. Truly these calculations are described as the fiery whirling wind, and why you should object to the name I don't know. It is just the name which fits it the best: "fiery whirlwinds."

Mr. Kingsland: The reason why that question was put is that Fohat is called a little later on, the "fiery whirlwind."

H.P.B.: Yes, sir, and so it is explained here. Fohat may be called anything you like.

Mr. B. Keightley: There is one point you might ask there, Kingsland, as to whether the cosmic dust when undergoing the process of collection is self-luminous, or like the dust you are comparing it to, by virtue of the light.

H.P.B.: By virtue of all your respective Mayas and nothing else. Because there is nothing luminous except the sun. All is borrowed light, and it is by virtue of the optical illusion and Maya.

Mr. B. Keightley: I thought that was the case, because it has been proved possible to photograph the nebulas. Consequently, if that is the case, they must be visible, I should think, by reflected light, not by dark light.

Mr. A. Keightley: On page 108, Fohat is called the "fiery whirlwind" (as mentioned in the previous sloka), and is referred to as the vehicle of the Primordial Seven. In what sense is Fohat identical with the fiery whirlwind of Sloka 1?

H.P.B.: Fohat is everything, he is the life principle, the vital air we breathe. He is in all the elements. Fohat is the symbol of the root of manifestation, and as such is necessarily the fiery whirlwind in synthesis. Fohat, in short, is the root and soul of motion. What do we call Fohat? It is not entity. It is called an entity. Fohat is not a gentleman of means or a young man of beauty or anything of the kind. Fohat is simply a force in nature. We may use, as the ancients did, all kinds of euhemerization, but it does not mean Fohat. It is anything, really. Fohat you have in your blood, every one of you. Fohat is the primal motor of everything, from the beginning of the Manvantara. That is what we are taught.

Mr. Kingsland: Then Fohat is a generic term, like Dhyan-Chohan.

H.P.B.: No. Without Fohat, the Dhyan-Chohan would not be much, anyway, for it is the cohesive force of everything; and it is the vivifying force and the force of vital action. Will somebody help me and give me a better word?

Mr. B. Keightley: You express that very well. You say somewhere in *The Secret Doctrine*, you say, actually, that Fohat is, and you say it is an entity, of which our electricity is the emanation.

H.P.B.: Is the universe that you see an entity, since it is?

Mr. A. Keightley: Do you see the universe?

H.P.B.: Well, that which you see, never mind; is it an entity or not? What is an entity, will you tell me? Something that is. Will you give me the etymology and definition of entity, before you criticize?

Mr. B. Keightley: Yes. Strictly and etymologically, it means something which is.

H.P.B.: Well, then what have you got to protest for? If Fohat is not, it is no use speaking about him or it or whatever it is. And if Fohat is, I call it entity — and why should I not? Invent some other words I may use. I am blessed if there are words enough in the English language to express the quarter or the millionth part of the ideas that are given in the occult teachings. The English language is inadequate. I don't say there is another better, because they are all in the same predicament.

Mr. B. Keightley: That is why we raise these questions.

H.P.B.: The Sanskrit language is a thousand times richer than the English language, and yet Sanskrit is full of symbols and figures of speech. Why? Because human language has not grown to say that which is in the human mind. The human mind is far more developed than the language. Thought, I mean.

Mr. Atkinson: Is Fohat in the Chinese represented by two Chinese syllables?

H.P.B.: It is from those parts something I have been asking many times. *Fo* means brilliant.

Mr. Atkinson: I know the root and the character of the Chinese syllable "Fo." If you could get the Chinese characters, I could turn it up in the Chinese dictionary.

H.P.B.: And in the Japanese, too. I don't think it is a real word, because some of them call it Fohat.

Mr. Atkinson: It would be "Ho" in Japanese. And it would represent the idea of "Ho," as "Ho" was a [...] part of the phoenix. If it is the same as the Chinese, I mean. It becomes "Ho" in Japanese, and then becomes the "Ho" of the phoenix, as part of the compound name of the phoenix.

H.P.B.: Fohat is also a relation to the cycles, because the intensity of this vital force changes with every cycle.

Mr. Atkinson: It is in the celestial cosmogony of China. It is in the celestial beginning and the cosmogenesis.

H.P.B.: I wish you would look somewhere where you could find it, because I have been looking for it in India.

Mr. Atkinson: If you will only give me the Chinese characters, I will find it at once.

H.P.B.: I have got it somewhere, but not in the Chinese.

Mr. A. Keightley: Question 4. What are the sparks (atoms) which Fohat joins together?

H.P.B.: The particles of the Fiery World-stuff, or dust of which we just spoke, nothing else.

Mr. B. Keightley: You might ask about what is really meant by the epithet "Fiery," if it is not the idea of being self-luminous.

H.P.B.: Oh, don't be so very dogmatic, for I cannot tell you anything, I am a poor, ignorant old woman, I cannot say anything at all. I cannot come and invent for you whether it is self-luminous or non-luminous. I don't care, I have not been at its birth, and I tell you I don't know.

Mr. B. Keightley: If you would explain it in any degree — the sense in which the word "fiery" is used — it would be helpful.

Mr. Kingsland: It is purely occult there.

H.P.B.: Fiery is fiery because it is not watery.

Mr. B. Keightley: Exactly, I see.

H.P.B.: Do you!

Mr. A. Keightley: Question 5. Are we to regard the atoms as purely metaphysical conceptions, even on the lowest material plane?

H.P.B.: I have just explained this very point. Now let me, if you please, remind you of what I read last Thursday, because I see I read one day, and then the following Thursday you forget it. This is what we said on Thursday: "The atoms, whether as representing Monads of Leibniz or the eternal, indestructible mathematical points of substance, can neither be dissolved during Pralaya nor reformed during Manvantara. The atoms do not exist as appreciable quantities of matter on any plane." When they come here they are not atoms, they are erroneously called atoms, "they are mathematical points of unknown quantity here, and whatever they are or may be on the seventh plane, each is and must be logically, as Leibniz says, an Absolute universe in itself, reflecting other universes. This is to say that each is Mahat or Divine Ideation," etc, etc. This I need not read any more, because I told you last time.

Mr. Kingsland: Just before, you speak of the atoms Fohat joined together as particles of the atoms of cosmic dust.

H.P.B.: Have patience and it will be here explained to you. Those atoms that we speak about do not exist, at least for us. They are simply mathematical points. There is not a man of science who can come and say to you that he saw the atoms or that he traced them, or that he smelt them or touched them or anything; it is a perfect impossibility. Now, what they call atoms they will find out are not atoms. If they ever find out, in I don't know how many thousand years, a little bit of homogeneous molecule or elements, they will be very happy. To this day they don't find a single speck or element. They have, I suppose, between sixty and seventy elements, and have they ever found molecules that are homogeneous? I do not think they have. Did they, Mr. Atkinson?

Mr. Atkinson: I think not.

H.P.B.: Very well, then; what is the use of calling them atoms and putting false noses on things, simply to confuse and perplex the mind? Why should we call elements that which are not elements and may be divided *ad infinitum*, and yet the chemist won't know what it is? They will come and mount on stilts and say we know everything. Elements, what are elements? There is one element, and it is the most tremendous conceit of modern science, such as I have never heard or read the like of in my days. They dogmatize and do everything, it appears. I am not at all learned, I have never studied; what I know is simply what I had to read in relation to the book that I had to write. But I say that, really, they give names which are positively ridiculous; they have no sense. Why should they go and call elements that which does not exist? And why should they go and pitch into the ancients about the four elements, speaking of earth, air, water and fire, saying we were all ignorant fools when our modern men of science act a thousand times more foolishly? They had not a *raison d'être*[1] except only their fancy and whim. Now, do somebody take the part of the men of science. What silence! Well, 6.

Mr. A. Keightley: In what sense is electricity atomic?

H.P.B.: Electricity as an effect at work must certainly be atomic. Nothing that exhibits energy is non-atomic, or can be. Atoms confined to our world system are not what they are in space, or mathematical points. These latter are certainly metaphysical abstractions, and can only be considered in such terms; but what we know as atoms on this plane are gradations of substance, very attenuated. This will be easily understood by those who think over the occult axiom which tells us that spirit is matter, and matter spirit, and both one. Those who study esoteric philosophy will understand this better than those who do not. Now spirit does not become suddenly a lump of matter, any more than vapour becomes suddenly a lump of ice. To use again an illustration: the clairvoyant who can distinguish always, will see an occult atomic effect in any energetic, intense feeling in man or animal — such, for instance, as anger, fear, joy, etc. But these things are non-atomic to our sensuous perception. And if they are not such, how can science explain, for instance, the effects produced on persons and animals

---

[1] **Raison d'être** (*French*) — a reason for being.

by various patients in their neighbourhood? If, for instance, anger, love, joy or anything, any passion expresses in the most intense way, if that were not atomic, how is it that it produces effects not only on men, but in animals? How is it that the man who is very reserved and won't show his anger, and will be perfectly calm in his bearing and his features, won't show his passion or anything, yet you feel that this man is terribly hurt, and that he is angry or that he is rejoiced? Don't you feel it, is it through your eyes you see it; and how is it sometimes anger affects a person in the most terrible way, though it is not even directed against that person? This may seem a foolish question; but I ask you, how can anything be felt without it being an energy — atomic — I mean atomic in the occult sense, not in your sense of being molecular?

Mr. Kingsland: As I understand you, then, you say it is atomic as soon as a primordial substance begins to differentiate. Then you call it atomic.

H.P.B.: No, I called it atomic, perhaps before, because what I call atoms are the whole on the unmanifested plane. It would be mathematical points as soon as it is on the manifested plane. You cannot call it atoms; you call it world-stuff, or anything you like. You have a definite idea of the word molecules, and therefore I cannot use that word.

Mr. B. Keightley: Material particles, you might say.

H.P.B.: Let it be material particles — the infinitesimal, but they have size.

Mr. Kingsland: We have got altogether out of the metaphysical conception.

H.P.B.: I don't want to do that, because on the physical plane your men of science are a great deal wiser than our metaphysical teachers, assuredly. They know all on the external plane. Now, whether they know as well that which underlies, I doubt.

Mr. B. Keightley: Now, on that analogy of anger, you call it atomic; it is more of a vibration?

H.P.B.: Vibration of what? What is that which vibrates spirit?

Mr. B. Keightley: That is what I want to get at.

H.P.B.: Nothingness vibrates. If there is something to vibrate, it is something.

Mr. Kingsland: And that must be atomic.

H.P.B.: Most assuredly. Now listen to the end. Another illustration. How would science have explained twenty years ago the contagion of disease? Now they have found out bacteria and bacilli, one of the most attenuated forms of matter, but atomic still. In another twenty years, perhaps they will discover the contagion of mental passions. Some people call it magnetism, a mesmeric power. Speaking of a lecturer, they say he electrifies his audience; we say that this electrification is purely atomic. The clairvoyant whose senses are opened in advance to the physiological, psychic condition of his age will perceive the stream of atoms proceeding from the lecturer to the audience, which will be coloured in various hues, according to his inner condition, and assuming different hues as it comes in contact with the various individuals in the audience, according to inner conditions and temperament. Do you see? Now, you will see a preacher who will be preaching most intensely about something; he will be preaching something, and he will be electrifying. They say Spurgeon produces a most extraordinary effect upon his hearers. Now, take the Salvation Army. Once that there are hundreds of thousands of them who will begin dancing and emanating all kinds of emotionalisms and everything, do you suppose it is not atomic? It sets the people crazy, it is infectious, it psychologizes them, it makes them lose all power over themselves, and they are obliged to think as General Booth,[1] once that they become perfectly under the influence. And they will give money, and believe in Jesus or anything you like. If General Booth went and preached instead of Jesus, H. P. Blavatsky once, everyone would believe in me, everyone would be a Blavatskyite. I can assure you he has the power, it is simply because it is a magnetic power. I wish I were friends with him. It is a good idea of making him preach me, and they would all come and believe in me.

Mr. Kingsland: Somebody must volunteer to become a General Booth.

Mr. ——: Then you hold that this atomic energy which emanates from the preacher has the same power upon all persons he addresses.

---

[1] **William Booth** (1829–1912) — an English Methodist preacher, who founded the Salvation Army, a Protestant Christian church, and became its first General.

H.P.B.: Oh no, there is a great difference, some won't be affected at all. Now, some of us will go there and laugh. He could not affect us, because we have not got the temperament of others to be affected by his preaching. Those it would affect in an extraordinary way, and especially sensitive people.

Mr. Kingsland: And then they in their turns psychologize the others.

H.P.B.: It is an immense inter-psychology all around.

Mr. B. Keightley: You get a very good analogy from a lot of tuning forks varying in key. If you struck one it would be taken up by the whole mass, and get at last a whole volume of sound.

Mr. ——: Is that so? I think not.

Mr. B. Keightley: I think there is something of that kind, or how do you get a reverberation?

Mr. ——: One tuning fork will strike its octave.

Mr. B. Keightley: But I am supposing the other forks are on the same key.

Mr. ——: Oh, yes.

Mr. B. Keightley: I was thinking of the intensification of the sound, for instance as a sounding board intensifies. You put a tuning fork onto a sounding box, the sound becomes much louder.

Mr. A. Keightley: Stanza 5, Sloka 3, page 118. In speaking of the six directions of space, is the term direction used in its ordinary sense, or does it mean here a property or attribute of space?

H.P.B.: Simply figuratively, it means the macrocosm is divided in occult philosophy, just as the microcosm. That is to say, into six principles, synthesized by the seventh. And space here is not limited to any particular area.

Mr. A. Keightley: Then space is used in its widest metaphysical sense.

H.P.B.: In its widest metaphysical sense. I would speak manifested. Every time I say space without the word manifested, it means in its widest metaphysical sense. If I want to speak about space in this universe, I would say manifested space, or something like that, just to make some qualification.

Mr. A. Keightley: Question 8. Are the six directions the six rays of the Logos?

H.P.B.: Just as I have explained. Just the same.

Mr. A. Keightley: Question 9, Sloka 4: "Fohat traces spiral lines to unite the six to the seventh."[1] Is there any special meaning in the word spiral, and is spiral action specially connected with Fohat?

H.P.B.: It is. Now in order that the neutral line, or zero point as Mr. Crookes calls it, and the centrifugal and centripetal must be made to run spirally, otherwise they would be entirely neutralized. I don't know how otherwise to call it. The neutral point can be destroyed. Now, see, if you please, in this volume, page 550, where the Caduceus[2] of Mercury is represented. Now, anyone who wants to know the explanation, let them read it. This spiral is represented in the Caduceus of Mercury. If you have a central point or a central line, for instance, like that (drawing), this must be the central line. As soon as you touch it, anything that is differentiated becomes undifferentiated again, and falls into the perfect Absolute. Then certainly, you must have the spirals go in such a way. One force goes in such a way (illustrating), and this is the Caduceus of Mercury which produces those miracles and marvels in the hands of [...]. You look at this, and you will see that the healing powers and everything, that is what it means. And now Mr. Crookes finds — he speaks about number 8, perhaps you read it — he speaks about number 8, that he has found out that these forces go like that and make the figure 8, and the middle line is the central

---

[1] *The Secret Doctrine*, vol. 1, p. 118.

[2] **Caduceus** (*Greek*, "herald's wand") — a staff entwined by two serpents and surmounted by two wings; an attribute of Hermes Trismegistus. The Greek poets and mythologists took the idea of the Caduceus of Mercury from the Egyptians. The Caduceus is found as two serpents twisted round a rod, on Egyptian monuments built before Osiris. The Greeks altered this. It is a cosmic, sidereal or astronomical, as well as a spiritual and even physiological symbol, its significance changing with its application. Metaphysically, the Caduceus represents the fall of primeval and primordial matter into gross terrestrial matter, the one Reality becoming Illusion. Astronomically, the head and tail represent the points of the ecliptic where the planets and even the sun and moon meet in close embrace. Physiologically, it is the symbol of the restoration of the equilibrium lost between Life, as a unit, and the currents of life performing various functions in the human body.

line. Therefore, there we are perfectly at one with ordinary science, of which I feel very proud. This is page 550.

Mr. A. Keightley: Then does that mean that by reason of a centrifugal and centripetal force, any force affected by that force must move in a spiral line?

H.P.B.: I believe it is a law that everything proceeds spirally, it never goes in straight lines. Science says something about gravity that goes on direct lines.

Mr. B. Keightley: That is one of the points I wanted to ask.

H.P.B.: I would never believe it. I can't give you my reasons, but I, knowing occultism, say it is impossible. There is nothing in this world that can proceed otherwise than in spirals, or on such things as that, but never in the direct line, never.

Mr. B. Keightley: Then the same thing would be true as to the conception of the action of the two forces of attraction and repulsion. You would not think of them as acting in direct lines, but always in spirals. I don't mean to say the effect, but as an abstract conception.

H.P.B.: Not only as an abstract conception, but I think you will find it in physical science that they must act something like that. They cannot act on direct lines.

Mr. B. Keightley: That is the effect they produce.

H.P.B.: Now look at the pranks that electricity plays with you. Put it on a sounding board. Does it do every straight line? A straight line is a thing unknown in the laws of Nature. Because that is why Pythagoras never would admit the straight line or number 2 — because he says number 2 is not a creature that ought to exist in the Universe. We know the point which is not a point, but the point which is everywhere and nowhere, because it is absolute and universal, or it is the Triad or the Trinity.

Mr. B. Keightley: This is where the scientific idea comes in. They say the effects would be spiral. I think I would ask Mr. Kingsland if he agrees with this. The scientists would conceive as an abstract conception of the centripetal and centrifugal as acting in straight lines, combining together that would produce the spiral action — even in the abstract conception. I should think that occultism would stick to the spiral idea, if considered as abstractions.

Mr. Kingsland: They would not be conceived of as straight lines, and the two combined would produce the spiral.

Mr. B. Keightley: The abstract idea is, of course, the force acting in a straight line.

Mr. Kingsland: Oh, I see. In that sense, it is.

Mr. B. Keightley: Or any of the forces acting in a straight line. Suppose a force occupying a given point. It would be conceived to act upon any other point situated anywhere else in the room along the straight line joining the two points.

Mr. Kingsland: That is, for mathematical purposes.

H.P.B.: Whether for that or for anything else, I don't believe in it. That is all.

Mr. A. Keightley: Question 10. "If Fohat is the uniting power, while at the same time differentiation is going on, what is the disintegrating force which is at work; or is Fohat bipolar, *i.e.*, does he produce both attraction and repulsion?"

H.P.B.: He does. I would like you to find me, as I said before, anything in this world that would not produce this bipolar action. Everything in creation is bipolar. Is there anyone very religious in the room, because I have to talk about personal God? Who of you is very religious?

Mr. ——: I am.

H.P.B.: You are not, I never would believe it, that is a blank denial. I want to say even your personal God is shown one moment infinite, and all kindness and mercy, the Creator and Preserver, and at another moment one of infinite anger, the destroyer and the annihilator. All this is bipolar, all this cannot be without, and if you take the God of your conception to be such a bipolar being, then how there can be any force, or anything that is not, I don't know. You cannot have a force absolutely good or absolutely bad, there is no such thing in Nature, therefore they must be bipolar. You take a little speck of something you will find the two poles in it, the negative and the positive.

Mr. A. Keightley: Then does that mean to say that the action of Fohat on any substance is alternately first one, and then the other — first constructive, and then destructive?

H.P.B.: I told you that. Take the trinity of the Hindus. There is Brahma the Creator, Vishnu the Preserver, Shiva the Destroyer, and all the three are one; and if you can conceive of one without the two others, then there remains no God but the flapdoodle, not good for anything. That which you call destruction is simply renovation, it is simply that. Well, I have explained it to you so many times: there is no such thing as death, there is transformation. Now, if you sow a seed, as St. Paul says, in order — I forget how he says it.

Mr. B. Keightley: "In order that the seed may bear fruit it must fall into the ground and die."[1]

H.P.B.: Yes, that is perfectly true. That is to say, it must be transformed. It will not die, because there is no such thing as anything that is destructible, because it simply passes into something else. This even science has discovered 20 or 30 years, it is the conservation of energy, and this is the greatest truth and the greatest thing they have discovered; really, the greatest truth that they ever will, because this is the law on which everything is based. The whole of occultism it is that nothing is lost and everything transformed. They found it 20 or 30 years ago. I advise you to take the books which existed 400 or 500 years ago, and there the conservation of energy is positively proven, because, it is said plainly. Or look in the *Anugita*, where it is said that nothing is lost, that Vishnu transforms himself and becomes [...] in humanity, but it will become always Vishnu; that every atom becomes something else, but it is still the sole atom, it is still the same thing. I cannot repeat it, because I have not got a good memory, but if you read the several pages, I am sure you will find that the conservation of the energy is perfectly well described there, 300 or 400 years ago. Let it be 100 years before science, I am perfectly satisfied it is proven that they knew it, and that they know it now. I don't care whether it was many thousand years old. We speak about the manuscripts.

Mr. A. Keightley: Then is the idea of Vishnu, the Preserver in that Trinity, is that the idea of the conservation of energy?

H.P.B.: It is. He preserves everything, but he can preserve nothing without Shiva. Remember that Shiva must come and transform one thing into another, and he is, so to say, the helper of Vishnu, and every time that Vishnu is left in the lurch, as is shown in the Puranas,

---

[1] A paraphrase of 1 Corinthians 15:36 and John 12:24.

they call Shiva to his help. And it is Vishnu he must come and help to transform one thing into another.

Mr. B. Keightley: And if I remember aright, Brahma is always appealing to Vishnu for help.

H.P.B.: He cannot move or do anything without Vishnu. You may say what you like, but it is highly philosophical, I assure you.

Mr. A. Keightley: Sloka 4, continued. "They (the Lipika) say: 'This is good.'"[2] Question 11. What special meaning is this phrase of the Lipikas intended to convey?

H.P.B.: Why should not the Lipikas say this is good, when the Lord God in the first chapter of Genesis says it is good several times? And if he can say it, why cannot the Lipika say it?

Mr. B. Keightley: Certainly they can. It is not an objection. It shows that phrase has some special meaning, or it would not appear both in the old source from which you have taken the stanza and the Bible of the Jews. And the question is what is the special meaning?

H.P.B.: In the Bible, you know, there is as much philosophy as anything else, though half of it was thrown out. If you could have the whole Elohistic chapters you would see, if you please, what the philosophy is; but out of perhaps fourteen there remain now only one and a half, or something.

Mr. B. Keightley: The question is, what is the meaning?

H.P.B.: That this is good. What meaning do you want more? If it were bad they would not say a word, but they would proceed to correct their mistake and create it better.

Mr. Kingsland: But they might find out their mistake afterwards.

H.P.B.: Well, so did God also find his mistake afterwards, because he repented that he made man. Even a God repents, so why should not a Dhyan-Chohan?

Mr. Kingsland: Then it is only good, relatively?

Mr. A. Keightley: Is the "Chhaya-loka"[3] — explained here as the shadowy world of primal form, or the intellectual — the same as what is called in the diagram on page 200 as the "Archetypal World"? Or is it what is there called the intellectual or creative world?

---

[2] *The Secret Doctrine,* vol. 1, p. 118.

[3] **Chhaya-loka** (*Sanskrit*) — the Shadowy World of Primal Form; Kama-loka.

Diagram 1. Seven Planes

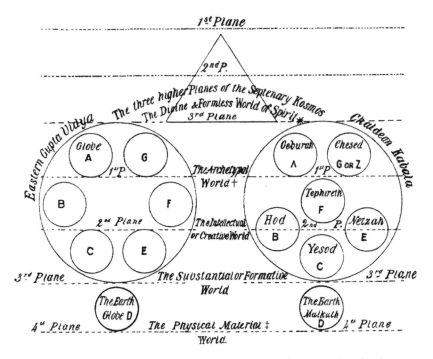

* The *Arupa* or " formless," there where form ceases to exist, on the objective plane.

† The word "Archetypal" must not be taken here in the sense that the Platonists gave to it, *i.e.*, the world as it existed *in the Mind* of the Deity ; but in that of a world made as a first model, to be followed and improved upon by the worlds which succeed it physically—though deteriorating in purity.

‡ These are the four lower planes of Cosmic Consciousness, the three higher planes being inaccessible to human intellect as developed at present. The seven states of human consciousness pertain to quite another question.

H.P.B.: The Archetypal World and the intellectual world; and of that, you can see in the Kabbalah, it shows four planes. Take Mathers' *Kabbalah*,[1] there it is shown. Don't show it to me. I know it by heart. The Archetypal World may be compared to the thought of man that precedes action; this is the kind of individual Manas in the light of the universal intelligence. The artist conceives his idea first of all, before he begins to work, but before he can paint his picture he has to gather and prepare his materials in accordance with the plans that are in his mind. He stretches his canvas and grinds his colours. This

---

[1] See S. L. MacGregor Mathers, *Kabbala Denudata: The Kabbalah Unveiled* (London: Kegan Paul, Trench, Trubner & Co., 1887).

is on the intellectual or creative world. Then he roughly sketches his idea on the canvas, and this may be compared to the presentment in the substantial or formative world. If you will follow there, you will see what I mean. He fills in all the details and the picture is ready. In the physical aspect there, they are the four planes. So it is in nature. I do not speak about the three higher, because they cannot be expressed in human language. The universal mind is above what they call the Divine ideation. This is a thing which cannot be expressed, but this Divine ideation falls, so to say, from the beginning; and when I say from the beginning, it means there is no beginning and no end. And the light of it will fall on the Archetypal World where are the antetypes or prototypes of everything. There would be nothing, not even this old carpet, if there was not an antetype or prototype. You understand my idea?

Miss Kenealy: Yes, I think that is very clear.

Mr. A. Keightley: Stanza 5, Sloka 5. Question 13. What are the influences proceeding from the four quarters of the world? Why are some, such as that from the East, injurious to life?

H.P.B.: Because it is; and do not ask me any more questions. They have been asking me a thousand times. It means North and East are good, West and South are bad. West is bad because the Egyptians and the Hindus and all the Chaldeans and the Phoenicians[2] and everyone had the idea that the Devil came from the West; why it should be, I don't know, because it is the presentment of western civilization in the present century. The Devil comes from the West in the Egyptian sacred books, in the Chaldean, in the Phoenician; in all he comes from the West. And everything that is good comes from the East, because the Sun is the regenerator and comes every day at the appointed time; and the Sun is our creator and friend and everything.

Mr. A. Keightley: If the evil influence is supposed to come from the West, and if the East is supposed to be good merely because the Sun, which is the regenerator, appears from there, what is the meaning of the Sun disappearing in the West? Is there any connection there? Is it merely an absence of good, or an actual presence of evil?

---

[2] **Phoenicians** — an ancient seafaring civilization of the eastern Mediterranean, primarily located in the coastal regions of present-day Lebanon, Syria and northern Israel.

H.P.B.: It appears there, from whence comes darkness.

Mr. A. Keightley: But darkness does not come from the West.

H.P.B.: No, but light disappears in it, and therefore I suppose they made it bad. But they must have had some other occult influences. There is not a country that did not have West in their abomination positively, so that you must be mighty proud, all of you!

Mr. B. Keightley: Yet the islands of the blessed were always supposed to be in the West.

H.P.B.: Geographically. But it is quite a different thing really. Just as it speaks of the east wind in London, and he asks me, "How is it the east wind is the most pernicious wind, and all good comes from the East?" I say it is geographically. It may be so in your little island, but it is not so in space universal.

Mr. A. Keightley: Then what is the meaning of it in space?

H.P.B.: In space there is neither East, West, North, or South, if you take infinite space; but if you take a limited space, nature has so ordained it that everything evil comes from the West.

Mr. A. Keightley: Take the solar system. What is the meaning of it?

H.P.B.: I don't know.

Mr. A. Keightley: Then what are the four corners?

H.P.B.: It is flapdoodle, because there are no corners in that which is spherical.

Mr. B. Keightley: I am afraid, Arch, your cross-examination won't bring you much.

H.P.B.: I am not afraid of cross-examination, to tell you the truth.

Mr. A. Keightley: What is the meaning of the evil influence coming from the West?

H.P.B.: Because evil influences are illnesses, and it appears they thought the Devil lived there.

Mr. A. Keightley: Why should it be the West and the South which are bad?

H.P.B.: From the South Pole come all the evils of the world; that is why you are not allowed to go to the South Pole, it is evil. To the North Pole you are not allowed to go because it is the Land of the Gods. And if you went there you would be desecrated. Seriously speaking, there is some magnetism, something magnetic coming from the South and the West, that is a very bad magnetism, the magnetism of the emanations of the earth. It depends on the earth. Now, let us speak of the earth. Why is it that the Hindus tell you to sleep in a certain way, with your heads so and so, that the magnetism should pass through you in a certain direction? I have read several men of science who say that it is not at all a foolish idea. There is such a thing as terrestrial magnetism. When you have calculated where it comes from, then you will see there is some philosophy in the way the evil influences come from the West and the good ones from the East.

Mr. A. Keightley: But supposing, for instance, you placed your body in the direct currents of magnetism, which are supposed to proceed from the magnetic pole in the North? That is not in the actual axis of the earth.

H.P.B.: I never said it was. What do you want to know? What are you driving at?

Mr. A. Keightley: I wanted to find out where these magnetic bad influences come from, with regard to the earth.

H.P.B.: When you are older you will know more; you need not come and burden your young brain with that, because you could not retain it, and it would become like a sieve and it would run through.

Mr. Atkinson: Is it magnetic North, or the geographical North?

H.P.B.: No, magnetic.

Mr. Atkinson: Because they are opposite to the other.

H.P.B.: I tell you more. I have just had the honour of telling you we don't believe in anything going in straight lines. Now, if you put 2 + 2 together, you will see what I mean; it does not go in straight lines. Therefore, you may say what you like, but unless you know occultism and all the points and everything you cannot know from where it comes and what is meant by it. There is simply the statement that it comes from such and such a thing. It is not meant for those who have not learnt occultism and who do not know there remained so many points into which the occultists divide the earth. And whilst you do not know it, how can you know how it passes, when it always goes either in a diagonal line or like that, in spirals, and never in a straight line? Therefore, it is extremely difficult to answer it; it is impossible.

Mr. A. Keightley: Then there is some special relation to the currents meant by the words East and West.

H.P.B.: Maybe there is, and maybe there is not. This is the sort of thing I am subjected to each Thursday. They will come and cross-examine me and pump out everything they can till Doomsday. I cannot say more than what I know.

Mr. A. Keightley: But you don't say all you do know.

H.P.B.: That is a different thing; you have no right to ask it.

Mr. A. Keightley: Question 14. Have the four Maharajahs and the four elements a special terrestrial application, as well as a cosmic one?

H.P.B.: Except in karma, nothing at all. The four Maharajahs produce karmic effects, certainly, because there the Lipika Maharajah is a title they have, simply.

Mr. A. Keightley: What is the meaning of the four elements, then?

H.P.B.: In what respect?

Mr. A. Keightley: As related to those four Maharajahs.

H.P.B.: I don't know what you are talking about. I didn't see the last question. I don't understand what you mean.

Mr. A. Keightley: We had better ask another time.

H.P.B.: I told you to take out the 15th.

Mr. A. Keightley: That is all there is, then.

H.P.B.: I think that my fate or my karma is to live all my life surrounded by points of interrogation. Sometimes I have the nightmare, and it seems to me I am surrounded by points of negation.

Mr. ——: Points of admiration, I hope, as well.

Mr. A. Keightley: Well, you should not convert yourself into such a perpetual conundrum.

H.P.B.: I am a very simple-minded old woman. I come here and offer to teach you what I can. You accept, very well; I cannot teach you more than I can, you know.

Miss Kenealy: You say so much we want to know.

H.P.B.: You all are discreet. It is immediately in the house. I am sorry Dr. Williams is not here. He puts questions beautifully.

Miss Kenealy: I think you are rather hard on us all.

H.P.B.: In the first place, you ask sometimes questions that trespass on forbidden ground. What is the use of my telling you one thing, and then shutting the door in your face? It will only be vexation of spirit, and it won't teach you much. And I cannot say certain things. I tell all that is permitted me to give. It may be very foolish, very exclusive, very selfish. You may think what you like; I have not made the rules, I never made the laws. I have not so received it, nor shall I so impart. What I promised not to reveal I cannot, it is impossible.

Miss Kenealy: You know so much that what is very simple to you is often very hard to us.

H.P.B.: You see, you always continue to ask things that really I cannot give fully. So what is the use of saying it by bits?

Mr. Kingsland: We have a dim perception there is something behind, so we keep pegging away.

H.P.B.: You cannot complain, because you have the explanation of many things.

Mr. Kingsland: I am speaking now generally, for the company.

4 APRIL 1889

Mr. A. Keightley: Stanza 5, Sloka 6, Commentary. Question 1. How do the "Recorders of the Karmic ledger"[1] make an impassable barrier between the Personal Ego and the Impersonal Self?

H.P.B.: Now, it seems to me it is very easy to understand that. I think that whoever understands the real nature of Nirvana, or even of the Christian Kingdom of Heaven, where it is said no one marries or is given in marriage, etc., ought to see very well what is the meaning of it. Because, what is Rupa? What is "Personal"? It is always something objective or material, and how can it then pass there beyond the point where everything is formless and Arupa? I think it is not given in symbolical language, but quite plainly. Now, I ask you: who is it that goes into the state of Devachan? Is it spirit, spirit-soul, or the monad loaded with spiritual consciousness and intelligence, or is it the lower principles of the personal man? Which is it that goes? You know perfectly well that the "Personal" was the Kama-loka, therefore they cannot go even on this plane. The principles remain to fade out in time and Kama-loka. The Lipika is said to circumscribe within the egg — which is the magnetic aura or manifested Cosmos — man, animal or any concrete object in the universe, or those objects which have form. It is an allegory, and is stated in allegorical language, this enchanted ring or circle. No such ring exists in nature, but there exists the plane of matter and spirit and consciousness. The Personal Self consists of a triangle in a square, man's seven principles, of which only the upper Triangle is left; it cannot pass beyond the plane of even the primitive differentiated matter. Every atom of the seven principles — even the refulgence of Atma-Buddhi, for refulgence is an attribute and related to absoluteness — every atom must remain outside the portal of Nirvana. Alone divine ideation — the consciousness, the bearer of Absolute memory, of its personalities now merged into the one impersonal — can cross the threshold of the Laya point, which lies at the very gate of manifestation, of the human soul and mind in which facts and events, past, present and future, were alike fixed during their joint pilgrimage. There remains, as it is said at the dawn of the great day, but that which is left of the various foods in a copper vessel when the latter

---

[1] *The Secret Doctrine,* vol. 1, p. 129.

is well washed out and dried. This is a quotation from the book. But if this is so at its dawn, what shall we say becomes of the same soul and mind during the great day itself? Why, that which remains of the said copper vessel when it is melted — the memory alone. You understand there is an enormous difference between Devachan and the Great Day, or that plane which only is reached during the Maha-Pralaya after all the cycle of existence is done away with. How is it possible, then, that anything personal should come into it? We are unable to represent to ourselves such an entirely formless, atomless consciousness. During ecstasy we can imagine something approximate to the fact. We say the subject in this state of Samadhi is beyond his everyday world of limits and conditions, and now all is one motionless day and state for him. The past and the future being all in his present, his spirit is freed from the trammels and changes of the body. The highest and most spiritual parts of his Manas only are united to his own particular monad, which, like the monad of Leibniz, reflects that and is the whole universe in itself. The yogi, we say, is become the partaker of the wisdom and omniscience of the universal mind; but can we say that of the mind when it crosses beyond the Laya point? If you can, gentlemen of Oxford and Cambridge, I cannot. For I cannot speak the language of the gods, and if I could you would not much understand me, I suppose. There is a question, and for the life of me I cannot make out what you mean by it. Who put such a question? What does it mean — to draw the line between the personal and the impersonal? You all of you ought to know it.

Mr. Kingsland: Is the state of Nirvana beyond the Laya point?

H.P.B.: Most assuredly; why, the Laya point is simply only for the planes of matter. This is the Laya point, as we call it, which goes beyond the material manifestation.

Mr. Kingsland: You would not say Devachan was beyond the Laya point?

H.P.B.: Most assuredly not. Devachan is one thing, and "the Great Day Be-With-Us" is another. For it is not simply planetary Pralaya, it is universal Pralaya.

Mr. Kingsland: We are to call that Nirvana, are we not?

H.P.B.: No, it is Para-Nirvana; para,[1] which means Meta.[2]

Mr. Kingsland: In the state of Samadhi, that is only Nirvana?

H.P.B.: It is simply Nirvana.

Mr. Kingsland: There is a certain amount of individuality attached to that.

H.P.B.: There is an individuality of spirit and soul, Atma-Buddhi.

Mr. Kingsland: You say the highest part of the Manas is assimilated with the Monad; you cannot say that of Nirvana.

H.P.B.: Most assuredly, you cannot. I explained it afterwards there, further on, because there are many places where you say things which I cannot make out. I cannot make out how you, who know all about the personal remains in Kama-loka, don't apply the same thing when you speak of the "Great Day Be-With-Us." I don't mean at all about our partial, short, little lives here. That is quite a different thing. You see, if I had some of those who put the questions to be there when I answer them, it would be a different thing.

Mr. A. Keightley: It is said here the esoteric meaning of the first sentence is that those who have been called Lipikas and the recorders make an impassable barrier between the personal ego and the impersonal self.

H.P.B.: Certainly.

Mr. B. Keightley: The phrase almost looks as if it were the line of demarcation and division between the four principles and the three. I think there is a question after that on that.

H.P.B.: I think you have a very erroneous opinion about the three principles or the upper triangle. You don't take into consideration, or make a difference, when we apply the seven principles on this plane as in man or in Devachan, or the same seven principles after the cycle of life is finished — which is a perfectly different thing, entirely different.

Mr. Kingsland: There is nothing in that Stanza to guide us to that.

H.P.B.: I could not write more than there is there.

Mr. B. Keightley: That is why these questions are asked.

---

[1] **Para** (*Sanskrit*, "infinite," "supreme") — the final limit. *Param* is the end and goal of existence; *Parapara* is the boundary of boundaries.
[2] **Meta** (*Greek*) — beyond.

H.P.B.: Don't you see very well that the Lipika, "the Great Day Be-With-Us," means when everything — when the cycle is finished? I am perfectly sure there must be some reference to it.

Mr. B. Keightley: That is plain; but then is there anything that can be spoken of as a "personal self" still remaining?

H.P.B.: I will tell you a thing which will settle the whole difficulty. This is what volume?

Mr. B. Keightley: The first.

H.P.B.: How is it called.

Mr. B. Keightley: Cosmogenesis.

H.P.B.: Then why should you make me speak of Anthropogenesis? The "personal self" is quite a different thing. This is a thing which has a relation, but no personal gods will have anything to do with it. It does not mean personal in the sense of our personality. It means objective individuality.

Mr. B. Keightley: Yes, but that is different from what the phrase would suggest.

Mr. A. Keightley: Question 2. Does "personal ego" here stand for the Upper Triad, Atma-Buddhi-Manas,[3] or for the lower Quaternary?[4]

H.P.B.: There it is. It would stand for all, if the principles of a still living man on Earth were meant; it stands for none in the case of the Lipika. It is said — I quote further — they circumscribe the triangle, the first one; the cube or quaternary, the second one; therefore all the seven contain in the triangle three, the quaternary or four within the circle. This is quite plain. No principles can cross the Ring "Pass-Not," only the memory of these in the eternal divine ideation, which ideation itself from something manifested becomes the Absolute on that "Day Be-With-Us." Therefore it is.

Mr. A. Keightley: Question 3. By "manifested plane of matter," do you here mean the four lower planes of the diagram on page 200, *i.e.*,

---

[3] **Atma-Buddhi-Manas** (*Sanskrit*) — the higher Triad of man, consisting of Spirit, Soul and Mind.

[4] **Quaternary** — the four lower principles in man, those which constitute his *personality* (*i.e.*, Body, Astral Double, Prana or life, organs of desire and lower *Manas*, or brain-mind), as distinguished from the Higher Triad, composed of the higher Spiritual Soul, Mind and Atman (Higher Self).

the four planes of the globes of our chain, or only the lowest of the four, that of our Earth?

H.P.B.: I mean what I say. Nothing manifested or having form or name or number can cross beyond the ring which divides the mutable and the manifested from the ever-present and immutable. Now, do put this into your wise heads, my dear children. There is the difference between the mutable and the manifested, and the ever-present and the immutable; and you cannot cross this line and you cannot — it is impossible — nothing that is within this domain can pass into the other, the beyond. It is impossible, at least in our philosophy; I don't know how it is in your conceptions, but in our philosophy, it is impossible. Where does our miserable atom of dirt, which gossipy conceit called the Earth, stand, once the Pralaya and universal destroyer and disappearance of the whole universe — the ideal as much as the physical — is concerned? How can I mean the Earth in one breath with absoluteness? Is it not said of the abstract elements on page 130 (which, please, look up) that even they, when they return into their primal element, or the one and secondless, can never cross beyond the Laya or zero point? Isn't it as plain as can be? Why do you torture me, then? There are seven meanings to every symbol. Astronomically, the ring "Pass-Not"[1] means one thing, and metaphysically, quite another.

Mr. A. Keightley: You state here — you quote from the *Visisht-advaita Catechism.*[2] [Reads from *The Secret Doctrine*, vol. 1, p. 132.] Question 4. Can you explain the esoteric meaning of the sentence: "Then it goes through a dark spot in the Sun"?

H.P.B.: Now, do you know what a Visishtadvaita[3] is? They believe in a personal, in a personal God, and they are dualists. They are Vedantins, but they have got no right to the name of Vedantins. There are

[1] **Ring "Pass-Not"** — the circle within which are confined all those who still labour under the delusion of separateness. The Lipika separate the world (or plane) of pure Spirit from that of Matter. Those who "descend and ascend" — the incarnating Monads, and men striving towards purification and "ascending," but still not having quite reached the goal — may cross the Circle of "Pass-Not," only on the Day "Be-With-Us." The Ring "Pass-Not" is not a locality, nor can it be measured by distance, but it exists in the absoluteness of Infinity.
[2] See N. Bhashyacharya, compiler, *A Catechism of the Visishtadwaita Philosophy of Sri Ramanuja Acharya* (Madras: The Theosophical Society, 1887).
[3] **Visishtadvaita** — one of the three schools of Vedantic philosophy. The two other schools are the Dvaita (dualistic) and the Advaita (non-dualistic). The ▸

three sects among the Vedantins: the Dvaita dualists, the Visishtad-vaita, which are more than dualists, and the Advaita, who are human-itarian, so to say, who believe only in one science. Therefore, I answer to this that you had better ask the [...], because I don't understand what it means. The "dark spot in the Sun" must be on a par with the Angel standing on the Sun. I could never understand what was meant. I even took the trouble of writing to the Pundit himself,[4] and I com-missioned Harte to ask him what it meant, and he could not tell me; so that what can I do?

Mr. B. Keightley: Then you cannot blame us for asking the question.

H.P.B.: I cannot, I don't know myself what it means. I have a dim idea, because for them the Sun is that Parabrahm; they don't know any better; and I do think, you know, that it means the heart of the Sun.

Mr. A. Keightley: Does it correspond at all with the point in the circle?

H.P.B.: I quote that simply to show the different systems in the Hindus. I don't blame you. I simply quote it to show what it says. Now comes a pretty question — number 5!

Mr. A. Keightley: Question 5, page 135. Can you tell us anything more as to the esoteric meaning of the 3,000 cycles of existence?

H.P.B.: Oh, immediately! Yes, of course! In the first place, I am not a mathematician — I say there it is perfectly impossible for me to go into figures. Secondly, you know perfectly well, as Mr. Sinnett has written already in his *Esoteric Buddhism*, that the powers that be and who have in their pockets the secret wisdom don't like to go into figures; they never do. The 3,000 cycles may mean any number of figures; it all depends upon the duration of each 3,000 cycles, which is, in short, the period of the whole Manvantara.

Mr. A. Keightley: Maha-Manvantara or minor?

H.P.B.: No, Manvantara; that is to say, when the seven rounds are accomplished.

Mr. A. Keightley: But is there any meaning attached to the idea of 3,000?

Advaita was founded by Sankaracharya, the greatest of the historical Brahmin sages.

[4] **N. Bhashyacharya** — the director of the Oriental Section of the Adyar Library of the Theosophical Society.

H.P.B.: I don't know; it may be.

Mr. A. Keightley: I am not asking the question numerically, but what is the idea?

H.P.B.: They say in many places 3,000; it has a Devachanic meaning, that is all. Every defunct who goes and crosses the Nile in the boat (you remember that ceremony) is Osirified, he becomes his own spirit, and the spirit goes into the field of Aanroo.[1] That is what it means.

Mr. A. Keightley: Question 6. Stanza 6, Sloka 1 (page 138). Can you further amplify this explanation as to the four kinds of Vach?

H.P.B.: In other words, can you analyse Subba Row's two lectures and once that it is published, to have all the blessed [...] on my head. It is a quotation from his lectures in the [...], he divides [...] and speaks of four forms, as a Vedantin who lays stress on the four-faced Brahma, the one who manifests on our plane and who is identical with Tetragrammaton also. If not four-faced, then the four numbered. He divided Vach into seven parts, and speaks of the seven faces of our Avalokitesvara,[2] that is to say, the seven forces manifested in nature. Our Vach is the female Logos. Now read *Vishnu Purana*; and I need not ask you, because I know you have read this several times. Or again, in Manu, or in any other work in which Vach is mentioned, and you will find that Brahma had divided himself into two persons, male and

---

[1] **Aanroo** (*Egyptian*) — the second division of Amenti (the kingdom of Osiris divided into fourteen parts, each of which was set aside for some purpose connected with the after state of the defunct). The celestial field of Aanroo is encircled by an iron wall. The field is covered with wheat, and the "Defunct" are represented gleaning it, for the "Master of Eternity"; some stalks being three, others five, and the highest seven cubits high. Those who reached the last two numbers entered the state of bliss (Devachan); the disembodied spirits whose harvest was but three cubits high went into lower regions (Kama-loka). Wheat was, with the Egyptians, the symbol of the Law of Retribution or Karma. The cubits had reference to the seven, five and three human principles.

[2] **Avalokitesvara** (*Sanskrit*, "on-looking Lord" — in the exoteric interpretation, he is Padmapani (the lotus-bearer and the lotus-born) in Tibet, the first divine ancestor of the Tibetans, and the complete incarnation or Avatar of Avalokitesvara; but in esoteric philosophy, Avaloki (the "on-looker") is the Higher Self, while Padmapani is the Higher Ego or Manas. The mystic formula "Om mani padme hum" is specifically used to invoke their joint help. While popular fancy claims for Avalokitesvara many incarnations on earth, and sees in him, not very wrongly, the spiritual guide of every believer, the esoteric interpretation sees in him the Logos, both celestial and human.

female, and they created the seven Manus. Now this is the exoteric version of the esoteric, or that which I have taught you many times. We are Vedantin, so far that we maintain seven, Vach being the female aspect of the seven Logoi. You must understand what it means. They are all androgynous. Even the first one, ethereal as he may be, might be made out of nothingness, but still he is androgynous — he has the feminine aspect in him, and because he emanates the second logos. Now the following question will give you more.

Mr. A. Keightley: Question 7. In speaking of the "Seven Sons of Light and Life" as being beyond the Laya centres, do you refer only to what may be termed the "relative" Laya centres which limit our solar system? For the term Laya centre seems usually to be used of the absolute limit of all differentiation.

H.P.B.: It is so, indeed, in the limit of differentiation in the manifested Cosmos. What is meant may be absolute darkness for us, but certainly it can be neither differentiation nor Laya, as we conceive of them, in that beyond. When I speak of the "Seven Suns of Light and Life" as being beyond the Laya centres, it only means this: they are subject neither to Laya nor differentiation — during the cycle of their life, at any rate, which lasts a Maha-Manvantara. If you had only remembered the order in which the Dhyan-Chohans emanate, or theogony, which is there explained in many places, you would not have asked the question. I thought you knew by this time that logos number one radiated seven primeval rays, which are as one, and are called the septenary robe of destiny; and that from that one is ultimately born logos number three, whose seven rays become the cosmic builders and whose aggregate is Fohat. How, then, can the sons of Light and Life, the septenary robe of immutable destiny, be otherwise than beyond the Laya centres? It is just what I had the pleasure of explaining to our dear President, Mr. Kingsland. I think it is very conceivable, that. You cannot take Laya as referring to anything but matter, manifested matter, differentiation, even finite manifested differentiation. And beyond this Laya point, which is the Zero point of matter, is matter which never differentiates, and nothing. It is not that it is a question of heat or anything, it is simply the within — how shall we explain this — as I have been explaining to you many times. Everyone of them is endless, shoreless, limitless, and yet there are seven. Well, there is a riddle for you! If not a mathematical one, it is not a physical one; and yet I suppose everyone ought to try and conceive of that — that it is not a question of right, left, up, top, below, or beneath. It is simply a question of the state of matter or state of consciousness. Matter is everywhere, because matter and spirit are one, but the Laya point, or beyond the Laya point, you cannot call that matter nor spirit; it is neither matter nor spirit, it is both and nothing.

Mr. B. Keightley: Then, really, that looks as if the Laya point would divide the four planes which you may call more especially manifested — the planes of the globe and solar system, and so on — from the three upper planes of which we have been speaking.

H.P.B.: They do not. The three planes and the four are just in one Cosmos as the seven principles are in you; but it is simply this: if we cannot understand or realize that we have these three principles in us, such as the higher intelligences, or Manas, and Buddhi, the spiritual soul, and Atma, the soul that is the synthesis — if we cannot realize this, how can you pretend to go and conceive that which is perfectly inconceivable for human intellect, the three higher intelligences? That is why I only give the four, because they represent the planes on which our planetary chain is. But I can't go beyond, because it would be perfectly incomprehensible; and moreover my knowledge of the English language would not tell me, nor any language, for I could not explain it.

Mr. Kingsland: You must look upon the three higher principles as differentiations of the Absolute one, whereas beyond the Laya point you have no differentiation whatever.

H.P.B.: That is just what it is.

Mr. B. Keightley: But you have the seven hierarchies.

H.P.B.: You have no seven. All is one after that.

Mr. B. Keightley: It was seeing the phrase used — "the Seven Sons of Light."

H.P.B.: Never mind what we use; we have a language to say many things, and we cannot say more than what the philosophy has evoluted. Try to understand it, if you please, that there are no differentiations, no spirit, nothing, it is the Absolute darkness for us. The highest Dhyan-Chohans could not tell you any more than could Mr. Herbert

Spencer. It is a thing on which human intellect cannot speculate. It is perfectly ridiculous and absurd for us stupid men and women to go and speculate upon such a thing as that. When I speak of stupid men and women, I include all those who possess the highest intellects in the world.

Mr. Kingsland: At the same time, do you not speak relatively of a Laya point of matter beyond which there are no differentiations?

H.P.B.: No, no.

Mr. Kingsland: Relatively.

H.P.B.: Look here. Try to understand me. We have seven planes of matter. On each of these planes there are seven again, and each has its Laya point. When we are on our plane, there is a Laya point which is the seventh of our plane; but when you have gone beyond those seven planes or seven divine ideations, as they are called sometimes, then there is nothing. You cannot speculate, because there, where there is nothing to grasp at, you cannot conceive of it; it is a perfect impossibility.

Mr. Kingsland: That is exactly what I meant, that there are certain relative Laya points.

H.P.B.: Yes, but those that come from the first Logos are beyond any Laya point, because they do not belong yet to differentiated Cosmos. They call it the septenary robe of destiny; I don't know why it is, but it is so. Mind you, though they are seven they are one; they are, so to say, the privations, the ideations of the seven that will be, of the second Logos — those that will be the seven from which will emanate the seven forces of nature. Please do ask me if you don't understand something, because I want to begin very seriously all these instructions.

Mr. A. Keightley: [Reads from *The Secret Doctrine*, page 138.] Question 8. Does Fohat stand in the same relation to the Hierarchy of Seven that Mayavi-rupa does to an Adept, *i.e.*, as the intelligent, formless, active thought power or energy?

H.P.B.: Whoever put the question has put an excellent definition. It is perfectly as you say. Who of you evoluted this? Let me give him the laurel wreath.

Mr. B. Keightley: It was Arch.

H.P.B.: Well, for once I must pay you the compliment; it is perfectly well defined. It is the Mayavi-rupa. You cannot make a better
illustration. [After a pause.] Now comes again a flapdoodle.

Mr. A. Keightley: Question 9. Sloka 3, page 140. After Maha-
Pralaya or any of the lesser Pralayas, does "Matter" remain in *status
quo* of progress, to re-emerge in Manvantara and take up differentiation and evolution at a corresponding point to where it was left at
Pralaya?

H.P.B.: Matter remains *status quo*, that is to say, in the form it
is found in at the hour of Pralaya, only with regard to the spheres
or globes of our chain. Then the globe, going into obscuration (as
Mr. Sinnett perfectly calls it, a name which has been given to him),
becomes, in the words of a Master, like a huge whale or mammoth
caught in the masses of ice, and frozen. The moment Pralaya catches
it, it remains *status quo*, everything. Even if a man happens not to
be dead, he will remain just as he is. But now listen. Otherwise, and
at the hour of any other Pralaya, save this planetary one in the solar
Pralaya, for instance, when our Sun goes into sleep, the matter of that
system which is to die and go out of existence is scattered in space
to form other forms in other systems. Every atom or molecule of it
has its Karma and its destiny, and everyone has worked out his way,
unconsciously, or according to the little intelligence it has; or it will,
if you please, go into other and higher systems when there begins
the new Manvantara. But the planetary Manvantara is the only one
where everything remains *status quo*. There are superb things in some
Sanskrit books, the description of it: when the Pralaya is near, when
you have to expect it, and all kinds of cosmic phenomena — most
magnificent. I quote a passage of it, but it is a long thing of about 17
or 18 pages.

Mr. Gardner: Is it in the Purana?

H.P.B.: It is not in the Puranas; it is in a philosophical book by
one of those Rishis. I have had it here, but I don't know what has been
done with it. I had one of the great pundits to translate it for me word
for word, and I was for about two weeks putting it down, because it is
a magnificent thing. I wanted to have it in *The Theosophist*.

Mr. Gardner: Do animals exhibit any peculiarities?

H.P.B.: There are not many animals left. There are what they call the Sishta[1] that remain, the seeds; they say they are great Adepts who become Manu when the time comes, when the obscuration is ended and this wave of life again reaches that particular globe or planet. Then they say they are the seed of life, the seed Manus.

Mr. Kingsland: Then the planet that is in obscuration will still be visible from other planets.

H.P.B.: Most assuredly, certainly; we see many dead planets.

Mr. Kingsland: The term obscuration gives us some idea, under the impression that in obscuration it would not be visible.

H.P.B.: It means from the standpoint of that which is on it, and not others.

A Lady: Is not the Moon in obscuration?

H.P.B.: No, it is not. The Moon is perfectly dead as a doornail.

Mr. Holt: Don't we understand obscuration by this paralytic condition?

H.P.B.: It is there that they are not asleep. "Not dead but sleeping."

Mr. Gardner: Suspended animation.

Mr. A. Keightley: There seem to be three stages then. There is obscuration, death, and dissolution.

H.P.B.: Yes.

Mr. A. Keightley: Progress towards destruction. There is the one you point out as the frozen state of paralysis; then there is the total death, like the Moon; finally the solar death, when the whole thing bursts up and goes on.

H.P.B.: But there are seven states, if you take not only planets but everything there is on them. Take sleep and take the trance state and take the yogi hibernation — for 40 or 50 days buried and then coming into life.

Mr. A. Keightley: Do the states of the planets correspond?

H.P.B.: Everything corresponds. There is nothing that happens to man that does not happen to everything else.

---

[1] **Sishta** (*Sanskrit*, "remnant") — the great elect or Sages, left after every minor Pralaya, when the globe goes into its night or rest, to become, on its re-awakening, the seed of the next humanity.

Mr. A. Keightley: Then what state does that sort of paralysis correspond to?

H.P.B.: Oh! This is not for you. Give your question. Don't you begin jumping.

Mr. Gardner: Can you tell us any of the planets that are in obscuration?

H.P.B.: We will tell you another day when you put the question. As the question is not there, I won't. Kindly learn a little more method.

Mr. B. Keightley: I think it is stated somewhere in *Esoteric Buddhism.* I think Mars is just emerging from obscuration and Venus is just passing into it. I don't remember exactly.

Mr. A. Keightley: Page 143. Can you give us a short sketch of "The Life and Adventures of an Atom?"

H.P.B.: That is the question I was expecting! "Can you give us a short sketch of the Life and Adventures of an Atom?" No, but I offer you two questions instead. Now you have to answer them. Which do you believe is larger, your body or that of the whole Cosmos? You will say, of course, it is the Cosmos.

Mr. A. Keightley: Well, wait a moment.

H.P.B.: And secondly, which of you has a greater number of atoms or molecules, you, or that Cosmos? Choose.

Mr. Holt: I should say exactly the same number.

H.P.B.: Do you? And how about men who are smaller and men who are a great deal bigger?

Mr. Holt: It is a matter of the size of the atoms.

Mr. B. Keightley: No, the distance between the atoms. That is, from the scientific point of view.

H.P.B.: Oh! But we are anti-scientists here.

Mr. A. Keightley: A man is commensurate with the whole of the Cosmos.

H.P.B.: I will tell you why I put this question. Now, supposing in view of the hopelessness of the task you offer me, and while I confess myself incapable of enlightening you with a sketch of the life and adventures of every atom, I seek to give you a biography of one of your personal atoms. Let us see now: am I generous and kind, that I consent to give you the life and adventures of only one?

Mr. A. Keightley: I asked for one.

H.P.B.: Now we will see if it is possible. How many years will it take me, do you think, to give you an accurate statement even about that one atom? For occult science teaches that from the moment of birth to that of death (and after death still more so) every atom, or let us say particle, rather, alters with every seventh fraction of something far less than a second; that it shifts its place, and proteus-like travels incessantly in the same direction as the blood, externally and internally, night and day. Now you are 28, 29, or how old are you? Thirty, let us say. Then let us say, if you please, that I will take an atom of your body, and from the moment of your birth I will begin giving you the life and adventures of that blessed atom in all its transformations, in all its gyrations, in all its metempsychosis. How long will it take me, gentlemen mathematicians? Tell me how much. Count and I will give it.

Mr. A. Keightley: Roughly, though; a short sketch.

H.P.B.: Go to bed!

Mr. Kingsland: If you ask a person to give a sketch of their life and history, you don't expect them to give the history of what they did every day of their time.

H.P.B.: An atom is not a man. An atom does not get into flirtations, and courtship and marriage, and pass through the Bankruptcy Court, and become a magistrate, and the Lord Mayor; nothing of the kind. An atom is a very well-behaved being, and what one atom does almost every other atom does. There are certain little variations, but it is nothing. But to come and tell you what I mean there, and give the life and adventures of an atom — which means, simply an impossibility. Because I said a chemist would be astounded and take it for the biggest nonsense for an alchemist to give him the life and adventures of an atom; and yet he comes and puts this question. Really and seriously, all of you, you must allow a margin, you must leave some possibility for a poor author to exercise his imagination.

Mr. Kingsland: We must have something to hang a discourse on.

H.P.B.: Oh, if it is only pegs you want, that is another thing.

Mr. B. Keightley: That question of atoms is consistently cropping up in *The Secret Doctrine.*

H.P.B.: It does, and I had the honour of telling you what I meant by atoms, that I used them in that sense of cosmogenesis. I said they were geometrical and mathematical points.

Mr. B. Keightley: Haven't you got something definite in your mind, when you write that?

H.P.B.: There are very many things I may have in my mind, and which I don't like to make public. There may be such.

Mr. Kingsland: I think Mr. Holt ought to tell us why he says there are the same number of atoms in the body as in Cosmos.

Mr. Holt: I was regarding the Earth and the solar system as but an atom; it was relatively. Each system might be regarded as but an atom of the whole Cosmos, just as we are but atoms of our permanent Earth with respect to our bodies.

Mr. Kingsland: Do you say every individual is an atom?

Mr. Holt: The mathematical idea of the atom is the least conceivable, not the least demonstrable — so that you see I am not begging the question. We may conceive the great and the small, and they are the same size in the noumenal. Are they not?

Mr. Kingsland: But when you compare the individual Cosmos, you are not working on that plane, you are working on the plane of manifestation.

Mr. Holt: I use it in that sense, but it was not until H.P.B. gave us her definition of the atom that I thoroughly understood what was intended. If it is the mathematical atom, then I say just as many. I mean metaphysically.

Mr. B. Keightley: The peculiarity of the mathematical point definition is, it has not got a size at all, neither bigness or smallness.

Mr. Holt: Therefore, it may be all or it may be nothing. So that is really why I said the man has so many atoms.

H.P.B.: You said it simply kabbalistically, as "the microcosm of the macrocosm."

Mr. A. Keightley: Question 11, footnote, "Force is a state of matter."[1] Are forces atomic and molecular, though supersensuous? The

[1] *The Secret Doctrine,* vol. 1, p. 143.

phrase used appears to imply Occultists make no distinction between force and matter. Is this the case? Please enlarge and explain.

H.P.B.: Still I say force as manifested on this plane is a state of matter. What would you call radiant matter, if not a state of matter? But the energy which produces the state of matter is perfectly the same as force. Call it force or energy, we consider it as a state of matter on this plane, for it cannot act without matter being present, and these two cannot be diverse. What force is on the other plane is quite a different thing, but I mean on this one. I say it is an electric state, that is what I say. Every force that is produced, to whatever it is applied, we call an electric force. It is a function of the whole universal electric ocean which acts. Do you understand my meaning?

Mr. Kingsland: Not thoroughly.

H.P.B.: As I don't know how science regards it this year, I am unable to make a comparison. I know how it regarded it last year, but it changes, you know, like an atom.

Mr. Holt: You admit of primordial substance, with the one absolute life moving or energizing in that substance?

H.P.B.: Most assuredly.

Mr. Holt: Then we may regard that as distinct ideal, but always co-existent and omnipresent.

H.P.B.: Certainly. I say that force on this plane is matter, a state of matter, at least; it has a function, a quality of matter — not of that matter on which it acts, but of the matter in general, of the Universal matter of the substance of the universal substance. Call it life, call it electricity, call it Fohat, call it whatever you like; it is always Fohat.

Mr. Holt: Would you then say that all cosmical force, as for instance planetary influence, is nothing else than the radiation of matter?

H.P.B.: It is the radiation of something, though for us it may not be matter, and we have no right to call it matter; yet it is matter on that plane, substance, call it if you like.

Mr. Holt: That would agree with the statement you made to me the other night, that everything is touch; thus, for instance, we might call light which is perceptible to the optic nerve, we might call it a force.

H.P.B.: I think it is more physical science, that wants to make the first one; but touch is something else than what is meant here. Who spoke to me about touch? I think Mr. Kingsland. One night here when we were talking about the first sense, which must be the touch.

Mr. Kingsland: Dr. Williams.

H.P.B.: But the way he explained it was not at all as we explain. It is touch, everything is touch. Taste and smell are touch, because everything must be touched in some way to produce or to put that particular sense into function or vibration, or whatever you call it — into activity. Therefore, I say that force is certainly a state of matter. And what objections have you to what I say? In that question I mean.

Mr. A. Keightley: What I wanted to understand is this. Supposing we see, for instance, a matchbox. That is force manifested on this plane, isn't it? It represents force.

Mr. Holt: It is force taking form, perhaps.

Mr. A. Keightley: But it is force.

H.P.B.: Nothing can manifest itself without force.

Mr. B. Keightley: Crystallized force.

Mr. A. Keightley: It is force, in the static state.

H.P.B.: You should say better as the Buddhist philosophers say, the concatenation of force and effect. It is force.

Mr. B. Keightley: You see, the ordinary idea of force is that which changes or tends to change. The state of matter which moves matter, shortly.

H.P.B.: This is the inherent energy, the inherent motion, which tends to change, and not at all force. Force is everything, because you cannot produce the smallest little effect without the cause of it being some force used — intellectual, moral, physical, psychical, any way you like. And what is force? It is the incessant action of what we call the one life, the one motion, the great motion which never ceases, which always goes on in the universe.

Mr. Holt: Then you would say it was always moving in primordial matter?

H.P.B.: Always. Even during Pralaya it is going on. There is no one to see it, or take notice of it, of how many vibrations, but still it is.

Mr. Kingsland: Now, take light, for instance, and radiant heat. Is that an actual movement of particles of matter from the object which emits the light and heat to us?

H.P.B.: I don't know. You see, our ideas of light are quite different.

Mr. B. Keightley: Let us leave light out and deal with heat.

H.P.B.: You have your own preconceived ideas furnished you by science. You have science as the grand priest, the high priest and initiator of all your ideas. You are obliged and in honour bound to accept everything that the Royal College or Royal Fellows tell you. We, on the other hand, are, so to say, the ostracized ignoramuses, the occultists; we have our own ideas, our own science; therefore I, being one of the humblest and most ignorant of those ignoramuses, cannot come and base what I tell you and give you always illustrations from science, because I don't know anything about it.

Mr. B. Keightley: But I think what Kingsland is driving at is this: we have certain erroneous ideas put into our heads, and we are obliged to use the same language which is familiar to us.

H.P.B.: But if I don't know it?

Mr. B. Keightley: What I think he wanted to get at was, wanting you to explain as far as you could, the way in which occultism would teach about this communication of heat, for instance, from, say, a red hot lamp or anything that is hot.

H.P.B.: Just in the same way as colour or sound is produced or any force which becomes manifested and apparent. We teach it as all coming from the Dhyan-Chohans.

Mr. ——: Isn't it molecular, though?

H.P.B.: It may be; everything is molecular if you call molecular that it is something. Of course I know what you mean by molecular, even in science.

Mr. Kingsland: What I wanted to get at was this: science conceives of the transmission of light as a transmission through a certain medium. Supposing you have a long stick, and you hit one end of it without the stick as a whole moving — you have the transmission of the knock from one end to the other. There is nothing transferred from this end to the other end. We wish to know whether it is the same in the case of light, or whether there is actually a transfer of particles from the radiant object to us.

H.P.B.: I say there is transfer of particles.

Mr. Holt: Are they transmitted as light shines through glass? Do these transmitted particles pass through the glass?

H.P.B.: These particles can pass through anything. All these things are nothing to them. It is just the same as the spirit passing through a wall.

Mr. Holt: It does not partake of the nature of matter. It is matter, but on another plane.

Mr. Gardner: Although it manifests on this plane.

H.P.B.: It manifests — not in particles, because they are not particles in our sense, but they are rays, they are radiant energies. It is very difficult to explain. They are emanations or breaths. I am afraid you won't understand me.

Mr. B. Keightley: There was a great dispute that went on between somebody and Newton, who had this theory, the corpuscular theory; he formulated it. Then that has been superseded in the opinion of modern science by the [...] theory of waves and vibrations along the stick.

H.P.B.: The corpuscular theory as it was presented by Newton, and the wave theory — the one that stands now through the ether that they were obliged to admit they took them from the ancients, however disagreeable it was for them — both of them are wrong. In both, according to occultism, there are right premises, and yet wrong conclusions. The thing is all muddled up both ways. It is excessively difficult, but perhaps in time we will come and coin words for things that you will have understood well; but until we have coined these words — upon my word, it seems almost hopeless to explain to you. For instance, I have had an idea perfectly clear and perfectly true to me; I know what it is. How can I explain it to you, even if I had at my command all the technical expressions used in physical science, and so on? I cannot, because there are not such expressions in existence.

Mr. Kingsland: No, but there are always analogies.

H.P.B.: But the analogy is very different for me. I am not at all of a scientific mind. I never learnt modern science in my life. All that I know is simply by reading, and sometimes not paying great attention to it. I know in some cases I had to learn, because I had to refute and I had to disprove it. But in general, I don't know; it does not interest me, because I know it is a flapdoodle, which will change tomorrow. Why should I go and cobweb my brain by learning all the lucubrations? Every day they invent something else, and on the following day you have to modify it or make away with it, or insult it in some way or other. I don't want to learn anything more, because one has the trouble of learning and unlearning. For you men of science who follow it, it is very easy — you remember the things you give up — but upon my word, I have too much of the occult theories that I have to learn and explain to you to go and bother myself with the physical science, which I hate.

Mr. Holt: May we pass on to the second part of that question, and ask whether this matter in its various forms is contactable on any plane, providing we have the requisite senses? And then I may supplement the question by: "Do we have the relative senses, even in the Nirvana?"

H.P.B.: Well, for the Nirvanic effect, certainly; but they call it Nirvanic. What does it mean? It means "a flame blown out" — *Nirvana*, no more, nothing. It is like a wind that passes and blows out everything. There is an entire disappearance of everything like the matter we know of on earth — not only matter, but even of our attributes, functions, feelings, everything. Nothing of the kind can go on in Nirvana. Therefore, they misunderstood the thing and they said it was annihilation, which is perfect nonsense.

Mr. Holt: But there is individual consciousness still retained, is there not?

H.P.B.: Not the individual consciousness of the present, but universal consciousness, in which the individual consciousness is a part. You see, it is quite a different thing, that. When you reach Nirvana you are the whole, the Absoluteness.

Mr. Gardner: But you are differentiated, all the same.

H.P.B.: Absolute differentiates? My goodness!

Mr. Holt: Then what is Para-Nirvana?

H.P.B.: Para-Nirvana differs from Nirvana because we are in the Absolute, which is just beyond the plane where differentiation begins. And Para-Nirvana is something which is beyond the Meta, of which you can know nothing. You come from Nirvana back into a new

Maha-Manvantara, when there is Para-Nirvana. Then there is the end of all; and nobody has ever calculated what shall be afterwards. That is the whole difference, philosophically.

Mr. Holt: What is the Buddhist name of the state where individual consciousness first manifests itself, coming out of Nirvana, towards the plane of matter?

H.P.B.: I don't know what you mean.

Mr. Holt: You say that individual consciousness is annihilated, except as it is preserved in the Absolute. So far as individuality is concerned, the sons of the "I am" that is apart from the Absolute, that is annihilated in Nirvana?

H.P.B.: Certainly it is annihilated. The "I am that I am," that is to say, I am all, I am absolute. You are not then old, but you are every blessed thing that there ever was, is, or will be; for what is it? You just make for yourself an idea of Absoluteness.

Mr. Holt: Does the identity merge itself into the Absolute?

H.P.B.: On our conceptions, it is no longer, but it is identity. It is a very abstruse metaphysical problem, this. You must understand this. If you conceive of deity as Absoluteness, or if you conceive of deity with attributes, then this deity cannot be infinite — it would be everlasting. It had a beginning and it had an end. Such are the Manvantaric Gods, those which are during the life cycle. The Absoluteness is that which is, to our minds, at least, immutable — which never had a beginning nor will ever have an end, which is omnipresent, which is absolute everything. And when we say of that Absoluteness that it is absolutely unconscious, absolutely without any desire, without any thought, it is because we mean and must mean that it is absolute consciousness, absolute desire, absolute love, absolute everything. Now you see how difficult is this thing to conceive. Those who have been brought up in a theology which limits and conditions everything, and makes and dwarfs everything that there is — the grandest things in the world — and those who, like the men of science, don't believe in anything but the limited and conditioned — they cannot conceive of anything which is not that. Therefore, occultism has to struggle with science and with more materialistic theologies yet, because the man of science holds to his department and he does his duty. He says: "I am incapable of understanding or believing; I am going to hold to that which my five senses show to me"; but the theologians who, at the same time claiming that God is infinite, God is endless, and God is absolute mercy and justice, gives to that absolute attributes, makes his God to be revengeful and make mistakes, repent that he has made man, do all kinds of things, and yet he will call him absolute and endless. This is where comes in this terrible, unphilosophical and illogical thing, which has neither head nor tail, which is a perfect, flat contradiction of everything. If you want to have it in a philosophical way, you have to take the Vendantin way of seeing things, but if you come to the theologians of the West, you are lost.

Mr. ——: Those are accommodations of truth.

H.P.B.: Not they, because you can do just the same as they do in India: they had to make accommodations for the minds of the poor Hindus, who are ignorant but there are no such contradictions. They say God. One will worship Vishnu, the other Shiva, the other anything you like, but they will never say these gods are endless and never had a beginning or an end. They will say the gods die, and Brahma at the end of Manvantara goes into Pralaya, and there remains only the one, to which they don't give a name, but they call "That," because, they say, "we cannot give it a name, it is that which ever was, is and will be and cannot not be." So you see how philosophical they are, much more philosophical than we are. I cannot understand even Herbert Spencer, speaking of the one deity and then calling it the "first cause" and calling it the "supreme cause." How is it possible?

Mr. ——: They are trying to comprehend things that are beyond the plane of their capacities.

H.P.B.: Most assuredly. That which is absolute, which is infinite, cannot have any attributes or anything; it is perfectly unphilosophical to speak of it in such a way as that. You cannot come and give any relations to that which is absolute, because the Absolute positively can have no relations and nothing to do with the conditioned; all this must be a thing entirely apart. When they ask me how is this, that this emanated, I say it emanates not at all, because if the supreme or the Heavenly father wants to emanate, it is simply because it is the Eternal law, the law of nights and days, as they speak of Brahma. There it is the breath, that principle, that law — and there is something which appears, the universe appears. I say it is a most magnificent and sublime conception of the Deity.

Mr. ——: The highest conceptions of the truth we have are not absolute truth. We can only take in what we are capable of taking in.

H.P.B.: That is why I say there is no one thing that is absolute and that we cannot speculate upon.

Mr. ——: And we are trying to talk about things about which we have no words.

H.P.B.: On this plane it may be speculation, but that which has no relation whatever to any ideas we have in our heads it is a perfect impossibility to speculate upon. That is why the Hindus call it "That"; they call it the one darkness, when it manifests in it but the rays. Then there is the manifestation and the creation, as they call it, the evolution of the world.

Mr. A. Keightley: Question 12. "Seven small wheels — one giving birth to the other."[1] In view of the diagram on page 172 of Earth and Lunar chains, does this mean that globe A gives birth to globe B within our planetary Ring?

Diagram 2. Earth and Lunar Chains

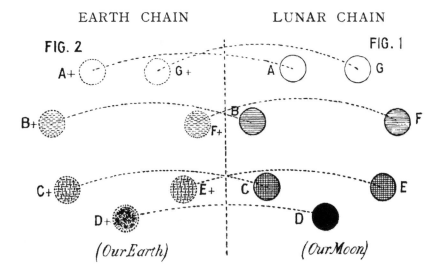

EARTH CHAIN   LUNAR CHAIN

FIG. 2   FIG. 1

A+   G+   A   G

B+   F+   B   F

C+   E+   C   E

D+   D

(Our Earth)   *(Our Moon)*

---

[1] *The Secret Doctrine*, vol. 1, p. 140.

H.P.B.: It does most decidedly. One principle goes out after another from the dying planet and generates a globe, as each principle generates another, except the physical body; for both are the productions of the Lunar Kama-rupa. Now that which I mean to say is, it means our planetary chain. And in *Esoteric Buddhism*, you will find that this wave of life, as he calls it, as it passes on, and when one is formed, then the other begins forming; and then one goes into obscuration, and they go one after the other. They emanate, because, if you have to believe what the occult sciences teach, namely, that our Earth is a production of the Moon that is a little bit of mud — well, it is a question of preference. But if you have to believe the occult doctrine, then every principle goes one after the other. There comes the first principle, that leaves when the Moon begins dying, which produces globe A; then the other can produce globe B, and so on. It goes in a round, the middle one being the Lunar Kama-rupa, that is to say, the seat of material things.

Mr. B. Keightley: You see the diagram as it is drawn; you remember how it is, the two chains side by side. Then A projects its principles into A of the Earth chain. But the phrase used there in the commentary seems to suggest that instead of going that way, that A being established, then from A came the next planet on our chain B and A of its own plane.

H.P.B.: A produces A, B produces B, and so on.

Mr. B. Keightley: The words of the Stanza seem to suggest that A produces B.

H.P.B.: It must have been done by some of you six or seven editors.

Mr. B. Keightley: It is the words of the Stanzas, but there are no alterations made. It looks as if in English it meant each wheel of a succeeding wheel.

H.P.B.: Don't be so very fine. I may give it, and then you can change it if you like.

Mr. B. Keightley: It was only to find out whether anything wanted explaining.

H.P.B.: No; one wheel it means, one globe giving birth to the other.

Mr. B. Keightley: In two successive chains?

Mr. A. Keightley: Question 13, page 145. With reference to what was said last Thursday about nebulas being collectively Fohatic affinity, what is the relation of a Laya centre to such nebulas?

H.P.B.: Here comes Laya centre again. None whatever. A Laya point is a little absoluteness of its own and can have no relations to differentiated things, so far as I know. It is a state in a point, moreover. It is neither a point nor a triangle nor any geometrical figure at all. It is simply called the Laya point to show the Laya state. It is a state — Laya — and not at all anything that can be indicated by any geometrical figure whatever.

Mr. A. Keightley: Question 14, "…four and one Tsan (fraction) revealed — two and one half concealed…"[1] Is there a distinctive separation into two parts of manifestation of the fifth element, corresponding to the separation of the Higher from Lower Manas?

H.P.B.: Yes there is. But you know this is a very abstruse question, in which you cannot go tonight. This is a thing which certainly it is, because if there is any analogy in nature it must be so; but we certainly cannot go into it tonight.

Mr. ——: Were the occultists aware that there were eight planets?

H.P.B.: They knew a great deal more. They simply speak about seven planets. They took the Earth and the Sun as substitutes, because they had planets of which our science now has vaguely and dimly an idea. There is one of the most sacred planets, the second one, which corresponded to that body which they take Mercury for. And it is the one between Mercury and the Sun.

Mr. ——: Is there one there?

H.P.B.: Most assuredly there is. And they searched for it, and they suspected it, and they cannot find it.

Mr. ——: That is to say, it is not visible to the physical sight.

H.P.B.: It is visible, but it is in its last obscuration. It will be seen from Mercury. It will be a moon, when there will be some other planet produced. There are figures for it.

Mr. Gardner: By what name was it known?

---

[1] *The Secret Doctrine*, vol. 1, p. 140.

H.P.B.: Oh, you would like to know it! Ask your instructor. I don't know it, so I cannot tell you. They wanted to call it Vulcan; they say that they suspected. I don't know what some of them said; others deny it.

Mr. Gardner: When the eclipse came?

H.P.B.: They thought there was something. I don't think it is anything.

Mr. ——: Does that make it invisible, being in obscuration?

H.P.B.: It may come again, you understand, but it is in its last brightness. It is as the Moon was before, because the Moon was far less visible than it is now. Now it vampirizes the Earth, but before it didn't have to vampirize anything; and it was in its last degree of consumption.

Mr. Holt: I don't think its luminosity would have anything to do with its visibility to this Earth. The darker it were the better for us, because we should see it against the Sun's disc.

Mr. B. Keightley: But they do fancy they caught a glimpse of it during the eclipse.

Mr. Gardner: Do you say the Moon vampirizes on us?

H.P.B.: Certainly, it does. All the moons and all the parents vampirize on their children in this space.

Mr. Gardner: Saturn's moon and Jupiter's too?

H.P.B.: They are all the same; no altruism among them. It is the survival of the fittest in nature. It is only men who ought not to have this.

Mr. ——: Have you any theory as to the numerous minor planets?

Mr. B. Keightley: 178 or more of them. Planetoids, it is.

H.P.B.: There is not the smallest star that is not personified. You may believe how many when even exoterically they give 330 million of gods, and every one of these gods, is a star — a visible star or planet.

Mr. B. Keightley: And has a story.

H.P.B.: Now the astronomers have not got more than 60,000 stars.

Mr. B. Keightley: They have got some millions.

Mr. Holt: Taking the zodiac, 218,000,000.

H.P.B.: And the Hindus have 330,000,000, and every one of them has its history and its place and space.

Mr. Kingsland: Has its life and adventures.

H.P.B.: Yes; I bring it in, because every god is connected with a star, that is why. Oh, they knew all; I can assure you they are a wonderful people. Why is it that they knew perfectly, without any telescopes or instruments, the seven Pleiades — the seventh sister which now has disappeared, and you can hardly see it with the best telescope? And they knew it perfectly, and it had not disappeared in their day. Therefore calculate how many thousand years they must have had this astronomers' knowledge.

Mr. B. Keightley: Their tables for the Moon's motion, which have been absolutely proved to have been obtained by independent data, are more accurate than the very best modern tables.

H.P.B.: Surely, it is wonderful, and they have no telescopes. What had they? The most rudimentary things, yet see how they knew it, because in the temples and the hierophants, the twice-born, they had all the things a thousand times better than we have now. But they don't speak of it; it is gone. It was sacred with them. They did not make a speculation of it simply on the material plane, as they do here. It was their religion, their most sacred doctrine. Certainly they did not give it to the *hoi polloi*.

Mr. Holt: They would not have needed telescopes to see these things. Could not they have seen them astrally?

H.P.B.: In the Pleiades, they disappeared. You cannot see them now without a telescope.

Mr. Holt: It has its astral counterpart. It is double. Then they could see.

H.P.B.: They can see not only that. They had their seers, but they had astronomers likewise.

Mr. Gardner: They had their instruments, as well.

H.P.B.: They are what Proctor[1] writes about — of the knowledge of the Chaldeans and the Egyptians.

Mr. Gardner: Did they have any force like Keely's force?

H.P.B.: That is not much. I suppose every yogi could produce Keely's force.

---

[1] **Richard A. Proctor** (1837–1888) — an English astronomer.

Mr. B. Keightley: There is not anything well-confirmed about this idea. I think it is flapdoodle. He might use it in some way to increase the power of perception, but I don't see how he can use his vibrating ether as a telescope. Somebody asserted that Keely could make use of his vibratory forces as a telescope.

Mr. A. Keightley: Hartmann said he had seen it. He said that he could just be looking down the tube after reflecting this force or getting it in some way on to it, he could make a bacillus the size of an orange.

Mr. Gardner: What magnitude is that?

Mr. A. Keightley: I don't know how many thousandth parts of an inch it measures, I mean the microscope. If you can get Keely's power to magnify that sort of size, you can surely apply the same principle to a telescope.

Mr. B. Keightley: Yes, if you can do it.

Mr. Holt: I don't see the application of it.

Mr. A. Keightley: Hartmann said he had seen it.

H.P.B.: He says only one thing that has attracted your attention, and he says one thing which sounds very much like our theory, only he expresses it in other words. He says that the Sun is a dead planet. I say that it looks very much like that that we say. The Sun, nobody has ever seen; it is simply the shadow of the real Sun, which is perfectly invisible and certainly in this sense, you can call it dead. You have the rays of light, and the shadow is strong.

Mr. ——: It throws up enormous fountains of molten matter.

H.P.B.: He gives his reason for it, and I say that which occultism teaches. I say, it is not the Sun we see; we see the shadow, the screen, the phantom; the real Sun is not seen at all.

11 APRIL 1889

Mr. B. Keightley: Page 142, line 7 of *The Secret Doctrine*, you say: "Neither Water, Air, Earth (synonym for solids generally) existed in their present form, representing the three states of matter alone recognized by Science; for all these are the productions already recombined by the atmospheres of globes completely formed — even to fire — so that in the first periods of the Earth's formation they were something quite *sui generis*.[1] Now that the conditions and laws ruling our solar system are fully developed; and that the atmosphere of our Earth, as of every other globe, has become, so to say, a crucible of its own, Occult Science teaches that there is a perpetual exchange taking place in space of molecules, or of atoms rather, correlating, and thus changing their combining equivalents on every planet." Question 1 (a): This long sentence requires further elucidation. What, for instance, must we understand by "the productions already combined"? How recombined? How do the atmospheres of globes effect this recombination? Why "even to fire"? In what aspect are they *sui generis* in the first periods of the Earth's formation?

H.P.B.: Why do you ask such long questions? Can't you put them like that — you know, A, B, C, D — as you used to do before?

Mr. B. Keightley: Because it is really all referring to the same subject.

H.P.B.: I will answer about the productions. The productions referred to are the differentiations of the primordial elements, water, air, fire, matter or earth, etc., which have all been very naturally combined in new forms in the atmosphere of the many globes they came in contact with — globes certainly anterior to our Earth by long æons of time. That is how they were recombined. How recombined, you ask? By the special crucible of each particular globe, recombined by heat, of course, by the internal fire latent in every form of every element, whether on this or the highest plane. Fire is spirit, the soul of things, whether in the form of Fohat or electricity or that magneto vital force which makes the plant grow. The term atmosphere in occultism does not mean the air we breathe; it applies to that Fohatic radiation or aura, which extends far beyond the limits of respirable air. This atmosphere is almost homogeneous, being the purest ether, or the seventh

---

[1] **Sui generis** (*Latin*) — of its own kind; unique.

principle of that which on our Earth is the first or lowest principle, namely, breathable air. Well?

Mr. B. Keightley: Question 1 (b): How is the atmosphere of our Earth a crucible of its own?

H.P.B.: Between any two planets — say between the Earth and the Moon — there is a regular gradation of density and purity in the etheric atmosphere which lies between the two. It commences on a planet with the densely material air, which is the rupa, or body of ether, and is as opaque to the light of its higher principle as the body of man is to the light of the Divine Spirit. From that material darkness the etheric atmosphere shades off gradually, till it reaches a point of — say, the perfect brightness or luminosity. This is the Laya point, or line on our plane, of the atmosphere between two planets. It is the condition of Laya which preserves the due equilibrium between the planets and prevents them being precipitated one upon the other. Therefore, in occult science it is impossible for anything in the shape of a material body to pass from one planet to another. From the occult standpoint, the fallacy of the meteorite theory is great indeed. Now have you got any questions, if you understand that which I said?

Mr. Kingsland: It would almost appear from that first answer to that question that the chemical elements as we know them now have not been differentiated, so to speak, but they have gone through a lot of processes on other globes.

H.P.B.: Most assuredly. I believe these diagrams drawn by Crookes are very fine on this plane, but certainly they have no rapport at all, no relation to the first differentiation from primordial matter. This I have never regarded.

Mr. Kingsland: Our idea — or rather mine — has been that the chemical elements have been differentiated from the cosmic fire mists *in situ*, so to speak, on this globe.

H.P.B.: No, not on this globe; every one of them has passed. Matter is eternal, and all this whatever-it-is that goes and whirls about is once concerned with one globe, then with another body on this plane, on the other and so on, until it goes down to our plane, which is the lowest.

Mr. B. Keightley: So that all the matter that we know and perceive practically has passed through an endless series of combinations before it reaches our plane of perception state?

H.P.B.: Most assuredly, because you could never see it; you could never perceive or sense it.

Mr. B. Keightley: Even, for instance, when Thomas Vaughan[1] said: "no man had ever seen Earth," he was not speaking of earth in the sense of the primordial differentiation.

H.P.B.: He was speaking about here. "No man had seen Earth." Don't forget that — that it has to pass from the seventh or the highest to the lowest, which is our Earth, to the first. Why, our Earth was created — this planetary chain — milliards and milliards after others. This is one of the things; and you see how many millions they give in the occult science. If you look at their calculations of the Yugas in the Manvantara and so on, why it makes the brains whirl, so to say, and get giddy to read those things.

Mr. Kingsland: On the last plane of all, take iron, for instance. Has that become iron on this globe, or was it iron before this globe?

H.P.B.: Take iron or take anything you like, it was, and all comes from, one and the same essence. One has become iron in reaching our globe, and another thing has become something else, and the third something else, and so on. But all these were the same thing. The essence of iron is no more than the purest ether.

Mr. Kingsland: But the material substance only became this on this globe?

H.P.B.: Yes, it can only be within our atmosphere. Therefore, the occult sciences say, it is a perfect impossibility, the speculation of this science, that the meteorites fall sometimes from a planet, because they cannot pass the Laya point. There is the thing which begins: it is dense, it is as black as night in comparison; it is between the Moon and this Earth. It begins quite black, then grey, then lighter and lighter, and lighter, until it reaches the Laya point. And from the Laya point it begins to be darker and darker and darker, until it becomes as black as possible. Therefore, between every planet there is the atmosphere and that which is beyond — not the breathable air, but the atmosphere.

---

[1] **Thomas Vaughan** (1621–1666) — a Welsh philosopher and great alchemist. His Rosicrucian name was Eugenius Philalethes.

Nobody breathed it, because you could not. If you went into a balloon you could not pass a certain point; there would be a certain stage where you would immediately die and be suffocated.

Mr. Kingsland: Then the "atmosphere" there is used in the purely occult sense, whereas, naturally, anyone reading it would take it as the ordinary atmosphere?

H.P.B.: I try to put in the words that everyone would understand. I did not use occult words there.

Mr. Gardner: Then we really see the stars through this atmosphere?

H.P.B.: But we don't see them as they are; it is a Maya. It is a regular Maya of vapours and things that prevent us seeing. It is all nothing but hallucination and illusion.

Mr. Gardner: Are not they really the distance off that the astronomers say?

H.P.B.: I don't believe in it.

Mr. Gardner: How about these meteoric signs?

H.P.B.: Have patience, and I will tell you. The meteors are, as a general rule, fragments of broken planets or comets. Once a planet is broken up, the Laya centres, which separate it from other planets, or the Laya line rather, I would say, disappears. It shifts its position so as to find itself between two planets which remain intact. You understand? You put our Earth, then there is a planet and then there is a third planet; the atmosphere begins dense here; it comes here, and there is the Laya between the line, and then it becomes dark here [illustrating]. Then this is broken up, and immediately it goes and will form this between other planets, the next planet and the Earth.

Mr. Kingsland: It will spread out on the Laya point?

H.P.B.: It shifts its position so as to find itself between two planets which remain intact. The result is that some fragments of the broken planet remain in the old orbit of the destroyed planet. Thus, of course, when the Earth crosses the former orbit of that planet, any fragments that are brought within its attraction fall to the Earth as meteors. Did you understand, Mr. Old?[2]

---

[2] **Walter Richard Old** (1864–1929) — an English astrologer and author who wrote under the pen name Sepharial. He held H.P.B.'s hand when she passed out on 8 May 1891.

Mr. Old: I merely wish to ask whether this planetary disruption, which is the cause of cometary masses, is contrary to the general rule? It appears that the general rule is, in the formation of a body, gradually to transfer its vitality to another and thus to die out; but here we have a case where a planet coming between the equilibrating forces upon both sides goes into a state of disruption and splits up. This is contrary to the general rule, is it not?

H.P.B.: No, it is not. Because, the Moon it will happen to, as soon as it has nothing more — no force even to try to vampirize the Earth. The Moon will be just in that position; then it will be disrupted. It is most probable that the Earth will have some other moon, or we will go without, so that the poets will not be able to compose their pretty verses to their beloved, and everything will go on as usual.

Mr. Gardner: Some of the pieces of the Moon will come down on this Earth.

H.P.B.: I hope it will not come on my nose. I will be dead and gone by that time, though.

Mr. B. Keightley: As a rule, the cometary state of a planetary body is before it becomes a planet.

Mr. Old: Yes, but we are talking of the meteors now, not of the comets.

H.P.B.: You see, it differs so much from real, official science that really, a man of science, a physicist, or an astronomer, if he were here listening to us, would say we are all lunatics. But I teach you the occult doctrine, and I think it is on the whole — if you learn it from A to Z — you will find it is certainly worth the speculations of science, and that it gives far more rational explanations, and even fills up all the gaps and missing links.

Mr. B. Keightley: There is one point about the meteors. You find in meteorites exactly the same minerals, metals and so on that you find on Earth, and indistinguishable by any of the tests that chemistry, at any rate can apply, or spectroscope analysis.

H.P.B.: You will remember the passage from *The Secret Doctrine*, that a planet only breaks up afterlife has entirely left it, when it is even more dead than the Moon is now; that is to say, only after Seventh and last Round. Witness the Moon. Mind you, it is long æons after the

Seventh Round; not directly. This accounts for the complete absence of any traces of life, or organic remains in the meteor; is it that that you want?

Mr. B. Keightley: You said a little while ago, in speaking about the elements, that they were so completely differentiated from any of our terrestrial elements. When a meteor falls to the Earth, you find it contains its constituents, the minerals and so on, and they are almost without exception the same as we find on Earth.

H.P.B.: Most assuredly, because as soon as they get on the atmosphere they change, and there is a kind of correlation, transformation — say what you like. This is what the Master taught Mr. Sinnett, of all these things. As soon as it comes, it goes beyond our atmosphere; it comes within the advantages of our atmosphere, and this atmosphere is a crucible — to which you just objected — because it changes everything that comes within it.

Mr. Old: When a planet is disrupted — and you say part of it may remain in the same orbit after the other planet died — does it continue to revolve round in just the same way as the original planet did, this fragment that remains?

H.P.B.: Yes, it has a motion of its own, but I don't think it dies; it falls in a kind of chaotic whirl.

Mr. Gardner: Supposing, for example, Jupiter was to come within the orbit of this disrupted meteor. That would leave a certain portion of it, the same as it does here.

H.P.B.: What applies to our planet applies to every planet.

Mr. Gardner: Would they have the same chemical combination?

H.P.B.: This I don't know. I cannot tell you what I don't know.

Mr. B. Keightley: The point raised before was that the elements — the substance of the matter — differed from one planet and the other.

H.P.B.: They will be remodeled according to the atmosphere.

Mr. Gardner: It does not change very quickly through the Laya point.

H.P.B.: Through the Laya point they cannot go; it is impossible. That is why I say that this theory, "that Mars fell down from some planet," is from the standpoint of occultism perfectly untenable, for it cannot pass the Laya point. If it did, it would be dissolved, it would exist no more. In the Laya point it cannot move, it is a negation of all movement.

Mr. Gardner: I cannot see that. You have potash and lime, and so on.

Mr. B. Keightley: Why should not they perform in the Earth's atmosphere?

H.P.B.: There is the occult student [Mr. B. Keightley], ask him.

Mr. B. Keightley: If you take a mineral out of a smelting furnace, you find all sorts of chemical combinations, lime and all sorts of things formed there, which are formed out of other substances which have been exposed to violent heat. Well, you get combinations, all sorts of combinations, formed out of what are to us unknown elements.

Mr. Gardner: You get different metals in these meteorites.

Mr. B. Keightley: Which enter into the material of the Earth. It is not a pot made of fire-clay, you know. It has the function of a crucible.

Mr. Hall: Then these meteors may be said to have in them certain potentialities, which, when they come within the crucible of this Earth, produce the metals that we know?

Mr. B. Keightley: Precisely. At least, that is the way I understand that.

Mr. Gardner: Then, if they get into the crucible of another planet?

Mr. B. Keightley: They would form others.

H.P.B.: There is something I took from the first question. "In what aspects are elements *sui generis*?" I answer, first, because no one period resembles the other, and secondly, because the First Round of every chain differs entirely from the subsequent that will appear subsequently. There is a greater difference between the First and Second Rounds of a Manvantara than between any two subsequent rounds. Then question (b) is: "How is the atmosphere of our Earth a crucible of its own?" That has already been answered as far as it can be done, so that this settles the first question.

Mr. Keightley: Had you anything more about the meteors which you have not read?

H.P.B.: No, I have read everything about the meteors; I just answered as much as there was there.

Mr. Hall: Will you give any explanation of the reason why there is so much more difference between the first and second Manvantara?

H.P.B.: No, I won't, because it will take us till tomorrow morning.

Mr. B. Keightley: It comes into the thing we go into about the Moon later on. Question 2. (a) Can you give us any instance of the atoms correlating and thus changing their combining equivalents? (b) What is meant by "combining equivalents," in this sense?

H.P.B.: I use the word "atoms" here not in the occult sense, but in that given to it by physical science, which speaks of an atom of iron, of hydrogen, and so on. *The Secret Doctrine* is not an occult book, as I told you, but a printed work for the public. What is meant by the terms "correlating," or "molecules changing their combining equivalents," is that the relations between what science calls atoms and molecules of our elements differ from planet to planet; therefore "b" in question 2 is also answered. That is all I can tell you. Has anyone to ask any questions — some of the physicists? Mr. Williams, have you nothing to say? Mr. Williams does not.

Mr. Williams: No, thank you, I have no questions to ask. I thought you were speaking of the other Mr. Williams, the doctor.

Mr. B. Keightley: Question 3. Page 143, line 10. Can you explain at all what is meant by "a current of efflux"?

H.P.B.: Which means that I am sat upon for using the word efflux.

Mr. B. Keightley: No, no, you are asked to explain what you mean.

H.P.B.: In physical science a current of efflux is a current of matter on one and the same plane, whatever its attraction. In occult science a current of efflux means a current passing from one plane to another, whether higher or lower. This efflux is not an objective movement in our third dimensional space, but a change of state from space without to space within, or vice-versa. Do you understand that? You see, in occult language it means quite a different thing.

Mr. Kingsland: It is change in differentiation.

H.P.B.: It is change from one plane to another.

Mr. B. Keightley: Question 4. Is the Laya centre that condition of primordial substance at which, or in which, Absolute Motion takes the specific name of Fohat? Or is Fohat the sum of the seven radical forces, in the same sense that Mahat is the sum of the seven intelligences of the Manvantara, called the "Seven Sons"?

H.P.B.: The Laya centre of primordial substance has everything else the side of it, or is the reflection of Absolute Motion, which adjective implies that it is equally Absolute Rest or Non-Motion. In occult philosophy the Absolute can have no attributes; therefore the adjective, Absolute, permits of no nouns. Fohat is the collective radiation of the Seven Sons, but the Seven Sons are themselves the third degree of manifestation. Fohat is not the synthesis or the sum of the seven radical forces, but their collective radiation. That which has a right to the name, or the synthesis of the sum of seven radical forces, is the second Logos, considered as the unity of the seven Logoi, or the seven primordial rays, which we call the Seven Sons. Mahat, in its turn, is a reflection on a higher plane of the divine ideation; on a lower one, Mahat corresponds to the higher Manas in man, and divine ideation is Buddhi. One is the mind, whether of cosmos or man, the cosmic and human soul; the other the spiritual soul in the universe, the macrocosm of man, its microcosm. Now, ask questions about that, because I see you do not understand that, Mr. Old.

Mr. Old: I had conceived, from my reading of *The Secret Doctrine*, the idea that Fohat stood in the same relation to the seven radical forces as Mahat did to the seven Rishis or Logoi.

H.P.B.: So it does on this plane, but on the others not, because I say to you that Fohat is simply not the synthesis, he is the collective radiation of the seven — what we call Builders. But on the higher plane, Fohat is no more that. He is also a collective radiation, not of the Builders, but of the Seven Sons of Mahat. What is Mahat? It is the intelligent — how shall I say — reflection of what we call divine ideation, that which Plato calls divine ideation, just in the same sense, because Plato gives the purely esoteric oriental doctrine. So you understand, now, the difference. If you ask a question, you must always ask whether it is on this plane or any other, because on every plane it changes, it alters its name, its functions and everything; that is why it is so difficult for someone who does not know the things.

Mr. Old: It was understanding that which made me ask the leading question: Is it at the Laya point of this sphere that Fohat is called Fohat, or is it called so on any higher plane?

H.P.B.: It is so called everywhere. About the Laya point, I am going to answer you here.

Mr. Old: There is something else attached to that.

H.P.B.: It is question 5.

Mr. B. Keightley: Question 5. Why are the Laya centres called "imperishable" (page 145)? For if the Laya centres are "conditions," they must, as such, perish in passing into the conditionless — as in the Maha-Pralaya — must they not? Are they so called only in relationships to any given Manvantara?

H.P.B.: You see, there is again a mistaken notion, not a mistake, but a mistaken notion about the thing. The Laya centres are imperishable and eternal, because they are no manifestation, but simply rents in the veil of Maya, or manifestation. Do you understand? The Laya centres are that which are no reflection, but the reality, the one Absolute substance, so to say, which has all the negative qualities and none of the positive, which is Absolute all, the Absoluteness; therefore it is the Laya point.

Mr. Old: It is merely a relative matter as to how you use this.

H.P.B.: Now, mind you, everything has a Laya point. If you want the Laya point in this matchbox you will find it. There is nothing in this world that has not got its polarity and its seven principles, from the highest to the central one, which is the Laya point. Not that it is somewhere inside, within, but, as I say to you, everything has so many degrees. If you take the thinnest thing that you can conceive of, say the cobweb, it will have its seven planes. You see the one that is visible, which answers to our perceptions, which is sensed by us; and the second, which will be less sensed, and so on, until you do not see anything. And the last one will be the Laya point. It is not a thing that one is without and larger and the other is within and smaller. It is simply the degree of density and of state of the substance, of the universal substance.

Mr. Old: Yes, I understand now, thank you.

H.P.B.: The Laya *centres* are not conditions *per se* any more than the Absolute is a condition; but it is said of objects, subjects, men and things that they pass into the Laya-like condition. You see, much depends also on the way. In some places it ought to have been written more explicitly. The universe, strictly speaking, doesn't emerge or re-emerge from or into the Absolute Laya, which is only another name for the Absoluteness of Parabrahm, after [...] or Manvantara, but it is reflected in you from the eternal root on the now differentiated substance. You see what I mean.

Mr. Old: But it was reading the sentence where you tried to explain what the "Laya centres" was. You said it is not any point at all, but a condition, and therefore you qualified it with the idea opposed to the conditionless. I quote the passage.

H.P.B.: I must say I had too many editors for it. Now, I have re-marked a mistake today, that it is said there "it is thrown into the Laya." You cannot throw anything *into* the Laya; I ought to have said "*onto*" the Laya — around the Laya, you understand. There are many such things that there may be. I am not English and I do not perceive immediately the mistake; and afterwards when I read it with a little more attention, I see there is something which might have been ex-pressed better. You know very well under what difficult conditions I wrote this book. I asked two or three there and they helped me; they had to type it out. You had better put a mark for the second edition, "onto" and not "into."

Mr. Old: We shan't complain so long as it draws forth so much intelligent instruction. Even mistakes give rise to intelligent interest.

H.P.B.: My dear ladies and gentlemen, if I knew English, I would hold meetings. I have not got the talent for the gab. If I could only put into Olcott's head that which I know, or have his eloquence (because he speaks beautifully), I could do something.

Mr. B. Keightley: You might take each chapter of *The Secret Doctrine* as it stands and make a volume of it, and not go further than explain the things you say in good English. Question 6. In what sense are the seven sons of Fohat also his seven brothers (page 145)?

H.P.B.: There we come to a most metaphysical thing; that is a thing I want you to remember well, now. I will tell you better than that, that the sons of Fohat are not only his brothers; they are his aunts, his grandmothers, his mothers-in-law, everything, because I am going to prove to you what it is; why they use this phraseology in the Oriental metaphor, in the Oriental philosophy. In that sense they were sons, brothers, fathers, mothers, etc., only in our evanescent and personal states on this Earth and plane. In our origin we are all one essence, therefore at once fathers, mothers, sons, brothers, what you like. Thus we find in Indian, Egyptian, and other cosmogonies that wives of gods, such as Isis and Aditi and others, called their mothers and daughters. Take the Egyptian cosmogony, or pantheon; you will see that Isis is called the Mother of Horus, the wife; she is the mother of Osiris, the wife and sister and everything. That is just the reason why, because they are all and everything. You understand it is only on this plane that we assume personalities and play our parts in this world of Maya and become something to somebody else; there we are all one.

Mr. Old: But don't you think when you use a qualificative term like "sons," you immediately set this said Fohat in relation to some other part of itself?

H.P.B.: Most assuredly; and I will give you the explanation. I have given you a rather lengthy thing about Fohat.

Mr. B. Keightley: Question 7. Can you explain more fully what is intended by the expression "Fohat is forced to be born again time after time whenever any two of his son-brothers engage in too close contact, whether an embrace or a fight"?[1]

H.P.B.: Now remember what I have given you two Thursdays ago, about the two forces, the two opposite forces, and what I told you about the centripetal and centrifugal forces. Now I am going to explain to you. Fohat is the symbol of universal, unpolarized electricity, you understand, his sons being the seven radicals of electro-magnetism, which are polarized forces. Electricity on this plane of visible Fohat is thus their brother of his sons. But relatively to that he is non-polarized, since he contains them all, and therefore he is their father. Now is this sufficiently explained to you?

Mr. Kingsland: It is all a question of the aspect in which you look at it.

H.P.B.: The Fohatic brothers are everywhere, one in each kingdom of nature. Now, take a piece of glass. To produce electricity you have to rub it with an animal or vegetable product. Then two of Fohat's sons are brought into close contact, and their father, Fohat, becomes now their son, because he is generated by them. Is not it so? He is the father on another plane, or in another aspect. And when you come to that

---

[1] *The Secret Doctrine*, vol. 1, p. 145.

friction business — take anything you like — then where electricity is generated, he becomes their son.

Mr. Old: Then Fohat is really not only electricity.

H.P.B.: He is unpolarized electricity, universal; it is the radiation of the seven highest Logoi of those seven rays that come from the second Logos, as we call it, or this manifestation that comes from the never-manifested.

Mr. B. Keightley: The more I think about it, the more I think that the English word which best translates the word Fohat is Energy.

H.P.B.: Energy is everything.

Mr. B. Keightley: So is Fohat.

H.P.B.: In the Kabbalah you have grand expressions. I have never met a good Kabbalist that wouldn't understand the real philosophical things.

Mr. Hall: Why not call Fohat the agent?

H.P.B.: Because you are an insurance agent we must call him agent! Why not call him prime minister? I won't, I have too much respect for Fohat.

Mr. B. Keightley: Fohat is all force, he is the causer, the mover, the radiator, everything. The only expression we have in English with anything like such a wide range is Energy.

Mr. Hall: Energy is what you might call the unapplied force. He is the applier of Energy.

H.P.B.: My dear sir, I will kick this thing and it will be energy that I use. Is it Fohat? Not at all. If I rub it, it will produce Fohat. You can't call that energy which applies to many other things. Energy is simply a force used. The word, Fohat, is the only one I have found.

Mr. Kingsland: Call it unpolarized electricity.

H.P.B.: Yes, but it means also the self-moving and that which forces to move; the brightness or the radiancy that moves and moves everything. This is the real, long translation of the word, Fohat.

Mr. Hall: Activity.

H.P.B.: Activity! No, your European languages will never express that which is expressed in Sanskrit.

Mr. Old: Five simple letters convey a great deal to you, but to us it is far from expressive under the name of Fohat.

H.P.B.: I explained it to Mr. Sinnett seven years ago. Rome was not built in one day. You have got to learn. There are thousands and thousands of things there, but if I were to come and speak in relation to these two forms there would be ten volumes and nobody would buy it, and they would put me into a lunatic asylum.

Mr. Keightley: You say here — speaking of the death and rebirth of planetary chains — you describe at the end of the Seventh Round on a planetary chain how the planets die, one after the other, and their principles and energies are thrown out from the dying planet and thrown upon a Laya centre, and then proceed to evolve round that Laya centre a new planetary chain. And you give, as an instance, that the Earth proceeds, so to speak, from the Moon in that way — that the Earth is the child of the Moon. The question asked is this: Question 8, page 155. Under what law may we account for the production by the Moon of a child (the Earth) much greater in point of size than its parent?

H.P.B.: I have seen sons that were six-footers from very small parents. This is nothing. But it is not the question. What do you want to know?

Mr. B. Keightley: Is it that in the transfer of the astral principles from the material body of the Moon to that Laya centre which becomes the Earth there is produced a falling in upon itself of the gross matter of the lunar body? And if so, may we say that the life-current, passing from the Laya centre of the parent to that of the offspring, contains the potentiality which is afterwards manifested in the development of the child-orb?

H.P.B.: The materials of the Earth were there in undifferentiated condition, for substance is eternal. There was never a moment when they were not a substance, the materials of which the Earth now is created, the whole chain; there was never a time when it was not. They were only awakened by the Moon's principles when one after the other they were transferred from the Moon to the nascent Earth when its turn came in the awakening of the chain. The phrase would run better in *The Secret Doctrine*, where it is said, all this, "the Moon's principles are sent out *onto*,"[1] instead of "*into*" the Laya centre, because a Laya centre is just as I told you, not differentiated, though everything around it can be differentiated. The Laya centre is the Atma, in this case, of the body that forms. The Moon shrinks after the loss of her principles as the dead body of a man shrinks after its vital and other principles have quitted it. And as it is so, the occultists say that, of course, the life current of the parent carries with it a potentiality of all that will be developed in the new planet. In the Moon there are no more principles, there is a kind of — how shall I say it? It is ridiculous to say vegetable — the life planet. There is a kind of a shadowy life. That is to say, you just think about a body in a trance condition: some of those bodies that are for 20, 30, or 40 days and live. There is the kind of life going on, but everything is dead to all appearances. Only there is something in the body that keeps up the vitality, and if certain substances are brought in contact with that body, that body will absorb it notwithstanding, by osmosis. You can perfume a body which is in such a condition as that. If you go and burn incense then the body for many hours afterwards will smell, which shows it absorbs. Now a thing which is perfectly dead will not, it will absorb nothing. Therefore, the Moon in the same way is said to vampirize. Now look at the terrible illnesses that are produced through the Moon. Look at the effects produced when you are in the Red Sea. Not a single sailor is allowed, when it is full moon, to sleep on deck without covered head, because he is sure to have his face paralysed and burnt. I have seen two cases like that. I have seen a man become perfectly insane, and he kept so for five or six months; simply moonstruck during the passage in the Red Sea.

Mr. Gardner: Is there no remedy to obviate that? Is there nothing in nature?

H.P.B.: Certainly Nature herself will perhaps restore her equilibrium. The doctors don't know anything. The yogis have a plant, the moonplant. They will use it and of course restore the man. I have seen the Lascars,[2] but then you must go to a yogi who knows it, a European doctor will not know anything at all.

---

[1] *The Secret Doctrine*, vol. 1, p. 172.
[2] **Lascars** — sailors from India, who were employed on British ships during the colonial era.

Mr. Hall: Then the Moon is cataleptic?

H.P.B.: It is something like that. It is very wicked.

Mr. ——: Is that a sort of reactory effect it has?

H.P.B.: See what an effect it has on vegetation. It has an enormous effect. There is not a plant, not a body in heaven that exchanges so much, or interchanges effects so much as the Moon and the Earth. There are not two such planets. It is always interchanging, that is going on, and there the Laya point won't prevent it; it is quite a different thing. This is a most occult thing.

Mr. ——: But the Earth in the end has greater power over the Moon than the Moon over the Earth.

H.P.B.: Certainly, because the Earth is a moving thing, and the Moon is a dead one, or is dying — it is in a cataleptic condition.

Mr. ——: Does that apply to other planets, as well?

H.P.B.: Just the same. As above, so below, at least on the same plane to everything visible — stars and suns, and fixed stars and planets and everything.

Mr. Old: I might just mention that with respect to that vampirizing influence that the Moon has upon the Earth, it is strange that just those principles, or rather those elements, which it lacks, it most powerfully attracts from the Earth, for instance, the atmosphere and water. It has plenty of dense matter, of course, but has little influence upon the dense objects of this Earth, far less than the solar influence. But upon the water and upon all fluids in the human system, it is known to have a most powerful effect; and hence the determination of the fluids, the humors to the head in the case of lunatics, and in the case of those who are moonstruck.

H.P.B.: But it is a most extraordinary thing in the occult science. I have been putting the question several times to the Masters, I have asked: "How is it possible, if these meteors cannot pass or anything, how is it that the influences pass the Laya point?" They say it is quite a different thing. The conditions are given by the radiation of the moonlight, which shows to you that it passes with its seventh principle, and not with the first — not with the bodily elements of the principles, but with the seventh, you understand.

Mr. B. Keightley: And therefore passes through the Laya point in the same order.

Mr. Gardner: Then its first principles do pass through it eventually?

Mr. B. Keightley: No, no. The influence passes, not the matter; you may call it matter, in the same sense that everything is matter.

Mr. Kingsland: In the same sense that one magnet affects another, there is nothing that passes between them materially.

H.P.B.: You can put between two magnets a dead wall, a glass wall for instance, an iron wall, and yet it will pass. Put any wall you like it will pass, and it does not prevent it.

Mr. B. Keightley: Did you ever see a very curious experiment showing the presence of something, whatever you can call it, between the poles of a magnet? If you get a copper disc, so arranged that it is between the poles of a powerful electro-magnet, and there is no electricity passing, therefore, it is not a magnet, it is just a plain piece of iron. You can make the disc revolve as fast as you please; the disc feels as if it were passing through butter, and it will become heated red hot, if you force it to revolve between the poles of the magnet, just as if there were actually matter between. Don't you know that?

Mr. Kingsland: I think a very good illustration of the Laya point, a practical illustration, would be that common experiment of scattering iron filings over a glass plate under which you have two poles of a magnet. The filings arrange themselves in circles; there is a certain influence circling round the one and the other. They separate, as it were, they won't coalesce; you see distinct dividing lines; that would illustrate the Laya point between the two planets.

H.P.B.: That is a good illustration.

Mr. B. Keightley: What is there between the poles of a magnet in an experiment of that kind? Can you answer that question?

H.P.B.: Don't you ask me, if you please, things which pretend to your physical science, because I have told you hundreds of times I don't know anything. I don't say I feel proud of it, but I feel perfectly indifferent.

Mr. B. Keightley: I can say with perfect confidence you can answer, if you like. Question 9: From what source does the Earth draw its active vital principle in order to persevere in its own line of physical development, and at the same time to meet the vampirizing demands of its lunar parent?

H.P.B.: It draws its life from the universal and all-pervading ocean of life and also from the Sun, the great life giver. The child receives its first stroke of life from the mother, but once born, it grows and develops by assimilating life from everywhere around it. The child could not grow and live, did it depend only on the incipient life principle which it derives from the mother. It receives a certain thing; she starts him in life with a little capital, and then he goes and makes speculations himself. Doesn't everything live? We live in the ocean of vitality. It is only the men of science who will tell you that life is not at all an entity, or something separate, but simply a certain combination of organs. Oh, heavens! There is Grant Allen![1] I wish you could see this new book of his, *Force and Energy*,[2] and the flapdoodle that the man says about the birth of the first man, and how he was born from the Earth, and some gasses and other things. Why, it beats anything I have ever heard in my life. *The Pall Mall Gazette*[3] laughs at him in the most extraordinary way. You ought to go and get his book.

Mr. Kingsland: I think that is a point that ought to be enforced a little more. There is rather a tendency to suppose the Earth became fully formed by the influence from the Moon.

H.P.B.: It received its principles, my dear sir; it is not said as you say. Once that it was started and was born, so to say, then it began to live; just the same as a child, it receives its first vital principle from the mother. Once it is born, it has to receive its influence and to be taken into the air and be promenaded. It takes its life from everything, from the air it breathes, and the food it eats.

Mr. Kingsland: It shows that the person who put that question seemed to think that the Earth ought not to be bigger than the Moon.

H.P.B.: No, I suppose he wanted to elicit an answer. No. The size is nothing.

---

[1] **Grant Allen** (1848–1899) — a Canadian science writer and novelist.

[2] See Grant Allen, *Force and Energy: A Theory of Dynamics* (London: Longmans, Green & Co., 1888).

[3] *The Pall Mall Gazette* — a London evening newspaper, published from 1865 to 1923.

Mr. Hall: Even the child before it is born, isn't it nourished by outside influences?

H.P.B.: It is what I said, but I am not going to speak about this question now. Why should I?

Mr. B. Keightley: Question 10. Page 155, line 7. As suggested by the analogy of the planets with man, does the female ovum constitute a Laya centre, and the fructifying male element correspond to the energy and principles thrown out by a dying planet?

H.P.B.: There is a Laya centre in the ovum, as in everything else, but the ovum itself represents only the undifferentiated matter surrounding this point, and the male germ corresponds to the vital principle of the dying planet. As above, so below, again; the Laya point is there, and it remains. The Laya point cannot be touched, but it is the matter around it. The Laya point, for instance, is there, where the principles of the Moon will migrate or pass; transfer this from a planet that is dying, it goes and falls into another, just like a woman who has a child and dies. Just in the same way the planet will transfer its principles, but it is not *into* the Laya centre, but on the matter which is around that. The Laya centre is not seen, it is there. It is again my fault to have said *into* instead of *onto* it. It is very difficult.

Mr. B. Keightley: Onto would not express the thing.

Mr. Kingsland: Around.

H.P.B.: Around means that the Laya centre is smaller, and it is not. There's again a difficulty. It is not, as I told you, like a Chinese nest — that one is smaller than the other and another still smaller. It is not that. It is all one.

Mr. Kingsland: It is the metaphysical point in the circle.

H.P.B.: It is simply the degree — the same thing on another state of consciousness, on another plane.

Mr. B. Keightley: Now the eleventh. You say a bit further on, speaking about the Moon and the satellites and so on — you explained this. Question 11, page 165. Can you give us any further explanations as to the meaning of a planet's two or more satellites?

H.P.B.: Well, I am going to answer you that which will make you, not laugh, but think I have avoided the question. Now, really and indeed I cannot answer any better than what is. Prepare to laugh, if you like — because, I suppose, one planet has more magnetic attraction than the others. Just as a medium will attract spooks, which become his satellites, according to the degree of his mediumistic powers, so a planet may, besides its parent when the parent is not dead and faded out, have similar parasites attached to it. They are what I call poor relatives, the genteel hangers-on. I cannot tell you anything else, because it depends on the magnetic attractions. There are those planets that will attract more, and those that do not attract so many. Now the Earth has got only one, because the Earth is not capable of attracting anything. There is too much sin on it, and fibs. Mars is a powerful fellow, and he has more.

Mr. Gardner: Saturn has seven.

H.P.B.: He may have as many as he likes. He would have more if the law permitted, but it doesn't.

Mr. Keightley: Then the other question is practically the same. Question 12. Can you give us any explanation as to why Mars has two satellites, to which it has no right?

H.P.B.: It is the same thing, ditto. I tell you, what can I answer you? Will you give me an explanation why England has, besides India, Burma?[1] She has no right to India any more than to Burma, and yet she has them. Can you give me an explanation? Or why Russia has Poland and Siberia, and she has no right to them?

Mr. B. Keightley: They happened to be handy and she took them.

H.P.B.: Might is right. And so it is in this world. A planet which is stronger will have more satellites and more things.

Mr. Kingsland: Are all these satellites in a similar condition to the Moon? Are they all dead?

H.P.B.: Not all. Some are more alive, some are ready to die. The Moon is dead, because she has passed her principles; the others appear to us moons, but they are simply forming something.

Mr. ——: What are the rings of the planet Saturn?

H.P.B.: It is nothing objective — at least, objective it is; it is nothing solid.

Mr. Gardner: Is it gassy?

H.P.B.: I suppose it is; I could not tell you what I have not learned.

---

[1] **Burma** — the official name of Myanmar, a country in Southeast Asia, until 1989.

Mr. B. Keightley: More optical.

H.P.B.: I don't believe they exist at all. It is all Maya. Mars is a fiery, strong planet which attracts to itself more than the others do. Once we accept the occult statement, it is easy to account for the rest. What is difficult and almost impossible is to make a European trained in physical science see that the occult sciences are far more logical and satisfactory than the former. Well, have you got anything else to ask?

Mr. Old: I should like to have asked, without intruding on time, whether these other satellites attached to the different planets are in the same relationship to these centres — that is to say, when they serve as satellites, as our Moon is to the other?

H.P.B.: I think they are the same, but not that they have any influence. I think they are fed by some planets, but they do not give out the interchange of influences on the Moon.

Mr. Old: They are not fading, the planets?

H.P.B.: No; it is only those who are parents, so long as they are not dislocated and disrupted, that have such influence. But the others, as far as I remember, are fed, so to say, on meteors. That is why I spoke about the power of the parents.

Mr. Old: It would be illogical to say that any one planet had half a dozen parents.

Mr. B. Keightley: Two are quite enough for any respectable planet.

H.P.B.: Quite enough!

Mr. Old: The case is different, then, with regard to the Moon, which is not only our satellite, but our parent.

H.P.B.: Yes, it is.

Mr. Gardner: Is that the only case in which we have them in a dual capacity? Are some of Jupiter's moons?

H.P.B.: Most assuredly. One of them is a parent. Now, it depends on the priority of the planets; it depends on their age. Some of the planets' fathers and mothers died long ago, as with Venus, and faded out entirely, in the case of one of them. It is said it was one of the sacred planets that disappeared, and this was the mother or father of the Moon. I am not sure — either the Moon or Venus; I think it is the Moon. This is a thing that I did not learn, since it doesn't exist. I was very anxious simply to learn about the existent.

Mr. Gardner: How about that other planet between Mercury and the Sun?

H.P.B.: Ask Tyndall or Huxley. Proctor is dead — well, somebody else.

Mr. Gardner: Is the parent dead of Mercury?

H.P.B.: I don't know. I know one thing, that there is a very funny thing in *The Path*[1] which I think you had better read to them, and then we will just talk about it. There is something that is said from the Purana. Where he gets it from I cannot understand. "The Origin of the Planet, Mercury" it is called. It is in this month's *Path*.[2]

Mr. B. Keightley: [Reads the extract referred to.]

---

[1] *The Path* — a Theosophical magazine, published by William Quan Judge in New York from 1886 to 1896.

[2] See "Culled from Aryan Science," *The Path*, vol. 4 (1889–1890), p. 6.

18 APRIL 1889

Mr. B. Keightley: Question 1 (a). In connection with the seven *relative* Laya points, are we to conceive of matter existing *simultaneously* on all the seven planes, or does it pass through the seven Laya centres from one state to another, actually? Or only relatively to our perceptions, or to the perceptions of beings on the other planes?

H.P.B.: During Maha-Pralaya there are no planes of matter, of course, since nothing exists. For the absolute Laya point is infinite. It cannot be. Who put that question?

Mr. Kingsland: I did.

H.P.B.: During Manvantara the seven planes of matter emanate, the one from the other in a regular order and succession, and embraces very naturally untold series of æons, with the exception of Manvantaric deities — a mystery, if you please. The beings on other planes must come down in the natural order of evolution, and to our plane, someday. All beings begin and end at the Laya point. Happy those who merge into it (I wish to goodness I was one of them!), for they will have no rebirth during that Manvantara. They begin on the highest plane and descend in regular sequence from plane to plane, the planes of all being *pari passu* with their descent. And let us add these planes of divine substance and consciousness are but the creations of these very beings. Now do you understand, from the first or highest, to the seventh or lowest state of consciousness? It is the divine being, the macrocosm, which ends in the man form, which is the creation of the corresponding plane of the microcosm. For the whole universe of matter is, as philosophy teaches, but an illusory reflection — as you know. Now, are there any questions to this?

Mr. Kingsland: There is another question relating to the same thing.

Mr. B. Keightley: Yes. Question 1 (b). For instance, take a piece of iron, this is perceived by us on this plane as iron. Is it perceived by a consciousness acting on other planes as something else than iron, or is it absolutely non-perceptible?

H.P.B.: Now, how can it be? Most assuredly, there cannot be the same piece of iron for every plane; otherwise, why should we not perceive as easily beings from every other plane, and they us? I mean the globes of the planetary chains. Or why should the globes of our chain be concealed from us? The usual way of measuring the spiritual development of an Adept among the disciples is to ask what plane of consciousness or perception he has reached; and this perception embraces the physical as well as the spiritual. This is the thing when you want to know what degree an Adept belongs to, how far he has developed; what plane of perception is his. That is a kind of Masonic formula. But how can we see a piece of iron in the same way?

Mr. Kingsland: Not in the same way, but in a different way. What I wanted to elucidate was in reference to Laya centres, which we had before. You stated there are seven relative Laya centres — that is to say, corresponding to the transition from one plane to the other.

H.P.B.: So there are, on every one of the seven planes. Only, of course, the Laya centre is Laya in accordance with the perception of that plane. That is to say that our plane being the grossest, the Laya point which exists for us would perhaps, be there no Laya point at all, and would be something a great deal more gross and perceptible. The Laya point is, of course, more refined on the following plane, and so on.

Mr. Kingsland: Then we may say that on the next plane, for instance, the iron is non-existent.

H.P.B.: Absolutely non-existent in the shape in which we see it here, because their perception is quite a different kind of perception. No comparison can be established.

Mr. Kingsland: But is it not perceived as something else?

H.P.B.: It may be, but I cannot tell you what.

Mr. B. Keightley: It would be translated into the terms of our consciousness.

H.P.B.: Matter is matter, and substance is substance, but it takes such various forms that certainly, that which would appear iron to us, may appear gooseberry jam on the other plane.

Mr. B. Keightley: It must exist on every plane, because we know the smallest atom existed on every one of the seven planes.

H.P.B.: But it exists in an atomic scattered condition. Once that you suppose a thing may fall from one planet to another, passing through the atmosphere of our Earth, it would change chemically all its constituent parts. It would become quite a different thing. It would become a thing of this plane; in fact, we could not see it if it didn't.

Mr. Kingsland: In fact, it exists, as substance but not as matter.

H.P.B.: Perfectly. And not as a definite form, or the definite form that it takes on our plane; it is quite a different story.

Mr. B. Keightley: Question 2. On page 150, it is stated that "each atom has seven planes of being or existence." Are we right in supposing that each corresponds with one of the seven globes of a planetary chain?

H.P.B.: No, sir, most assuredly not. These seven globes are on four planes only, as you know.

Mr. B. Keightley: Question 3. In connection with this, how is it that in the diagram on page 153, the seven globes are represented as existing on only four planes?

Diagram 3. **Human Principles and Planetary Division**

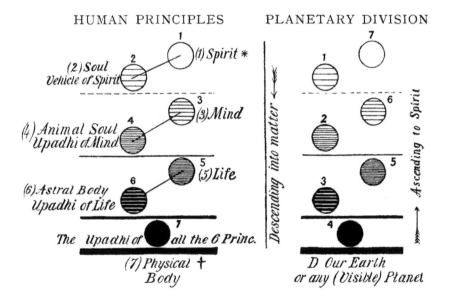

HUMAN PRINCIPLES   PLANETARY DIVISION

(1) Spirit *
(2) Soul Vehicle of Spirit
(3) Mind
(4) Animal Soul Upadhi of Mind
(5) Life
(6) Astral Body Upadhi of Life
The Upadhi of all the 6 Princ.
(7) Physical † *Body*

Descending into matter   *Ascending to Spirit*

D Our Earth or any (Visible) Planet

* As we are proceeding here from Universals to Particulars, instead of using the inductive or Aristotelean method, the numbers are reversed. Spirit is enumerated the first instead of seventh, as is usually done, but, in truth, *ought not to be done.*

† Or as usually named after the manner of *Esoteric Buddhism* and others: 1, Atma ; 2, Buddhi (or Spiritual Soul) ; 3, Manas (Human Soul) ; 4, Kama Rupa (Vehicle of Desires and Passions) ; 5, Linga Sarira ; 6, Prana ; 7, Sthula Sarira.

H.P.B.: There you are, because the triangle, the quaternary or square are the symbols of the microcosm, or man. The globes are seven, but out of seven there are three pairs, or what the Gnostics call Syzygies, the couples, male and female — positive and negative, respectively. Our globe lies solitary on the fourth, or seventh, or first plane — just as you like to give the numbers; combines in itself the material by dual nature. The form of the globe of our planetary chain corresponds exactly to the esoteric diagrams of the principles, as every esotericist here knows — of the human principles, I mean. Atman stands for the triangle, remember, and the physical man for, firstly, the globe; secondly, the quaternary; and, finally, the pentagon, the five-pointed star. You must try to find out the eternal riddle of the Sphinx,[1] without being blinded for it like Oedipus.[2] Do you see what I mean by it, why it is so, why the seven are on the four planes?

Mr. Kingsland: Simply because they correspond to the quaternary in that respect.

H.P.B.: First there is our Earth, then comes the second plane, and there, too, they are couples; then come two again, and then two again — six in all.

Mr. Yeats: Are these the material, astral, sidereal planes of the diagrams?

H.P.B.: Yes; call them what names you like, I know it is. Ours is the lowest plane; then comes the more ethereal, and more ethereal, and still more ethereal, until no human conception can conceive of the three planes. And therefore we leave them alone, because it is perfectly ridiculous with our finite intellects to try to understand and unriddle the infinite. It is quite enough to take what the seers can see.

Mr. Yeats: Are not the seven planets that exist only on four planes, a microcosmic representation of the whole seven?

H.P.B.: They are. Most assuredly, they are. Now, if you take the principles of man in a diagram, you see just the same thing as that;

---

[1] **Sphinx** (*Greek*) — a mythical creature with a human head, a lion body and eagle wings. In Greek mythology, the Sphinx guarded the entrance to the city of Thebes in Greece with a riddle: when travellers failed to solve her riddle, she devoured them.

[2] **Oedipus** (*Greek*) — a tragic hero in Greek mythology, who answered the riddle of the Sphinx and became the king of Thebes by marrying the widowed queen. However, upon learning that he had married his own mother, he blinded himself.

you see the physical body of man; then comes the vehicle of light and life; then comes the Manas and the Kama-rupa — the lower Manas, I mean — then comes the higher Manas, and Buddhi-Atman. I speak for you who know better, not for those who are exoteric, but for all those who have studied esoterically. You know Atman is not a principle in fact.

Mr. Yeats: There was a sense, then, in which the seven planets were represented as existing upon the seven planes.

H.P.B.: They exist on four planes.

Mr. Yeats: Do they correspond to the seven planes?

H.P.B.: Yes, but still it is four and seven.

Mr. Yeats: I was simply trying to get that clear, that they did not exist...

H.P.B.: The globes pretend to matter, to form, and to shape, and there is nothing that exists on the third, remember, or higher planes that can have form or shape: they may have it, but not according to our conceptions. It does not exist in Nature, there are not any such things, as though you would put staircases, or ladders, or rungs. All this is metaphysical, and all this is symbolical; but still, to come and to try to precisely give a form, shape, to that which we cannot understand, is perfect nonsense.

Mr. Yeats: The whole seven correspond to the seven planets, not only four.

H.P.B.: They do.

Mr. Kingsland: I put that question in order to elucidate that point a little more. It is stated that these planets did correspond to the states of matter.

H.P.B.: Seven states of consciousness, yes, and not to the seven states of perception.

Mr. Yeats: You have again confused me. Though they do not exist on the plane, yet they correspond?

H.P.B.: In the first place, we cannot think with our lower four states of consciousness. We can hardly begin perceiving them with the fourth, and then come the others; therefore it is a perfect impossibility. You cannot see with your physical eyes, you cannot see with the state of consciousness which is located in the [...], can you? You cannot, till you come to the upper Manas, to the fifth, so to say; then you can perceive them. But not with the lower Manas, or the Kama-rupa, or any of those principles, because these are purely physical…

Mr. B. Keightley: And pertain entirely and exclusively to the Earth, in fact.

H.P.B.: Certainly.

Mr. B. Keightley: Question 4. "What is the relation of these four planes to the seven states of matter?"

H.P.B.: None, except that each of the four planes has its own seven states of matter. That is all. For instance, it seems to me that all these questions are the same, under various forms. If they are made under the impression that the seven states of universal substance are identical with the planes of the globes in our chain, then I answer, it is not so. I don't know, you see, what your thoughts are. They are correspondential, but not consubstantial; the one belongs to a tiny solar system still denser in the degree of their materiality; the others are universal. It is our system which is still denser.

Mr. B. Keightley: Question 5, page 172, footnote. "Can you give us any idea of the states of consciousness corresponding to the various Pralayas: *viz.* between two globes, between two Rounds, and after seven Rounds?"

H.P.B.: There I am asked to deliver the keys of esoteric philosophy in about five seconds, on two pages, and on a Thursday! Now suppose we first studied thoroughly the nature of the Pralayas on our present plane, and within the limits of our present states of consciousness. How can one understand anything about states of consciousness without the limits of purely physical consciousness, when even the latter is in a state of most chaotic confusion as to itself and its own capacities? Don't you think we are often trying to mimic those frogs who wanted to become bulls, and they "busted up"? I don't want to bust up; I know I can go and speculate upon things that are within the possibility; but how can we? Sometimes they make such questions that positively I open my mouth and say: "Really now, what is that?" I look at them about 4 o'clock, and I say, "What can I answer?" So I leave them to the grace of God. This is very flattering, you know, because it shows you think I know more than I do. I cannot speak about things which it is impossible to speculate upon.

Mr. B. Keightley: [Reads from *The Secret Doctrine.*] "The Monadic hosts may be roughly divided into three classes," etc. Question 6, page 174. "Do the highest class of Monads, which attain the human stage on globe A in the First Round, appear at once in the human stage on that globe in the Second Round, or do they have to pass through any lower forms?"

H.P.B.: I cannot answer anything more than what I said in *The Secret Doctrine.* Pass on to question 7. Then I have something for you.

Mr. B. Keightley: Question 7, page 174. "Does the first class of Monads here mentioned consist of those who attained Adeptship[1] on the Lunar chain, or simply of the intellectually developed races of that chain?"

H.P.B.: How can anyone know whether there are Adepts on the Moon? If there were Adepts, they would call themselves lunatics, that is a fact! I ask you if it is possible? How can we know that? How can I answer you, so as to satisfy you? Now listen well to this, because it is very important. Of all the mysterious globes in our present Manvantara, the Moon is the most mysterious — not in relation to her physical formation, but to her psychic and spiritual functions. Now, do you remember, any one of you who read *Five Years of Theosophy*, that there are some questions by an Englishman,[2] and how poor Mr. Sinnett was snubbed for this moon question? So never touch questions of this kind. There are many mysteries that they don't want to speak about; it is the most mysterious of all. The Moon is our sidereal power of silence and the Venetian Piombi[3] thrown into one. Better never ask anything about the Moon, except that which relates to its half-dead body. Now pass to the eighth, because there is a continuation.

Mr. B. Keightley: Question 8. "What law is it that determines to which of the three classes named, a particular Monad will belong?"

---

[1] **Adeptship** — the role, position, or status of an Adept, one who has attained true knowledge and mastered the Laws of Spirit and Matter, reaching the stages of Initiation and thus becoming a Master of Esoteric Philosophy.

[2] **Frederick W. H. Myers** (1843–1901) — a British poet, philologist and a founder of the Society for Psychical Research. See "Some Inquiries Suggested by Mr. Sinnett's *Esoteric Buddhism*," *Five Years of Theosophy* (London: Reeves and Turner, 1885), pp. 230–235.

[3] **Piombi** — a former prison in the Doge's Palace, the residence of Venetian rulers.

H.P.B.: I suppose Karmic law, of course. What law is it which determines whether a child will be born the eldest son of a lord, and thus grab all the family estates, or as a penniless younger son having to take refuge in a family living, or to try to make money out of Jesus, as they generally do? Karma, of course. Yet very often the younger sons inherit all the brains of the family, whilst the former are but brainless bags of money. Therefore there is no law except Karmic law. What law can it be? It is simply an accident brought on by past incarnation; by merit or demerit, who knows? There are so many thousands of things. We see the most terrible injustice done in this of birth. You see men who ought really to be on thrones, and we see them starving miserably, and we see them kicked. And we see the biggest fools, and they are royalty and dukes and all kinds of things. Look at our emperors. Look at the Russian emperors. Oh, Lord! They were nice fools, all of them.

Mr. Yeats: How far does the collective Karma control the individual beyond his own actions? Can an individual receive results he does not deserve, which are forced upon him by the Karma of the race?

H.P.B.: I suppose I do understand you, but it seems to me that the Karma of everyone and everything affects you just the same. You may be an excellent man and not deserve to have the measles, but if you go near a person who has it, you may have it, too.

Mr. Yeats: How far the Karma of another may affect it is what I wished to know.

H.P.B.: You cannot touch pitch without being black. You cannot come into rapport with a person that can give you some disease without catching it. You will be rewarded for that injustice and the other man may not be punished, because it is not his fault. You see, the Karma is a question of such difficulty; it is such an abstruse thing that if we begin talking about Karma, we must not ask other questions. It is too abstruse, Karma.

Mr. Mead: Then that question with regard to the first Monads that come in?

H.P.B.: You will find it there.

Mr. B. Keightley: There are some questions on that subject. Keep your question clear in your head to the end, and if it is not answered then, you might mention it. Question 9 (a). Will a Monad belonging to one particular class always belong to that class?

H.P.B.: Certainly not. How can it be that? Because, if nature were stationary and never moved, it would be a different thing; but how can it be in this case? Because, there would be neither progress nor Karma nor anything, if it were such a thing as that.

Mr. Mead: I suppose that question means, would a Monad go on evolving in its own class?

Mr. B. Keightley: That, I think, is a fair question — whether a Monad in its evolution would remain together with the other Monads that formed the same class, or is it free to get ahead of the others or drop behind them?

Mr. Kingsland: Only during one cycle.

Mr. B. Keightley: If not, what law determines his rate of evolution, or the length of time he remains in that class?

H.P.B.: Again, Karma. I cannot answer you anything more. His own actions and previous existence; the collective existences of nations and races, of persons that are around — of everything.

Mr. B. Keightley: Question 10, page 175. Can you explain what is meant by the Monad's "skipping two planes and getting direct into the third"?

H.P.B.: The Monad, though meaning strictly one, is in its manifestation always Trinitarian — being one only in Nirvana. When it is in its Laya state every ancient philosophy proves it to be so. Now remember the Monad of Pythagoras having to descend and form the first triangle, after which it subsides again and disappears in darkness and silence. Take, for instance, the Kabbalistic Sephirothal tree; you find that first it forms the triangle. Just the same in the Pythagorean Tetraktys; it produces the triangle and then leaves it to do the further business. So it is in the Kabbalah, just in the same way; there is the first, Kether, Chokmah, and Binah; or the crown, wisdom, and understanding. Wisdom and understanding are on the same horizontal plane. It cannot be otherwise than Trinitarian. How can Monad manifest, unless it is Trinitarian and capable of acting only on the third plane, as the second and the first are too spiritual to be regarded in our perceptions as planes of any activity? Take the human septenary. Atma alone is nothing; it is not only not a breath, but it is simply an idea, nothing, because it is absoluteness; it is the essence of Ain-Soph or Parabrahm; Buddhi is its vehicle, and yet Buddhi, even in conjunction with Atma, is still nothing on this plane. In Sankhya philosophy, Atma is represented by Purusha,[1] who has no legs; he has to mount on the shoulders of Prakriti, which is Buddhi, who has legs but no head, to form a manifested Monad with the potentiality of becoming rational and self-conscious. This is a most beautiful allegory, showing Purusha, who cannot walk; who, having no legs, is obliged to mount on the shoulders of Prakriti, and therefore the two produce a rational being.

Mr. Yeats: Does the allegory refer to the silent one?

H.P.B.: It is Prakriti that gives the legs. Therefore it is said that the Monad skips the first two planes and gets direct into the plane of mentality.

Mr. Kingsland: Skips the two highest planes, that is. I think the question has been put on the supposition that it was kept to the two lower planes.

Mr. B. Keightley: No, it was the meaning of the phrase — why two higher planes are used. That is all in the questions about the Monad.

Mr. Mead: "Further, when globe A of the new chain is ready," etc. [Reads from *The Secret Doctrine,* vol. 1, p. 173.]

H.P.B.: We will come to that further on. It comes here.

Mr. B. Keightley: Question 11, page 176, last paragraph. Can you name the "ten stages" here referred to? And what stage do you call "the first really manward stage"?

H.P.B.: I can. I name the first really manward stage when the Third Race, being at the threshold of the Fourth, the racial stage, as it is called, becomes a potential septenary through the incarnation in it of the Manas, or sense of wisdom. Hence with the three sub-elemental, or the sub-mineral kingdoms, we have certainly ten, all the ten that are mentioned there. Man is a septenary; arrived at the end of the Third Race, entering upon the Fourth, he is potentially septenary. The fifth yet is not quite developed in us; it will be because we are only on the Fifth Race, and with every race there is one higher and higher that develops. But still it is potentially a septenary, and this, with the others, we say are ten.

Mr. Yeats: The fifth, you say. Is that counting from above or below? You say it is not yet fully developed.

---

[1] **Purusha** (*Sanskrit,* "man") — heavenly man; the Spiritual Self.

H.P.B.: It is the Manas.

Mr. B. Keightley: Page 181: "It now becomes plain that there exists in nature," etc. [Reads from *The Secret Doctrine.*] Question 12. Does the fully developed man embody the perfection of each of the three schemes of evolution? Please enlarge on this idea.

H.P.B.: Certainly, for a perfect man has to be: 1, perfect in physical form, as regards the organism and health; 2, perfect intellectually; and 3, perfect spiritually. At any rate, he must have all the schemes of evolution sufficiently represented to produce perfect equilibrium. An absolutely healthy man, full of vitality, but deficient in intellectual powers, is an animal, not a man. A perfectly spiritual man with a sick limb, or weak body, is no man, but a spirit imprisoned, looking out of the window. A perfectly healthy, intellectual, well-developed man, without corresponding spiritual consciousness, is — his intellect notwithstanding — an empty shell, and nothing more. If all three qualities are present, so as to produce equilibrium, the man himself will be a perfect man, on his particular plane, I mean — meaning by the latter not the universal planes, but his own personal or individual plane of the septenary scale of perfection. Do I explain it to you sufficiently well, this?

Mr. Kingsland: Yes.

Mr. B. Keightley: For each man, so to speak, as an individual, will have seven planes of activity, or seven degrees. Well, he may be perfect on one plane. He is a perfect man on that plane, but if, in his development, he has not reached one of the higher planes, he is not on that plane at the time you are considering.

Mr. Mead: I understand this about the harmony.

Mr. B. Keightley: You can take that perfect equilibrium on the plane in which a man happens to be, for the time being.

H.P.B.: Let me read to you, again, this thing. A perfect man is not. He can be a perfect man on the first and the second and the third plane; it is a degree of perfectibility. Now, what I say is, that to make a perfect man, he is to be: 1, perfect in physical form, as regards his organism and health; 2, perfect intellectually; 3, perfect spiritually. All these must be equilibrized. At any rate, he must have all these three schemes of evolution sufficiently represented to produce perfect equilibrium. An absolutely healthy man, full of vitality, but deficient in intellectual powers, is an animal, as I say, not a man. A perfectly spiritual man with a sick limb and a weak body is not a man, but a spirit imprisoned, looking out of the window — an unfortunate spirit. A perfectly healthy and intellectual, well-developed man, without the corresponding spiritual consciousness, is — his intellect notwithstanding — an empty shell and nothing more. If one of these things, there is no equilibrium, if all these three qualities are present so as to produce equilibrium, the man himself will be a perfect man on his particular plane — I mean. Meaning by the latter, not the universal planes, but his own personal or individual plane of the septenary scale of perfection. Now that is very easily understood.

Mr. Mead: I understood it perfectly up to the last.

H.P.B.: Why, look here — we have seven planes of perfection, everyone individually; every man has seven states of consciousness. A man may be, if he have all these three equilibrized in him, a perfect man in his own plane. If he is still more so, he will be a perfect man on the second, and then on the third and fourth, and so on.

Mr. Mead: I understand.

Mr. Yeats: These three things — intellectual, physical, and spiritual — of course correspond to three of the four planes quaternary, do they not? Which, then, will the fourth be?

Mr. B. Keightley: Those three are taken as representing the body, soul, and spirit.

H.P.B.: You mix up the planes in the most terrible way. We spoke about the four planes of the globes — of the seven globes.

Mr. Yeats: This is my difficulty. Of course, I see perfectly plainly that a man must have a triple harmony; I am not confusing it in that way. I know the triple harmony applies to each separately. That triple harmony itself, does it not correspond to the three planes of the four. In Blake's[1] system it does.

Mr. B. Keightley: How can it? Because the spiritual is the highest, the intellectual is the Manasic, and the physical is the lower.

Mr. Yeats: But Blake has it in his.

H.P.B.: I don't know anything about Blake. I never read a single word about him. I am sorry, you know, that we disagree with him.

---

[1] **William Blake** (1757–1827) — an English poet and painter.

Mr. Yeats: He considers it is the fourth plane which is higher.

H.P.B.: I speak about the Eastern system.

Mr. B. Keightley: Question 13, page 182. Do the "Sishta," the Seed-Humanity, remain on a globe during its Pralaya, while the rest of humanity has passed on to the next globe?

H.P.B.: The esoteric books say they do, and esoteric philosophy corroborates it. Otherwise, the Monads — or egos rather — would have to recommence again, in the same Round, every time they reached a new globe, the same process of evolution through the lower kingdoms as they did only on the First Round. Let us not misunderstand the thing. I mean by egos only those first class of Monads which reached the human stage of globe A and become Lunar Pitris on the fourth, and those later arrivals who reached the human stage before the middle of the Fourth Round; all the egos of the Third and Fourth Races, I mean, and not any others. Because after the Fourth Race — after the middle of the Fourth Race, there stops everything; there are no more Monads coming for this Manvantara. These are the younger sons we have just been speaking about. You said that Mr. Sinnett was interested in the Sishta. You came out very cunningly, you remember, with that "Noah's ark theory," as you call it.

Mr. B. Keightley: Question 14. Is the suggestion correct that, even during the depths of Pralaya, life remains *active* around the North Pole — the Land of the Gods?

H.P.B.: If you mean the Planetary Pralaya, then I say, "yes," esoteric science teaches us so; but not in every Pralaya. I mean that while one globe is in obscuration it remains, but when there is the whole chain certainly it does not; because they are all dissipated then.

Mr. Yeats: Does esoteric philosophy imply that, as the Greeks believed, Mount Meru[1] is inhabited at this moment?

---

[1] **Mount Meru** (*Sanskrit*, "navel") — the name of a mountain in the centre (or "navel") of the Earth, where *Svarga*, the Olympus of Hinduism, is placed; another name for Shambhala — the Imperishable Sacred Land, the first and ever-present continent of the planet Earth. Mount Meru contains the cities of the greatest Gods and the abodes of various Devas. Geographically accepted, it is an unknown mountain north of the Himalayas. In tradition, Meru was the Land of Bliss of the earliest Vedic times. It is also referred to as *Hemadri* ("the golden mountain"), *Ratnasanu* ("jewel peak"), *Karnikachala* ("lotus-mountain"), *Amaradri* and *Deva-parvata* ("the mountain of the gods"). The Occult teachings ▸

H.P.B.: We see in the esoteric philosophy there is a Meru. What the Indians mean by the Meru is one thing, and what the Greeks mean is another. They call it the thigh, and they said that Bacchus was born in India, because he was born out of the thigh of his Father Jupiter;[2] he is the Motherless, and that is Miros, which means the thigh in Greek; therefore, being born on Mount Meru, he was an Indian.

Mr. Yeats: I know nothing of the Indian at all, so I think I must be right. They suppose a region existed in the North Pole inhabited by a blameless people.

H.P.B.: Blameless people! Why, it is the gods. You read it in *The Secret Doctrine*, and you will find it all. You read it in the second volume. In the second volume I have got all that — the Eternal Land, the one infinite that never goes down.

Mr. Yeats: Is it meant to be actually, physically located in the North Pole?

H.P.B.: We won't talk about it; it will take us into too high metaphysics.

Mr. B. Keightley: Question 15. Can you tell us anything more about the Sishta?

H.P.B.: The Sishtas are the highest Adepts which happen to be on a globe when Pralaya reaches it. They sacrifice themselves for universal human good and cosmic purposes, too esoteric to discuss now. Let it be known only that they are the living and now objective Nirmanakayas — that is to say, that when the hour of the Pralaya strikes, some of the highest Adepts, whether living objectively or subjectively, become the voluntary custodians of the sleeping planet. When it is morning dawn then these Terrene Pitris play the same parts as the Lunar Pitris did in the Fourth Round (that is to say, when there is the

---

place it in the very centre of the North Pole, pointing it out as the site of the first continent on our Earth, after the solidification of the globe. However, it should be borne in mind that there have been frequent changes of the poles over the entire history of the Earth. Therefore, the original North Pole is where Shambhala is located nowadays.

[2] **Jupiter** (*Latin*) — from the same root as the Greek Zeus, the greatest god of the ancient Greeks and Romans, adopted also by other nations. His names are among others: Jupiter-Aërios; Jupiter-Ammon of Egypt; Jupiter Bel-Moloch, the Chaldean; Jupiter-Mundus, Deus Mundus, "God of the World"; Jupiter-Fulgur, "the Fulgurant," etc.

dawn for the globe). They surrender or give their three lower principles as a ready, prepared vehicle for the incoming egos of the new
round; then only are their Monads reached. They have done their duty
and won a long, long rest. They will remain in Nirvanic bliss until the
Manvantara of the successor in this planetary chain, until the dawn
strikes for the successor in this chain. The successor will be the two
globes on our plane above which will unite and form the androgynous
earth of the new chain. For then the two uppermost globes will have
descended to the plane which is now below them. Another planet
shooting its principles into the Laya of the empty place will give birth
to a globe which will replace one of these two, and still another to
replace the second. There is certainly a mystery, and *raison d'être* of
which mystery it is too early for us to know anything. Nor will the
principles of the Earth be lost. As the egos, I mean, are incarnated
on Earth, so are the principles of egos or departed globes incarnated
in sidereal space. As above so below. As with the Moon, so with the
Earth; and as with Father, so with Son. These are immutable lines of
nature. Now, this is a thing I tell you perfectly new to you.

Mr. Kingsland: That is the most interesting thing we have had for
a long while.

H.P.B.: I had very many interesting things for you.

Mr. Sinnett: I should like afterwards to see what passed before I
arrived.

H.P.B.: I will read it again. It is very difficult to tell much more
about it, because it is such a vast, but such a mysterious thing, that.

Mr. Sinnett: The point there is about the reincarnation of the Earth
principle.

H.P.B.: Well, listen again. The Sishtas are the highest Adepts which
happen to be on a globe when Pralaya reaches it. Now, those who will
be the highest are the voluntary — how shall I say — self-immolators
or self-sacrificers. Do you remember what I say in *The Secret Doctrine*?
They sacrifice themselves for human good, and cosmic purposes, too
esoteric to discuss now. Let it be known only that they are the living
and now objective Nirmanakayas. You know what that means? Nirmanakayas means, for instance, you become a great Adept. You don't
want to live any more, but you are not selfish enough to go into Nirvana (because it is selfish: you will benefit no one by it but yourselves,

and this selfishness is to be avoided); therefore, instead of going into Devachan (you cannot go into Devachan, because it is yet an illusion for an Adept; for mortals as we are, but not for a high Adept), therefore he leaves his body, and lives in all his six principles. Wherever he lives, of course, it is subjectively and in space; but he lives and helps humanity, and sometimes he will inspire people, or communicate with them, and so on. I know several cases like that. Very rarely of course, but it is because they do not generally go for individuals; but they will protect a nation, or protect a community, or something like that, and help as much as Karma permits them. That is to say that when the hour of the Pralaya strikes, some of the highest Adepts, whether living objectively or subjectively, as Nirmanakayas become the voluntary custodians of the sleeping planet, etc. [Reads as before.] The Moon gives its principles; so will every planet do it. It goes with a great harmonious succession. There is not a single gap in Nature.

Mr. B. Keightley: From that it would follow, I think, that there are no Sishta until the Fourth Round. Until after the Fourth Round, really.

H.P.B.: Active Sishta, those that have to act, certainly, because man begins only on the Fourth Round. There are in the Third Round all kinds of astral shapes and things that we cannot speak about, or know anything about. The regular men, as we know them, begin on this round only. I don't suppose there were any Adepts there before. I don't know. An Adept has a definite meaning for us — it is on this plane, and that which is within our conception. How can we know they are Adepts there?

Mr. B. Keightley: It again brings out into prominence the great importance which the Fourth Round plays.

H.P.B.: The Fourth Round is the adjustor; it adjusts all the things and brings matter and spirit into equilibrium. It is that which in the middle of the Fourth Round makes everything settled. And already, instead of spirit falling into matter, it is matter which begins to evolve into spirit.

Mr. B. Keightley: Question 16, page 184. What are we to understand by the phrase, "astral human forms (or the highest elementals)" in the following: Monads of the anthropoids, "the highest mammals after man ... will be liberated and pass into the astral human forms (or the highest elementals) of the Sixth and Seventh Races, and then into the lowest human forms in the Fifth Round."

H.P.B.: By the time the Sixth Race comes on the scene, all the animal egos now inhabiting the highest anthropoid forms will have been liberated and will exist. Some exist now in sidereal spaces in astral human forms, as I say. This is what I call here the highest elementals — they have not been human yet. These will incarnate in the lowest men of the Sixth Race. The young men of the Darwinians truly have dreamed dreams, and their old men seen visions, for their founder must have caught from the astral a glimpse of that which will be; and forthwith dragging it down to his own material plane, he made of it that which has been in his own imagination. This is the most curious thing, and I don't think it is Darwin; I think it is Haeckel who took the astral forms. The Master says himself there were gigantic astral forms in the Third Round. They were like gigantic apes. But they were not speaking of the dumb animals — they were men, ape-like, from which individuals evolved the apes. Millions and millions of years after, when there came the reversion to the primal type again, they produced the monsters for which they fell.

Mr. B. Keightley: What happens to the anthropoids is, when they die, they remain as semi-human elementals until the Sixth Race begins to come.

H.P.B.: They are not yet human, because they were not human.

Mr. B. Keightley: The elementals that will be human.

H.P.B.: Just as the egos of men are their past elementals.

Mr. Kingsland: But that is not in the Sixth Race, it is in the Sixth Round.

H.P.B.: There will be a few already in the Sixth Race. Like the chimpanzees, they do not come from space, but these are already imprisoned.

Mr. Kingsland: You don't call them human Monads, yet.

H.P.B.: They are semi-human, because they are due to that Fourth Race. Do you suppose, really, that they are men? It is all very fine to listen to our missionaries, who say all the savages are our brothers. They are not. They have the potentiality; the mineral has the potentiality. But the savages are not — especially some of those who died out — they are not the same as we are.

Mr. Kingsland: Then they will come in at the Sixth Race?

H.P.B.: Yes. What I say is, that not a single Monad will come any more from space, so to say, unless it is here: that all that which had the time to settle in some of the higher shapes, till the middle of the Fourth Race, these will remain on this Earth till the end of the Manvantara, but certainly not afterwards. If you go and believe this absurd thing, that for every child that is born, there is a new soul breathed and created — that I cannot understand at all.

Mr. Kingsland: Then as a matter of fact, the Monads of some of the anthropoids are sufficiently near the human point to come within the Sixth Race.

Mr. B. Keightley: The exception is expressly made here, and insisted upon. I speak of the class of Monads that one expresses as emphasized.

Mr. Yeats: The population of the world is unchanging.

H.P.B.: The Monads are unchanging in the middle of the Fourth Race.

Mr. B. Keightley: You may have any number of Monads in Devachan, and so on.

H.P.B.: It is unchanging. Otherwise, there would be no Karmic possibility of adjustment.

Mr. Yeats: Take any time in the history of the world, and contrast it with any other period of 3,000 years. There must, of course, be variations; but still, go back — according to that theory, the population of the world was then the same as it is now.

H.P.B.: You don't know anything at all about population. What it was, and what I have learned, is that the population was almost twice as great as the one we have now — nearly twice as great. There was not a corner on the globe that was not populated, and that is why sometimes it must come, that some of you must be drowned. Look at China; it is the most providential occurrences, those tidal waves.

Mr. B. Keightley: And everywhere in the Atlantean[1] times was twice as populated as China is now.

---

[1] **Atlantis** (*Greek*) — the continent that was submerged in the Atlantic and the Pacific Oceans according to the secret teachings and Plato. The Atlanteans were the ancestors of the Pharaohs and the forefathers of the Egyptians. Plato heard of this highly civilized people, the last remnant of which was submerged 9,000 years before his day, from Solon, who had it from the High Priests of Egypt. ›

H.P.B.: Not twice; a great deal more than it is now. I remember one thing: there was a time when Africa was all inhabited (in times after that, when it had emerged from the ocean). And now, why, how many parts of Africa are inhabited? I suppose not a twentieth part. You cannot call those savages inhabitants, those that Stanley[1] has been meeting with.

Mr. B. Keightley: A very sparse population ever, at that. But Yeats' point is a curious one.

H.P.B.: They say the continents were greater. Look at the continent that went from India to Australia. It was one continent unbroken, and now it is all seas and seas.

Mr. B. Keightley: What I want to get at is, look at the population of the Earth now: The population of the Earth then was very much greater. It follows that a large number of the Monads which were then on Earth at the Atlantean period, incarnated, are still in Devachan.

Mr. Sinnett: I don't think it necessarily follows. Assume for the moment that a Devachanic period was 200 years, instead of 2,000. The change from a condition of things in which there were simply 200 years spent, to a condition in which you have 2,000 spent, would reduce the population to a tenth of what it was, without giving any Monad a period of longer than 2,000 years.

Mr. Kingsland: That is to say, the general period then was shorter than the general period is now.

Mr. Yeats: That explains that so many of the greatest nations of the world have been very small in number.

H.P.B.: We had last time a very interesting thing about the planets, and I think Dr. Berridge[2] was very much interested. It was all about planets and stars and astronomy in their astronomical bearing.

Mr. Sinnett: Taking the chimpanzees, the chimpanzee monad would be a more advanced creature than some of the human savages. For he belongs to the Fourth Race, and the savages belong to others.

The Atlanteans (our Fourth Root Race) made their appearance in Egypt. It was in Syria and in Phrygia, as well as Egypt, that they established the worship of the Sun.

[1] **Henry Morton Stanley** (1841–1904) — a Welsh explorer and journalist, known for his expeditions to Africa.

[2] **Edmund William Berridge** (1843–1923) — a medical doctor and homoeopathist.

H.P.B.: If you took the savage and brought him up as a chimpanzee, he would develop intellect just as much as a chimpanzee. It is because they remain there, entirely shut out from all civilization or anything to see, that they are ignorant. And the chimpanzee, when we take him, he sees the world, he lives in cultured localities, and so on, and becomes very intelligent. So would the poor savage be. Mind you, the savages will be more intelligent in the Sixth Race than these are now. I don't think we shall have one soon remaining from the old race; they are all dying out. I mean the direct ones, such as the flat-headed Australians were.

Mr. Sinnett: Some of the Chinese are a very early race.

H.P.B.: Some, but they are in the mountains. They are not really Chinese; they are extraordinary creatures.

Mr. Yeats: There was that curious tribe in Southern India. In *Isis Unveiled* you have something about them.

H.P.B.: I say that the Todas[3] were the most mysterious race in all India. And I say what I said in *Isis Unveiled*, because there were three men who assured me of the same. I knew that they were that, and they assured me of it. They had lived years with them. They are very dirty, if you like, but they look like Grecian gods. It is about 70 years ago that they were discovered, and in these 70 years they found six or seven hundred of them. They are now the same number. They never vary. Notwithstanding the panthers and the tigers and the leopards, they never lose a single buffalo. The buffalos of others will be stolen every night, especially by the leopards, but never one of their cattle. They have not got arms, they have not got even a knife. They sit there with a little thing like a kind of wand in their hands. I have watched them for years, when I was there with Mrs. Morgan.[4] They are the most extraordinary people you ever saw, and there is not a bit of the Indian

---

[3] **Todas** — a mysterious people of India found in the unexplored fastnesses of Nilgiri (Blue) Hills in India, whose origin, language and religion are to this day unknown. They are entirely distinct, ethnically, philologically, and in every other way, from the *Badagas* and the *Mulakurumbas*, two other races found on the same hills. See H. P. Blavatsky, *The People of the Blue Mountains* (Wheaton, IL: Theosophical Press, 1930).

[4] **Ellen Henrietta Morgan** (1828–1899) — a founder with her husband, Major-General Henry Rhodes Morgan, of the branch of the Theosophical Society in Ootacamund, India.

in them. You see the round Dravidian[1] race, and the flat-nosed, and all kinds of types; this type is the most pure type that you can find. They are tall; they have got most regular features, most handsome; and their women are ugly. Did you see them, Mr. Sinnett? Now, the missionaries did everything in creation to try and convert one. They never converted a single one.

Mr. B. Keightley: Don't you say that their wives are taken from the Dravidian tribes?

H.P.B.: No one knows what it is. Sometimes there are women that come there that are not of that tribe. A missionary went there, and he prided himself that he was the first one to have learnt the language of the Todas. He remained with them 18 or 20 years. When he came out he began talking with a Toda and he said, "Where have you learnt [...]? Isn't it the [...] language?" Now, they don't work, they don't sow, they do nothing whatever, except have buffalos, live on milk and cheese, and so on. It is the Badagas[2] who are their voluntary tributaries; they bring them everything, corn and the first fruits of the Earth, etc. They do everything for them. They serve them just as priests would serve the gods, if the gods came on Earth. They are afraid of them, those Mulakurumbas;[3] and they are the vilest race of dwarfs that you can meet with. They are the embodiment of fiendish cunning. Ask Mrs. Morgan and General Morgan, who lived for years there. It is something awful, their black magic. They will do the most atrocious things. Mrs. Morgan lost about 23 men in one month, the best of her labourers and workmen. One would come and point out a man, yet never approach him; and in a few days he would be a dead man. There was a commissioner who never believed in them. The Mulakurumbas are fearfully afraid of the Todas; when they see them they will run away; they are just like a frog under the look of certain serpents; it is something terrible. Now Mrs. Bachelor,[4] whom we went with, speaks all these languages beautifully; and we went with Mrs. Morgan, and we passed days there. I have watched them, and it is something extraordinary. They don't pay any attention to you. With the long hair they have, they look like Roman senators in togas. For

---

[1] **Dravidians** — a group of tribes inhabiting Southern India; the aborigines.
[2] **Badagas** — the largest tribe in the Nilgiri Hills.
[3] **Mulakurumbas** — a dwarf tribe in the Nilgiri Hills.
[4] **Rhoda Bachelor** — the daughter of the Morgans.

a painter, it is the most beautiful thing in the world. Such grace and dignity — well, they look like gods.

A Lady: Are they great magicians?

H.P.B.: They say they are good men, and that the Mulakurumbas are mortally afraid of them.

The Lady: They have superior magic then?

H.P.B.: They have the most extraordinary power. There was 30 years ago a terrible lawsuit there. There were the Mulakurumbas who had done such awful things that the Badagas went and made a conspiracy to burn them, and they roasted them in their village. And it was said that they could not burn their houses unless there was a Toda present. The legend goes that they brought a Toda with them, though they swore always that they never did that, because I don't think in 70 years there was one Toda who was ever imprisoned, except on the testimony of one of these women. I have read all the things General Morgan gave me. This Toda disappeared, and nobody knew where he was gone to, and that was the only Toda who was in prison. You may put millions of money, coins and everything in their way — they never were known to take a thing. You never saw such honesty as they have.

Mr. B. Keightley: Are they intellectually intelligent?

H.P.B.: General Morgan said to me: "They are very intellectual." Claude Vincent says they are amazingly intellectual, that they will talk on everything; but their dignity and manner and way is something extraordinary.

Mr. B. Keightley: I think you hinted somewhere that they are really of Greek descent?

H.P.B.: No, they are of Lanka[5] descent, not Greek. They have got their own things. I have written all these legends that they gave me

---

[5] **Lanka** (*Sanskrit*) — the ancient name of the Sri Lanka island formerly called Ceylon. It is also the name of a mountain in the South East of Sri Lanka, where, as tradition says, was a town peopled with demons named Lankapuri. It is described in the epic of the *Ramayana* as being of gigantic extent and magnificence, "with seven broad moats and seven stupendous walls of stone and metal." Its foundation is attributed to Visva-Karma, who built it for Kuvera, the king of the demons, from whom it was taken by Ravana, the ravisher of Sita. The *Bhagavat Purana* shows Lanka as primarily the summit of Mount Meru, which was broken off by Vayu, god of the wind, and hurled into the ocean.

themselves, and what I heard of all these I have written in Russian.[1] They say by the calculation of the Moon it comes to something like 22,000 years that they came on the hills, the blue hills of the gods, and that their forefathers were in the service of Rama.[2] This is their story, and that they come from Lanka; but it was not what it is now. It was enormous. It was a part of the continent of the Atlanteans when it sunk. But they are the most mysterious race. I wish you had an opportunity to see them, what handsome men, all with long, beautiful wavy hair, even their old men.

Mr. Sinnett: Do they speak other languages besides their own?

H.P.B.: They speak [...]. Nobody in the world would know their rites, that they have — some of the rites, that they perform in their crypts, that they do in every one of their little houses, which are just like beehives, with a little door where they must come out bending. They have their buffaloes there, and among the buffaloes there is a leader with the silver bells, and one of them has golden bells, and he is a superb animal; but tell me how it is that never a tiger or leopard touches them? This is a thing Webster told me. His father was one of the first to go there 70 years ago, when it was discovered. A man who was in trouble a few years ago in Madras[3] — he was on the Council of the Governor together with Webster there, and his father was one of the first who went there, so he has enormous narratives of them. He was born there, and he has been telling me many things. And he says never was there a case known that one of their cattle was carried away. But these Badagas number about 10,000; the Mulakurumba are many thousands; but the Todas never vary between 600 and 700.

Mr. Sinnett: Do they come under the operation of the census?

---

[1] See H. P. Blavatsky, *From the Caves and Jungles of Hindostan* (Wheaton, IL: Theosophical Publishing House, 1975). This edition by Boris de Zirkoff is the only full translation of the book. All other editions contain the incomplete translation by Vera Johnston, Blavatsky's niece, originally published in 1892.

[2] **Rama** (*Sanskrit*) — the seventh *Avatar* or incarnation of Vishnu; the eldest son of King Dasaratha, of the Solar Race. His full name is Rama-Chandra, and he is the hero of the *Ramayana*. He married Sita, who was the female *Avatar* of Lakshmi, Vishnu's wife, and was carried away by Ravana, the Demon-King of Lanka, which act led to the famous war.

[3] **Madras** — the former name of Chennai, the capital city of the Tamil Nadu state of India.

H.P.B.: They are nomadic people. But how can you call them nomadic, when they go from one place to another and they have their own chief priests — those that are set apart, and who never marry, and who have got some ceremonies for the burials and the cremation, such customs as nobody knows of, entirely *sui generis* — and they say their forefathers served Rama, and went to Lanka, and after that were rewarded for services rendered to Rama. When [...] was killed, they sent them there to take possession of the blue hills of the gods. And they say even the most curious thing, that the Government tried to coax from them — and they would not give — a kind of stone. Morgan tells me he saw it several times in his youth, and it was all with the most extraordinary characters. Nobody had the key to it. And this was the thing given to them by Rama and others.

Mr. B. Keightley: Will they go on living and living there until something happens?

H.P.B.: I know this man was the only one. When they roasted about 40 men, they said they had to have the Toda to preside over the operation, or else they could do nothing. They hung a good many of those Badagas; but that single Toda that was there disappeared. Speak [...] of the curious nations, I can assure you, that there are nations that are very little known in India. Those who served them are the Badagas, and the others are the Mulakurumba. Mrs. Morgan knows all about them, and they like her very much, and they treat her to magnificent milk and buffalo cream, and so on. Very rarely they eat meat; they don't do anything; they are kept and served by the Badagas, who work for them perfectly voluntarily.

Mr. Kingsland: Do they practise some kind of yoga?

H.P.B.: No, they don't, not apparently. I never heard of one. I know they have got their men who know a good deal — I suppose they are priests. I conversed with some of them, but only through an interpreter. I don't know their language. Two of them always looked at me with a kind of grin and with a good-natured smile, and I returned the compliment. And when I went away they gave me a kind of a petrified fig, and he said, "Keep this because it is a good thing if you ever have fever," and so on. I lost it.

25 APRIL 1889

Mr. B. Keightley: Question 1. Why should rotation cease on a dead planet?

H.P.B.: Because the life of a body as a whole is nothing but motion, a reflection of that one life which is called in *The Secret Doctrine* absolute motion. When a man dies his body as a whole ceases to move, although the individual activity of its cells, and ultimately of its molecules, increases enormously. This is proved by the rapid and violent changes that take place in a decomposing corpse. In the same way when a planet dies, its rotatory motion about its own axis ceases, though its activity in its constituent particles is increased rather than diminished. Now, if I am asked if the Moon moves — it is in relation to the Moon that this is asked — if I am asked why the Moon moves in an orbit round the earth, I reply that this is caused by the vampirizing action of the Moon upon the earth — not as science teaches, owing to an attraction exerted by the earth upon the Moon, but rather the reverse: the Moon is so saturated with the magneto, vital emanation of the earth that she is carried along by it like an over-full sponge in a current of water. It is not the water that attracts the sponge in the case, but the sponge is carried along by the stream in its own movement. Does this explain satisfactorily, or did you want to know something very occult?

Mr. Kingsland: No, I only wanted to know why the mass of the Moon should cease to rotate as a mass of matter when the principles had left it — what was the relation between the principles having left it and the mass of the matter of the Moon ceasing to move.

H.P.B.: It did not cease to move; it moves.

Mr. Kingsland: But, as a whole, on its own axis.

H.P.B.: Because it cannot move, because the spirit is fled, because the principles are gone; so how can it move?

Mr. B. Keightley: I think you are answered by the analogy.

Mr. Kingsland: It is only removing the difficulty one step further.

Mr. B. Keightley: When a man is dead, when his principles have left him, the body as a whole does not move.

Mr. Kingsland: That is to say, that a man is walking consciously.

H.P.B.: It is not consciously that they move. They don't know what they are about. Take an idiot, a complete idiot: he will be moving and running and grinning and jumping, but he will not know what he is about.

Mr. Kingsland: Then it is purely internal force.

H.P.B.: It is simply vital impulse.

Mr. B. Keightley: The scientific idea of the thing is that it is a purely mechanical movement, because the large mass of matter having once been set spinning, there is no friction and nothing to stop it.

H.P.B.: Don't speak to me about science, because science and I are on cool terms.

Mr. Kingsland: The astronomical idea is that there is friction.

Mr. B. Keightley: Well, it is so slow that no calculation has found any trace of it.

Mr. Kingsland: They have found traces of it.

Mr. B. Keightley: It is supposed to take 300,000,000 of years to make the difference of 1/2 hour.

Mr. Mead: Are you right in saying the Moon does not move at all? Doesn't it revolve once?

Mr. B. Keightley: Not on its own axis; I don't think there is any rotation of the Moon about its own axis.

H.P.B.: It rotates (revolves) because it vampirizes and is carried away.

Mr. B. Keightley: Swept along, so to speak, in the current.

H.P.B.: It vampirizes — not by conscious action, but there is a kind of dead matter, which by its own inherent attribute or quality attracts.

Mr. B. Keightley: You cannot say a sponge absorbs water consciously, but it absorbs.

H.P.B.: Yes, it is carried up by the current.

Mr. Mead: In another way that is rather analogous, because it does rotate for some time — for instance, near the rocks.

H.P.B.: There are no rocks in space.

Mr. Kingsland: That gives us rather a different idea as to the planetary motion — the planets revolving by means of their own inherent force. If anything revolves in that way it must have something to revolve against, so to speak.

H.P.B.: One is a satellite, and the other an independent entity.

Mr. Kingsland: I mean to say it must be able to pull itself round by something, unless it is set going at the beginning, and goes on until it gradually stops by means of friction or some force acting upon it from outside. A man cannot lift himself by his own waistbelt, and you can hardly conceive of a planet revolving, and continuing to revolve, by means of its own axis.

Mr. B. Keightley: Has it ever occurred to you that the Laya centre is really, if you come to follow it out, the idea of rotatory motion, the centre of a vortex.

H.P.B.: It is.

Mr. Kingsland: This Laya centre does not correspond to the centre of the planet.

Mr. B. Keightley: There is a Laya centre. It is not in three-dimensional space, of course, but it must be the centre of the planet.

H.P.B.: The Laya centre is the Atman, so to say, the spirit of the Atman.

Mr. Kingsland: It is not a mathematical centre of a circle.

Mr. Old: There must be such a mathematical centre, I think, must there not?

Mr. B. Keightley: It must be the centre of rotation of the earth. That is to say, if you locate it anywhere, then of course the Laya centre is not a point in our three dimensional space.

H.P.B.: It is out of space and time, the real Laya centre.

Mr. Ingram: Each atom of the whole world has it own Laya centre?

H.P.B.: It has.

Mr. B. Keightley: Each body as a whole is formed of such particles.

Mr. Kingsland: Do the globes revolve in virtue of the circulation of their principles?

H.P.B.: I believe so; I could not tell you with certainty.

Mr. Kingsland: Take the analogy of a globe of some kind of substance — metal, or anything you like, immersed in water; that globe could not revolve in the water if it were only exercising an internal force. But if it emitted something that acted against the water, then it could cause it to revolve.

Mr. B. Keightley: All the planets are exercising attractive and repulsive forces upon each other.

Mr. Mead: In the present state of affairs, it would be impossible to introduce any internal power to make it revolve. It would be outside all experience. Take the case of a sphere revolving in water. You could not introduce an internal rotary motion into such a sphere.

Mr. Kingsland: The sphere as a whole could rotate if you had some gas which emanated from it. That is the conception I want to get at.

Mr. Old: We have such cases in mechanics where a body revolves for a long time after the cause of its revolution has ceased, as for instance the flywheel of a large piece of machinery. Or take the ordinary peg-top of our youth. After the first lash, after it is delivered from its cause of motion, it goes on manifesting that cause for a long time after the immediate cause has ceased. It seems to have a mediate cause in itself, a potency to retain the same motion.

Mr. Kingsland: That does not correspond to the planets; they are continually revolving in virtue of an inherent force. When the Pralaya comes, the planet will continue to revolve for some considerable time after its principles had left it.

H.P.B.: When the real Pralaya comes, the planets won't exist at all, because they will all disintegrate and fly asunder.

Mr. Old: And in the case of the Moon, which is considered as a satellite to us, it has a Pralaya, you know, its individual planetary Pralaya. And it has ceased to have any axial motion. The Moon has ceased to have such a motion on account of those principles having discharged themselves.

Mr. Kingsland: What is it — what are those principles, and what is the action that causes a life planet to revolve?

H.P.B.: I suppose the light, but there is a great difference between planets and the moon; the Moon is a dead planet.

Mr. Kingsland: And that is why it has ceased to revolve.

H.P.B.: It has ceased to revolve, and therefore it is carried on by induced motion, so to say, from that emanation from the Earth.

Mr. B. Keightley: It is swept along in a current of the Earth, in fact.

H.P.B.: Yes, where the Earth goes it will go. That is what I understood. As far as I remember what I have learnt, it is so.

Mr. Old: There is the ordinary circulation of the interplanetary plenum. Is that taken into consideration by you, Mr. Kingsland, in your thoughts?

Mr. Kingsland: That is what I want to get at and elucidate.

H.P.B.: Do you mean that there is nothing but stillness in space? Why there is a tremendous hurricane of all kinds of rotary motions going on, even outside of any visible planets, or existing planets, because all these currents of air are always in motion; there is the eternal breath which never ceases.

Mr. B. Keightley: You have not got an empty place full of a sort of semi-rigid jelly.

H.P.B.: Certainly not. It is all alive with all kinds of currents and counter-currents, and wheels within wheels and rotary motion, and so on. This is that which certainly may help to solve the difficulty.

Mr. Ingram: In some part of *The Secret Doctrine* it is treated of at length, the genesis of rotary motion, and the different scientific hypotheses.

Mr. B. Keightley: In the first volume, I think it is.

Mr. Mead: Is not the original rotary motion part of the original life of a planet? And doesn't it gradually decrease?

H.P.B.: Certainly, but this has nothing to do with the first impulse which is given to that which goes on and becomes a comet, and after a comet it becomes all kinds of things. The first thing is given to that particle which starts by Fohat.

Mr. B. Keightley: Fohat says, he collects the fiery dust and forms them into balls.

H.P.B.: And this Fohatic force is outside the planets, not only inside, as I explained in the case of centripetal and centrifugal forces — space is full of that.

Mr. B. Keightley: You always have that element which must apply equally to man as to everything else, the two forms: the internal force, which is limited and confined, so to speak, which is always seeking to free itself; and then the free force outside, which is again acting upon the body all the time, and, as it were, in correlating with the confined force. That, of course, would tend to produce a rotative motion.

Mr. Ingram: Then there are forces at work now, producing the rotary motion of the Earth?

Mr. B. Keightley: Well, of course — not solely because of the rotation must be kept up. Clearly we know, if we take the analogy and follow it out strictly, that a human being does not go on living and moving and expending energy simply in virtue of the life impulse which he receives from his parents, but he grows, and is nourished and takes in food and assimilates it and keeps up his strength in that way. And some process analogous to that must take place in the case of a planet.

H.P.B.: Certainly. I cannot tell you anything more, because I don't know anything about science.

Mr. Kingsland: I think there is something in *Lucifer*[1] this month which bears upon that by Keely about the magnetic circulation of the Earth. Has the rotation of the Earth anything to do with these magnetic currents that are always circling around it?

H.P.B.: Most assuredly.

Mr. Kingsland: And these currents cease when the Earth is dead?

H.P.B.: They won't cease, but the Earth won't be able to feel them any more because there will be no receptive hold upon them. They never cease; they are always going on, but the Earth cannot receive any more. Just the same if you have a hurricane, and it comes to Lansdowne Road,[2] and if you have got a dead cat there, the dead cat will be swept away. But once it touches it when it is dead, it cannot do anything.

Mr. Mead: And the Moon is unresponsive to these forces?

H.P.B.: No, because I have just explained why the Moon moves.

Mr. B. Keightley: The Moon is unresponsive to these forces, to the magnetic currents, but the Moon is swept on, carrying on a sort of vampirized life through absorption from the Earth.

---

[1] See C. J. B-M. [Clara Jessup Bloomfield-Moore], "Comments of John Worrell Keely on Dr. Schimmel's Lecture," *Lucifer*, vol. 4 (March 1889–August 1889), pp. 137–140.

[2] H.P.B. lived at 17 Lansdowne Road, London, where the meetings of the Blavatsky Lodge were held.

Mr. Mead: It does not receive whatever it has of motion from the influences from the Earth.

H.P.B.: It is not entirely dead. It is paralysed. It has no more its principles. They are gone.

Mr. B. Keightley: It is dead, but not corrupted yet.

H.P.B.: Therefore, there is the motion, but not its particles. Sometimes the motion is so great in a dead body that you will find it turned; and then some will say: "the man was not dead," and came to himself — which is nothing at all but the work of the disintegrating forces.

Mr. B. Keightley: Question 2, page 171, last paragraph. What are the seven classes of monads here mentioned? Are they simply the mineral, vegetable, animal, etc.? Can you give them seven distinctive names by which we may refer to them afterwards in the order of their appearance on a chain of globes?

H.P.B.: The seven classes here referred to are the seven classes of Lunar Pitris or fathers, all of which have reached the human stage of development on the lunar chain. They are therefore not the monads, or rather elementals, of the seven kingdoms of nature, but are the subdivisions of what we may term the lunar mankind — the lunar lunatics. Of course, when they first arrive on the Earth chain they are very nearly in an undifferentiated condition, and as they descend into matter they differentiate even more and more, till at last they form seven distinctly marked types or classes. Therefore, how can we give them distinct names when these names indicate their attributes, and these are perpetually changing? They may be described by the names of the seven lower Sephiroth of the Kabbalah, or by the seven Amshapends[1] of Zoroaster;[2] but this is only in their primitive differentiation

---

[1] **Amshaspends** or **Amesha Spentas** (*Avestian*) — the six angels or divine Forces personified as gods who attend upon Ahura Mazda, of which he is the synthesis and the seventh. They are one of the prototypes of the Roman Catholic Seven Spirits or Angels with Michael as chief, or the Celestial Host; the "Seven Angels of the Presence." They are the Builders, Cosmocratores, of the Gnostics and identical with the Seven Prajapatis, the Sephiroth, Dhyan-Chohans, etc.

[2] **Zoroaster** or **Zarathustra** (*Avestian*, "golden shining star," "golden Sirius") — the great law-giver, and the founder of the religion variously called Mazdaism, Magism, Parseeism, Fire-Worship, and Zoroastrianism. Like Manu and Vyasa in India, Zarathustra is a generic name for great reformers and law-givers. The hierarchy began with the divine Zarathustra in the *Vendidad* (a part of the ▸

from homogeneity. Every time they are transformed they go down lower on the hierarchy, or higher. They change names.

Mr. Kingsland: These human monads, lunar monads, have to pass through the mineral kingdom, have they not?

H.P.B.: Yes, on the globe A.

Mr. B. Keightley: On globe 2.

Mr. Kingsland: On the whole of the first round?

H.P.B.: Yes. They don't pass anymore on globe B; it is only the latest arrivals. Still, there are some monads, and they will be those who will come. And at the threshold of the Fourth Round and the fourth globe, which is ours, they are perfectly ready. And after that, having evolved their astral images, and so on — which are those images which become men, hereafter — they merge into that mankind. It is they themselves. It is not that they create, like the Lord God out of nothing, but it is simply that they evolve their Chhayas, and little by little they evolve into it.

Mr. Kingsland: Take the first class of Lunar Pitris. They have to go through the first round on our planetary chain, in one of the elemental kingdoms.

Mr. B. Keightley: No, they go through the three elemental kingdoms — mineral, animal, vegetable kingdoms — up to the human stage, and just enter it on globe A. Then they repeat the same process on globe B, on globe C, D and all round through the first round. The second class of monads arriving from the Lunar chain are a stage behind. They don't reach the human stage, they stop one stage short of that all through the first round; the third class of monads, a stage still later, and so on. So that if you take the Second Round, the first class have reached the human stage already, but the remaining classes each have one or more stages to complete in that round or subsequent rounds.

Mr. Kingsland: It is rather difficult to follow.

Mr. B. Keightley: That is the way it seems to be stated here.

Mr. Mead: But if all these seven classes of Lunar Pitris had reached a man stage on the Lunar chain, had they — all the seven classes — reached a human stage, so to speak?

Avesta), and ended with the great, but mortal, man bearing that title and now lost to history.

H.P.B.: The human stage on the Moon is far inferior to that of the Earth, because every time that the principles of a plane go to form another plane, it is always on a higher scale.

Mr. Ingram: But they had, all of them, reached that stage, but they differed from themselves in order of merit.

H.P.B.: You don't think that the principles shot from the Moon in one day created the whole chain? It certainly required millions and millions of years to do such a thing as that. Once that globe A was ready, then the Lunar Pitris of the globe A passed into it. Then the others remained yet there during the time that the second, B, was produced; then the principles began shooting out from globe B of the Lunar chain, on to our earthly chain, and then the second ones came in. During the First Round, when it comes to the last globe, then only it is that you can say the whole lunar chain is at an end, you understand, that it is dead, as it is now. But to the last moment they come.

Mr. B. Keightley: You say in *The Secret Doctrine* that only when the first or highest class of the monads leave the last globe of the lunar chain, that is the moment of death of the first globe.

H.P.B.: That is what I say. It is all explained there.

Mr. Mead: Yes, but I don't understand it.

H.P.B.: What don't you understand there?

Mr. Mead: The first class on the lunar chain have passed off the whole of the lunar planetary chain into a Laya centre, have not they?

H.P.B.: I beg your pardon; the monads go when the globes are ready.

Mr. B. Keightley: The monads are not the principles of the globe.

Mr. Old: Is it stated how long since the Moon ceased to give off monads to the Earth?

H.P.B.: I could not tell you. You are a mathematician: reckon. I cannot tell you, because they don't give the correct figures at all; they say simply it is 300,000,000 of years since life appeared on this Earth, and there they stop. I speak to you about the Hindu chronology. And then they leave you to whistle and infer for yourselves. They won't give it to you. Mr. Sinnett tried it several times and he met a Chinese wall. You must go by the Brahmanical calculation, and it gives a Manvantara of 15 figures. It gives it to you certainly quite correctly. It is given in the second volume. Everything is given — how long it is since the universe was evolved; how long it is that such and such a thing happened; how many years the Manvantara consisted of, and the Pralaya, and when the Manu period was. It is 18,000,000 of years — that is to say, 18,000,000 of years is given to the appearance of the real man, and not the Chhaya. It begins, therefore, in the Fourth Round — or rather, in the middle of the Third Race. This is when they begin their 18,000,000 of years, so you may count. Our Fifth Race is a million of years; take into consideration, if you please, that there are several kinds of Pralaya, that Pralaya is not only that which you think, when everything is dissolved and disappears. There are several kinds of Pralayas, and unless you learn all these, it is very easy for you in reading the *Vishnu Purana* to take one Pralaya for another. And they don't go to the trouble of qualifying the Pralayas, and they let you lose yourselves as much as you like. That was always a game of the priests.

Mr. ——: With regard to the first class of the Lunar Pitris, directly it leaves the seventh globe, does it incarnate?

Mr. B. Keightley: No, it passes into Nirvana.

H.P.B.: And then it comes in time for the Second Round, because between every life and evolution there is a temporary Pralaya between them — an obscuration. And then take into consideration that after every round there is the same period, the same duration, that lasted, for instance, for the Manvantaric day of the chain. It will be the same Pralaya, you understand: the night will be as long as the day. Mind you, I don't speak about the cosmic days; I speak simply about the days of the chain.

Mr. B. Keightley: That is to say, between the going to sleep of the last planet-chain, and the re-awakening, you have the time of the awakening of the whole chain.

H.P.B.: If you are a mathematician you can go and do it very easily. For instance, if you take a given period of time approximately, and be guided by the Hindu chronology, you can do it. They say to you that 12,000 human years and 12,000 divine years make quite a difference, and they give you a proportion of how much more it is. There are divine years and human years and Manvantara years and all kinds of years. So if you are a good mathematician, you won't be lost in it.

Mr. ——: The first class goes on through the different kingdoms right up to the human stage, and following after the steps come other classes in such a way that when the first class leaves the first globe A, the seventh class appears on the first globe and passes on.

Mr. B. Keightley: Passes into the interplanetary.

Mr. ——: Do they all follow it and go into the two planets?

H.P.B.: Yes, but now comes algebra — that the duration of the lunar days and nights are in proportion a great deal shorter than those of the Earth, and that during, for instance, four and a half rounds, the whole seven come. That is a very great thing: the whole seven have the time to have their Pralayas, so that of the four rounds there is not a single Monad that can come. Every one of us is a Monad of the true blue stock; there is not a single Monad that has come since then. It is only, you see, the pious people who teach that God breathed a soul into every baby that appears. We say: "Fiddlesticks!"

Mr. Mead: These seven classes incarnated, we have said. When the first class leaves the globe A, does the sixth class — or rather, will the next one after it, the second class, which has reached the sixth kingdom, stop short of the human stage, because that class does not go into the human stage till the Second Round? Therefore, it leaves that planet and goes into the Pralaya or the animal kingdom.

H.P.B.: It seems to me, if my recollection is right, that the first class of Pitris, those who become the Lunar Pitris, have passed through all the kingdoms on globe A, and they don't pass through all the kingdoms on globe B.

Mr. B. Keightley: You are mistaken in your recollection.

Mr. Mead: If that is so, and they being the pioneers, when they incarnate they — being the first, into what kingdom do they go straight away? Into the human kingdom?

H.P.B.: That is what you have got to read. I have simply written and tried, without a single mistake, to give that which is in *The Secret Doctrine.* But when it comes to those calculations, after a time I don't want to remember it, even.

Mr. Kingsland: There is one point which is making a little confusion all through. The first class comes over from the lunar chain to globe A and they are followed by the second, third, fourth, and so on.

Now, are all those seven classes on globe A at the same time, before the first class goes on to globe B?

Mr. B. Keightley: What is stated here is this, in this paragraph which we are just passing. [Reads from *The Secret Doctrine*.]

Mr. Kingsland: Has that first class been all round the chain by this time?

H.P.B.: No. It must be placed so that he who would like to know the time and calculate, would have to take into consideration the greater shortness of the Pralayas and of the Nirvanic state of the lunar classes. That is what you have to do.

Mr. Kingsland: You see, from that statement, class one are leaving globe A just when class seven are coming onto it; therefore, in the meantime, two, three, four, five and six are all on globe A.

Mr. B. Keightley: But, you see, when the Pralaya comes, as far as I can understand from this, the development of the several kingdoms is stopped short at the point they have reached for that time, and then they have to go on all round the chain.

Mr. Mead: I want to know if it is at the moment of that Pralaya when the last monad of the first class is passed on.

Mr. B. Keightley: That is not stated.

Mr. Kingsland: Does that obscuration come before all the classes have passed on globe B?

H.P.B.: No. There are those who remain, the last ones, and then they come after that, because they have only just come in, and it must be timed in such a way that the seven come into the space of the rotation or formation of the first globe, of the future humanity. Till the Fourth Round they are not really humans.

Mr. B. Keightley: This is what seems to be implied here, that the development of the other classes, as it were, reaches a point when the obscuration sets in in which they cannot go any further. On that globe the hour of the obscuration has struck, and they are developed on that globe and everything is stopped. Then they have to go on to globe B and repeat the process, and so on all round the chain.

Mr. Kingsland: We ought to have a board with seven rows and seven heads, as they have in the schools.

H.P.B.: And what good would it do to you? It would be loss of time, and nothing else.

Mr. Kingsland: My difficulty is to see how it is that a half of these do not come in in time to reach the human stage. Isn't that your difficulty, Mead?

Mr. Mead: No, I understand that. My difficulty is when this Pralaya, this obscuration, overtakes it. When does it?

Mr. B. Keightley: It comes at a moment, and then all these Monads who are cycling have to leave that planet.

Mr. Mead: In a rush?

Mr. B. Keightley: At that moment, apparently.

H.P.B.: It is so timed that they all enter into their Nirvanic state, their time of rest, between the two planets. Nature does not make mistakes in this case.

Mr. B. Keightley: Her timepieces do not require cleaning, you know.

H.P.B.: You see, in mathematics, I was never a Newton in my life.

Mr. Mead: If this first class goes through all the kingdoms up to man, the second class will have been worked up once with the first class, so that the seventh class coming in, it will have been six times differentiated by the six classes that have gone before.

Mr. B. Keightley: So that it is able to work up by degrees. That is how it is that all the seven classes reach the human stage of the Fourth Round.

Mr. Ingram: Have we been Lunar Pitris?

H.P.B.: We are the Lunar Pitris.

Mr. Ingram: Then we are talking of ourselves when we are talking of these?

H.P.B.: It is "we," if you please, but we do not remember it. To think that we have been angels and have become — what — such pumpkins, knowing nothing at all! To think we have been ornamented with beautiful wings and pinions, and where are they? Gentlemen, you are very much addicted to questioning, and you really ought not to pry into the mysteries of God!

Mr. B. Keightley: Question 3, page 172. What are the seven principles of the globes which are transferred one after the other to the globes of the new chain?

H.P.B.: Each globe has seven principles which are correlative with the seven principles in man; but this must not be understood to mean that the seven principles are represented by the Monads which are performing their cyclic pilgrimages through the seven kingdoms of nature. For example, the seventh or highest principle of the planet is not the Monads which have reached the human stage of development, but the planet as a whole has its own seven principles, as any other body has. To make it clear. The Earth has its physical or material body, its astral body, its life principle, its animal nature, its instincts, or lower Manas, its higher intelligence which it imparts to and shares with some of the animals, its Buddhi, composed of the gnomes, or earth elementals, and its Atman, represented by an intelligence called the spirit of the Earth, which some Kabbalists have identified with Jehovah. This latter belief was a dogma with the Valentinians and the Ophites,[1] who said that the God of the Jews was simply the spirit of the Earth. You will find this if you read the Valentinians. They all say that the God was the spirit of the last terrestrial plane which created this, and then you can read the corrections that are there, with this Bahak-Zivo,[2] and Fetahil[3] and so on. Did you ever read this? It is the most interesting thing in the world, only, unfortunately, it is not translated and you can only get it in Latin.[4] It is one of the oldest gospels, and one of the most interesting.

---

[1] **Ophites** (*Greek*, "serpent") — a Gnostic Fraternity in Egypt, and one of the earliest sects of Gnosticism, or *Gnosis* (Wisdom, Knowledge), known as the "Brotherhood of the Serpent." It flourished early in the 2nd century, and while holding some of the principles of Valentinus, had its own occult rites and symbology. A living serpent, representing the Christos-principle (*i.e.*, the divine reincarnating Monad), was displayed in their mysteries and reverenced as a symbol of wisdom, Sophia, the type of the all-good and all-wise.

[2] **Bahak-Zivo** — the "father of the Genii" in the *Codex Nazaraeus*. He called the world into existence out of the "dark water."

[3] **Fetahil** — the lower creator in the *Codex Nazaraeus.*

[4] **Codex Nazaraeus** (*Latin*) — the Book of Adam, the latter name meaning *anthropos*, Man or Humanity. See M. Norberg, translator, *Codex Nazaraeus "Liber Adami" appelatus Syriace transcriptus* (London, 1815).

Nazarenes (*Hebrew*, "set apart") — a pre-Christian sect. The same as the St. John Christians. They settled on the banks of the Jordan river 150 years BCE.

Mr. Mead: Would you mind reading that again? Not the explanations of the principles, but the last principles of the Earth upwards.

H.P.B.: [Reads again, "The earth has its physical," etc., etc.]

Mr. Kingsland: Then what we have been calling the planetary spirits in the previous discussions are simply the Atman of each of the planets?

H.P.B.: Some of them. Because they are again divided into seven. This is the great mysterious number of this Manvantara, so you had better not mix up too many things, because you will be terribly confused, that is sure.

Mr. Kingsland: Then are we to understand that the Monads, although independent of these seven principles, are necessary for the completion, so to speak, of the animal life of the planet?

H.P.B.: Certainly.

Mr. Kingsland: Of the individual animal life of the globe or planet?

H.P.B.: You mean the elementals which precede the other kingdoms?

Mr. Kingsland: I mean the Monads in their whole career.

H.P.B.: Certainly, they are necessary.

Mr. Mead: Wouldn't it be convenient to give some name to these three sub-kingdoms?

H.P.B.: Call them Smith or Brown or anything you like, because I am not going to bother myself. They called me by a pet name when I was young, but they would not call me by that now, I have changed.

Mr. Kingsland: Can you tell us at all in what way the seven human principles are necessary for the completion of these seven principles?

H.P.B.: Because it is a link. Because every one of them radiates something which corresponds in some other principle, in anything, in any being. If you break one link, the whole goes to nothing.

Mr. Kingsland: But they are not identical.

Mr. B. Keightley: As far as I gathered, as far as I inferred, it was that the development of the earth, of the principles of the earth, is assisted and carried on, or very largely assisted by the development of humanity after it has once made its appearance on a globe.

H.P.B.: Most assuredly, because the sins of humanity affect the earth, and the joys of humanity affect the earth. And you will see that when humanity is at its worst, then they will have neither harvest nor anything growing, and the earth will be in perfect sterility and despair.

Mr. B. Keightley: You must have this intimate connection between man and the earth, or else you would have no relation at all.

H.P.B.: The ancients were wise when they called the earth the mother of man.

Mr. Kingsland: What is the difference between the mineral kingdom before these Monads have come over from the other chain and after?

Mr. B. Keightley: Greater perfection.

H.P.B.: Everything grows. That which we see now certainly has not existed at the beginning of the Round; and that which was at the beginning of the Round did not exist and was entirely different at the Third Round, and so on. As we go on, when we reach the point at the Fourth Round, then everything is adjusted. There is a totally complete adjustment of matter and spirit. And then, till that point we were falling into matter, but from that point, once it is reached, it is matter that goes and ascends into spirit.

Mr. ——: Has not the worst point of human life been passed, yet?

H.P.B.: I do not know, physically. I say we will have worse days than we have had yet, because we have been sinning so much.

Mr. ——: Then we have not reached the lowest point, yet?

H.P.B.: We have not reached the lowest point.

Mr. B. Keightley: The greater the responsibility, the heavier the sin. While we were falling into matter, and while the spiritual consciousness was entirely obscured by matter, we had not anything like the responsibility that we have now, not in the same way. Because now we passed that point to a considerable extent, and we are beginning to become more spiritualized. With that comes at the same time a possibility of much more far-reaching sin or breach of the law, which would be very much farther reaching in its effects, and something more serious.

H.P.B.: This is perfectly logical and comprehensible.

Mr. Ingram: Isn't there, at the same time, on the other side, a greater acquiescence and obedience to law, as against the disobedience? Isn't there a larger part of mankind that obeys the law and whose accumulated Karma neutralizes the bad Karma of the others?

H.P.B.: I do not know. I do not think so. Nothing can neutralize the bad Karma of individuals. Collectively there may be some equilibrium, but I am afraid it is all the wrong way. You see, evil predominates everywhere. It is not good. Go where you like, you find there is not a thing that is done that is not done with selfish motives and so as to benefit all one's self, or nation, or individual, and that the others would be the losers thereby. It is something terrible when you come to look at the present state of business, of life, and of civilization. This civilization is the cancer of humanity; it will be the ruin of humanity in the way it is conducted. I do not say civilization as it ought to be. It is the most gigantic development of selfishness that ever was known. And I can assure you that the Fifth Race will go out with a great flourish of trumpets, which will be other than the trumpets of the war cry.

Mr. Ingram: Is the selfishness greater now than it was in the Fourth Race?

H.P.B.: A thousand times worse, because they are just descending into matter, and they cling to matter with the utmost desperation, that is why.

Mr. B. Keightley: Question 4. Are these principles all transferred from each of the globes of the lunar chain to the earth chain, and the latter made complete in all the seven principles of each of the seven globes, *before* the *Monads* emerge from the Nirvana into which they pass after leaving the lunar chain? Or does the evolution of the new chain, as regards the transfer of the principles and the evolution of the Monads, proceed *pari passu*?

H.P.B.: The question is answered in *The Secret Doctrine*, so why should you ask? Of course the principles of the globe of the lunar chain are all transferred, each septenary, to its corresponding globe of the earth chain. And the earth chain globes have attained their full septenary constitution before the first Monads make their appearance on globe A. From that time onwards the evolution of the globes and the Monads proceed *pari passu*, not before.

Mr. B. Keightley: That is to say, each globe in its turn has attained its full septenary constitution before any Monads make their appearance on it.

Mr. Kingsland: But that is only the starting point of the evolution of the globe; it is not the obtaining of these seven principles, but something further beyond.

Mr. B. Keightley: The child attains his full septenary constitution at the age of seven years, but you can't say the evolution of the man is complete.

H.P.B.: You can't say the evolution is complete, ever. It is complete only an instant before the final Pralaya. Nature is always evoluting, always transforming itself and going higher and higher and higher. Once Nature stops it is death, it is stagnation.

Mr. Kingsland: In what does the evolution of the globes consist, apart from the evolution of the Monads?

H.P.B.: In its own external evolution and everything.

Mr. B. Keightley: It has got to form itself into a globe. Of course, it has to be done up to a certain point, so there is a complete septenary.

H.P.B.: The evolution must proceed.

Mr. B. Keightley: Question 5. "Nature, the physical evolutionary power."[1] What does "Nature" represent?

H.P.B.: "Nature, the physical evolutionary power," stands here for all the forces which are innate in the four lower Cosmic principles, or the Cosmic quaternary. For Cosmos has got its seven principles, as we have — *e.g.*, my hand in conjunction with my brain makes signs on this paper which convey an intelligible meaning (I am not sure of it, though!). But if my brain were partially paralysed, as has been observed in certain cases of disease, my hand may still, by sheer force of habit, make signs on this paper, or pretend to write, but these signs would convey no meaning whatever. In the latter case, only the lower quaternary or physical evolutionary power is acting. This, I suppose, answers sufficiently. That is what I mean by it.

Mr. B. Keightley: Question 6. What class or classes of intelligences are included here under the term "Nature"?

---

[1] *The Secret Doctrine*, vol. 1, p. 181.

H.P.B.: The four lower classes or principles, as I have just said. There is no need to repeat it.

Mr. B. Keightley: Question 7. "The Chhayas of the Lunar Pitris."[1] What is a Chhaya?

H.P.B.: Did I not tell you 29,000 times, Chhaya is a Sanskrit word, meaning shadow, or image, or what we call astral body? Sanjna,[2] the wife of Surya,[3] the Sun, becoming tired of the too ardent love of her husband, left him her handmaiden, Chhaya, that is to say, her own astral image, or body, and took herself off to the jungles to become a yogi. So runs the tradition. Somehow or other, as *Vishnu Purana* narrates, the Sun, deceived by the likeness, managed to have two children from this astral body — so it is stated in *Vishnu Purana* — and that is the origin of Chhaya, the astral body.

Mr. B. Keightley: Question 8. Has a planet an individuality as a man has an Ego?

H.P.B.: It has. Its ruling spirit, or governor, as it is called in *Pimander*,[4] is self-conscious. Any questions to that?

Mr. Kingsland: That has been partially answered before.

Mr. B. Keightley: Question 9. Is there any analogy between the Monad of man and the vital essence of a planet?

H.P.B.: You do offer very funny questions! Certainly not. There is an analogy — I would call it a perfect correspondence — between the Monad of a man and the ruling spirit or governor of a planet. But the vital essence of that planet corresponds to the vital essence of man, therefore to the Kama-rupa. For Prana (or life) has, strictly speaking, two vehicles, as Manas is double: Linga-sharira, or astral body, is the vehicle of the life principle, or spirit life; while Kama-rupa is the vehicle of the physical or material essence. In other words, the three higher principles of the septenary of Prana reside in the astral

---

[1] *The Secret Doctrine*, vol. 1, p. 181.

[2] **Sanjna** (*Sanskrit*) — Spiritual Consciousness; the wife of Surya, the Sun.

[3] **Surya** (*Sanskrit*) — the Sun, worshipped in the *Vedas*. The offspring of Aditi (Space), the mother of the gods. The husband of Sanjna, or spiritual consciousness. The great god whom Visvakarman, his father-in-law, the creator of the gods and men, and their "carpenter," crucifies on a lathe, and cutting off the eighth part of his rays, depriving his head of its effulgency and creating round it a dark aureole. A mystery of the last initiation, and an allegorical representation of it.

[4] **Pimander** or **Poimandres** (*Greek*) — the first treatise in the *Corpus Hermeticum*.

body, while the four lower principles have their seat in Kama-rupa. You have learnt something new tonight, because I discovered, to my great surprise, that Mr. Bert Keightley did not know what I meant, that Kama-rupa was the vehicle of the life essence and that there was a difference between it and Prana, which has seven principles. Therefore, as Kama-rupa is the vehicle of the grossest of that form, that Prana the astral body has got is a vehicle of the spirit of the life principle, because it is connected with the higher principles of the triad and not with the quaternary.

Mr. Kingsland: That is certainly a new idea.

H.P.B.: I did not know it was a new idea at all.

Mr. B. Keightley: Nobody had ever stated it in any theosophical work.

H.P.B.: My dear sirs, I say to all you, "Not guilty," who do not live in the house; but those who live in the house and from morning to night speak and live and have their being in occultism ought to know it. I absolve everyone who does not live here, but not Mr. Bertram Keightley, because he ought to know.

Mr. Kingsland: It has not been done in any published work so far.

H.P.B.: My dear sir, it was said to Mr. Sinnett before he wrote *Esoteric Buddhism* (whether he put it there, I don't know), but it is a thing which is an axiom, and it has been put, I am perfectly sure, in *The Theosophist* — that there is not a thing in nature which has not got its two poles and its seven principles. That is one of the fundamental axioms of the occult sciences and the esoteric doctrines, that every blessed thing has its seven principles and its polarity.

Mr. Kingsland: If you can divide each principle into seven you get 49, which is confusing.

Mr. ——: And then divide each of those 49 into seven.

Mr. Mead: One understands that everything is subdivisible into sevens like that, but that Prana principle having two vehicles is difficult to follow.

H.P.B.: Prana in man has two vehicles because there is a spiritual life and there is a material, physical life. Now, that which is in the Kama-rupa is the grossest sub-principle, so to say, and all that, but that which is in the astral body is the pure spiritual life. Now, if you do not understand this, how will you understand the 49 fires of occultism? If you don't understand them, you are simply a flapdoodle, and he who wants to be a flapdoodle, let him neglect the 49 fires. That is all I can tell you. The astral body being the shadow or the image of man is in direct communication with the higher principles, whereas Kama-rupa is the animal. It is the seat of everything animal.

Mr. B. Keightley: If you look at the diagram of the planet in the human principles which is given a few pages back, you will find you get exactly the explanation of the two vehicles.

H.P.B.: You cannot expect me to give everything; something must be left to the intuition and to human intelligence. If I had written everything I would have had to make 25 volumes and it would not have been enough. I told you hundreds of times, stick to analogy here.

Mr. B. Keightley: If you look at page 153, you get it. That diagram gives the key if you make that substitution, if you put it in its proper order.

H.P.B.: I have remarked you must not number them. The number "one" is that principle which is predominant in man. Now, if you happen to have your fourth principle predominant, it will be the first. They want to have everything put straight for them. They won't shake their own brains.

Mr. B. Keightley: Question 10, page 192: "The holy youths refused to multiply…" If these "sons" could once refuse to inhabit the Chhaya-rupas,[1] why could they not continue to refuse? And what was the necessity which finally compelled them to incarnate in even less pure rupas?

H.P.B.: Because they were not independent Englishmen, but simply poor celestial beings, and they were not as obstinate as your nation is. And what prevented them was Karma. Not a single word more can I say. Let us not forget that there is a limit to the freedom of action of every differentiated being in the whole universe. Karma, being the absolute adjusting law, whether in heaven or on earth, says to the proud waves: "So far shalt thou go and no farther."[2] If it says this to the waves, it says it to the angels, and anything you like. It is Karma, and they cannot go against Karma. It is the whole thing. They may

---

[1] **Chhaya-rupa** (*Sanskrit,* "shadow-form") — the astral body.
[2] Job 38:11.

kick as much as they like, but they have to do it. Instead of pure and wholesome bodies, they had to enter into defiled bodies.

Mr. Mead: Then free will is always circumscribed?

Mr. ——: Did these beings that refused to incarnate know they were doing wrong?

H.P.B.: I suppose they did, but it was disagreeable to imprison themselves into those bodies once more, and they delayed and delayed. And if you read *The Secret Doctrine*, you will see what occurred.

Mr. ——: How did the law of Karma act on them?

H.P.B.: It acts on everything that is differentiated under the Sun — not our Sun, but the Spiritual Sun.

Mr. B. Keightley: All these classes and hierarchies of divine beings are these evolutions of previous Manvantaras, and they have an infinite line of Karma behind them.

H.P.B.: They do not come created by anything or make a simultaneous appearance with the universe.

Mr. B. Keightley: Question 11, page 193: You say that the Jewish Kabbalists argue "that no Spirit could belong to the divine hierarchy unless Ruach[3] (Spirit) was united to Nephesh (living soul)." That is to say that "it is necessary for each ego to attain full self-consciousness as a human, *i.e.,* conscious being."

H.P.B.: They do belong to the divine hierarchy, because they had been men in the preceding Manvantara. Now, whether it was on this earth or on other earths, I do not know; never mind they were men or human beings. I do not know whether they had two arms and two legs and a head, but they were Manus — thinking beings. As the sons of divine hierarchy, which will represent divine creators in the Manvantara to come, will be those men of this earth who will have attained the highest perfection, everyone of us, ladies and gentlemen, has before him or her a chance. If we behave well we will become, every one of us, one of these gentlemen — the Kumaras, they call them, the youths. Perhaps they too will in their turn hesitate to inhabit very unsavoury bodies and be imprisoned in them; but they will have

---

[3] **Ruach** (*Hebrew,* "spirit") — the Spirit, one of the human principles (Buddhi-Manas).

to do it in order to atone for the unpaid bills of the total of their past existence. Every one of us has to act according to law and Karmic law.

Mr. B. Keightley: Question 12 (originally question 14), page 194: "Bahak-Zivo … is ignorant of Orcus."[1] What does "Orcus" symbolize? You say in *The Secret Doctrine* that it is the "rebellious angels," those who refuse to create, that are the intellectual saviours of mankind, and you prove that the fall through pride is only a theological libel on these, our true deliverers from ignorance. Yet what you have just said in answer to question 10 seems to imply this latter view. Please explain.

H.P.B.: It is true they have fallen in one sense, but not through pride; only through unwillingness to imprison themselves, as I have just said, in finite and limited form. But this is quite a different thing from what the theologians say. They aver these angels sought to become gods and dethrone gods, which is an absurdity. We say they were gods whom the law of evolution compelled to descend into matter, that is to say, to fall, but instead of submitting quietly to the law and incarnating at the proper time, they delayed until man had brutalized himself in his ignorance, and thus defiled themselves and the bodies which the law compelled them to inhabit. Theologians now speak of a hell into which they were hurled; and the occultists say the hell means simply the human body, and there is no other hell than earth. The fact that Christ and so many other solar gods — Hercules,[2] etc. — descended into hell is an allegory pointing to just such imprisonment in the physical body. They are certainly our saviours, because without them we would be simply senseless animals. Therefore, what the theologians say is a perfect libel. They speak of angels who wanted to become gods.

Mr. ——: Is there no limit to the cycle of necessity after the egos attained the state Nirvana? Is there a possibility of having to go through succeeding rounds?

H.P.B.: The universe that they will inhabit will be immeasurably higher than the one they have inhabited, and therefore it is one more step to perfection — more and more and more.

Mr. B. Keightley: One question that suggests: When there is one more step to perfection, does it mean to carry with it the idea that as

---

[1] **Orcus** (*Latin*) — the bottomless pit in the *Codex Nazaraeus*.
[2] **Hercules** — a legendary hero in Greek mythology known for his great strength and celebrated for completing the Twelve Labours assigned to him.

it is analogous to this universe, so, on the higher universe, there will be pleasure and pain?

H.P.B.: As the Absolute has never taken me into his confidence (for which perhaps he is to be blamed), I cannot answer such questions as that.

Mr. B. Keightley: The question is whether pleasure and pain are really limited to our plane of consciousness.

H.P.B.: I would ask you, if you please, what is pleasure and pain? Is it an eternal entity, or eternal entities?

Mr. B. Keightley: Why I put the question was this. For instance, we know there is differentiation…

H.P.B.: We know there is differentiation? We *understand* there is differentiation and are very proud of it, but whether there will be a differentiation of the same kind or another in other Manvantaras, this remains a secret. Even between the Absolute and the Logos.

Mr. Kingsland: Isn't it possible that during another Manvantara everything may be arranged into nines or sixes, instead of sevens?

H.P.B.: It may be in the following Manvantara that two and two may not make four any longer, but it may make twelve. Something will happen we cannot expect.

Mr. ——: Has there ever been number one evolved?

H.P.B.: Number one would be a difficult thing. It does not yield to any combination, it is unity. We must have two, at least, and two will never make a figure. Two is a despised number. Despised by the Pythagoreans. They were two straight lines, which started from nowhere, and did not know where they went to. Two we must not take, also.

Mr. ——: Then three is the lowest number?

H.P.B.: It is the first one from which you can make anything. You cannot make of one anything, or of two. One is unity. It may be endless and infinite.

Mr. ——: That is all from the point of view of the seven?

Mr. ——: Unless it is a circle.

H.P.B.: The circle, if you please, is "the," the root of number one, which is no number.

Mr. B. Keightley: You speak a good deal about various Gnostic systems; there are one or two points that wanted clearing up a little. Question 13, page 194: If Fetahil, as stated later, represents the host of the Lunar Pitris who created a senseless man, and if he is "a still purer spirit" than Bahak-Zivo, what does the latter correspond to?

H.P.B.: The Nazarene business is not at all plain, and is full of metaphor, chiefly directed against the God of the Jews, and their opponents. Therefore it is so mixed up that nobody will know which is which. He is represented sometimes as a higher spirit, and sometimes as a lower. Bahak-Zivo corresponds sometimes to Christ, and sometimes to other things. I have been bringing this in, not at all that you should come and ask me to learn it, because everyone can go and read it in the original, who reads Latin. But why I have quoted it here is, to show that in every system, high or low, the "Secret Doctrine"[1] was repeated, and there were things which were all based on truth. But you need not go out of your way to make me teach you the Nazarene system.

Mr. B. Keightley: Question 14, page 194: "Bahak-Zivo ... is ignorant of Orcus." What does "Orcus" symbolize?

H.P.B.: Orcus symbolizes many things: Death, Hell; it symbolizes what the Buddhists would call Mara[2] — many, many things. Orcus is a place of Darkness and Desolation, and since Bahak-Zivo was not acquainted with Orcus, that is to say, with the corresponding contrasted pole of life, he could not create beings, because he could not make a finite being. It is just the same as the thing which Shiva throws out, which is more necessary than the Prince of Denmark to "Hamlet."[3]

Mr. B. Keightley: That is all in the questions.

Mr. Old: I was trying to evolve that idea which was generated with me, which you call wisdom. A thought did strike me a short time ago, that was in respect to the numerical basis of a Manvantara, or order of creation. There was the number seven as the root basis

---

[1] **Secret Doctrine** — the general name given to the esoteric teachings of antiquity.
[2] **Mara** (*Sanskrit*, "destruction") — the god of temptation, the *Seducer* who tried to turn away Buddha from his Path. He is called the "Destroyer" and "Death" (of the Soul).
[3] **Hamlet** — the Prince of Denmark in William Shakespeare's tragedy of the same name.

of this Manvantara. Do you speak of our limited Manvantara, or the Maha-Manvantara?

H.P.B.: Of all the Manvantaras that the Hindus speak about. Maybe it is of the solar system only.

Mr. Old: You speak of it in *The Secret Doctrine* as the root number of nature.

H.P.B.: In this Manvantara.

Mr. Old: You say in another Manvantara we may have five.

H.P.B.: Most assuredly we may, because Nature changes entirely in her manifestations and forms. Now go and see, if you please, and ask medicine, ask botany — you find in every department the septenary everywhere. Even the diseases can be septenary, 7, 14, 21, and so on. Here is a doctor; he will tell you everything is in seven. Take the flakes of snow, you will find in it the septenary number. You find six little spots, and a seventh in the middle. You take a drop of water, it splashes, and becomes a pentagon, and a six-pointed star. See what Tyndall writes about it. Once we had a discussion about it. There is not a thing where you can escape it. All this goes by the weeks of the Moon, weeks by septenates and everything.

Mr. Old: Of course that is quite true, but our scope of observation is so limited, that it is tied down to this plane.

H.P.B.: Then extend it. Try to see it with your third eye, and don't look only with your two eyes. And try also to think with your spiritual brain.

Mr. Old: I want to identify myself with somebody or some Monad outside our solar system altogether.

H.P.B.: You cannot fail to identify yourself because *it* will identify you if you don't. Every one of us, we were before and will be afterwards — not in our personalities, but in our higher selves. We may defy those selves as much as we like, yet they remain immortal. We cannot get rid of them, but they can get rid of us. Every and each consciousness of ours will feel it, and will see that it is entirely linked to it. It cannot be separated.

Mr. Old: Then the number of changes in mere units for the basic number would be seven. 2 you do not count, 1 is Absolute, 2 is nothing, and you have 3, 4, 5, 6, 7, 8, and 9 as possibilities, that is to say, you have 7 possibilities.

H.P.B.: But the 7 are the principal forces in Nature. The 7 are all the 7 planets, the 7 planes of consciousness. It is the great mystery number. Take the Kabbalah; you know yourself how the name is written, even the name of Tetragrammaton. If you put it in the Jewish letters, you make of it 3 and 4. Out of these, the 4 represent the 7 lower Sephiroth, and the 3, the 3 higher Sephiroth. If you add Shekhinah[1] and Ain-Soph, you will have 9, not the 12, because the 3 are apart. Even the year is divided, because it divides itself naturally. Everything is divided into that.

Mr. Old: Then the term Nature — does that apply to everything in the solar system, or right away to infinity?

H.P.B.: It occurs in our solar system. At all events, I can't say to anything outside of it, and you won't find high Adepts who will tell you much outside of the solar system.

Mr. B. Keightley: You said just now number 7 is found in the solar year. I don't see quite how it comes in. It does not divide into 365.

H.P.B.: Ask Old, he'll tell you.

Mr. Old: There was a difference. It was a matter of 360, the difference between 360 lunar, and 370 solar — that is to say, reckoning by digits or the degrees in the zodiac, apparent degrees — mathematical degrees, I should say. And the difference between these two was 365, which gives a solar circle roughly.

H.P.B.: Very roughly, because in the tropical year it won't agree.

Mr. B. Keightley: The true solar year is 365 and a quarter, about, and a fraction less than a quarter; but then I don't think that divides into 7.

Mr. Old: No, certainly not. Not unless we proceed to minutes or seconds. I don't know how it would work out then.

Mr. B. Keightley: I don't see the 7.

Mr. Old: I will try and work it out.

---

[1] **Shekhinah** (*Hebrew*, "dwelling") — a title applied to Malkuth, the tenth Sephira, by the Kabbalists, but by the Jews to the cloud of glory which rested on the Mercy-seat in the Holy of Holies. As taught, however, by all the Rabbins of Asia Minor, its nature is of a more exalted kind, Shekhinah being the veil of Ain-Soph, the Endless and the Absolute; hence a kind of Kabbalistic Mulaprakriti.

H.P.B.: You will have 7 always, because 7 Manvantaras go in that, and the 7 in the tropical year, and the 7 in the solar year and the cycles. Well if you reckon or calculate you will see that the cycles come to number 7. They are septenates, the cycles, that is sure.

Mr. ——: Just now, madam, you were speaking of the word Nature as applying only to the solar system. Do you mean the planetary chain?

H.P.B.: No, the whole of the system.

Mr. ——: Then surely it includes the other ever-invisible planet.

Mr. B. Keightley: Certainly I think so.

Mr. ——: That is divisible by 7. 365 days, 4 hours, 49 minutes, 49 seconds.

Mr. Old: The latest calculation is 365 days, 5 hours, making nearly 6 hours. And if you add one leap day, you get beyond this, so that in about 213 years you would require to drop a day.

H.P.B.: That shows that you have got to calculate as the Hindus do, because they calculate, and sometimes they drop out, and sometimes they bring in. They always bring them into sevens. Look at their old astronomical works, the buildings in Benares,[2] and in the old cities, they are all worked on that system. They were most curious machines for their buildings, instruments, and so on. The chief constellations are all septenaries. The seven Pleiades and the Great Bear and every-where are all seven. When I come to think about this blessed Sabbath and the seventh day and rest that is taken bodily from the periods, the Manvantaric periods, the seven Races and so on, I say they don't understand it. That is the day of rest, that is to say, the Pralaya. They come and they make in this blessed England a regular Pralaya on the Sundays, so that everyone is ready to go and cut off his head and die; because to begin with the ancient Jews did not have a week at all, they did not have names for days of the week. They had only one, it was the seventh day they knew, and nothing else. They were calculating by the Moon, the lunar calculation.

Mr. Old: How far back do the Jews' days date? We have 300 B.C., we have the seven days of the week given according to the planets. I suppose it would be a period quite anterior to that you refer to?

H.P.B.: They never had a week.

---

[2] **Benares** or **Varanasi** — the holy city in India on the Ganges river.

Mr. Old: Was it the Assyrians?

H.P.B.: The Chaldeans had. The Athenian week was ten days, the Roman eight days. It was only the Hindus who had seven days, and had a planetary name for each day of the week, and it is from the Hindus that it comes. They went and began calculating, and took the names of the solar angels, which belong to the solar calculation, and they shoved them and stuck them on the weeks which belong to the lunar calculations, so they made a mess of it. It is a terrible mess in astronomy; they have mixed up the colours, the metals, they have mixed up everything, as you know yourself.

2 MAY 1889

Mr. B. Keightley: You quoted this passage: "And there was war in heaven." etc. [Reads from *The Secret Doctrine*, vol. 1, p. 194.] Question 1. "Michael and his angels fought against the Dragon and his angels." What is the "Dragon," exactly?

H.P.B.: The "Dragon" is so many things, my beloved brethren, that my answer depends on what you mean by the question. In which of the seven symbolical meanings do you want me to explain it? If your answer refers to Revelation, then I cannot answer it, as I would have to tread on forbidden grounds — not because I am a Christian — St. John's Revelation is not a Christian work, but is simply the Christianized form of prophecy, which is universal — and I can assure you it is one of the most occult things for anyone who understands it. Now, astronomically, of course, in one sense — for there are several — the "Dragon" is the Moon producing an eclipse over the Sun. This you all know, and astrologists more than any anyone else. Mystically, in general, it is matter or the lower self. It was called the "Dragon" over which the Sun's spirit, or the higher self, triumphed during the trials of initiation. Now the third meaning, also an occult meaning, is in *The Secret Doctrine*, and in connection with the allegorical "fall." The "Dragon" symbolized the sons of wisdom incarnating in humanity, and thus hurled into the Hell of matter, which is our bodies, because there is no Hell outside of our own dear persons here. It is humanity, and on this Earth, that is Hell, and nowhere else. Four, in esoterical allegorical history the "Dragon" represents the secret wisdom which was obscured and driven from the field by the dead letter of dogma in ritualism; while five, Christian theology has availed itself of all these Pagan legends to build up the dogma of "Satan," the foremost pillar of the Christian religious scheme, because if there were not devils there would be no Christian religion. Take away the Devil, and what will remain? Why should Christ come to have saved, and who would he have saved? So that the Devil really is the great prop of Christianity, and so you must, everyone of you who feels like it, have a great reverence for the Devil. This is my advice to you all; I do not suppose any of you will accept it.

Mr. B. Keightley: Then further on you compare the cosmogony of the old Gnostics with that of the "Secret Doctrine," and you speak about the "Seven Stellars." Question 2, page 195: The "Seven Stellars," being the product of the Astral Light and blind Matter, must be evil. Is, then, the influence of the seven planets all evil as far as man is concerned?

H.P.B.: I do not think so. Why should you go and insult the poor planets? The term planets here does not refer to the seven sacred planets at all, but means simply they are planetary bodies within our system. If the expression is erroneous or leads to any equivocation, in the second edition you have only to make a mark there and change it. But this is what it means. The seven bad Stellars are the progeny of Saturn and the Moon. That is to say, corruptness in the Nazarenes representing in one sense blind, frantic matter ever devouring its own progeny, is identical with Saturn; while [...], the mother of that [...], in the Nazarenes is the Moon, at the same time that she is the lower Astral Light. Some mystics assert that these seven bad Stellars are represented by seven moons, though there are eight. There is an old Coptic[1] legend which related how the mother, or the Moon, after her union and junction with her son, Saturn, in order to prevent him from devouring his own children cast him down on to the earth, where they became the seven capital sons. It is they who are credited with the building of everything material on the Earth. Even western astrologers are familiar with the evil effects of the junction of Saturn with the Moon. Now, Mr. Old, tell us something about that. In what way is it bad?

Mr. Old: It has so many renderings, and the influences are so various, it depends entirely upon the radical tendency to take that particular form of evil — as for instance, the corrupt tendencies at birth, which you understand is nothing less than the Karmic horoscope. If the tendency were towards martial or inflammatory evils and diseases and rash precipitous forms of mind, then of course they would not come in the same degree under the influence of Saturn. But if you were predisposed to melancholia and so catch cold and so suffer all those evils which arise out of adjustment and contraction, frigidity, then you would come remarkably under the influence of Saturn at the time of this junction and according to the position in your own Karmic map,

---

[1] **Copts** — an ethnoreligious group primarily indigenous to Egypt and Sudan, one of the oldest Christian communities in the world.

then you would suffer accordingly. So that you see it depends entirely upon the angular distance with respect to the space of the birth, and then also the sign of the zodiac from which it transpires.

H.P.B.: In astrology I believe there are many good things, only somehow or other they do not reckon as we do. Of course it comes to the same results; but there is a difference.

Mr. B. Keightley: Saturn is regarded in astrology as the most evil-producing of all the planets.

Mr. Old: Certainly. And at the same time, you know, it has been said that the origin of the name is [...], the pure fire. So that he has a reverse aspect also; whereas he is the great evil, he is also the great good, in this sense.

H.P.B.: Just like the Hindu Shiva. He is destructive because he is the regenerative power; because a seed cannot come to life unless it first perishes, he destroys only to regenerate.

Mr. Old: I noticed that particularly when you spoke of the Dragons — that is to say, the [...], the eighth sign of the zodiac, which corresponds to the eighth house of death; and you know eight is a very bad number.

Mr. B. Keightley: Well! It is all matter, matter, matter.

Mr. Old: And while you said that, I have no doubt they also noticed it was also the symbol of archaic wisdom.

H.P.B.: Well, the "Dragons" are, which I will give you here by and by — all the "Dragons" were the emblems. They called the sons of the "Dragons," the initiates. In China, also where the "Dragon" is the symbol of power and the symbol of the Imperial family, the "Dragons" are considered very high beings. It is an allegory.

Mr. Old: I suppose the New Testament assertion is a Gnostic assertion? [Quotes from the Testament.]

H.P.B.: Most assuredly.

Mr. B. Keightley: Question 3, page 199: "The older wheels rotated downward and upward..." Does the expression "rotated downward and upward" refer to the outbreathing, which occupies the first half of any Manvantara, and the "inbreathing," which takes place in its second half? Or does it refer to the direction of the rotation which takes place about the Laya centres, upon which the wheels are formed?

H.P.B.: It refers to neither and to both and so much more, which I cannot give out now. You will have to wait for it. Have patience a little.

Mr. B. Keightley: Question 4. You say that man must awaken the three "seats" to life and activity. Do you mean by this phrase that the three "seats" have no life and activity on their own planes, *i.e. per se*, or, merely, that our human consciousness on this plane must be awakened to perceive and reflect their activity?

H.P.B.: It refers to what is said in *The Secret Doctrine*, and very plainly; whatever the three higher "seats" in cosmos may be, the three corresponding higher "seats" in man — whether we call them states or seats of consciousness, or principles — have to be awakened before they can be attuned to the three higher planes in cosmos. And once they are so attuned, the knowledge will reveal sufficiently what their sources and *fons et origo*[1] are. It is knowledge enough. Besides which, *The Secret Doctrine* teems with this. And I am not going to answer things that *The Secret Doctrine* explains. If you who put the questions do not choose to read *The Secret Doctrine*, I am not going to repeat it like a poll parrot, because it is perfectly useless asking me questions that are impossible of explanation. Ask me questions that are dark then I am perfectly ready and at your service, but not to say things which have been a great deal better put in *The Secret Doctrine* than I can give you.

Mr. Old: You see, H.P.B., I had some little hand in formulating that question. You see, it leaves us in the dark to a certain extent; because, although perhaps reference is found and full information given elsewhere, still in confining ourselves to respectable limits for one evening it did not give me the idea that there was any activity *per se*.

H.P.B.: Where? In the human "seats," or the cosmic "seats"?

Mr. Old: In the human, because you speak of that being awakened.

H.P.B.: Certainly, there are none. But once that they are awakened, they must be attuned to the seats of the cosmic planes, or else I can assure you it won't produce good results, because the man will

---

[1] **Fons et origo** (*Latin*) — the source and origin of something.

become a Frankenstein Jr.[2] — everything that is horrid. For those are the rare cases when the higher powers are awakened and put to bad use by matter, which is so intensely stronger that it forces a man into the worst of vices and black magic and therefore he ends in Avichi. These are the rare cases that are spoken about in *Esoteric Buddhism*.

Mr. B. Keightley: It is what Sinnett calls "evil spirituality."

Mr. Old: Does the elevation of the spiritual consciousness precede or come after the awakening? Or is it the cause of the awakening?

H.P.B.: The cause of awakening depends a good deal upon the higher Manas, and how it perceives the universe, and how it can discern right from the wrong — for the man has the faculty in him of discerning, really, that which is wrong universally (I do not mean about Mrs. Grundy's code of honour). Then he can attune his seats with those on the higher cosmic plane. And then he becomes at one with Nature; he becomes a co-worker with Nature, he helps Nature, and therefore Nature helps him. But, gentlemen, unfortunately, the three — excepting persons who lead very high lives — this certainly don't awaken. There is the higher Manas, the intelligence in man in the physical brain. We see plenty of intellectual men, but they are nothing but — they are higher intellectual animals. They have no spirituality in them.

Mr. Old: Would not you rather say then it is the men, the individuals, who don't awaken to the existence of these three higher principles — not the principles which awaken?

H.P.B.: I never said the cosmic seats have to be awakened. Perhaps it is badly put; it is the fault of the editors. You see, I don't understand the value of the English language, and I had about six or seven editors, and they have made a nice mess of it. For me it is perfectly written. Now, if I happen to have written it in such a way as to lead into error, it is the right thing to make a sign or mark and correct it in the second edition.

Mr. B. Keightley: I think it is to a certain extent expressed, because she says here: "It remains with him to attune the three higher states

---

[2] **Frankenstein** — a scientist in Mary Shelley's 1818 novel, *Frankenstein or the Modern Prometheus*, who creates a monster that eventually destroys him. People often refer to the creature as Frankenstein, too.

in himself. ... But before he can attune these states he must awaken the "seats" to life and activity."[1]

H.P.B.: It is not the "seats" at all in cosmos. It is just the same as if you told me that a mosquito could influence the Himalayas.

Mr. Old: You mean to say their correspondences on this plane have to be awakened.

H.P.B.: Most assuredly.

Mr. Kingsland: If you said, instead of "seats," "sense" or "principles," there would be no confusion. I don't think seats is quite a good word.

H.P.B.: Why don't you put it for the second or third edition.

Mr. Kingsland: Even "sense" would be a better word than "seats."

Mr. B. Keightley: It is the occult words.

H.P.B.: "Seats" means vehicles.

Mr. B. Keightley: It is put in converted commas.

Mr. Old: We are quite right in saying that whether we know it or not, these three principles — Atman, Buddhi, and Buddhi-Manas — all have activity on their own planes.

H.P.B.: They have, but not with respect to man. They don't influence, so to say, the lower quaternary, which is the personal man. They have certainly their activity, but it does not influence, and therefore the lower quaternary remains the animal, the personality, that is for eating and drinking, and selfishness and money-making, and political things and so on. I wish them joy.

Mr. B. Keightley: Question 5, page 200: In the diagram, Hod[2] and Netzach[3] are figured as lying on two planes at once, which is not the case for the corresponding "globes" in the eastern system. Is this intentional?

H.P.B.: It is done not intentionally, but because it was a thing of necessity. We live in a three-dimensional space, and a certain limited set of geometrical figures are given to us. The Hod and Netzach are not on two planes at once; but as a sphere cannot be well put

---

[1] *The Secret Doctrine*, vol. 1, p. 199.
[2] **Hod** (*Hebrew*, "splendour") — the eighth of the ten Sephiroth, a female passive potency.
[3] **Netzach** (*Hebrew*, "victory") — the seventh of the ten Sephiroth, a masculine active potency.

astride on a straight line otherwise than by seeming on two planes, how could I do it? The diagram could not be done otherwise, if the orthodox Kabbalistic arrangement had to be retained at all. I tried to retain it, and I could not do otherwise. Mind you, I take the seven lower Sephiroth, I do not take the whole ten. I leave others, as I don't mention them here. They put the whole ten on four planes: the archetypal world, the intellectual, and so on; I could not do it because we have a thing of seven, therefore I had to come and cram these in. Moreover, remembering that the Sephiroth letter is on four planes, and composed of ten Sephiroth and in the Kabbalah, how could one arrange the thing otherwise, when only the seven lower Sephiroth were used? The Chaldean Kabbalah, moreover, the Book of Numbers, agrees perfectly with the eastern arrangement, and disagrees with the present orthodox Kabbalah in its diagrams. This is no fault of *The Secret Doctrine*. Now, look here: I had a rabbi who had the real Book of Numbers — and there is another; I have only seen two in my life, and I don't think there exist more. He had fragments of the Chaldean Kabbalah. With that, when I came to take notes (I had large books), when I came to compare with the Rosenroth[4] translation, I saw they had changed it in the most wonderful way. How can you have the Kabbalah of […], when the Kabbalah was entirely lost in the 13th century? Moses de Leon,[5] who is accused of forgery — which is perfect nonsense — took all he could find. What did he do? He had, as so many links were missing, and so many things were lost, to go to the eastern Christians, and to the Chaldean Gnostics to ask them to help, since they had their own Kabbalah. And the result is, you find more of Christian eternity — the Virgin Mary, Joseph, etc. — than the wisdom of the old […]. That is the result. Now, in the Chaldean Kabbalah, in the Book of Numbers, you have the wisdom of the Hebrew initiates, but you have not got it in this; they have been so interfering with it, that Mr. Isaac Myer may say what he likes, and Mr. Mathers also; I say there is more flapdoodle than truth. There is a thing just

---

[4] **Christian Knorr von Rosenroth** (1636–1689) — a German Christian Kabbalist, who translated Hebrew texts into Latin and published them in the two-volume *Kabbala denudate* [Kabbalah Unveiled]. Its partial English translation was made by S. L. MacGregor Mathers in 1887 under the title *The Kabbalah Unveiled*.

[5] **Moses de Leon** (1240–1305) — a Spanish Rabbi and Kabbalist, who published the *Zohar*.

as Isaac Myer says; did you hear about him, Mr. Cobb,[1] of Mr. Isaac Myer, who wrote the *Qabbalah*?[2]

Mr. Cobb: I did not.

H.P.B.: He writes perfectly truly that the Kabbalah written there is one of the 11th century, which is written by Ben Judah. They thought the man an Arabic philosopher. Very well, he has these things perfectly. Many of his fragments are perfectly Kabbalistic, and just the same as the Chaldean Kabbalah; whereas you don't find it, if you compare it with the other. I say it is more than that.

Mr. Mead: These Chaldean Gnostics, are they the Gnostics of [...]?

H.P.B.: Yes, they had dogma enough to throw everything into confusion, and that is why you find now that by the methods, by these Gematrias, you can do anything you like; you can find in the Kabbalah Washington and the President of the United States: you can find anything in the Kabbalah.

Mr. Kingsland: Are there any more questions with reference to this diagram?

Mr. B. Keightley: There is a question relating to the note to the diagram. Question 6. (Note to diagram.) Can you define more clearly the term "Cosmic Consciousness"?

H.P.B.: It is an easy question, this. "Cosmic Consciousness" has been defined hundreds of times in *The Secret Doctrine* as the collective or aggregate consciousness of those Dhyanis, or Dhyan-Chohans, called the builders of the universe, physical and spiritual, or that which the Masons call — making a plurality of unity — the architects or the G.A.O.T.U., so that the Cosmic Consciousness will come after.

Mr. Kingsland: There is a question which I had here.

Mr. Keightley: Page 199, last paragraph. You have spoken of "these seven planes (which) correspond to the seven states of (human) consciousness in man," and in the note, the second note to the diagram, you say "the seven states of human consciousness pertain to quite another question." Speaking of the diagram you say, "these are the

---

[1] **John Storer Cobb** (1838–1904) — a lawyer and the treasurer of the Theosophical Society in New York. In 1878, he organized the first local division of the Society in London.

[2] **Isaac Myer** (1836–1902) — an attorney and the author of *Qabbalah* (Philadelphia, 1888).

four lower planes of Cosmic Consciousness … the seven states of human consciousness pertain to quite another question." These two quotations appear to contradict each other. What then is the connection between the seven planes as given in the diagram, and the seven states of consciousness? And what is the "other question"?

H.P.B.: Ah! But you see, you want me to give you three volumes, and I cannot give it to you. Remember only one thing, that the seven states of consciousness in man are not only states of consciousness as Herbert Spencer understands it, but also the feeling, the consciousness of the ego. For instance, I am smoking a cigarette, and I am pitching into you, and so on. There are many states of consciousness. Those states of which I speak belong to one order, and others to another. I don't mean to say they are not the same, but there is an infinite gradation in all of them. Now, there are the higher states of metaphysical consciousness. Can you compare it with the consciousness I have of having taken a cigarette, and smoking it?

Mr. Kingsland: What is the order of those states of consciousness, which refer to those seven planes? It will all come in analogy. If you read it afterwards, you will find it all dovetails.

Mr. B. Keightley: I don't know whether this is legitimate, but it is what struck me. The seven states of human consciousness are practically seven states of consciousness on the terrestrial plane.

H.P.B.: There is a consciousness while we sleep — during sleep, and a consciousness while we are awake. There is a consciousness when we look mechanically at something. There is one consciousness that takes in external objects, and the other goes wool-gathering. There are many degrees of consciousness; you cannot go and call consciousness all one.

Mr. B. Keightley: Yet get to this, the seven planes of Cosmic Consciousness.

H.P.B.: There is consciousness that I am positively in India with this lamp, and here I am in the North Pole.

Mr. B. Keightley: I think there is where the distinction lies, that the seven human states are analogous to the seven cosmic states, but they cover a very much smaller range.

Mr. Kingsland: The fact of the matter is, there are seven states of consciousness on each of the seven planes.

H.P.B.: You remember what Cobb said the other day. He began to give us the mathematical series that never ended. There was some seventh question that I got mad over, and which has been asked hundreds of times. I said this has been stated very clearly in *The Secret Doctrine*, and I refuse to answer questions that have been already in previous writings, and are in *The Secret Doctrine*, and have been stated on Thursdays. I refuse to pass time on Thursday nights in more repetition.

Mr. B. Keightley: Well, question 8. Question 8, page 200: In occultism, are the terms "seed" and "atom" synonymous?

H.P.B.: There, there! Isn't that the same thing?

Mr. B. Keightley: You give a hint there as to the question we have been hunting after a good deal: the real meaning of the word "atom."

H.P.B.: You are the most inquisitive people I ever met. If it were not your unmentionables that protect you, you would all be Mother Eves, every one of you! You are the most inquisitive people I ever saw in my life, and you are the most impertinent. You cannot come and ask one thing after another, Tuesday after Monday, Wednesday after Tuesday, and so on. You want to jump from Monday to Saturday and from Saturday to Halifax. Upon my word, I have no patience.

Mr. B. Keightley: Question 9, page 201: Can you give us some more definite idea — *e.g.*, an analogy on the physical plane — of what is meant here by "Cosmic Desire" which "evolves into absolute Light"?

H.P.B.: Now there is a question for a modest young woman. The answer is found even in Hesiod's[1] cosmogony. What is the use of attempting to learn occultism and eastern esoteric philosophy, if one is not acquainted with the exoteric classics? The reply to this is stated in *The Secret Doctrine*. Now I am going to examine you. Have you read Hesiod's cosmogony, Old?

Mr. Old: No.

H.P.B.: Have the goodness to go to the British Museum, and read it. Mr. Cobb has read it. If you have not read it, what can I do?

---

[1] **Hesiod** — an ancient Greek poet and philosopher who lived around the 8th century BCE. His major work, *Theogony*, describes the genealogy and myths of the Greek gods and also expounds cosmogony.

Nevertheless, I will attempt to explain it again in a few words. Take Hesiod, and try and understand what he says, and better still, [...] Phoenician cosmogony. There you will find that what [...] calls pure force is the principle of creation. It is identical with Brahma's will to create, which you have read many times in the *Vishnu Purana*. In the primitive world cosmogonies, Chaos is not what it became later on, or that on which the Spirit of God moved on the waters. It is not the [...] of Ovid,[2] matter in its inert and confused or chaotic state. Chaos was space, according to Aristotle, gaping space or the void — *kenon*,[3] and after Hesiod, Chaos is absolutely limitless, it is the dark shore-less cloud of vapours, which gives birth to the universe. Now, if you remember that the first of the three primordial elements at the first flutter of differentiation were and are with Hesiod, Chaos, and, with Eros,[4] elements that were never conceived (as they were co-existent potentiality in all eternity), you will perhaps understand that which I say, that no more than primordial Venus was Eros — that which both became in later ages. Now Eros means simply human love, and

---

[2] **Ovid** or **Ovidius** (43 BCE–17/18 CE) — a Roman poet who wrote *Metamorphoses*, a narrative poem that chronicles the history of the world.

[3] **Kenon** (*Greek*, "empty") — a pure void, *e.g.* nothingness.

[4] **Eros** (*Greek*, "love") — Hesiod makes of the god Eros the third personage of the Hellenic primordial Trinity composed of Ouranos (Uranos), Gaia and Eros. It is the personified procreative Force in nature in its abstract sense, the propeller to creation and procreation. Exoterically, mythology makes of Eros the god of lustful, animal desire; hence, the term *erotic*. Esoterically, it is different. Eros is the same as Kamadeva, the god of love in the Hindu Pantheon. As the Eros of Hesiod was degraded into Cupid by exoteric law, and still more degraded by a later popular sense attributed to the term, so is Kama a most mysterious and metaphysical subject. The earlier Vedic description of Kama alone gives the keynote to what he emblematizes. Kama is the first conscious, *all embracing desire* for universal good, love, and for all that lives and feels, needs help and kindness; the first feeling of infinite tender compassion and mercy that arose in the consciousness of the creative One Force as soon as it came into life and being as a ray from the Absolute. Says the *Rig Veda*, "Desire first arose in *It*, which was the primal germ of mind, and which Sages, searching with their intellect, have discovered in their heart to be the bond which connects Entity with non-Entity," or *Manas* with pure *Atma-Buddhi*. There is no idea of sexual love in the conception. Kama is pre-eminently the divine desire of creating happiness and love; and it is only ages later, as mankind began to materialize, by anthropomorphization, its grandest ideals into cut and dried dogmas, that Kama became the power that gratifies desire on the animal plane.

worse; but then it meant the most solemn metaphysical and divine thing. Eros was not at the beginning the wily God of Love and passion with wings and arrows to wound the hearts of sentimental ninnies with. There were no such fools, nor yet men enough; but he who is now God of human love was simply an abstract idea, and image of the Divine creative force — that universal force of attraction which causes particles to congregate, combine, and correlate, and to produce a triad. Well, that creative force is our Fohat, who neither creates, nor does he produce anything *per se* and by himself, but in virtue of his action, elements, as well as beings, seek to unite in polarity; from which unison results life. Remember that in the first cosmogony out of Chaos are born Erebus[1] and Nox,[2] primordial and already differentiated darkness divided into two principles, male and female, from which two emanate the other two, Æther[3] and Hemera,[4] in the light of the superior regions and that inferior or terrestrial atmosphere. Light is born of darkness number two, darkness on the differentiated plane, and that darkness begets light under the influence of creative love, or that which is called there "cosmic desire"; or again Fohat, the electric creative principles which make of all one, and which produces the three, the correlation.

Mr. B. Keightley: What you have said there is very good, and it is a great deal more than you have said anywhere in *The Secret Doctrine.*

H.P.B.: But I thought you stood there over me when I was writing.

Mr. Mead: Eros was always first-born of the Gods.

H.P.B.: Eros is the first-born — he is not the first-born, he is coeval. Chaos, Eros and Gaia[5] are coeval, therefore none of these three elements are conceived, they are simply co-existent in eternity; only at the moment of differentiation they manifest themselves. That is to say,

---

[1] **Erebus** (*Greek*, "gloom") — the personification of darkness in Greek mythology.

[2] **Nox** (Greek, "night") — the goddess and personification of night in Greek mythology.

[3] **Æther** (*Greek*, "brightness") — the personification of the light of the superior heavenly spheres in Greek mythology.

[4] **Hemera** (*Greek*, "day") — the personification of day and of the light of the inferior or terrestrial regions in Greek mythology.

[5] **Gaia** (*Greek*, "earth") — Primordial Matter in the cosmogony of Hesiod; Earth, as some think; the wife of Ouranos, the sky or heavens. The female personage of the primeval Trinity, composed of Ouranos, Gaia and Eros.

out of the subjective and the non-being comes being, and then after that they begin to come on each other and react. This is the polarity, this electrical force, to which belongs our blood and life and anything. It is life, in short. This is cosmic desire.

Mr. Mead: Cupid[6] is simply the lower aspect.

H.P.B.: Take Hesiod's cosmogony, and see the enormous difference there is between what Hesiod says and what later on the mythologies have invented. Even a few hundred years before our era, then it was a most sublime thing, and pretended to the mysteries. And now they made of it — I don't know what.

Mr. ——: How can Gaia be said to be coeval?

H.P.B.: Ask Hesiod; take him by the beard.

Mr. B. Keightley: It means the abstract.

H.P.B.: The female portion in Chaos.

Mr. Mead: The Earth that no one has seen.

Mr. Old: There was just that word "absolute" that I have not, and if they made it in connection with that, this absolute appears to be the effect of cosmic desire. Well now, the idea of the absolute as we postulate it…

H.P.B.: Why do you use the word absolute?

Mr. B. Keightley: It evolves into absolute light.

H.P.B.: On the manifested plane; if we take it metaphysically again, I say the Christians can make it into perfect light. When I say "Absolute" I quote it or underline it. But when I put absolute, I just use the expression as perfect.

Mr. B. Keightley: Absolute light of the manifested plane.

Mr. Old: But Eros, or Lucifer,[7] any one aspect, is that light?

H.P.B.: Certainly it is.

---

[6] **Cupid** (*Latin,* "passionate desire") — the god of desire and love in Roman mythology.

[7] **Lucifer** (*Latin,* "Light-Bearer") — the bright "Morning Star." Before Milton, Lucifer had never been a name of the Devil. Quite the reverse, since the Christian Saviour is made to say of himself in Revelation 22:16: "I am … the bright morning star" or Lucifer. One of the early Popes of Rome bore that name; and there was even a Christian sect in the 4th century which was called the *Luciferians.*

Mr. B. Keightley: Then you go on to say this: "now light without any shadow would be absolute light," etc. [Reads from *The Secret Doctrine*, vol. 1, p. 201.] Question 10. The idea of "Fire" has usually been associated in mystic writings with *Spirit* rather than *Matter*. Can you tell us why you associate it here with the latter?

H.P.B.: Because I am not a mystic writer, and I try to make you understand things a little less misty than they are. And you instead of thanking me, criticize me. The physical, or the material and finite universe, is the shadow thrown upon the screen or illusion or Maya by eternal light, or the universal fire. It symbolizes with every nation the creative deity. Primordial matter is not our dense matter, but spirit; hence the spirit of creative fire, or heat, or cosmic desire again. How can you dissociate fire from matter, any more than spirit from matter? Can you do it, when the latter spirit or matter is materialized spirit, and spirit is potentially matter? That is what we say in occultism. If mystic writings held less to poetry and fantastic imagery, and a little more to plain statement of fact, they would be less misty, and those who study them more positive than they are now about the real end of things. Fire is spirit and fire is matter, and if a particle of the London slush can be found without the two qualities, fire and spirit, then mankind had better accept at once the anthropomorphic idea of the Church Fathers, and the dead letter of the Bible, and not its philosophy. You cannot come and say what the mystic writers could write in those days, when for every truth it was said there was immediately an inquisition, and so many cardinals to burn and roast you. Now you won't find mystic writers; now it is time to state plain facts, because there is no one to burn them any more — except after death.

Mr. B. Keightley: In this little extract from the commentaries, speaking about the world germs and so on, you say... [Reads from *The Secret Doctrine*.] Question 11. It is said that "the older (bodies) attract the younger, while others repel them."[1] What are these "others" here spoken of, and why should it be the *older* bodies that attract?

H.P.B.: I suppose they are wiser, less green than others. On this I can say no more than is given in *The Secret Doctrine*. There is such a thing as attraction and repulsion, and in occultism it stands in the place of gravity, the scientific teachings about which we reject. This

---

[1] *The Secret Doctrine*, vol. 1, p. 201.

belongs to occult physics, before the turn of which comes for us on Thursday evenings the 20th century must have dawned. I give you everything I can give; don't you ask me for more.

Mr. Old: Then I suppose occultism recognizes an attraction which has no relation to bulk. It overthrows the accepted Western idea.

H.P.B.: If I have one thing well in my memory it is the 20, 30, perhaps 100 conversations we had with Mr. Cobb, sitting there. When it came out here with the fourth-dimensional space — which was ridiculous, because the fourth-dimensional space, taken simply, means the fall of matter through matter, the impenetrability of matter — and we had many conversations; and he knows perfectly well in occultism no one believes in this gravity question. We believe attraction and repulsion. Is it not so, Mr. Cobb?

Mr. Cobb: I believe it is so.

H.P.B.: You remember what conversations we had in New York? And you were the first one who said it.

Mr. Cobb: I do not know about that, I am sure.

H.P.B.: You said always it was attraction and repulsion.

Mr. Cobb: I did not know I was the first, at all.

H.P.B.: Well, it is the old occult axiom.

Mr. B. Keightley: Question 12, page 202: In these pages you distinctly state that, even in the higher phases of cosmic evolution, there rages a "struggle for existence." Now it is on this struggle for existence, regarded as a universal law, that the materialists base their justification of human selfishness. We would therefore ask: (a)

Where does this "struggle" for existence" cease: (1) in reference to the cosmos; (2) as regards humanity? (b) How is it that this cosmic law is suspended by that of altruism in the case of human beings?

H.P.B.: The struggle for existence rages universally in sidereal as in terrene spaces. This is the first fundamental law in nature, the visible effects of which materialistic science has called correlation of physical forces in matter. But this applies only and solely to differentiated matter; it has nothing to do with individual or even personal units, which ought to be, if they are not, guided by the higher laws of the upper triad and not by the instinctual impulses acting on the plane of the lower quaternary. The struggle for existence begins with the physical molecules and ends with those animals which are quite irrational. This is therefore no justification for human selfishness, as man is an animal on a higher plane of being and consciousness than is the animal. The man is a higher animal and on a higher plane of consciousness than the animal; even the most abject savage is. I answer with regard to physical cosmos; the struggle will come to an end only with the coming of Pralaya. With respect to its living and conscious beings, however, the [...] ceases to operate at that human stage where consciousness and reason make their appearance. It is in man alone that the higher divine triad may be fully active, but this triad is trinity in unity, and unity or homogeneity characterizes the plane of its action. In the four lower planes of cosmos, on the contrary, it is the law of diversity and heterogeneity which reign supreme. Hence those beings who are endowed with the higher triad come under its laws, not under those of the lower quaternary, which act only upon those beings, atoms or things in which rationality is still an underdeveloped potentiality. Therefore, since true law of being is unity, the higher self in him, it follows that the individual human being can only attain his complete and perfect development by acting in perfect unity, that is to say harmony, with all other men. Now (b). The struggle for existence which exists today among men proves only that firstly, man has not yet fully emerged from his savage animal condition, his Manas not yet being fully developed in this our Fourth Round, for it will be only in the fifth; and secondly, that the great men of learning who proclaim selfishness as the great law of human life are, their learning and intellect notwithstanding, not on a much higher plane themselves. In other words, these learned gentlemen are still animals. Whoever wants to go and tell them, let them. What have you got to say? Are you going to take up the defense of the men of learning — of the F.R.S's[1] and so on?

Mr. Kingsland: There is a question of mine that rather bears upon that, if I might read it.

H.P.B.: Do please.

Mr. Kingsland: Is it the case that no human being, Adept, or initiate can progress during the present round beyond what humanity will be at the close of the Seventh Race, or can they progress as far as what

---

[1] F.R.S. stands for Fellows of the Royal Society, the British national academy of sciences.

humanity will be at the close of the Seventh *Round*? Is there not some
limit beyond which they cannot progress as individuals, but must wait
for the development of humanity as a whole?

H.P.B.: Assuredly, the Seventh *Round*. They cannot — the greatest
Adepts cannot. When I say the word Adepts in the plural, it is too
bumptious. I have heard of one only, or two — one at the beginning
of each age that may progress and be in that state in which man will
be in the Seventh Round; beyond that they cannot. No one can go
beyond his Manvantara, not the highest Adepts.

Mr. Kingsland: Then that is really the basis of everyone helping
humanity. It is really helping themselves?

H.P.B.: Most assuredly. It is the most logical thing and the plain-
est in the world. People will not understand that by hurting their
neighbours they hurt themselves. If it is not now, it will be in another
incarnation. Of course if you don't believe in it, it is another thing.
But if you believe in it, it will be so, because if I hurt this finger the
whole of my body will feel it. I may neglect it, but it may come in five
years, because not the smallest little things remain without effects.
Our universe is a concatenation of causes and effects. There is not
the smallest thing that we can do to our brothers or neighbours —
or even persons — that we won't suffer for, and the whole humanity
also. It is just the same when you disturb an enormous pool of water;
if you disturb but in one place, then every drop of water in that pool
will feel it; there will be reaction. I say that this selfishness of races,
of individuals; of diversity of religion; of everything, this is the great
curse not only of the 19th century, but it will last so long as we do not
change or become a little better than we are. But this humanity here,
nothing can be compared with. No imagination can create devils in
hell as bad and as wicked as humanity is on the whole. Every race hates
the other. One race goes and spits on the other; another says: "I am
the one." It is something terrible to look at. Man, instead of becoming
better spiritually every day, becomes worse and worse and worse. This
selfishness that you think — "everything for me" — it is a thing which
hurts you first and most; this will be proven to you logically as 2 and
2 make 4; it cannot fail to do so. When they come and speak to me
about a struggle, I say, the materialists go and say: "The struggle for
existence is the great law; therefore let us go and annex a country, as

the Russians go and annex places"; but you begin by putting stuff in your guns and shooting out of them at these unfortunate people — as they did last year in Burma, where about 200 were shot. That is the brotherly love; and they call themselves Christians. Good Heavens! Why, they are devils, all of them! They are not human beings, all those who go and make war and kill people and hurt everyone.

Mr. Old: But apart from any efforts that we may make either individually or as a race, is there not a law in the human universe which prescribes our making a certain advance? Is there no law which limits our advance during a certain age?

H.P.B.: There are certain boundaries; you cannot go further. Nobody expects you to become omniscient gods all at once, or angels and the kindest men; but there are limits, that the more civilization progresses the more man becomes wicked and selfish and the more it is the poor who suffer on account of the rich. The misery and the suffering never was greater on this Earth than it is in the 19th century, which is the accursed age among all ages.

Mr. Hall: I suppose there will be a reaction?

H.P.B.: And the reaction will be a terrible one. Look at the socialists. It is the highest and the noble-minded; notwithstanding their efforts, it is the anarchism that is produced. And when the time comes that the people starve wholesale everywhere, I can assure you there is no law that will be able to impede the movement.

Mr. Hall: Do you think it will ever come?

H.P.B.: You have great faith in your 10,000 policemen. Fortunately the time has not come yet. If they go on as they do it is something terrible. I don't mean England alone. Show to me the country where people are not starving. With every new invention that comes, there are several who become millionaires, and in proportion there are so many thousands who starve. That seems to be the law.

Mr. Hall: I should not think the reaction will be quite so severe as that. It will be met through legislation.

H.P.B.: I invite you to read my editorial in *Lucifer*.[1] I have poured all my heart there, and I can assure you I did not pay them compliments.

---

[1] See H. P. Blavatsky, "Our Cycle and the Next," *Collected Writings*, vol. 11 (Wheaton, IL: Theosophical Publishing House, 1973), pp. 186–202.

They may abuse me as much as they like. For me and for every Theosophist there ought to be no distinction between races, colour, creed, ideas or anything.

A Lady: There ought to be.

H.P.B.: But there is, unfortunately. Look at the Anglo-Indians;[2] look at the supreme contempt they show for the Hindus who are intellectually and spiritually a thousand times higher than we are. "Inferior race." Inferior for what? Why, Englishmen were not even in the state of molecules in space when India was old with wisdom, and they come and speak about the Hindus being an inferior race! Now this is that pride of which it is spoken in the Bible, and I verily believe all you English say you were the fallen angels. Every one of you are devils from your wickedness.

Mr. Kingsland: Is it not possible for the different races to incarnate in another race? May we not have been Indians on previous incarnations?

H.P.B.: Yes; or you would not be as you are. You are sure to be, all of you who are so proud — I tell Sinnett every day that I see him, he is sure to be an outcast in India for his sins. And he does not like it at all.

Mr. B. Keightley: Question 13, page 204: The nuclei of cosmic matter after generation take elliptic and parabolic courses. The former, owing to their inferior velocity, are generally absorbed by suns, whereas the latter escape absorption by their greater velocity. Can any explanation be given of this original difference of velocity, on which the whole future evolution of the "nucleus" depends?

H.P.B.: The velocity with which a nucleus starts on its sidereal career depends in the first place upon the "hour" of its birth. By hour I mean the stage or period of the universal life cycle at which it starts upon its life pilgrimage. Of these stages there are seven to which the Brahmins refer as the seven creations, and which in Genesis are called the six but ought to be called the seven days of creation. Now, if you ask me why the seven days and not the six, I answer because the seventh day which is described in Genesis as the day of rest really represents the seventh stage of creation. It is not one of full rest or inactivity, but simply represents that period when everything has been harmonized and came into equilibrium, and when the evolutionary impulse has

[2] **Anglo-Indian** — a person of British descent or birth living in India.

slackened down to a uniform rate of motion and everything assumed
an orderly and uninterrupted and regular course, as is exhibited to us
in the regular succession of years, seasons, months, weeks, days, etc.
All those chaotic forces which have been in their impulse struggling
for life came down and settled; and there is the first day of rest when
everything went in the orderly way. This is what I mean. Now, the
seventh day, really, taking it occultly, means the seventh Manvantara;
that is, the day when everything has evoluted in this life cycle, and
everything will come to a point and everyone will be as good as the
other, and there will be no more backbiting and no more hitting of
each other's noses, and we will be decent people, then. The Pralaya is
the seventh day. The Pralaya is called generally the evening of the day
of the Seventh Round; and then it will last as long as the whole. If you
go and read the old rabbinical books and all those things of Babylonia,
you will find the idea stated perfectly well. Why is it that the Sadducees[1] did not believe as the Pharisees did? Because they were learned
occultists and kabbalists; they observed Sabbath, but they understood
what the meaning of Sabbath was perfectly philosophically. Because
look at this Babylonian treatise and you find that it means the seventh
period and that it means — well, it is a perfectly astronomical thing,
but it is just what the Brahmins called the seventh creation, as it is
seventh day and nothing else.

Mr. Kingsland: In Genesis it says the evening and morning were
the seventh day.

H.P.B.: It is the Manvantaric dawn and Pralaya, as well.

Mr. Kingsland: Just the same as we count the day as the day and
the night.

Mr. B. Keightley: Have you not got something more?

H.P.B.: The creative impulse has settled down to quiet family life
for a time. Consequently, the initial velocity of the nucleus depends
upon the place it occupies in the series of descending generations from
the primordial mother or matter. Mother and matter are the same,
and now some dark disciples who know what I mean may explain
further. There is one [pointing to Mr. B Keightley] who has learned

---

[1] **Sadducees** (*Hebrew*) — a sect of the learned men of Jerusalem, who held the
highest offices, such as of high priests and judges.

enough to have forgotten half of it, but I would like to know if he has forgotten the other half.

Mr. B. Keightley: What that means is this: if you take the very beginning of the Manvantara, you get from the descendants of primordial matter the first animated cosmic nuclei; then after that they pass through their Manvantara, and they become, first comets, then suns and then planets; then they die and their principles are transferred to a fresh Laya centre, which are like the children of the first generation. Then they pass through their series of evolutions and are reborn again as the grandchildren, and so on through innumerable generations.

H.P.B.: You had better to have also about the mother-in-law!

Mr. B. Keightley: In each of these stages the impulse, as it were, gradually diminishes to a certain extent so that the velocity with which the Laya centre or cosmic nucleus starts on its career is diminished.

Mr. Mead: What was puzzling there was the elliptical and the parabolic orbit.

Mr. B. Keightley: Many comets have elliptical orbits. It is simply a question of the velocity, as it is stated here. Entirely a question of the initial velocity with which a nucleus starts. There are comets which have both elliptical and parabolic orbits.

H.P.B.: In the beginning there is always the impulse, and it goes quicker.

Mr. B. Keightley: There are several comets the return periods of which are well-known. They expect them back at certain periods, and look out for them. They have very elongated elliptical orbits of enormous concentricity. Other comets have arrived in parabolic orbits, and we shall never have the pleasure of seeing them again; they are gone. Look at any map of the Sun.

H.P.B.: I would like them to understand why the impulse is greater at the beginning and then slackens — because it sets into respectable form, and there are laws; and periodically it goes on seasons and years and so on which it did not before. Therefore it slackens. The motion is always there.

Mr. B. Keightley: "'The abodes of Fohat are many,' it is said," etc. [Reads from *The Secret Doctrine*, vol. 1, p. 204.] Question 14. "The ancients made the polar circles seven instead of two." Are we to assign four of these to the North Pole, and three to the South; or are the seven lokas counted from the equator, north and south?

H.P.B.: If I were you I would, every one of you, go and ask to become a critic in *The Saturday Review,*[1] because you are so crotchety. I now say this is not my fault, but as the proverb says: "seven cooks spoil the broth," so I had seven editors. I wrote and wrote and they took it and corrected; and so, if you please, there would be no mistakes. And the result is that they have allowed to pass such flapdoodles and corrected some that were well written, only "to better the English," and they have made a flapdoodle of it. And this is one of the flapdoodles, because it is not in this way that it ought to read. The sentence should be: "The ancients counted seven circles and at each pole" instead of one at each — instead of two; or to have said: "at every pole there is one"; but the Brahmins have counted seven at each.

Mr. Kingsland: Counting from the equator?

H.P.B.: The seven circles which are the seven steps of Meru are the seven below — are the seven hells, as they call them.

Mr. Mead: The seven silver ones down, and the seven golden ones up.

Mr. B. Keightley: They divide the twenty-eight degrees from the Pole to the Arctic Circle into seven sets, each four degrees apart, which is not the whole space from the equator to the pole. From 0° to 28° latitude, that space is divided into seven circles, each four degrees apart.

Mr. Kingsland: I understood H.P.B. to say from the equator.

H.P.B.: The seven in the north and the seven in the south; not at the equator, at the poles.

Mr. B. Keightley: I will tell you where the expression is derived from. She is really referring to speculations by a man named Mackey.[2] Where you speak about Mackey is another place in *The Secret Doctrine.*[3]

---

[1] *The Saturday Review of Politics, Literature, Science, and Art* — a London weekly newspaper, published from 1855 to 1938.
[2] **Sampson Arnold Mackey** (1765–1843) — a Norwich self-taught astronomer, the author of *The Mythological Astronomy of the Ancients Demonstrated* (Norwich: R. Walker, 1823).
[3] See *The Secret Doctrine,* vol. 2, pp. 362, 431.

H.P.B.: It is written in such a way that it leads to entirely another thing. Modern science gives one ring, or pole, and the Brahmins gave seven to the top and seven to the South Pole. The southern pole represented the seven Narakas[4] in Patala;[5] but their idea of hell was not our idea. There it was a place of rejoicing. When [...] went to hell he said he never had a more pleasant time, just like one going now to the Paris Exhibition;[6] and he learned his wisdom, his astronomy there from Shesha,[7] the serpent of eternity on which Vishnu sleeps; and that serpent gave him hospitality and taught him astronomy magnificently. That is where you ought to go and learn.

Mr. Old: I want to know something about the division of the globe by the Hindus. Do they count five of our degrees to one of theirs, making 72 degrees instead of 360? Are you counting from the equator to the pole according to our degrees?

---

[4] **Naraka** (*Sanskrit*, "hell") — in the popular conception, a hell, a "prison under earth." The hot and cold hells, each eight in number, are simply emblems of the globes of our septenary chain, with the addition of the "eighth sphere" supposed to be located in the moon. This is a transparent blind, as these "hells" are called vivifying hells because, as explained, any being dying in one is immediately born in the second, then in the third, and so on; life lasting in each 500 years (a blind on the number of cycles and reincarnations). As these hells constitute one of the six *gati* (conditions of sentient existence), and as people are said to be reborn in one or the other according to their Karmic merits or demerits, the blind becomes self-evident. Moreover, these Narakas are rather purgatories than hells, since release from each is possible through the prayers and intercessions of priests for a consideration, just as in the Roman Catholic Church, which seems to have copied the Chinese ritualism in this pretty closely. As said before, esoteric philosophy traces every hell to life on earth, in one or another form of sentient existence.

[5] **Patala** (*Sanskrit*, "that which is below the feet") — the nether world, the antipodes; hence, in popular superstition, the infernal regions, and philosophically the two Americas, which are antipodal to India. Also, the South Pole, as standing opposite to Meru, the North Pole.

[6] **Exposition Universelle of 1889** — a world's fair held in Paris from 5 May to 31 October 1889, which attracted more than 32 million visitors. The Eiffel Tower was created for the exposition.

[7] **Shesha** (*Sanskrit*, "one who remains") — *Ananta*, the great Serpent of Eternity, the couch of Vishnu; the symbol of infinite Time in Space. In the exoteric beliefs, Shesha is represented as a thousand-headed and seven-headed cobra; the former the king of the nether world, called Patala, the latter the carrier or support of Vishnu on the Ocean of Space.

Mr. B. Keightley: Yes. You know the present Arctic Circle is 28 degrees. That space they divide into spaces of four degrees each; this is according to Arnold Mackey.

H.P.B.: But Mackey is perfectly wrong there. He is only right about the seven. But this fourteen is a flapdoodle, because he takes fourteen Manus, and these Manus have nothing to do with it. It is the seven steps of Meru.

Mr. B. Keightley: Mead has an idea in his head that these are counted from the equator. They are counted from the Pole.

H.P.B.: It is the Land of Bliss — and after that, when Asia was entirely formed, the last races of the Third Race, those that separated into males and females.

Mr. Kingsland: It was at that time the North Pole.

H.P.B.: It was simply the Meru, the Land of Bliss, the Land of the Gods, and you find references to this in Hesiod, where Apollo is said to go to Eternal Light and Eternal Day. It was a tropical country then. Where Greenland is now you had palm trees, laurels, and I don't know what.

Mr. B. Keightley: Remember this, Kingsland, that the axis of the Earth relatively to the Sun is fixed; it has the inclination to the ecliptic.

Mr. Kingsland: The inclination you thought [...] the tropics.

H.P.B.: All this changes twice every tropical year; everything is shifted, if you please. Every 12,500 or 12,600 years it changes.

Mr. Mead: Twice every tropical year, do you say?

H.P.B.: Yes, sir. Every 12,500 or 12,600 years.

Mr. Kingsland: Does this change take place gradually?

H.P.B.: Gradually! To what do you attribute the fact that the seas more and more encroach upon the earth? All this is that action. That there are continents that are sinking and the sea that is rising.

Mr. Kingsland: That is why we always get spring a month later.

H.P.B.: 12,000 years ago, the Earth was not as it is now.

Mr. Kingsland: I think twelve years ago it was not, either.

H.P.B.: Now it goes very rapidly. And it is time it should go and rest and give room to something better.

Mr. Mead: How much does this angle change by?

H.P.B.: This I could not tell you. I am not learned enough.

Mr. B. Keightley: Four degrees, I think, every sidereal year of 25,000 years.

H.P.B.: Old has studied it well.

Mr. Old: I gave it as well as I could in the [...]. What Mackey says would agree, because there are 28 degrees to be divided.

Mr. B. Keightley: Question 15. "As soon as a nucleus of primordial substance in the Laya state is informed by the freed principles of a just deceased sidereal body, it becomes a comet, then a sun, then a world."[1] Is the term "sidereal body" used in a general sense, as applying to all bodies in cosmos, or technically, to distinguish it from a planetary body?

H.P.B.: I use the term "sidereal body" in a general sense, as applying to bodies in cosmos in general. I do not give it any technical or special signification.

Mr. B. Keightley: Then page 205 you have a very important note about the stages in the evolution of the cosmic bodies. [Reads from *Secret Doctrine.*] Question 16, page 205, note. In the order of evolution of globes with respect to their material transformation, does the Laya state correspond to (1); the cometary to (4); the solar to (5)? If so, to what do (2) and (6) correspond?

H.P.B.: Now, look here. You just answer me a question frankly and sincerely, as I would to a mother-in-law. Do you ask me these things because it is so obscurely put in *The Secret Doctrine*, or is it that you want to pump me out?

Mr. B. Keightley: It is for this reason, to make quite certain that we get a right basis of correspondence and analogies to go upon. Because if we get that wrong, we shall go making mistakes all through.

H.P.B.: You corroborate that statement, Mr. President?

Mr. Kingsland: I think so.

Mr. B. Keightley: If we once get a wrong idea, we continue to go wrong.

H.P.B.: It seems to me you want to pump me out.

Mr. Old: You don't suspect us of wanting to know anything, do you?

---

[1] *The Secret Doctrine*, vol. 1, p. 203.

H.P.B.: Yes! I do. Well, the Laya state corresponds to the atomic or ethereal, and the solar to germinal and the fiery.

Mr. B. Keightley: That being so, what do the second and the sixth and seventh, that is to say, the aeriform and the radiant or gaseous — well, that first.

H.P.B.: The aeriform or gaseous transformation does not write a distinct stage in the cosmic evolution; but, rather, a link connecting the homogeneous with the nebulas or curd-like stage, a correlation of one into the other.

Mr. Mead: That is what you call matter in a critical state.

H.P.B.: Yes, sir. The fourfold vapour represents the stages through which the Earth has passed to reach its present condition. The earth is materialized vapour, as ice is materialized steam. The seventh or depending stage describes the stage the Earth will reach at the end of the Seventh Round. Then men will depend on no other sustenance than their own divine natures. There will be no need of food or drink; they will have no more clubs or lawn tennis, or anything. The principles of the Earth will have almost entirely left her physical body, save the upper triad, just as this Moon had done at the close of the lunar Manvantara; and its principles will be ready to shoot, each in its turn, on to a new Laya centre to form a new globe, which will be the Earth's Septenary Only Begotten Son. Do you want to know anything more? You are the biggest pumpers I have seen in my life. My notes are at an end, and I open my brains to you, and you may ask what you like.

Mr. Hall: Will this new earth be constructed and worked on the same principles as the old one?

H.P.B.: Behave yourself, Hall. We had a very great philosopher in Russia, some of whose aphorisms and axioms I have been translating for Bert's gratification, and he is called Kozma Prutkov.[1] Well, Prutkov has got a magnificent aphorism, and he says: "Plug thy fountain, if thou hast one, because even the fountain needs a little rest." That is one of the best things I have read. So I wonder when anyone of you will know when to plug your fountains and to give a little bit of rest?

---

[1] **Kozma Prutkov** (1803–1863) — a fictional Russian author, a collective pen name used by four Russian satirical poets: Aleksey Tolstoy (1817–1875) and the brothers Aleksey Zhemchuzhnikov (1821–1908), Alexander Zhemchuzhnikov (1826–1896) and Vladimir Zhemchuzhnikov (1830–1884).

Mr. Kingsland: They rest for six days; they are only open on Thursdays.

Mr. Hall: It is always leaking at other times.

Mr. Kingsland: I have got one question that has not been asked. It would appear from analogy that there should be seven chains of planets (each consisting of seven planets — total 49) in which humanity develops, the lunar chain being one, and our Earth chain another. Is this so, and is our chain the fourth in the series, lunar chain being the third?

H.P.B.: It may be. I am not sure of it, but I would not destroy your illusions.

A Lady: I thought it was good to destroy illusions.

H.P.B.: Yes, because everything is illusion on this plane of existence. I have been thinking myself about this.

Mr. Kingsland: Are the seven sacred planets, the planets which correspond to our Earth, in the above-named seven chains?

H.P.B.: No, I don't think so. Really, I do not know. There are very few things that I know, really.

Mr. Hall: What is the meaning in the fable of Jason[2] going to fetch the Golden Fleece, and his having to sow the Dragon's teeth?

H.P.B.: What does he mean?

Mr. B. Keightley: You know, the fable of Jason and the Argonauts.[3] One of the labours he has to undertake is to sow Dragon's teeth. First of all he has to plow the ground with fiery bulls; then, having plowed the ground, he sows the Dragon's teeth from which grow a crop of armed men.

Mr. Mead: Cadmus[4] does the same.

Mr. B. Keightley: Hall wants to know what the interpretation is.

H.P.B.: Exercise your own imagination. You know what a "Dragon" is; I told you just now.

---

[2] **Jason** (*Greek*) — a hero and leader of the Argonauts in Greek mythology.

[3] **Argonauts** (*Greek*) — a group of heroes in Greek mythology, who accompanied Jason in his quest for the Golden Fleece.

[4] **Cadmus** (*Greek*) — a hero and the founder of the ancient city of Thebes in Greek mythology. He is also credited with introducing the Phoenician alphabet to Greece.

Mr. Hall: It was in connection with that, that I asked the question.

H.P.B.: I don't know. I could not tell you.

Mr. Hall: Is it a symbol of initiation?

H.P.B.: I have plugged my fountain. It may be.

Mr. Mead: The armed men that spring up from the teeth Cadmus sows all fall to fighting one another.

Mr. Hall: That is only because he tricks them.

Mr. Mead: They straight away fall to work to fight one another.

Mr. B. Keightley: He throws an enchanted helmet among them.

H.P.B.: I have been on that spot,[1] and if you want an interpretation of it, there are again seven legends, each relating to one of the keys.

Mr. Mead: Simon gave one in the…

H.P.B.: Take the alchemical, if you please, in connection with the expedition of the Argonauts. All alchemy is there, if you could only understand it; the philosopher's stone[2] and everything is in that expedition of the Argonauts, there in the Golden Fleece.

Mr. Hall: I wish I could understand why Jason deserts Medea?[3]

H.P.B.: If we begin about these allegories, we will never end.

---

[1] **Colchis** (*Greek*) — the destination of the Argonauts, as well as the home to Medea and the Golden Fleece, in Greek mythology. It is located on the eastern coast of the Black Sea, the present-day western Georgia.

[2] **Philosopher's Stone** — an alchemical term also called the *Powder of Projection*, which is a mysterious substance possessing the power of transmuting the base metals into pure gold. Mystically, however, the Philosopher's Stone symbolizes the transmutation of the lower animal nature of man into the highest and divine.

[3] **Medea** (*Greek*) — the daughter of King Aeeta of Colchis who helped Jason in his search for the Golden Fleece. Once the quest was completed, they fled together and married. However, ten years later, Jason abandoned Medea to marry another woman.

16 MAY 1889

Mr. B. Keightley: This is an attempt to put forth in plain and simple language the principal ideas of Theosophy, what we believe in and what we don't believe in, in the form of question and answer between a Mystic and an Enquirer. It is just divided into sections — fourteen sections — each of which again is subdivided under headings — not numbers — but headings with titles, just to indicate the subjects that are dealt with. The whole idea of the thing is to make it practical, simple and straightforward, and not very metaphysical or abstruse. It is more of the nature of a popular book.

H.P.B.: You see, the people ask such extraordinary questions. Anyone who speaks of Theosophy will ask you if you are a Buddhist. Theosophy is not a religion, it is not a sect, and nobody is forced to believe or not believe. A Theosophist may belong to any religion, and to no religion, if he likes. What does it matter? He may be a very good man and justify his name of Theosophist more than anyone else; but people will not take this in their heads, they will come and say all of them that we are esoteric Buddhists, without understanding what esoteric Buddhism means. So it is time to give them answers to the most simple questions as to what we believe and don't believe, and this thing is one of the chapters. Of course, it is impossible to read the others, but I have taken one of them — for instance, "Theosophical Duties" — and I want everyone to suggest what will be the needed thing. What questions are the most necessary? All of you go about, and you ought to know what it is that which the public misunderstands the most, what is that which will do the most good; because it is something terrible, the misconceptions that are in the world about Theosophy. They do not seem to know what Theosophy is.

Mr. B. Keightley: I think the best plan would be that as I read it, anybody who has suggestions to make should stop me — because they will not be able to follow me, otherwise. The section, as a whole, is called "What is Practical Theosophy," and the first subdivision is on "Duty." [Reads from a manuscript.][4]

Mr. Williams: Is it proposed that this should be circulated about?

Mr. B. Keightley: This is part of a book that H.P.B. has written.

---

[4] See H. P. Blavatsky, "What is Practical Theosophy?" *The Key to Theosophy* (London, Theosophical Publishing Company, 1889), pp. 227–231.

H.P.B.: I will finish it in a day or two. It has been announced yesterday, *The Key to Theosophy.* Everyone complains that *The Secret Doctrine* is so abstruse and difficult, that we will give this and perhaps they will say this one is too difficult. I don't know what to say. I am putting all the questions I have had over and over again; therefore, I am answering these.

A Lady: I think that is most useful.

H.P.B.: But now we must have suggestions, if there is anything more to say; because, when it goes to press we cannot put anything more, and we have to explain as much as we can all that Theosophy is and is not. Afterwards, people may come and say, why didn't you put this and that? And then it will be too late.

Mr. Old: There is a statement that the attainment of freedom of individual progress and eventual happiness can only be attained by life experience. Might this not be logically proven without going very far into words?

H.P.B.: How would you do it?

Mr. Old: You need a logical necessity. It is a bare statement, and not satisfactory, perhaps, to the inquirer. It has to be shown how individual happiness — which, in the altruistic sense, of course, is based in the happiness of the whole body, of which that ego is only an atom — it has to be shown how this happiness can be attained only by life experience. For myself, I should first go to show that the earth plane upon which we live — or perhaps, this would be entering rather deeply into the matter — by showing this earth is the ultimate of spiritual action, it is that plane on which action ceases and reaction commences, and therefore the dual action is only manifest here. That is to say, the descending and ascending, and therefore it is the only point at which evolution can take place. There is a decided motion or progress of spirit towards matter from the standpoint of the spiritual planes; that is, they are all downward, and there is — or, as H.P.B. puts it in *The Secret Doctrine* — the angel has desired to be man, and man desired to become an angel. You can quite see what I mean, perhaps? The personality, the incarnating ego, is the only point of differentiation — of individual differentiation — at which mankind are interblended; and, therefore, co-mingle and produce individual evolutions.

H.P.B.: Would you put this there?

Mr. Old: Do not put my words.

H.P.B.: We avoid putting metaphysics. This is the complaint of everyone, that they don't understand half or two thirds in *The Secret Doctrine.* What I have tried to avoid was metaphysics in this little book, because if you do put metaphysics it will confuse them, and they won't understand anything, and there will be complaints again. These things, as I put them, are as plain as can be.

Mr. Kingsland: I think you want a little more connection.

Mr. B. Keightley: Your statement is open to this objection: on the three planets preceding our own, there must be evolution of some kind. You must be careful not to land yourself in subsequent [...].

Mr. Kingsland: What he said is very valuable, but does not touch that point in reference to the question which has been asked, it is in reference to incarnation. The questioner may grant all that, and then say: "well, the man has passed through his earthly life into another plane."

Mr. B. Keightley: The drift of the question is this: a man finds no satisfaction or peace as the result of his life. He has left unsatisfied. Then he asks, where is the necessity for reincarnation, if you don't attain peace during one life? Then the answer is, because it is only attainable by a series of life experiences.

Mr. Kingsland: That is the point Old wants to prove.

Mr. Old: I was a bit too metaphysical, perhaps.

Mr. Williams: It would be a good thing to give examples of lives that have not shown any experience.

H.P.B.: I do not think I have ever met a truly happy man. To everyone life is a burden, there is something they cannot find — any interior satisfaction, or peace of mind. I have never met one man yet who was perfectly satisfied.

Mr. B. Keightley: The conclusion to be drawn from that would seem to be that no permanent satisfaction is possible in material life.

H.P.B.: If evolution progresses in such a way as that, then they will most certainly go *pari passu* with physical evolution; and what matters it, now that we have all the joys and blessings of civilization? They come and say to us: Christianity has softened the customs. I say, did it? Why, the more civilized a country is, the more cant it has, and the more miserable are the people. Look at England. Where is there more wealth, and every blessing in the world? If they only thought a little bit about the people! Where is there more misery than in England?

Mr. B. Keightley: That is not a direct answer to this question; your assertion is perfectly general here, that the final goal, or peace, can only be reached through life experiences. That applies broadly all round, whether you speak about a civilized country or a Buddhist country. Then you want to give a general answer.

H.P.B.: I do not answer it on the paper. As we speak now, it is quite a different thing. I simply answer to that: there is no man that is satisfied; because, civilization brings outward blessings, but that civilization shows there is every day more and more immorality, corruption, and selfishness. And what does selfishness lead to? It leads to the thing that half of mankind have become: the Cains of the others, which are the Abels.

Mr. B. Keightley: Would you say you have found amongst the Buddhists, people who would say they were perfectly happy?

H.P.B.: Perfectly. They die with as great serenity as they get up in the morning.

Mr. B. Keightley: But are they happy?

H.P.B.: I never saw happier people than in Ceylon where they don't believe in god or soul. They believe in incarnation simply. They don't think anything of the previous man passes into this. They are perfectly incapable of talking metaphysics; and, yet, see the effect it produces upon them. Every man is taught that whatever he does he will be either punished or rewarded for. Whatever the cause he produces, it will have the same effects; therefore, he knows if he does something bad, he will have bad results; if he does anything good, then good results will ensue from it, whether it is in this life or another. Now, look here! You just ask every one of yourselves — you have all been little boys — is it not a thing, that when you know you have deserved something, that you don't murmur as you would otherwise? You don't feel this terrible feeling of injustice. Don't you know that, every one of you?

Mr. B. Keightley: That is absolutely and entirely true.

H.P.B.: You may swear at it and be angry, but you will say I have done it. This is the only thing that can lead people to happiness. I don't know what you are driving at now.

Mr. B. Keightley: What Old is after is the purely general statement here: that the goal of peace is only to be attained by life experience.

Mr. Old: Might I have another try? I think it might be done on the *ad absurdum*[1] principle, by proving that happiness cannot be attained elsewhere. For instance: a person dies; he hopes to go to heaven. Ask him his definition of heaven. He says: "the place of happiness." Ask him what "happiness" is; he says: "it is a relative thing." Happiness, I suppose, in heaven would be to have everything you want, and nothing you don't want. Consequently, it is nothing else than an expression or full realization of Kama, desire, of individual desire. Can this be a condition of progress?

H.P.B.: Even Devachan is a state of exalted selfishness, but this is finite. It is not as theology says, that because a man has been "goody-goody" he will be given a golden harp and be very happy for eternity; there is no logic in it. A man says very well, if I only believe what I am told, I may have the golden harp and sit — I don't know what they do there; I think, recline on the soft clouds! This is the most absurd thing in the world. A man is taught thus to believe: that, do what he may, if he only believes that because another man has been put to death on his account, his sins are pardoned to him. I say it is the most pernicious doctrine in the world. It forces every man to lose self-esteem and self-reliance. It makes him lose sight of this terrible injustice, that because I may go and steal cherries another will be flogged for me. This is an absurdity.

Mr. Old: Moral responsibility is lost sight of.

H.P.B.: However, I want you to hear to the end, and after he has read all this, then we will have a general conversation, because I want you to see if anything is forgotten.

Mr. B. Keightley: The second section is on "Self-sacrifice." [Reads.]

Mr. Old: That section is very beautiful.

A Lady: I don't think there is anything to be added to it.

H.P.B.: Did I make it comprehensive enough?

---

[1] **Ad absurdum** (*Latin*) — to the point of absurdity.

A Lady: Perfectly clear.

Mr. Johnson: I thought the attack on the Roman Catholics was rather severe, madam, to single them particularly.

H.P.B.: The priests are self-sacrificing. It is not against any particular priest, but such a pernicious system.

Mr. Kingsland: Say simply missionaries, not Roman Catholic missionaries.

Mr. Old: Call them Christian missionaries.

Mr. Kingsland: I think you are quite right not to single out one particular sect.

H.P.B.: Were there any Christian missionaries who were killed in China?

Mr. Old: Any amount of them.

H.P.B.: This Damien, I tell you I was going to start for a collection among we Theosophists just to send him, and the poor man dies.[1] I just got some shillings, and he died. Let him be any religion, such a man is the highest Theosophist possible. I am perfectly sure the Roman Catholic Church will not recognize it. They recognize Labre,[2] who for forty years allowed himself to be devoured by vermin. I say it is positively ridiculous. They make a saint of this Labre, and the unfortunate Damien they won't make anything of. You won't find a Jain[3] who does not lie in the sun and allow vermin to come upon him, because they say: "They are our younger brothers." They allow all the vermin to come upon them, fleas, and all the less comely animals.

Mr. B. Keightley: It is carrying the point too far.

H.P.B.: We have Jains among our Theosophists in India, and they plead to me, saying it is a very sinful thing that I permitted our Malay to kill cobras. But, I say I am not going to allow the cobras to sting.

---

[1] **Father Damien** (1840–1889) — a Roman Catholic priest from Belgium, canonized in 2009.

[2] **Benedict Joseph Labre** (1748–1783) — a Catholic saint canonized in 1881.

[3] **Jainas** (*Sanskrit*) — a large religious body in India closely resembling Buddhism, but who preceded it by long centuries. They claim that Gautama, the Buddha, was a disciple of one of their Tirtankaras, or Saints. They deny the authority of the Vedas and the existence of any *personal* supreme god, but believe in the eternity of matter, the periodicity of the universe and the immortality of men's minds (*Manas*), as well as that of the animals.

Mr. Kingsland: Better a dead cobra than a dead Theosophist.

H.P.B.: He says: why don't you throw some powder? He wants me to throw salt on his tail. They could not pardon me, and many of them left because I had two or three cobras killed.

Countess Wachtmeister:[4] Mr. Johnson thought you had taken the Jains' advice when we saw all the cockroaches about here.

Mr. B. Keightley: I am afraid that is illegal; that would not stand before law.

H.P.B.: We laugh at this, but really it is a most sublime thing — because they are so sincere, they would not breathe. They wear those things so as not to breathe the air and swallow those unfortunate insects, those animalcules; and they sweep as they go along not to walk by chance on some insect. It appears ridiculous; but, really, if you analyse the thing, it is the most sublime thing. They do it with the greatest discomfort in the world, and they believe in it.

Mr. Kingsland: The principal thing is to force out how Altruism, like everything else, can be abused. And the only question for us to decide is whether that is pointed out forcibly enough, or whether anybody can suggest a more forcible illustration.

A Lady: I think it is the most forcible you can find.

Mr. Kingsland: I don't know anything about Labre, but the majority of people won't know.

H.P.B.: He is the last saint who was beatified. For forty years he was sitting on the Piazza di Spagna.[5]

A Lady: I read a piece in the American newspaper about him. A Nonconformist[6] was calling him over the coals so cruelly because he was not a Protestant, because he was a Catholic, and would not recognize his work.

H.P.B.: You see how these Christians love each other? Just as much as Theosophists love each other.

A Lady: As much as you love the Roman Catholic.

---

[4] **Constance Wachtmeister** (1838–1891) — a close friend and co-worker of H.P.B.; the author of *Reminiscences of H. P. Blavatsky and The Secret Doctrine.*
[5] **Piazza di Spagna** (*Italian*, "Spanish Square") — a square in Rome, Italy.
[6] **Nonconformist** — a Protestant in England, who does not conform to the doctrines and practices of the Church of England.

H.P.B.: I speak against the system, not against the Roman Catholics. I say, pitch into systems but don't touch personalities. We have quite enough to do with pitching into systems, because systems are abominable.

Mr. B. Keightley: Then this is on "Charity." [Reads.]

Mr. Kingsland: I think it is better to eliminate all reference to any special sect or creed whatever, and I should eliminate Spurgeon's name.

H.P.B.: Oh Lord! I must not, because it is a personality, but I do despise the fellow. Very well, we will take out "Spurgeon" and put simply "Fashionable Preacher." Now I have made two concessions. I have taken out for Mr. Johnson the "Catholic," and for you, "Spurgeon."

Mr. Old: Someone will ask you to take out Buddha's name, presently.

H.P.B.: "The Most Popular Preacher."

Mr. Kingsland: I think if you refer to the "Asbestos Soul," everyone will know who it means.

Mr. Keightley: "Theosophy for the Masses." [Reads.] Then the last is: "How Members Can Help the Society."

H.P.B.: This is where you have to give your suggestions.

Mr. B. Keightley: [Reads.]

H.P.B.: Give us suggestions what to put more, because I put only that which comes into my head, and I may forget hundreds of things which you Theosophists ought to think about, and see what could be added. Mr. Cobbold[1] came too late, and did not hear the beginning.

Mr. Kingsland: Mr. Cobbold as a practical Theosophist will give us his views.

H.P.B.: What can Theosophists do?

Countess Wachtmeister: Theosophists should try and not backbite their neighbours.

Mr. Old: I think there is a negative aspect to action, H.P.B. I was thinking the same as yourself, Countess. I thought there was a negative side to Theosophical duty — what the Theosophist should *not* do; that is to say, he should not create any obstructions — which

---

[1] **Arthur Westhrop Cobbold** — a member of the Theosophical Society in London.

very often he does, unconsciously through ignorance, or consciously through spleen.

H.P.B.: Personality is the curse in the Theosophical Society, as it is everywhere.

Countess Wachtmeister: I don't think it is put strongly enough there, that every evil springs from personality, and that personality is the great curse.

H.P.B.: You have not heard the whole thing. This is only a chapter, and I have eleven more.

Countess Wachtmeister: The first duty of a Theosophist is to try and forget his personality.

H.P.B.: Exactly. How few do it. You just make a footnote, and mark it there. Are not these Buddhist precepts beautiful! I can assure you, if I one day translate them, you will say they are splendid.

Mr. Old: They are very poetical.

H.P.B.: And written so beautifully.

A Lady: They are indeed sublime.

Mr. Johnson: It says there that "attacks made on the Society should be defended by any means in one's power." I think that is rather loose.

H.P.B.: We cannot oblige anyone to do anything. We cannot create penances.

Countess Wachtmeister: I think Mr. Johnson meant "legitimate means," that is what he meant.

Mr. Kingsland: Not in the doctrine of the Jesuits.[2]

H.P.B.: Now, gentlemen, please, some more.

Countess Wachtmeister: You put down your negative points, that Mr. Old was just saying, of what Theosophists should not do. That is later on in the book.

H.P.B.: I have covered all the tenets of Theosophy. I have spoken about Karma and Devachan and the states of afterlife — not that we are obliged to believe in it, but only Theosophists who study Occultism believe in it. This is what I have been putting. A Theosophist may believe in anything he likes.

---

[2] **Jesuits** — a Roman Catholic order, also known as the Society of Jesus, founded by Ignatius of Loyola in the 16th century.

Mr. B. Keightley: Another thing which has been slightly touched upon is a thing which I have very often been asked, whether vegetarianism is a tenet of the Theosophical Society, and whether abstention from alcoholism, and so on?

Countess Wachtmeister: And then, also, you should distinctly state that Theosophy has nothing to do with Spiritualism.

Mr. B. Keightley: That is stated.

Mr. Kingsland: I think, in reference to this objection, this must be fully answered. He thinks all the literature is not of much practical value. I think I would point out that right thinking is the basis of right acting, and we are not a Charity Organization Society to merely alleviate misery on the surface. Each one does that as much as he can. We believe that by promulgating these doctrines that that will in time naturally work out on the physical plane.

H.P.B.: I say literature will reach ten thousands, where all the money we can get will reach one hundred.

Mr. Kingsland: The Charity Organization, and even legislation, is only working on the surface of things.

H.P.B.: We don't take any concern in politics, because what is the use of making political reforms with men who are not yet reformed? Let them be Conservative or Liberal, it is six of one, and half dozen of the other.

Mr. Johnson: Theosophy cannot be preached to a man who has an empty stomach.

H.P.B.: Among Theosophists there are far more with hardly filled stomachs, and yet they try to do what they can. I know many of them who have hardly money enough to get food.

Countess Wachtmeister: They would starve in India to enable them to join the Theosophical Society. On joining formerly they had to pay a certain fee. Some of these Hindus have starved themselves for a week, so as to enable them to join the Theosophical Society. They have done it, not only once or twice, but again and again.

H.P.B.: What I want to put are the rules of the Theosophical Society at the end — rules and so on. A selection, of course.

Mr. Kingsland: You mean the objects?

H.P.B.: No, the rules as they are in India.

Mr. B. Keightley: Only a selection.

H.P.B.: Then to give how many branches we have and their names, and everything.

A Lady: I think that would make a very good impression, the immense number of people that have joined the Society, and the number of branches.

H.P.B.: You see, we have one-hundred and seventy-three branches, but in India alone there are one-hundred and twenty-nine or one-hundred and thirty. Now, in America we have about twenty-four, and six which are forming; here, we have six or seven branches in England. It is growing very rapidly, and really, there are as many Theosophists who don't know what the Theosophical Society is as there are outsiders.

Mr. Johnson: I think that book will do splendid work for the cause.

Mr. Kingsland: Most undoubtedly.

Mr. ——: What is the Theosophical Society good for? Well, we might say to promote Altruism, the answer to that would be. A Christian has done the same thing, taught the same thing.

H.P.B.: They speak a good deal of it in Christianity, but they act mightily little.

Mr. ——: And that puts a stop to progress.

H.P.B.: These people would be just as good Buddhists.

Mr. Old: It is the best thing they know of.

Mr. B. Keightley: They all go in for this fallacy, that their idea of helping other people is almost in all cases confined to the physical. They don't try to give them actual moral stamina; it is always, "your sins have been wiped out and washed in the blood of Jesus," and so on.

A Lady: They teach them sectarianism.

Mr. B. Keightley: They teach them hardly anything which has any basis in it.

Mr. Old: The man who trained the fleas to do tricks did a good deal more than Labre, because the one only educates the physical idea...

Countess Wachtmeister: And the other develops the intelligences.

Mr. Old: It shows there is a ray of intelligence in the smaller parts of humanity.

H.P.B.: The Roman Catholic Church did not have that superb contempt for animals always that it has now, saying they have no souls. Read the *Golden Legend*:[1] you will see any number of wolves who have been converted, a dragon who had some sore in his eye, and some saint drew it out of his eye, and he immediately shed tears and became a Christian. It is a fact — animals of all kinds, wolves, dragons, and hyenas.

Mr. B. Keightley: There is the story of St. Francis's[2] preaching to the animals.

A Lady: And the Jackdaw of Rheims[3] became a saint.

Mr. Kingsland: When the ban was removed.

Mr. Old: I have seen a more Christian spirit in some faithful dogs, than I have seen in man.

H.P.B.: They are the most respectful fellows I have ever met with. Under any circumstance they will remain faithful.

A Lady: Even with a master as bad as Bill Sykes.[4]

Mr. Old: Martin Tupper[5] says: "What if they cannot rise so high? They can't fall so far." Which is quite true.

H.P.B.: What are we to do more? Because there are two sections more, representing 30 or 40 pages.

Mr. Old: I think something might be said as to what constitutes happiness.

H.P.B.: With me, to sit and never move.

Mr. Kingsland: And never have anyone asking questions.

H.P.B.: This young creature sitting here cannot live without air, and air kills me.[6]

---

[1] **Golden Legend** (*Legenda aurea* or *Legenda sanctorum*) — a work by Jacopo de Voragine (c.1230–1298), an Italian chronicler and archbishop of Genoa. It is a collection of Christian legends and lives of the saints, written in Latin around 1260.

[2] **Francis of Assisi** (c.1181–1226) — an Italian saint and mystic.

[3] **The Jackdaw of Rheims** — a poem by the English novelist and poet Richard Barham (1788–1845), in which a jackdaw steals a cardinal's ring and is made a saint. The poem was included in *The Ingoldsby Legends*, published under his pseudonym Thomas Ingoldsby.

[4] **Bill Sykes** — a malicious criminal in the Charles Dickens novel *Oliver Twist*.

[5] **Martin Farquhar Tupper** (1810–1889) — an English poet and novelist.

[6] H.P.B.'s health was vulnerable to drafts and therefore she had to keep her windows closed.

Mr. Old: That is not happiness. I think a person who has suffered physically, intense tortures, may still be happy.

H.P.B.: One man is very fond of money.

Mr. Old: It depends where the individual consciousness happens to be gravitating for the time being. If it is in the body, physical ailments cause misery. But otherwise he would still be happy.

Mr. B. Keightley: There is a certain amount of truth in the old saying: "What philosopher was ever able to bear the toothache?"

H.P.B.: Now what are you going to do with this Burgoyne,[7] who writes a book against us? It shows to you the perseverance with which they act against the Theosophical Society. I have just received this. Burgoyne as a young man, Mr. Johnson will tell you about him, was two and a half years away for some swindling.

Mr. Johnson: He had to quit the country. He victimized me; he was two years in Bradford Gaol.[8]

H.P.B.: I have got a portrait of him that was sent from Scotland Yard,[9] and he has got on the handcuffs; and there he was taken before he was handcuffed, where he appears very smiling, and there he appears with handcuffs — well, he doesn't smile — and this is the bright and shining light of esotericism in America.

Mr. Johnson: I know perfectly well he is an enemy of the Society, and especially about you.

Mr. Kingsland: How long is it since he was in England?

Mr. Johnson: Three and a half years ago.

Countess Wachtmeister: He had to leave the country quickly.

Mr. Kingsland: For the country's good.

Countess Wachtmeister: The police said it would be the greatest swindle England had ever known. They were collecting money to purchase land out in America, and the whole thing was a bubble, and they went off to America with all they had collected. They intended to swindle the Theosophist out of his land, and not pay for it.

---

[7] **Thomas Henry Dalton** (1855–1894) — a Scottish astrologer who assumed the name Thomas H. Burgoyne. He had been imprisoned in Leeds, England, in 1883.
[8] **Bradford Gaol** — a prison in Bradford, England, 14 km from Leeds.
[9] **Scotland Yard** — the British police force.

Mr. Old: I think the best thing the "Theosophist" can do is to prepare a counterblast.

Countess Wachtmeister: There are numbers of people who lost money.

H.P.B.: But this is *The Religio-Philosophical Journal.*[1] It is the same paper that for years and years has been putting in letters about my habitual drunkenness. You know, they said that I habitually every morning danced on a tightrope for an hour — I never even tasted liquor in my life, because I hate it: there is no virtue in it at all.

Mr. Kingsland: I would like a few suggestions as to letting Theosophists know as to these scandalous things. For instance, there are the monthly papers, there will be some notice of it in these journals, but all Theosophists do not take these journals.

Mr. B. Keightley: There is this objection to be raised against it, that you only advertise a book of that nature.

Countess Wachtmeister: Yes, everybody goes and purchases it. I think the best plan is to take no notice.

Mr. B. Keightley: The thing that will be done, if Judge is wise, is to simply not to refer to the book, but show up Burgoyne as a fraud.

H.P.B.: Then, if there are the same laws in America as here, you told me the more a statement is true, the more it is libelous, and he may bring an action against Judge. It seems if you speak the truth you are taken up as a confederate. You are always nicely situated.

Mr. Old: I think if Judge were to just write to some of the local papers and make a thorough *exposé*[2] of the man, and just conclude by saying he proposes to publish a book — which will be his book — you could still mention the book, and everybody would fly at it, but they would know how to take the contents in the face of these facts.

Mr. B. Keightley: I don't think anybody will take any notice of the book.

Mr. Kingsland: Unless any paper puffs it up; then we should write a counterblast.

---

[1] *The Religio-Philosophical Journal* — a weekly spiritualist journal, published in Chicago from 1865 to 1905.

[2] **Exposé** (*French*) — an exposure of something discreditable.

Mr. Old: I think the great question in America today is, what is a Theosophist? Here is this man and that man, all pseudo-theosophists, who claim to be *the* Theosophists, representative members of a society which does not exist, but which nevertheless is Theosophical. I don't wonder at all at the Americans raising the question, what is a Theosophist?

H.P.B.: Hiram Butler[3] founded the Esoteric Society, and allowed people to believe he was a Theosophist. Now he has been pounced upon by the police for all kinds of very queer-looking tricks, and he had to run away from Boston, and he went to California.

Countess Wachtmeister: I think all Theosophists ought to protest when they see anything of the kind.

Mr. B. Keightley: They say some astrologers used to say that the stars ruled human destinies and were active agents in controlling human destinies. Others put it that that was not the case, but that there was a sympathetic relationship between human beings and the stars, so that they moved parallel to each other; that you can predict the conditions under which a human being would find himself from the stellar aspects, but it was not inferred that there was any cause of relationship between them. Those are, broadly speaking, the two different views put forward by the astrologer. The old one is the orthodox.

Mr. Old: There is almost a third class of thinkers on this question. That is those who believe in the planetary spirits — you know, that there are legions under them who directly influence the minds of us, the thoughts, desires, and actions of individuals. But my own personal opinion is — and also that which seems to me to be reflected dimly in the Hindu works on the subject, in both North and South Hindustan[4] — that there is a relationship between the terrestrial body, of which man's body is but a differentiation, and the material bodies of all the planets. There is also a sympathy between his astral body, and the whole astral plane to which he belongs, in which — or of which, I might say — and the astral principles animating the planetary bodies. Themselves are the composites, that is, that the astral bodies of planets and of men all enter into and are integral parts of the universal astral plane. Material atoms either collectively or individually make up the

---

[3] **Hiram Erastus Butler** (1841–1916) — an American fraud.
[4] **Hindustan** (*Persian*) — a historic name for India.

material universe; so with respect to the individual or collective astral. Now, it would appear that the life current, called by the Hindus Prana, radiates, permeates, acts and moves in this astral plane, and that it is in passing through this astral that it becomes stranded, as it were, and thrown off, just as a ray of light.

Mr. B. Keightley: Reflected?

Mr. Old: Well, I don't mean that exactly; spread out, I mean, into its different parts or principles.

A Lady: Refracted?

Mr. Old: And this severance of the one Pranic ray causes the different aspects of life. Thus we might have a single ray of light coming from the sun entering the earth, and, as you know, immediately stranded off into so many other rays — refraction is the word, of course. So it is with the universal life, which has no particular reference to our visible sun, which is in the material universe, and is part of it, although it is the most sublimated kind of matter; but it is with respect to the Pranic plane, that is to say, the plane above the astral plane. Then they say that the various astral planets corresponding to the material planets receive the rays of the sun and reflect to the earth, first of all to the astral plane, then precipitated on the plane where the astral planets receive the life rays of the sun. I am speaking of the sun on the Pranic plane. And the astral planets receive these rays and reflect them to the astral body of this earth, which is in the astral plane, and thence they are precipitated on to the earth, and so into individuals. Now as every person is born [...], as it is said, well through the astral plane, it hence follows that the moment of birth is that time when the individual existence commences, and the person is brought under an individual law, and in the general law which controls the revolution of the planets, both in the astral plane and in the physical plane. And I believe myself that planets only exert an influence upon us through the astral plane itself — that is to say, that it is not the material planet, Saturn, Jupiter, Mars, or any other — which affects us, except physically. But we know they do affect us in our desires; for it can be without a doubt predicated that at any particular time a person will be actuated by desires which are, to a certain extent, foreign to the general tenor of that person's life. If that can be done — and it certainly can — that at certain times people shall be moved by influences not generally a characteristic of theirs, then we can refer these, of course, to a plane which is certainly higher than the material plane. And therefore these forces — not being physical forces, but psychic forces acting on the psychic plane on the individual and of nature — must necessarily originate in the psychical plane. That is to say, in a plane higher, at least, than the physical plane. And thus its seems there is a necessity for planets existing in planes higher than the material plane, and yet corresponding to the material planes which are visible to us on this physical plane. I think you will see that necessity yourself, because life in itself is homogenous. It has but one quality and that is life; it is only when it becomes refracted or differentiated that it has a quality, that it can be said to have any particular quality. The modifications of life, hence, would be what constitute individual life, very much like, of course, the colours on the prism: they are all light, but it is the aggregate of all degrees of colours, all tones in equal proportions, that would make up the white. It is when one predominates that the white becomes tinged with a tone or a distinct colour. Thus, if more pink were in the aggregate, then the white would be no longer white but it would be pink; so, whatever principle happens to be in excess in an individual, so that person is called either Saturnian, Jovian,[1] Marsian etc. I am speaking, of course, of the ultimate effects of planetary influences upon individuals and how it would operate.

H.P.B.: Occult astrology says that, just as you explain it, but that colours having, each of them, a particular tendency or a faculty of impressing one way or the other what ray that individual will be, so are his passions or desires affected. It is the colour of the ray that impresses. For instance, if such a colour comes from Saturn or Venus, if he happens to be born under this planet, then certainly every time that a certain colour — by passing through this astral plane that you have been talking about, and passing through other certain things — assumes a certain colour, this colour it is which affects the individual mentally, and psychically, and spiritually, and all kinds of ways. Is it like that?

Mr. Old: Yes. Of course, we know that we individually are impervious to certain colours. Thus, some people show an instinctive liking

---

[1] Jove — another name for Jupiter.

for this colour, and a distinct hatred for the other; at any rate, they feel a psychic influence arising from the presence of these colours.

A Lady: What do colour-blind people feel, a psychic influence?

H.P.B.: No. It happens to be a colour which is of a planet which is perfectly contrary to theirs.

Mr. Old: They would feel it on a psychic plane.

Mr. B. Keightley: All that colour-blind means is that there is something wrong with the physically registering apparatus. A man cannot be occultly colour-blind.

H.P.B.: This is the keynote of Occultism, to know the true relation of sounds, colours, and numbers. There are so many. There are seven rays, but what are they? They have got seventy-seven thousand times seven, all kinds of combinations; it takes a lifetime to learn them, and you cannot do it by registering all these in your physical memory. It is a perfect impossibility. You have to use your intuition, and your psychic memory, the memory of your ego, of the astral. You have to register it on your astral form.

Mr. Cross: It appears to me the books you circulate on astrology are rather written above the heads of the people. As an outsider, I can tell you that really, the people who want to know about Theosophy want to know the first steps, rather than these advanced theories. These are very well for your own Society; but, if these books which come out from time to time are supposed to spread the doctrine, I don't think, speaking from experience, that they really do so much good. They come out along with the others.

Countess Wachtmeister: Could not you give us a series of questions, such as outsiders ask themselves?

Mr. Cross: I should like to know why the person who so very clearly answers the questions so clearly is called a mystic.

H.P.B.: There you are. Mr. Keightley wanted "Mystic." I said put "Q" and "A." I wanted to put "Theosophist," but that is such a name which is arrogant.

Mr. Kingsland: Put "Teacher."

H.P.B.: No! No! No! It is worse, yet.

Mr. Cross: That is really the objection that outsiders have, that it is vague. Does not the use of the word "Mystic" go to build up that idea?

Mr. B. Keightley: You are perfectly correct.

H.P.B.: What name would you suggest?

Mr. Cross: Why won't you put your own name?

H.P.B.: "H.P.B." stinks in the nostrils already.

Mr. Cross: But people look to you as the kind of oracle of the movement.

H.P.B.: There is my name there already; everyone would know I have written this. But I would like throughout the book not to put so many times my name. I know that "Mystic" was not good. Now please give me some good advice.

Mr. B. Keightley: "Q" and "A" as an alternative would be good.

Mr. Cross: I suppose there is an objection to using "Theosophist"?

Countess Wachtmeister: Explain what Theosophist is, H.P.B.

H.P.B.: It is very arrogant, because "Theosophist" we call men who are really holy, saintly men, whoever they be, whatever nation they belong to, or whatever religion. Now, I don't think myself holy, good, or even learned enough to call myself a "Theosophist."

Mr. Cross: If you are not a Theosophist, who are the Theosophists? Are we going to do away with the term Theosophist, simply because nobody can live up to the ideal? "Theosophist" is an ideal, not what he really is, the same as Christian might be.

H.P.B.: I think "Theosophist" is better than "Mystic." They will only say it is very mystic. Let it be "Theosophist."

Mr. Cross: I feel I am not competent to speak, not knowing enough.

Mr. Kingsland: Then you can just give us advice.

H.P.B.: We are so immersed in this Theosophical Society business that we cannot see things as those who surround us can. The heads of outsiders are a great deal clearer.

Mr. Cross: It would be better if you could have a line drawn — a more definite line — between Occultism and Theosophy.

H.P.B.: We have it, a very great line. I am going to have a chapter on the difference between Occultism and Theosophy. Theosophist may be any member of a Theosophical Society. They may study or not as they like; it obliges to nothing; you have not to change your religion, or give up anything. But those who study Occultism, who study esoteric Theosophy, those have, of course, to believe. They must have one belief. Certainly Theosophy and Occultism are different, for an Occultist must be a Theosophist if he would not be a black magician, but you may be a Theosophist without being an Occultist.

Mr. Cross: But why do you bring out these books together? Now, I got hold of a book called *The Higher Science*; that did me a great deal of good. Another time I had a book called *The Black Art*, and it was something I knew nothing about.

H.P.B.: If you know about the light side, you must know the dark side. If you know anything about night, you must know what day is.

Mr. Cross: You are handicapping yourself before the British public by bringing these things together, because we know that astrology in the ordinary man is a good deal connected with fraud. No doubt there is a great deal of truth in these old sciences, but you are really doing yourself harm. You are handicapping yourself, so to speak.

Mr. Kingsland: You cannot help that, because Theosophy is based upon Occultism. Occultism is the theoretical study of the laws upon which Theosophy as an exoteric thing is based.

H.P.B.: And the laws of nature.

Mr. Kingsland: You must have some law to which you can point as the reason for your Theosophical tenets, and that is Occultism. It is necessary for those who are the leaders in the movement to have this in our knowledge, so that they may meet the opponents of Theosophy on all planes, on the intellectual as well as on others.

Mr. Cross: Then pray let us have it in plain terms. We want no such scientific terms, we want everything clearly defined.

Countess Wachtmeister: Learning Theosophy is not like going to a schoolmaster. Learning Theosophy is by developing your intuition; it is not like having your lesson, just made easy. What Theosophy really is, is the development of the inner man.

Mr. Cross: True. But before you know anything about composition you must learn grammar. What I say is we should know something about the more simple things.

H.P.B.: I have tried to put it in as simple language as I could. Everyone throws it at my head; the outside public certainly does not.

I took it into my head to write this *Key to Theosophy*; two weeks ago I began it, and I am finishing it; it will be about 250 pages.

Mr. Cross: Let us have books on astrology, by all means. Let us have books on Occultism, but begin at the ABC.

Mr. Kingsland: There are ABC theosophical books. We are sending out books which are both ABC and the most metaphysical books.

Countess Wachtmeister: There are so very different minds.

Mr. Kingsland: If a man wants only the ABC of Theosophy, a Theosophist will tell him: "what you want is such and such a book." Another man comes and says I want to find the scriptural basis of things; there is *The Secret Doctrine* for him. The only practical way is for a man to go to a Theosophist.

H.P.B.: Theosophy is a very easy thing if you happen to meet a Theosophist who can give you an exposition of it clearly, well, so as to make you understand; but sometimes you happen to meet a Theosophist who will appal you with all kinds of metaphysical terms. Now, for instance, for myself I speak very indifferent English, but still I am accustomed to use Theosophical terms that every Theosophist will understand. But other people will look at me and take me for a lunatic. For us it is perfectly comprehensible. And you must understand that a person accustomed to talk a certain language cannot come and speak to children. Take a mathematician: he could not. It is extremely difficult for a Theosophist to come and speak plainly to those who have never heard of Theosophy, and therefore, there is the difficulty. I wrote *The Secret Doctrine*. It seems to me every word is comprehensible; many of our Theosophists understand it, and that which they cannot they come to me about and I explain to them. Every Thursday I explained that which was not clear enough. But look at those newspapers; they don't understand it, they say it is all bosh.

Mr. ——: You must not take any notice of what *The Telegraph*[1] says.

H.P.B.: Now, has *The Saturday Review* even given a single word?

Mr. ——: You must take into consideration it is their business.

H.P.B.: What, to sit on every book that appears?

Mr. ——: It is not a fair criticism, and you must not take it as such. If you write anything new in music or art they sit on it, because they

---

[1] *The Telegraph* — a British daily newspaper, published in London since 1855.

like a thing that they know. That is why music is so popular, because it is like so very many other things.

Mr. Kingsland: Mr. Cross's contention is perfectly valid; but it seems to me there is a remedy for it. It is not supposed you could select what you could best read, but you will find that you will want to read these very books that you are now condemning.

Mr. Cross: I want a book that will tell me what to read.

Mr. Kingsland: Only someone who has been over the ground can help you.

30 MAY 1889

Mr. Old: The first question this evening is: *Jiva* is sometimes used as synonymous with *Prana*, or simply "life"; but it appears also to be used in the plural as synonymous with the Monads, and in some other senses in the Commentary on this and the following sloka. Please throw a little more light on the meaning of the word "Jivas" in *The Secret Doctrine.*

H.P.B.: Well, I said many times that there are six schools of philosophy in India; each school has its own terms, and uses them sometimes in a different sense. What a Vedantin of the Visishtadvaita sect will call "Jiva," that, for instance, the Advaita, also belonging to the Vedantin school, will say is a great heresy, because they call "Jiva" "One," which cannot be plural — that is to say, which is Parabrahm; it is the one universal principle. Therefore, it is very difficult to know which to use, and you must know in the light of what philosophy you use it, otherwise there will always be confusion. "Jiva" is really the incarnating ego, the fifth principle, in our school, in the esoteric school.

Mr. Kingsland: Jivas in the plural are very often used for the Monads.

H.P.B.: No, you cannot use Monad, because Monad is one thing and Jiva is another. If you take Atma-Buddhi-Manas, then, it will be another thing; but, if you use them in distinction, it is impossible to say that, because Monad is Atma, what is Monad?

Mr. Kingsland: It appears often to be used there in the same sense.

H.P.B.: The Monad is from Greek, "One," the unit, whatever it is. If we call it Monad, it is simply because it is with Buddhi. And that Atma in reality is not a unit, but the one universal principle, and it is simply a ray. That which uses Buddhi as a vehicle is that ray of that universal principle. Therefore, in reality it is Buddhi which is the Monad, the one unit.

Mr. Kingsland: The Monad. But it is used in reference to the Monad in the lower forms of life.

H.P.B.: That is a different thing. Leibniz uses it in quite a different way.

Mr. Kingsland: But, is not it used there in the same sense as in *The Secret Doctrine?*

H.P.B.: The Monad is that which incarnated in the Chhaya, in the image, in the first image projected by the Lunar Pitris; but, it is perfectly senseless, because it has not got the cementing link, so to say, the Manas which comes after that. One comes in the First Race, and the other in the Third. So you see the difference.

Mr. Old: In reading through *The Secret Doctrine* I have been led to conclude that Jiva was always used in the sense of the individual life principle.

H.P.B.: You must pay attention to what part of the book it is used in, and when. For instance, if you see that I quote something there from some sectarian book, then it will be a different thing; or if I quote Leibniz, I will say the "Monads"; but I don't think you will find that it is used simply when I speak from my own philosophy, that I mix them up, because it is impossible to mix up the two.

Mr. Old: May we conclude, then, that Jiva is the individual expression, and Prana the universal?

H.P.B.: Prana is simply physical life, that in which animals and men and all the animal kingdom and the vegetable kingdom are; but Jiva can only be applied to the one universal principle, that is to say, the unknowable Parabrahm. Prana is the Sanskrit for the life principle. There are no "Pranas," for you cannot use it in the plural. Life is indivisible; but it is used sometimes as a synonym for Jiva, when Jiva is applied to the one life or the universal living essence — another term for the unknowable, yet self-manifesting and evident principle, the first emanation, or that which you ordinarily call the first Logos — not the second, the manifestation from the one universal.

Mr. Kingsland: Are not the Jivas synonymous with what are called the "Devourers," later on in the stanza?

H.P.B.: Every life has a Jiva in it. Every little insect has a Jiva. Every microbe, every speck of dust will have its Jiva, but that is a different thing. "Jivas" mean "the lives."

Mr. Kingsland: That is identical with Leibniz' idea of the Monads.

H.P.B.: Yes, well, but it is not that. It can be called the same. The Monads of Leibniz are quite a different thing. In one sense it is, because Leibniz calls the Monads, every atom; so there is a great difference.

Mr. Old: Whether your Monad has intelligence or not, of course it has a sentient intelligence of its own, peculiar to its degree.

H.P.B.: There is a great difference between Monad, a unit, like an atom, and a Monad which is an intelligent Monad. Such a one as reflects the whole universe is the Monad of Leibniz. One is on the plane of manifestation, and of gross matter, and the other is on the plane of pure spirituality. The two planes are quite different. You take the two, and at one end of the pole is pure spirit and at the other pole there is the gross matter. So you see you cannot mix it up. You must always see in what sense it is used. One is the Unknowable, as I say, and the other is what I have said. This is a mistake which is very often made.

Mr. Old: Question 2. You speak of the Unknowable. "Is the Unknowable of Occultism the same as the Unknowable of Herbert Spencer?"

H.P.B.: Well, that is just what I want to tell you, because there is a very great difference. It is not. Herbert Spencer's "Unknowable" is that which we Occultists would simply call the "unknown," or that first invisible and intangible, yet logically necessary, existing principle which some call the first cause. Now, the Unknowable of Herbert Spencer is that which he calls the first cause, and we would never call the first cause, but the first Logos. We do not call Parabrahm the first cause, because Parabrahm is the all-cause, the universal cause, or the causeless cause, which is quite a different thing. The first cause has a cause preceding it, and from which it emanates. The causeless cause has no cause, because it is the Absolute Cause itself. The Unknowable or Parabrahm of the Vedantin philosophy cannot manifest, since it is Absolute, hence the immutable; it can undergo no change whatever. To understand this Occult doctrine one would do well to study critically the quarrel between Harrison,[1] the Positivist,[2] with Herbert Spencer, in regard to this term. Now, as I understand it, Unknowable, which to Harrison means Unknown — has anyone of you read this thing between Harrison and Herbert Spencer?

---

[1] **Frederic Harrison** (1831–1923) — a British jurist and historian.
[2] **Positivism** (*Latin*) — an approach that emphasizes using empirical evidence and the scientific method to understand and explain the world, rejecting metaphysical or supernatural explanations.

Mr. Burrows:[1] Yes.

H.P.B.: So you know it then. You will tell me, if you please, if it is as I understand it. The "Unknowable" Harrison would replace by the word "Unknown." Neither Spencer nor Harrison makes this abstract doctrine any clearer by their discussion and coined terms, for both of them are right, and both are wrong. It is as if one insisted that the diurnal period of 24 hours should be termed day, and the other would insist upon calling it night; it is both a day and a night that make up in our perception that period, and one without the other would at once become meaningless. It is both the Unknowable and the Unknown. If then you blend together the Unknowable of Herbert Spencer and the Unknown of Harrison, the sum total will give you a relative idea of what we Occultists mean by the term, and why the words Jiva, Prana, Monad — the latter in its universal application of aggregate — are in reality all one; but yet on this plane of manifestation we are obliged to differentiate them and give a name to each and not mix them up. Now, Herbert Spencer thinks that the final aim and expression of the deific idea is an unconditioned and illimitable absoluteness, and he is right. For us there exists only one absolute certitude, *viz.* this: that the human spirit or consciousness finds itself constantly, uninterruptedly in the presence of infinite and eternal energy, whence emanates — or rather, radiates — all that which exists, or is. Is the idea of Herbert Spencer this?

Mr. Burrows: Yes, in the main.

H.P.B.: This is then the Unknowable, and this contains more than a simple negation. It is the confession of our human ignorance; but also the tacit or virtual admission that within man there is that which feels that energy which is the universal substance; it is fabric, so to speak. Now, Spencer repeats very often that Unknowable is that energy which manifests itself simultaneously in the universe, and in our consciousness, and that it is the highest existing reality, only concealed in the ever-changing progress of physical manifestation; and yet spirit for Herbert Spencer is simply the invisible cosmic cause of these phenomena. As I understand him he does not see in spirit anything more. He attributes to this essence, as we do, unity, homogeneity, and a limitless existence outside space and time, whose means of activity are

---

[1] **Herbert Burrows** (1845–1922) — a British socialist activist.

universal laws. We say so, too, but we add that above that essence and plurality of the laws whose manifestations are only periodical, there is the one eternal law, the causeless cause, as we call it. Spencer places the Unknowable face to face with the abstract and the cosmic phenomena, and sees in this Unknowable the cause of the manifestation. The Positivist, on the other hand, while admitting the existence of a certain fundamental or basic energy, speaks, nevertheless, of the Unknowable as being simply a negative quantity, which is a contradiction in terms. Now, you understand the idea. One calls it the Unknowable, and the other the Unknown. It is positively a contradiction in terms, and both mean quite a different thing; and yet, the same thing. Because Herbert Spencer calls that which we would call the First Logos — or the first manifestation, the radiation from the eternal — he calls it the first cause; and then he speaks about the Unknowable. The other one speaks of the Unknown and wants to make of the Unknown the Parabrahm. You understand? But the Parabrahm is entirely unconsciousness, that is to say, a negative quantity, as he calls it. Now, what we Occultists say is that neither Spencer nor Harrison offers anything like a complete philosophy. The Unknowable or the Unknown could not exist for our perceptions, nor could our perceptions for it. It is the Unknown, or the Invisible manifesting the Logos, which we place face to face with every phenomenon — abstract, physical, psychic, mental, or spiritual — because the Unknown will always contain in itself some portion of the Unknowable, that is to say, some of the laws and manifestations which elude our perception for a time. On the other hand, Unknowable, being the sum of all that which owing to our finite intellectual organization may elude forever our perceptions, is the Parabrahm, or the causeless cause. Now, if I have succeeded in making myself understood, then I say if you study Spencer's Unknowable, and take Harrison's Unknown, instead of accepting either one or the other, seeing the necessary complements of each one life, then our one abstract Monad, and our one universal Prana, whose eternal, immutable, causeless cause is our Vedantic Parabrahm at one end of the line, and the great being, the human race or humanity at the other, then you will have the true idea of what the Occultists mean. You see it is this humanity and each unit in it which are, at one and the same time, the Unknowable, the Unknown, and the To-Be-Known. This is what Occultism says: as it is impossible for the human mind to know anything definite even of the unknown essence, so let us turn our whole attention to its highest manifestation on earth, mankind, and say as is said in the Bible: "In it we live and move and have our being"[1] — "Illo vivicuus movemur et sumus."

Mr. Old: There is one point that I don't quite understand — perhaps it is not understandable — but that was that the Unknowable could not differentiate.

H.P.B.: I should say it could not, if it is the Absolute.

Mr. Old: But that Absolute, as the Absolute, is this, and that, and everything.

H.P.B.: Yes.

Mr. Old: Well, we are a differentiation, certainly; we are the being in that non-being. Humanity is the being, the one end of the line of life, and Parabrahm is at the other, and yet Parabrahm comprehends them both. He is not only the centre, but the radius and also the limitless circumference. It looks like a contradiction in terms.

H.P.B.: I will say, if you please, the Absolute cannot differentiate. You don't take the philosophical idea. You cannot say in philosophy that the Absolute differentiates, that the unconditioned has any relation whatever to the conditioned, or the finite; the infinite can have no relation to it. So you cannot, in thinking about cosmos, or the universe in its manifestations — perhaps you may use your argument — you cannot, if you talk pure philosophy and Vedantin philosophy, fix it up and say the Absolute can differentiate.

Mr. Old: Of course I see in the true idea of absolute being is lost in non-being.

H.P.B.: We say that Parabrahm is perfect, absolute unconsciousness. By saying that it is absolute unconsciousness, we say it is absolute consciousness. Now, can you imagine absolute consciousness? The Vedantins will. If it is absolute unconsciousness, it must be absolute consciousness; but, as it is absolute, it can have no relation to the finite consciousness or to finite unconsciousness. Do try and understand that difference. You see those enormously difficult and abstruse ideas in the Occult philosophy.

Mr. Old: I think it is high reasoning, which our language scarcely portrays at all.

---

[1] Acts 17:28.

H.P.B.: Herbert Spencer has tried it, and made a mess of it, because he takes the Unknowable for a kind of transcendental first cause, which appears a little less than anthropomorphic. It is simply invisible, and he does not give it a personality. I don't think that he is at all a Vedantic philosopher.

Mr. Old: I believe that the pure idea can be conceived, but I do not think it can be expressed.

H.P.B.: Everyone must feel it, certainly. Let me tell you, and perhaps it will help you. The Unknowable, as absoluteness, is eternal, immutable; had neither beginning, nor will it have an end. The Unknowable, as a manifestation, is periodical. The one is immutable, outside of space and time; the other is finite, because it is periodical — that is why the Parabrahmic period or the Manvantaric period is separated or divided into days of Brahma and nights of Brahma. The days are the periods of activity, in which this periodical manifestation, or the Unknowable manifested, puts in an appearance; and the night of Brahma is a period when everything merges in this one non-entity. Now, when the age of Brahma has finished the hundred years — which are not our human hundred years, but which it takes about 17 or 18 figures to express, milliards and milliards, I think about 15 figures — then it is a period which will take as many years as it took years of activity. Do you understand this division? The Unknowable is always the absolute unknowable, the abstract unknowable, or what Harrison calls the negative quantity — which, for our perceptions, it may be.

Mr. Old: Then you might say that the unknown is, in reality, that which is to be known.

H.P.B.: The unknown cannot be; because the unknown has always some potentiality of the unknowable in it, whereas the unknowable cannot have such a potentiality.

Mr. Old: But I, like yourself, distinguish here between the words "unknown" and "unknowable." I should call Herbert Spencer's first cause "unknown."

H.P.B.: Harrison is perfectly right. But, don't you call it Unknowable, because that is what we call Parabrahm.

Mr. Kingsland: It is the difference between Brahma and Parabrahm.

Mr. Old: Question 3. In reference to the whole of paragraph (e), and to some points which were raised last Thursday, it would be as well to devote a little more time to the subject of reincarnation. And then there are several clauses which I think it would be well to read separately. Unfortunately, the paragraph is omitted.

Mr. Kingsland: "The fourth order are substantial entities, etc." [Reads paragraph e, *The Secret Doctrine*, vol. 1, p. 218.]

Mr. Old: (a) For example, we have been accustomed to think of the "Imperishable Jivas," or "Monads," as the Atma-Buddhi-Manas (exoterically), and that this "Monad" incarnates at some period or other in the newly-born child — not, however, fully incarnating until seven years after birth.

H.P.B.: I told you that "Imperishable Monads" are not at all what you think. It is that which I have told you already, that the "Imperishable Jivas" are the incarnating individualities, not personalities; and they are not the Monads. The Monads take immediate possession of the astral images, the Chhaya of the Lunar Pitris; the Jivas or Manasa-Putra, only at the end of the Third Race. With the child it is just as it is with the First Race. The Monads, Atma-Buddhis, are said to have fully incarnated only when full consciousness is developed in the child mankind — that is to say, the Third Race — and so it is with the child unit, or man. Take always analogy, then you will find invariably the key to the occult explanation. As it is with the First Race to the Third Race, so it is with the child, because the child is microcosmos of the macrocosm, and it repeats, stage by stage, everything. The whole evolution of the universe is found in the evolution of the fetus and of the child. That is a well-known fact, which the Occultists ought to know, more or less.

Mr. Old: Then you say that the Monad does not incarnate.

H.P.B.: The Monad incarnates the Monad, so to say, of a shadow. It is not united, because Chhaya — or this image, the astral form — is not conscious of the presence of the Monad, because there is no Manasic element to appreciate or to be conscious of that Monad in it. Therefore, it is just as though he did not have it. So it is with the child.

Mr. Old: It is merely the vehicle of the individual life.

H.P.B.: Nothing else. But when the Manas comes, or the mind, then there is the union of all the principles, and all the principles appear all about between seven and eight years when the child becomes conscious.

Mr. Old: Manas is a connecting link. Then (b). It was suggested by Mr. Sinnett last Thursday, and also apparently by the paragraph before us, that the Monad is really necessary as a potentiality denominating, and being in fact the "germ" which causes the development of the entity from the germinal cell onwards. But can we really say that the Devachanic entity or upper triad has anything to do, as an entity, with the purely physical evolution of that form in which it will presently incarnate? Are not the four lower principles derived entirely from the parent and following broadly what we usually call heredity? And may we not say that this affects the four lower, but not the three higher principles?

H.P.B.: Now, I will try to answer you *seriatim*.[1] Mr. Sinnett probably calls Monad that which we call the image, Chhaya, unless he misunderstood the teaching — which I don't think, because he understood it well. And I think you misunderstood Mr. Sinnett. He did not say this about the Monad, because it is the first thing that is taught, that the Monad does not come but at a certain stage of the life of the child — the Buddhi, especially.

Mr. Old: He has prescribed that seven years in his *Esoteric Buddhism*.

H.P.B.: The germinal cell contains the seed or astral form only. The father plants the seed in the soil of matter. This seed is like a flame without wick or fuel: it neither decreases nor increases, and whether he has one or a hundred children, each of these children will be like a rush candle[2] to which was imparted a light from the same inexhaustible flame. There is a thing which goes for millions and millions, from the time when mankind began. It all passes from father to son, from father to son, and so on. You understand the meaning, and certainly it cannot decrease.

Mr. Old: But for how many principles is the human parent responsible?

H.P.B.: I will tell you all this which is written here. The Monad overshadows the fetus only in the seventh month, and enters fully the

---

[1] **Seriatim** (*Latin*) — one after another.
[2] **Rush candle** — a candle made from the pith of a rush plant, typically dipped in wax or animal fat for illumination. These candles were used in the past for lighting purposes before the widespread use of modern candles.

child after he reaches consciousness. The Devachanic entity envelops, so to speak, the new entity, lights it up, but begins its process of assimilation only after the first ray of consciousness, say at seven or eight months. Thus, it does not enter it. It begins to overshadow it, it is there, it is led by Karmic law to it, but it cannot enter immediately. It is perfect nonsense to say the child has a soul, and is a human being before it is born.

Mr. Kingsland: Then it is attracted by the astral shadow?

H.P.B.: Just in the same way.

Mr. Old: It is rather dangerous against the law of infanticide.

H.P.B.: It cannot be taught to the masses and the people. But unfortunately the Hindus know it, and therefore they get rid of their children very easily. But this is certainly Karma. But whether the child has got a will or not, it is a human being, and there are other laws in the code of philosophy which prevent infanticide; that will always be a crime. From the parents the child receives only the astral and physical bodies and the Kama-rupa, the animal soul. It receives life from no one. It does not receive life from father or mother; it is born, and therefore it is in life. I ask you, do you receive the ocean? Can it be said that you receive the ocean when you bathe in it, or does the sponge receive it? You and the sponge have your being, and that ocean because you are in its waters. Now, suppose that the waters penetrated you entirely, that is life, the water. The child receives life from no one. The life is there, it is the universal principle. Of course, science will tell you it is nothing of the kind. It is nonsense, that life is not an entity. Life is just that deity of which we know nothing.

Mr. Old: You think the physical parents have the power of focusing this life and bringing it into distinct channels.

H.P.B.: The form is made which, as soon as it is born, receives, or as soon as it begins developing, receives life; just the same as you breathe air unconsciously. Nobody gives you the air that you breathe. Without air you would die, that is all.

Mr. Old: Then you really mean to say that the endowment of life is the result of certain physical development which has led up to that stage when the reception of life is a necessity.

H.P.B.: Most assuredly. You are born, you are formed to come into being, and you live because life is there. You are in life. When you die, it is not that life leaves you; you are in the life. It is you who leave the life, and not life that leaves you.

Mr. Kingsland: Life begins to function and manifest through you.

H.P.B.: And once that your organs are destroyed, it won't function. It is like the force in the clock. You wind it up; so long as it is wound up it will work, but once that this force is exhausted — not the force that made it — but once the thing has been wound up and runs down, there is an end of it, it cannot function. And this force cannot function where there are no conditions.

Mr. Kingsland: It is more like a tree moving about in the wind. You see the effect of the wind by the tree, but if you take away the tree, the wind is blowing past there, just the same.

H.P.B.: The three higher principles are the human trinity, the three in one. They do not come to the child from the parents. If somebody objects to this and asks: how about the heredity intellect and its absence? You know, as they said the other time when somebody here thought the heredity the all. I say it is perfect nonsense. Neither this heredity intellect or dullness rests with the higher ego or Manas at all. Their degrees are dependent upon our physical organism and brain, the size of which, by the bye, does not always go *pari passu* with the quality of the brain. Now, some persons will say: "He has got an enormous brain, and it shows the intellect." Not at all. I have been reading things in the medical books. The pig has a far larger brain than the man, and yet it is not quite so intellectual.

Mr. Old: They say the depth of convolutions, rather.

H.P.B.: No, they weigh the brain. Such a one has got so many ounces or pounds or tons. I say it is the quality, not the quantity. If the father or the mother were intellectual people, they will sometimes pass by inheritance an organism as theirs was to the child. Thence the son will have the same capacities of receiving into and reflecting in his physical brain the same amount of light from Manas or the mind principle. But how often do we find stupid sons of intellectual parents, and vice versa? This is not heredity. Do you understand this? The parents may give by heredity their organism, their convolutions, or whatever it is, the physical material, which will have the same capacity of reflecting the light from Manas as they had, therefore the child will be as intellectual; but Manas is not at all that. It is always the same, it is omniscient. It becomes dull or stupid only in its personalities and incarnations upon earth. You can't say of Manas that one ego is more intellectual than the other.

Mr. Kingsland: Does not one ego bring back more Manases from the Devachanic state than another?

H.P.B.: Not at all. One ego will have a better Karmic development than another, but it does not bring back at all. Once it is past its period of illusion in Devachan — when it is in Devachan or anything, it becomes the omniscient ego.

Mr. Kingsland: But that portion which we have always understood to be assimilating, is not that brought back again?

H.P.B.: It is. But in Devachan it is not itself. It is very difficult to explain; it reflects the human personality, because if it did not do that, it could not have the bliss that it has, because Devachan, after all, is an illusion, the Fool's Paradise.

Mr. Kingsland: But then that portion of Manas surely develops with every individual.

H.P.B.: It does, because the personality differs, but the Manas *per se* is the incarnating ego.

Mr. ——: Manifestation depends upon the perfection or the imperfection of the instrument.

A Lady: It would really be, then, from the parents you have a certain development or non-development of mechanism. And it is according to that the Manas is able to manifest itself in ordinary life. And that is where heredity will come in.

H.P.B.: The Manas is always the same. It is the stem, the eternal stem around which cling the personalities, so to say, those that come and go, and so on. It is called the Sutratma, the silver thread on which are strung those pearls as personalities — you know the expression. In its own inherent nature, or essence, it is omniscient, for it is part of the Divine Mind. But once that it has been brought to incarnate on earth, it takes up all the materiality and all the finite attributes, so to say, and the qualities of the personalities it incarnates in. And moreover, these personalities are subject to the imperfections of the material form.

A Lady: Supposing during the human life, the spiritual nature has been developed up to a very considerable extent, and then death comes. When that Manas returns to a fresh incarnation, will the progress that has been made in the past life settle the type of humanity that it will then take up, so that its past life will carry it on further?

H.P.B.: Certainly. If the Karma was good, it will go higher and higher, and all the experiences of the past life will come in this life, because, when you find children who are not at all like their parents — no musicians in the family — and you see little boy phenomenons, Hofmann,[1] or some such things, this is a thing which comes from the previous life. It comes to him as easily as water to a duck.

Mr. ——: How does it happen that the mechanism he gets from his parents does not retard that? Because, if his parents are non-musical, then their mechanism, so far as regards music, must be stronger than his.

H.P.B.: It overpowers blind matter.

Mr. Kingsland: In many cases, I fancy it is retarded?

H.P.B.: Look at little, blind Tom,[2] who is in America, a little nigger[3] of four years, who is perfectly blind, and yet see the wonderful things that he does.

A Lady: Would it be attracted, rather, towards the musical mechanism?

H.P.B.: Heredity is a Karmic effect. Therefore, if an individuality has to incarnate in Karma in a person, then the frame will be given to him, which will give to him this musical mechanism.

A Lady: There will be a sort of affinity?

Mr. Old: And then has not an astral body the power of impressing its own image upon the gross matter supplied by the physical parents?

Mr. Kingsland: The other way about.

Mr. Old: The antitype which exists previous to the child's birth.

---

[1] **Josef Hofmann** (1876–1957) — a Polish-American pianist, composer and inventor. He gave a debut piano concert at the age of 5 in Warsaw, Poland.
[2] **Thomas "Blind Tom" Wiggins** (1849–1908) — an American pianist and composer.
[3] Please note that this word was used in 1889, when it was not considered offensive.

H.P.B.: This astral is nothing at all with the Manas that incarnates. This belongs to the lower matter, and this is given by the father and mother, by the parents, and around this astral then forms the physical child. But this astral is nothing to do with that. It is nothing to do with the ego, which is one and continuous, unbroken.

Mr. Old: The Monad, in incarnating, projects its shadow Chhaya.

H.P.B.: No, no, not at all.

Mr. Old: Does not it overshadow? It is said to overshadow the child.

H.P.B.: It overshadows the child that has its astral self in it, and its body. Then it begins overshadowing when the child is born. The Monad Buddhi, this immortal principle, gets into the child and over-shadows it as soon as the child begins to be conscious — as conscious as a kitten, for instance. It is there already, but the Manas is called a different thing. The Manas is mind. That is why the child will never become intellectual before five or six years. It depends upon how pre-cocious he is. Read in the second volume of *The Secret Doctrine* and see how the Lunar Pitris project their Chhayas. And having projected their Chhayas, this is the vehicle of the Monad.

Mr. Old: That is just what I understood, and it carries it towards the child — the as yet unintelligent child.

H.P.B.: I tell you again that till the Third Race, it does not link itself entirely.

Mr. Kingsland: It has nothing to do with the development of the germ, either physically or astrally, but it is attracted afterwards at a certain period to the already partly developed germ.

Mr. Old: How much of the individuality, then, shapes the organism?

Mr. Kingsland: That is the point I don't think has been quite elucidated yet. Where does the individuality of the reincarnating Monad come in?

H.P.B.: The individuality is the reincarnating ego, the Manas. Manas is a thing, it is Sutratma. The personality and individuality are quite different. You make the same thing out of personality and individuality.

Mr. Kingsland: Where does the musical quality come in? How does that belong to it?

H.P.B.: It belongs to it because every personality that passes gives a certain colour, and gives more and more and more to the incarnating ego; and then it remains, this talent for music, and it brings it back. Very well. All that remains on the individuality, on the ego being reincarnated, is brought back on earth, and therefore it is an inherent soul quality.

Mr. Kingsland: I understood you just now, the intellectuality does not depend upon Manas at all, but upon physical qualifications.

H.P.B.: Intellectuality and music are quite different things. I have known idiots who played beautifully. I said the parents did not give to the child anything but the form, and certainly there is the lower Manas and the higher Manas. If they made the form fit enough to receive this higher light, or to have untrammelled this light from the Manas, he will be intellectual. If the Kama-rupa, or the lower Manas, predominates too much, then he won't receive, because he will be dull. There will be no light coming from Manas. Manas, itself, depends upon Buddhi.

Mr. Kingsland: Then, as a matter of fact, there is a large portion of everyone's Manas, that does not incarnate at all, that always remains undeveloped, unrepresented, in the present personality of the person.

H.P.B.: Remember that we are in the Fifth Race and only at the end of the Fifth Race will Manas be entirely developed, and we are yet on the Fourth Round only. I cannot tell you all that I would like to. There are three more rounds.

Mr. Kingsland: Take the case of the person who has got this inherent quality. Suppose he doesn't find the physical conditions?

H.P.B.: Then he won't be a musician. There is Karma that will always find that.

Mr. Kingsland: Surely the whole of your Karma does not find all the development. Where is it during the present incarnation?

H.P.B.: I can't understand what you mean.

Mr. Old: I can understand your question, because it was one that arose in my mind.

Mr. Kingsland: Instead of saying music or intellectuality, let us say the character. Isn't it the Manas or distinctive quality that gives character to the person?

H.P.B.: To give character to the person, do you mean that the Manas would have to change and become a different Manas every time? Where would be, if you please, the incarnating ego, the Sutratma?

Mr. Old: Then you think character is only an expression of mind?

H.P.B.: I only know one thing. Let us say this pair of spectacles is the Manas. It is always for ever eternally the same. Now, I put the spectacles in mud; something will remain on it of this mud. Then I will put them in jam, there will be some jam left. Then I will put it in something else. Every incarnation gives to the Manas some personality, and at the end of the Manvantaric round, that is to say, at the end of the cycles of incarnation, there will be the Manas with all the experiences it has acquired. For personality dies. It is only the secret of spirituality, of the spiritual qualities, of the eternal qualities, that will survive. You read *Esoteric Buddhism*, and *Esoteric Buddhism* is well-enough written. You read it, Dr. Berridge, I can't explain it any better.

Mr. ——: Putting it into very bold English, supposing you always dropped them into jam?

H.P.B.: They will be very sweet then.

Mr. ——: Taking an analogy of jam and music — supposing it will be always music — Josef Hofmann will have so much by and bye that it will be bound to come to the front.

H.P.B.: Certainly I like somebody who can speak plainly.

A Lady: He will also incarnate into a body in which the mechanism is likely to go towards music.

H.P.B.: I say that, in the karmic sense, heredity is governed by Karma. Therefore, when the musical entity is to reincarnate, then certainly this law will take care that the body will be musical and fit for it — that they should not be born with stumps instead of fingers.

Mr. Old: You would say, really, that individual character is nothing else than expression of mind through different organisms, and that the organisms control the expression of character?

H.P.B.: For instance, you put some intelligence under blue glass. It will appear to you blue, or under red, and so on. It will go on like that.

Mr. Kingsland: If that is so, if Manas as we find it here depends upon the quality of the organism that it functions in, where does the development of Manas come in?

H.P.B.: It develops through the personality. Manas does not come to be happy and to be developed. Manas comes because it is too pure; and being too pure, it has neither merit nor demerit. Therefore, it must come and suffer a little bit, and have the experience of everything that can be got in this cycle of incarnation. And therefore, the same experiences will make it fit to merge in the Absolute. It contains all the experiences in this blessed world, and the worlds that have been and will be.

Mr. Kingsland: It appears from that, that Manas is something that is to be, still qualified by the individual lives with no life.

H.P.B.: Most assuredly. In *The Key to Theosophy* I give all this. Read *The Key to Theosophy*. It will come out in two or three weeks. I think I answer every question there. It is extremely difficult for me, "unaccustomed as I am to public speaking," to come and explain this. Really, I want to say one thing, and I say quite a different thing — or you take it as such.

Mr. Old: The next paragraph clears it up, I think. Question 3 (c). According to this view, the "spiritual plasm" referred to in the paragraph in question[1] is not the Devachanic Entity, though it is liable to be confounded with it. There is, of course, a mystery within a mystery here, but it is very desirable that we should have a clear view of the matter, in connection with the more immediate derivation and evolution of the seven human principles.

H.P.B.: You see what I said. You are right, and Mr. Sinnett or somebody else spoke also of this heredity business as being an obstacle. Do you remember, Mr. Burrows, who spoke about it, that it was an obstacle?

Mr. Burrows: I don't remember.

H.P.B.: It is just that which enters into Karmic attributes. Heredity is governed by Karma, in short. Therefore, you see, Karma will take care to bring it into a musical physical body.

Mr. Old: Then we may say that the law of heredity applies to the four lower principles, and the law of Karma operates in the plane of the three higher.

---

[1] *The Secret Doctrine*, vol. 1, pp. 219, 224.

H.P.B.: The law of heredity has nothing to do with life. Remember what you learn, if you please, apart from the Thursdays. Exoterically it is, not esoterically.

Mr. Old: (d) From what is said on page 224, line 10, the above view would appear to be supported, with the further addition that the parent is also responsible for Manas — perhaps we should say, some portion of Manas?

H.P.B.: Now, how can the parent be responsible for Manas? You will say next it is responsible for Atma.

Mr. Old: It is the animal mind we refer to, perhaps?

H.P.B.: It is the reflection from the higher mind. We say it is dual simply because on this plane the full Manas cannot manifest; and in relation to its lower Manas, it is just the same as Parabrahm's relation to the first Logos. It radiates. Very well. And the rest depends upon the more or less perfect organisms, on education, on environment, and on everything, on the vices that are inculcated; all these things that come, and are so many obstacles.

Mr. Kingsland: Then Manas stands there in the same way as Prana does in reference to the lower, to the life on the physical plane. It is universal, so to speak.

H.P.B.: The Manas is universal. These are distinct entities which incarnate, which in other Manvantaras have finished their cycle, and it is their time to incarnate in this cycle.

Mr. Kingsland: It says here the five lower principles in the four.

H.P.B.: It is not the five principles of the seven, it is the five principles of the lower principles. It is perfectly correctly said there. Man must have the fruition of all the five, it is said, and this fruition carries within it no responsibility to anyone. You look there on the page that you have been mentioning, page 224, line 20. You find there the phrase I have quoted: "Man must have the fruition of all the five," and this fruition carries with it no responsibility to anyone. How can the parents be responsible for Manas, where Manas is a defined and independent entity? The parents may in some way be karmically responsible for the physical organism of the child, but certainly not for Manas.

Mr. Kingsland: Not responsible for Manas any more than they are responsible for Prana.

H.P.B.: Most assuredly.

Mr. Old: Question 4 (page 233). Since each round, globe, etc., is under the guidance of a "Creator," "Builder," or "Watcher," can you tell us what part, if any, these Manus play in polity of nations on the terrestrial plane?

H.P.B.: None at all. The "Watchers" or "Builders" are commissioned by law to guide and animate, so to say, the elements of which our globe is composed; but they have no power to interfere with Karmic law, because they are not anthropomorphic gods. They are simply powers, cosmic powers, of which we have no ideas. Not what you men of science and naturalists would call cosmic powers, but what we Occultists would call cosmic powers.

Mr. Old: Question 5. During the reign of one Manu or Race, have the other six any *direct* influence on human affairs?

H.P.B.: Well, I would say to you with the French. When the king dies they say: "The king is dead; long live the king!" How can the six Manus have anything to do with the Manus now? When an age or race has passed away, nothing that has caused the Nidanas, or the concatenation of causes of the previous, act on the new one. It is only the Karmic effects that develop. When Victoria dies, and you have your next royal — ninny, shall I say — shall the four Georges[1] have any direct influence on the forces of England? You see, I am a very great Republican.

Mr. Old: Question 6, page 238, Sloka 5: "Sacred Animals." Elsewhere you explain the term "Sacred Animals" as referring symbolically to the signs of the zodiac. How is this meaning of the term connected with the explanation given here of it as "the first shadow of physical man"?

H.P.B.: How many times shall I have to repeat that each symbol has a septenary significance? Did I tell you one, or twenty, or a hundred times, that everything has seven meanings? In astronomy, the "Sacred Animals" mean the zodiacal signs; in geology, they mean the globes, which are also the planets (which may be taken astronomically), or geologically, as worlds; in zoology, they are sacrificial animals; in anthropology it is physical man. It has, in every department, some meaning, just as you apply it.

---

[1] **Four Georges** — the four kings of Great Britain who reigned from 1714 to 1830.

Mr. Old: Question 7, page 250: It would be interesting to have a clearer definition of the three "waters" — "solid water," "liquid mist, watery," "third world-element water"; also, to know the order of the development of the senses in the races of the Fourth Round. We are in the Fourth Round, but Fifth Race, and therefore are developing a sense which cannot reach its full expansions till the Fifth Round: 1. Fire (sight); 2. Air (touch); 3. Water (taste); 4. Earth (smell); 5. Ether (sound); 6. Akasha (intuition); 7. Kundalini[1] sense (includes all others).

H.P.B.: We are, for the first time, in this Fourth Round; and we are, for the first time, men. In the three previous Rounds we were mere intangible phantoms; then ethereal, fluidic creatures; then jelly-like animals; and only in the Fourth Race we have become real physical men, haven't we? Then, take the analogy, and look what I have written there, and go to bed. You must ask this question with your initiation of the Masters, not of me (see footnote on page 252). You put me questions that are — well, extraordinary. All this is esoteric, but I don't mind telling you something of it. If you have air in seven states of density, why cannot you have water in such seven states of degree, and everything else, including fire? I ask you the question. Of course, if we represented and analysed them, we shall find in each all the other elements, in one form or the other. Now, let us take earth, and we will find in it that we divide it into seven. We find in its lowest and most material end granite rock, the hardest that you can think of, which will become softer and softer as it passes through each of its states until it becomes mud, and what you would call simply dirty water. It will be matter, still. Now, in the rock, matter, or earth, you will find fire concealed. That is to say, it contains fire potentially, as it contains air and everything else. The same with air, which begins at the third stage above radiant matter, and ends with ether and Akasha, and so on. All this will show to you that, whether four or seven, these

---

[1] **Kundalini** (*Sanskrit*, "curled in the form of a snake") — the "Serpent Power" or mystic fire, also named the "World-mother." It is *Buddhi* considered as an active instead of a passive principle (which it is generally, when regarded only as the vehicle, or casket of the Supreme Spirit *Atma*). Kundalini is called the "Serpentine" or the *annular* power on account of its spiral-like working or progress in the body of the ascetic developing the power in himself. It is a fiery electric occult or *Fohatic* power, the great pristine force, which underlies all organic and inorganic matter. This creative and electro-spiritual force, when aroused into action, can as easily kill as it can create.

are called elements, are correlative, and each becomes a definite element only on our plane of perception and by one of its seven aspects, because that aspect which predominates over the others will give that qualification to that element. We call it water because that aspect is more developed than air, or fire; but, you will find all the seven in every element occultly, in reality, in their final essence. And on the plane of manifestation, they are all one element. And when they have achieved their cycle of evolution in the world of manifestation, this one disappears and they merge back into their primal cause, and from the one element they become no element again, absoluteness. I did not create the world. I cannot explain this to you. I must not.

Mr. Old: Question 8 (page 260 — end of second paragraph). If our globe is in its Kama-rupic state, in what state was it during the First, Second, and Third Rounds?

H.P.B.: That is a modest man, and he asks very easy things, to which extremely easy answers can be given. Count from what you will, it is always the Kama-rupic state, since it is right in the middle. From above or below it will become rupa. It is the middle thing; but, if we count from the races — for the evolution of the globes has to begin by the highest, or seventh — the second will correspond to the second, and so on. We call it Kama-rupic because there are no words to express the corresponding states. If from round we turn to races, it will be easier, and it is explained in *The Secret Doctrine.* Everything is explained there, how with every race you acquire new facility. In the Fifth Race we have attained the highest intellectuality in this round; but in the Sixth Round or the Fifth Round, the Fifth Race will be a thousand times more intellectual yet. Take it all on analogy. Now, gentlemen, let us have questions, and I am ready to answer you.

Mr. Old: What is the meaning of the second plane mentioned here (page 262 note)?

H.P.B.: That is what I say. You ask me in three years that! Now, you had better ask questions, and we will make the conversation general.

6 JUNE 1889

Mr. Old: These are questions such as would come from a person beginning to search out Theosophical truth, and I thought myself that it would be a leader to the issue of this new book, *The Key to Theosophy*. I thought a consideration of some of the elementary questions would not only fill up a very pleasant evening, but, at the same time, would excite some interest in the book which is now approaching completion. They are mere elementary questions on Karma, Devachan, and Reincarnation; the How, When, and Where of Theosophy. Question 1. What is Karma?

H.P.B.: Am I really expected to answer this?

Mr. Old: You are.

H.P.B.: Karma is the law of retribution. Now, Mr. Bertram Keightley, go on.

Mr. B. Keightley: They would much rather listen to you than to me. However, Karma is, as H.P.B. began to say, the law of retribution — that which is recognized by modern science as the law of cause and effect. But although that law is absolutely universal, the law of Karma is more frequently used in a narrower sense as applying more particularly to the law of cause and effect acting on the moral plane. Literally, it means simply action, and it expresses the idea that every action is productive of consequence, and so the chain of causation goes on infinitely. But, it is not simply that causes operate blindly, because in the Theosophical view the law of Karma is absolute intelligence; and it also has to be remembered that the law of Karma applies to the individual. It is not merely that a man performs certain actions.

H.P.B.: Stop. You say that the law of Karma is intelligent.

Mr. B. Keightley: I said "intelligence."

H.P.B.: I say it is not. It is neither intelligence nor non-intelligence.

Mr. B. Keightley: It is absolute intelligence.

H.P.B.: Because you will make of it immediately a personal god, and I protest against that. That is to say, that everything that falls under the sway or the influence of that ever-present law will have certain effects, as in the physical world there is a concatenation of causes and effects always. For instance, if I do like that, I will just hurt my hand; the pain I feel in my hand will be the effect of having done that;

so it is in the world of moral causes. But you cannot and must not say it is intelligent or intelligence. Is it simply the absolute harmony, absolute — well, call it intelligence, wisdom, anything you like. There again I am stuck for a word.

Mr. B. Keightley: It is true to say it acts with intelligence.

H.P.B.: It does not act. It is our actions that act, and that awaken into all kinds of influences. Look here, if you say that Karma acts and you say it has intelligence, immediately you suggest the idea of a personal god. It is not so, because Karma does not see and Karma does not watch, and does not repent as the Lord God repented. Karma is a universal law, immutable and changeless.

Mr. B. Keightley: But you cannot conceive of a law which does not act.

H.P.B.: Well, I say it does not act. In my conception, it does not act. Well, Karma does not act any more than water drowns you.

Mr. B. Keightley: But water does drown you.

H.P.B.: Water does not drown you. You drown yourselves in the water. Don't go into the water and you won't get drowned.

Mr. Old: Is it possible to get outside the law of Karma, then?

H.P.B.: You cannot.

Mr. Old: The analogies scarcely fit.

H.P.B.: I beg your pardon. It does, as much as it can fit in this world of physical symbols — or whatever you may call them — because it is the way that you act. It is not because you act wickedly or sinfully, or with or without a motive, you produce an effect. You strike a note in the universal.

Mr. Sneyd: Is not ignorance the cause of all evil action?

H.P.B.: It is, but Karma does not take stock of it, does not concern itself whether you do it from ignorance or from too much learning. It is simply if you do a certain thing, so the effect will be on a similar line. For instance, you will strike one note, and you know perfectly well what will be the consequence of that note. That is why I simply wanted to stop Mr. Keightley, because he said it was intelligent and it acted. Certainly we must say that it acts; but, I want you at the same time to understand that in saying it acts, we use the same expression as if we said the sun is setting. The sun does not set at all.

Mr. Burrows: If our action is a note which we strike, that really is the echo of some previous note which has been struck somewhere in the universe.

H.P.B.: Certainly, it is not the first time that you struck this note. Whether you strike it in the ordinary way, or otherwise, it depends on that whether it will be flat, sharp or something else.

Mr. Kingsland: Karma is, so to speak, the absolute equilibrium; and however we act we disturb that equilibrium one way or another, and Karma adjusts.

Mr. B. Keightley: The analogy that dwells in my mind is this — it almost presents itself to me under this form: If we conceive ourselves as beings absolutely surrounded and penetrating everything in fluid of such a nature that every action we make in that fluid produces a series of vibrations which eventually react upon ourselves. If you imagine a body suspended in a perfect fluid, no movement is possible without disturbing the fluid. That sort of pressure pressing in upon you from all sides, that substance — if you like to call it that — is Karma. Or rather, Karma describes the relation of that subject.

H.P.B.: There is simply one way of getting outside the influence of Karma. It is the yogis who do it only — it is by merging oneself more and more in the Laya state. That is to say, that you are just like in a vessel out of which air has been pumped — a perfect vacuum. In that vacuum, of course, you cannot go either left or right or any way; there is no point of attraction, and there you are. You understand the analogy?

Mrs. Besant:[1] Then it would always be the striving after equilibrium?

H.P.B.: Certainly! Every action produces a Karmic effect on the spiritual plane, on the psychic, on the spiritual, and everything. And the only thing is to be in this neutral point where there is no differentiation, where there is no action.

Mr. Old: Then we understand Karma to be the law of equilibrium.

H.P.B.: It is perfect harmony and equilibrium.

---

[1] **Annie Besant** (1847–1933) — a British social rights activist and campaigner for Indian independence; the President of the Theosophical Society from 1907 to 1933.

Mr. B. Keightley: I think you want to add to it one thing. People get an idea very often that Karma only applies to bad actions. Karma is simply the action, the law of the consequence of action of all kinds, whether good or bad, and it is, entirely apart from that, the inevitable sequence of cause and effect. It will fall upon you whether the action is good or bad.

Mr. Sneyd: But would not you say that all that arose — every evil consequence which decreased happiness — arose from ignorance on the part of the conscious being that did the action? However learned a person may be, supposing he does an action which results in the decrease of his happiness, should not you say that action was caused by his ignorance in some respect?

H.P.B.: But ignorance won't save you from the effects of Karma.

Mr. Sneyd: Don't you think ignorance is the cause of bad Karma?

H.P.B.: It is.

Mr. Sneyd: And that knowledge is the cause of all good Karma? Supposing you did a thing and it increased your happiness; would not it be the reason of that would most likely be that you had done something with knowledge, as it were?

Mr. B. Keightley: I don't think so, because the effects produced by a given cause are not always of the same character. You see, a man who uses his knowledge to do good, to make good Karma for himself, acts fundamentally from a selfish motive, which is again a wrong motive, at the back of his good action.

Mr. Sneyd: Would not the reason be that he was ignorant in so far as he did not know the interest of one conscious being was the interest of all?

H.P.B.: Wait a moment, there is another question about Karma here.

Mr. Old: I thought it would not do to let each question go too far into the discussion, otherwise it might overlap some of the other questions. The second question is: How far does this law operate in this life, and how far in Devachan?

H.P.B.: In Devachan, it does not operate at all. It is the law of Karma which sends a man to Devachan with a programme already prepared beforehand, which programme is the consequence of his suffering and of the miseries that he had in this world, and it is already there; it is cut and dried for him. Karma waits on the threshold of Devachan at the moment of reincarnation, and then it pounces upon the individual when he is rewarded. There is no punishment in the hereafter, in the other world, as you call it.

Mrs. Besant: It only works then, really, in this world?

H.P.B.: It is the hell, and the purgatory, and everything, and the paradise.

Mr. B. Keightley: The good effects are reaped in Devachan.

H.P.B.: Reaped for those who want a consolation, and want a rest, and bliss, and care for it; those who don't care for it won't have it.

Mr. Gardner: The fool's paradise.

H.P.B.: For instance, you are perfectly indifferent to everything.

Mr. Kingsland: There is a question which might be put with reference to very wicked people who don't go into Devachan.

H.P.B.: They are born almost immediately after a kind of sleep in which they won't have very nice dreams.

Mr. Kingsland: That is what I wanted to say.

H.P.B.: There is nothing, you see, like Devachan; there is Avichi, but that is quite a different thing.

Mr. Kingsland: In the state of Kama-loka.

H.P.B.: There it is no more the man, the entire man. He has been left and abandoned by one of his principles. He has no more of the Atma over him; he has simply his intelligence and his consciousness. That is why I say those creatures that you see in the séance rooms are so very dangerous. It is not the man, it is the shadow of the man, and his reflection; but with all the wickedness and with all the wicked influences, the utmost fear of all that which he has committed in this life. And certainly he will inoculate it in those present as though a living man came with the smallpox and gave it to you all. All this idea of spiritualism is perfectly ridiculous.

Mr. Old: Then Karma does not operate, or has no active operation, only a reflex operation, in Devachan?

H.P.B.: Merely sends a man into Devachan and stops on the threshold. Allegorically speaking, it waits when the man comes out of the state of bliss, during which he will be rewarded for all the unmerited suffering and all the things he had — for after all, a man is a very miserable creature. A man does not want to be born, and does not know he is born.

Mr. Burrows: Is there such a thing as unmerited suffering?

H.P.B.: If you suffer from causes you produce, it is merited; but very often you have sufferings through causes generated by other persons, of which you are not guilty at all.

Mrs. Besant: For instance, national Karma.

H.P.B.: Very often you suffer for things you have never committed, but you simply happen to fall under this current, and there you are. You suffer tremendously, and you suffer that which is not merited, and then you have to have an adequate bliss and reward for it.

Mr. B. Keightley: That is the personal Karma. The suffering man has a conscious personality — Mr. Smith or Mr. Brown, who is not aware he has committed any of these crimes, how shall we say? Take for instance now, this accident in America;[1] it will be a very good instance. Now, you could not suppose that all the people that have been drowned or have suffered in various ways, and all the children in that catastrophe, were all, as it were, brought under its influence by their personal Karma, so to speak, would you, H.P.B.?

H.P.B.: No. It is just that, you know.

Mr. B. Keightley: There a dam bursts and these people are swept away.

Mr. Sneyd: Would not you say it was the result of a sort of ignorance on the part of those people being there and not knowing the train would come to a smash?

Mr. B. Keightley: Of course it is, in one sense.

Mr. Old: This is what you call diffused Karma. A person comes under it by virtue of being an atom of a body. He cannot have a law separate from the body to which he belongs.

Mr. B. Keightley: The distinction I drew between the personality and individuality of a man is of special importance, because as a personality he has not perhaps a responsibility for that; he is one of a race, and he suffers the Karma of the race.

Mr. Burrows: And then the justice comes in afterwards.

---

[1] **Johnstown Flood** — the flood which occurred in Pennsylvania on 31 May 1889 due to the collapse of the South Fork Dam, killing more than 2,200 people.

Mr. B. Keightley: Because he has suffered personally more than he has merited, he receives his reward in Devachan in the shape of a personal reward. Is not that so, H.P.B.?

Mr. Old: Then our third question is: How far can this law of Karma be diverted, deferred, or prevented — diverted in the sense of turning off one track, onto another?

H.P.B.: You meddle with Karma, and then it will be just a thousand times worse. You can defer it and you can stop it for a while, but it will come always.

Mr. Old: You cannot prevent it, then?

H.P.B.: You cannot. It will become worse.

Mr. B. Keightley: Can you divert it in the sense of changing the character of its manifestation? Can you neutralize bad Karma by subsequent good action?

Mr. Old: Can an individual take on the Karma of half a dozen people?

H.P.B.: He cannot. No, sir.

Mr. Kingsland: But you can make new Karma for half a dozen people.

H.P.B.: Yes, but you cannot *take* it any more than you can take the illness of a half a dozen persons. Now, if it is not Karmic, of course you may stop it — this thing which has been produced by someone else — but if it is Karmic, nothing will stop it.

Mr. Old: A person who alleviates suffering only generates good Karma for himself.

H.P.B.: He does temporary good to the persons, but the Karma must come in some other shape.

Mr. Old: Because I was wondering how far Karma was worked out, or worked off, in physical suffering.

H.P.B.: Who told you that? I don't know what you mean.

Mr. Old: Well, you know, some people suffer tremendously in this world, they undergo physical suffering. Well, I presume that is one of the effects comprehended under the law of Karma.

H.P.B.: Or perhaps the Karma of your parents.

Mr. Old: Well, that is a diversion of Karma.

H.P.B.: But you can't take it voluntarily. Your parents have been creating a bad Karma for you in the shape of heredity, disease, and therefore for this you are going to be rewarded in Devachan, and consoled for it, and your parents when they are incarnated will have to pay for it. For instance, there is one kind of Karma that nobody thinks of: it is for statesmen and kings and all the blessed autocrats. If they wanted to do any good, they ought to do the following: to have the strictest laws not to permit diseased persons, consumptive people, those with anything like insanity or scrofula[1] in them, to get married and to have children, because this is the greatest crime that can be. They have no right to do it, and this is the thing that brings the worst Karma, and changes whole populations. I know I was forty years ago in England, and I saw of every ten men, there were seven or eight who were magnificently and stoutly built. I come here now, if you please, and I see the population altered. Look at the army. You have no more of those men you had forty years ago, there are none, it is changing entirely. You see sometimes tall men, and that is all; but certainly it is not what it used to be.

Mr. B. Keightley: How far is it that the Karma of the reincarnating egos in those diseased and unhealthy bodies — how far does their Karma attract?

H.P.B.: I suppose it does attract them, but sometimes it does not. It is very difficult to come and tell you of these workings of Karma.

Mr. B. Keightley: It is one of the very great points.

Mr. Old: I want to know if it is any good alleviating suffering.

H.P.B.: It is good if you distribute suffering, so that you will have a little today and a little tomorrow. When you suffer terribly, you lose your head; but on the other hand, you get accustomed to suffering. Now, I don't remark my pains and aches, but if I had them all at once, I don't know what I would be.

Mr. Kingsland: Is there not all along the tendency to refer Karma too much to the physical plane? All we are making that mistake, I think.

H.P.B.: Surely.

Mr. Kingsland: People are apt to imagine that you do an act, and that that act produces a certain effect in the next incarnation. Well that

---

[1] **Scrofula** — the tuberculosis of the lymphatic glands.

act, as an act on the physical plane, can only produce a physical result on the physical plane. What is carried over in the next incarnation, which becomes your Karma, is the effect which is produced in you. The state of consciousness, so to speak, in doing that act; it is not the act itself. The mere act of killing a man is a physical act on the physical plane, and won't result in Karma on the physical plane.

H.P.B.: But see the moral effect it produces — and that goes for a thousand times more than the physical act. The man that dies today, dies instead of dying two or three days later, but he may leave orphans. By the act of killing, the generations will be thrown entirely in a new track. They will be scattered. Every one of them will go into other creations they never thought about. Others will go into other parts. Physically it is nothing; only, the physical produces moral effects and results.

Mr. Sneyd: Supposing we say there is a man that is blind, and he runs in the way of a railway train, that train runs over him. Is not that the result of a sort of ignorance, or absence of knowledge and perceptions?

H.P.B.: Again this may be merited or unmerited, as the case may be.

Mr. Sneyd: Supposing we say that the driver stopped the train in time?

Mr. B. Keightley: The driver saw him and stopped the train?

Mr. Sneyd: How would it be then?

Mr. B. Keightley: It was the man's Karma to be saved.

Mr. Sneyd: You could not say that he was ignorant, then, to a certain extent?

Mr. B. Keightley: Oh yes. He was not saved by his own act, but by the act of somebody else.

Mr. Old: Question 4. How far does the general belief in Karma operate towards the acceptance of fatalism?

H.P.B.: If you are ignorant, you see fatalism.

Mrs. Besant: But the way it comes from outsiders sometimes is, that supposing you believe in these evils, why should you go against them?

H.P.B.: That is what the Easterners do. We don't do it, but the Eastern people do it.

Mr. B. Keightley: Is it right to do that?

H.P.B.: Not always. When it is done as the Muslim does it, it is bad, because it is crass fatalism.

Mr. B. Keightley: Take the people in Burma. They practically, until they were brought under the influence of Olcott and yourself, sat down under the state of things.

H.P.B.: They accepted it not on account of Karma, but on account of [...].

Mr. B. Keightley: Well that is Karma in another form. It is really an important question, what is the right spirit to develop, to cultivate in yourself in reference to the action of Karma.

H.P.B.: To do your duty on this plane. Not to go and kick against Karma, any more than what a Christian will tell you — don't fly into the face of Providence, to a certain extent. But it is your duty when you see any evil to try and avoid it, not only for yourself — which would be very little — but for anyone else.

Mrs. Besant: And try to help other people out of it.

H.P.B.: Yes, more than you help yourself.

Mr. Burrows: Is not the true solution that we should separate "it" from humanity?

Mr. B. Keightley: Here you get this: Before the last 25 years, the population in India, broadly speaking, sat down and submitted to European rule and domination — I am speaking very broadly — but now what they do is to try and wake themselves up from their sloth and apathy, and to reorganize and to start a fresh current of activity in which the Theosophical Society has had a very large share. They are reacting, and are doing their best to react against the condition into which their past history in Karma had brought them. Is that right or is that wrong?

H.P.B.: It is right, because a life of inaction is worse than a life of action.

Mr. B. Keightley: If a man feels the impulse in himself, it is a part of the law working through him.

Mr. Old: It is like Bailey's[1] definition, "Free will in man is necessity in play."

H.P.B.: Individually, there is free will, but once you take it collectively, there is no free will. It operates only with personalities. But speak of a nation or think of a nation, what kind of a free will has it? It is simply a dry leaf that is blown hither and thither, and sent by the wind everywhere. You have no right to sit and do nothing. You are obliged to be co-workers with Nature. But otherwise, as is said in the Apocalypse, "Nature will spew you out of the mouth."[2]

Mr. B. Keightley: The law of progress is as much a part of the law of Karma. The thing to get out of the idea of Karma is not the idea that you have to sit down and accept things as they are — though you should not resent things — but you should strive your best to make those things right, without the feeling of bitter resentment.

Mr. Burrows: If we try to alter them now, it will be better in the future. It is not selfishness.

Mr. B. Keightley: Then that again is productive of evil.

Mrs. Besant: So that really you strive against the evil.

Mr. B. Keightley: Yes. Without resentment.

Mr. Burrows: That is a very important point, because the tendency now is get angry and bitter.

Mr. Sneyd: How do you say about free will? How can one prove there is such a thing, when everything is the result of cause and effect? I don't say that exactly. Well, I can see one thing, I suppose you the cause — the individual himself is the cause.

Mr. B. Keightley: Yes, the primary cause. The conditions under which he operates the Karma, so to speak, that is working out. As an individual, he is a cause.

Mr. Burrows: But would it be right to say that we can really create fresh causes?

H.P.B.: Most assuredly. Every one of you creates fresh causes from morning to night. That is where the free will comes in, because if there were no free will you would not create causes, you would simply be under the thrashing of this law.

---

[1] **Philip James Bailey** (1816–1902) — an English poet.
[2] A paraphrase of Revelation 3:16.

Mr. B. Keightley: Under the blows of the law.

Mr. Gardner: The results of past Karma. If the actions are happening by accident, they are the result of past Karma.

H.P.B.: The accidents are commas and semicolons. That is all they are.

Mr. B. Keightley: Yes, the accidents are the punctuation of life.

Mr. Old: Things from which we measure off theories.

H.P.B.: Accidents are not things that are preordained, if you please.

Mr. Old: Then we branch off on to the subject of death.

H.P.B.: That is why we say we are our own punishers and rewarders and saviours.

Mr. Old: Then come questions on Devachan. It opens up with the orthodox question: What is Devachan — a state, a place, or both?

H.P.B.: A state. It is no more a place than your dreams.

Mr. Old: Has it any corresponding loka?

H.P.B.: No, it has not. We may be in Devachan, I can be in this chair, and you can be on yours. It is a state, not a locality.

Mr. B. Keightley: That is one of the things that strengthens its analogy to sleep.

H.P.B.: It is a dream — the most vivid, so vivid that even in this life there are dreams that sometimes you awaken and are not sure whether it was reality or not. You just imagine yourself a dream as vivid as life.

Mr. Kingsland: Now we think of an entity in Kama-loka, which is attracted at certain times to a séance room.

H.P.B.: They are not entities, they are reflections, they are spooks.

Mr. Kingsland: For the time being, they are to a certain extent individualized. We have been accustomed to talk of the Devachanic entity.

H.P.B.: Yes, because it is the three higher principles; but would you think of an entity of a personality? You would not call the reflection of a personality in the looking glass an entity.

Mrs. Besant: But the one in Devachan is the three higher principles.

H.P.B.: It is consciousness.

Mr. B. Keightley: The three higher principles, at any rate, have some sort of Upadhi, or basis. Where is the Upadhi of the three higher principles during the Devachanic period?

H.P.B.: Upadhi is the consciousness of it and nothing else. It is the Manas.

Mr. Old: Is there no form under which this Monad is identified?

H.P.B.: No form at all. It has a form in your own consciousness, and everything else that it sees are forms, created by the consciousness.

Mr. B. Keightley: Can you say that your thought is anywhere? That is the analogy.

Mr. Old: No, but you can embody it.

H.P.B.: No, you cannot.

Mr. B. Keightley: If the thought or Manas is the Upadhi of the Devachanic entity, then you can't say your thought is located anywhere.

H.P.B.: "Remembrance" will not express the thing. It is the recollection of your personality, the feeling of the ego, that you were the personal ego; and that is the Upadhi of Devachan. Because if you are Mr. Smith, Mr. Smith will be in Devachan as Mr. Smith and will have the little Smiths around him, if he loved them, and his Mrs. Smith and everything. Therefore the Upadhi is the consciousness of this personality for the time being. After it leaves Devachan, it is no more Mr. Brown.

Mrs. Besant: But would Mr. Smith be visible to a higher intelligence?

H.P.B.: Why should a higher intelligence look at him, what is there to see in the consciousness of another personality? The higher intelligence has got something better to do. What do you mean, Mrs. Besant, by higher intelligence — a Deva, a god?

Mrs. Besant: Yes, in all those higher instances.

H.P.B.: We are not concerned with them. During the Devachanic period the personality becomes, for the time being, so to say, merged in the individuality. It is immortal, for the time of the cycle of life and, so to say, the individuality plays the part of that personality that he or she was during the life period. And this is the Upadhi — this is the basis upon which the whole Devachanic experiences and thoughts of bliss go and act.

Mrs. Besant: Suppose we take it as a state of sleep. A bystander would see the person, but not the mind. Then if that body is gone, there is nothing left to see.

H.P.B.: Certainly that is what it is. It is consciousness, just that.

Mr. B. Keightley: I suppose you could only say it was the centre of consciousness in the Akasha?

H.P.B.: Now what has Akasha to do with it? Neither Akasha, nor ether, nor air has anything to do with it. It is simply a state of consciousness. It is a state, and not a locality.

Mr. Kingsland: But it is an individualized state of consciousness.

H.P.B.: Yes, for a person that is in a Devachanic condition. My Devachan won't be yours, and yours won't be mine. It is that a person dies and suddenly finds itself in Devachan, where the separation of the principles takes in a moment — or several days or weeks or months. All this depends upon the previous life of the personality, on the statement, on the degree of intellectuality, on the degree of everything.

Mr. Burrows: Then if Mr. Smith has Mrs. Smith there, it does not follow of necessity that Mrs. Smith has got Mr. Smith?

H.P.B.: Yes. If Mr. Smith loved her he would have Mrs. Smith, but if he did not, he won't even remember her.

Mr. Burrows: But suppose Mrs. Smith did not love him.

H.P.B.: That is another thing.

Mr. Burrows: He will have her, and she won't have him.

H.P.B.: It is that which we loved. In Devachan there is a perfect oblivion of everything that was disagreeable or that caused any pain, or of anything but an eternal bliss — which must be, by the way, exceedingly monotonous and stupid.

Mrs. Besant: It is really, then, the fruition of our desires.

H.P.B.: All the aspirations you had which were unsatisfied, all that which you could not have here through divers circumstances, you will have in Devachan. You will have all your desires realized, everything that you loved and could not have — perhaps that from which you are separated — but spiritually. Nothing that pretends to the earth. For instance, if you had some vicious love or something like that, you will have nothing of the kind there.

Mr. Burrows: Supposing three or four people had the same desire.

H.P.B.: Every one of them will have it, so long as it is not vicious. Now, for instance, a man who drank himself to death will certainly not have his whiskey there.

Mrs. Besant: It is only Buddhi-Manas that goes.

H.P.B.: Atma is nothing; it is all absolute, and it cannot be said that it is this, that, or the other. It is simply that in which we are — not only that we live and breathe and have our being, but in the whole universe, and during the whole Manvantaric period. Therefore, Atma is said to have Buddhi for a vehicle, because Buddhi is already the first differentiation after the evolution of the universe. It is the first differentiation, and it is the Upadhi, so to say, of Atma. Then Buddhi is nothing, *per se*, but simply the first differentiation. And it is the consciousness in the universal consciousness, but it is non-consciousness in this world. On this plane of finite consciousness it is nothing, for it is infinite consciousness. Understand me, Atman cannot be called infinite consciousness. It is the one Absolute, which is conscious non-consciousness. It contains everything, the potentiality of all; therefore, it is nothing and all. It is Ain-Soph, and it is the Parabrahm and so on; many names you can give it. It is "No Thing," you understand? Therefore, Buddhi being the first differentiation, the first ray, it is universal consciousness, and could not act on any one plane, especially on the terrestrial plane. And to be conscious of something, of somebody, it must have Manas, that is to say, the consciousness of this plane. If you read *The Secret Doctrine* you will see that men had nothing of the kind until the Manasa-Putra (the sons of the mind) incarnated in the forms that were projected by the Lunar Pitris. There was nothing but matter, and the nothingness of Buddhi and Atma; therefore, they had to be cemented, so to say, between this Buddhi and themselves. They had to have this Manas, which is the finite consciousness of our plane of existence and their incarnating ego. This incarnating ego, which goes from one personality to another, collects the experiences of every life. After having collected all the experience of millions and millions of incarnations, then, when the Manvantaric period ceases, and this world goes into dissolution, this ego, having had all this experience, approaches more and more of the Absolute, and, at the end of I do not know how many Manvantaras, certainly it will become — before it merges into the one, it must have the experience. Then it approaches more and more and more that which is all and nothing. Finally it emerges. When we say that we speak about the state of Nirvana, that is nothing. It is Para-Nirvana that we are speaking about. Nirvana is simply a high Devachan.

Mr. Burrows: When does the memory come in of all the previous incarnations?

H.P.B.: To have a memory you have to live. You can have the memory of what? If you have never been anything, you cannot have a memory. You must have a memory of something.

Mr. Kingsland: Mr. Burrows asked at what point it came on.

H.P.B.: Every life is a peg on which you hang that memory.

Mr. Burrows: When does the universal memory come in?

H.P.B.: That is a thing which is during the whole Manvantara; it is the Mahat, as they call it. It is the universal intelligence, and all these incarnating egos are simply rays of that.

Mr. Keightley: When the ray has succeeded in merging itself into the universal mind, it then recovers the knowledge.

H.P.B.: When there is an end of all, there is the Maha-Pralaya — not what will come after our little earth is destroyed. Then Mahat itself disappears and is merged in Parabrahm, and is merged in the All.

Mr. Burrows: Then does reincarnation go on again in the higher plane?

H.P.B.: Yes. You see, the butterfly will never become the chrysalis and the grub again. It goes on, and nature never goes back, but always goes progressing higher and higher. It may become, for instance, mentally, and in its acts, a thousand times worse than it was before, but it will be higher on the plane of physical manifestation — physically.

Mr. Old: What gave me the opinion that the Devachan had some particular form and a place corresponding to its state was this. I think on page 157, Volume 1, where those tables are given and the scheme of the different schools of thought in the East,[1] it says: Upadhi is a basis and in a corresponding system of philosophy it is translated by the word *kosha*,[2] which means a sheath. That word is very confounding, especially when we see that opposite Manas. Thus: one of the Devachanic principles is put [...], or [...], the causal basis or sheath. You see, that is what gives one an incorrect opinion.

Mr. B. Keightley: Are not you confusing the idea of basis with the idea of form? They are not the same. For instance, the water you

---

[1] See Table 2 on page 76.
[2] **Kosha** (*Sanskrit*, "sheath") — the Vedantic name for five principles in man; the sheath of every principle.

may consider the basis of something, but you could not say it has a form, *per se.*

H.P.B.: You consider gas the basis of something.

Mr. B. Keightley: Upadhi and form are not the same things.

Mr. Old: Has this monad a diffused consciousness into the whole universal Devachan? Has it a locus? Has it a distinct place? Has it a limitation?

H.P.B.: It has not. Consciousness has no limitation.

Mr. B. Keightley: How can it have, when three belong to the Arupa world?

H.P.B.: Of which two are nothing.

Mr. B. Keightley: I was quoting *The Secret Doctrine.*

H.P.B.: You take the three systems of philosophy,[1] one of which shows what the Theosophists give, one what the Taraka Raja Yoga give, and the other what the Vedantins give; it is not at all that it corresponds. It corresponds to one as a sheath, and the other does not. It is only our [...], or the occult system, because that is a thing which is confined to the three principles, and we are dividing it into seven principles, because it is a great deal easier to explain. The Vedantins have got five sheaths and the sixth, the Atma and the Buddhi, of which they don't speak at all, because what they mean by [...] does not mean at all the Buddhi, but simply the astral form.

Mr. Old: The next question is: What determines the length of the Devachanic state?

H.P.B.: Your actions.

Mr. Old: In the previous life?

H.P.B.: In the previous life.

Mr. Old: It is not, then, the aggregate?

H.P.B.: It is not the aggregate, unless there is some surplus that has to be worked out.

Mr. Old: Then you consider that at the end of Devachan, we are quits?

H.P.B.: We are quits with that personality of Mr. Smith and Mr. Brown, and there is the end of it.

---

[1] See *The Secret Doctrine*, vol. 1, p. 157.

Mr. Gardner: Still, it is possible to spread it over a series of Devachans. For instance, Napoleon Bonaparte's Devachan — that would be spread over several.

H.P.B.: Yes. I think he will have a nice Karma for the people he has killed.

Mr. Old: It is such an accumulation of energy. It is quite an event to have a man like Bonaparte in the world, and in order to have reaction in the next life, it would be quite a different thing.

H.P.B.: I don't suppose he has much to do in Devachan. He was the most materialistic man that ever was. He had no Devachan. If he had a Devachan after his own mind he would have all you English and try that you should have one head, and cut it off.

Mr. Gardner: I suppose he was the embodiment of the nation?

H.P.B.: No.

Mr. Old: What seems to determine the length in my mind is the activity of the nature, the rate at which the monad runs.

H.P.B.: The intensity of your aspirations or desires, and the degree of your sufferings unmerited — those that you have not deserved directly, but through the Karma or the bad actions of somebody else — that is what determines it.

Mrs. Besant: The more desires you have, the longer you will be there?

H.P.B.: Yes. But if you have desires that were perfectly on the spiritual plane, then you are sure to be a spook.

Mr. Sneyd: When the individuality becomes merged in Parabrahm, then in that state, why do they call it the nothing, if it is the reality?

Mr. Old: It is not called nothing; it is *no thing.*

H.P.B.: It is the All.

Mr. Sneyd: But they only mean when they say nothing, no thing.

Mr. Old: Nothing is the wrong pronunciation; it is *no thing.*

Mr. Sneyd: It seems a contradiction.

H.P.B.: Ain-Soph — No thing.

Mr. Sneyd: It is, really, I suppose, the state of intense happiness?

H.P.B.: That cannot be, unless you feel intense unhappiness — a contrast. Parabrahm is not to be either happy or unhappy, and does not feel, because feeling is a finite thing.

Mr. Sneyd: Then why should we wish for it?

H.P.B.: I suppose on account of our stupidity, which is great.

Mr. B. Keightley: Or because we have learned that you cannot have happiness apart from suffering. Why do you go in for differentiated existence? Why do you desire pleasure, or happiness? You desire by that very fact the corresponding pain or suffering, the two being differentiated aspects.

Mr. Old: Everything exists by relation of its own opposites.

Mr. Sneyd: For instance, I can go to a beautiful picture gallery.

H.P.B.: You won't have them in Devachan.

Mr. Kingsland: The more your mind is attuned to happiness, the more it is subject to the shock of discord; and the more intense your pains are in one direction, the more pleasure in another.

Mr. Sneyd: Why should we say that is Parabrahm?

Mr. B. Keightley: May I put this question to you? Can you imagine this condition as lasting permanently? Can you really suppose every desire that you conceive of, gratified? You will find it uncommonly slow when you try it on for about five minutes, because the very fact of having a desire produces suffering until it is fulfilled.

H.P.B.: To have a desire is already suffering, because it is something ungratified. The fact of desiring is suffering.

Mr. Sneyd: But you know you would have it soon, that there is something new coming, something coming on extra, as it were. You are satisfied with what you have got, but you are very glad of this extra.

Mr. Kingsland: You can go piling the extras up until there was nothing left of extras.

Mr. Old: Parabrahm is a state of absolute indifference.

H.P.B.: Please don't call Parabrahm happiness, because it is lowering to the idea of the happy god who sits and rejoices and something smells sweet to his nostrils.

Mr. B. Keightley: If you think about it you will see you cannot have one without the other, really and truly.

Mr. Sneyd: But why should we wish for it? Supposing we say it is absolute indifference. Why should we wish for it?

Mr. Kingsland: You think that over, and in the meanwhile we will go on.

Mr. Old: What is the impulse which determines the Devachanee to incarnate?

H.P.B.: It is Karma that makes him incarnate. He won't have more than he deserves. There is no impulse in him, but he dies out. His dream is at an end.

Mr. Old: When a man takes a meal, he satisfies his hunger. When the Devachanee has assimilated the experiences of his past existence, then there is reaction which takes place.

Mr. B. Keightley: I think that gives the impression on the mind that the Devachanee is actually desiring reincarnation, which is not the case.

Mr. Kingsland: He has no choice.

Mr. B. Keightley: If he did, you do away with one of the first great causes.

Mr. Old: But you must get rid of the sense of individual desire, because the monads have no such desire. Then how would you define that impulse?

H.P.B.: There is no impulse on the part of the Devachanee; it is no impulse at all. Karma takes him by the nape of his neck, and there is no impulse at all, just as when a policeman comes and takes you.

Mr. B. Keightley: In which case, there is a strong impulse to take to your heels and run away.

Mr. Burrows: Does he know that he is going to be reincarnated at all?

H.P.B.: Well, it is a poetical expression.

Mr. Sneyd: I think you said it had no effect, in Devachan?

H.P.B.: There is no new effect produced. It has placed the Devachanee into the state of happiness; it gives him his fill of what he deserves and stands and whistles at the door. When that is finished, Karma takes him by the nape of the neck and puts him into the new body.

Mr. B. Keightley: Then you come to the question which Mr. Burrows raised — when the Devachanee knows he is reincarnated.

H.P.B.: You will see it in *The Key to Theosophy*. There are two moments when the reincarnating ego returns to its pristine omniscience, because, since it is Manasa-Putra (meaning the son of wisdom or the universal intelligence), it is omniscient — or it is at the moment of death, just at the moment when a man dies. When he is dead, he is dead, and it is finished, and he sees everything.

Mr. B. Keightley: He sees the life he is going to enter into.

H.P.B.: He is really himself and knows everything.

Mr. Gardner: Does he see his past lives?

H.P.B.: Most assuredly he does; it is what the Buddha saw.

Mr. B. Keightley: He does not forget, but the impression is not transferred.

H.P.B.: It cannot be transferred, because the instrument cannot receive it. Sometimes you have it, in moments of high vision. What is it, for instance, the states the sensitive persons have? It is simply by some circumstance, some physiological cause or reason or nervous condition. The faculties that were impeding the man to receive this light from his Manas, from his higher ego, are suddenly taken away.

Mr. B. Keightley: Occasionally the light is reflected upon our physical brain.

H.P.B.: It is like a cobweb. For a moment he says: that is what it is, because the ego is omniscience *per se*, not omniscience in the body. It is an extremely interesting thing, if only one could put it into language. If I had your gift of speech, I can assure you I would make all London Theosophists. It is one thing to be plain, because I sit and explain, and another to say in one sweeping, magnificent phrase the whole thing. I have not got "the gift of the gab."

Mr. Old: Is it possible to escape Devachan, say from pure aversion to its useless inactivity?

H.P.B.: Most assuredly. Don't desire anything and you won't have Devachan. You will have nothing to hang your consciousness on. You will be asleep and snore and have no dreams.

Mr. Old: That is worse than ever. Let us dream out of preference.

H.P.B.: But there are persons who reach to such wisdom that once they are dead they are perfectly done with. I have taken off my dress and here I am. What am I going to do? Shall I go to sleep, and so on. And the person shall do as he likes.

Mr. Old: Could you predetermine those which should be your experience?

A Lady: Then you want another body.

H.P.B.: You live in your five principles.

Mrs. Besant: You keep on getting in your five principles.

H.P.B.: That is just what the Adepts do. They have a perfect right to Nirvana, but they won't go. They think it is selfish to do so, and they won't go. They refuse the Nirvanic condition. That is just like Gautama did. He wants to be present, but he has no right to interfere with Karma.

Mr. Burrows: That would be the highest form of unselfishness.

H.P.B.: Most assuredly, because it is suffering. Every Nirmanakaya suffers, because it is terrible to be there, and see the misery and sufferings of people, and not to be able to help them.

Mrs. Besant: Still, you are a force for good.

H.P.B.: Most assuredly. This is the most glorious thing, and that is what they say that Buddha did and many of the Adepts.

Mr. Old: It is called the great renunciation.

H.P.B.: Yes. Remember what I speak about with reference to the Silent Watcher. This has got a very profound occult meaning.

Mrs. Besant: That is the great sacrifice.

Mr. Sneyd: Is not Gautama now in Nirvana?

H.P.B.: The orthodox Buddhist will tell you he is, but he is not.

Mr. B. Keightley: Besides the Nirmanakayas, others escape. There are numerous cases of speedy reincarnation without Devachan.

H.P.B.: For instance, children who died before the age of reason. Immediately they are reincarnated. Persons who did not have a glimpse of spirituality in them. It is a degree of consciousness. If he is Gautama, of course he will have a kind of Devachan of his own, but there are children who have had no consciousness at all.

Mr. Burrows: What form will their incarnation take?

H.P.B.: A child who dies is but a mistake of nature, a failure.

Mr. Gardner: It is sometimes the same with parents.

H.P.B.: I don't think so.

Mrs. Besant: Suppose you had a very noble type who had not evolved sufficiently to refuse Nirvana. Would he be obliged to reincarnate? He who had not reached quite far enough to remain?

H.P.B.: An Adept who has not even reached and who may not reach Nirvana may remain as Nirmanakaya. He may refuse the higher state of Devachan, simply if he reached that point of consciousness in which there is no illusion possible for him — that he knows too much.

Mr. Old: I thought perhaps there was a middle way.

H.P.B.: No sooner they are dead than there are some who step into another body where they can do good.

Mr. Burrows: And the more we eliminate desire the more we escape from Devachan?

H.P.B.: Certainly.

Mr. B. Keightley: The man I was thinking of was Dramard.[1] I think I heard you say he would incarnate very speedily.

Mr. Old: This is the last question on Devachan. Physical rest may be accomplished in the same and even less time than the period of wakeful consciousness and activity. Why then should Devachan extend to twenty or more times the short span of life?

H.P.B.: You had better ask Karma this question, for I cannot answer you.

Mr. Old: Is not there any theory then in the Vedanta philosophy?

H.P.B.: I teach you the occult philosophy. Really, I don't know; it is too difficult.

Mr. Old: Then we go on with questions on reincarnation. Can any reason be given for the necessity of reincarnation?

Mr. B. Keightley: The first great reason is, on no other hypothesis can you account for the inequalities of life — not only of condition and of circumstances under which a man is born, but inequalities in the actual inborn faculties and powers of the man himself, his mental powers, his moral force, his development in all respects — unless you have some antecedent existence. In the first place, whether you assume it to be on this earth or some other state, unless you assume some other existence for the man, it is impossible to account for the varying conditions of life, with any appearance of justice whatever.

Mr. Burrows: You will never get your equilibrium.

---

[1] **Louis Dramard** (1848–1887) — the President of the Isis Lodge of the Theosophical Society in Paris, France.

Mr. B. Keightley: The great thing to my mind is, you don't account for the different stages of development in which the people are obviously born. If neither preexisted, how does that difference come in? I have always thought the fundamental idea of the Christian heaven was injustice in this respect. They say there the poor man, the man who has had little or no chances, is to be rewarded by heaven for the very little good he has done; the man who has had very little or no temptation owing to his low state of development. But a very highly developed man is exposed to much more temptation, yet he is to be weighed, so to speak, in the same scale as the other man.

Mr. Burrows: They take the other side of it though — they rather teach the poor that because of their suffering they are going to be rewarded by and bye. Of course, that is the pastoral idea.

Mr. B. Keightley: If you make an eternal idea, where is the proportion?

Mr. Sneyd: Supposing we say Parabrahm is a state of indifference. Do you think it is a state to be desired? Do you think a state which is not a happy state is a state we should desire?

H.P.B.: I can't understand this. How can you be happy, if you are not unhappy? You won't appreciate happiness unless you have the contrast. Happiness or unhappiness is a thing which is of very little moment indeed, which begins this moment and ends three moments afterwards. How can you have such transitory and such evanescent ideas, which can have no relation whatever to the infinite?

Mr. B. Keightley: Anyone who studies the facts of their own consciousness must have found his active, definite consciousness is neither happiness nor unhappiness.

Mr. Sneyd: Is it to be desired?

Mr. B. Keightley: It is eminently to be desired, because it is a great deal more permanent and useful condition than either happiness or unhappiness.

Mr. Sneyd: It is a quietude, a sort of peace.

Mr. B. Keightley: I should not call it quietude or peace. It is a thing for which we have not got any very good expressions in the English language.

Mr. Old: How do you account for the association of persons on this earth plane as an apparent result of reincarnation?

Mr. B. Keightley: Karma.

Mr. Old: Then we may always presume that we have met before.

H.P.B.: You may.

Mrs. Besant: And does the mental condition influence that at all? Supposing people have reached something of the same mental state, will there be a tendency, then?

H.P.B.: Don't you always experience when you meet a person for the first time whether you like that person, whether you are drawn towards him or have an antipathy? Even the dogs have their sympathies and their antipathies. It must be some reason, some cause.

Mr. Old: It must have been a past cause, if you have not met before. Then can a person of strong will, by a persistent effort, determine the conditions of the next incarnation?

H.P.B.: You go, my dear sir, into the domain of the Adept, into the region of creation.

Mr. Old: That is the only person who has the strong will?

H.P.B.: Of course, desire has a great deal to do with it. An intense desire creates the circumstances, and creates the conditions.

Mr. Old: Then the last question is: "How far do the psychic, mental, and spiritual attainments of the past incarnations advantage the ego in its new life?"

H.P.B.: There is always the reflection that if you worked you cannot become an Adept in one life. It is impossible. You must have begun desire for Adeptship and for knowledge many, many previous incarnations before, because you may have a great desire for it, and you may be born in a man whose circumstances and conditions make him forget that and lose sight of that desire. You will be incarnated ten times, and then these desires and longings for knowledge come in. Then again you go perhaps to a life where it cannot be gratified. There are no conditions to develop this thing, and then you become all that which you had in the previous life, and it all comes in the present life.

Mr. B. Keightley: Until you go to several successive lives in which by effort the man has worked himself into a favourable condition.

20 JUNE 1889

H.P.B.: Now you have got to study for yourselves. The only thing I can give you is just to put the "Key" in your hands and say: "This opens this way, and this that way," and so on. You understand that whereas one person will understand well, another will understand less.

Mrs. Gordon:[1] Because you must have the possibility of understanding transcendental ideas.

H.P.B.: No, it is not that. You have been many years in India and yet you have never taken any pleasure in those ancient religions; others have given their practice to the study of it. Now, if all these Orientalists were not such terrible materialists, with the knowledge they have — I speak about the Max Müllers, not the Sir Monier-Williams,[2] because he has no more spirituality in him than this chair — but about him and others, they would understand perfectly; but they won't, they are materialists. Even that which they understand they would not accept. They would not permit themselves. But I don't see what there is that you don't understand. Mr. Kingsland, you have summarized it beautifully. What are all complaining of?

Mr. Old: That is a broad question, H.P.B.

H.P.B.: You will end by saying it is all flapdoodle, and that there is nothing to understand.

Mrs. Gordon: I don't think we can expect to understand it all.

H.P.B.: But these ladies and gentlemen who have been here Thursday after Thursday for, I suppose, a year, I don't see that you don't understand it. How is it possible?

Mrs. Gordon: You may accept things intellectually without saying you understand them. You may accept them as being true theories.

H.P.B.: Take it vice versa. Take it there are persons who feel it is a truth, and yet intellectually, on scientific grounds, they would not take it.

Mr. B. Keightley: Take the one point Kingsland touched on.

H.P.B.: You have to use your high faculty; intellect has nothing to do here. Materialistic science would step in.

---

[1] **Alice Gordon** — a member of the Theosophical Society, who was the President of the Ladies' Theosophical Society formed in Calcutta, India.

[2] **Monier Monier-Williams** (1819–1899) — a British scholar and professor of Sanskrit at Oxford University, England.

Mrs. Gordon: It is a spiritual conception, as it were.

Mr. B. Keightley: Take that point you touched upon, Kingsland, for instance, how to conceive of the relation between these celestial hierarchies of Dhyan-Chohans and the physical forces, or what we call physical forces, if you like, with which we are ordinarily familiar. Of course, these physical forces, according to *The Secret Doctrine*, are the effects produced on the plane of Maya, the plane of objectivity, proceeding through or caused by these hierarchies; but the difficulty is how to understand, how to form to one's self a conception of what that means.

Mr. Kingsland: I confess I have not been able to form a conception. I have only got the general idea.

H.P.B.: Every hierarchy relates to some force in nature. There are seven fundamental forces in nature; there are seven hierarchies. Now, to come and say that I will undertake to explain to you every one of the seven, which may be subdivided *ad infinitum*, is impossible. In the first place, if I know what it means, I am not scientific enough to come and give you the correspondences in scientific terms. I only know that not only every hierarchy and the Dhyan-Chohans, but every one of those that have been mentioned, correspond; and it may be shown how they correspond to the forces in nature. That would necessitate ten volumes, not two.

Mr. B. Keightley: Take, for instance, this question: There is a well-known property of matter which is called chemical affinity, the combining power which varies from substance to substance; certain things you can take hold of and touch and our physical senses respond to them. How to conceive corresponding relations of things on the next plane above our own, to the next plane behind the objective plane? Because those combinations, I take it, in the objective plane — say, of oxygen and hydrogen to form water — can only take place because the things on the next plane behind ours are also related in some way which corresponds to the relation that we see in the physical substances of oxygen and hydrogen, and so on.

H.P.B.: To whom did you address this speech? To Mr. Kingsland, or me?

Mr. B. Keightley: To you and Mr. Kingsland.

H.P.B.: I did not hear half of what you said. I want a definite question, and I cannot afford to answer about two pages of uninterrupted speech. This may sound very pretty, but I want to have a definite question. Otherwise, before you end, I forget what you began.

Mr. Kingsland: These forces, what we call natural forces, are simply emanations from one or other of these hierarchies. That is the term you use — "emanations."

H.P.B.: I have not any better word.

Mr. Kingsland: How can we dissociate that as an emanation from a hierarchy?

H.P.B.: With physical means, you cannot. Mr. Crookes has done the best he could, and certainly he is the greatest chemist in the whole world.

Mr. Kingsland: Bert has taken one particular thing, chemical affinity. How are we to connect that with an intelligent entity on a higher plane?

H.P.B.: Well, look here! If you are prepared to tell me that everything that shows some action is an action which has its laws, and a scientist may tell you beforehand how such and such a thing may become definite and fixed affinity; if you are prepared to tell me there are no intentions behind it, I will say alright. I say there is not the smallest thing in the universe — there is not the contact of two atoms, take any two things in nature — there is certainly an intelligence in them, behind them, and they act through intelligence, in intelligence, and we are all immersed in intelligence.

Mr. B. Keightley: That is what we believe is at the basis, but Kingsland's difficulty is how to think intellectually of the relation between that intelligence and the physical facts that we observe.

H.P.B.: To drop entirely your scientific and your inductive methods and become not a physician but a metaphysician, that is the only thing I can tell you. Once that you become instead of a metaphysician a physician, and take it from the standpoint of physical nature and mix up orthodox science, you will never arrive at anything.

Mr. B. Keightley: I don't think that is what Kingsland was doing.

H.P.B.: By knowing better than you do everything from the first beginning, from the first flutter of differentiation. Learn it just as I learned. I am not a scientific person at all. I am simply a metaphysician. I have been looking at it; I know it, I feel it in me, I see it before me. I could not put it in scientific terms, because I am not scientific enough; but I say that it is the easiest thing in the world to trace it if you begin by the beginning. But if you do as the men of science do, and begin by the tail, and by that which appears here on this plane of illusion, you will never arrive at anything.

Mr. Sargeant: It seems the question is very simple. If there is no correspondency between the seven hierarchies and the manifestations of these physical forces on the physical plane, then there can be no correspondency between cause and effect. We know effect proceeds from cause; and we should know that the seven manifestations on this physical plane must proceed from one of the hierarchies.

Mr. Kingsland: You can't always trace the effect to a theological cause.

H.P.B.: Shall I tell you a mistake, gentlemen, that you fall into? It is because you take independently all these causes that you want to call intelligent, that you take them one by one, instead of taking the whole. You cannot come and take this affinity. Let us take the Fohatic hierarchies, which are all for the electrical phenomena. You must take them in conjunction with all others, and take them as a whole; because, you see, science is perfectly right from its physical standpoint to say that they are blind forces of nature, because science does not see farther than its nose, and it does not permit itself to go farther than its plane of physical manifestations. But, if we go from the beginning, and if we imagine to ourselves this one life, this eternal, omnipresent homogeneity, that which underlies every phenomenon in nature — which underlies nature itself — which I won't call spirit, because it is far more than spirit. Spirit is something definite, in our language it has no name; it can have only existence in our perception, and then only when we are perfectly divorced from matter. But you have to take the whole thing and then proceed from the universals to the particulars. Otherwise you cannot grasp the thing. It is impossible. You have to skip many things, or to embrace it in a general sense, and then begin it in the first manifestation that you can; otherwise, you cannot make to yourself a clear representation. To me it is as clear and intelligible as can be. It may be because I am an innocent fool, but it has never presented to me any difficulty.

Mr. Sargeant: Is it because ladies and gentlemen must first seek the kingdom of heaven?

H.P.B.: I don't know, but it is quite on a different plane.

Mr. Sargeant: That would be from universals to particulars.

H.P.B.: If there is anything like a middle heaven, then it must be in the clouds, represented by those seraphs with the golden harps. That is what I understand by the kingdom of heaven.

Mr. Sargeant: Unfortunately, *that* in twelve hours time will be the kingdom of hell, because it will be below.

Mr. Old: It is not the general law that causes do proceed into effects that we wish to know.

Mr. Sargeant: Call it a fortuitous combination of circumstances.

Mr. B. Keightley: What Old was after was that here are a lot of effects; well, when we talk about the higher intellectual hierarchies, they are only represented to us by words, at the present moment.

H.P.B.: They cannot be represented by words. They must be represented by the feeling of intuition. If they are represented by words, you have nothing, you have a flapdoodle. You have to represent them to yourselves in your intellectual perception, in your spiritual perception. It is impossible. It is with your higher self that you must understand, and not with your brains and intellectual perceptions, which are all sensuous perceptions, and will not help you. You have to reach to that point when you feel yourself one with the whole, and perfectly inseparable from it — from the one and the eternal, which has no end and no beginning. Otherwise, it is impossible.

Mrs. Gordon: The higher consciousness.

H.P.B.: Well, the higher consciousness. Maybe I speak to you Greek and Hebrew, but to me it is perfectly clear, and I don't know how to explain it better.

Mr. B. Keightley: The thing has to be understood by direct consciousness, the direct contact — your consciousness having been attuned to the universal consciousness. Then you are in direct contact with those hierarchies, and you perceive them or sense them.

H.P.B.: Why should not you put yourself as these hierarchies?

Mr. Kingsland: Which in fact you are.

Mrs. Gordon: Then we have a dual consciousness. The higher consciousness, it is, that we must cultivate, and in some way bring it *en rapport* with our inner consciousness. That is what, of course, the men in India do — they bring their higher consciousness into outer consciousness.

Mr. Sargeant: Are not all higher truths which can be perceived through the universe perceived through the automatic flow of thought?

H.P.B.: I don't think so. I don't believe it.

Mr. Sargeant: It is a thought of which we are partially conscious on the higher plane, but not on the lower plane.

Mr. Kingsland: But what is that but the intuition? You are only giving it another name. It is intuition, is it not?

Mr. Sargeant: I don't think we can call it so. We may intuitively know a thing without understanding it.

H.P.B.: You may intuitively know a thing without being able to give it expression, but you must understand it. You understand it in your spiritual understanding, but very likely you cannot give it an expression, because the European languages cannot convey it; not even Sanskrit, which is certainly a thousand times richer. These are things you have to use your soul language for, as it is called — the inner perception and the unspoken language.

Mr. Sargeant: May we not intuitively know that a certain cause will yield a certain effect, without knowing the way in which that effect will be yielded?

H.P.B.: Certainly there is not the smallest effect that can be produced without a cause, and certainly if there is an effect there must be a cause.

Mr. Sargeant: Then intuition can exist with partial knowledge?

Mr. Old: I don't think you can call that the inner aspect of Manas or the mind, because, you see, we identify the faculty of intuition with Buddhi, which is a separate principle.

H.P.B.: Not quite; it is Manas that you have to identify first.

Mr. Kingsland: It is the essence of all your reincarnations.

Mr. Old: Manas is?

Mr. Kingsland: No, intuition is.

H.P.B.: It passes through the incarnating ego.

Mr. B. Keightley: If you had Buddhi by itself, without any conjunction with Manas on this plane, you would have no intuition at all.

H.P.B.: The mission of Buddhi is simply to shadow divine light on Manas, otherwise Manas will be always falling into the Kamic principle, into the principle of matter; it will become the lower Manas, and act as the lower Manas or mind. But the incarnating ego is certainly the mind, the Manas.

Mr. B. Keightley: And intuition is the recollection.

H.P.B.: Of all the past accumulated experiences.

Mr. Old: But they would be sublimated.

Mr. Kingsland: How is it that one man's intuition will make a Theosophist of him, and another man's will make a Roman Catholic of him?

Mr. Sargeant: Because a Roman Catholic is a Theosophist. It must necessarily be so, if Theosophy embodies all the wisdoms of known religions. All the Roman Catholics are really Theosophists.

H.P.B.: So far, I know only of one real Theosophist among the Roman Catholics: it was poor Father Damien. But not at all because he was a Roman Catholic, but because he was a real Christ-like man.

Mr. Old: Don't you claim St. Aloysius[1] as such?

H.P.B.: Fanaticism we cannot believe in, and we must not believe in. We say there is truth in everything, for it is impossible a thing should exist without having some leaven of truth.

Mr. Sargeant: And consequently there is Theosophy in everything, even in fanaticism.

Mr. B. Keightley: Fanaticism is the negation of the first principle of Theosophy, which is universalism.

H.P.B.: Fanaticism is nothing but concentrated selfishness and vanity. A man says: "I believe in it, and therefore it must be so. I am *the* one wise man and everyone else must be a fool." He who is a fanatic shuts himself out of the universal truth. He simply sticks to a little thing like a fly sticks to one of those medicated papers. It is just that and nothing else.

---

[1] **Aloysius de Gonzaga** (1568–1591) — an Italian Jesuit.

Mr. Sargeant: What about Peter the Hermit,[1] whose fierce preaching stirred up the whole of Europe? Was he a Theosophist?

H.P.B.: Not a bit of it. He was an anti-Theosophist. He forced people to make fools of themselves and led them to death, and made them ridiculous to posterity. He represented to them the goose as the Holy Ghost.

Mr. Sargeant: And yet with the views these people came back with from the Holy Land, Christianity became something grand. Our ancestors never knew the principle of toleration on the battlefield until Saladin[2] taught them.

H.P.B.: There was more Theosophy in Saladin than there ever was in Peter the Hermit. Perhaps you will say Louis XI[3] was also a Theosophist. You are a paradoxalist.

Mr. Kingsland: It is a universalist. But then you must make a distinction in terms.

Mr. Sargeant: There is no distinction in spirit.

Mr. B. Keightley: But you see, we are not in the spirit, but in the flesh.

Mr. Sargeant: The great error of today is that man imagines he is a body possessed of a spirit, instead of a spirit possessed of a body.

H.P.B.: My dear Sargeant, you would appear to me the embodiment of wisdom, if you spoke in a way that I could hear.

Mr. Sargeant: If it is that I speak low, it is because of those internal breathings.

H.P.B.: You are a humbug! Perhaps he will say there is real Theosophy in humbug.

Mr. B. Keightley: Perhaps I might quote the lines of Olcott: "There's a spirit above, and a spirit below; A spirit of love, and a spirit of woe; The spirit above is the spirit divine; The spirit below is the spirit of wine!"

Mr. Sargeant: And yet the "spirit of wine" is only an expression of the "spirit divine." If you read your esoterical works, you will see what affinities there were between these things.

---

[1] **Peter the Hermit** (c.1050–1115/1131) — a Roman Catholic priest.
[2] **Saladin** (c.1137–1193) — the first sultan (ruler) of Egypt and Sudan.
[3] **Louis XI** (1423–1483) — the King of France from 1461 to 1483.

H.P.B.: Now this man's intuition tells him you are trying to humbug me; he does not understand English, and yet his intuition tells him that. You are trying to tease me, he says.

Mr. Old: I wanted to say I didn't think I was agreeable to the proposition. But unconscious thought, cerebration — no, ratiocination — not the physical action which is called cerebration, but the higher, the metaphysical correspondence — this unconscious thought is not in itself intuition, because, reasoning from analogies, we have these two things represented on the lowest plane which we can apply to every one of the seven principles. There is in nerves — the automatic arc of nerves and the influential arc of nerves — the voluntary and involuntary. Exactly the same with the vital process; there is the voluntary and involuntary. There are functions over which we have voluntary control, and there are those over which we have none, except in strange, complex cases like Captain Townsend and others who are able to control the vital processes as well as the muscles. Seeing there is the unconscious and the conscious, the dark and the light side of every bifacial monad, might we not argue that there is the conscious and the unconscious cerebration, both identified with Manas? Because I have seen instances precipitated in the form of automatic writing where a person has been holding a conversation on one subject and writing on another.

Mr. Kingsland: Supposing we say that intuition is the unconscious action?

Mr. Old: I wish to say it is not.

Mr. Kingsland: You take the unconscious vital action, for instance. The action goes on without your will. How does that come about? Is not that the accumulation of numerous past experiences?

Mr. Sargeant: No.

Mr. Kingsland: What is it, then?

Mr. Sargeant: It is simply owing to the action of a universal flood on nerves which are termed involuntary. They affect these nerves in such a manner that they restore any equilibrium which has been lost.

Mr. Kingsland: How does it arise that we have certain physical functions? You are simply tracing it back. I say those functions develop through innumerable ages by means of evolution; these things act through the Kama-rupa experience of past action.

Mr. Sargeant: You don't mean that the past experiences are the very causes that set these influences at work?

Mr. Kingsland: I don't. I carry that analogy up to what Old says about the conscious and the unconscious ratiocination. I say that the unconscious is simply that same result. By analogy you can put it in the same way: that your intuition is the result of all the past stages you have gone through in the stages of consciousness — in fact, your evolution.

Mr. B. Keightley: I think it works out from the known experience of the training of the muscles. You learn to do certain very complicated muscular actions at first with great pain and difficulty, such as writing. Gradually the thing becomes automatic; you do it without thinking of the different steps. You think of the sense you are going to express, and you do not think of the individual movement of your hand.

Mr. Kingsland: There is nothing you can do at the present moment but what is the result of your past experiences.

Mr. Old: I can trace it in what the physicists call inhibited action. If one gets into the way of nursing his thumb in his pocket, it is a strange thing how this will become habitual. First of all, it is generally voluntary, but it becomes a habit, and it is then called an inhibited action. And the seat of the cerebral forces is the cerebrum; it is supposed to be the lieutenant of the thinking brain. Then, when you have decided to walk home, you don't have to think of putting more than the first foot foremost; the rest follow. What I wish to say is this: I find some difficulty in tracing this inhibited action which has once been voluntary action. How can you say that vital action was ever inhibited, was ever involuntary? If you can prove that each pulsation of the aorta of the heart was controlled voluntarily, then you prove the case.

Mr. Kingsland: Your present physical body is the result of several influences which can be traced back to a previous incarnation.

Mr. Keightley: The point is this: whether, for instance, the involuntary action of the muscles — as in the beating of the heart — is the result of evolution. I contend it is the result of the evolution of the molecules forming the heart.

Mr. Old: But not of conscious experiences.

Mr. Kingsland: Not in your present lifetime.

Mr. Old: I merely wish to show, reasoning by analogy, just as there was the conscious and unconscious action of the physical body, and there were conscious and unconscious systems of nervation and so forth on the physical plane, so there was in every principle this conscious and unconscious, this dark and light side.

H.P.B.: I think you confuse the material things with the spiritual.

Mr. Old: We know every one of those principles has a manifesting and an unmanifesting side.

H.P.B.: If you speak of one of the acquired habits, as nursing your thumb, it is a different thing. It is not a thing which is natural and normal. The beating of the heart is a thing which pretends to the physical, the habits of men. This has nothing to do with acquired things.

Mr. Kingsland: It has nothing to do with the acquired habits in this incarnation. But you can trace back the beating of your heart, which takes place automatically; you can trace that back to the evolution, where it was first.

H.P.B.: Certainly.

Mr. Old: I cannot go so far as that.

Mr. Kingsland: Suppose we take your analogy?

Mr. Old: Reasoning from this by analogy, on this line I wanted to show that there would be conscious and unconscious thought, both identified with and peculiar to the Manas.

Mr. Kingsland: Very well, let us say that. Then I say that the conscious thought you are going through now is your present intellectuation.

Mr. Old: We have already identified intuition with Buddhi. Now you wish to identify Buddhi with the higher aspect of Manas.

Mr. B. Keightley: You are taking that from Sinnett, Old.

Mr. Old: Is not Buddhi the sixth principle, and is not intuition the sixth sense?

H.P.B.: You argue on the line of what? Do you bring the thing as it is given to you in the Esoteric Instructions, or the exoteric? There is the difference. You know what I mean. Exoterically, there is another thing. Of course, the Buddhi will be the sixth, for the Buddhi is quite a different thing, exoterically. The Buddhi, *per se*, has nothing to do with any qualification of anything; it is simply the vehicle of Atman, of spirit; and spirit is nothing. It cannot be said it is something. It is that which has neither beginning nor end. It is the *one thing*.

Mr. B. Keightley: Old's identification of the Buddhi's intuition is derived from Sinnett's *Esoteric Buddhism*.

H.P.B.: That is certainly not esoteric.

Mr. Kingsland: You cannot identify Buddhi with intuition, because intuition, after all, is only the intellectual process of the very highest order.

Mr. Old: I understand there are two facets to Buddhi?

H.P.B.: One thing you may say about Buddhi. Intuition is in Manas for the more or less light shed on it by Buddhi, whether it is assimilated much or little with Buddhi.

Mr. Kingsland: It must pass through Manas. It is derived from Manas.

Mr. Old: Ultimately it is from the brain; it can flow down. The brain is the instrument of thought.

H.P.B.: My poor Old! I never thought you were as materialistic as you are.

Mr. Old: You have put me off the track by asking me the question whether I was speaking esoterically or exoterically. I was talking on my ground, and you told me to get off.

H.P.B.: Was I wrong?

Mr. Old: No, you were right.

H.P.B.: There are esotericists here, and exotericists. The esotericists will be terribly confused if we speak in this way, and the exotericists still more.

Mr. Old: I ought not to have mooted it.

H.P.B.: Buddhi by itself can neither have intuition, nor non-intuition, nor anything; it is simply the cementing link, so to say, between the higher spirit and Manas. What goes into Devachan? What reincarnates? It is certainly the ego, the Manas, the higher portion of Manas. Once in Devachan we call it the eternity, but it has no eternity at all, because Buddhi and Atma are nothing but obstructions, in the strict sense of the word. It is the reincarnating Manas that goes; and therefore intuition belongs to Manas, because it brings it through all the reincarnations that it passed through. All this is more or less defined through the amount of light shed on Manas by Buddhi, but so far as regards this life. You understand? Because the intuition is one. You have learned enough about that, Mrs. Gordon.

Mr. Old: What is your distinction, Kingsland, between unconscious cerebration and intuition?

Mr. Kingsland: Unconscious cerebration is a thing belonging purely to the physical plane, and the other thing is different.

Mr. Old: So is unconscious thought, then?

Mr. Kingsland: Take the extreme case of the lad who could solve the most difficult mathematical problems that were given him immediately without any reference to figures at all. That you will say was a purely intellectual process. He must have had it in previous times; he had assimilated that knowledge at some time or other, and it was owing to certain combinations of astral influences that he was able to make use of that information, for the time being, in that rapid manner. His physical senses overclouded this, in time.

Mr. Sargeant: That is the product of unconscious thought.

H.P.B.: Unconscious cerebration is something that was suggested to the brain unconsciously to yourselves, though perhaps you heard it or saw it and had no remembrance of it; and there it comes out. But, intuition is a different thing.

Mr. B. Keightley: I don't think such a term as "unconscious thought" can mean anything.

Mr. Sargeant: Then "unconscious cerebration"?

Mr. B. Keightley: "Unconscious thought" — what meaning can you attach to the phrase?

Mr. Old: Call it ideation, if you like.

Mr. B. Keightley: It is conscious enough on the right plane.

Mr. Old: There is nothing unconscious, as a matter of fact. Because, if you only identify your consciousness for the time being with that plane, you would be perfectly conscious you were so engaged; therefore, I think the term is a bad one, and I only wish to use it relatively, in contradistinction to relative thought.

Mrs. Gordon: It seems to me that the experiments that have been made in regard to hypnotism show that there is this higher consciousness which may be brought forward occasionally under exceptional circumstances — that is, with exceptional natures. It is not everyone in whom it can be developed. Don't you think so, madam? I am speaking of the latent soul. The other half which is not unconscious can be, as it were, more or less exhibited under some forms of hypnotism, in which the higher self becomes clairvoyant, and the other faculties always develop.

H.P.B.: Don't you use the term "higher self." That is the Atman.

Mr. B. Keightley: Say the higher ego. In most cases, that consciousness or ego refers to the personality in the third person speaking, for instance, of the name.

Mr. Kingsland: I take it in this way: that we have stored up, so to speak, in our Manas an enormous amount of experience that we have passed through in past incarnations, and we are not able by certain reasons of our physical constitution to assimilate and give expression to all that in our present lifetime. But the act of making use of your intuition is simply the act of getting at this storehouse that you have already in your Manas. And what it is that clouds our intuition is our connection with the physical plane. And if we can get rid of that, we can make use of our intuition.

H.P.B.: It is the amount of weeds and parasites that we have collected in our life which makes us positively fools.

Mrs. Gordon: You always see children much more intuitive than adults. Children have the intuition much more prominent than we who live in the world and are more of the world, and our minds are exercised in connection with worldly things.

Mr. Kingsland: I think that also is the case.

Mrs. Gordon: I have seen it myself, among friends of my own. They had a sixth sense, as I may say. They lived in another atmosphere altogether, you see.

Mr. Kingsland: There are a great many cases in which that is brought forward — abnormal cases, such as I have mentioned. Take the case of Josef Hofmann, the young pianist. Where does his musical knowledge come from? It is nothing but intuition. He is able to give expression to that on the physical plane through his physical body.

Mrs. Gordon: Of course the child has not learned it intellectually. He has not brain enough to do it. He has brought it with him.

Mr. Kingsland: The basis of all our actions is simply intuition.

H.P.B.: Is it your Buddhi, Old, that made you what you are?

Mr. Old: It is my Atma.

H.P.B.: You have got no Atma, distinct from others.

Mr. Old: There is the divine spark in me.

H.P.B.: It is not yours; it is common property. It is your ego, and your incarnating ego. It is that which you were in past lives that makes you what you are, a young man of 25 that has such a wonderful capacity of grasping all these things.

Mr. Old: There are certain things — as, for instance, these abstract meditations — which are not the result of experience. What experience, what self-consciousness have I when I am in Devachan? I have no relative consciousness except my own that forms the creation in my own mind.

Mr. Kingsland: And yet you believe that Devachan is the result of your experiences that you have passed through in your previous life.

Mr. Old: Certainly. But there are other abstract problems which are thinkable and cognizable by me which it is perhaps impossible to formulate, but which I can feel; and I say that these laws, this consciousness, belongs to Atma. It is related to Manas by its vehicle Buddhi, and therein this absolute consciousness is, to a certain extent, capable of being appreciated by the Manas, the monad.

H.P.B.: You are a heretic, because you speak entirely against not only the occult philosophy, but against the Vedantin philosophy.

Mr. Kingsland: Does Atma accumulate experiences?

Mr. Old: No! But you have got hold of the idea that it is only accumulated experience that we know.

Mr. Kingsland: It is only accumulated experience which is our intuition.

H.P.B.: How can you give experience to that which is absolute? How is it possible to fall into such a philosophical error as that? The Atma no more belongs to you than to this lamp. It is common property.

Mr. Old: Every higher self is, so to speak, the manifested end of a ray.

H.P.B.: It is not. It is the Manas itself.

Mr. Old: There is the individual logos, as well as the universal logos.

H.P.B.: Not at all. It is simply that Atma and Buddhi cannot be predicated as having anything to do with a man, except that man is immersed in them. So long as he lives he is overshadowed by these two; but it is no more the property of that than of anything else.

Mr. Old: This is identifying Atman with Jiva.

H.P.B.: I beg a thousand pardons. Jiva and Atma are one, only Jiva is this end, and Atma at the highest end; but you cannot make the difference in England. It would have a meaning for the Sanskrit, but not in the European languages, or any of them, because there is but one essence in the universe, and this has neither beginning nor end, and the various shadows or rays of that absoluteness during the period of differentiation, this is that which makes it the final essence of everything, and of man.

Mr. Old: Then would you say that all this which is written of Nirvana, of Brahma, of Para-Nirvana, of Parabrahm, is the result of experience?

Mr. Kingsland: All that you can understand of it, that is the result of experience.

Mr. Old: I take it as the result of intuition.

H.P.B.: It is simply a symbol expressed in the best language in which man is capable of expressing it, that is all.

Mr. B. Keightley: Try to formulate your idea more clearly by explaining what kind of meditation you refer to, because I think you will find that the very highest meditation you can conceive of is really Manasic, and nothing more. Manas and experience are not synonymous.

Mr. Old: Kingsland wishes to identify intuition with experience. According to Kingsland, intuition is one aspect of Manas.

H.P.B.: Look here, you Europeans ought never to have been given the seven principles. Well, perhaps in a hundred years you will understand it. It would be a thousand times better to hold to the old methods, those that I have held to in *Isis Unveiled*, and to speak about triple man: spirit, soul, and matter; then you would not fall into the heresies, in such heresies as you do. Why do we divide this into seven parts or aspects? Because ours is the highest philosophy. But, for the general mortal, certainly it is a great deal easier to understand if they say man is triple: he has got spirit, soul, and matter. What is spirit? Spirit then becomes the ego. Soul is simply the Nephesh, the living soul of every animal, that is to say, the lower Jiva, and matter is his physical body. Now, we, having divided it, as all esoteric philosophies divide it, have simply confused the European mind, because it has not been trained in that direction. It is too early for them, and there are very few men who will really understand the seven divisions. And, therefore, we are called lunatics or frauds — one of the two — and nobody will understand what we mean. I say it is a thousand times better not to understand it, and not to go and speak about this septenary number, and simply take it on the old ground of spirit, soul and matter. There would be no heresy, then.

Mr. Kingsland: It has been broached abroad now, this seven principle, and we have to clear our ideas of it.

H.P.B.: You must never say: "my Atma"; you have no Atma. This idea is the curse of the world; it has produced this tremendous selfishness, this egotism [...] we say "we are," "*my* Atma," "*my* Buddhi." Who are you? You are nobodies; you are something today, and tomorrow you are not. Even that disappears at the end of the Manvantara in the one.

Mr. B. Keightley: To go back to what Kingsland was saying. Intuition as we know it is defined in this way: the memory, the action or the reflection on our lower plane of the hierarchies. It is not the higher aspect of the hierarchies, nor does it exhaust the Manas.

H.P.B.: The incarnating principle simply. It is not something that is an individual or entity. It is simply the highest mind.

Mr. Old: That incarnating ego consists of what?

H.P.B.: What do you want it to consist of? Plums, or oranges, or what?

Mr. Old: How do you formulate it? Do you say it is Atma-Buddhi?

H.P.B.: I say it is Atma-Buddhi, certainly. Because, in every incarnation, it is under the direct ray of Buddhi, if he wants to assimilate. If he does not want to, it is his look out; his personality will drop out. It is only in the case which assimilates Buddhi that it really lives throughout, and will belong to that string of personality which forms consciousness after the Manvantara is at an end — the direct, immortal ray.

Mr. Old: I thought I was quite right in saying Buddhi was a ray from Atma; it is that vehicle.

H.P.B.: You would not call this lamp a ray of the flame that burns in it, would you?

Mr. Old: Certainly not.

H.P.B.: That is Buddhi, if you please — the vehicle. It is not a ray; it is only that through which that ray passes. It is the agent of that light that it throws on Buddhi. How is that we read in all those books about Nirvana and Atma, when they say: "Does Parabrahm exist? It does not. Then Parabrahm is not. Yes it is, but it does not exist."

Mr. Old: You say the incarnating ego consists of Buddhi-Manas, or rather Atma-Buddhi.

H.P.B.: It consists only of itself.

Mr. Kingsland: In the aspect in which we are discussing, it is simply the assimilation of the higher Manas.

Mr. Old: What assimilates it?

H.P.B.: Consciousness. It is universal consciousness, which falling into matter becomes personal consciousness in its last manifestation on earth. And when it gets rid of all the matter that impedes it, when it becomes more and more pure, and finally it reaches its highest manifestation, or whatever you call it, then it gradually falls into the universal consciousness; it is again reabsorbed into universal consciousness. That is what Manas is. But as it falls lower and lower, it would be nothing but a material entity — I don't mean material physically, but material *de facto*, nothing but a bundle of nothing — if it were not under the ray of this Atma-Buddhi. But Atma-Buddhi certainly does not follow the reincarnating ego. Simply, once it is reincarnated, they are again in the region of the universe in which there is Atma and Buddhi. Therefore, we say that Atma and Buddhi exist in every man.

Mr. Old: It is a contradiction between the undifferentiated Atman and Buddhi.

H.P.B.: It is simply that Atma is beyond the seventh plane. Buddhi is one of the planes; you understand that. Therefore, if Atma, which is beyond the seventh plane, falls on the ego through seven planes, it will fall a great deal weaker. You understand what I mean? It depends on our ego to draw it immediately on itself, or to have a kind of wall between it and the other planes. This depends on the degree of assimilation. I don't know if you understand my meaning.

Mr. B. Keightley: Yes, you put it very well.

H.P.B.: Well, it is extremely difficult to do so, because those who don't understand what I mean by planes will not understand me. It has seven degrees of spirit-matter, and certainly it depends on the force or degree, the intensity with which it assimilates. And if it is too opaque, and too dull, then certainly it won't reach it.

Mr. B. Keightley: I don't know whether you ever studied that problem, Old, the definition of liberation. There is always that rather puzzling explanation: "the soul is neither bound, nor is it ever liberated." It is a very intricate problem, which has never been really satisfactorily explained.

H.P.B.: What do you take Purusha to be on this plane? Which of the principles? To which of the principles does it belong?

Mr. B. Keightley: They talk about Purusha mounting on the shoulders of Prakriti.

H.P.B.: Prakriti is simply a body, and therefore the body would be a perfectly blind animal if Purusha were not there; and Purusha without the body could not manifest. Purusha emanates from Brahma, and from [...], or from [...], whatever school he belonged to.

Mr. B. Keightley: I could show passages in which Purusha is not taken in that sense, but in the higher sense.

H.P.B.: If you speak about mind, Purusha corresponds with the ego. If you take it in the universal sense, then it corresponds to the universal soul, to the Anima Mundi.

Mr. Kingsland: I think you might look at it in this light: by analogy, it is exactly the same as the way in which we require to postulate for the descending scale of manifestation — first the manifesting spirit, then the first Logos, and then the second. Isn't it the same?

Mr. Old: Who is your first Logos in this case?

Mr. Kingsland: It is Buddhi, and the second is Manas.

Mr. Old: A short time ago I ventured the remark that Buddhi was the Logos, and I was told that I was incorrect.

Mr. B. Keightley: You spoke of an individual Logos.

Mr. Old: Of an individual ray — because Atma has to radiate in order to function any particular...

H.P.B.: Atma has to radiate! It cannot radiate anything. Atma, if you take it of the third Logos, then yes, but not Atma in the universal sense of Parabrahm.

Mr. Old: We are not teaching Parabrahm here. If we entered Parabrahm, or if we entered into the consideration of Parabrahm, here would come in that intuition which I speak of.

H.P.B.: I thought I knew pretty well the philosophy, and I don't think I know it. I never said that Atma or Parabrahm could radiate. If you take it in the sense of the third Logos, then I admit it radiates.

Mr. Kingsland: Correspondentially, Atma is Parabrahm.

Mr. Old: There is a source of confusion to an occidental mind; just the same with your juxtaposition of the two words Jiva and Prana, which throws everybody into confusion. I mean to say, your repetition of the language.

Mr. B. Keightley: The juxtaposition was sensed, and nobody ever took it up.

H.P.B.: The Brahmins have given it to us, and they all fell on me as to why I permitted Sinnett to do this. Sinnett never asked me my permission, and I did not know until *Esoteric Buddhism* came out. It is not my fault.

Mr. Old: Oh! No; only, in some parts of *The Secret Doctrine* it is difficult to tell if Jiva is to be taken on the noumenal plane or on the phenomenal.

H.P.B.: When you speak about the objective things then it is Jiva. At least it is Prana. When you speak about the universal life, then it is Jiva. In some schools of philosophy they call it Jiva; the Vedantins will call it Jiva; the Sankhya will never call it that, and the six schools are entirely distinct. That which the Vedantins call Jiva, others will call Prana, and vice versa.

Mr. Old: One conceives of abstract ideas apart from the formula. The formula is the matter of experience; it belongs to Manas.

Mr. B. Keightley: Don't you conceive that it is the Manas which conceives the abstract ideas? Because, how do they exist, otherwise?

Mr. Kingsland: You cannot conceive of abstract ideas without the experience. That is just my point.

Mr. Old: Who was Hermes?

H.P.B.: If you mix up the Greek gods with the philosophy, then we are lost.

Mr. Old: I will bear it.

Mr. Kingsland: But our brains won't.

H.P.B.: Let us leave in quietude all these analogies.

Mr. Old: But this is our only key.

Mr. B. Keightley: Your argument is open to this reply. If abstract ideas can only be received in virtue of experience, how do you ever get your chain started?

Mr. Kingsland: By the first emanation. When you first emanate from the Absolute, it is when you begin your cycle of experiences.

H.P.B.: There is a potentiality of everything: past, present, and future.

Mr. Old: That is better. This is not experience.

H.P.B.: If you take the present Manvantara for the only one, then, of course, granted you are right.

Mr. Old: This is making two square walls meet, that the past, present, and future are comprehended in the now. It is a matter of experience. There are the future Manvantaras.

H.P.B.: What do you make of the past Manvantaras? If you were in the first, you would be right.

Mr. Old: You have no individual consciousness, in Parabrahm, in which you enter at the Maha-Pralaya. I mean in Nirvana.

H.P.B.: You don't understand what Nirvana is. It is absolute consciousness.

Mr. Old: There is no individual consciousness. How do we know anything about Nirvana?

Mr. Kingsland: Do you believe that the future Manvantara will be an improvement upon the present one, or not?

Mr. Old: Yes! I do, because my experience has told me from what little I have seen that the law of nature is progression.

Mr. Kingsland: Is not that the same as saying it is experience?

Mr. Old: Plus analogy.

Mr. Kingsland: I am drawing the analogy now. I say you can carry it not only from your past life to the present, but from the past Manvantara to the next Manvantara.

Mr. B. Keightley: If you ever read Froude,[1] he talks about the faculty of apprehending abstract ideas. H.P.B., answer this, if you can, from the point of view of exotericism. Is the apprehension of highest abstract ideas the function of Manas, or of Buddhi?

H.P.B.: Buddhi can have the apprehension of nothing.

Mr. B. Keightley: There you are answered, Old.

Mr. Old: Yes! Certainly.

H.P.B.: If we argue or discuss about the universe we had better leave the first two things — Parabrahm, and the first Logos, call it; and when we speak of men, let us remember that it is a perfect analogy — that that which we call Parabrahm in the first Logos is in man, Atma, and Buddhi. Then as we begin by the third or second Logos, so we must begin by Manas, because there it is where the point of differentiation begins. Otherwise you are lost. You will only make confusion, otherwise.

Mr. Old: It is having to keep parallel texts before you all the time. Knowing certain teachings on the one side of the book, and trying to keep them parallel.

H.P.B.: He will come and reproach us that he knows too much.

Mr. Old: I refer to esoteric teaching.

H.P.B.: Most assuredly. Therefore, every time you put this question, I say, do go to bed, let us talk of something else. Let us talk about exoteric subjects, of which we can discuss as much as you like. But the others — well, it is very difficult to speak of that which we had better keep silent about.

---

[1] **James Anthony Froude** (1818–1894) — an English historian, novelist and biographer.

HELENA PETROVNA BLAVATSKY
(1831-1891)

by Charles Johnston[2]

"I understand, Socrates. It is because you say that you always have a divine sign. So he is prosecuting you for introducing new things into religion. And he is going into court knowing that such matters are easily misrepresented to the multitude, and consequently meaning to slander you there."

— **Plato**

I first met dear old "H.P.B.," as she made all her friends call her, in the spring of 1887. Some of her disciples had taken a pretty house in Norwood,[3] where the huge glass nave and twin towers of the Crystal Palace[4] glint above a labyrinth of streets and terraces. London was at its grimy best. The squares and gardens were scented with grape-clusters of lilac, and yellow rain of laburnums under soft green leaves. The eternal smoke-pall was thinned to a grey veil shining in the afternoon sun, with the great Westminster Towers[5] and a thousand spires and chimneys piercing through. Every house had its smoke-wreath, trailing away to the east.

H.P.B. was just finishing her day's work, so I passed a half-hour upstairs with her volunteer secretary, a disciple who served her with boundless devotion, giving up everything for her cause, and fighting her battles bravely, to be stormed at in return, unremittingly for seven years. I had known him two years before, in the days of Mohini Chatterji,[6] the velvet-robed Brahman with glossy tresses and dusky

---

[2] **Charles Johnston** (1867-1931) — an Irish-American writer, journalist and Sanskrit scholar; the founder of the Dublin Lodge of the Theosophical Society, whose members were the poets William Butler Yeats and George William Russell (Æ). He was married to H.P.B.'s niece, Vera Vladimirovna de Zhelihovsky.

[3] **Norwood** — an area of south London. When H.P.B. arrived in London in 1887, she first stayed at Maycot, Mabel Collins' home, situated at 77 Elgin Crescent, Crownhill, Upper Norwood, London.

[4] **Crystal Palace** — a monumental glass and iron structure to house the Great Exhibition of 1851 held in London's Hyde Park. It was destroyed by fire in 1936.

[5] **Westminster Towers** — the two towers of the Palace of Westminster in London. These towers are the Victoria Tower and the Elizabeth Tower, which houses the famous Big Ben bell.

[6] **Mohini Mohun Chatterji** (1858-1936) — a Bengali attorney and scholar.

face and big luminous eyes. So we talked of old times, and of H.P.B.'s great book, *The Secret Doctrine*, and he read me resonant stanzas about Universal Cosmic Night, when Time was not; about the Luminous Sons of Manvantaric Dawn; and the Armies of the Voice; about the Water Men Terrible and Bad, and the black magicians of Lost Atlantis; about the Sons of Will and Yoga and the Ring Pass-Not; about the Great Day Be-With-Us, when all shall be perfected into one, reuniting "thyself and others, myself and thee."

So the half-hour passed, and I went downstairs to see the Old Lady. She was in her writing-room, just rising from her desk, and clad in one of those dark blue dressing-gowns she loved. My first impression was of her rippled hair as she turned, then her marvellously potent eyes, as she welcomed me: "My dear fellow! I am so glad to see you! Come in and talk! You are just in time to have some tea!" And a hearty handshake.

Then a piercing call for "Louise," and her Swiss maid appeared, to receive a voluble torrent of directions in French, and H.P.B. settled herself snugly into an armchair, comfortably near her tobacco-box, and began to make me a cigarette. The cuffs of a Jaeger[1] suit showed round her wrists, only setting off the perfect shape and delicacy of her hands, as her deft fingers, deeply stained with nicotine, rolled the white rice-paper round Turkish tobacco. When we were comfortably alight, she told me a charming tale of Louise's devotion. She had got away from her base of supplies somewhere, in Belgium I think, and things were rather tight for a while. A wealthy gentleman called to see the famous Russian witch, and tipped her maid munificently. As soon as he was gone, Louise appeared, blushing and apologizing: "Perhaps madame will not be offended," she stammered, "but I do not need money; *enfin — madame consentira…*"[2] and she tried to transfer the *douceur*[3] to her mistress.

Louise's entry cut short the story, and H.P.B. turned with a quizzically humorous smile to another theme: "Of course you have read the S.P.R. Report? — The Spookical Research Society — and know that I am a Russian spy, and the champion impostor of the age?"

---

[1] Jaeger — a British fashion brand.
[2] **Enfin — madame consentira…**" (*French*) — "in short, will madam agree…"
[3] **Douceur** (*French*) — sweetness; a gratuity.

"Yes, I read the Report. But I knew its contents already. I was at the meeting when it was first read, two years ago."

"Well," said H.P.B., again smiling with infinite humour, "and what impression did the frisky lambkin from Australia make upon your susceptible heart?"

"A very deep one. I decided that he must be a very good young man, who always came home to tea; and that the Lord had given him a very good conceit of himself. If he got an opinion into his head, he would plow away blandly, and contrary facts would be quite invisible. But your case was not the first on the list. They had a paper on modern witchcraft, at which another of your accusers proved that pinches and burns could be sent by thought-transference to a person miles away. It was quite gruesome, and suggested ducking-stools. Then you came on. But as far as I could see, the young Colonial had never really investigated any occult phenomena at all; he simply investigated dim and confused memories about them in the minds of indifferent witnesses. And all that Mr. Sinnett says in *The Occult World*[4] seems to me absolutely unshaken by the whole Report. The Poet, the third of your accusers, came down among us after the meeting, and smilingly asked me what I thought of it. I answered that it was the most unfair and one-sided thing I had ever heard of, and that if I had not already been a member of your Society, I should have joined on the strength of that attack. He smiled a kind of sickly smile, and passed on."

"I am glad you think so, my dear," she answered in her courtly way, "for now I can offer you some tea with a good conscience." Louise had laid a white cloth on the corner table, brought in a tray, and lit a lamp. The secretary soon joined us, receiving a tart little sermon on being unpunctual, which he was not. Then we came back to her friends, the Psychical Researchers.

"They will never do much," said H.P.B. "They go too much on material lines, and they are far too timid. That was the secret motive that turned them against me. The young Colonial went astray, and then the bell-wethers of the flock followed in his wake, because they were afraid of raising a storm if they said our phenomena were true. Fancy what it would have meant! Why it would practically have committed

---

[4] *The Occult World* — the name of the first book which treated Theosophy, its history, and certain of its tenets; written by A. P. Sinnett, then editor of the leading Indian paper, *The Pioneer*, of Allahabad, India.

Modern Science to our Mahatmas and all I have taught about the inhabitants of the occult world and their tremendous powers. They shrank at the thought of it, and so they made a scapegoat of this poor orphan and exile." And her eyes were full of humorous pity for herself.

"It must have been something like that," I answered, "for there is simply no backbone in the Report itself. It is the weakest thing of the kind I have ever read. There is not a shred of real evidence in it from beginning to end."

"Do you really think so? That's right!" cried H.P.B.; and then she turned on her secretary, and poured in a broadside of censure, telling him he was greedy, idle, untidy, unmethodical, and generally worthless. When he ventured an uneasy defence, she flared up and declared that he "was born a flapdoodle, lived a flapdoodle, and would die a flapdoodle." He lost his grip, and not unnaturally made a yellow streak of egg across her white tablecloth.

"There!" cried H.P.B., glaring at him with withering scorn, and then turning to me for sympathy in her afflictions. That was her way, to rate her disciples in the presence of perfect strangers. It speaks volumes for her, that they loved her still.

I tried to draw a red herring across the track — not that there were any on the table. We were limited to tea, toast and eggs.

"The funny thing about the Psychical Researchers," I said, "is that they have proved for themselves that most of these magical powers are just what you say they are, and they seem to have bodily adopted, not to say, stolen, your teaching of the Astral Light. Take the thing that has been most made fun of: the journeys of Adepts and their pupils in the astral body; you know how severe they are about poor Damodar[1] and his journeys in his astral body from one part of India to another, and even from India over to London. Well, they themselves have perfectly sound evidence of the very same thing. I know one of their Committee, a professor of physics, who really discovered thought-transference and made all the first experiments in it. He showed me a number of their unpublished papers, and among them was an account of just such astral journeys made quite consciously. I think the astral traveller was a young doctor, but that is a detail. The point is, that he kept a diary of his visits, and a note of them was also kept by the person he visited, and the two perfectly coincide. They have the whole thing

---

[1] **Damodar K. Mavalankar** (1857–1885) — an Indian Theosophist.

authenticated and in print, and yet when you make the very same claim, they call you a fraud. I wonder why?"

"Partly British prejudice," she answered; "no Englishman ever believes any good of a Russian. They think we are all liars. You know they shadowed me for months in India, as a Russian spy? I don't understand," she went on meditatively, yet with a severe eye on her secretary, "I don't understand how these Englishmen can be so very sure of their superiority, and at the same time in such terror of our invading India."

"We could easily hold our own if you did, H.P.B.," ventured the patriotic secretary, pulling himself together, but evidently shaky yet, and avoiding her eye. She was down on him in an instant:

"Why!" she cried, "what could you do with your poor little army? I tell you, my dear, when the Russians do meet the English on the Afghan frontier, we shall crush you like fleas!"

I never saw anything so overwhelming. She rose up in her wrath like the whole Russian army of five millions on a war footing and descended on the poor Briton's devoted head, with terrific weight. When she was roused, H.P.B. was like a torrent; she simply dominated everyone who came near her; and her immense personal force made itself felt always, even when she was sick and suffering, and with every reason to be cast down. I have never seen anything like her tremendous individual power. She was the justification of her own teaching of the divinity of the will. "But H.P.B." — hesitated the secretary. But she crushed him with a glance, and he desperately helped himself to more buttered toast only to be accused of gluttony.

Again I attempted a diversion: "There is one thing about the S.P.R. Report I want you to explain. What about the writing in the occult letters?"

"Well, what about it?" asked H.P.B., immediately interested.

"They say that you wrote them yourself, and that they bear evident marks of your handwriting and style. What do you say to that?"

"Let me explain it this way," she answered, after a long gaze at the end of her cigarette. "Have you ever made experiments in thought-transference? If you have, you must have noticed that the person who receives the mental picture very often colours it, or even changes it slightly, with his own thought, and this where perfectly genuine transference of thought takes place. Well, it is something like that with the precipitated letters. One of our Masters, who perhaps does not know English, and of course has no English handwriting, wishes to precipitate a letter in answer to a question sent mentally to him. Let us say he is in Tibet, while I am in Madras or London. He has the answering thought in his mind, but not in English words. He has first to impress that thought on my brain, or on the brain of someone else who knows English, and then to take the word-forms that rise up in that other brain to answer the thought. Then he must form a clear mind-picture of the words in writing, also drawing on my brain, or the brain of whoever it is, for the shapes. Then either through me or some chela with whom he is magnetically connected, he has to precipitate these word-shapes on paper, first sending the shapes into the chela's mind, and then driving them into the paper, using the magnetic force of the chela to do the printing, and collecting the material, black or blue or red, as the case may be, from the Astral Light. As all things dissolve into the Astral Light, the will of the magician can draw them forth again. So he can draw forth colours of pigments to mark the figure in the letter, using the magnetic force of the chela to stamp them in, and guiding the whole by his own much greater magnetic force, a current of powerful will."

"That sounds quite reasonable," I answered. "Won't you show me how it is done?"

"You would have to be clairvoyant," she answered, in a perfectly direct and matter-of-fact way, "in order to see and guide the currents. But this is the point: Suppose the letter precipitated through me; it would naturally show some traces of my expressions, and even of my writing; but all the same, it would be a perfectly genuine occult phenomenon, and a real message from that Mahatma. Besides, when all is said and done, they exaggerate the likeness of the writings. And experts are not infallible. We have had experts who were just as positive that I could not possibly have written those letters, and just as good experts, too. But the Report says nothing about them. And then there are letters, in just the same handwriting, precipitated when I was thousands of miles away. Dr. Hartmann received more than one at Adyar,[1] Madras, when I was in London; I could hardly have written that."

---

[1] **Adyar** — a neighbourhood in south Chennai (formerly Madras), India.

"They would simply say Dr. Hartmann was the fraud, in that case."

"Certainly," cried H.P.B., growing angry now; "we are all frauds and liars, and the lambkin from Australia is the only true man. My dear, it is too much. It is insolent!" And then she laughed at her own warmth, a broad, good-natured Homeric laugh, as hers always was, and finally said:

"But you have seen some of the occult letters? What do you say?"

"Yes," I replied; "Mr. Sinnett showed me about a ream of them; the whole series that *The Occult World* and *Esoteric Buddhism* are based on. Some of them are in red, either ink or pencil, but far more are in blue. I thought it was pencil at first, and I tried to smudge it with my thumb; but it would not smudge."

"Of course not!" she smiled; "the colour is driven into the surface of the paper. But what about the writings?"

"I am coming to that. There were two: the blue writing, and the red; they were totally different from each other, and both were quite unlike yours. I have spent a good deal of time studying the relation of handwriting to character, and the two characters were quite clearly marked. The blue was evidently a man of very gentle and even character, but of tremendously strong will; logical, easy-going, and taking endless pains to make his meaning clear. It was altogether the handwriting of a cultivated and very sympathetic man."

"Which I am not," said H.P.B., with a smile; "that is Mahatma Koot Hoomi; he is a Kashmiri Brahman[2] by birth, you know, and has travelled a good deal in Europe. He is the author of *The Occult World* letters, and gave Mr. Sinnett most of the material of *Esoteric Buddhism*. But you have read all about it."

"Yes, I remember he says you shriek across space with a voice like Sarasvati's peacock. Hardly the sort of thing you would say of yourself."

"Of course not," she said; "I know I am a nightingale. But what about the other writing?"

"The red? Oh that is wholly different. It is fierce, impetuous, dominant, strong; it comes in volcanic outbursts, while the other is like

---

[2] **Kashmir** (*Sanskrit*) — a valley in northern India, surrounded by the ranges of the Himalayas.

Brahman (*Sanskrit*) — the highest of the four castes in India, one supposed or rather fancying himself, as high among men, as Brahman, the Absolute of the Vedantins, is high among, or above the gods.

Niagara Falls.[1] One is fire, and the other is the ocean. They are wholly different, and both quite unlike yours. But the second has more resemblance to yours than the first."

"This is my Master," she said, "whom we call Mahatma Morya. I have his picture here."

And she showed me a small panel in oils. If ever I saw genuine awe and reverence in a human face, it was in hers, when she spoke of her Master. He was a Rajput[2] by birth, she said, one of the old warrior race of the Indian desert, the finest and handsomest nation in the world. Her Master was a giant, six feet eight, and splendidly built; a superb type of manly beauty. Even in the picture, there is a marvellous power and fascination; the force, the fierceness even, of the face; the dark, glowing eyes, which stare you out of countenance; the clear-cut features of bronze, the raven hair and beard — all spoke of a tremendous individuality, a very Zeus in the prime of manhood and strength. I asked her something about his age. She answered:

"My dear, I cannot tell you exactly, for I do not know. But this I will tell you. I met him first when I was twenty — in 1851. He was in the very prime of manhood then. I am an old woman now, but he has not aged a day. He is still in the prime of manhood. That is all I can say. You may draw your own conclusions."

"Have the Mahatmas discovered the elixir of life?"

"That is no fable," said H.P.B. seriously. "It is only the veil hiding a real occult process, warding off age and dissolution for periods which would seem fabulous" so I will not mention them. The secret is this: for every man, there is a climacteric, when he must draw near to death; if he has squandered his life-powers, there is no escape for him; but if he has lived according to the law, he may pass through and so continue in the same body almost indefinitely."

Then she told me something about other Masters and Adepts she had known — for she made a difference, as though the Adepts were the captains of the occult world, and the Masters were the generals. She had known Adepts of many races, from Northern and Southern India, Tibet, Persia, China, Egypt; of various European nations, Greek,

---

[1] **Niagara Falls** — a group of waterfalls located on the Niagara River, on the border between the United States and Canada.

[2] **Rajput** (*Sanskrit*, "son of a king") — also called Thakur, a member of northern India's warrior caste.

Hungarian, Italian, English; of certain races in South America, where she said there was a Lodge of Adepts.

"It is the tradition of this which the Spanish Conquistadores found," she said, "the golden city of Manoa or El Dorado.[3] The race is allied to the ancient Egyptians, and the Adepts have still preserved the secret of their dwelling-place inviolable. There are certain members of the Lodges who pass from centre to centre, keeping the lines of connection between them unbroken. But they are always connected in other ways."

"In their astral bodies?"

"Yes," she answered, "and in other ways still higher. They have a common life and power. As they rise in spirituality, they rise above difference of race, to our common humanity. The series is unbroken. Adepts are a necessity in nature and in supernature. They are the links between men and the gods; these 'gods' being the souls of great Adepts and Masters of bygone races and ages, and so on, up to the threshold of Nirvana. The continuity is unbroken."

"What do they do?"

"You would hardly understand, unless you were an Adept. But they keep alive the spiritual life of mankind."

"What does it feel like, to go sailing about in your astral body? I sometimes dream I am flying, and I am always in the same position; almost lying on my back, and going feet foremost. Is it anything like that?"

"That is not what I feel," she said; "I feel exactly like a cork rising to the top of water, you understand. The relief is immense. I am only alive then. And then I go to the Master."

"Come back to what you were saying. I ought not to have interrupted you. How do the Adepts guide the souls of men?

"In many ways, but chiefly by teaching their souls direct, in the spiritual world. But that is difficult for you to understand. This is quite intelligible, though. At certain regular periods, they try to give the world at large a right understanding of spiritual things. One of their number comes forth to teach the masses, and is handed down to tradition as the Founder of a religion. Krishna was such a Master; so

---

[3] **El Dorado** or **Manoa** — a legendary kingdom, located somewhere in the Americas.

was Zoroaster; so were Buddha and Shankara Acharya,[1] the great sage of Southern India. So also was the Nazarene.[2] He went forth against the counsel of the rest, to give to the masses before the time, moved by a great pity, and enthusiasm for humanity; he was warned that the time was unfavourable, but nevertheless he elected to go, and so was put to death at the instigation of the priests."

"Have the Adepts any secret records of his life?"

"They must have," she answered; "for they have records of the lives of all Initiates. Once I was in a great cave-temple in the Himalaya mountains, with my Master," and she looked at the picture of the splendid Rajput; "there were many statues of Adepts there; pointing to one of them, he said: 'This is he whom you call Jesus. We count him to be one of the greatest among us.'

"But that is not the only work of the Adepts. At much shorter periods, they send forth a messenger to try to teach the world. Such a period comes in the last quarter of each century,[3] and the Theosophical Society represents their work for this epoch."

---

[1] **Acharya** (*Sanskrit*, "teacher of ethics") — a spiritual teacher, Guru. A name generally given to Initiates, etc., and meaning "Master."

Shankara Acharya (*Sanskrit*) — the great religious reformer of India, and teacher of the Vedanta philosophy — the greatest of all such teachers, regarded by the Advaitas (Non-dualists) as an incarnation of Shiva and a worker of miracles. He established many *mathams* (monasteries), and founded the most learned sect among Brahmans, called the *Smartava*. The legends about him are as numerous as his philosophical writings. At the age of thirty-two, he went to Kashmir, and upon reaching Kedaranath in the Himalayas, entered a cave alone, from whence he never returned. His followers claim that he did not die, but only retired from the world.

[2] Jesus Christ.

[3] Please note that the Masters of the Himalayan Brotherhood live according to the calendar of Shambhala — the Kalachakra (*Sanskrit*, "Wheel of Time") calendar. Its "century" consists not of a hundred years, but of sixty. This is why the messenger promised by Blavatsky appeared not at the end of the 20th century, but much earlier. Blavatsky could not speak about the correct periods in writing, but she did impart them verbally to her closest colleagues. However, this entrusted information was misinterpreted: instead of waiting for a new disciple, as mentioned by Blavatsky herself, there arose an anticipation of a "World Teacher" in a physical body. Yet this "anticipation" was scheduled not in 1975–2000, as Blavatsky stated in writing, but in the 1920–1930s that coincided with the completion of the next 60-year cycle. This suggests that Blavatsky did convey to her closest colleagues that the following disciple must be sent by the Masters much earlier than the timeframe she was permitted to mention ►

"How does it benefit mankind?"

"How does it benefit you to know the laws of life? Does it not help you to escape sickness and death? Well, there is a soul-sickness, and a soul-death. Only the true teaching of Life can cure them. The dogmatic churches, with their hell and damnation, their metal heaven and their fire and brimstone, have made it almost impossible for thinking people to believe in the immortality of the soul. And if they do not believe in a life after death, then they have no life after death. That is the law."

"How can what people believe possibly affect them? Either it is or it isn't, whatever they may believe."

"Their belief affects them in this way. Their life after death is made by their aspirations and spiritual development unfolding in the spiritual world. According to the growth of each, so is his life after death. It is the complement of his life here. All unsatisfied spiritual longings, all desires for higher life, all aspirations and dreams of noble things, come to flower in the spiritual life, and the soul has its day, for life on earth is its night. But if you have no aspirations, no higher longings, no beliefs in any life after death, then there is nothing for your spiritual life to be made up of; your soul is a blank."

"What becomes of you then?"

"You reincarnate immediately, almost without an interval, and without regaining consciousness in the other world."

"Suppose, on the other hand, you do believe in heaven, say the orthodox El Dorado?"

"Your fate after death is this. You have first to pass through what we call Kama-loka, the world of desire, the borderland, in which the soul is purged of the dross of animal life; of all its passions and evil desires. These gradually work themselves out, and having no fresh fuel to keep them burning, they slowly exhaust themselves. Then the soul rises to what we call Devachan, the state which is distorted in the

---

publicly. This promised mid-20th-century disciple who continued the mission of Blavatsky was Helena Roerich. She gave the highest form of yoga, *Agni Yoga*, to the world in co-operation with the Master Morya. It is especially essential today, when new fiery energies are incrementally arriving on the Earth from the Spiritual Sun. These energies cause climate change, while humanity's inability to assimilate them results in natural disasters. *Agni Yoga* is designed to help in this by teaching how to master the Fire, which manifests itself both in human beings and throughout the Cosmos.

orthodox teaching of heaven. Each soul makes its own Devachan, and sees around it those whom it most loved on earth, enjoying happiness in their company. If you believed in the orthodox heaven, you see the golden city and the gates of pearl; if you believed in Shiva's paradise, you find yourself in the midst of many-armed gods; the Red-man sees the happy hunting grounds, and the philosopher enters into the free life of the soul. In all cases, your spirit gathers new strength for a fresh incarnation."

"Must you come back? Is there no escape?"

"If your material desires are unexhausted at death, you must. Desires are forces, and we believe in the conservation of force. You must reap the seed of your own sowing, and reap it where it was sown. Your new life will be the exact result of your deeds in your preceding life. No one can escape the punishment of his sins, any more than he can escape the reward of his virtues. That is the law of Karma. You must go on being reborn till you reach Nirvana."

"Well, it seems to me that all that is more or less contained in the orthodox beliefs, only a good deal distorted."

"Yes," she answered; "that is just it. The orthodoxies do contain the truth, but their followers do not understand it; they put forth teachings which no intelligent man can accept, and so we are all drifting into atheism and materialism. But when we Theosophists show them how to interpret their teachings, it will be quite different. Then they will see how much truth they had, without knowing it. The stories in Genesis, for instance, are all symbols of real truths; and the account of the Creation there, and of Adam and Eve, has far more real truth than Darwinism,[1] once you understand it. But that can only be done by Theosophy."

"How would you, as a Theosophist, set about it?"

"Well," she answered, "in two ways: first, by giving out the truth, as it is taught today in the occult schools, and then by the comparative method; by setting people to study the Aryan and other Eastern scriptures, where they will find the other halves of so many things that have proved stumbling-blocks in the Bible."

"For instance?"

"Take that very teaching of heaven and hell and purgatory. The sacred books of India light up the whole of it, and make it a thoroughly

---

[1] **Darwinism** — a theory of evolution developed by Charles Darwin (1809–1882).

philosophic and credible teaching. But you must study the Oriental religions before you can fully understand what I say. Remember that in the Old Testament there is absolutely no teaching of the immortality of the soul, while in the New Testament it is inextricably confused with the resurrection of the body. But the Upanishads have the real occult and spiritual doctrine."

"Well, I can thoroughly understand and sympathize with that; and to put forth any such teaching at a time like this, when we are all drifting into materialism, would seem a big enough work for any school of Adepts and Masters. I can see how the teaching of rebirth would make life far more unselfish and humane, and therefore far happier. What else do you teach, as Theosophists?"

"Well, sir! I am being cross-examined this evening, it would seem," she answered with a smile, and rolled me another cigarette, making herself one also, and lighting up with evident relish. "We teach something very old, and yet which needs to be taught. We teach universal brotherhood."

"Don't let us get vague and general. Tell me exactly what you mean by that."

"Let me take a concrete case," she said; and glanced meditatively at her secretary, who had been listening quietly and with serious and sincere interest to all she had been saying, even though he had heard much of it from her, time and again. He began to grow a little uneasy under her gaze, and she noticed it and instantly fastened upon him.

"Take the English," she said, and looked at him with those potent blue eyes of hers, as though he in his own person must answer for the sins of his race.

"H.P.B.," he said, rising with a sigh from the table; "I think I had really better go upstairs and go on copying out the manuscript of *The Secret Doctrine*"; and he disappeared.

"Do you think he will?" said H.P.B. with a smile of infinite good-humour. "Not he; he will cuddle into his armchair, smoke endless cigarettes, and read a blood and thunder novel." She was mistaken, however. When I went upstairs to say goodbye, he was in the armchair, serenely smoking, it is true; but it was a detective story. He sat upon it, and said something about getting to work.

"Take the English," she repeated. "How cruel they are! How badly they treat my poor Hindus!"

"I have always understood that they had done a good deal for India in a material way," I objected.

"India is a well-ventilated jail," she said; "it is true they do something in a material way, but it is always three for themselves and one for the natives. But what is the use of material benefits, if you are despised and trampled down morally all the time? If your ideals of national honour and glory are crushed in the mud, and you are made to feel all the time that you are an inferior race — a lower order of mortals — pigs, the English call them, and sincerely believe it. Well, just the reverse of that would be universal brotherhood. Do them less good materially — not that they do so very much, besides collecting the taxes regularly — and respect their feelings a little more. The English believe that the 'inferior races' exist only to serve the ends of the English; but we believe that they exist for themselves, and have a perfect right to be happy in their own way. No amount of material benefit can compensate for hurting their souls and crushing out their ideals. Besides there is another side of all that, which we as Theosophists always point out. There are really no 'inferior races,' for all are one in our common humanity; and as we have all had incarnations in each of these races, we ought to be more brotherly to them. They are our wards, entrusted to us; and what do we do? We invade their lands, and shoot them down in sight of their own homes; we outrage their women, and rob their goods, and then with smooth-faced hypocrisy we turn round and say we are doing it for their good. There are two bad things: hypocrisy and cruelty; but I think if I had to choose, I would prefer cruelty. But there is a just law," she went on; and her face was as stern as Nemesis; "the false tongue dooms its lie; the spoiler robs to render. 'Ye shall not come forth, until ye have paid the uttermost farthing.'"

"So that is what the Adepts sent you forth to teach?"

"Yes," she answered; "that and other things; — things which are very important, and will soon be far more important. There is the danger of black magic, into which all the world, and especially America, is rushing as fast as it can go. Only a wide knowledge of the real psychic and spiritual nature of man can save humanity from grave dangers."

"Witch-stories in this so-called 19th century, in this enlightened age?"

"Yes, sir! Witch-stories, and in this enlightened age! What do you call it but a witch-story, that very experiment you told me of, made by my friend the Spookical Researcher? Is it not witchcraft, to transfer pinches and burns, pain and suffering, in fact, though only slight in this case, to another person at a distance? Suppose it was not as an experiment, but in dead earnest, and with dire malice and evil intent? What then? Would the victim not feel it? Could he protect himself? And would not that be witchcraft in just the sense that sent people to the stake and faggot all through the Middle Ages? Have you read the famous witchcraft trial at Salem? Yes, sir! Witchcraft in this very enlightened age — the darkest, most material, and unspiritual that the world has ever seen."

"Oh, but sending pinches by thought-transference can do no great harm?"

"You think not? Well, you don't know what you are talking about. That is the privilege of the young! Once the door is open for that sort of thing, where do you think it is going to be shut? It is the old tale; give the devil an inch, and he will take an ell; give him your finger, and he will presently take your whole arm. Yes, and your body, too! Do you not see the tremendous evils that lie concealed in hypnotism? Look at Charcot's[1] experiments at the Salpêtrière![2] He has shown that a quite innocent person can be made to perform actions quite against his or her will; can be made to commit crimes, even, by what he calls Suggestion. And the *somnambule*[3] will forget all about it, while the victim can never identify the real criminal. Charcot is a benevolent man, and will never use his power to do harm. But all men are not benevolent. The world is full of cruel, greedy, and lustful people, who will be eager to seize a new weapon for their ends, and who will defy detection and pass through the midst of us all unpunished.

"Yes, sir! Witch-tales in this enlightened age! And mark my words! You will have such witch-tales as the Middle Ages never dreamt of. Whole nations will drift insensibly into black magic, with good intentions, no doubt, but paving the road to hell none the less for that!

---

[1] **Jean-Martin Charcot** (1825–1893) — a French neurologist, who worked on hypnosis.

[2] **Pitié-Salpêtrière Hospital** — a charitable hospital in Paris, where Jean-Martin Charcot worked for 33 years.

[3] **Somnambule** (*French*) — a sleepwalker.

Hypnotism and suggestion are great and dangerous powers, for the very reason that the victim never knows when he is being subjected to them; his will is stolen from him, and mark my words: these things may be begun with good motives, and for right purposes. But I am an old woman, and have seen much of human life in many countries. And I wish with all my heart I could believe that these powers would be used only for good! Whoever lets himself or herself be hypnotized, by anyone, good or bad, is opening a door which he will be powerless to shut; and he cannot tell who will be the next to enter! If you could foresee what I foresee, you would begin heart and soul to spread the teaching of universal brotherhood. It is the only safeguard!"[1]

"How is it going to guard people against hypnotism?"

"By purifying the hearts of people who would misuse it. And universal brotherhood rests upon the common soul. It is because there is one soul common to all men, that brotherhood, or even common understanding is possible. Bring men to rest on that, and they will be safe. There is a divine power in every man which is to rule his life, and which no one can influence for evil, not even the greatest magician. Let men bring their lives under its guidance, and they have nothing to fear from man or devil. And now, my dear, it is getting late, and I am getting sleepy. So I must bid you goodnight!" And the Old Lady dismissed me with that grand air of hers which never left her, because it was a part of herself. She was the most perfect aristocrat I have ever known.

It was long after that, before we came back to the question of magical powers. In August 1888, H.P.B. had a visit from her old chum, Colonel H. S. Olcott. He was writing, at a side table. H.P.B. was playing Patience, as she did nearly every evening, and I was sitting opposite her, watching, and now and then talking about the East, whence Colonel Olcott had just come. Then H.P.B. got tired of her card game, which would not come out, and tapped her fingers slowly on the table, half unconsciously. Then her eyes came to focus, and drawing her hand back a foot or so from the table, she continued the tapping movement in the air. The taps, however, were still perfectly audible — on the

---

[1] H.P.B.'s prediction came true in less than fifty years. Some of the techniques of hypnotism and suggestion were used by Adolf Hitler to rule the German people. However, nowadays, similar psychological technologies are also widely used in the media and social media to manipulate people and to pass off black for white.

table a foot from her hand. I watched, with decided interest. Presently she had a new idea, and turning in my direction, began to send her astral taps against the back of my hand. I could both feel and hear them. It was something like taking sparks from the prime conductor of an electric machine; or, better still, perhaps, it was like spurting quicksilver through your fingers. That was the sensation. The noise was a little explosive burst. Then she changed her direction again and began to bring her taps to bear on the top of my head. They were quite audible, and, needless to say, I felt them quite distinctly. I was at the opposite side of the table, some five or six feet away, all through this little experiment in the unexplained laws of nature, and the psychical powers latent in man.

No experiment could have been more final and convincing; its very simplicity made it stand out as a new revelation. Here was a quite undoubted miracle, as miracles are generally understood, yet a miracle which came off. But at our first meeting, Madame Blavatsky did not even approach the subject; none the less, she conveyed the sense of the miraculous. It is hard to say exactly how, but the fact remains. There was something in her personality, her bearing, the light and power of her eyes, which spoke of a wider and deeper life, not needing lesser miracles to testify to it, because in itself miraculous. That was the greatest thing about her, and it was always there; this sense of a bigger world, of deeper powers, of unseen might; to those in harmony with her potent genius, this came as a revelation and incentive to follow the path she pointed out. To those who could not see with her eyes, who could not raise themselves in some measure to her vision, this quality came as a challenge, an irritant, a discordant and subversive force, leading them at last to an attitude of fierce hostility and denunciation.

When the last word is said, she was greater than any of her works, more full of living power than even her marvellous writings. It was the intimate and direct sense of her genius, the strong ray and vibration of that genius itself, which worked her greatest achievements and won her greatest triumphs. Most perfect work of all, her will carried with it a sense and conviction of immortality. Her mere presence testified to the vigour of the soul.

THANK YOU FOR READING!

Helena Blavatsky's wisdom remains as relevant and enlightening today as it was during her own time. Her insights and knowledge, revealed through conversations with her young students, have illuminated the pages of this book, and we hope they have similarly illuminated your mind and spirit.

If you've enjoyed her profound teachings and if they expanded your understanding of our nature and the Universe, we kindly ask for your support. Your thoughts and opinions matter, and they can make a significant impact. If you could spare a moment, we would greatly appreciate it if you could leave a review wherever you bought the book and share your experience with your friends on social media.

Not only will your feedback help fellow seekers of eternal truths discover this treasure, but it will also contribute to the ongoing legacy of H. P. Blavatsky — a woman whose self-sacrificing heart reshaped our world.

We sincerely thank you for embarking on this enlightening journey back in time to meet the enigmatic H.P.B. in person.

If you would like to be the first to know about our new releases, please subscribe to our newsletter through this link and receive a free bonus:

radiantbooks.co/bonus

COSMIC EVOLUTION

SEVEN STANZAS FROM
THE SECRET BOOK OF DZYAN

The reader has to bear in mind that the Stanzas given treat only of the Cosmogony of our own planetary system and what is visible around it, after a Solar Pralaya. The secret teachings with regard to the Evolution of the Universal Cosmos cannot be given, since they could not be understood by the highest minds in this age, and there seem to be very few Initiates, even among the greatest, who are allowed to speculate upon this subject. Moreover, the Teachers say openly that not even the highest Dhyan-Chohans have ever penetrated the mysteries beyond those boundaries that separate the milliards of solar systems from the "Central Sun," as it is called. Therefore, that which is given, relates only to our visible Cosmos, after a "Night of Brahma."

The history of cosmic evolution, as traced in the Stanzas, is, so to say, the abstract algebraical formula of that Evolution. Hence the student must not expect to find there an account of all the stages and transformations which intervene between the first beginnings of "Universal" evolution and our present state. To give such an account would be as impossible as it would be incomprehensible to men who cannot even grasp the nature of the plane of existence next to that to which, for the moment, their consciousness is limited.

The Stanzas, therefore, give an abstract formula which can be applied, *mutatis mutandis*,[1] to all evolution: to that of our tiny earth, to that of the chain of planets of which that earth forms one, to the solar Universe to which that chain belongs, and so on, in an ascending scale, till the mind reels and is exhausted in the effort.

The seven Stanzas given in this volume represent the seven terms of this abstract formula. They refer to, and describe the seven great stages of the evolutionary process, which are spoken of in the Puranas as the "Seven Creations," and in the Bible as the "Days" of Creation.

Stanza I describes the state of the *One All* during Pralaya, before the first flutter of re-awakening manifestation.

A moment's thought shows that such a state can only be symbolized; to describe it is impossible. Nor can it be symbolized except in

---

[1] **Mutatis mutandis** (*Latin*) — with the necessary changes having been made.

negatives; for, since it is the state of Absoluteness *per se*, it can possess none of those specific attributes which serve us to describe objects in positive terms. Hence that state can only be suggested by the negatives of all those most abstract attributes which men feel rather than conceive, as the remotest limits attainable by their power of conception.

The stage described in Stanza II is, to a western mind, so nearly identical with that mentioned in the first Stanza, that to express the idea of its difference would require a treatise in itself. Hence it must be left to the intuition and the higher faculties of the reader to grasp, as far as he can, the meaning of the allegorical phrases used. Indeed it must be remembered that all these Stanzas appeal to the inner faculties rather than to the ordinary comprehension of the physical brain.

Stanza III describes the Re-awakening of the Universe to life after Pralaya. It depicts the emergence of the "Monads" from their state of absorption within the One; the earliest and highest stage in the formation of "Worlds," the term Monad being one which may apply equally to the vastest Solar System or the tiniest atom.

Stanza IV shows the differentiation of the "Germ" of the Universe into the septenary hierarchy of conscious Divine Powers, who are the active manifestations of the One Supreme Energy. They are the framers, shapers, and ultimately the creators of all the manifested Universe, in the only sense in which the name "Creator" is intelligible; they inform and guide it; they are the intelligent Beings who adjust and control evolution, embodying in themselves those manifestations of the One Law, which we know as "The Laws of Nature."

Generically, they are known as the Dhyan-Chohans, though each of the various groups has its own designation in the Secret Doctrine.

This stage of evolution is spoken of in Hindu mythology as the "Creation" of the Gods.

In Stanza V the process of world-formation is described: First, diffused Cosmic Matter, then the fiery "whirlwind," the first stage in the formation of a nebula. That nebula condenses, and after passing through various transformations, forms a Solar Universe, a planetary chain, or a single planet, as the case may be.

The subsequent stages in the formation of a "World" are indicated in Stanza VI, which brings the evolution of such a world down to its fourth great period, corresponding to the period in which we are now living.

Stanza VII continues the history, tracing the descent of life down to the appearance of Man; and thus closes the first volume of *The Secret Doctrine*.

The development of "Man" from his first appearance on this earth in this Round to the state in which we now find him will form the subject of Volume II.

STANZA I
THE NIGHT OF THE UNIVERSE

1. The Eternal Parent, wrapped in her Ever-Invisible Robes, had slumbered once again for Seven Eternities.

2. Time was not, for it lay asleep in the Infinite Bosom of Duration.

3. Universal Mind was not, for there were no Ah-hi to contain it.

4. The Seven Ways to Bliss were not. The Great Causes of Misery were not, for there was no one to produce and get ensnared by them.

5. Darkness alone filled the Boundless All, for Father, Mother and Son were once more one, and the Son had not yet awakened for the new Wheel and his Pilgrimage thereon.

6. The Seven Sublime Lords and the Seven Truths had ceased to be, and the Universe, the Son of Necessity, was immersed in Paranishpanna, to be outbreathed by that which is, and yet is not. Naught was.

7. The Causes of Existence had been done away with; the Visible that was, and the Invisible that is, rested in Eternal Non-Being — the One Being.

8. Alone, the One Form of Existence stretched boundless, infinite, causeless, in Dreamless Sleep; and Life pulsated unconscious in Universal Space, throughout that All-Presence, which is sensed by the Opened Eye of Dangma.

9. But where was Dangma when the Alaya of the Universe was in Paramartha, and the Great Wheel was Anupadaka?

STANZA II
THE IDEA OF DIFFERENTIATION

1. Where were the Builders, the Luminous Sons of Manvantaric Dawn? In the Unknown Darkness in their Ah-hi Paranishpanna. The

Producers of Form from No-Form — the Root of the World — the Devamatri and Svabhavat, rested in the Bliss of Non-Being.

2. Where was Silence? Where the ears to sense it? No, there was neither Silence nor Sound; naught save Ceaseless Eternal Breath, which knows itself not.

3. The Hour had not yet struck; the Ray had not yet flashed into the Germ; the Matripadma had not yet swollen.

4. Her Heart had not yet opened for the One Ray to enter, thence to fall, as Three into Four, into the Lap of Maya.

5. The Seven were not yet born from the Web of Light. Darkness alone was Father-Mother, Svabhavat; and Svabhavat was in Darkness.

6. These Two are the Germ, and the Germ is One. The Universe was still concealed in the Divine Thought and the Divine Bosom.

STANZA III
THE AWAKENING OF COSMOS

1. The last Vibration of the Seventh Eternity thrills through Infinitude. The Mother swells, expanding from within without, like the Bud of the Lotus.

2. The Vibration sweeps along, touching with its swift Wing the whole Universe and the Germ that dwelleth in Darkness, the Darkness that breathes over the slumbering Waters of Life.

3. Darkness radiates Light, and Light drops one solitary Ray into the Waters, into the Mother-Deep. The Ray shoots through the Virgin Egg, the Ray causes the Eternal Egg to thrill, and drop the non-eternal Germ, which condenses into the World-Egg.

4. The Three fall into the Four. The Radiant Essence becomes Seven inside, Seven outside. The Luminous Egg, which in itself is Three, curdles and spreads in milk-white Curds throughout the Depths of Mother, the Root that grows in the Depths of the Ocean of Life.

5. The Root remains, the Light remains, the Curds remain, and still Oeaohoo is One.

6. The Root of Life was in every Drop of the Ocean of Immortality, and the Ocean was Radiant Light, which was Fire, and Heat, and Motion. Darkness vanished and was no more; it disappeared in its own Essence, the Body of Fire and Water, of Father and Mother.

7. Behold, O Lanoo, the Radiant Child of the Two, the unparalleled refulgent Glory — Bright Space, Son of Dark Space, who emerges from the Depths of the great Dark Waters. It is Oeaohoo, the Younger, the * * *. He shines forth as the Sun, he is the Blazing Divine Dragon of Wisdom; the One is Four, and Four takes to itself Three, and the Union produces the Sapta, in whom are the Seven, which become the Tridasha, the Hosts and the Multitudes. Behold him lifting the Veil, and unfurling it from East to West. He shuts out the Above, and leaves the Below to be seen as the Great Illusion. He marks the places for the Shining Ones, and turns the Upper into a shoreless Sea of Fire, and the One Manifested into the Great Waters.

8. Where was the Germ, and where was now Darkness? Where is the Spirit of the Flame that burns in thy Lamp, O Lanoo? The Germ is That, and That is Light, the White Brilliant Son of the Dark Hidden Father.

9. Light is Cold Flame, and Flame is Fire, and Fire produces Heat, which yields Water — the Water of Life in the Great Mother.

10. Father-Mother spin a Web, whose upper end is fastened to Spirit, the Light of the One Darkness, and the lower one to its shadowy end, Matter; and this Web is the Universe, spun out of the Two Substances made in One, which is Svabhavat.

11. It expands when the Breath of Fire is upon it; it contracts when the Breath of the Mother touches it. Then the Sons dissociate and scatter, to return into their Mother's Bosom, at the end of the Great Day, and re-become one with her. When it is cooling, it becomes radiant. Its Sons expand and contract through their own Selves and Hearts; they embrace Infinitude.

12. Then Svabhavat sends Fohat to harden the Atoms. Each is a part of the Web. Reflecting the "Self-Existent Lord," like a Mirror, each becomes in turn a World.

STANZA IV
THE SEPTENARY HIERARCHIES

1. Listen, ye Sons of the Earth, to your Instructors — the Sons of the Fire. Learn, there is neither first nor last; for all is One Number, issued from No-Number.

2. Learn what we, who descend from the Primordial Seven, we, who are born from the Primordial Flame, have learnt from our Fathers.

3. From the Effulgency of Light — the Ray of the Ever-Darkness — sprang in Space the reawakened Energies; the One from the Egg, the Six, and the Five. Then the Three, the One, the Four, the One, the Five — the Twice Seven, the Sum Total. And these are the Essences, the Flames, the Elements, the Builders, the Numbers, the Arupa, the Rupa, and the Force or Divine Man, the Sum Total. And from the Divine Man emanated the Forms, the Sparks, the Sacred Animals, and the Messengers of the Sacred Fathers within the Holy Four.

4. This was the Army of the Voice, the Divine Mother of the Seven. The Sparks of the Seven are subject to, and the servants of, the First, the Second, the Third, the Fourth, the Fifth, the Sixth, and the Seventh of the Seven. These are called Spheres, Triangles, Cubes, Lines and Modellers; for thus stands the Eternal Nidana — the Oi-Ha-Hou.

5. The Oi-Ha-Hou, which is Darkness, the Boundless, or the No-Number, Adi-Nidana Svabhavat, the $\bigcirc$:

I. The Adi-Sanat, the Number, for he is One.

II. The Voice of the Word, Svabhavat, the Numbers, for he is One and Nine.

III. The "Formless Square."

And these Three, enclosed within the $\bigcirc$, are the Sacred Four; and the Ten are the Arupa Universe. Then come the Sons, the Seven Fighters, the One, the Eighth left out, and his Breath which is the Light-Maker.

6. Then the Second Seven, who are the Lipika, produced by the Three. The Rejected Son is One. The "Son-Suns" are countless.

STANZA V
FOHAT — THE CHILD OF THE SEPTENARY HIERARCHIES

1. The Primordial Seven, the First Seven Breaths of the Dragon of Wisdom, produce in their turn from their Holy Circumgyrating Breaths the Fiery Whirlwind.

2. They make of him the Messenger of their Will. The Dzyu becomes Fohat: the swift Son of the Divine Sons, whose Sons are the Lipika, runs circular errands. Fohat is the Steed, and the Thought is the

Rider. He passes like lightning through the fiery clouds; takes Three, and Five, and Seven Strides through the Seven Regions above, and the Seven below. He lifts his Voice, and calls the innumerable Sparks, and joins them together.

3. He is their guiding spirit and leader. When he commences work, he separates the Sparks of the Lower Kingdom, that float and thrill with joy in their radiant dwellings, and forms therewith the Germs of Wheels. He places them in the Six Directions of Space, and One in the middle — the Central Wheel.

4. Fohat traces spiral lines to unite the Sixth to the Seventh — the Crown. An Army of the Sons of Light stands at each angle; the Lipika, in the Middle Wheel. They say: "his is good." The first Divine World is ready; the First, the Second. Then the "Divine Arupa" reflects itself in Chhaya Loka, the First Garment of Anupadaka.

5. Fohat takes five strides, and builds a winged wheel at each corner of the square for the Four Holy Ones ... and their Armies.

6. The Lipika circumscribe the Triangle, the First One, the Cube, the Second One, and the Pentacle within the Egg. It is the Ring called "Pass-Not" for those who descend and ascend; who during the Kalpa are progressing towards the Great Day "Be-With-Us." ... Thus were formed the Arupa and the Rupa: from One Light, Seven Lights; from each of the Seven, seven times Seven Lights. The Wheels watch the Ring.

STANZA VI
OUR WORLD, ITS GROWTH AND DEVELOPMENT

1. By the power of the Mother of Mercy and Knowledge, Kwan-Yin — the Triple of Kwan-Shai-Yin, residing in Kwan-Yin-Tien — Fohat, the Breath of their Progeny, the Son of the Sons, having called forth, from the lower Abyss, the Illusive Form of Sien-Tchan and the Seven Elements.

2. The Swift and the Radiant One produces the seven Laya Centres, against which none will prevail to the Great Day "Be-With-Us"; and seats the Universe on these Eternal Foundations, surrounding Sien-Tchan with the Elementary Germs.

3. Of the Seven — first One manifested, Six concealed; Two manifested, Five concealed; Three manifested, Four concealed; Four produced, Three hidden; Four and One Tsan revealed, Two and One-Half concealed; Six to be manifested, One laid aside. Lastly, Seven Small Wheels revolving: one giving birth to the other.

4. He builds them in the likeness of older Wheels, placing them on the Imperishable Centres.

How does Fohat build them? He collects the Fiery-Dust. He makes Balls of Fire, runs through them, and round them, infusing life thereinto, then sets them into motion; some one way, some the other way. They are cold, he makes them hot. They are dry, he makes them moist. They shine, he fans and cools them. Thus acts Fohat from one Twilight to the other, during Seven Eternities.

5. At the Fourth, the Sons are told to create their Images. One-Third refuses. Two obey.

The Curse is pronounced. They will be born in the Fourth, suffer and cause suffering. This is the First War.

6. The Older Wheels rotated downward and upward. The Mother's Spawn filled the whole. There were Battles fought between the Creators and the Destroyers, and Battles fought for Space; the Seed appearing and reappearing continuously.

7. Make thy calculations, O Lanoo, if thou wouldst learn the correct age of thy Small Wheel. Its Fourth Spoke is our Mother. Reach the Fourth Fruit of the Fourth Path of Knowledge that leads to Nirvana, and thou shalt comprehend, for thou shalt see.

STANZA VII
THE PARENTS OF MAN ON THE EARTH

1. Behold the beginning of sentient formless Life.

First, the Divine, the One from the Mother-Spirit; then, the Spiritual; the Three from the One, the Four from the One, and the Five, from which the Three, the Five and the Seven. These are the Three-fold and the Four-fold downward; the Mind-born Sons of the First Lord, the Shining Seven. It is they who are thou, I, he, O Lanoo; they who watch over thee and thy mother, Bhumi.

2. The One Ray multiplies the smaller Rays. Life precedes Form, and Life survives the last atom. Through the countless Rays the Life-Ray, the One, like a Thread through many Beads.

3. When the One becomes Two, the Threefold appears, and the Three are One; and it is our Thread, O Lanoo, the Heart of the Man-Plant called Saptaparna.

4. It is the Root that never dies; the Three-tongued Flame of the Four Wicks. The Wicks are the Sparks, that draw from the Three-tongued Flame shot out by the Seven — their Flame — the Beams and Sparks of one Moon reflected in the running Waves of all the Rivers of Earth.

5. The Spark hangs from the Flame by the finest thread of Fohat. It journeys through the Seven Worlds of Maya. It stops in the First, and is a Metal and a Stone; it passes into the Second, and behold — a Plant; the Plant whirls through seven changes and becomes a Sacred Animal. From the combined attributes of these, Manu, the Thinker, is formed. Who forms him? The Seven Lives and the One Life. Who completes him? The Fivefold Lha. And who perfects the last Body? Fish, Sin, and Soma.

6. From the First-born the Thread between the Silent Watcher and his Shadow becomes more strong and radiant with every Change. The morning Sunlight has changed into noon-day glory.

7. "This is thy present Wheel," said the Flame to the Spark. "Thou art myself, my image and my shadow. I have clothed myself in thee, and thou art my Vahan to the Day 'Be-With-Us,' when thou shalt re-become myself and others, thyself and me." Then the Builders, having donned their first Clothing, descend on radiant Earth and reign over Men — who are themselves.

THE LAND OF THE GODS
BY H. P. BLAVATSKY

Hidden in plain sight for 135 years, Blavatsky's story is a beautifully written account of an exceptional journey into Shambhala. Immersive and engaging, this profound book will provide you with a unique outlook on the deeper side of life, exposing our true nature, interior powers, and ultimate destiny. It explains grand, spiritual ideas more thoroughly and swiftly than any book you'll ever read.

THE SECRET WORLD GOVERNMENT
BY HELENA ROERICH

A secret for many years, this book provides the first-ever evidence showing how the Secret World Government, known as Shambhala, helped the United States during the Franklin D. Roosevelt presidency. It outlines profound principles for becoming a true leader who can guide any nation to prosperity by building just relations between the people and the state.

THE TEMPLE OF MYSTERIES
BY FRANCIA LA DUE

Bridging spirituality and science, this classic work is a true gem of the world's esoteric legacy. The Master Hilarion, the Protector of America and Europe, transmitted it through Francia La Due, intending to assist humanity in resolving the challenges of modern civilization and guide us toward unity with the cosmic forces that shape our existence. *The Temple of Mysteries* will illuminate your path to self-realization and help you find answers to the most pressing questions that trouble your soul.

THE MYSTERY OF CHRIST
BY THALES OF ARGOS

Eye-opening and heart-touching, *The Mystery of Christ* brings a fresh perspective, an uncommon insight, and spiritual depth to the dramatic events which occurred two thousand years ago. As you read the profoundly stirring pages of this beautifully crafted narrative, you will comprehend the unequalled mission of Christ and the innermost secrets of Mary, culminating in an unexpected encounter with the new mystery of the Cosmos named Sophia.

BECOMING WHAT YOU ARE
BY TWO WORKERS

Drawing on timeless spiritual wisdom, this book will take you on a journey toward self-realization and inner awakening. Its inspiring messages and practical advice will show you how to cultivate the qualities necessary for spiritual growth. It will help you align your actions with your highest potential and ultimately become what you are — a radiant and awakened being.

THE SEVEN LAWS OF SPIRITUAL PURITY
BY TWO WORKERS

Providing a profound and eye-opening perspective on achieving true spiritual purity, this thought-provoking and straightforward book draws practical advice from ancient wisdom to show you how to purify your mind, body, and soul. It is a passionate plea for a better world — a world in which humanity no longer has to accept and deal with the consequences of many sufferings but instead prevents their very causes.

THE KINGDOM OF WHITE WATERS
BY V.G.

For a thousand years, this secret story could be told only on the deathbed, for it revealed an inaccessible garden paradise hidden in the Himalayas — Shambhala, a place thousands of people searched for, but always failed to find. Each carrier of this secret story took a vow of silence that could be broken under only two conditions: when facing imminent death or in response to another's persistent requests for knowledge about the mythical Kingdom of White Waters.

Terrestial Existance.
Accept life as the only conscious
existance.
2 kinds of conscious existance -
        terrestial + spiritual